Sixth E

A HISTORY AND PHILOSOPHY OF SPORT AND PHYSICAL EDUCATION

From Ancient Civilizations to the Modern World

Robert A. Mechikoff
San Diego Christian College

Connect
Learn
Succeed™

A HISTORY AND PHILOSOPHY OF SPORT AND PHYSICAL EDUCATION: FROM ANCIENT
CIVILIZATION TO THE MODERN WORLD, SIXTH EDITION

Published by McGraw-Hill, a business unit of The McGraw-Hill Companies, Inc., 1221 Avenue of the Americas,
New York, NY, 10020. Copyright © 2014 by The McGraw-Hill Companies, Inc. All rights reserved. Printed in
the United States of America. Previous editions © 2010, 2006, and 2002. No part of this publication may be
reproduced or distributed in any form or by any means, or stored in a database or retrieval system, without the
prior written consent of The McGraw-Hill Companies, Inc., including, but not limited to, in any network or
other electronic storage or transmission, or broadcast for distance learning.

Some ancillaries, including electronic and print components, may not be available to customers outside the
United States.

This book is printed on acid-free paper.

3 4 5 6 7 8 9 10 QVS/QVS 20 19 18 17 16 15

ISBN 978-0-07-802271-5
MHID 0-07-802271-1

Senior Vice President, Products & Markets: *Kurt L. Strand*
Vice President, General Manager, Products &
  Markets: *Michael Ryan*
Vice President, Content Production &
  Technology Services: *Kimberly Meriwether David*
Executive Director of Development: *Lisa Pinto*
Managing Director: *Gina Boedeker*
Senior Brand Manager: *Bill Minick*
Marketing Specialist: *Alexandra Schultz*
Managing Development Editor: *Sara Jaeger*
Editorial Coordinator: *Adina Lonn*
Director, Content Production: *Terri Schiesl*
Project Manager: *Erin Melloy*
Buyer: *Nicole Baumgartner*
Media Project Manager: *Sridevi Palani*
Cover Designer: *Studio Montage, St. Louis, MO*
Compositor: *S4Carlisle Publishing Services*
Typeface: *10/12 Times*
Printer: *Quad Graphics*

Cover Image: *Imagestate Media (John Foxx);
Getty Images/RF; Library of Congress Prints
and Photographs Division [LC-USZ62-78070];
U.S. Air Force photo by Staff Sgt. Desiree N.
Palacios; Royalty-Free/Corbis; © Library
of Congress Prints & PHotographs Division
[LC-DIG-ppmsca-08935]; Wesley Hitt/Getty
Images/RF; Olivier Renck/Getty Images/RF;
© Library of Congress Prints & Photographs
Division [LC-USZ62-27663].*

Library of Congress Cataloging-in-Publication Data

Mechikoff, Robert A.
  A history and philosophy of sport and physical education: from ancient civilizations to
the modern world / Robert A. Mechikoff. —6th ed.
    p. cm.
  Includes bibliographical references and index.
  ISBN 978-0-07-802271-5
  1. Physical education and training—History. 2. Sports—History. 3. Physical education
and training—Philosophy. 4. Sports—Philosophy. I. Title.

GV211.M43 2014
796.09—dc23   2012042580

www.mhhe.com

CONTENTS

SECTION III

The Historical and Philosophical Development of Sport and Physical Education in America 195

CHAPTER 9

Sport in the Colonial Period 196

CHAPTER 10

Changing Concepts of the Body 207

CHAPTER 11

The Impact of Science and the Concept of Health on the Theoretical and Professional Development of Physical Education: 1885–1930 235

CHAPTER 1 2

**The Transformation of Physical Education:
1900–1939 261**

SECTION **IV**

The American Approach to Sport
and Physical Education in the
Twentieth Century 279

CHAPTER 1 3

**The Evolution of Physical Education:
1940 and Beyond 280**

CHAPTER 17

After the Cold War: 2008–2012 401

This edition, unlike the previous five editions, has been reorganized to reflect the chronology of historical and philosophical content as opposed to the thematic approach utilized in the previous five editions. While Sections I and II remain the same (Chapters 1–8) the rest of the text has been revamped and a new chapter has been added.

Chapters 3 and 4 Ancient Greece and Rome, have new photos and new information. Of particular note is the new information about Greek and Roman sport as seen from the perspective of the Jews during this time. This insightful and revealing account is taken from the Roman historian Josephus who was a Jew and fought the Romans on more than one occasion before he decided to become a Roman.

Section III, The Historical and Philosophical Development of Sport and Physical Education in America begins with Chapter 9, which has not changed in regard to content, and ends with Chapter 10. This chapter has new material relating to pragmatism and how segregation was a fact of life in American society and was rampant in sport, especially baseball. New information about African-American baseball teams and players are found within this chapter.

Section IV, The Theoretical and Professional Development of American Physical Education, is where the reorganized chapter sequence comes into

play. In previous editions, the chapter titled The Impact of Science and the Concept of Health on the Theoretical and Professional Development of Physical Education: 1885–1930, was Chapter 9. It is now Chapter 11. This chapter uses original documentation that was written over 100 years ago to warn early physical education professionals about the charlatans and quacks who would exploit the profession for the soul purpose of making money while claiming to be credible.

The "old" Chapter 10, The Transformation of Physical Education: 1900–1939 is now Chapter 12, and remains essentially the same relative to content. In this edition, Chapter 13, The Evolution of Physical Education: 1940 and Beyond, is brand new and provides the reader with the status of physical education and sport during World War II and beyond. During this time, long before Title IX was enacted, physical education departments in schools and colleges were segregated by gender and many men and women wanted to keep it this way. It was also a time when physical education came under attack at the University of California, Berkeley by university faculty who saw little if any value in the degree and worked very hard to eliminate it. This assault on the credibility of the physical education degree was partly due to the Conant Report which is discussed in this chapter along with the contributions of Franklin Henry, who campaigned for the academic discipline of physical education at the expense of the profession of physical education and the All American Girls Professional Baseball League

Chapter 14, Sport in the Twentieth Century (formerly Chapter 13) has new content about women's basketball. Students will learn about the Flying Queens of Wayland Baptist University, and Coach Pat Summitt of the University of Tennessee.

Section V, A Social and Political History of the Modem Olympic Games, (Chapters 15–17) has been updated to reflect the latest research and the story of the 2010 Vancouver Winter Olympic Games.

When appropriate, new discussion questions are introduced along with a few new Internet sources and suggested readings. The online learning center contains PowerPoint presentations, extensive photos that cannot be accommodated in the text, plus additional resources that should inspire and stimulate the reader.

My inspiration is derived from multiple sources; however, a few of the more inspirational people and institutions who have made a great contribution to my life and consequently, my way of thinking deserve to be recognized.

Orange Coast College (OCC) provided me with an excellent educational experience and the opportunity to continue playing football after I graduated from high school. While I am certain the students and faculty who study and teach there today are stellar, my enduring appreciation goes to the 1967 and 1969 OCC football team, the students and professors who opened my eyes to all sorts of new ideas and experiences, and especially the OCC football coaches: Dick Tucker, George Mattias, Jack Fair, and Dale Wonacott.

To the Martot family: Kelly, David, Anna, and Yuri for their encouragement and support, and to all my students and colleagues at home and abroad, your questions, insights, and conversations continue to be a profound influence.

Robert A. Mechikoff, Ph.D
Professor and
Chair—Department of Kinesiology
San Diego Christian College

SECTION

I Ancient Civilizations

History and Philosophy of Sport and Physical Education

O B J E C T I V E S

Upon completing this chapter, you will be able to:

- Understand the rationale and purpose of historical study in general.
- Appreciate the historical contributions that sport and physical education have made to society.
- Apply selected definitions as they relate to the concept of play, games, and sport, and understand the need for these definitions.
- Discuss selected methods of historical study.
- Describe modernization theory and how it applies to the study of the history of sport and physical education.
- Recognize how urbanization and industrialization affected the development of sport and physical education.
- Understand the rationale and purpose of philosophical inquiry and its utility to comprehending the philosophical positions that the human body has been assigned throughout history.
- Understand the nature and application of metaphysics to the study of sport and physical education.
- Understand the nature and application of epistemology to the study of sport and physical education.
- Apply fundamental philosophical processes and terms.
- Recognize the impact that metaphysical dualism has had on the historical development of sport and physical education.
- Understand the difference between dualism and monism and their influence on epistemology specific to the use of the body/senses as a source of valid information for acquiring accurate knowledge.
- Identify selected philosophies of the modern world, and discuss their impact on perceptions of the worth or value of the human body and consequently the utility of sport and physical education.

Before we begin describing the process of "doing" history, a basic question needs to be asked and answered: Why study history? It may not be immediately obvious that the study of history in any area, including sport and physical education, can lead to a more enlightened and productive life. Many people argue that knowing history is irrelevant to their lives. One aspect of our character is the prevailing belief that we are headed "into the future," and the most obvious aspect of history is that it is in the past—and so, over. Making things even more problematic is that the study of history (even sport history) is sometimes perceived as boring, repetitive, and not connected in any immediate way to the lives of those who read about history. As the argument goes, because the players and events in history are behind us, these events and people have no relevance in our lives.

This skeptical perspective relative to the study of history can be at least partially dismissed with a few observations. Students of history have found that it often provides an illuminating perspective on why we behave and think in the present and offers a basis for forecasting the future. History is not, however, *the only* answer as to why we think and act as we do, nor is it *the only* manner in which we can forecast what will happen. History provides a particular perspective—and when done well, an enlightened perspective—on why we think and behave the way we do and how we ought to think and behave in the future. This argument for understanding history was put most eloquently by philosopher George Santayana (1863–1952): "Progress, far from consisting in change, depends on retentiveness. . . . Those who cannot remember the past are condemned to repeat it."[1] The eminent scholar and journalist Norman Cousins (1915–1990) held a similar view: "History is a vast early warning system."

Apart from Santayana's and Cousins' prophetic belief, there are additional reasons to study history. Historical study/inquiry can serve as a dramatic source of inspiration and motivation. Epic achievements and accomplishments—as well as disappointments and defeats—brought about by individuals, groups, or entire civilizations provide exciting testaments to courage, bravery, and sacrifice in the name of monumental achievements—and colossal failures. Your ability to "think outside the box," a skill prized by employers and one of the hallmarks of intellectual achievement, is largely dependent on your understanding and application of the critical thought process. Understanding and applying the lessons of history—especially the history of ideas and their track record of success or failure—will serve to demonstrate your analytical ability to think outside the box and go beyond the status quo.

The study of history is replete with examples of ideas, beliefs, social experiments, and architecture that have either been consigned to the dustbin of history because they failed or have withstood the test of time to the extent that they (ideas, beliefs, and so on) remain as vital and beautiful today as when they were first created. In many cases, timeless ideas and approaches that we use today were developed centuries or even millennia ago. For example, the ancient Greeks employed the term *stadion,* which in the beginning was actually a unit of measurement, about 600 ancient feet. The inventive Greeks then instituted a foot race that covered 600 feet and, as you may have guessed, referred to this race as the "stadion" (sometimes called the "stade race"). Not long after, the term *stadion* was used to identify the location where the race was held. Over time, the stadion became known as a venue where athletic competitions took place—and the rest, as they say, is history!

Another tradition that has been carried over from the ancient to the modern world is found in horse racing. This sport was very popular in antiquity, especially in Rome. In the chariot races, often held in the 250,000-capacity Circus Maximus, teams were represented by four factions or syndicates that could be identified by their respective colors: the Reds, Blues, Greens, and Whites. The drivers wore these colors so the fans who wagered their money on the outcome could watch the progress of the races and cheer their drivers or jockeys on to victory. And today, jockeys wear silks of various colors that identify the horse and its owner.

In this sense, some things may never change if the original idea is sound. These ancient ideas and practices that have withstood the test of time remain just as appreciated today as the day they were introduced. The great works of literature, such as *The Iliad* and *The Odyssey;* the thoughts and ideas of ancient philosophers like Socrates and Plato; great architectural monuments like the pyramids of Egypt, the Parthenon in Athens, or the Colosseum in Rome—all are part of the rich social and cultural fabric that is both history and inspiration.

Of course, history can mean different things to different people. Although we are utilizing history to study sport and physical education, history is also widely used to study politics, theology, warfare, weather science, economics, and other fields and disciplines that influence the human race and planet Earth. Historians, anthropologists, sociologists, and archaeologists study men and women who have played a significant role in shaping the course of history, ancient and modern. Do you believe there is any truth to the adage "The more things change, the more they remain the same"? As we shall see later in this book, many of the same concerns, goals, hopes, and dreams that most of us have today were shared by men, women, and children who lived five centuries or even four or five millennia ago.

There is some comfort in knowing that men, women, and children who lived long ago enjoyed many of the same sports that we do today. Ancient athletes competed in wrestling, boxing, swimming, horse racing, discus and javelin throw, and footraces, among other events. Today's athletes have much in common with the athletes who competed for fame, glory, and riches in the ancient world. What may be particularly illuminating is that the "extreme sports" that have become so popular in the twenty-first century pale in comparison with the competitions and athletic prowess of the ancients. After reading Chapters 2–4, you can draw your own conclusions about the extreme sports and

athletes of the modern world as compared with the competitions that drew hundreds of athletes and tens of thousands of fans to huge stadiums in the ancient world.

Assuming that the arguments given support the importance of the study of history, can these arguments be applied to sport and physical education? The answer would seem to be yes. Sport and physical education can be understood through the methods of history, as can any other human activity. In so doing, we understand how past events shaped the present and how future events in sport and physical education will be affected by "current events." Furthermore, understanding how a culture plays tells us much about how that culture operates outside of sport and physical education. Play, in the form of games and sport, can be seen as serving certain functions in a culture, what Brian Sutton-Smith calls "buffered cultural learning" (learning necessary survival skills in a safe environment) to the expression of specific cultural values (such as discipline and teamwork).[2] Sociologist Jacques Barzun observed that "whoever wants to know the heart and mind of America had better learn baseball."[3] Barzun argued that baseball and its rules, the way we interact with the game, and its importance to our culture over the past 150 years tells us much about how we think and behave today.

DEFINITIONS

It will be helpful if we define commonly used words and concepts so that our discussions of history and philosophy can begin from some common basis. We will begin with a brief definition of the concept of "sport" because the word will appear frequently throughout this book. Sport is a modern term first used in England around A.D. 1440. The origins of the word *sport,* or its etymology, are Latin and French. In French, the word *de(s)porter* has its roots in the Latin word *deportare,* which means "to amuse oneself." Over time, the meaning of the term *sport* grew from merely "amusing oneself" to an interpretation that was used extensively throughout England, referring to competition in the form of games, individual athletic exploits, and hunting.

Sport cannot be understood, however, without understanding something about the nature of play and the nature of games, for play is a larger domain than sport. While it can be argued that all sport is play, it does not follow that all play is sport. Johan Huizinga, who wrote the classic *Homo Ludens (Man the Player),* developed the general hypothesis that play is precultural and permeates all facets of life.[4] Huizinga argued that play is a "significant function," that there is some sense to it, and that this aspect of human existence—play—defines the nature of being human and the nature of culture. In short, one of our defining characteristics as human beings is that we are playful and seek activities that are fun. According to Huizinga, play is

> a free activity standing quite consciously outside "ordinary" life as being "not serious," but at the same time absorbing the player intensely and utterly. It is an activity connected with no material interest, and no profit can be gained by it. (p. 13)

Huizinga's work has withstood the test of time and has been added to by Roger Caillois,[5] Brian Sutton-Smith,[6] and others.

As you might expect, achieving complete consensus on what constitutes play is unlikely. While many scholars who study the phenomenon of play agree on certain aspects of its nature, there are points of departure; this is also true for sport, games, physical education, dance, and athletics. For example, although Huizinga and others have reached somewhat complementary definitions of play, J. Levy further refines these definitions, arguing that play has three fundamental characteristics:

1. *Play is intrinsically motivated.* We are born with the desire to play; we don't have to be taught to do this. Huizinga also agrees with this tenet.

2. *Play involves the temporary suspension of normal/typical reality and the acceptance of alternative realities.* We can be so immersed in the "play experience" that we enter a reality that is highly personal and out of the norm.

3. *Play involves an internal locus of control.* We believe that we have control over our actions and outcomes while engaging in various forms of play.[7]

You may be wondering about the heavy emphasis on the definition of play (several more definitions will follow in this chapter) and other seemingly abstract issues. This is a reasonable question. The necessity of this information is based on the intellectual level of study—the sophistication and nature of the area of study—as well as the opportunity and ability to develop, expand, and engage in critical thought. The level or status of your intellectual and personal growth as a college student will be determined, to a large extent, by exposure to different schools of thought and the opportunity to engage in the process of critical thinking—to assess the value of the information you obtain through readings, research, lectures, discussion, and reflection. After examining the material/information, as a critical thinking-student, you must determine whether it is significant, insignificant, or somewhere in the middle. For example, the various definitions and characteristics of play help to illustrate the level of interest in this area, as well as the fact that the initial definition by Huizinga has been modified by others. In addition, play, games, sports, and athletics are essential elements within the realm of human movement and are one of the cornerstones of the scholarly study of kinesiology and physical education. It is imperative that students of kinesiology and physical education have a basic understanding of these terms.

Definitions are critical to the study of specific academic areas or issues. If individuals are not "on the same page" relative to the meaning of various concepts, confusion is likely to result, and the educational value and critical-thinking opportunities will likely have been squandered. In short, the level of academic rigor and the intellectual demands of the area that is under study—such as kinesiology and physical education—can significantly enhance the interested student's intellectual, personal, and professional growth. In contrast, if the academic rigor and intellectual and physical demands reflect low expectations or weak/minimal content, the student has been cheated out of "elevating his or her game and going to the next level," to use a sports metaphor. At the risk of moralizing, I believe that this latter situation is both untenable and unethical; do you agree? Accepting the rationale for presenting and understanding definitions that are integral to the study of sport and physical education, we will proceed with a few more essential definitions.

A *game* is a somewhat more organized effort at play, where the organized and playful elements of the activity become more evident. All of us have "played games," so we have a good idea of what to expect when we do so. This structuring of the playful impulse leads to the following definition of a game:

> a play activity which has explicit rules, specified or understood goals . . . , the element of opposition or contest, recognizable boundaries in time and sometimes in space, and a sequence of actions which is essentially "repeatable" every time the game is played.[8]

Arriving at a definition of sport based on play and games, however, is not without its difficulties. This is because when factors such as religion, social class, and historical period are considered, sport may not easily fit into a universally accepted definition. For example, throughout history, dependent upon one's socioeconomic status, one person's sport may have been another person's work. Kings and noblemen would often hunt on their private reserves for the enjoyment of the sport, while their peasants worked at developing their skills as hunters in an effort to put food on the table and survive one more day.

Another example of differing viewpoints is how sport was conceived and practiced by the ancient Greeks. The Greeks strove to achieve *arete,* a unique Greek concept. Greek athletes, under the watchful eye of their coaches, underwent rigorous training striving to achieve individual (not team) excellence. What is even more striking is that the ancient Greeks did not encourage team competitions in everyday athletics, in the Olympic Games, or in any of the four great Crown Games: Olympia, Nemea, Isthmian, and Delphi. Rather, the emphasis was on individual excellence and performance to honor specific gods, city-states, and families. Tens of thousands of fans would travel to the great athletic festivals of antiquity to watch their favorite athletes compete. In this respect, little has changed from ancient times to modern times.

The ancient Romans, who eventually conquered the Greeks in 146 B.C., did not have the cultural belief in individual excellence to the same extent that the Greeks did—if at all. Roman sport, if we can call it that, took place in massive arenas (much bigger than anything ever built by the Greeks) that held up to 250,000 fans, who were entertained by watching bloody gladiatorial combats in which hundreds of fighters and animals would be slain in a single day. Another form of mass entertainment took place in the infamous Colosseum, where hapless "enemies of the state" were fed to lions, tigers, bears, and crocodiles or consigned to other horrific deaths in front of 50,000 Romans and others. The vast majority of Romans were bored with the Greek version of sport, even as most Greeks were repulsed by the Romans' forms of entertainment.

For our purposes, a general definition of sport will include the following characteristics: continuity, division of roles, dynamic interaction with an audience, and a supporting establishment.[9] Continuity refers to the longevity of a game. For instance, American football has been played in its current form for over 100 years and as such meets the criteria of continuity. In philosopher Paul Weiss's words, a game is an occurrence; a sport is a pattern. The pattern of the game of football is one characteristic that defines it as a sport.

We have provided a definition of sport that will be used throughout this book. However, as a critical thinker, there are other definitions that you may want to consider. Betty Spears and Richard Swanson have fashioned the following definition:

Sport will be considered to be activities involving physical prowess and skill, competition, strategy and/or chance, and engaged in for the enjoyment and satisfaction of the participant and/or others. This definition includes both organized sport and sport for recreational purposes. It includes sport as entertainment and also encompasses professional sport.[10] According to the definition used by Spears and Swanson, would you agree that what the Romans enjoyed watching in the Colosseum and other venues qualifies as sport or mass executions?

Professor John Charles of The College of William and Mary observes that "contemporary analysts disagree as to whether the history of [American] college sport may be characterized more accurately as pluralistic or as hegemonic in nature."[11] Professor George Sage, a distinguished sport sociologist, describes the differences between these two models:

In the pluralistic model, sports and physical recreational activities are seen primarily as innocent, voluntary social practices that let people release tension and enjoy themselves. . . . [In] the hegemonic perspective, sport is viewed as promoting and supporting the social inequality endemic to capitalism. This is seen in class, gender, and race social relations and the control, production, and distribution of economic, political, and cultural power in sport.[12]

It should be apparent that Sage's explanation has sport serving either as a voluntary recreational and entertainment activity for college students or as a vehicle to promote capitalist ideas of social inequality and related topics of domination and social control.

Roberta J. Park, professor emeritus of the University of California and one of the premier historians in our field, suggests that, viewed broadly, sport is "a category term that includes, at the least, agonistic (characterized by the struggle of competition) athletics, vigorous recreational pursuits, and physical education, and intersects with aspects of medicine, biology, social reform, and a host of other topics."[13] This broad definition of sport introduces elements of medicine, social reform, and biology.

A number of definitions of sport have evolved from the academic disciplines of history, sociology, archaeology, philosophy, physical education, kinesiology, and classical studies, to name but a few.[14] The study of sport is not limited to scholarship in physical education and kinesiology. Indeed, the history of sport and physical education and related fields (dance, exercise science, and so on) has a storied past. Sport and physical activity served as a central focus of ancient cultures long since buried under the sands of time. In modern times, individuals, groups, and nations continue the worship of athletes that started long ago. As a universal construct, the societal and cultural impact of sport and physical education has been nothing less than profound. The magnitude of sport in the twenty-first century may have eclipsed the importance of art, music, and religion as the icon of the masses. Or has it? At some point in the future, historians will weigh in on this issue. We turn our attention to the methods of history in general and to how sport history is "done" in particular.

"DOING" HISTORY

Having defined sport, play, and games, we are ready for a definition of history that can guide us in our studies. *History* is the study of change, or the lack of change, over time. Therefore, sport history is the study of how sport has changed (or not) over time.[15] Looked at in this way, sport, play, and physical education as we know them are the latest rendition of all of the changes that have occurred in the past. To study these activities as they have been practiced and viewed in the past is to understand what sport and play are now. This textbook can help kinesiology and physical education students understand our current attitudes and behaviors in sport and play by understanding how these attitudes and behaviors evolved. The following example of how sport has changed, and how we understand sport as a result of this change, will illustrate this point.

Michael Oriard in *Reading Football* tells the story of the development of the game of football and how our attitudes toward it came to be.[16] Students at American colleges played football for decades before the first intercollegiate game between Princeton and Rutgers in 1869. Football was played primarily because it was fun, but it also served the purpose of hazing new freshmen on campus and was a popular form of interclass rivalry. The game most students played, however, was more like soccer than what we now know as football. Only Harvard used rules that we would recognize today as something like modern football, which allows for running with the ball and tackling.

In 1876, Harvard and Yale, which played both games, agreed to use what they called the "Concessionary Rules," rules similar to those governing the Harvard rugby style of football. In November 1876, representatives of Harvard, Yale, Princeton, and Columbia met to formalize these rules and to create the Intercollegiate Football Association. These new, formalized rules distinguished American football from its soccer and rugby counterparts, and these differences remain with us for the most part.

While this change that occurred in the 1870s tells us much about how football evolved from rugby and soccer, it also tells us much about being an American in the nineteenth century. Why did Americans change the rules of rugby to make a distinctly American game? Specifically, Oriard asks why Americans ran with the ball from the line of scrimmage instead of playing rugby as their British ancestors did and why they began to use judges and referees:

> The interesting question is, why these most basic alterations? The evolution of football's rules has left a fascinating record that demands interpretation. Why Americans' initial preference for the running and tackling rather than the kicking game? [And] why our insistence on amending the Rugby Union code once adopted? (p. 27)

Why, Oriard wonders, did these changes occur? Football changed from something like soccer or rugby to something like the contemporary American game. What can these changes tell us about Americans and American sport? Among other things, Oriard argues that referees were needed because Americans had a different attitude toward rules than did our British ancestors. British amateur athletes operated on a code of honor associated with the peculiarities of their elitist social class, a code that was as old as the games they played. Adherence among upper-class British boys to the code of honor was enforced by the captains of each team, and in so doing, both the social nature of the contest and the social status of the players were supported.

Americans, in contrast, had no such social understanding—Americans argue to this day that we are of the "middle class" and so have no code of honor to break. This difference in culture is reflected in our games, and Oriard argues that Americans wish to exploit the rules of the contest as much as they wish to adhere to them. The American attitude toward rules, then, is reflected in the change from the British games of soccer and rugby to the American game of football. Oriard concludes that

> this attitude toward rules—a recognition of the letter but not the spirit, a dependence on rules in the absence of tradition yet also a celebration of the national genius for circumventing them—expressed an American democratic ethos, a dialectical sense of "fair play" [embracing both "sportsmanship" and

"gamesmanship"] that was very different from the aristocratic British version. (p. 30)

The point is not to describe the development of the modern American game of football, at least not yet. Rather, it is to show that sport history can be understood in a way that demonstrates how and why sport has changed. In so doing, we can understand a variety of changes that occurred: the evolution of football rules, the different attitudes that cultures and nations have toward sport, and the ways in which all of these changes are manifested in the American character.

Interpretive Versus Descriptive History

The previous example of how sport has changed uses a basic assumption—that the changes that have occurred can be interpreted. Not all written histories are interpretive, however. The two basic types of traditional historical research are descriptive and interpretive.[17] *Descriptive history* describes objectively and in as much detail as possible, what happened in the past. Descriptive history tries to provide the who, what, when, and where of the past, and it tries to do so without injecting ideas, values, and judgments from the present onto the events of the past. Many early historical works are descriptive and are literally records of the past.

Interpretive history evaluates the evidence and attempts to explain the how and the why of events that happened in the past. For example, Oriard sought to discover how football changed from its rugby origins and why it changed in the manner it did. What makes interpretive history different from descriptive history is that an interpretive history introduces the narrator's perspective into the interpretation, and the history is no longer "just the facts." Using a particular perspective does not, however, make interpretive history less valuable. On the contrary, the use of some perspective allows much of the fullness and the richness of history to come forth and makes the historical explanation more open to discussion. Between descriptive and interpretive histories,

one is not better or worse than the other; they are merely different accounts of what occurred.

To write either descriptive or interpretive history, we must have access to different types of information, and two main sources are used in historical research. The first is a *primary source,* one that was part of the event being studied. Examples of primary sources include an eyewitness account of an event, a contemporary newspaper story, a picture or painting made at the time of the event, a video recording of the event, a record of the event kept by an observer, and an ancient inscription or account of the event. *The Iliad* and *The Odyssey,* epic poems by Homer, are frequently used as primary sources. Primary sources, then, are firsthand accounts of historical events. *Secondary sources* of historical research are written by those who did not participate in or observe the event being studied. Examples include some magazine articles, many history textbooks, and other accounts of the event, like Hollywood movies. In 2007, *300* premiered in cinemas around the world. The movie was a loose account of the Battle of Thermopylae. Some parts of the movie were historically accurate, but most of it was rubbish. *300* would not qualify as a primary or secondary source.

As stated earlier, this textbook is an attempt to understand how and why sport, play, and physical education have changed (or not changed) over time. As such, it is much more of an interpretive history than a descriptive one, although we use many who, what, when, and where descriptions of historical events. The perspectives used most often to explain how and why sport and physical education have changed involve the concepts of modernization, urbanization and industrialization, and, finally and most importantly for understanding the first half of this textbook, metaphysics. None of these perspectives provides a complete or perfect explanation for how and why behaviors and attitudes toward sport, play, and physical education changed as they did. Rather, the variety of these four perspectives, and the ways in which they are applied, determine the quality of this written history and aid in your comprehension.

Modernization

One interpretive device used is known as *modernization theory,* an organizational scheme that helps to describe how culture tends to change from "premodern" or "traditional" to "modern" characteristics.[18] Premodern culture is stable and local, is governed by men at both the family and political level, has little specialization of roles, depends on muscle power, views time as cyclical (by the seasons), and operates on myth and ritual. Modern culture is the opposite: It is dynamic, cosmopolitan, meritocratic, and highly specialized, and it depends on technology, views time linearly (by the clock), and operates on the idea that it is rational. Historians who interpret history from the perspective of modernization theory use these characteristics to explain or interpret how and why a particular culture changed the way it did. Sport and physical education, as part of culture, can be interpreted as either premodern or modern, and historian Melvin Adelman argues that sport changed from its "premodern" form into its current "modern" form between 1820 and 1870.[19] Table 1-1 lists the key characteristics of the premodern and modern ideal sporting types.

The concept of modernization can be used to explain and interpret many changes in American culture, including the manner in which sport and physical education changed. However, modernization is not a cause of change. Americans did not want to become "modern" in the nineteenth century any more than they wanted to be "premodern"; indeed, Americans in 1850 did not know what "modern" meant. Modernization merely explains and interprets, from the perspective of an agreed-upon set of rules, the changes that took place in

TABLE 1-1	The Characteristics of Premodern and Modern Ideal Sporting Types	
	Premodern Sport	**Modern Sport**
Organization	Either nonexistent or at best informal and sporadic; contests are arranged by individuals directly or indirectly (e.g., tavern owners, bettors) involved.	Formal; institutionally differentiated at the local, regional, and national levels.
Rules	Simple, unwritten, and based on local customs and traditions; variations exist from one locale to another.	Formal, standardized, and written; rationally and pragmatically worked out and legitimated by organizational means.
Competition	Locally meaningful only; no chance for national reputation.	National and international, superimposed on local contests; chance to establish national and international reputations.
Role Differentiation	Low among participants; loose distinction between playing and spectating.	High; emergence of specialists (professionals) and strict distinctions between playing and spectating.
Public Information	Limited, local, and oral.	Reported on a regular basis in local newspapers, as well as national sports journals; discussed in specialized magazines, guidebooks, etc.
Statistics and Records	Nonexistent.	Kept and published on a regular basis; considered important measures of achievement; records sanctioned by national associations.

Source: Melvin Adelman, *A Sporting Time: New York City and the Rise of Modern Athletics, 1820–70* (Urbana: University of Illinois Press, 1986), 6.

American sport more than a hundred years ago and continue to occur in many countries in the world.

Urbanization and Industrialization

Another way to interpret the changes in sport and physical education involves where people live—in the country or the city—and how they go about providing for themselves—with muscle power or with technology. Like modernization, urbanization and industrialization patterns explain changes that happened primarily during the nineteenth century. In the early 1800s, most Americans lived in the country, providing for themselves by farming the land, and their farming practices used either their own muscle power or that of their livestock. In the 1820s, cities in the United States began to grow faster than did the agrarian population, beginning the shift from a farming nation to an urban nation. Americans simultaneously experienced a technological revolution that radically changed the way they worked. These changes in living patterns had a significant impact on the sport and physical education patterns of Americans. As historian John Betts noted,

> Telegraph lines went up all over the landscape, the railroad followed the steamboat from the East to the Midwest and the South, and by 1860 a network of over thirty-thousand miles of track covered the United States. An immigrant tide helped populate midwestern states, and Cincinnati, St. Louis, Chicago, Milwaukee, and Detroit gradually became western metropolises. The reaper and other new tools slowly transformed farm life; agricultural societies sprouted up; journals brought scientific information to the farmer; and the agricultural fair developed into a prominent social institution.[20]

These changes facilitated a shift from an isolated and remote farming lifestyle to a more city-oriented lifestyle, and the changes that occurred in sport and physical education reflected this change. For instance, it was difficult to have team games when people lived far apart because of their farming

lifestyles. The railroad changed this. In addition, sporting activities could not safely be held at night until the invention of the electric light made large, indoor events possible. These and many other changes can be explained through interpretations that take into account urbanization and industrialization.

Metaphysics

Metaphysics is the area of philosophical study concerned with the nature of reality. A metaphysical question would be "Are ideas real?" or "Which is more real, the body or the mind?" At first glance these questions seem silly. Many of us would argue, "Of course ideas are real! Of course bodies are real!" On the other hand, have you ever held an "idea" in your hand? More will be said about metaphysics as part of philosophy in the next section of this chapter, but here we will briefly outline how metaphysics can be used to understand changing attitudes toward the human body.

Why is it important to understand how past cultures viewed the reality of the human body? Once we assume a metaphysical position, one type of knowledge becomes more "real" than another. Similarly, what we value is based on our metaphysical assumptions. If, to take an extreme example, we assume that humans are merely biological computers, then all education can be considered physical education. Education is the act of programming the body to get the right behavior. If, on the other extreme, we take the position that what makes us human is our intellectual capacity (as the name *Homo sapiens*—"man the thinker"—implies), then education becomes the process of developing our intellectual capacities. And, with regard to the topic of this textbook, the phrase "physical education" makes no sense. Philosophers over the ages have debated the questions we just asked and many more. The answers to these questions have a significant bearing on the role and scope that sport, play, and physical education occupy in a culture.

Two examples may help make these positions more clear. The ancient Romans assumed that the human body and the senses were primary means of knowing and understanding reality. One thousand years later, the monks of the Middle Ages viewed the reality of the human body in different terms. The monks often practiced ascetic, or self-denying, behaviors that were a result of a philosophy that valued the eternal soul much more than the physical body, which they considered evil. Consequently, sport and physical education were not seen as important because they focused on the body and not the soul.

Some of these attitudes toward the human body are still with us, especially in the institution of education. In your experience, which is treated as more important, the mind or the body? What would most of your instructors value, the training of the mind or the body? For which classes in your program of study do you receive more credit, theory classes or physical activity courses? Is a philosophy course worth more credit hours than an activity class in football? If so, why? After all, both classes require hard work.

These and other questions can be answered when we use metaphysics to interpret how sport and physical education have changed. Figure 1-1 will help make these changes more explicit. However, there have been many deviations from this model.

PHILOSOPHICAL PROCESSES

The discussion of metaphysics can be used to help you understand the role of the mind and body in culture. However, there are many more aspects to philosophy than using it to interpret history. A more thorough understanding of philosophy can enrich your understanding of how sport, play, and physical education have changed because values toward sport, play, and physical education change with each philosophy.

Many philosophies can be used to understand physical education and sport, and we will discuss several of those that are most relevant to this text.

High emphasis on the body

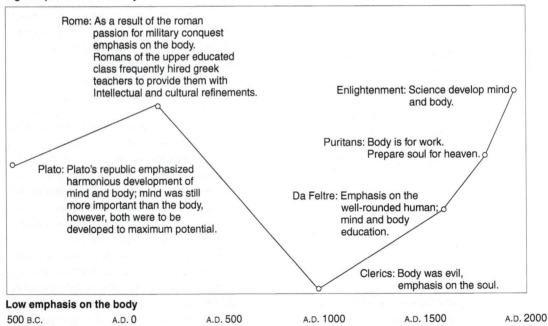

Low emphasis on the body

500 B.C.   A.D. 0   A.D. 500   A.D. 1000   A.D. 1500   A.D. 2000

Figure 1-1
Ontology chart.

This discussion is not exhaustive by any means. Our purpose is to demonstrate that philosophy can be a useful guide and tool in our personal and professional life.

Philosophy is derived from the ancient Greek word *philosophia,* which means "love of wisdom." *Philosophy* can be defined as the systematic investigation of reality, knowledge, and values, which should lead to the acquisition of wisdom. In other words, it is the study of what we believe and why. Philosophy also provides the foundation from which nearly all other inquiries originate.

For most people, philosophy represents abstract ideas that originate within the minds of tortured academics and other overly cerebral types. Philosophers often appear to take great delight in engaging in mental gymnastics that are confusing to most of us. Although this type of philosophical inquiry does go on, it represents only a part of the philosophical process. You should understand the links among religion, science, and philosophy, because doing so will enhance your understanding of sport and physical education.[21]

Many students are surprised to find that philosophy, religion, and science have in common certain assumptions or starting points.[22] Indeed, most Americans tend to believe that science is "fact," whereas philosophy represents mere "opinion." However, if we look closely enough, we will find that science, philosophy, and religion have similar origins. This does not, contrary to what you might believe, devalue any of the three. Rather, we describe the foundations of those areas of knowledge to point out that all of them can be discussed as human creations.[23] As the overall framework for our discussion is philosophical, the following points should help provide a basic understanding of the process of philosophy and the ways in which philosophy and religion differ from science:

1. Although philosophy and religion may share similar purposes and common questions, religion is grounded in blind faith and belief. In contrast, science operates from a set of rules called a "paradigm," and philosophy is grounded in reason and logic.[24] Some philosophers and theologians have tried to show a relationship between religion and philosophy, but their efforts have been futile.[25]

2. Science strives for objectivity and rejects subjective value judgments.[26] Philosophy, in contrast, accepts the idea of subjective value judgments and studies the nature of values in an area known as *axiology.* So philosophy can be used to make value judgments, whereas science cannot.[27]

3. Questioning lies at the core of both philosophy and science. In philosophy, however, the focus is as much on the process as it is on getting the answers to questions. More often than not, philosophical inquiry results in more questions than absolute answers. Science, on the other hand, seeks to prove or disprove hypotheses based on material data and scientific experiments.

4. The role of the philosopher traditionally has been to raise and examine the more profound questions arising out of the human experience. Philosophers have sought to understand in rational terms the meaning of life. Scientists, however, are concerned with the material, objective, observable universe and are less concerned with meaning than they are with measurement.

Basic Philosophical Terms

It will be helpful to define the most commonly used terms found in philosophical inquiry. Much of philosophical inquiry is concerned with reality, knowledge, and value. For this purpose, the following list describes these areas of study and their main subtopics:

Metaphysics: the study of the nature of reality and the nature of existence

> *Ontology:* the study of the nature of being, especially human existence
>
> *Theology:* the study of the nature of God in the Judeo-Christian sense or as God exists in Islam and other organized and established religions

Cosmology: the study of the nature of the universe

Epistemology: the study of the nature of knowledge and how we acquire it e.g. can accurate knowledge be acquired via the bodily senses or is intellectual evaluation and analysis the only path to knowledge and wisdom?

Axiology: the study of the nature of values

Ethics: the study of the nature of good; establishment of a code of values to live by

Aesthetics: the study of the nature of beauty and the beauty of the human form/body

Politics: the elements and ideas that make for a good and just society

One important area of philosophy not mentioned above is *logic,* the art and science of reasoning, and an area that describes the ability to think accurately and systematically. Our analysis, as well as any other historical process that uses a set of rules to interpret change over time, assumes that logic will be central to the process. Indeed, using logic is one of the central tasks of a liberal arts education, and you will need to apply logic to understand both the process of doing philosophy and the process of interpreting history.

Axiology, the branch of philosophy that seeks to determine the nature of values, is central to understanding concepts such as fair play. Aesthetics addresses the nature of art and beauty and can be applied to such forms of human movement as in dance, gymnastics, and figure skating, in which beauty and grace of movement many times represent art. Ethics is concerned with issues of right and wrong, and with correct and incorrect behavior. The concept of fair play abiding by the rules, is representative of good ethical behavior.

Metaphysics and Ontology

Metaphysics is the branch of philosophy that attempts to determine the nature of reality and to distinguish between the real and the unreal or imagined. Metaphysical questions and inquiry are profound and speculative. The nature of human existence, or the nature of mind and soul, are metaphysical issues that have perplexed philosophers, scientists, and theologians for thousands of years. Ontology is a branch of metaphysics that studies the nature of existence relative to humans; does the mind provide a more accurate representation of reality than revealed by the senses? This discussion is an old one, and understanding the argument and its implications are central to understanding the Western world. What is more "real," an idea or the physical, tangible, material world? Plato's "Allegory of the Cave" illustrates his argument that reality is an "idea,"[28] and he used this allegory to describe the relationship between the material world and the perfect, never-decaying ideal world.

In Plato's allegory, prisoners were chained to the wall of a cave. As their captors walked across the mouth of the cave, the shadows of the captors could be seen by the prisoners on the opposite wall. That is all the prisoners had ever seen; it was their reality, and so they believed that the shadows were "real."[29] However, we know that there is more to reality than the shadows on the wall and that there is a whole world apart from the mouth of the cave.

Plato argued that you and I are like the prisoners in the cave: There is a whole world apart from the reality we experience with our bodies and our senses. This is the world of ideas or, in Plato's words, the "reality of forms" and of God and an ideal, perfect place such as "heaven." In this reality, there exists perfect knowledge, and souls in this "heaven" have access to and understanding of perfect knowledge. This reality is more real because it is perfect and never decays. Using Plato's logic, isn't an idea that will remain the same for thousands of years more real, and thus of greater value, than a body that will decay after a number of decades?

Plato's argument is logical; the question is whether it accurately describes reality. The idea that the material world will change but a timeless idea will not, and an idea is therefore perfect and so more real, has a certain plausibility. Other philosophers, however, would argue that the material world is real and an idea is not. Which is right? It depends on your metaphysical position; what you perceive as "real."

A fundamental theme of this book is that metaphysics, especially ontology, has an enormous impact on the value of physical education and sport. If the material, corporeal world is real, or at least more real than the visionary concept of an ideal world, then it will be highly valued. If it is highly valued, then activities like sport, play, and games will be highly valued. The converse is also true: If the mind and soul are more valued or real than the physical body, then sport, play, and games will be less valued. If we can understand the significant metaphysical and ontological positions of a culture, then we can gain perspective on that particular culture's views of sport and physical education. It also follows from this position that if we study the cultures that significantly affected the development of Western civilization and helped determine our contemporary metaphysical and ontological positions, then we also gain an understanding of why we view sport and physical education the way we do.

Metaphysical Dualism

Philosophy in the Western world has its roots in ancient Greece. The civilization that began in roughly 1200 B.C., prospered during the Golden Age of Greece (480–338 B.C.), and eventually became a subject nation of Rome (146 B.C.) was spectacular by any standards. Ancient Greek civilization is a primary source for the philosophical forces that helped to shape and define Western civilization. In addition to starting Western philosophy, the ancient Greeks gave birth to Western ideas about physical education and athletic competition.

The Greeks developed philosophical positions that provided rational explanations of human nature and of the universe. For example, Anaximander (610–545 B.C.), generally recognized as one of the first philosophers,[30] developed a theory of adaptation to the environment similar to Charles Darwin's theory of evolution as described in his *On the Origin of Species* (1859). Plato (427–347 B.C.) developed a theory of being, or ontology, similar to that found in the Christian Bible, and his "Allegory of the Cave" was one of the first examples of this philosophy.

Plato and the Bible share an explanation of the nature of reality that is central to Western philosophy. Both argue that all of reality is divided into two parts: matter—the physical realm—and ideas—the thoughts and concepts formed by the intellect and soul. This approach to metaphysics is known as *dualism*. Plato and the Bible are Western in their understanding of how we should understand what a person is, and this early Western approach still defines, for many, "correct" attitudes toward the body, physical education, and sport. Most importantly, these early Western philosophies shared the idea that the soul and mind are the most important aspects of a person, much more important than the body. While many philosophers who followed Plato disagreed with his position on the soul, mind, and body, all philosophers who followed him had to deal with his metaphysical dualism in one way or another; this is sometimes called the *mind-body problem.* This division of reality into two parts is of critical importance to students of sport history and philosophy, for this concept can be used to explain many of the attitudes and behaviors we have in the twenty-first century regarding sport, physical education, and play. For example, in your opinion, what does our society value more, the education and nourishment of the mind or the body?

Epistemology

Epistemology is the branch of philosophy that examines the nature of knowledge and how we come to know things. It is relevant to physical education in that different ways of knowing have different consequences for the mind and the body, and consequently, for how we value the mind and the body.[31] For each metaphysical position, there is a corresponding epistemology. For example, if the mind is more real more discerning, than the body, as Plato held, then we learn through intellectual activity. If, on the other hand, the body and the senses are considered to be the best means of gathering knowledge, then our metaphysical position will reflect this epistemology.

Finally, what is perceived as real is valued by a culture, so there is a corresponding axiological position—cultural value, to the metaphysical and epistemological positions. Epistemology does not come first, nor does metaphysics or axiology. Rather, they correspond to each other.

Certain questions fall within the realm of epistemology: Is knowledge and the nature of reality more easily known through intellectual activity, or can we better acquire accurate and valid knowledge through our bodies via the senses? Is the information we acquire through the five senses valid all of the time? For example, is the information we obtain through sight and hearing completely reliable, or must this knowledge be subject to analysis and evaluation in our mind to ensure that it is valid? This question is particularly important to physical education teachers, because if knowledge can be acquired only through the mind, or if the mind is the essential vehicle in the formation and acquisition of knowledge, then the body is not valued as highly as the mind and at best is of secondary importance as articulated in Plato's opus, *Phaedo*.

The nature of "knowing" is not limited to the mind-body debate. How many ways of knowing do you have at your disposal? Most of us can identify a subject—the human body, for example—and study and "know" it through science, theology, history, philosophy, and other ways of knowing. Do you employ and evaluate a subject or issue by multiple "ways of knowing," or are you wedded to a single school of thought or belief? In reality, which approach is more erudite?

FROM DUALISM TO MONISM IN THE WESTERN WORLD

The Mind-Body Relationship

The mind-body relationship is important to physical educators because, to a great extent, what we know and how we teach is determined by our philosophy and corresponding position about the mind-body relationship, and this position is usually determined by our culture.[32] We also argue

that if a given culture considers the mind and body to be integrated and whole, as opposed to being divided into two parts, the body will have esteem and value.[33] In such a culture, sport, play, and physical education will be valued more highly.

In the coming chapters, we will examine the relationship of mind and body from different philosophical perspectives, so we will not go into detail here regarding philosophies that were developed prior to the 1800s. These philosophies range from Plato's and René Descartes', which have in common the view that the mind and body are separate and distinct entities, to Thomas Hobbes's *empiricism,* a philosophy arguing that there is only the material world (there is no spiritual world) and in it, physical bodies. While these Western philosophies represent extremely different metaphysical positions, they concur *a priori* (meaning "prior to experience"), in beginning with a metaphysical position, usually one that is dualistic and that emphasizes either the mind or the body.

Another characteristic of most Western philosophies is that they emphasize the mind and spirit and try to explain how these two aspects of a person control the body. "Mind over matter" would be a good way of describing these philosophies, and this particular relationship is to a great extent what makes the Western world "western." Occasionally, as with Thomas Hobbes and other empiricists, the senses of the body are the primary source for knowing reality. As a rule, though, the history of Western philosophy can be understood as an attempt to explain reality through the framework of the mind controlling the body and the evil that results when individuals become slaves to their bodies and seek sensory pleasure.

As we noted earlier in our discussion of interpretive history using metaphysics, there have been different philosophies that emphasize either the mind or the body. In *The Republic,* Plato argued for harmony between mind and body. Roman philosophers such as the epicureans and stoics emphasized the senses. The Scholastics, in reaction to the excesses of Roman culture, emphasized the soul and mind but did not neglect the body. Renaissance philosophers were influenced by classical Greek and

Roman thought and argued for a balance between mind, body, and soul.

In the 1500s, a secular trend began that is evident in modern philosophy as well as contemporary culture. There is an increasing emphasis on the here and now, on understanding the material world and how bodies react to it. In the sixteenth and seventeenth centuries, Galileo, Newton, Descartes, and other philosophers developed new philosophies, including science, to try to better explain the material secular world. In the nineteenth and twentieth centuries, American philosophers developed transcendentalism, a philosophy that would "transcend" the limitations of the mind and body by focusing on experience. What these philosophies had in common was an attempt to explain our embodied experiences. Some began with mind, and some with the body, and some tried to transcend the distinction between the two. They all were concerned with our material existence and how to explain it.

Pragmatism, phenomenology, and existentialism can be seen in this light. These three philosophies seek answers to profound and abstract questions such as these: What is the nature of the material world? What is the nature of consciousness and awareness in the material world? How does the awareness of movement fit into this picture?

The transition from Plato to more modern philosophies was not smooth.[34] Over the centuries, philosophers developed radically different metaphysical positions to describe the rules that govern human experiences and to explain the relationship of ideas and matter, of minds and bodies. There has always been a problem with metaphysical dualism, though. Philosophies that emphasize the mind cannot adequately explain the relationship of the body. The same is true for philosophies that emphasize the body: They cannot adequately explain the relationship of the mind.

In the last 170 years, philosophers have argued that the assumption of metaphysical dualism that philosophers begin with actually causes many of the problems philosophers try to solve. Again, dualism argues that reality is composed of two parts: matter—the material, physical world—and ideas—the realm of the mind and soul. By rejecting this assumption, contemporary philosophies "unify" the mind and body. With respect to the fields of kinesiology and physical education, a philosophy that unifies the mind and body will place a greater value on physical activity than will a dualistic philosophy that emphasizes the superiority of the mind over the body. Having noted this, we must contend that educational philosophy in the West currently elevates the education of the mind over that of the body. Were your high school physical education classes used to determine your GPA for admission to college? Why or why not?

Philosophies of the Modern World

We will describe several modern philosophies in some detail, as they represent some of the most recent attempts to explain our physical experiences. The philosophies we discuss developed in the twentieth century in the West (in Europe and the United States) and are based on a monist, not dualist, view of reality. These philosophies value the body as well as the mind. Thus, monist philosophies such as pragmatism, existentialism, and phenomenology view human beings as an integrated whole. Mind and body are not separate components; rather, both are part of the same thing—a person—and what is valued is the whole person. These philosophies are rooted in the assumption that knowledge does not exist only in the mind or only in the body, but exists in the entire person. The focus of these philosophies is on the different ways a person experiences reality.

Pragmatism

Pragmatism is one of the first philosophies to reject metaphysical dualism. In the late 1800s and early 1900s, pragmatists argued that humans' physical experiences, and therefore the body, are where they begin to come to know reality. Pragmatists also argued that humans are embodied entities. By embodiment, pragmatists mean that the mind, or spirit, is of the body, and that mind and body are integrated into one entity.[35] As Carolyn Thomas argued,

Pragmatism was the first position to view the body as having value in and of itself [existential value] rather than just serving the mind. The idea that all knowledge is based on experience of a person suggests an integration of mind and body. This testifies to the value of the body as a source of knowledge.[36]

The philosophy of pragmatism evolved from the desire to do two things: (1) to determine the differences between the many philosophies developed in the preceding 2500 years and (2) to develop a practical method for dealing with the social unrest generated by the rapid changes in American society. Consequently, pragmatism can be seen as a philosophical response to changes (urbanization, industrialization, and so on) that occurred earlier in the nineteenth century. As philosopher Philip Smith noted,

> Old ways [philosophies] were unable to deal with this situation. The result was that people found themselves in a vacuum on many significant matters, matters that were of intellectual as well as practical concern. The progressive movement originally gained in public support because it appeared to fill this void on both counts. And, truly, it was suited for the American scene. Born and bred in the United States, it had none of the shortcomings of imported schemes from Europe. From the start it was designed to reintegrate American culture, and by 1900 had been finely fitted out specifically for this purpose.[37]

The importance of pragmatism as a philosophy in American culture, or, perhaps more boldly, the philosophy *of* American culture, cannot be overestimated. Pragmatism evolved at the same time as, and was a product of, the demographic, technological, and philosophical influences previously described. It was also a product of one of the most powerful scientific advances of all time, the seminal work on genetics of Charles Darwin. The value of Darwin's work to physical education may not be obvious at first, yet his influence on the modern mind is widely recognized in historical and philosophical circles. In short, Darwin revolutionized thinking by arguing that biological

systems—specifically, our bodies—are the response to some change in the environment. Consequently, the moving human body can be seen as a response to a changing environment.

With pragmatism, the possibility of studying the human body, and any other aspect of the human condition, becomes much easier. We can create knowledge of how the body functions under physiological stress and what physical forces shape the body and control movement, and use all other methods of science to understand human movement.

Existentialism

The beginnings of existentialism and phenomenology can be traced to Søren Kierkegaard (1813–1855). For well over a century, the philosophy of Kierkegaard was largely unknown outside Scandinavia because of the inability of most English-speaking people to read Danish. Kierkegaard's philosophy, like that of George Berkeley, argued for the existence of God. Kierkegaard suggested that religion would be useless if we had the capacity to reason our way back to God. That is, God would no longer be omnipotent, the supreme creator, if all knowledge could be completely understood and comprehended by humans.

The essence of his philosophy rests on the belief that there are three stages of life experience: (1) aesthetic, (2) ethical, and (3) religious. Kierkegaard's existentialism argued that some of us will progress from one stage to the next, whereas others will remain in the first stage forever. The third stage, however, is superior to the first two. For Kierkegaard, all three stages reflected the attempt to win salvation and achieve satisfaction or "life's greatest good, while it remains in reach to be all you can be in an individual sense." What makes Kierkegaard an existentialist was his emphasis on life experience as a means of saving the soul. This emphasis distinguished him from previous philosophers who first considered the essence of the soul and from this understanding of soul determined how people should live their mortal life.

Shortly after Kierkegaard's philosophy became known, Friedrich Wilhelm Nietzsche

(1844–1900) argued that the transcendent ideals of Judeo-Christian ethics, and thus the position of Kierkegaard, were nonsense. In a sense, Nietzsche began with Kierkegaard's emphasis on existence but abandoned Kierkegaard's quest for knowing the Christian soul. Nietzsche argued that science "proved" that there is no spirit or such things as God and sought a reworking of all existing values. Nietzsche asserted that the Judeo-Christian system of morality, developed over centuries of Western civilization, had given way to the forces of materialistic, modern culture.[38] A new system of morality was needed to replace it—one that emphasized the values found in nature.

Most historians have concluded that Nietzsche was a proponent of Darwin. Dirk R. Johnson (2010) does not believe there is a convergence in their thinking. Johnson credits Darwin for influencing Nietzsche's philosophy but also notes the antagonistic nature of their relationship to the point when Nietzsche becomes, more or less, anti Darwinian.[38A] Both Darwin and Nietzsche believed that strenuous and extreme physical challenges would benefit the individual and the survival of the human race. (Figure 1-2) Nietzsche spoke in favor of maximal physical and intellectual development and the expression of animal, or natural, instincts. In *Thus Spake Zarathustra,* Nietzsche described the ideal man, the "Superman," whom he contrasted with the average man of the common herd.[39] The body, to Nietzsche, was a vital component of the Superman. Nietzsche described his Superman as one who is "beyond good and evil," who creates his own set of values and rejects other so-called moral frameworks based on, for instance, religion. Nietzsche has been criticized for his position, but usually by those who do not understand it. As Esar Shvartz argued,

> When read superficially, [Nietzsche] seems to be an extremist, an anti-Semite and a German nationalist. But for anybody who bothers to understand, his writings reveal that he was an anti-anti-Semite, an anti-German nationalist, and one of the most humane thinkers.[40]

Figure 1-2
Friedrich Nietzsche (1844–1900). Library of Congress; Bain News Service 1910.

The abandonment of religion as a means of knowing right and wrong implies an emphasis on one's physicality. Nietzsche's philosophical position advocated physical fitness as a priority, as a component of individualism and power. Nietzsche's general reasoning rested on the belief that the body occupies a central role relative to existence. Therefore, claimed Shvartz, Nietzsche can be described as the "philosopher of fitness."

In *The Will to Power,* Nietzsche argued that "the belief in the body is more fundamental than the belief in the soul. The latter arose from unscientific observations of the agonies of the body."[41] Consequently, Nietzsche advocated that bodily health should become a priority and be taken more seriously. According to Nietzsche, the greatest enjoyment of life is to be had by living dangerously, an approach that necessitates superb health. Nietzsche would have been a big fan of extreme sports and "over the top" physical challenges.

The following is a brief view of *existentialism* and how this philosophy might be used to approach physical education and sport:

1. Existentialism begins with the belief that the individual is at the center. Everything "outside" the individual is subordinate to, and evaluated by, the individual.

2. "Existence" precedes essence—the origin for the term "existentialism."[42] This means that each individual creates him- or herself through choices and experiences, and that a person is the sum of all his or her choices and experiences. For everything in the world that is outside the individual, essence precedes existence.

3. Every person should have full opportunities to make choices and decisions. Without the opportunity to make legitimate choices, the individual loses some of his or her existence.[43] Individuals will personally determine what value an activity or experience holds. With respect to sport, Harold Vanderzwaag argued that

> if any group proceeds to claim the values of sport, the individual has already lost some of his opportunity to make a decision. Values are specific to each individual, and they grow out of the experiences of each person. There are no eternal values so to speak. . . . Consequently, nothing could be worse than to require people to participate in sport.[44]

4. The individual is responsible for his or her actions and behavior. This freedom, however, does not allow the individual to ignore his or her responsibilities. The burden of responsibility that existentialism demands is enormous. Each person is responsible not only for him- or herself but for other people as well. "The responsibility for others does not mean dictating to others or attempting to limit their freedom in any way. It does mean that one's decisions will also influence and affect others."[45]

5. The focus on individualism necessitates a commitment to authenticity. The authentic individual is truly an individual, not one who seeks approval from others or who desires to conform to the dress, language, and destination of the "in crowd."

6. The concept of ambiguity is an essential component in understanding how existentialism operates. Abraham Kaplan argued that

> Existentialism emphasizes . . . possibilities. There must be alternative possibilities of action or choice would be meaningless; and there must be alternative possibilities of existence, or it would be predetermined by essence. This manifold of possibility gives meaning to the final basic existentialist category: ambiguity. . . . Choice is continuous as we go through life, and with each choice some possibilities vanish forever while others emerge for the next choice. We are continuously making something of life, but we can never make it out: life is inescapably ambiguous.[46]

Existential doctrine is highly individualistic and ambiguous, yet as Nietzsche stated, it demands that individuals "become who you are!" His philosophy is for the strong and courageous, yet he also advocated an extreme humanism. Nietzsche's existentialism is attractive to sport philosophers because it calls for "a doctrine of action, a refusal to surrender to human weaknesses and falsely human institutions, a call for excellence in every aspect of human endeavor."[47] Although not a systematic philosophy, existentialism demands that we take responsibility for our behavior and actions. Striving to perform at our best, refusing to concede defeat, and seeking complete victory are existential concepts embraced by Nietzsche and the vast majority of elite coaches and athletes.

Jean-Paul Sartre's (1905–1980) arguments illustrate the monistic view of being that is held by existentialists. In *Being and Nothingness*,

Sartre argued that there are three dimensions of the body:

1. The body as being-for-itself
2. The body as being-for-the-other
3. My body as body-known-by-the-other

Sartre's three dimensions of the body provide insight into the nature of movement and the manner in which bodies are viewed. They also distinguish between the body as object and the body as subject. When the body is viewed as an object, having its own laws and defined from the outside, it is difficult to connect or link the material body with a mind or consciousness that is personal and subjective.[48] However, when the body is experienced or lived on a personal/holistic level (treated not as an object), the subjective "being-for-itself" dimension manifests itself. The following quote summarizes existential thought on the mind-body relationship:

> In the objective mode, I have a body, I train it, I use it, and in this regard "IT" can be viewed as separate from me. But this same body in the subjective mode means that I am my body and that my consciousness is embodied, or integrated, in this subjectivity.[49]

Phenomenology

Phenomenology, like existentialism, can be described as a tool or method that can be used to gain insights into questions that arise from "being in the world."[50] As a movement, phenomenology can be traced back to the works of Franz Brentano (1838–1917) and Carl Stumpf (1848–1936). Perhaps the originator of phenomenology was Edmund Husserl (1859–1938). In addition, a number of Husserl's students who fled to the United States to escape Hitler's Germany in World War II helped introduce and spread phenomenology throughout the country.

Husserl was interested in epistemology, the study of how we come to know things. He concluded that current epistemological beliefs, including the methods of science, are not valid. It was Husserl's contention, noted Seymour Kleinman, that

the immediate phenomenon, that which is directly given to us in experience, has been largely ignored by the traditional empiricism of contemporary science. Husserl called for a return to the things themselves. Thus, phenomenology began as a protest which called for a departure from crystallized beliefs and theories handed down by a tradition which only too often perpetuates preconceptions and prejudgements.[51]

Phenomenology, like existentialism, is not comfortable with "preconceptions and prejudgements," because these beliefs and values have been predetermined, preventing the individual from deciding these things for him- or herself.

From a metaphysics/monistic standpoint, the body is viewed as the means of fundamental access to the world, the instrument of communication with the world.[52] The body is not an instrument of the mind or the enemy of reason, but is the individual's avenue to worldly experience and related knowledge. The phenomenologist's view of the body is similar to that of the empiricist but goes further in that the quality of mind comes into play:

> The empiricists would explain that the reason one becomes aware of himself, or others, is due to a constant stream of data being delivered to the sense organs of the body. The phenomenologist, however, sees no reason to restrict himself to sense data alone. His [the phenomenologist's] experience of the phenomenon itself tells him that there is more involved than that [sense data]. . . . Every experience comes loaded with meanings and qualities, none of which can be explained by a sense organ's reception of stimulus. It is the task of phenomenology to deepen and enlarge the range of immediate experience, which we see to be much richer than the limited empirical view of it, i.e., experience.[53]

The objective of phenomenology is to go directly to the experience and relish it for what it is. What the experience represents will be decided by each individual. Because each of us experiences things and events differently, our feelings about and knowledge and understanding of a particular event or experience will in all probability vary greatly, even if several people engage in the same activity simultaneously. To the phenomenologist, you are your body, and your body is your "being in the world."[54]

From a phenomenological viewpoint, the body and the world of experiences available to the physical/athletic individual have value. There is no need to justify or defend bodily, physical experiences and whatever attendant epistemological outcomes are revealed through human movement. The body becomes a source of knowledge and personal growth, not an enemy of reason and a hindrance to knowledge as depicted in some dualistic philosophies. Kleinman continued:

> For the phenomenologist, to understand the body is to see the body not in terms of kinesiological analysis, but in the awareness and meaning of movement. . . . Movement becomes significant not by knowledge about the body, but through an awareness of the self. . . . From the phenomenological view, it becomes

the purpose of the physical educator to develop, encourage, and nurture this awareness of, and openness of, self—this understanding of self.[55]

Phenomenology and existentialism offer physical educators the opportunity to promote subjective experiences that can enhance the human condition. This can be contrasted to traditional physical education programs that many times encourage conformity. In so doing, coaches and teachers can overcome the prevailing philosophical ethos that encourages and promotes conformity and reliability at the expense of responsibility. The key question seems to be this: Are there components of existentialism and phenomenology compatible with the activities and purposes of physical education and athletic competition? Put another way, can some of the beliefs of existentialism and phenomenology contribute to the betterment of physical education and sport? The answer to these questions would appear to be yes. To some extent, these philosophies may be used to help us improve and better understand our sport and physical education experiences.

SUMMARY

We first defined the terms *sport, play,* and *games.* These concepts, so commonly used in contemporary culture, have many different meanings. An agreement on what these words and concepts mean is necessary prior to doing any type of history or philosophy.

We then defined history to be the study of change over time and described the type of history that we will be doing. We also described some of the people, events, times, and places important to our understanding of history. We examined how history has moved from pre-modern to modern characteristics, how moving to the city and coming to rely on technology has changed sport and physical education, and how various cultures have viewed the nature of being and how these views have had an impact on sport and physical education. We discussed briefly the process of "doing" philosophy and, in so doing, introduced to you the idea that a critical examination of history can help reveal how and why changes have occurred or not occurred in sport and physical education.

Pragmatism, existentialism, and phenomenology represent three of the more powerful philosophical movements of the nineteenth and twentieth centuries, but they are not the only movements. Logical positivism; Eastern philosophies such as Zen Buddhism, Confucianism, and Taoism; constructivism; deconstruction; and other philosophies are having an impact on Western civilization as we move further into the twenty-first century. The effects of these philosophies on contemporary attitudes toward the mind and body, and on sport and physical education, are reshaping the types of experiences all of us will have in human movement activities. What seems to be the common thread during the last hundred years is the theme of the unified mind and body, a monistic view of human experiences that include sport and play.

These additions to the philosophical movements that are in place illustrate how quickly the contemporary world is changing. Rather than a single philosophy that will explain the mind-body relationship and a single approach to sport and physical education, there seem to be an increasing number of philosophical explanations. What we can expect, then, are even more changes in the future. As twenty-first century culture becomes more diverse, there will be more explanations for this diversity. What will remain consistent is the desire of these many cultures, in their many ways, to explain in a philosophical way how their playful activities have changed over time and how they benefit cultural norms and expectations.

The primary reason for presenting the information in this chapter, and the entire text, is to impress upon physical education and kinesiology students the revealing insights that history and philosophy provide into our discipline. Physical education and sport have a rich heritage that spans thousands of years. The exploits of male and female athletes captured the attention of tens of thousands of fans in the ancient world in the same way that the feats of modern athletes leave us yearning for more. To study the scope and stature of sport and physical education through the medium of history and philosophy will enrich your personal and professional lives. After all, how many events have withstood the test of time as well as the Olympic Games? Which mere mortals have been glorified as much as athletes? Throughout history, what were the justifications that required men and women to develop such superb, aesthetically pleasing physiques? These and many other discussions are presented in this book. We believe you will find that the study of history and philosophy of physical education and sport is well worth the effort.

DISCUSSION QUESTIONS

1. How is sport different from play? How are these two different from physical education?

2. What is the difference between an interpretive history and a descriptive history? What makes interpretive history subjective?

3. What makes traditional philosophies different from those developed in the nineteenth and twentieth centuries? How does this have an impact on sport and physical education?

4. Given the trends in the United States since the 1800s, what might be the trend for sport in the twenty-first century with respect to the mind and body?

5. To what extent might modern fans and athletes relate to their counterparts in the ancient world?

6. To what extent has philosophy focused on the relationship between the mind and body?

7. There is enormous interest among scholars across many disciplines relative to the study of sport and physical education. Why do you think these topics receive so much attention?

8. Do you agree with Nietzsche's philosophy? Why or why not?

9. To what extent, if any, have existentialism and phenomenology influenced your philosophical beliefs of exercise and athletic competition?

10. Is there any truth to the concept that the study of philosophy is the study of what we believe about beliefs?

11. To what extent do philosophy and theology differ? What do they have in common?

INTERNET RESOURCES

Heldref Publications: Historical Methods Journal
www.heldref.org/hm.php
Contains *Historical Methods: A Journal of Quantitative and Interdisciplinary History* and other related social science journals; is a good source for information from the perspective of quantitative and interdisciplinary history research.

Research Methods Resources on the Web
www.slais.ubc.ca/resources/research_methods/
    history.htm

An excellent site developed by the School of Library, Archival, and Information Studies at the University of British Columbia; features methods utilized in historical research, as well as related links.

Historical Approach to Research
www.gslis.utexas.edu/~palmquis/courses/
    historical.htm
Provides explanations of how historical research is conducted, as well as excellent links to related sites.

Philosophical Terms and Methods
www.princeton.edu/~jimpryor/general/vocab
Provides terms and vocabulary utilized in philosophy, as well as an excellent discussion about how to argue using methods of philosophy.

Philosophical Method
**www.fact-index.com/p/ph/philosophical_
method.html**
Introduces readers to methods of philosophical inquiry.

Pragmatism Cybrary
www.pragmatism.org
Discusses pragmatism and provides an extensive set of links.

American Philosophy: Pragmatism
www.radicalacademy.com/amphilosophy7.htm
Provides good sources for discussions about pragmatism and other philosophical schools and philosophers.

Critical Thinking Community
www.criticalthinking.org
Includes resources and forums related to critical thinking.

Ayn Rand Institute and the Ayn Rand Society
www.aynrand.org
www.aynrandsociety.org
Presents the philosophy, writings, and ideas of Ayn Rand.

A Historiography of American Sport
www.oah.org/pubs/magazine/sport/riess.html
Contains an excellent article by Steven A. Reiss reprinted from the *Magazine of History,* published by the Organization of American Historians.

Visit the *History and Philosophy of Sport and Physical Education* Online Learning Center (www.mhhe.com/mechikoff6e) for additional information and study tools.

SUGGESTIONS FOR FURTHER READING

Hyland, D. A. *Philosophy of Sport.* (New York: Paragon House Publishers, 1990).

Kleinman, S. "Pragmatism, Existentialism, and Phenomenology." In *Physical Education: An Interdisciplinary Approach,* ed. Robert Singer et al. New York: Macmillan, 1972.

Kretchmar, R. S. *Practical Philosophy of Sport and Physical Activity,* 2nd ed. (Champaign, IL: Human Kinetics Publishers, 2005).

Ousterhoudt, R. C. *Sport as a Form of Human Fulfillment: An Organic Philosophy of Sport History.* (Victoria, BC, Canada: Trafford Publishing, 2006).

Selleck, G. *Raising a Good Sport in an In-Your-Face World: Seven Steps to Building Character on the Field—and Off.* (St. Louis: McGraw-Hill, 2002).

Shvartz, E. "Nietzsche: A Philosopher of Fitness." *Quest,* Monograph VIII (May 1967).

Singer, R. N., P. R. Lamb, J. W. Loy, R. M. Malina, and S. Kleinman. *Physical Education: An Interdisciplinary Approach.* New York: Macmillan, 1972.

Thomas, C. E. *Sport in a Philosophic Context.* Philadelphia: Lea & Febiger, 1983.

Vanderzwaag, H. J. *Toward a Philosophy of Sport.* Reading, Mass.: Addison-Wesley, 1972.

NOTES

1. George Santayana, "The Life of Reason," quoted in J. T. English, *A Garden Book of Profundities, Atticisms, and Smartaleck Sayings,* 9th ed. (Tacoma, WA: School of Education, University of Puget Sound, 1905), 60; Thought-of-the-Day archives at www.refdesk.com.

2. Brian Sutton-Smith, *The Folkgames of Children* (Austin: University of Texas Press for the American Folklore Society, 1972).

3. Jacques Barzun, "God's Country and Mine," quoted in English, *A Garden Book of Profundities, Atticisms, and Smartaleck Sayings,* 5.

4. Johan Huizinga, *Homo Ludens: A Study of the Play-Element in Culture* (Boston: Beacon Press, 1955).

5. R. Caillois, *Man, Play, and Games* (New York: Free Press, 1961).

6. Sutton-Smith, *Folkgames of Children.*

7. J. Levy, *Play Behavior* (New York: John Wiley, 1978). See also John Charles, *Contemporary Kinesiology: An Introduction to the Study of Human Movement in Higher Education* (Englewood Cliffs, NJ: Morton, 1994), 63.

8. L. P. Ager, "The Reflection of Cultural Values in Eskimo Children's Games," in D. Calhoun, *Sport, Culture, and Personality* (Champaign, IL: Human Kinetics, 1987), 47.

9. Calhoun, *Sport, Culture, and Personality.*

10. Betty Spears and Richard Swanson, *History of Sport and Physical Education in the United States,* 3rd ed. (Dubuque, IA: Championship Books/Wm. C. Brown, 1988), 1. A number of sport historians have researched nineteenth- and twentieth-century boxing. Excellent work can be found in the following journal articles: Andrew M. Kaye, "Battle Blind: Atlanta's Taste for Black Boxing in the Early Twentieth Century," *Journal of Sport History* 28, no. 2 (2001): 217–32; Dennis Brailsford, "Morals and Maulers: The Ethics of Early Pugilism," *Journal of Sport History* 12, no. 2 (1985): 126–42; and David K. Wiggins, "Peter Jackson and the Elusive Heavyweight Championship: A Black Athlete's Struggle against the Late Nineteenth Century Color-Line," *Journal of Sport History* 12, no. 2 (1985): 143–68.

11. Charles, *Contemporary Kinesiology,* 149–50.

12. George H. Sage, *Power and Ideology in American Sport* (Champaign, IL: Human Kinetics, 1990), 25–26.

13. R. J. Park, "Sport History in the 1990's: Prospects and Problems," in *American Academy of Physical Education Papers,* vol. 20, pp. 96–108 (Champaign, IL: Human Kinetics, 1987), 96.

14. For a provocative definition/explanation of the genesis of Greek sport, see David Sansone, *Greek Athletics and the Genesis of Sport* (Berkeley: University of California Press, 1988). In this brief but illuminating book, Sansone rejects the approaches and ideas of many scholars, arguing that sport must be defined as the ritual sacrifice of physical energy. The key concept seems to be that the fundamental nature of sport—its essence—is that of a sacrificial ritual. He rejects the widely accepted interpretations about the origin of sports in ancient Greece and makes a profound statement that there is no significant difference between modern sport and the type of sport that earlier cultures participated in. Since modernization theory looks upon history as how things changed, or did not change, over time, Sansone's thesis is quite controversial.

15. N. Struna, "Sport History," in *The History of Exercise and Sport Science,* eds. John Massengale and Richard Swanson (Champaign, IL: Human Kinetics, 1996).

16. Michael Oriard, *Reading Football: How the Popular Press Created an American Spectacle* (Chapel Hill: University of North Carolina Press, 1993).

17. J. Thomas Jable, "The Types of Historical Research for Studying Sport History," in *Getting Started in the History of Sport and Physical Education,* ed. William H. Freeman (Washington, DC: History of Sport and Physical Education Academy, 1980), 13–14.

18. Melvin Adelman, *A Sporting Time: The Rise of Modern Sport in New York City, 1820–70* (Champaign: University of Illinois Press, 1986).

19. Ibid.

20. John R. Betts, *America's Sporting Heritage: 1850–1950.* (Reading, MA: Addison-Wesley, 1974), 31–32.

21. S. Estes, "Knowledge and Kinesiology," *Quest* 46, no. 4 (1994): 392–409.

22. For a wonderful discussion of the assumptions that undergird science and how science is used in kinesiology, see R. Martens, "Science, Knowledge, and Sport Psychology," *The Sport Psychologist* 1 (1987): 29–55.

23. Religion, by definition, is a creation of God, but it can be discussed using the rational methods of philosophy.

24. See Thomas Kuhn, *The Structure of Scientific Revolutions,* 2nd ed. (Chicago: University of Chicago Press, 1970). Kuhn argued that scientific *paradigms* change over time, reflecting that what various cultures identify as "knowledge" changes over time as well.

25. Perhaps the best-known example of this, and one of the first, was that of Thomas Aquinas, who tried to reconcile the methods of philosophy with the dogmas of the Catholic Church.

26. R. Martens, "Science, Knowledge, and Sport Psychology," *The Sport Psychologist* 1 (1987): 29–55.

27. For example, sociology and political science can objectively analyze and investigate the Nazi Holocaust using the methods of science. However, because the doctrine of science does not recognize value judgments, a strict scientific perspective would reject approving or disapproving of Hitler's policies. Instead, scientists would focus on the consequences of his policies in terms of lives lost, atrocities committed, and so on. Many scholars disagree, however, with this strict approach to studying social phenomena. Many sociologists now argue that there is no such thing as "value-free" research and instead try to place their values in perspective by alerting the reader to them.

28. Plato, *The Republic,* trans. Desmond Lee (London: Penguin Books, 1987). In terms many of us might be more comfortable with, Plato defined "reality" to be something like "heaven." This "reality" is where ideas are perfect and where souls have perfect knowledge.

29. This situation seems absurd to us in modern times, but it was not as far-fetched in Plato's time. The wars that occurred in his life taught him that humans can be incredibly brutal.

30. The other two philosophers considered "founding fathers" were Thales (624–546 B.C.) and Anazimenes (585–528 B.C.).

31. Estes, "Knowledge and Kinesiology."

32. J. R. Fairs, "The Influence of Plato and Platonism on the Development of Physical Education in Western Culture," *Quest* 11 (1968): 12–23.

33. Ibid.

34. Note that we are using a *very* broad brush in painting all philosophers in an era as having the same metaphysical views. We recognize that there were philosophers who rejected the dominant philosophies of their time, as there are now. The philosophies we select are those that seem to be good representatives of cultural attitudes toward mind and body, as well as recognized philosophies in Western civilization.

35. Carolyn E. Thomas, *Sport in a Philosophic Context* (Philadelphia: Lea & Febiger, 1983), 31.

36. Ibid., 32–33.

37. Philip Smith, *Sources of Progressive Thought in American Education* (Lanham, MD: University Press of America, 1981), 4–5.

38. See Alasdair MacIntyre, *After Virtue: A Study in Moral Theory* (Notre Dame, IN: University of Notre Dame Press, 1981).

38a. Dirk R. Johnson, Nietzsche's anti-Darwinism. (New York: Cambridge University Press, 2010), 240.

39. Esar Shvartz, "Nietzsche: A Philosopher of Fitness," *Quest,* Monograph VIII (May 1967): 83.

40. Ibid.

41. Friedrich Nietzsche, *The Will to Power* (London: T. N. Foulis, 1913), 18.

42. Harold J. Vanderzwaag, *Toward a Philosophy of Sport* (Reading, MA: Addison-Wesley, 1972), 211.

43. Ibid.

44. Ibid., 212.

45. Ibid.

46. Abraham Kaplan, *The New World of Philosophy* (New York: Random House, 1961), 117.

47. Schvartz, "Nietzsche."

48. Seymour Kleinman, "Pragmatism, Existentialism, and Phenomenology," in *Physical Education: An Interdisciplinary Approach,* ed. Robert Singer et al. (New York: Macmillan, 1972), 353.

49. Thomas, *Sport in a Philosophic Context,* 34–35.

50. Kleinman, "Pragmatism," 352.

51. Ibid.

52. Ibid., 352–53.

53. Ibid.

54. Thomas, *Sport in a Philosophic Context,* 34.

55. Kleinman, "Pragmatism," 355.

CHAPTER 2

Sumer, Egypt, China, and Mesoamerica

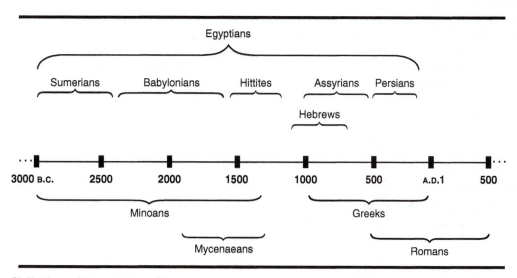

Civilizations of the ancient world.

OBJECTIVES

Upon completing this chapter, you will be able to:

■ Appreciate the cultural contributions of non-Western civilizations to society and the influence they had on the development of Western culture.

■ Appreciate the social and cultural significance of sport and physical activity in ancient Sumer, Egypt, China, and Mesoamerica.

■ Identify selected play, games, and sports that were unique to these ancient civilizations.

■ Identify similarities in play, games, and sports that were shared by these ancient civilizations.

General Events

Sumerian and Egyptian civilization contribute to beginnings of ancient Western world

Sumer, ancient civilization, established circa 4000 B.C.

Sumerians introduce cuneiform writing

Egyptian civilization established circa 3000 B.C.

Egyptians introduce writing in form of hieroglyphics

First of Egypt's thirty dynasties founded between 3200 and 3000 B.C. by Menes (also known as Narner)

As first pharaoh, Menes founds the city of Memphis

Period from 3100 to 2686 B.C. known as the Early Dynastic Period

With rise of Third Dynasty in 2700 B.C., ancient Egypt divided into three prominent historical eras and some lesser ones:
  1. Old Kingdom: 2700–2200 B.C.—great pyramids built
  2. Middle Kingdom: 2000–1800 B.C.—economic and political power solidified
  3. New Kingdom: circa 1600–1100 B.C.—peak of power reached

The Late Dynastic Period: 1085–341 B.C.

Egypt divided; Solomon's temple destroyed; Egypt invaded by Nubians and Assyrians

The Ptolemaic Period: 332–30 B.C.

Alexander the Great conquers Egypt

When Alexander dies, one of his generals establishes Ptolemaic Dynasty

China

Chinese civilization predates Christianity by about 2500 years

China's recorded history begins about 1500 B.C.

Over 2400 years, ten major dynasties rule China:
  Shang Dynasty: 1500–1000 B.C.
  Early Chou Dynasty: 1000–600 B.C.
  Late Chou Dynasty: 600 B.C.–A.D. 221
  Ch'in Dynasty: A.D. 221–206
  Han Dynasty: A.D. 206–220

■ Identify play, games, and sports that were established in these ancient cultures and that still are played in the modern world.

■ Understand the role, scope, and religious significance of ball games in these ancient cultures.

■ Appreciate the architectural venues that were built in Mesoamerica to accommodate athletic competitions.

■ Explain the link between sport and religion.

INTRODUCTION

Athletic ability, physical fitness, competition, and play have been a significant cultural component of civilization since the dawn of time. Civilizations that perished long ago, as well as those civilizations that still exist, share this characteristic. Historians, sociologists, archaeologists, and anthropologists who study our primitive ancestors and ancient civilizations have long noted the importance of physical ability and physical expression. It may manifest itself as play, dance, sport, or a means of survival. One conclusion that we may draw from these observations is that the quest for survival during ancient times—and modern times—was and is in some way facilitated in our desire to play. In modern times, this desire to play serves as a catalyst for the current emphasis on physical fitness and helps explain our cultural attitude toward sports.

It is arguable, then, that the human race evolved because, in part, our ability to adapt to our surroundings was facilitated by the playful characteristics manifest in human nature—our being. This play impulse is central to our ability to survive. During prehistoric times, dinosaurs ruled the earth. They were large and strong, had sharp fangs, ran fast, and were aggressive. These animals could not adapt to the changing environment and eventually became extinct. The English scientist Charles Darwin studied the evolution of plants and animals in the nineteenth century and popularized the phrase "survival of the fittest." Humans survived and, slowly but surely, grew stronger and faster with each successive generation. From the dawn of time to the present, humans, like any other species, competed against the elements and each other for survival. Contemporary sport reflects this Darwinian maxim as athletes strive to defeat their opponents and emerge victorious, whether it is against the clock, another individual, or another team. In doing so, they play out the contemporary version of learning life skills through play.

Initially, humans hunted for food as individuals, but soon they found it more effective to form groups and hunt as a team. Once again, humans adapted to the environment and survived. Perhaps the individual who stood out as the best hunter was admired by those around him for his skill and bravery, and the activities that served to make one a better hunter were in all probability playful activities that emulated hunting. During the prehistoric era, honor and respect were given to those who had the courage and athletic skills necessary to ensure victory over the elements. Each day was a contest for survival. Over time, the desire to survive, to compete for honor, and to claim victory has become a part of culture and is symbolized in many ways through games and sports.

Survival and the necessity to triumph over one's adversaries were prominent themes in ancient times, when the lands were ruled by kings, queens, pharaohs, emperors, warlords, and tyrants.

Warfare was a routine occurrence. As one group sought to exercise dominance over another for political, religious, or economic gain, it became necessary to form an army that would conquer the enemy. This required a rigorous and demanding physical training program that would produce warriors capable of defeating the enemy in hand-to-hand combat. This need for trained soldiers exists to the present day. In the twenty-first century, physical skills such as endurance running, wrestling, swimming, and other related fitness activities required for military combat are a curricular component of physical education programs for men and women during times of war and peace.

To repel invaders, cities formed military units. Soldiers throughout the ancient world received roughly the same types of training. Wielding weapons, wrestling, boxing, riding horses, driving chariots, and racing across rugged terrain on foot required the ancient warrior to be in superb physical shape and possess athletic abilities that would ensure his survival and the survival of his village or city.

As a consequence of the need for physical training, young men in the ancient world engaged in various combat sports, some of which are still evident in the modern world. These ancient sports manifest themselves in some of the events in track and field, wrestling and other martial arts, equestrian events, and dance. We know that the javelin throw originates from spear throwing contests and ancient warrior athletes engaged in footraces. In addition to spear-throwing contests and foot races, archery contests and boxing and wrestling competitions were popular in the ancient world. The opportunities for women to participate in sport and physical education in Sumer, Egypt, China, and Mesoamerica were considerably fewer than the opportunities available to men. Cultural and religious beliefs were major barriers that, more often than not, precluded women from participation in sport. It was not unusual for men to enter into competitions where women were among the prizes.

Combat sports remain popular today and can be found in physical education and sports programs in schools, colleges, and universities, as well as the Olympic Games. For example, the modern pentathlon was developed to promote military skills needed in the late nineteenth and early twentieth centuries. In the 1912 Olympiad held in Stockholm, Sweden, a young U.S. army officer named George S. Patton, Jr., placed fifth. He would later achieve fame as a tank commander and highly decorated General in World War II.

Although combat sports have their genesis in ancient civilizations, they have endured and remain a significant activity in modern culture. Why have these ancient sports remained such a significant part of our culture? Perhaps

Three Kingdoms Dynasty: A.D. 220–265
Western Chin Dynasty: A.D. 265–316
Northern and Southern Dynasties: A.D. 316–589
Sui Dynasty: A.D. 589–618
T'ang Dynasty: A.D. 618–907

it is because we still possess the innate need to persist and persevere, to compete against each other, to prove that we can survive. The characteristics used to ensure the survival of individuals and their culture live on in these competitive sporting situations. However, the reason these contests and games endure may not be solely because they teach survival skills.

The children who lived long ago were not much different from those of today. They played ball games, amused themselves with dolls, wrestled, and enjoyed rough-and-tumble activities. While the need to ensure our survival, to compete, to emerge victorious, and to play is a common thread woven through all civilizations, past and present, there may be other explanations about the nature of play. Perhaps Johan Huizinga, who defined play in his classic work *Homo Ludens,* is right: The reason we play and partake in games is that we enjoy it; it is fun.

After reading Section I, ask yourself how much (if any) the direction of sport and physical education has changed in comparison with the way it was practiced several thousand years ago. Do you think the recent phenomenon of extreme sport would have appealed to the athletes and fans of the ancient world? As you read the chapters to come, think about what lies at the core of our desire to compete or attend events where physical and athletic prowess is displayed.

To introduce you to some of the salient historical and philosophical themes that have shaped sport and physical education throughout the ages, we will examine other modes of thought and philosophical positions present in the ancient non-Western world. In addition to information about sport and physical activities in the non-Western world, we will also discuss sport and culture in Mesoamerica, especially the ball games and venues where the games were contested.

SUMER

The Sumerians lived in an area historians identify as Mesopotamia; we know it today as Iraq. Geographically, Iraq is situated in the Middle East.

Mesopotamia is known as the "cradle of civilization" because, over 5000 years ago, the Sumerians created the world's first known civilization. The Babylonians and the Assyrians also established great cities in this region. Mesopotamia was situated between two great rivers, the Tigris and the Euphrates. Like the inhabitants of present-day Iraq, the inhabitants of Mesopotamia endured a climate that was very hot and dry. There are numerous references to Mesopotamia in the Old Testament. The prophet Jeremiah said of this land, "Her cities are in desolation, a dry land, and a wilderness, a land wherein no man dwelleth, neither doth any son of man pass thereby."[1] Today, the ruins of Sumer, Babylonia, and Assyria are buried in the harsh desert of the Middle East. Archaeologists work to uncover these civilizations that perished long ago, but it remains "a dry land, and a wilderness . . . wherein no man dwelleth."

The Sumerians developed cuneiform writing, which revolutionized the way people communicated. The age-old practice of committing ideas, conversations, and records to memory was replaced with a written form of record. Researchers have uncovered thousands of inscribed clay tablets written in the wedged-shape cuneiform style, and these records—primary sources for doing history—reveal a great deal about life in ancient Sumer. There were proclamations by Sumerian kings, inventories of the contents of merchants' holdings, literary works, and admonitions to wayward sons (some things never change).[2]

The various cultures in Mesopotamia used religion to explain the mysteries of life and to define what it meant to be human. In this regard, not much has changed. The Sumerians believed that the universe was created by powerful and immortal gods. Initially, it was understood that the gods created men as servants—to serve the gods. Men were at the mercy of these gods, and their only purpose in life was to obey the commands of the gods. Vera Olivova notes that this particular view of the world, as seen though the eyes of ancient Mesopotamian cultures, helped to establish the religious beliefs of the Jews, Christians, and Muslims.[3] Change is inevitable, and this was the case with religion in Mesopotamia. As time passed, the rulers found reasons to break free from complete subordination to the gods, and instead of serving these gods, the rulers became representatives of the gods. As more time passed, the rulers became affiliated with the gods, a much better situation than being a representative of the gods. In this context, the mortal rulers believed they were "kings" of the earth. To solidify this position, an annual wedding was established, a sacred event that married the kings to the goddess Inanna. This sacred ritual secured the position of the mortal kings with the immortal gods. As a result of religious beliefs and custom, the great civilizations of Mesopotamia believed that only gods and kings had a right to express their individuality; ordinary people were of no value and so were expendable. This is not to say that the Sumerians lacked a high level of civilization. Archaeologists have uncovered the ruins of magnificent cities replete with beautiful temples and palaces. These ancient people built an infrastructure and paid attention to hygiene by constructing sewer systems and drains.

Given the Sumerian belief that ordinary humans had no value, it should not come as a surprise to learn that their philosophical view of the body was negative. If ordinary people had no value, the body certainly did not have value. But what about the kings? How did they rationalize their corporeal existence? The kings married the goddess Inanna each year, which removed them from the realm of mere mortals—they were "god-like" and had value. Their physical presence was elevated over that of mere mortals and had a spiritual quality. Kings were portrayed in art as larger than life, but the human body was rarely the subject of a sculptor or artist. According to Olivova, "Nakedness expressed humiliation and subjection. . . . A naked woman's body was even less often depicted and the Greek historian Herodotus tells us that it was typical of the people of the Near East to be ashamed to be seen naked, men as well as women."[4]

Although the body as the subject of art was of minimal interest, the Sumerians did pay attention to the body in matters of personal hygiene. Ancient artifacts show them bathing, washing clothes, and washing their hands. The kings enjoyed the riches of their office and lived in luxury. These rulers enjoyed the company of many beautiful women and indulged themselves in pools filled with fragrant oils and perfumes. Physical beauty was an asset in a king and was coveted by heirs. However, it was not the naked body that was beautiful; it was how the king was adorned. Beautiful clothes were essential for the kings of this era, and a handsome face was important as well. Kings paid attention to their appearance, and the women of the palace used perfumes to smell good and colored powders to highlight their eyes—has anything changed? Kings participated in sports reserved for royalty while the ordinary people found time to engage in the "blue-collar" sports and pastimes of the day.

The city of Sumer was surrounded by villages, and an intricate economic and political system developed. Trade, travel, and entertainment were routine activities, as was warfare. The struggle to retain and extend power was important to the people of Sumer. As a result, skill as a warrior was important, and skill was largely dependent upon athletic ability and physical fitness. One of the most famous Sumerian kings was Gilgamesh, believed to have ruled in the twenty-seventh century B.C. Legends have been uncovered about this man that relate epic feats: He slays lions, leads his armies into battle where he kills many of the enemy and triumphs over superhuman opponents. There is some speculation that Gilgamesh may have been the model for the Greek hero Herakles.[5]

Not to be outdone by Gilgamesh was the Assyrian warrior-king Assurbanipal, who reigned over an empire in 7 B.C. that extended from present-day Egypt to Iran. He led his troops into battle and was quite a hunter. His palace was at Nineveh, where archaeologists have discovered many reliefs and sculptures, in addition to numerous odes and citations to his skill as a hunter and warrior:

> I am Assurbanipal, King of the universe, King of Assyria, for whom Assur, King of the Gods, and Ishtar, Lady of Battle, Have Decreed a Destiny of Heroism. . . . The God Nergal caused me to undertake every form of hunting

on the plain, and according to my pleasure . . . I went forth. . . . On the plain savage lions, fierce creatures of the mountains rose against me. The young of the lions thrived in countless numbers. . . . They grew ferocious through their devouring of herds, flocks, and people. . . . In my sport I seized . . . a fierce lion of the plain by his ears. With the aid of Assur and Ishtar . . . I pierced his body with my lance.[6]

This inscription reveals more than a king with an ego; it demonstrates the ritual connection that religion had with sport, one that existed into the 1800s: "The God Nergal caused me to undertake every form of hunting." Sport and spirituality will be frequently connected until sport becomes "modern" and is governed by attitudes based more on reason than ritual. In a relief that illustrates the rituals of a lion hunt, King Assurbanipal is depicted wearing a ceremonial robe and pouring wine over the dead lions. Apparently, the king is able to

exhibit his strength and virtue by removing the forces of evil (lions).

The archaeological evidence obtained from sites in Mesopotamia indicate that lions were a constant menace to the safety of the inhabitants. As sensational an athlete as King Assurbanipal appears to have been (Figure 2-1), one Assyrian king who preceded Assurbanipal must have been a better hunter because he claimed to have killed 1,000 lions![7] Lion hunting was a popular sport for the rulers. There were armies of huntsmen who accompanied the king because it was thought that lion hunting prepared men for the dangers and challenges of war. Bravery in battle was expected, and the lion hunts enabled the king and his officers to instill bravery and other virtues. The process of teaching courage and bravery was simple but harsh: Men were selected to form a circle around the lions to "fence them in" and prevent them from escaping. The king could then enter the area and

Figure 2-1
King Assurbanipal of Assyria demonstrating his skill as an archer and hunter by slaying a lion.

kill the trapped lions. It is not known how many men were mauled by lions attempting to escape. However, it seems logical that the men who survived this ordeal were indeed courageous. Or perhaps the really brave men were mauled while the others held back.

Archaeologists have discovered artifacts that provide evidence of sports and games during the Early Dynastic Period of Sumerian civilization (3000–1500 B.C.).[8] Artifacts that depict combat sports such as boxing and wrestling date from around 2000 B.C.[9] With the ever-present threat of war, it is understandable that combat sports existed and probably had many participants. The most well-known artifact of wrestling is a copper statuette of two figures, heads interlocked and hands gripping the belt on their opponent's hips.[10] On the head of each wrestler appears to be a large pot, and this has been the subject of much discussion. Some have maintained that the object of the contest was to knock the pot off the head of the opponent, while others say that the pots served as ornaments.

According to Maxwell Howell and Reet Howell, "Archaeological evidence related to warfare allows the sport historian to make inferences about the possibility of play activities. If an individual [Sumerian] is to master a chariot, it is easy to envision challenge races."[11] Within this context, we can also assume that there were contests in archery, running, swimming, and other sports that would help ensure one's survival in war.

The Sumerians also fished and boated extensively.[12] This practice was a necessity to put food on the table; however, it may have been a form of recreation as well. Board games also were played in Sumer. Gaming boards with drawers to hold the pieces[13] have been discovered in the royal graves at Ur. In addition to these board games, children's toys have been found in the form of toy chariots and boats.[14]

EGYPT

When we think of Egypt, we think of a vast country in the Middle East with pyramids, mummies, and giant statues. Egypt is a land that boasts an extensive

array of historical artifacts and enjoys a rich history. So prominent is the place of Egypt in the history of civilization that a significant part of the Old Testament of the Holy Bible is devoted to this land.

More than 10,000 years ago, people began to inhabit the land along the Nile River (Figure 2-2). Over time, the villages grew in number and the collective population began to prosper. Geography favored Egypt, as desert barriers ringed the Nile River valley, which discouraged invasion. In about 4000 B.C., Egypt emerged as a political and economic entity, ruled by pharaohs, that would last for the next twenty-seven centuries. According to Wolfgang Decker (1992), "Sports were a means by which the most famous Egyptian monarchs presented themselves to their people. . . . His obligatory and, in the ideal case, actual physical strength was that of a warrior, and a hunter as well as an athlete."[15]

And as Ahmed Touny explains,

There are numberless representations [sports] on tomb and temple walls, but none is more striking than the oldest document relating to sport. It is a unique mural, not only because of its historical date, but also through its social implications, for it depicts the Pharaoh himself, Zoser the Great, the founder of the third dynasty nearly 3,000 years before Christ. This mural shows Zoser participating in the running program of the Heb Sed festival, a symbol of the significance of physical fitness of the Ancient Egyptians. The artist has brought out, with a thorough knowledge of anatomy, the harmonious play of muscles. The positions of Zoser's arms, trunk and legs denote an expertise of technique and movement which only advanced development can achieve.[16]

Egyptian queens were no less aware of the importance of sports in the culture. On a wall of her sanctuary in the Karnak Temple, Queen Hatshepsut of the eighteenth dynasty had herself represented in a similar attitude in the Heb Sed festival. Hardly any of ancient Egypt's rulers during the thirty centuries under view failed to have themselves depicted as sporting figures in the

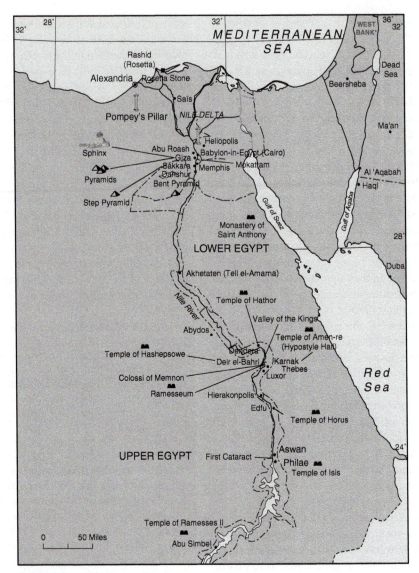

Figure 2-2
Ancient Egypt.

Heb Sed festivals, where athletic competition was the highlight of the event.[17]

Touny notes that even the most famous of the pharaohs, Seti and his son Ramses II, who fought Moses and eventually lost, are depicted as athletes in their temples located at Abydos and Abu Simbel, respectively. Touny also points out that it

is difficult to think of a sport which the Ancient Egyptians did not practice. The Benni Hasan rock tombs [ancient archaeological site] are a show place for most sports such as athletics [track and field], swimming, wrestling, dancing, gymnastics, hockey, yoga, and many others.[18]

To grasp the significance of Egyptian history, recognize that the ancient Greeks and Romans considered Egypt as "ancient." To explain how old Egyptian civilization actually is, Cleopatra (69–30 B.C.) is actually closer in time to us today than she was to the time when the great pyramids were built![18A] It was an established nation with grand palaces, monuments, and streets and thriving commerce a thousand years before the Minoans of Crete constructed their opulent palaces. It should be noted that while the Testament of the Holy Bible tells us that Moses would lead the Israelites out of Egypt nearly 900 years after Egypt became an imposing civilization. There is not much in the way of archaeology discoveries that support the Exodus. The Greek historian Herodotus toured Egypt in 5 B.C. and remarked on "wonders more in number than those of any other land."

The science of medicine may have its origins in Egypt. The ancient Egyptians used "magic" to cure disease because, they believed, sickness was more often than not delivered by the gods. However, their skill as doctors and surgeons was known throughout the ancient world. The Greek physicians Hippocrates, considered the "father of medicine," and Galen, whom some consider the "father of sports medicine," spoke about the work of the Egyptians.

Much of what we know about the ancient Egyptians and their lifestyle and sporting activities is revealed in the paintings found in tombs and in the countless artifacts that have been discovered. The paintings in the tombs (the wealthy and the nobility were the only ones who could afford such a grand burial place) portray their expectations of life in the next world, which reflected those activities that they engaged in when they were alive. Death was considered to be merely another journey for which they must prepare. To what extent does Judeo-Christian theology and other religions reflect this same belief?

The aristocracy enjoyed a life of luxury, and their tombs were elaborately furnished. Paintings depict wealthy Egyptians boating on the Nile, hunting fowl in the marshes, having picnics with their families, and enjoying beverages in the garden.[19] Interestingly, there is little evidence of ideas that reflected the beliefs of Hebrew ethics, Greek philosophy, or Roman law. The objective of the aristocracy in Egypt was to become "socialites" and gain power and influence in the court. Success was measured in a material manner; how much land individuals owned and how many cattle they could call their own were the standards of material success. The most important statement that a wealthy Egyptian could make was constructing an impressive tomb that would be the envy of Egyptian high society.

To a degree, the good life was available for most Egyptians to enjoy. The ancient Egyptians engaged in sports to train and strengthen their bodies, and also for pleasure and recreation. While the wealthy enjoyed festive parties in lavish surroundings, the less fortunate enjoyed life's little pleasures as well. Paintings show children engaged in playful activity while their parents worked the fields or engaged in other forms of commerce and trade. As well as a source of food, the Nile was the "highway" of Egypt. Skilled sailors navigated the Nile, moving people and commerce up and down the river to the great cities of Egypt. The Pharaoh Akhnaton (1352 B.C. to 1336 B.C.) started a royal regatta—a race between oarsmen, known as the Festival of the Oars. It took place on the Nile River. It is quite probable that this particular crew race was the beginning of the sport of competitive rowing. Swimming is an activity depicted in many paintings. It appears that it was a recreational activity; however, swimmers had to keep an eye out for the crocodiles who inhabited the area. The nobles did not have to worry about the crocodiles because it was not unusual for a member of the upper class to have his own swimming pool at home.

As advanced as Egyptian civilization was for its time, the demand for physical labor to build monuments, engage in trade and commerce, sustain agriculture, and provide for the defense was never-ending. The prevailing view among most historians is that thousands of slaves were used for the most difficult labors, such as working the mines and moving heavy stones for monuments or public buildings. However controversial, Egyptologist and archaeologist Dr. Zahi Hawass insist that Jewish slaves were not used per se to build the pyramids and other Egyptian monuments. Instead, Dr. Hawass claims that Egyptian citizens were used. It must be noted that Dr. Hawass is no friend of Israel and was very close to the former prime minister of Egypt, H. Mubarak who was arrested in 2011.

Away from the large cities, life was unusually harsh, and maintaining the health and vigor of individuals was necessary to ensure survival. Working the fields in the fertile Nile River valley required waking before dawn and getting as much work done as possible before midday, when the heat became unbearable. After the rest break, work resumed again until the evening. Each day was more or less the same—time moved in endless cycles, seasons following each other as they always had, in an endless, repeating pattern. Festivals and religious observations provided a break from the harsh demands of farming and fishing. Still, life was generally difficult, as can be seen in the following account of life in an Egyptian village thousands of years ago:

> Mice abound in the field, locusts descend and animals eat the crop. . . . What remains . . . is taken by thieves. The hire of oxen is wasted because the animals have died. . . . Then the scribe arrives at the riverbank . . . to register the tax on the harvest.[20]

Survival depended in large part on physical fitness, health, and luck.

Like the Sumerians, the Egyptians were superb warriors. Ancient documents reveal that when the time for war came, the pharaoh could mobilize the entire kingdom for battle. Scribes had records of soldiers; there were vast storehouses of food and armament. Conscription agents were sent into the land to draft men who were not yet on the rolls of the army scribes. Reserve soldiers were called up from their jobs and families to join the fight.

The following ancient account tells of the daily routine of an Egyptian soldier:

> Come, I will speak to you of the ills of the infantryman. He is awakened while there is still an hour for sleeping. He is driven like a jackass and he works until the sun sets beneath its darkness of night. He hungers and his belly aches. He is dead while he lives. But frightened and calling to his god, "come to me that you may rescue me," he fought. He fought with maces, daggers and spears on fields filled with charging chariots and bronze-tipped arrows.[21]

This account, written by a scribe long ago, stirs our imagination. To endure such harsh conditions and physical demands, the physical training of the Egyptian soldier had to be severe. In the event that a young boy aspired to be a soldier, he was removed from his family and placed in the barracks, where he was "pummeled with beatings." After completing the necessary training, he was allowed to live with his family between campaigns. The Egyptians also relied on foreign mercenaries and captured slaves to fill the ranks of the army.[22]

The young men of the aristocracy usually enlisted in the separately organized chariot corps. It was not unusual for a young, wealthy Egyptian man to show up with his own chariot, which he would take into battle. Contests among the chariot drivers enabled them to display their driving skills prior to battle.

The primary weapon of the Egyptian soldier was the bow and arrow and his foot speed. Skill as an archer was very important for personal survival, as well as assuring victory for the pharaoh. Archery contests were held to encourage young men to gain proficiency, but the contests were probably popular among the young men anyway. Archers were encouraged to be fit because of their place in the order of battle, and running contests pitted one archer against another. The archers, along with the chariot drivers, were the first wave to assault the enemy. The archers raced along with the speeding chariots and killed as many of the enemy as they could. They were followed by the infantry, who finished off the enemy in hand-to-hand combat. It is easy to understand why victory in combat sports was so important to the ancient Egyptians.

The Egyptians were excellent bookkeepers, and scribes accompanied the warriors on their campaigns. Their purpose was to record the quantities of sheep, cattle, oxen, or other spoils of war taken in battle. The Egyptian army severed the hand of a captured enemy soldier for each item recorded by a scribe. In this way, believed the Egyptians, an exact count of the spoils of war could be made. The spoils of war were dedicated to the god Amon.[23]

Although life was difficult for the Egyptians, they also knew how to enjoy themselves. Hunting was a popular sport among the Egyptians. The noblemen rode the countryside accompanied by trained hunting dogs to hunt gazelle and antelope. The peasants hunted also, but rarely for sport; it was a matter of survival. Skill with a bow and arrow was a means of securing food as well as warding off the enemy. Music, singing, and dancing were popular activities among all classes of Egyptians. Among the wealthy, feasts were a frequent occurrence, and musicians and dancers provided entertainment. Sometimes, wrestlers would provide entertainment during the initial phase of a feast, followed by dancing girls selected by the host from his harem. The dancers were skilled athletes and delighted the guests by performing acrobatic stunts, pirouettes, cartwheels, splits, somersaults, and backbends.[24] Archaeologists have uncovered tops, balls, dolls, hoops, marbles, and other assorted amusements still used by children the world over. Wrestling and "games of chance" such as dice were played. Ball games were especially popular among men and women of all ages.[25]

The ancient Egyptians were accomplished athletes, and sport played a prominent role in their culture. Touny believes that sport was not simply reduced to a recreational activity or used to train warriors. Rather, it was a serious aspect of Egyptian culture. They held competitions and organized championships, and they competed in international

events. They were proud that their officials, who worked the international contests, were impartial and held in the highest regard. Touny makes reference to a theory that the ancient Egyptians began the practice of holding international games on a regular basis at Akhmem in Upper Egypt. He also states that "it remains to be said that in Egypt, sport was born and flourished, and from there spread to Greece, Rome, and to the rest of the world."[26]

CHINA

The cultural history of China begins approximately 2500 years before the advent of Christianity. Like the Egyptians, the Chinese enjoy a rich history that predates Christianity. From the Shang Dynasty (1500–1000 B.C.) through the T'ang Dynasty (A.D. 618–907), China enjoyed the status of the most civilized and influential country in East Asia. During the T'ang Dynasty, it was not unusual to find that the standard of living and the level of cultural arts enjoyed by the Chinese surpassed those that existed in the West.[27] Archaeological evidence reveals that games and organized sport existed in China prior to the birth of Christ.[28]

The ancient Chinese political system was feudal, and a consequence of this situation was a divided China composed of city-states that continually fought one another. One object of contention was the water routes through the Yellow River valley and Yangtze River valley that fostered trade and commerce. Early Chinese leaders waged territorial wars and repelled "barbarians," meaning anyone who was not Chinese. Geographically, China is situated in the Far East.

Physical culture in China has been traced as far back as Peking Man, who lived over 500,000 years ago in the caves of Zhoukoudan. Archaeologists have discovered the skeletal remains of thousands of wild horses and deer. This is a strong indication that the ancient Chinese were swift runners and accomplished hunters. Cave paintings at Canhyuan, believed to be over 3,400 years old, show dancing and other physical activities. There is even historical evidence of a dance identified as *xiaozhongwu* (reduce-swelling dance), used in ancient times to treat diseases of the legs and feet.[29]

Military training was a necessity for warlords and emperors to retain their turf as well as to expand it whenever they could. Chinese knights rode into battle on chariots while wearing bronze helmets. These knights, armed with axes, spears, and daggers, rode chariots that were weapons of war as well as expressions of wealth; they were lavishly decorated with bronze ornamentation. The extent of chariot ornamentation probably depended upon the wealth of the knight. Each chariot was manned by a driver, a spearman, and an archer. Following the chariots were the infantrymen, who were almost always drawn from the ranks of peasant farmers.

The farmer who was drafted into the army in time of war held out little hope of ever returning home. The ordinary infantryman led a miserable, harsh existence and probably died on the hot sands of the northwestern deserts, repelling the barbarian hordes, or in one of the many civil wars. His prowess as an athlete, level of physical fitness, and skill in using the tools of war (and some luck) were about all he had on which to depend. If captured, the soldier or knight would probably be put to death, because

> victorious generals like to enhance their reputation for ferocity and to chill the hearts of future enemies by mass execution of prisoners. The First Century writer Wang Ch'ung reports that officers of the ancient state of Ch'in . . . buried alive 400,000 soldiers of a rival state.[30]

With the Mongol invasions came horses, and before long the Chinese developed a reputation as fine riders and fierce warriors. Hunting was a popular pastime as well. Falcons provided the nobility with an additional sport as these birds of prey were trained to hunt fowl. A royal hunt was a grand occasion. Men were sent in advance of the hunting party to act as "beaters"—people who flushed game into the open—in concert with hunting dogs. A commoner used falconry for purposes of survival and could take his trained hawk into the field with the hope that it would return with a rabbit or pheasant.

Captured slaves sometimes joined the court as servants, and women who danced were highly valued. Life in the court of Shih Hu, who reigned over the small northern state of Chao after the fall of the Han Dynasty, provides a revealing look at the opulence and flair of the ancient Chinese. Shih Hu was a violent man, a superb hunter, and a skilled archer. In his palace, he enjoyed the music of an all-girl orchestra; he also boasted a battalion made up entirely of women clothed in sable furs and carrying bows painted yellow. An interesting anecdote has it that as the years passed, Shih Hu gained a lot of weight and could no longer walk to the hunting grounds. Yet he enjoyed the hunt so much that he was carried to the hunt on a litter borne by twenty men. Once he arrived, he sat on a revolving couch so that he was able to shoot in any direction.[31]

Like the Sumerian and Egyptian nobility, the Chinese nobility enjoyed a life of luxury. By A.D. 9, wealthy families could inhabit a house equipped with baths, heaters, mechanical fans, water fountains, and rooms cooled with ice. One account tells of a guest who visited a monarch and was treated to a whirling fan that sprayed water behind the throne, which resulted in a cool breeze. The monarch invited the guest to sit on a stone bench cooled from within and enjoy an ice-cold drink![32] The ancient Chinese understood material comforts and from time to time indulged in corporeal delights as well.

Boxing became a popular sport after Buddhidharma came to China around A.D. 527. Initially, eighteen movements were taught and focused students on appropriate offensive tactics. Over time, the system was refined and expanded, and in approximately A.D. 1070, a boxing teacher named Chio Yuan Shang Jen incorporated more than 170 movements and wrote a set of training rules, which, among other things, espoused a vegetarian diet, self-discipline, and sexual control.[33]

The martial arts evolved from efforts like those of Chio Yuan Shang Jen and were a product of Chinese philosophy and the need for skilled warriors. According to Howard Knuttgen and colleagues, the most recognized form of martial arts is currently known as *wushu*.[34] However, in earlier times, it was called *wuyong,* which meant "military valor," or *wuyi,* meaning "military skill." The ancient Chinese appear to have used military skills that were more complex than those traditionally practiced by their contemporaries in the West. By the time of the Yuan and Ming Dynasties (A.D. 1279–1644), the movements and skills we in the West identify as martial arts had been refined and distilled into 18 types of military skills. These skills reflected the various elements of Chinese philosophy, such as yin and yang, the negative and positive forces that exist in nature. Over time, martial arts incorporated *jingluoxue,* the science of attending to the main and collateral channels found in the body. This concept is a traditional mainstay of Chinese medicine. The result of these influences is a system of martial arts that blends the physical aspects of existence with the philosophical, a highly sophisticated way of living that Westerners are only now coming to appreciate.[35]

Members of the upper class passed their time playing sports and parlor games, listening to music, and dancing. A form of football was played and was useful in military training. The game had rules of attack and was popular for centuries. During the T'ang Dynasty, the men and women of the aristocracy played polo, introduced by travelers from Persia (now known as Iran). The Chinese admired the equestrian skill of the Persians, and Persian horses were highly prized. Among the lesser sports were board and table games. Playing cards are believed to be a Chinese invention from the T'ang Dynasty, and games of chance were a popular activity in China, as was chess.[36]

MESOAMERICA

Spheres and other "round" objects have fascinated humans since the dawn of civilization. Throughout the ages, we have gazed at the planets, the moon, and the sun and made them an integral part of religion and science. Spheroids have been employed in art, architecture, mathematics, cuisine (pancakes, meatballs, scoops of ice cream), and, of course, sport. Apparently, the "perfect circle" in the form of a ball is at the core

of some of the most contested athletic competitions in both the ancient and the modern world.

Without the round or spheroid shapes we call "balls," there would be no baseball, basketball, tennis, cricket, table tennis, water polo, softball, bowling, handball, volleyball, squash, or golf. When we think about the millions of athletes worldwide who practice every day to develop skills and stamina in attacking the ball or defending against it (soccer, baseball, volleyball), we have to marvel at the power that this seemingly harmless object commands. As a cultural mainstay, ball games were very popular in antiquity, just as they are now. At this point, we leave the great civilizations of the Middle East, Africa, and Asia and turn our attention to Mesoamerica, where a ball game called *ulama* was truly a cultural and religious experience.

The term *Mesoamerica* is used to distinguish the inhabitants of a particular part of the Americas from the Indians who lived in neighboring areas. The geographical location of Mesoamerica extends from the desert region of northern Mexico southward to include Belize, Guatemala, and western Honduras and El Salvador.[37] Ulama was a ball game that was played with a rubber ball by the Olmecs, beginning about 1800 B.C., and continued, albeit with rule changes, to be played by the pre-Columbian Maya of the Yucatan, as well as the Totonacs, the Zapotecs, and the mighty Aztecs. An adaptation of ulama continues to be played in northwestern Mexico even today. The historical game contained religious, cultural, and competitive elements.

Kirchhoff observed that the natives of Mesoamerica shared a number of cultural characteristics:

1. Building steep pyramids as temples
2. Using a calendar that had one year designated with 365 days
3. Developing a written form of language
4. Learning to make a type of beer out of the agave plant
5. Using tortillas as a food staple
6. Playing a ritual ball game using a hard rubber ball.[38]

What is important here is that the Mesoamericans utilized a hard rubber ball—rubber was readily available from the abundant rubber trees. The Sumerians, Egyptians, and Chinese, in contrast, had little access to rubber. As students of critical thought, we can use interpretative history to make some comments about ulama. It seems reasonable to suggest that the inhabitants of Mesoamerica enjoyed a ball game that must have been very fastpaced and exciting, and probably caused significant pain if the athlete was hit with the ball; modern baseball players can relate to this particular occupational hazard. The velocity or speed achieved by throwing or propelling a hard rubber ball with the hip or buttocks, foot (sometimes this was a penalty), or arm is much greater than with balls made from animal skins stuffed or inflated with hair, air, or other material, as was the case in much of the ancient world. Ulama may have been the precursor to the modern game of jai alai, which is very popular in Mexico and Central America today and shares similarities with handball and racketball (Figure 2.3).

Figure 2-3

Jai Alai competition in Havana, Cuba 1904. Jai Alai athletes are dressed in white shirts and pants; because the ball travels so fast, modern day players wear helmets. Each player uses a "scoop" to catch the speeding ball and hurls the ball inside the scoop against the wall in the same manner handball and racketball players do.

When Columbus sailed to the Americas, he observed a ball game on a Caribbean island that utilized a solid rubber ball. And when he sailed back to Spain, he brought with him the first rubber ball ever seen in Europe.[39]

Initially, ulama was probably played on a level field without walls or earth barriers. Archaeological excavations near Chiapas, on the Pacific coast of Mexico, have revealed a ball court that dates from circa 1500 B.C. Two ball courts discovered in Guatemala date from 800 to 600 B.C. According to archaeological evidence (terra cotta figures, stone sculptures, Mayan vase paintings and wall paintings), several different types of games were played by the Indians of Mesoamerica. Pre-Columbian art illustrates ball players using sticks to strike the ball, as well as athletes using their hips and feet to propel the ball.[40]

Over time, magnificent courts called *tlachtli*—a word in Nahuatl, the language used by the Aztecs—were built. Chichen Itza is a well-known archaeological site and the location of an intact *tlachtemalacatl* (ball court) known as the "god's ball court." It is located in southern Mexico on the Yucatan Peninsula.[41] The court is oblong, with each end wider than the middle part, similar in shape to the letter I. In the postclassical period (A.D. 300–900), architectural changes were introduced, and a high, thick, ornamental wall was built. This wall was lower at each end but much higher in the central playing alley where the athletes mainly competed. Along the alley was a bench, and in the middle of each side wall, a stone ring, or tlachtemalacatl, was built that served as a goal. In Chichen Itza, the walls were built on a 90-degree angle (Figure 2-4). The size of the stone rings, which were situated high in the middle of each parallel wall, varied from 50 centimeters in diameter in Chichen Itza to 10 centimeters for the rings on exhibit in the National Museum of Anthropology in Mexico City. There were also different types of ball courts. Some were open-ended, and others were completely enclosed. The different sizes of the stone rings and the different ball court configurations suggest that the game was played in more than one way. One possibility is that the athletes used one wall to bounce the ball off,

Figure 2-4
Ball court at Chichen Itza.

Figure 2-5
Stone relief carving from ball court at Chichen Itza.

which marked one type of game, and in another variation, both sides were used.

The cultures of the Maya and the Aztecs utilized the game of ulama as a competitive sport with strong religious overtones. The cultural and attendant religious belief in human sacrifice as a core function of ceremonial ulama is especially noteworthy. Archaeological evidence suggests that some of the ball courts incorporated artistic representations and decorations along the playing alley (Figure 2-5). The artwork along the playing alleys shows human sacrifices, which implies that the game and attendant sacrifice of players or teams was intended to appease the gods and provide for a good agricultural crop. In the god's ball court in Chichen Itza, sacrifice involved ritual beheading. The blood that gushed from the sacrificial athlete was assigned to the seven serpents that adorned the walls; one of the serpents had an agricultural association. Thus, the ball game incorporated ritual religious themes with agricultural "hopes." At this venue, the human sacrifice theme is depicted six times, three on each bench (side). Similar artwork illustrating human sacrifice is found at ball courts throughout Mesoamerica. In the Casa Colorada ball court of Chichen Itza, a ball player/executioner is depicted standing between two players, who seem to be the captains of the two teams, holding a severed head in his hand. The winning captain lost his head while the captain of the losing team kept his for the time being. There also exists the

possibility that the entire winning team may have been sacrificed. The gods would be pleased that the best team was sacrificed in their honor, and a bountiful harvest could be the result.[42]

As you can imagine, there was a lot on the line for the ball players of Mesoamerica when they played ulama as part of a major religious ritual. The games could last a long time. The gods could only be served with the most precious thing humans possess—life itself. Using a modern sports metaphor, these athletes likely gave 110 percent, and then some, as the losers—and sometimes the victors—could pay with their lives. Although ulama was played for recreational reasons as well, it mainly represented a deadly ritualistic struggle that had profound religious and cultural significance. The scenes or tableaus that are depicted on a number of the ball courts represent "a dramatic representation of how to control the cosmic order, establish fertility, and obtain a good harvest in pre-Columbian Mesoamerica."[43]

Athletes who played ulama used many of the same types of equipment that soccer and baseball players use today, including gloves, loincloths (primitive athletic supporters), arm guards, and knee pads. The Mayans used a type of chest protector so the players could bounce the ball off their chests.[44] When the Spanish explorer Hernando Cortes (1485–1547) saw the Indians playing ulama, he was fascinated by their athletic ability. The variant of the game that Cortes observed did not include human sacrifice, although Cortes and the Catholic Church knew of the human sacrifices associated with Mayan and Aztec ball games. In the game that Cortes witnessed, the players used a firm piece of leather that covered their hips and buttocks. Even while offering protection from the hard rubber ball, the leather "uniform" was employed to propel the ball by using the hip to strike it. The players also used gloves but did not touch the ground with their hands. The ball was returned/hit from one player to the other until one player was not able to hit it back to the other; we

are not sure how score was kept. In any event, these ball players were so impressive that Cortes took two of them back to Spain, where they put on a demonstration at the court of Charles V in 1528.[45]

In sum, Mesoamerica has a long cultural history of glorious venues that featured the sport of ulama. The game was played by the Mayans and Aztecs not only for recreational purposes but also to curry favor with the gods; this latter included the sacrifice of athletes. Today's extreme sports pale in comparison to the high-stakes competitions that were part of the culture of the Aztecs and Mayans.

Modern athletes and fans share a number of similarities with the ancient Mayans and Aztecs relative to ball games. Like the Mayans and Aztecs, we build magnificent venues where baseball and basketball games are contested and players are immortalized. We use gloves, knee pads, and chest protectors, and we keep score. Fortunately, we have made the transition from the premodern and sometimes deadly sport of ulama to the modern sports of basketball and baseball; however, for many in the modern world, losing is still a matter of life and death in a metaphorical sense.

SUMMARY

The study of ancient civilizations reveals that the attitudes and behaviors found in Western civilization are similar to the modes of thought, cultural mores, and philosophical positions that reflect the beliefs and values of non-Western civilizations. These ancient civilizations flourished long before the birth of Christ and appear to have influenced our Western ancestors in ways that we may never discover. Of interest to the student of history are both the similarities and the differences: Certain aspects of these ancient civilizations that are similar to those found in the West reveal how all humans are similar. In contrast, those aspects that are manifest in these ancient civilizations that differ from what is believed and practiced in the West reveal the infinite variety of attitudes and behaviors that define our unique differences.

Although many of these ancient values and mores are very different from those that Westerners are comfortable with, links exist between all civilizations, past and present. The ancient civilizations that inhabited

Mesopotamia, Egypt, China, and Mesoamerica enjoyed many of the same sports and physical activities that we do today. The ball games of Mesoamerica have characteristics that are similar to modern-day basketball, racquetball, and squash. The equipment utilized by the athletes of Mesoamerica has similarities to that used in baseball, and their venues were magnificent. Like the people of today, the inhabitants of ancient civilizations linked sport and physical education with the spiritual as well as the secular world. Although long since vanished, these ancient civilizations left their mark on Western civilization in terms of science, architecture, and thought, and in sport and physical education. One of these ancient civilizations, Egypt, was in contact with ancient Greece and Rome. Exactly how much the Egyptians influenced the Greeks and Romans is subject to debate. However, one thing is certain: The ancient Greeks and Romans were beneficiaries of Egyptian medicine, science, and sports and games.

DISCUSSION QUESTIONS

1. How do you account for the association between the innate need in humans to survive and the growth of competitive sport in ancient civilizations?

2. In your estimation, why do the combat sports that were developed in ancient times continue to be practiced in modern times?

3. What were the similarities shared by the Sumerians, Egyptians, Mesoamericans, and Chinese concerning sport and physical activity?

4. How does martial arts training link the philosophical with the physical?

5. What types of sports and games do we engage in today that were just as popular in the ancient world?

6. Kings and other leaders in the ancient world involved themselves with so-called manly pursuits that revolved around physical skill and athletic competition. To what extent do the leaders of modern industrialized countries continue this practice? What examples can you provide?

7. To what extent did sport, ritual, and religion coincide in ancient civilizations?

8. Why was it necessary to have ritual sacrifices of athletes in Mesoamerica?

9. How easy or difficult was it to play the ball games of Mesoamerica? Do you think that the athletes of that era were equal to the athletes who compete today?

INTERNET RESOURCES

Sumer
ancienthistory.about.com/library/bl/bl_intro_sumer.htm
Provides articles related to the history of Sumer.

Ancient Mesopotamia
www.fidnet.com/~wied/Sumer.htm
Gives information about Mesopotamia and Sumer.

Virtual Egypt
virtual-Egypt.com
Contains articles, photos, and glyphs.

British Museum: Ancient Egypt
www.ancientegypt.co.uk
Lists British museum holdings and gives information about Egypt and other ancient civilizations.

Ancient Egypt
www.ancient-egypt.org
Is a site dedicated to ancient Egypt, developed by Egyptologists.

Minnesota State University EMuseum: China
www.mnsu.edu/emuseum/prehistory/china
Provides information about the culture and history of ancient China.

Condensed China
condensedchina.com
Gives an introduction to ancient China for beginning students.

China Online: Sports History of China
**chineseculture.about.com/library/weekly/
    aa032301a.htm**

Includes an article summarizing the sports history of China.

Ancient World Web: Daily Life
julen.net/ancient/Daily_Life/
Includes articles on the origin of sports in ancient China and ancient Egypt and related topics.

Ancient Egyptian Culture
**www.touregypt.net/magazine/
    ancientegyptculture.htm**
Includes articles about ancient Egypt, including information on sports.

Ancient Egyptian Sports
**www.sis.gov.eg/egyptinf/history/html/
    sport001.htm**
Gives information about ancient Egyptian sports.

Mayan Art and Books
maya_art_books.org
Is a source for information about sports and their position in Mayan culture.

Ancient Maya
**www.logoi.com/links/nativeamericans/ancient_
    maya.html**
Provides links to information about ancient Mayan sports.

Visit the *History and Philosophy of Sport and Physical Education* Online Learning Center (www.mhhe.com/mechikoff6e) for additional information and study tools.

SUGGESTIONS FOR FURTHER READING

Breasted, J. H. *A History of Egypt.* New York: Charles Scribner, 1912.

E. S. Eaton. "An Egyptian High Jump." *Bulletin of the Museum of Fine Arts, Boston* 35 (1937): 54.

Gahlin, L. *Egypt: Gods, Myths and Religion.* New York: Barnes and Noble, 2002.

Giles, H. A. *The Civilization of China.* New York: Henry Holt, 1911.

Lexova, J. *Ancient Egyptian Dances.* Trans. K. Haaltmar. Prague: Oriental Institute, 1935.

Leyenaar, Ted J. J. *Ulama—Ballgame from the Olmecs to the Aztecs.* Lausanne: Bartelsmann, 1997.

Littauer, M. A., and J. H. Crouwel. *Chariots and Related Equipment from the Tomb of Tut'ankhamun.* Tut'ankhamun Tomb Series 8 (Oxford: Oxford University Press, 1985).

Love, M. "Regatta on the Nile." *Aramco World Magazine* 32(4) (July–August 1981): 31–36.

Saad, Z. "Khazza Iawizza." *Annales du serivce des antiquites de l'Egypte. Cairo* 37 (1937): 212–18.

Stumpf, F., and F. Cozens. "Some Aspects of the Role of Games, Sports, and Recreational Activities in the Culture of Modern Primitive Peoples." *Research Quarterly* 18 (October 1947): 198–218.

NOTES

1. Jeremiah 51:43.

2. Samuel Noah Kramer, *Cradle of Civilization* (New York: Time-Life Books, 1967), 12.

3. Vera Olivova, *Sports and Games in The Ancient World* (New York: St. Martin's Press, 1982), 21.

4. Ibid., 22–23.

5. Kramer, *Cradle of Civilization,* 36.

6. Ibid., 64, 66.

7. Ibid., 67.

8. Maxwell L. Howell and Reet Howell, "Physical Activities of the Sumerians" (paper presented to the Research Section American Alliance for Health, Physical Education and Recreation, Milwaukee, WI, April 4, 1976); Denise Palmer, "Sport and Games in the Art of Early Civilizations" (master's thesis, University of Alberta, 1967), 3.

9. G. Contenay, *Everyday Life in Babylon and Assyria* (London: Edward Arnold, 1954), 3.

10. L. Woolley, *Mesopotamia and the Near East* (London: Methuen, 1961), figure 21.

11. Howell and Howell, "Physical Activities of the Sumerians," 6.

12. N. Kramer, *The Sumerians* (Chicago: University of Chicago Press, 1963), 25.

13. L. Woolley, *Ur Excavations: The Royal Cemeteries* Vol. 11 (Cambridge: Oxford University Press, 1934), 274–79.

14. *Iraq,* vol. VIII, 1946, photo VIII; Howell and Howell, "Physical Activities of the Sumerians," 8.

15. Wolfgang Decker, *Sports and Games of Ancient Egypt* (New Haven, Conn.: Yale University Press, 1992), 5. This book was originally published in German as *Sport und Spiel im Alten Agypten* by C. H. Beck'sche Verlagsbuchhandlung (Oscar Beck), Munich, 1987; C. E. DeVries, "Attitudes of the Ancient Egyptians Toward Physical-Recreative Activities" (Ph.D. dissertation, University of Chicago, 1960).

16. Ahmed D. Touny, "History of Sports in Ancient Egypt" (paper presented at the Twenty-Fourth Session of the International Olympic Academy, Ancient Olympia, Greece, July 4–19, 1984), 86.

17. Ibid.

18. Ibid., 86–87.

18a. The author would like to thank Professor Steven R. Murray of Colorado Mesa univ. for providing and excellent review and the time line example of Cleopatra, last Queen and Pharaoh of Egypt.

19. Lionel Casson, *Ancient Egypt* (New York: Time-Life Books, 1965), 35.

20. Ibid., 44.

21. Ibid., 63.

22. Ibid., 63.

23. Ibid., 68.

24. Ibid., 111.

25. Deobold B. Van Dalen and Bruce L. Bennett, *A World History of Physical Education,* 2nd ed. (Englewood Cliffs, NJ: Prentice-Hall, 1971), 11–12.

26. Touny, "History of Sports in Ancient Egypt," 90.

27. Edward H. Schafer, *Ancient China* (New York: Time-Life Books, 1967), 7.

28. Howard G. Knuttgen, Ma Qiwei, and Wu Zhongyuan, eds., *Sport in China* (Champaign, IL: Human Kinetics, 1990), 1.

29. Ibid., 4.

30. Schafer, *Ancient China,* 34.

31. Ibid., 40.

32. Ibid., 40.

33. Knuttgen et al., *Sport in China,* 5–6.

34. Ibid.

35. Van Dalen and Bennett, *World History of Physical Education,* 15–16.

36. Schafer, *Ancient China,* 41.

37. Ted J. J. Leyenaar, *Ulama—Ballgame from the Olmecs to the Aztecs* (Lausanne: Bartelsmann, 1997), 11, 13, 16. Publication from the exposition held at the Olympic Museum and Studies Center, Lausanne, Switzerland, June 26, 1997, to October 12, 1997.

38. Ibid., 16.

39. B. de las Casas, *Apologegtica Historia de las Indias* (Madrid: Nueva Biblioteca de Autores Espanoles 13, 1909), 159.

40. Leyenaar, *Ulama,* 18.

41. Ibid., 21.

42. Ibid., 27, 28.

43. Ibid., 31.

44. Ibid., 32, 33.

45. Ibid., 35. See also Ted J. J. Leyenaar, *Ulama: The Perpetuation in Mexico of the Pre-Spanish Ball Game Ullamaliztli* (Leiden: Spruyt, Van Matgem & De Does, 1978); Ted J. J. Leyenaar, *Trophy Heads, Coffee Bean Eyes and the Ballgame: The Mesoamerican Ball game,* ed. Gerard W. van Bussel, Paul L. F. van Dongen, and Ted J. J. Leyenaar (Leiden: Spruyt, Van Matgem & De Does, 1991); and Ted J. J. Leyenaar and Lee A. Parsons, *Ulama: The Ballgame of the Mayas and the Aztecs* (Leiden: Spruyt, Van Matgem & De Does, 1988).

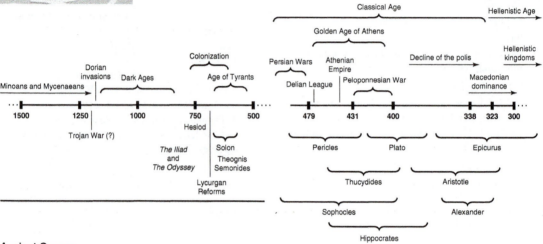

Ancient Greece.

CHAPTER 3

Greece

General Events

B.C.

c. 1600–1100 Mycenaean Period

c. 1184 Fall of Troy to Achaeans

c. 1100 Dorians and Ionians invade Greek peninsula, conquer Achaeans; end of Mycenaean Period, beginning of Hellenic civilization

c. 950–800 Period of Homeric epics

c. 800–500 Archaic Period

c. 776 First Olympiad; all Greeks compete in ceremonial games

OBJECTIVES

Upon completing this chapter, you will be able to:

■ Understand the magnificent cultural, philosophical, and athletic impact of ancient Greece on the development of Western civilization.

■ Identify cultural influences from other civilizations that shaped the development of Greek culture in general and sport and physical activity in particular.

■ Identify the philosophical views of the body that were important to Athens and elsewhere in Greece and that to this day affect the status of sport and physical education.

■ Understand the philosophical views of the body advocated by Plato and Socrates in the *Phaedo* and Books II and III of *The Republic,* and their impact on the historical and philosophical development of sport and physical education.

■ Understand the rationale put forth by Dr. Charles H. McCloy, advocating education *of* the physical, and the opposing view put forth by Dr. Jesse F. Williams, who advocated education *through* the physical, and discuss their impact on physical education and sport in America.

■ Explain the contributions of Aristotle to education, his belief in the necessity of a mind-and-body education, and his contributions to the Olympic Games of antiquity.

46

- Understand, appreciate, and possibly relate to the concepts of *agon* and *arete*.
- Appreciate the impact of Homer's *The Iliad* and the role of Funeral Games in the history of sport and physical education.
- Recognize that many of the sports and physical activities that the ancient Greeks enjoyed remain popular today.
- Discuss the role of sport on Crete.
- Identify some perspectives on the development of sport in ancient Greece.
- Identify and understand the significance and scope of the four major Panhellenic or Stephanitic athletic festivals.
- Understand the cultural and sporting differences between Athens and Sparta.
- Understand the differences that existed between Athens and Sparta relative to their programs of physical education and physical training.
- Discuss the access that women had to physical education and athletic competition in Sparta and throughout Greece.
- Discuss the role that religion played in athletic competition.
- Appreciate the timeless design of the architectural venues that were devoted to athletic competitions.
- Understand and appreciate the religious rituals and cultural functions that were at the foundation of the ancient Olympic Games.
- Recognize that in addition to athletic competitions, the Olympic Games featured competitions in the arts, as did other festivals.
- Identify the athletic competitions that took place at the Olympic Games.
- Discuss the philosophical arguments supporting and opposing a mind-and-body education.
- Understand the nature of dualist philosophy relative to the belief that the essence of human existence is that of mind/soul and matter/body.
- Understand the impact of Homer's epic poems *The Iliad* and *The Odyssey* on the development of the athlete as a hero.
- Understand that the great city of Troy did exist in antiquity and held athletic competitions at the temple of Athena and other nearby venues.

INTRODUCTION

As we move forward within the new millennium, there are a number of "timeless" activities and pursuits in which our society will continue to engage. The scholarly study of sport and physical education will continue to mature. As a profession, we will endeavor to make profound discoveries that contribute to the growth and betterment of society and the individual. We will fine-tune our knowledge of diet and exercise to help achieve peak performance. We will continue to investigate the link between exercise and health and, in this regard, will seek additional information to develop, as Plato advocated, a harmonious relationship between mind and body.

Our society will continue to build monuments to sport in the form of stadiums, gymnasiums, and arenas. Athletes will continue their quest to achieve victory, sometimes no matter what the cost. Their performances will inspire, entertain, and, from time to time, disappoint us. And virtually all of these monuments, achievements, and emotions that take place today have their origins in the legends and stories about the trials and tribulations of the athletes who lived in ancient Greece.

c. 494 Persians under Darius invade Greece
c. 490 Athenians defeat Persians at Marathon
480 Persians under Xerxes defeat Spartans at Thermopylae
Athens sacked and burned
Athenians defeat Persian fleet at Salamis
477 Delian League founded under Athenian leadership
c. 461–429 Pericles rules Athens
454 Delian League treasury moved to Athens
437–404 Peloponnesian Wars between Athens and Sparta
413 Athenians defeated at Syracuse, Sicily
404 Athens falls to Sparta; end of Athenian Empire
387 Plato founds Academy
335 Aristotle founds Lyceum

Architecture and Sculpture

c. 650 Ionic temple of Artemis built at Ephesus
c. 600 Kouros from Sounion carved
c. 550 Hera of Samos carved
c. 530 Archaic Doric temples built at Athens, Delphi, Corinth, Olympia
c. 489 Doric temple (Treasury of Athenians) built at Delphi
c. 468–457 Temple of Zeus built at Olympia
c. 460–440 Myron and Polyclitus active
450 Phidias appointed overseer of works on Acropolis
449–440 Temple of Hephaestus (Theseum) built
447–432 Parthenon built by Ictinus and Callicrates
Parthenon sculptures carved under Phidias
437–432 Propylaea built by Mnesicles
427–424 Temple of Athena Nike built by Callicrates
421–409 Erechtheum built by Mnesicles
c. 350–300 Lysippus active

Philosophers

c. 582–507 Pythagoras
500–428 Anaxagoras

c. 470–399 Socrates
c. 428–348 Plato
384–322 Aristotle

Historians

c. 495–425 Herodotus
c. 460–395 Thucydides
c. 434–355 Xenophon

Sculptors

c. 490–432 Phidias
c. 460–450 Myron active
c. 460–440 Polyclitus active
c. 390–330 Praxiteles
c. 350–300 Lysippus active

Dramatists and Musicians

525–456 Aeschylus
496–406 Sophocles
484–406 Euripides
c. 444–380 Aristophanes

A.D.

c. 100 Plutarch writes *Parallel Lives*
c. 140–150 Pausanias visits Athens; later writes description of Greece

The timeless interest in athletes, sport, and physical development continues unabated. However, as far-reaching as our current efforts in these areas are, we never cease to be amazed and humbled when we reflect upon the achievements of the ancient Greeks. The pursuit of individual excellence in mind and body that was emblematic of the Greeks during their Golden Age serves as an inspiration to the millions of physical educators and athletes who follow in their footsteps today.

The Influence of the Jews and the Phoenicians upon Greek Culture

The Greeks developed, quite possibly with Judaic and Phoenician influence, much of the Western world's philosophical orientation toward the body and physical education. Judaism predates the ancient Greeks. The Jews paid close attention to the care of the body as well as the significance of their corporeal existence. Their religion, culture, and philosophical views spread to some areas of the Greek world and may have been very influential. For example, during his trial, Socrates told the court that he believed in a god that was far higher than any of the gods worshiped by the polytheistic Greeks. His reference to a single, supreme deity may have originated from interaction with Jews or through reading the works of Jewish theologians.

The close proximity of Greece to the Middle East enabled the Phoenicians to establish trade with the Greeks (Figure 3-1). These ancient seafaring people, who inhabited present-day Lebanon, enjoyed sport and physical activity. Their influence upon the development of the Western world is significant. According to Labib Boutros, "The Phoenicians had developed in Antiquity a wide Civilization and had a significant role in the early development of European Culture."[1] Boutros states that Phoenician civilization was established prior to Greek civilization. To what extent did the Phoenicians engage in sport? We have two sources of information: mythology and archaeological research. In Phoenician mythology, the gods Baal and Mot engaged in a wrestling competition while the Phoenician hero Melkart was compared to the Greek hero, and great athlete, Herakles. Archaeological excavations at Amrit have uncovered ruins similar to those of Greek stadiums. According to Sophia Vakirtzi, "Athletism [sport] was, indeed, practiced in Phoenicia." However, this athletic activity cannot be characterized as "Phoenician" in origin and concept.[2] Vakirtzi suggests that the Phoenicians may have been influenced by other cultures in the region, such as the Egyptians, Mesopotamians, Sumerians, and Hittites during the Aegean Bronze Age (3000–1100 B.C.). It is probable that some of the rituals, sports, and physical activities enjoyed by the Phoenicians were adopted by the Greeks. According to Boutros,

> In fact, it appeared to me that Greek Sport was based on divinities and worship rites borrowed from the Phoenicians, and even the Greeks adopted Phoenician gods and rituals, almost completely, with only a change in

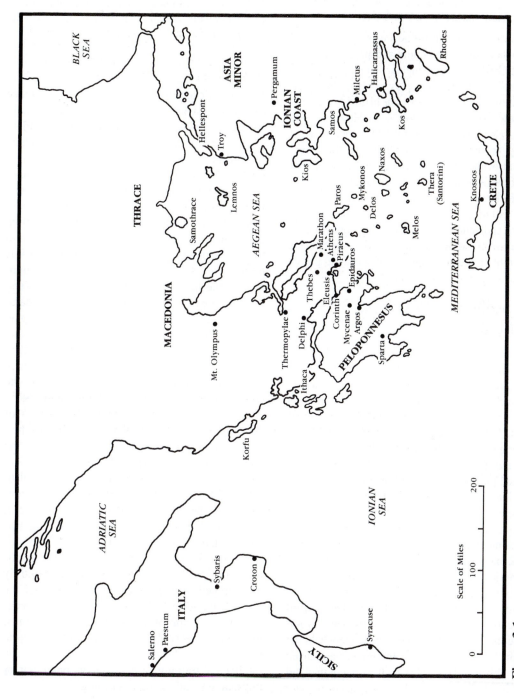

Figure 3-1
Map of ancient Greece.

49

the names of the divinities, which were clearly behind the establishment of the Olympic Games and other Athletic Festivals in Greece.[3]

The extent of the influence of the Jews and Phoenicians upon the beliefs and practices of the ancient Greeks remains unclear. There is evidence that these two cultures did play a role in the development of the Greek world, but historians are not sure how extensive this role was. However, one thing is clear: The idea that the Phoenicians were directly or indirectly responsible for the establishment of the Olympic Games and other Greek athletic festivals as reported by Boutros is sure to provoke lively debate. Nonetheless, the study of history is not an exact science. Over time, archaeologists and scholars in the field of sport history may uncover additional information that sheds more light on the development of sport and physical education in ancient Greece.

PHILOSOPHICAL POSITIONS OF THE BODY

There were two opposing ideas of physical education in Greece. According to John Fairs, "Each idea of physical education was the end product of a specific world view, or metaphysical position, and its corresponding cultural mentality [and] sociocultural system."[4] These two opposing metaphysical schools of thought were naturalistic and antinaturalistic. The *naturalistic* view held that man should have a balanced program that would incorporate physical education and intellectual education, because man was perceived to function as both a spiritual and corporeal being. This approach necessitated achieving a harmonious balance among the spiritual, intellectual, and physical. The *antinaturalistic* view held that physical education was a servant to the intellectual process. The learning mind and a behaving body were the end product of a worldview that rejected the material world in favor of the self-created world of pure thought.[5] The antinaturalistic view held the mind in higher esteem than the body; naturalistic philosophy held the body in higher esteem than did the antinaturalistic school. Both schools of thought held the mind in high esteem, but they differed on the position and subsequent importance of the body. The naturalistic view was far more popular than the antinaturalistic view. Is this still true today?

DUALISM

The dualistic approach to the problem of existence (ontology)—whether humans are essentially spirit or body—was classically described by Plato in the *Phaedo*.[6] Two of the greatest philosophers of all time, Socrates (c. 470–399 B.C.) and Plato (c. 428–348 B.C.) formulated philosophical views of the body based on metaphysical dualism,[7] and this argument decisively influenced the purpose and status of contemporary physical education. The separation of our being or existence into two components—the mind and the body—is referred to as *dualism* and is a critical component in the history of metaphysical thought and remains popular today. For example, the separation of mind and body in perhaps its most graphic form can be seen in the early philosophical and psychological orientation of ascetic dualism. Using a dichotomous approach, ascetic dualism held belief in (1) soul and (2) matter. Unlike the Greeks, who strove to develop the mind and to possess a magnificent physique, the ascetics of the Middle Ages (A.D. 900–1400) based their beliefs on the concept of original sin and the attendant total depravity of men, women, and children. The body was thought to be a tool of the devil to infect and pervert the soul. As a consequence, the training of the body was ignored; the body as a mode of being and existing was mortified, degraded, and held to be repugnant and repulsive. Had the ancient Greeks had the means to see into the future, they would have been truly discouraged by the beliefs and practices of the ascetic dualists. No doubt these same Greeks would have approved of the physical fitness movement sweeping across most of the world today and the devotion to health, exercise, and intellectual training emblematic of contemporary physical education and kinesiology.

CLASSICAL HUMANISM

Classical scholars such as William Fleming are comfortable identifying the ancient Greeks with the philosophy of *humanism,* which provides a system of human conduct among members of society. The philosophy espoused by Plato, however, may not lend itself readily to humanism. Throughout Plato's work, the preeminence of the mind or soul (that which is eternal) over the body (that which is temporary) is fairly clear, especially when his social class system is taken into account as told in *The Republic.* In his caste system, selected people who occupy the higher rungs of the caste hierarchy have less and less concern for earthly, humanistic concerns. Plato was not an advocate of democratic ideals, but instead believed that the masses should be ruled by philosopher-kings who have the wisdom, as a result of proper schooling, that ordinary citizens lack. Democratic voting as practiced in the United States and many other countries were not permitted in Plato's *The Republic.*

The primary focus of the Greeks was on their existence as humans. They had the same concerns that we do today: What is our place in nature and the universe, and what type of social relationships are we best suited for? These questions and countless others helped form the foundation for humanism, the philosophical school that takes the position that concern for one's total welfare is central.[8] In this respect, the Greeks saw their gods as idealized human beings. This can be seen in their art, which used the human form as a point of departure. The sculptures and artistic renderings of Zeus, Apollo, and Athena are often aesthetically perfect images of masculine and feminine beauty.

The Greeks were more thoroughly at home in the physical world than were the later Christian peoples, who believed in the separation of flesh and spirit. The Greeks greatly admired the beauty and agility of the human body at the peak of its development (Figure 3-2). In addition to studies in literature and music, Greek youths were trained from childhood for athletic competition. Because it was through the perfection of their bodies that

Figure 3-2
Greek wrestlers.

men most resembled gods, the culture of the body was a religious as well as a physical activity.[9]

SOCRATES' AND PLATO'S VIEW OF THE BODY

If Socrates left any written material, it has yet to be discovered. Our knowledge of Socrates primarily comes from what his pupil Plato wrote. By all accounts, Socrates and Plato were not only accomplished philosophers but excellent athletes as well, especially Plato!

Although most modern scholars do not believe that Plato won the wrestling competition at Olympia, there is a single recent source that claims he did. When the Olympic Games were held in 408 B.C., Plato would have been 19 years old. The wrestling champion of the 408 B.C. olympiad is not known, could it have been Plato?

Ancient sources provide us with enough information to reconstruct his wrestling career during his youth. His coach was Ariston of Argos and we know that Plato won the wrestling competition at Nemea and Isthmia. His writing is filled with wrestling metaphors and references. We do know that Plato attended the Olympics as a spectator, what we are not certain of is that he won the Olympic wrestling championship in 408 B.C.[10]

Socrates' and Plato's metaphysical position regarding the nature and reality of human existence is that of dualism, which divides us into a corporeal (bodily) existence and a spiritual/mental existence. This division culminates with the soul departing the body upon death. Throughout Plato's writings (*Phaedo, The Republic* Books II and III), the development and practice of philosophy (intellectual activity) that will nourish the soul is always elevated over the cultivation and training of the body. The manner in which Plato argued for the division of mind and body, or dualism, and the implications of his philosophy can be seen in the following passage from the *Phaedo,* the story of Socrates' last day in prison. During the course of the day, he discusses the immortality of the soul, the soul's capacity for pure knowledge, the establishment of the dualistic nature of existence, the grossness of the body, and the way the evil body infects and confuses the mind/soul. The importance of death and the role of death are explained, although only the true devotee of philosophy will understand the claim that death liberates the soul from the chains and limitations of the body. Once rid of the evils of the body, the soul (mind) has the capacity to know that which is pure (unadulterated knowledge). The passage reads:

> And the true philosophers, Simmias, are always occupied in the practice of dying [to release the soul from the limitations of the body], wherefore also to them least of all men is death terrible. Look at the matter thus: if they have been in every way the enemies of the body, and are wanting to be alone with the soul, . . . how inconsistent would they be if they trembled and repined, instead of rejoicing at their departure to that place where, when they arrive, they hope to gain that which in life they desired—and this was wisdom [knowledge]—and at the same

time to be rid of the company of their enemy [body].[11]

> What again shall we say of the actual acquirement of knowledge?—is the body, if invited to share in the enquiry, a hinderer or a helper? I mean to say, have sight and hearing any truth in them? Are they not, as the poets are always telling us, inaccurate witnesses? . . .

> Then when does the soul attain truth?—for in attempting to consider anything in company with the body she is obviously deceived. Then must not true existence be revealed to her in thought, if at all?[12]

This passage from the *Phaedo* describes the epistemological position of Socrates as well as his contempt for the body. Plato presented us with an epistemological issue: Can we come to "know things," to acquire knowledge, while in the body? To Plato, the mind was eternal. In his concept of transmigration of the souls, the eternal mind/soul had knowledge—knew things—that it forgot at birth. Knowledge (to Plato) was knowledge of the real (world of forms); belief was about the changeable, sensible world. Our earthly life is a process of rediscovering or uncovering all those things the soul/mind experienced as knowledge or truth before it inherited or was assigned to the body. The body, however, will constantly deceive us as to what is real or authentic. The body will fool us with inaccurate information; therefore, we should not trust our senses to reveal truth but rely completely on our mind/soul to reveal truth insofar as possible while in the company of the body. The ideas of truth and knowledge shaped by the mind/soul are far more accurate than the examples or representations of truth and knowledge represented in the physical-corporeal-material world, which, because of the ability of the body to deceive the mind, cannot be trusted.

This metaphysical position and attendant epistemology are damaging to physical education because the body is not valued. The body is viewed as the enemy of the mind. If this extreme epistemological position were ever supported as the foundation of contemporary educational philosophy, physical education and sport would never be components of the curriculum. The curriculum would be devoted to the exclusive training of the mind. In summary, Plato and Socrates believed that the training of the mind was crucial because the individual who developed intellectual prowess could make contributions that would be eternal—contributions to science, literature, architecture, poetry, and philosophy that would withstand the "test of time." Great ideas, great contributions, are eternal and never decay. The body, however, always decays. Why cultivate and develop the corporeal aspect of existence when it is guaranteed to decay? It is wiser to develop the mind, nurture creativity, and inspire individuals and civilizations to make contributions that are just as much appreciated today as when the mind conceived them! How much "truth" is reflected in this belief?

SOCRATES' AND PLATO'S VIEW OF PHYSICAL EDUCATION

Although the *Phaedo* describes a negative philosophical view of the body that is clearly understood within the traditions of Western civilization, it is not Socrates' and Plato's only position on this subject. The paradoxical nature of Plato becomes evident when we observe that although Socrates and Plato were athletes who trained hard for competition and cared for their bodies, they attacked the body as a "source of endless trouble" that prevents the mind and soul from attaining truth as long as "the soul is infected with the evils of the body."[13] However, in a radical departure, Plato provides us with yet another philosophical position of the body in Books II and III of *The Republic*. Although he continues to maintain his dualistic approach to the nature and reality of man, he argues that there must be balance and harmony in the education of his citizens:

> Come then, and let us pass a leisure hour in story-telling, and our story shall be the education of our heroes.
>
> And what shall be their education? Can we find a better than the traditional sort?—and this has two divisions, gymnastic for the body, and music for the soul.[14]

Figure 3-3
Plato and his students in the garden of the academy.

In *The Republic*, Plato attempts to construct the first utopia in literature. The education and training of the citizens in his utopia were of critical importance to Plato. Gymnastics and music were the two components of the curriculum (Figure 3-3). Of interest to physical educators is that these components, identified as "physical education" e.g. Gymnastics and "academics" e.g. Music reinforce and perpetuate the dualistic approach to education that remains in place today: One component educates the mind, and another component educates the body. However, the logic Plato used to incorporate gymnastics into his educational curriculum elevates the philosophical position of the body. Although the body will never be equal to the mind/soul, the body is now in a position of importance, even though it continues to be subservient to the mind. In *The Republic*, Book III, Socrates states:

> Gymnastic as well as music should begin in early years; the training in it should be careful and should continue through life. Now my belief is . . . not that the good body by any bodily excellence improves the soul, but, on the contrary, that the good soul, by her own excellence, improves the body as far as this may be possible.
>
> Then, to the mind when adequately trained, we shall be right in handing over the more particular care of the body.[15]

Figure 3-4
Greek athletes train for the boxing competition while their coach gives instructions. Greek boxers wrapped their hands with strips of tanned and softened oxhide called himantes which were a form of early boxing gloves. (Source: National Archaeological Museum, Athens, Greece. R. Mechikoff, 2005.)

Plato was concerned that the citizens of his utopia, especially its leaders (the philosopher-kings) and the warrior-athletes, receive a well-rounded liberal arts education (Figure 3-4). He recognizes that gymnastics can promote health, a significant departure from his views on health in the *Phaedo*. Perhaps more important, he recognizes the problem of excessive devotion to music or gymnastics, which can be seen in the following conversation between Socrates and Glaucon from *The Republic*, which uses the Socratic method of questioning. Socrates states:

> *Did you never observe, I said, the effect on the mind itself of exclusive devotion to gymnastic, or the opposite effect of an exclusive devotion to music?*
>
> *In what way shown? he said.*
>
> *The one producing a temper of hardness and ferocity, the other of softness and effeminacy, I replied.*
>
> *Yes, he said, I am quite aware that the mere athlete becomes too much of a savage,*

> *and that the mere musician is melted and softened beyond what is good for him. . . .*
>
> *And so in gymnastic, if a man takes violent exercise and is a great feeder, and the reverse of a great student of philosophy, at first the high condition of his body fills him with pride and spirit, and he becomes twice the man that he was.*
>
> *Certainly.*
>
> *And what happens? if he does nothing else, and holds no converse with the Muses, does not even that intelligence which there may be in him, having no taste of any sort of learning or enquiry or thought or culture, grow feeble and dull and blind, his mind never waking up or receiving nourishment? . . .*
>
> *And he ends by becoming a hater of philosophy, uncivilized, never using the weapon of persuasion,—he is like a wild beast, all violence and fierceness, and knows no other way of dealing; and he lives in all ignorance and evil conditions, and has no sense of propriety and grace. . . . And he who mingles music with gymnastic in the fairest of proportions, and best attempers them to the soul, may be rightly called the true musician and harmonist in a far higher sense. . . .*
>
> *You are quite right, Socrates.*
>
> *And such a presiding genius will be always required in our State if the government is to last.*[16]

The view of the body in the *Phaedo* is an extreme example of how the body could inhibit the development of the mind and the attendant acquisition of reliable information. Why did Plato change the tone of his philosophical belief in the *Phaedo*, where the body is the enemy of the mind, to that found in *The Republic*, where he asserts a harmonious relationship between mind and body?

When Socrates was put to death, he was 70 years old, but Plato was still quite young. Plato was a devoted disciple of Socrates and was probably easily influenced by his mentor. As a staunch supporter of Socrates, Plato believed that after Socrates was dead the authorities would be looking for him, so he fled Athens and stayed away for a long time. During his time away from Athens, Plato matured intellectually and began to form his opinions without the "help" of Socrates. Plato wrote

The Republic and argued for a mind-and-body education. Although the development of a harmonious relationship between the mind and body is a significant philosophical departure from the position espoused in the *Phaedo,* Plato remains a dualist in *The Republic.* Developing the mind is still more important than developing the body. Understand that a "harmonious relationship" does not imply equality. Many students have harmonious relationships with their professors, and athletes may have harmonious relationships with their coaches. These relationships are congenial and amicable—but not necessarily "equal."

The belief in the harmonious development of mind and body in *The Republic* is a "means to an end" for Plato. In his utopia, he needs warrior-athletes to guard it against its enemies. He will not accept a warrior-athlete who is strong in body but weak in intellect. He has a realistic concern about the possibility of a group of warriors overthrowing the government of the republic, ruled by philosopher-kings, if these warriors fail to understand the reason for the existing form of government. If he gives his warrior-athletes a mind-and-body education, they will have the physical skills to defend the city and the intellectual ability to appreciate and defend the government.

Plato is also concerned with the type of citizens who will inhabit his utopia. He wants only the best. As a consequence, Plato has no patience with athletes devoted to the training of the body while neglecting the mind. He refers to these individuals as dull and boring. Conversely, he has no use for the individuals who pay attention exclusively to the mind and neglect the body. He believes this type of behavior will make men soft and effeminate. He also observes that if the body is healthy, it will please the eye and not be susceptible to disease. If individuals can maintain their health through exercise and sports, the mind will not be hampered by illness and other ailments and can do its work more efficiently. A healthy body will not harm the intellectual development of the individual; it frees the mind to attend to matters of importance. The body will not contribute to knowledge, but it will impede the mind if it (the body) is sick.

Plato developed solid arguments in favor of a mind-and-body education, even if it was only a means to an end. Although Plato's philosophical arguments justifying a mind-and-body education in *The Republic* support the need for modern physical education programs, he remained steadfast in his view that the body does not contribute to the development of the mind.

In summary, Plato provides us with two views of the body based on his metaphysical dualism: The argument in the *Phaedo* is for the development of the soul almost to the exclusion of the body, whereas in *The Republic* the argument is for a harmonious, but not equal, relationship between the body and the mind/soul. The significance of Plato's dualism is tied into what knowledge is and how we acquire knowledge (epistemology).

EDUCATION THROUGH THE PHYSICAL VERSUS EDUCATION OF THE PHYSICAL

Plato did not trust the body, which has a significant impact on the two historically divergent positions embodied in American physical education: (1) education through the physical and (2) education of the physical. The impact of Plato's dualism can be best grasped by posing two questions:

1. Can "accurate" knowledge be achieved while in the body?
2. If the answer is no, how is it possible to become educated?

Philosophically, the discussion of physical education as "education of the physical" or "education through the physical" was and is a key distinction among approaches to physical education. These two positions were advocated by two of America's leading figures in physical education. Jesse Feiring Williams (1886–1966) in his excellent article "Education Through the Physical"[17] expressed his opposition to the dualistic nature of existence and instead supported the view of each individual as a unity of mind and body, with the soul seen as an essential element of the whole.

According to Williams, who obviously took exception to Plato's dualism, physical education was concerned with not only physical fitness but also personal relationships; emotional responses; mental learning; group behavior; and related social, emotional, and aesthetic outcomes via education through the physical. Charles H. McCloy (1886–1959) was a contemporary of Jesse Feiring Williams, but he held fast to the position that physical education was education of the physical (Figure 3-5). The thematic emphasis in McCloy's work was on the importance of physical characteristics—physical development. Like Williams and physical educators of today, McCloy believed that the nature of men and women is that of an organic unity. McCloy's position was that the physical dimension is a significant aspect of

(a)

(b)

Figure 3-5
(a) Jesse Feiring Williams. (b) Charles Harold McCloy.

our existence. In his book *Philosophical Basis for Physical Education,* McCloy states the classic position for supporting education of the physical:

> The psychological literature of late has spoken much of the fact of body-mind unity, but this same literature has usually gone on thinking and writing as though the child were all mind. We in physical education, with our growing overemphasis upon the educational aspects of physical education [education through the physical], are apt to fall in the same error. Our organism is more body than mind, and it is only through the adequate functioning of all of it that the most desirable functioning of even the brain occurs.[18]

McCloy believed that the development of the physical, not education through the physical, should be the priority of physical education. It is fascinating to speculate about the nature of a debate between Plato, Williams, and McCloy concerning their epistemological positions relative to the body: the dualism of Plato versus the organic unity of Williams and McCloy, and the education through the physical advocated by Williams vigorously opposed by the education of the physical espoused by McCloy.

Contemporary physical education professionals may look to Plato's *Republic* to articulate or defend the mission of physical education in the schools. The position that Plato argues for in *The Republic* is one that blends academics with movement. However, these same physical education professionals may be unaware of the philosophical view of the body presented in the *Phaedo,* in which the body is evil and subservient to the mind. The education of students in physical education is not complete without a basic understanding of the philosophical position of the body put forth by Socrates and Plato. The epistemology of Socrates and Plato relative to the body, their dualistic beliefs, and their views on the need for gymnastics/physical education continue to have a profound philosophical influence on physical education in particular and education in general. Plato viewed the world as an imperfect copy of the actual or "ideal" world that existed in the mind and would not trust his senses. But his best pupil did not agree with him: Aristotle believed that the world of the senses is real.

ARISTOTLE

Aristotle (384–322 B.C.), the son of the physician Nicomachus, went to study with Plato when he was 18. He spent the next 20 years with Plato and later became tutor to a 13-year-old boy who became famous as Alexander the Great. In 335 B.C., Aristotle started his own school, the Lyceum, also known as the Peripatetic School of Philosophy. His students were called Peripatetics (from the Greek word that means to walk or stroll, which is the manner in which he taught). Aristotle would stroll around the grounds of the Lyceum while he lectured and engaged in philosophical discussions. In 323 B.C., the Athenian authorities accused Aristotle of impiety, and remembering what happened to Socrates when he was accused of impiety, he left Athens and the Lyceum 12 years after he opened the school. Aristotle moved to Chalcis, where he died at the age of 62.

Aristotle is generally recognized as one of the preeminent philosophers of all time, as well as Plato's most gifted student. His influence on science and philosophy has been profound. The works of Saint Thomas Aquinas, René Descartes, Immanuel Kant, Georg Hegel, and others were strongly influenced by Aristotle, who divided philosophy into three parts: (1) theoretical philosophy consisted of mathematics, physics, and metaphysics; (2) practical philosophy concerned itself with the theoretical practice of ethics and politics; and (3) poetic philosophy focused on aesthetics. According to Aristotle, logic enabled humans to find truth rather than function as a compendium of truths, and it prepared them to study philosophy. Aristotle believed logic would enable them to find truth, which meant that knowledge would agree with reality; truth will exist when mental ideals or representations concur with things in the objective world.[19] In contrast with his mentor Plato, Aristotle believed that there is only one reality—that reality

is the natural world we perceive with our senses. Plato and Socrates did not value sense perception as an accurate representation of reality. But to Aristotle, the body was a valid source of knowledge.

The social and political philosophy of Aristotle is interesting. He believed that man must be extracted from the crude conditions he finds himself in by the state, which will then civilize him by providing the foundation of an ethical and intellectual life. The state is the mechanism that will allow man to achieve a life of virtue and happiness. Man is not capable of achieving this goal without the state, because man is a political animal by nature and therefore must exist within an organized society. The highest virtue for the individual is intellectual attainment and the pursuit of peace. Aristotle considered women, children, and slaves to be inferior and so excluded them from government. However, he felt that children should be provided with an education designed to instill virtue that would ensure responsible citizenship and motivate them to work toward the common good of the state. The educational curriculum Aristotle envisioned included grammar, gymnastics, music, and drawing.[20]

To Aristotle, it was important that the rational soul be educated because the health of the mind was dependent on the health of the body. Aristotle believed that athletics enabled youths to develop as strong, healthy citizens who would defend Athens in times of war and serve her in times of peace. He held to the belief that because the health of the soul/mind was contingent on a healthy body, physical education (gymnastics) was necessary. Aristotle was also a big fan of the Olympic Games. He conducted an extensive review of the list of Olympic victors and ended up writing a much better account of the victors at Olympia than that which previously existed.

HISTORICAL FOUNDATIONS OF SPORT AND PHYSICAL EDUCATION

The Acropolis of Athens and the birthplace of the Olympic Games are familiar symbols that we associate with both ancient and modern Greece. The history of ancient Greece is a story replete with myths, enslavement, wars, romantic poems, cultural activities on a grand scale, and the development of athletic competition and promotion of physical beauty—a story that continues to fascinate us 2000 years later.

Arete and Agon

Arete and *agon* represent ideals that resonated with every Greek. From a historical and philosophical perspective, these two ideals are important if we are to develop an understanding of Greek culture and the cultural importance of specific qualities that each Greek strove to achieve. This is not an easy task because a literal translation of the meaning of these two words into modern English is at best difficult. The *Journal of Sport Literature* notes that arete is possible only while one is striving; those who think they have attained arete have lost it and have passed into hubris (excessive pride). Stephen G. Miller, professor emeritus of classical archaeology at the University of California at Berkeley and an expert on sports in ancient Greece, provides the best explanation of arete: "Arete is inextricably connected to the athletics of ancient Greece and laden with a plethora of meanings."[21] Miller continues:

> A definition of arete would include virtue, skill, prowess, pride, excellence, valor and nobility, but these words, whether taken individually or collectively, do not fulfill the meaning of arete. Arete existed, to some degree, in every ancient Greek and was at the same time, a goal to be sought and reached for by every Greek.[22]

The understanding of arete by some scholars and most physical educators has too often focused on arete relative to the achievement of excellence in athletics, to the neglect of other cultural institutions in ancient Greece. Miller notes that "in antiquity, arete was not limited to athletes. Arete—incompletely understood—has thereby dimmed our picture of the realities of antiquity and has robbed us of many of the real lessons to be learned from ancient athletics."[23] In ancient Greece, arete was not limited to the extraordinary accomplishments of male athletes; public servants, poets, philosophers, and common citizens received arete as well. One example of arete is found in a document written almost 2000 years ago by Pausanias, who lived in the second century A.D. and traveled all over the Roman world. He spent time in Greece as well as Egypt and left behind detailed accounts of his observations. Much of what we know about the ancient world is attributed to the writings of Pausanias.

In approximately A.D. 170, he made reference to arete during a visit to the agora (marketplace) of Phigaleia. While in Phigaleia, Pausanias inspected a stone statue erected in tribute to Arrhichion, a great athlete who won three times at Olympia in the pankration (a combination of boxing and wrestling). According to Pausanias, the inscription on the stone monument to Arrhichion disappeared, but the account of his victory in the fifty-fourth Olympiad was legend. In the fifty-fourth Olympiad (564 B.C.), Arrhichion won in part due to the fairness of the Hellanodikai (judges) and in part because of his arete.[24] As Arrhichion was fighting his opponent, his adversary began to strangle him and also managed to wrap his legs around Arrhichion's belly. Arrhichion fought back and was able to break one of his adversary's toes. However, during the course of the competition, Arrhichion died from being strangled, but his opponent did not realize this and signaled defeat. When the Hellanodikai separated the two athletes, they discovered that Arrhichion was dead. It seemed that Arrhichion decided that it was better to have died as an Olympic champion than admit defeat. The Hellanodikai, inspired by Arrhichion's arete, proclaimed him the champion and crowned the dead athlete with the olive wreath.

The story of Arrhichion's victory and display of arete is but one example of arete, and a drastic one at that! Arete is a complex yet compelling concept that does not lend itself to easy definition. It reflects qualities and behaviors held in the utmost esteem by the ancient Greeks. We still make reference to arete in the modern world, albeit, more often than not, inaccurate references—such as limiting arete to sporting excellence. Remember, arete was not limited to sport and was available to all Greek men—athletes and nonathletes. It must be noted that there is no evidence that a connection existed between arete and agon relative to women. Arete is likely a purely male ideal, with the possible exception of Spartan women; however, this is speculation.

Miller and others have frequently observed that much can be learned from the ancient Greeks, especially Greek sport. Perhaps it is time that we rediscover the true meaning of arete and apply its principles to the enhancement of modern sport and society. Arete is a quality that is not easily defined in the modern world. We may not have the appropriate words to capture the meaning of arete, but we can understand its significance.

Although arete was available to all Greeks, it was an evasive quality, and not all Greeks attained it. Agon is less complex than arete. Homer makes reference to agon as a meeting place where athletic events were held. Over time, agon expanded to include not only competitions for athletes but also competitions in music, poetry, public speaking, and related events. For example, gymnikos agon was used to identify nude athletic competitions while mousikos agon referred to music competitions. The modern word agony is derived from agon. The agonistic process is usually in reference to the physical pain endured by athletes during the process of training and competition. Gymnos means naked in classical Greek. Over time the word gymnastes emerged and was equated with anyone who did something nude. Ultimately "gymnastes" was used to refer to coaches who trained athletes, usually in the gymnasion which literally meant, more or less, where nude instruction was given in developing both mind and body—a place of education.

The Iliad and The Odyssey—The Story of Troy

Homer's The Iliad and The Odyssey are actually epic poems. They were first told as oral narratives and attributed to the poet Homer who was supposedly blind. Later on, The Iliad and The Odyssey were preserved in written form at some time between 1100 B.C. and 700 B.C. Homer may have been

a single poet although there are some who believe that Homer represents the work of more than one person. In any case, these are great stories with a cast of famous Greeks whose names are as recognizable today as they were thousands of years ago: Helen of Troy; Agamemnon, King of Mycenae; Paris, abductor of Helen and Son of Priam the King of Troy; Odysseus, hero of The Odyssey and crafty Greek who came up with the idea of building the Trojan Horse; Hector, Son of Priam, older brother of Paris and greatest Trojan of them all who was killed by Achilles; and Menelaus, King of Sparta who demanded that his wife Helen be returned to him at once or else there would be war! And so it was.

The Iliad tells the story of the kidnapping of Helen, wife of Menelaus, King of Sparta, and the 10-year Trojan War, while The Odyssey depicts the adventures of one of the heroes of Troy, Odysseus, as he makes his way back home after the war ends. Troy and the Trojan War captivated the people of the ancient world. When Alexander the Great (356–323 B.C.) began his conquest of the Persian Empire, he stopped at Troy and paid homage to the heroes of Troy by running around the walls of the city naked, carrying the shield that was said to have belonged to Achilles. While at Troy, he prayed at the Temple of Athena. Most of the temple has collapsed, but the same floor that Alexander stood on is still there.

The Odyssey is the story of Odysseus, also called Ulysses, and his journey back home to Greece. It is another great story that should be read, and yes, Hollywood has made a movie of this epic adventure as well.

Troy and the saga of the Trojan War continue to hold us hostage in the twenty-first century. Hollywood movie moguls knew that the modern world continued to be fascinated by this fantastic epic and in 2004 released the movie Troy, starring Brad Pitt as Achilles. The movie, like Homer's poem, was a huge success. But did Troy actually exist? How much of The Iliad and The Odyssey, first told in the oral tradition thousands of years ago, is factual?

Troy did indeed exist. The Greeks had colonized Asia Minor, present-day Turkey, with majestic cities. After the Roman conquest of Greece in

146 B.C., the Romans usually "Romanized" the Greek cities and frequently made them more lavish than the Greeks had done. The Romans, like the Greeks, were captivated by Homer's poetry and inhabited the great city. More about this in the next chapter; back to Troy.

During the time Homer lived, Troy was known as Illium. The ruins of Troy are located in western Turkey near the Aegean Sea, about an hour's drive from Canakkale or a six-hour drive from Istanbul. The Trojan War began in the 13th century when Priam, King of Troy, sent one of his two sons—Paris—to Sparta on a diplomatic mission. The younger of two brothers, Paris made the journey to Sparta in order to cultivate the Spartans as allies. When Paris arrived in Sparta, he was introduced to the Spartan King Menelaus. It did not take Paris long to focus his attention upon Helen of Sparta, wife of Menelaus and the most beautiful woman in all of Greece.

Seduced by Helen's beauty, Paris abducted Helen from Sparta in the dead of night and sailed back to Troy with his conquest. Helen of Sparta would soon become Helen of Troy and wife of Paris.

As you might guess, the Spartan King Menelaus was outraged that the Trojan prince had kidnapped his wife and demanded that Paris return Helen. Paris was not about to return the love of his life even if it meant war. Menelaus consulted with his brother, the mighty King of Mycenae, Agamemnon. Before long, the Greeks assembled thousands of warriors to attack Troy and return Helen to Sparta. Helen became known as "the face that launched a thousand ships."

The war lasted 10 years. When all seemed lost, the clever Greek leader Odysseus came up with an idea to fool the Trojans who refused to give up Helen. A giant wooden horse was built. Inside the horse was a compartment that concealed Greek warriors. The "Trojan Horse" was left outside the walls of Troy as a "gift," or so it seemed. The Greeks led the Trojans to believe that they had given up and were on their way back to Greece. The unsuspecting Trojans gladly took the horse inside the city and shortly afterward, a huge victory celebration commenced. Drunken revelry ensued and by nightfall, the exhausted but happy Trojans went to sleep. Soon after, the Greeks who were inside the horse slid down a rope and opened all of the city gates to their fellow Greek warriors who had quietly returned. The Greeks put the Trojans to the sword, showing no mercy. Menelaus was searching for Helen, not to rescue her, but to kill her. However, when he finally found his Spartan wife, her beauty once again overwhelmed him (as it seemed to overwhelm just about every man she met) and he spared her. The phrase, "beware of Greeks bearing gifts" is from the Trojan Horse presented to the Trojans as a "gift." It has morphed into the name of a computer virus in today's language, but the meaning is the same, showing us once again the enormous impact of the ancient Greeks on the modern world.

For thousands of years, people had assumed that the story of the Trojan War was a myth. Heinrich Schliemann (1822–1890) was born in Germany and at an early age became fascinated with Homer's account of the Trojan War. So fascinated was Schliemann that he became convinced that Troy and the Trojan War must be real and not a myth.

Schliemann became very wealthy through astute business transactions, especially his business dealings in California. He could speak several languages with ease. His wealth enabled him to pursue his life's ambition, to find Troy. He spent several years studying the classics and archaeology at the Sorbonne in Paris but never did receive the Doctor of Philosophy degree. He managed to badger the officials at the Sorbonne to award him a certificate of study. Returning to Turkey, he received permission from the Ottoman government to dig up sites that he believed to be Troy. As a self-taught archaeologist—the worst kind of archaeologist—he destroyed several ancient sites in the course of his quest. However, on a large hill called Hiserlick, he discovered a site that held artifacts suggesting that he had found the legendary city of Troy.

As it turned out, a number of ancient cities had occupied this site. Excavations revealed nine ancient cities dating back to Troy I, circa 3000 B.C. Most archaeologists believe that Troy VI is the city described by Homer.

Schliemann had married a Greek named Sophie. According to his account, he saw what appeared to be the glimmer of precious metal. Could it be Priam's Gold? He quickly gave his workers the day off and sent them home. He dug up a horde of precious jewels. He identified a beautiful gold necklace as the one worn by Helen of Troy and photographed his wife wearing this magnificent necklace.

Never shy of publicity, Schliemann promptly notified the world press that he had indeed discovered the legendary city of Troy. There were many skeptics. However, as time went by and more and more archaeological excavations took place under the direction of trained archaeologists

such as Carl W. Blegen, the Troy of Homer's epic poetry came to life. Excavations at Troy continue today. The famous Turkish archaeologist Reyhan Körpe has been conducting research at Troy and the surrounding area, known as the Troad, for more than 20 years.[25] So far, archaeologists have not found any actual artifacts (evidence) from the original wooden horse of Troy. However, an artifact that depicts a wooden horse hiding Greek soldiers has been found. A huge model of this "Trojan Horse" is the first thing that greets visitors when they enter the archaeological site of Troy today (Figure 3-7).

Funeral Games

The poet Homer provides us with an account of the Funeral Games in Book XXIII of *The Iliad,*

Figure 3-7
This replica sits inside Troy. Its construction was based on an image taken from an ancient vase that depicts the Greek soldiers concealed inside the Trojan Horse.

written between 1100 and 700 B.C. along with *The Odyssey.* The Funeral Games described by Homer involve Patroclos, a friend and fellow soldier of the legendary warrior Achilles. Patroclos was killed during the battle of Troy, and Achilles, wishing to honor and mourn his friend, instituted the Funeral Games. The Greek warriors were seated around the body and enjoyed a funeral feast. The next day, Achilles placed the body on an altar of wood surrounded by four slaughtered horses and 12 unfortunate Trojan boys executed for the occasion. The altar, horses, and Trojans were burned. After the cremation, the Funeral Games took place, consisting of chariot racing, discus throwing, archery, wrestling, footraces, spear contests, and boxing.

The Funeral Games were not unusual, nor were they the sole domain of the Greeks. The Greeks, like other ancient cultures, were very religious and sought to honor and appease their gods such as Zeus (supreme god), Apollo (god of the sun; patron of music, medicine, and prophecy), and Athena (goddess of wisdom and the arts). In addition to honoring the deceased, the Funeral Games were thought to give pleasure to the gods, who were believed to watch and enjoy athletic competition. The Temple of Athena at Troy was also a venue for athletic competitions to honor the goddess. These athletic competitions were celebrated by both Greeks and Romans, depending on who was occupying Troy; it is important to note that Troy was the scene for epic battles and athletic contests.

THE INFLUENCE OF CRETE

Environmental factors played a significant role in the development of athletics. Located on the northern shores of the Mediterranean, Greece is blessed with abundant sunshine and warm weather. These ideal climatic conditions enabled the Greeks to pursue a vigorous outdoor life throughout the year, as compared with Scandinavian and Germanic peoples who stayed indoors much of the year because of the severe weather. Greece is a collection of numerous islands as well as the mainland,

which has an irregular, rugged coastline with beautiful harbors, serene bays, and scenic villages. The Mediterranean island of Crete, which flourished as a related but separate culture, also has magnificent ruins and monuments to sport, such as what appear to be arenas where bull jumping took place (Figure 3-6). In Crete, major Minoan palaces occupied the sites of Knossos, Phaestos, and Mallia, and within the ruins remain works of art in which athletes are depicted jumping over bulls, possibly using a vaulting device, in an arena that may have been located in the central court of the palace. Boxing and dancing were other popular sports engaged in by the people of Crete during the Aegean Bronze Age (3000–1100 B.C.).[26]

SOME HISTORICAL PERSPECTIVES ON THE DEVELOPMENT OF GREEK SPORT

The origins of Greek sport have not been clearly established by scholars. Greek mythology makes abundant references to the athletic prowess of gods and mortals. Homer's *The Iliad* recounts the story of Achilles and his legendary exploits of physical skill and courage. In *The Odyssey,* Homer extols the virtues of the hero Odysseus and his skill as an

Figure 3-6
Minoan bull jumping and acrobatics.

athlete. Prior to that (mythical) time, the Greeks of the Mycenaean era engaged in athletic contests that closely resembled a modern track-and-field meet. Although the actual origins of Greek sport are still debated, the rich tradition and historical legacy of Greek athletics have never been equaled. This is not to say that other civilizations have not tried. Boutros argues that the Phoenicians may have been largely responsible for the early development of Greek sport. However, this view does not represent the majority opinion. There are two predominant schools of thought on the development of Greek sport. The first explanation, the traditional view, is the rise-and-fall approach. Scholars who adhere to this romantic perspective believe that ancient Greek sport rose to glory during the sixth and fifth centuries B.C. and then endured a long decline due in part to the disdain the Romans had for Greek sport, the rise of Christianity, and the steady increase of professional athletes who ignored the original concepts of agon and arete.

According to the traditional view, Greek sport evolved primarily from the games described by Homer in *The Iliad* and *The Odyssey.* We know for certain that from the sixth century B.C. onward, the primary goal of the athlete was to compete in a "circuit" of four major national competitions designated as the Stephanitic Games because the victorious athlete was bestowed with a *stephanos,* or "crown," of olive, laurel, pine, or celery. The Stephanitic or Crown Games later became known as the Panhellenic (all-Greek) Games. The "circuit" was instituted in 573 B.C. with the inclusion of the Nemean Games. The Panhellenic Games were scheduled to ensure that one major contest was held every year. The Panhellenic Games consisted of the following:

1. Olympic Games—held every four years at Olympia to honor Zeus. These are the oldest and most prestigious of the Panhellenic Games. The first record of the Olympic Games appears in 776 B.C. Victors were crowned with an olive wreath.
2. Pythian Games—held every four years in Delphi at the sacred site of Apollo. Victors were crowned with a wreath of laurel.

3. Isthmian Games—held every two years near Corinth to honor Poseidon, the sea god. Victors received a wreath of pine from a sacred grove. For a short period of time, a wreath of dried celery was awarded.
4. Nemean Games—held every two years in Nemea to honor Zeus. Victors received a wreath of fresh celery.

The traditional view holds that the rise of professional athletics gave way to an age of specialization, rewards, and all the attendant ills that money and glory bring about. By the fourth century B.C., sport was nothing more than a spectacle, corrupted by money. There is some truth to this view.

However, modern sport historians view this traditional or romantic view as flawed, due in part to the influence of Baron Pierre de Coubertin, founder of the modern Olympic Games. The first modern Olympiad was held in 1896 in Athens, although the Greeks staged some "Olympic Games" in the nineteenth century prior to Coubertin's Olympics. The Wenlock Olympic Games in England predated the modern Olympics as well. Baron de Coubertin perpetuated the amateur ideal that, according to the traditionalists and romantics, epitomized the ideal of Greek athletic competition that was supposedly pure and emblematic of the virtues of agon and arete. However, the Greek ideal of "amateur" was created by self-serving groups that invented the concept as a means to an end.

Scholars who disagree with the traditionalists suggest that Greek sport originated as a result of contact with the established sporting communities of Crete and Near Eastern civilizations such as the Phoenicians and the Egyptians. According to the nontraditionalists, Greek sport did not develop along the ideal lines of amateurism described by the traditional school. H. W. Pleket, for example, maintains that our concepts of amateur and professional and our beliefs about prizes and other rewards are often anachronistic with regard to Greek sport.[27] According to David C. Young, there was no word for *amateur* or for *games* in the Greek language.[28] In support of Pleket, Cynthia Slowikowski states that "the ancient Greeks never had a word which meant professional, and moreover, they did not distinguish between amateur or other athletes in their competition."[29] Young also argues that the Greeks never considered themselves amateurs and that they never developed the idea. Allen Guttman goes so far as to say that the idea of amateurism was a nineteenth-century invention by British historians and was perpetuated as a weapon of class warfare to keep the lower classes from beating their upper-class counterparts in athletic competition.[30]

There will continue to be different interpretations of history and general disagreement among physical education and sport historians over what happened and why it happened with regard to the development of sport in ancient Greece. However, like the walls of the ancient Acropolis in Athens, the foundation of the romantic interpretation of the origin of Greek sport is crumbling. Unfortunately, this view remains popular with many physical education professionals and the sports media. There is still more historical and archaeological research to be done on Greek sport, and with time and new information, a clearer, more accurate picture should emerge, or we may arrive at a different interpretation of the same evidence.

ATHENS AND SPARTA: A TALE OF TWO CITY-STATES

Greece was composed of a series of city-states, a collection of regional cities and towns that banded together for mutual benefits such as commerce and defense. Greece was not a politically unified country; the city-states were ruled by kings who would often go to war against each other. Over time, these city-states merged into over 20 major leagues or coalitions directed by the dominant city in each league. Athens and Sparta are the two most famous city-states and will be discussed here because the contrasting nature of these two most powerful city-states in ancient Greece provides an illuminating and revealing cultural analysis.

Athens was a city of immense culture and fabulous architecture and was home to Socrates,

Plato, Aristotle, Aristophanes, and other famous poets, playwrights, and philosophers. In addition, Athens had advanced the furthest toward democracy. Sparta, in contrast, was a military power whose primary purpose was to rule all of Greece. As a result, the citizens of Sparta had but one goal: to be warriors. The Spartan king Lykourgos authored a code of laws that gave Spartan women more rights and freedom than Athenian women enjoyed. He also mandated that Spartan women undergo serious physical training and compete in athletic contests held in Sparta. Sparta imposed ironfisted discipline over her citizens and the lands she conquered. Because the Spartans were obsessed with military supremacy, they contributed minimally to the arts, sciences, literature, and philosophy of Greece, especially compared with the contributions of the Athenians. Physical education programs and athletic competitions were taken seriously by Sparta, Athens, and the rest of the Greek world, which included colonies in Italy, Turkey, and, thanks to the conquests of Alexander the Great, India, Afghanistan, and Pakistan as well (Figure 3-8).

Two Views on Physical Education

As discussed earlier, the Greeks pictured their gods as perfect physical specimens. The artwork and literature of the Greeks is replete with pictures and tales that depict Zeus, Herakles, and other gods possessing incredible physical beauty and athletic prowess. For the Greeks to properly pay homage to their gods, they sought to resemble them through the attainment and cultivation of physical beauty.

The cultural nourishment and support of athletic competitions, along with the desire to resemble the gods through the attainment of physical beauty, promoted an athletic culture and sporting heritage of unprecedented proportions. Physical education reached a pinnacle in Athens, where it had the utilitarian purpose of preparing soldiers for war and also exemplified the Greek ideals of beauty and harmony. The Athenian program was education through the physical, meaning that through

Figure 3-8
Athletic competition. Under the scrutiny of his coach, the athlete is victorious.

physical education Athenians were believed to acquire important virtues of citizenship, loyalty, and courage. The Athenians sought harmony of both mind and body, and consequently, physical education occupied a prominent place in the education program. In the Athenian gymnasium, both body and mind were developed. Athenians believed that if a person displayed an out-of-shape, flabby body, it was a sign of poor education and personal disgrace.

Because the purpose of physical education was so different in Sparta from that in Athens, their respective programs were not at all similar, although their results, from a physical standpoint, were both favorable. The Spartan approach of physical training (not physical education) was strictly education of the physical, meaning that the training of the body was for military purposes. The education of Spartan citizens was the responsibility of the state.

Each newborn infant was examined by a council of elders who determined if the infant would be of benefit to Sparta. Only the strongest and healthiest babies were allowed to live; the rest were left on Mount Taygetus to die. The male child stayed at home until the age of 7, when he was conscripted into military service, where he remained until the age of 50 (if he lived that long). The 7-year-old boy was housed in primitive barracks under the watchful eye of the Paidonomos, who supervised the educational program called the *Agoge*. It was here that the Spartan character was developed—one personified by iron discipline, obedience to authority, indifference to pain and suffering, and obsession with victory in battle or any type of competition; defeat was unthinkable.

Gymnastics were the primary means of military and physical training. Spartan exercise did not take place in the lavish gymnasia or palaistrai that were built in Athens. Spartan facilities were plain and functional. Spartan youths were instructed in swimming, running, fighting, wrestling, boxing, ball games, horsemanship, archery, discus and javelin throwing, field marches, and the pankration (a combination of boxing and wrestling). At the age of 20, each male took an oath of allegiance to Sparta and then went into combat.

Periodic testing and evaluations were done in Sparta by officials known as *ephors*. The ephors would observe the Spartan youths and comment on their progress, as can be seen in the following passage:

> And besides, it was written in the law that every ten days the youth stripped naked should pass in public review before the Ephors. Now if they were solid and vigorous, resembling the work of a sculptor or engraver, as the result of the gymnastic exercise, praise was accorded them; but if their physique displayed any flabbiness or flaccidity, with fat beginning to appear in rolls because of laziness, then they were beaten and punished.[31]

The well-educated Spartan was one who was physically fit and a fearless soldier. Spartan cultural mores were not broad-based, as in Athenian culture, but were directed to achieving military superiority, which their program of physical training reflected.

Athenian Physical Education

The physical education activities in Athens also commenced at about age 7 and began with general physical conditioning. As in Sparta, physical education included boxing, running, wrestling, dancing, javelin and discus throwing, and the pankration. If the family could afford it, chariot racing, choral training, and assorted ball games were also included.

In contrast to Sparta, the education of Athenian youths was the responsibility of the family, not the state. Athens, like the rest of Greece, had a rigid class structure that placed citizens in certain classes depending on birthright, education, and finances. Depending on the resources of the family, either the children would receive an education centered in the home, with parents as the teachers, or a tutor would be retained who could provide a more enriching educational experience. Nonetheless, Athenians believed that the education of both mind and body was absolutely essential, and a great deal of care was given to this area. The Athenians thought it necessary to perfect the military skills of citizens and also to teach the appropriate values, virtues, and methods for the continued progress of the city through education and cultural enrichment.

Physical education was a prominent feature of Athenian education. According to Deobold Van Dalen and Bruce Bennett,

> The Greeks gave physical education a respectability that it has never since achieved. They accorded the body equal dignity with the mind. They associated sport with philosophy, music, literature, painting, and particularly with sculpture. They leave to all future civilizations important aesthetic ideas: the idea of harmonized balance of mind and body, of body symmetry, and bodily beauty in repose and in action.[32]

The athletic facilities in Athens and the rest of the Greek world consisted of gymnasia and palaistrai. Located in Athens were three prominent gymnasia: the Academy, the Lyceum built by Peisistratus, and the Cynosarges. Early gymnasia were probably nothing more than a designated area located near water where the athletes could exercise and then bathe. Gymnasia gradually evolved not only into elaborate centers of athletic training but also into places where intellectual pursuits were encouraged and supported. As intellectual and refined as Plato was, he was also a dedicated athlete. Miller notes that Plato's Academy "was first and foremost a place of exercise for the body."[33] Rules were posted in every gymnasion. A stone was uncovered by archaeologists, and rules were identified, titled "Concerning those who are not to enter the gymnasium." Some of the rules were "No slave is to disrobe in the gymnasium, nor any freedman, nor their sons, nor cripples, nor homosexuals, nor those engaged in commercial craft, nor drunkards, nor madmen."[34]

The palaistra is commonly referred to as a center where wrestling activity occurred. However, Rachel Sargeant Robinson states:

> When gymnastic training was developed into a regular institution, subject to well-formulated rules, a slightly more elaborate athletic plant became necessary. A simple building, called Palaestra, seems to have been added to the exercise grounds' gymnasium. [and] . . . equipped for exercise used in training boxers and wrestlers.[35]

Male athletes would undress in the Apodyterion, similar in concept to a modern-day locker room, albeit with one exception: They did not adorn themselves with a uniform or sweats. They oiled their nude bodies and then proceeded to train and compete naked.

There were both public and private athletic facilities, and some of the wealthier Athenians had gymnasia built for their personal use. If the family had enough money, they could hire a *paidotribe*, a physical education teacher who owned his own palaistra and charged a fee, similar to today's private health clubs. Music was popular in the gymnasia and palaistrai of Greece, and flute music could often be heard. Pedagogues, or teachers, were citizens as well as trusted slaves who would accompany young boys as their guardian, tutor, servant, counselor, and, when need be, disciplinarian. Formal educational training in Athens was limited to citizens. Slaves and other noncitizens did not have access to schools, although the gymnasium of Cynosarges allowed non-Athenian parents to enroll their sons. The health fitness clubs and personal trainers available to us today are remarkably similar to the practices of the ancient Athenians.

Athletic Participation of Greek Women

We are well aware that Greek culture and custom mandated that males compete in sports. However, to what extent did Greek women compete in sports and engage in exercises that promoted physical fitness? As previously noted, Spartan women received extensive training in sports and participated in rigorous exercises. Spartan law giver Lykourgos believed that the primary function of women was to bear strong, healthy children for Sparta. He hypothesized that strong children are born to parents who are also strong. He knew that the training men received in Sparta would make them strong. But what could he do to ensure that the women would also be strong? To this end, he ordered that Spartan women should do no less bodybuilding than the men and proclaimed that making the women compete in races would be of significant benefit. According to Plutarch (c. A.D. 100), Lykourgos ordained that virgins in Sparta not only compete in footraces but also wrestle and throw the discus. Lykourgos also

> removed from them [virgins] all softness and daintiness and effeminacy and accustomed the girls no less than boys to parade nude and to dance and sing at certain religious festivals in the presence of young men as spectators. . . . The nudity of the virgins was not shameful, for modesty was present and intemperance was

absent . . . it imbued them with a noble frame of mind as having a share in arete and in pride.[36]

The Athenians, bitter rivals of the Spartans, were not impressed by the physical education program for women in Sparta. A famous Athenian, Euripides (480 B.C.–406), observed that "a Spartan girl could not be chaste even if she wanted. They abandon their houses to run around with young men, with naked thighs and open clothes, sharing the same race track and palaistra—a situation which I find insufferable."[37] Another famous Athenian, Plato, was impressed with some of the approaches used by the Spartans. In the *Republic,* Plato presents his educational philosophy:

> With regard to women there should be a stadium and a diaulos [a footrace that went from one end of the stadium to the other and back] and an ephippios [a longer footrace than the diaulos, covering four lengths of the stadium], for the girls under the age of puberty who are to be nude when they compete in the race itself; the girls above the age of thirteen should continue to participate until marriage or until the age of twenty at the most . . . but dressed decently when they are actually competing in these races.[38]

There was a way for women to take part in the Olympic Games. Although they could not show up and drive, if they were wealthy enough they could enter a chariot team to compete in the games. Kyniska, daughter of the Spartan king Archidamos, entered such a team in the Olympics and won two times, once in 396 and again in 392 B.C. She erected a statue at Olympia to celebrate her victory, with an inscription that said, in part, "Kings of Sparta were my fathers and brothers. Kyniska, victorious at the chariot race with her swift-footed horses, erected this statue. I assert that I am the only woman in all Greece who won this crown.[39] Belistiche, concubine of Ptolemy Philadelphos who was the king of Egypt, also is listed as an Olympic victor in the chariot race.

Pausanias reports that after the men completed the Olympic Games, Greek women held athletic competitions at Olympia to honor the goddess Hera, Zeus's sister as well as his wife. The Heraian Games included footraces for virgins. The athletic virgins were divided into three groups. The first group were the youngest. The second group consisted of slightly older virgins, while in the third group were the oldest virgins, who ran last. These athletes used the same Olympic stadium although the races were not as long as for the males. In addition to footraces, there were exhibitions of dancing. The Heraian Games were sponsored by 16 women who convened prior to the start of the contests to weave a robe for Hera. These 16 women were assisted by the Hellanodikai. The Hellanodikai and the 16 sponsors could not begin their rituals until they purified themselves with the ritual sacrifice of a pig. The purification ritual took place at a spring called Piera, located between Olympia and Elis.[40] Victors were awarded an olive wreath and part of the cow that had been sacrificed to honor Hera. The winners were permitted to attach a victory plaque to the columns of the Temple of Hera. Traces of these plaques can still be seen at Olympia today. Judith Swaddling reports that the victorious women preferred paintings that depicted their victory.[41]

The Eleans lived in the region of Elis where Olympia is situated and, more often than not, served as its administrators. They built an altar in the stadium at Olympia where a married woman representing the cult of the goddess Demeter Chamyne could watch the athletes. Although the Eleans did not prevent virgins from viewing the games, a law was in place that excluded married women from watching the Olympics. Swaddling notes that there is no written evidence to explain why the Greeks discriminated against married women. This discriminatory law may not have been stringently enforced or at various times may have been ignored because Dio Chrysostom observed that "even women of dubious character were allowed at the Olympic Games."[42]

If an "unauthorized" woman was caught watching the Olympics, the punishment was to be hurled from the cliffs on Mount Typaon to her death. There is an account of a woman who did manage to sneak into the Olympics to watch her son compete. She was dressed like a male trainer and may have gone undetected if she hadn't jumped over a fence and exposed her true identity. She was caught but allowed to live because she was a widow and the daughter of the legendary athlete Diagoras of Rhodes. It also helped her case that her brothers and son had been Olympic champions. To discourage women who might think of disguising themselves as trainers to watch the athletes, a new law was passed that required the trainers to attend the games in the nude, just like the athletes.

Other than the Spartans, few Greek city-states provided much of an opportunity for women to compete in sport or become physically fit. We can conclude that, apart from the Spartans, most Greeks did not promote or encourage athletic competition or physical fitness among their women. What little "sport" existed for females was largely insignificant compared to what was available for males.

The ancient Greeks enjoyed watching nude female acrobats performing somersaults and vaults that are still performed by gymnasts and acrobats today. Acrobats and tumblers were not considered athletes but as entertainers in antiquity. Acrobats performed at weddings, banquets, and funerals where the assembled crowds would marvel at the display of strength and death defying leaps.[43]

THE ANCIENT OLYMPIC GAMES

There are enough irksome and troublesome things in life; aren't things just as bad at the Olympic festival? Aren't you scorched there by the fierce heat? Aren't you crushed in the crowd? Isn't it difficult to freshen yourself up? Doesn't the rain soak you to the skin? Aren't you bothered by the noise, the din, and other nuisances? But it seems to me that you are well able to bear and indeed gladly endure all this, when you think of the gripping spectacles that you will see.

These were the questions and observations made by Epictetus, who lived in the second century A.D., to a friend who was about to begin the trip to Olympia to watch the ancient Olympic Games (Dissertations 16, 23–9). For almost anybody who has attended the modern Olympic Games as a spectator, the timeless questions of Epictetus remain valid today.

The Athenians built a stadium and held hundreds of festivals over the years that were mainly religious, as are the probable origins of the Olympic Games. In addition to the stadium and attendant games in Athens, beautiful stadiums hosted athletic contests in Argos, Sikyon, and Epidavros (the latter can be seen today; it is only an hour's drive from Athens). In fact, there were numerous athletic festivals in Greece; nearly every city-state and small town celebrated festivals in which athletic competition was a major activity.

The first recorded evidence of the existence of the Olympic Games dates to 776 B.C. According to Kleanthis Palacologos, "The Olympic Games were, in fact, not founded on a fixed date and this is the reason why there were no definite founders. The Olympic Games evolved year after year, sacrifice upon sacrifice, ritual upon ritual."[44] Coroebus of Elis had the honor of being recognized as the first Olympic champion.

The demise of the Olympic Games remains somewhat of a mystery. As far as an actual date is concerned, there is no consensus. It may have been in A.D. 393 when the first Christian emperor of Rome, Theodosius I, issued a decree that banned all pagan cults. Since Olympia was a place of pagan worship, the games may have come to an end at this time. Or they may have ended in A.D. 435 when the Temple of Zeus at Olympia was destroyed, along with all of the remaining pagan temples in the eastern Mediterranean, by order of Emperor Theodosius II of Rome. The most illuminating argument comes from Stephen Miller, who states,

> There is no evidence that the Olympic Games were ever officially ended. But when the Emperor Theodosius II formally forbade the use of old pagan religious buildings in A.D. 435, games that were tied to buildings like the Temple of Zeus certainly also ended. [At that

point in time,] Greek religion and Greek athletics, already relics, ceased completely to play any meaningful role in society.[45]

Recently, German archaeologists excavating an ancient latrine at Olympia uncovered evidence that the Olympic Games may have continued until A.D. 493 or later.

The origins of the Olympic Games are based on myths and religious festivals. However, it is known that around 1000 B.C. the small town of Olympia erected a shrine to Zeus, who, according to legend, lived on Mount Olympus with 11 other gods who composed the Olympic Council. Religious festivals that honored their gods were popular in Greece, and Olympia was no exception. Over time, Olympia became famous as a location where victories, both athletic and military, were celebrated. The Greeks believed that victory was ordained by the gods. Olympia began as a religious sanctuary to the gods who, the Greeks believed, enjoyed watching mortals compete in sport. The athletes competed to honor Zeus, the most important deity of the ancient Greeks, and had to take an oath and swear to Zeus that they would play fair. In the second century A.D., Pausanias wrote the following account of the oath to Zeus:

> But the Zeus in the Bouleuterion is all of the images of Zeus most likely to strike terror into the hearts of sinners. He is surnamed Horkios [Oath god] and in each hand he holds a thunderbolt. Beside this image it is the custom for athletes, their fathers and their brothers, as well as their trainers, to swear an oath upon slices of boar's flesh that in nothing will they sin against the Olympic Games.[46]

When the athletes were caught breaking the rules or exhibiting other unsportsmanlike conduct, they were assessed fines, which were used to fund very expensive bronze statues honoring Zeus. Although cheating was frowned upon, it did happen. In one instance, a father was so eager that his son emerge as an Olympic champion that he bribed the father of his son's opponent to throw the match. They were caught and heavily fined.

Over the years, the religious festivals at Olympia became very popular and attracted athletes and spectators from all of Greece.

The Panhellenic athletic festivals, especially at the Olympic Games, were a time for religious rituals, athletic competitions, and lectures by the intellectual elite of the Greek world. The ancient Greeks also enjoyed socializing and drinking wine.

Early Olympic Games had but one event, the *Stade,* a footrace of about 200 meters (Figure 3-9). By 724 B.C., another event was added, the *Diaulos,* a sprint of about 370 meters, and in 720 B.C., a "long run" of approximately 4800 meters was added to the program. Wrestling and the Pentathlon (which consisted of five events: jumping, the swift footrace, discus, javelin, and wrestling) (Figures 3-10, 3-11, and 3-12) were added in 708 B.C., chariot races in 680 B.C., boxing in 623 B.C., and the race in armor in 520 B.C. (Figure 3-13). The chronological order of Olympic events is listed in Table 3-1.

Athletic facilities during the early stages of development were rather primitive (Figures 3-14 and 3-15). Construction of permanent buildings began in approximately 550 B.C. and culminated with a stadium (seating capacity 40,000), gymnasion, palaistra, and hippodrome. A temple dedicated to Zeus was erected in the middle of the fifth century B.C., along with a treasury building that housed the gifts brought to honor Zeus. There was even a hotel that housed the officials and visiting VIPs. It was known as the Leonidaion, named after Leonidas of Naxos, who built it in 4 B.C.

Every fourth year, three heralds left Olympia and traveled throughout the Greek world to announce the commencement of the Olympic Games. A sacred truce, by order of the Delphic oracle, was to be observed that permitted athletes and spectators making their way to Olympia to travel in safety. Even Alexander the Great had to pay money to an Athenian robbed by some of his soldiers while traveling to Olympia. Female virgins could attend as spectators, but Greek males were the only athletes who could actually compete in the games. This changed when Rome ruled Greece; the Romans opened up the competition to just about

Figure 3-9
Starting blocks. Athletes would set their toes in the grooves and perhaps use a sprinter's start or upright start.

Figure 3-10
Bowl painting illustrating the Pentathlon.

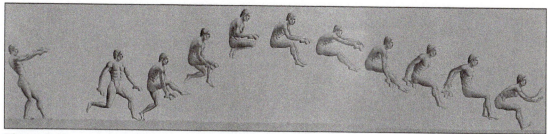

Figure 3-11
Sequence of the long-jump event, using halteres.

Figure 3-12
A haltere. Halteres were held in each hand; each
weighed about 4 to 5 pounds.

Figure 3-14
Aspendos was an ancient Greco-Roman city in Asia
Minor 40 kilometers east of the modern Turkish city of
Antalya. This coin, commonly called a Stater, was minted
to honor two Olympic athletes from the city, a wrestler
and a slinger (javelin thrower) circa 370–333 B.C.

Figure 3-13
Athlete competing in race in armor.

Figure 3-15
Ancient stadium of Olympia.

TABLE 3-1	**Introduction of Events into Olympic Games**	
Olympiad	**Year**	**Competition**
1	776 B.C.	Stadion
14	724 B.C.	Diaulos or double stadion
15	720 B.C.	Dolichos or long race
18	708 B.C.	Pentathlon and wrestling
23	688 B.C.	Boxing
25	680 B.C.	Chariot racing with teams of four—tethrippon
33	648 B.C.	Pankration and horse racing
37	632 B.C.	Footracing and wrestling for boys
38	628 B.C.	Pentathlon for boys (immediately discontinued)
41	616 B.C.	Boxing for boys
65	520 B.C.	Race in armor—hoplitodromos
70	500 B.C.	Chariot racing with mule (apene) held until 444 B.C.
71	496 B.C.	Race for mares (Kalpe) held until 444 B.C.
77	472 B.C.	Duration of festival and sequence of events legislated
84	444 B.C.	Apene and Kalpe abandoned
93	408 B.C.	Chariot racing with two-horse teams—synoris
96	396 B.C.	Competitions for heralds and trumpeters
99	384 B.C.	Chariot racing for colts with teams of four
128	268 B.C.	Chariot racing for colts with two-horse teams—synoris
131	256 B.C.	Race for colts
145	200 B.C.	Pankration for boys

Source: Maxwell L. Howell, "The Ancient Olympic Games: A Reconstruction of the Program," Seward Staley Address of the North American Society for the History of Sport, Boston, April 1975.

anybody who showed up. This was especially true in the later days of the Empire. There was one married woman who was allowed to watch the games. She would represent the Cult of Demeter, a Greek goddess who had a shrine at Olympia.

The rules of the Olympic Games were explicit: Athletes (and their trainers) had to arrive in Elis, a short distance from Olympia, no later than one month before the start of the games. They had to prove that they were citizens without a criminal record, they had to take an oath that they would compete fairly, and they had to swear to Zeus that they had trained for the previous 10 months.

You say, "I want to win at Olympia." . . . If you do, you will have to obey instructions, eat according to regulations, keep away from desserts, exercise on a fixed schedule at definite hours, in both heat and cold; you must not drink cold water nor can you have a drink of wine whenever you want. You must hand

*yourself over to your coach exactly as you
would to a doctor. Then in the contest itself
you must gouge and be gouged, there will be
times when you will sprain a wrist, turn your
ankle, swallow mouthfuls of sand, and be
flogged. And after all that there are times
when you lose.* (Epictetus, *Discourses* 15.2–5,
trans. W. E. Sweet)

The most visible officials of the ancient Olympics were known as the *Hellanodikai.* Their preparations began some 10 months prior to the start
of the games. They lived in a complex called the
hellanodikaion, located in the city of Elis, reserved
exclusively for them. These officials were chosen
by lot, and during most of the Olympics, there were
10 Hellanodikai on hand to oversee the games. One
of them was selected to act as a general supervisor,
and the others were assigned to the different events.
According to Swaddling, the first group of Hellanodikai were in charge of the equestrian competition,
the second group were in charge of the Pentathlon,
and the third group oversaw all of the remaining
events. They were in charge of assessing fines and
administering punishment for any infraction of the
rules. These punishments could be harsh. Both athletes and their trainers could be publicly flogged by
the *mastigophorai* (whip bearers) if their failure to
play by the rules was especially sinister.[47] These
officials wore the purple robes of royalty because
of their lofty position and authority. They took an
oath to be fair in their judging and to never reveal
anything they learned that would give one athlete
an advantage over another.

For a minimum of one month prior to the
start of the Olympics, the athletes were required
to live in Elis and train under the watchful eyes of
the Hellanodikai. These judges made sure that the
athletes were qualified to compete. Chariots and
horses were examined to make certain they were
within the rules. The training was harsh, for the
ancient Greeks did not taper off or rest immediately before competition as do today's athletes.
The Greek athletes were careful to obey every
command of the Hellanodikai and had to follow a
strict diet as well.[48]

Two days prior to the start of competition, the
Hellanodikai left Elis and, along with the procession of athletes, made their way to Olympia. Following the athletes were the coaches, trainers,
horses and their owners, jockeys, and chariots. This
must have been an imposing and inspiring sight,
watching all these Olympians march along the
Sacred Way toward Olympia. Along the way, they
stopped at the Fountain of Piera, situated at the border between Elis and Olympia, to conduct religious
rituals. At the end of the first day, the participants
spent the night in Letrini.[49] The next morning, they
followed the Sacred Way through the valley of the
Alpheios to Olympia, where they were greeted by
thousands of spectators.[50]

With both opening and closing ceremonies,
the atmosphere surrounding the Olympic Games
was a spectacle. Vendors sold food; businessmen
arranged "deals"; delegations from various city-
states discussed political matters; and fortune tell-
ers, souvenir sellers, musicians, and dancers, along
with pimps and prostitutes, did a brisk business.

In 472 B.C., the Olympics were reorganized
into a five-day event,[51] and they remained virtually
unchanged for the next 800 years. Two and a half
days were devoted to competition, and the remaining days were primarily religious in orientation.
Table 3-2 shows a typical sequence of events.

The importance of athletic ability in Greek
culture and the legendary display of athletic prowess at Olympia were topics of conversation for centuries. In the second century A.D., Lucian wrote:

If the Olympic Games were being held now
. . . you would be able to see for yourself why
we attach such great importance to athletics.
No-one can describe in mere words the
extraordinary . . . pleasure derived from them
and which you yourself would enjoy if you
were seated among the spectators feasting
your eyes on the prowess and stamina of the
athletes, the beauty and power of their bodies,
their incredible dexterity and skill, their
invincible strength, their courage, ambition,
endurance, and tenacity. You would never . . .
stop applauding them.[52]

TABLE 3-2	**Ancient Olympic Festival (472 or 468 B.C.)**

FIRST DAY

Morning: Inauguration of the festival; oath-taking ceremony; contests for heralds and trumpeters
Afternoon: The entire program of competition was written and posted for all to see.

SECOND DAY

Boys' events in the stadium
Equestrian events

THIRD DAY

Equestrian events and Pentathlon
Evening: Ritual banquet

FOURTH DAY

Ceremony to honor Zeus
Men's events—footraces
Heavy events (wrestling, boxing, pankration)
Hoplite race

FIFTH DAY

Prize-giving ceremony
Banquet in Prytaneion to honor the victors

Sources: Ludwig Drees, *Olympia: Gods, Artists, and Athletes* (New York: Drager, 1968); Panos Valavanis, *Games and Sanctuaries in Ancient Greece—Olympia, Isthmia, Nemea, Athens* (Los Angeles: J. Paul Getty Museum, 2004).

Boxing then, as now, was a brutal and bloody sport. Primary source material from thousands of years ago paints a gruesome picture. The bronze boxer at the Terme Museum in Rome and a relief on a tombstone at the Kerameikos Museum in Athens show scarred faces, broken noses, and cauliflower ears. Vase paintings of boxing matches show bloody noses. Ancient sources claim that boxers became so disfigured their dogs did not recognize them and they could not claim inheritances:

When Odysseus returned safely to his home after 20 years, only his dog Argos recognized him when he saw him. But you, Stratophon, after you have boxed for four hours, neither dogs nor your fellow citizens can recognize. If you will be so kind as to view your face in a mirror, you will affirm with an oath, "I am not Stratophon." (Lucillius, *Greek Anthology* 11.77, trans. W. E. Sweet)

O Augustus, this man Olympikos, as he now appears, used to have nose, chin, forehead, ears, and eyelids. But then he enrolled in the guild of boxers, with the result that he did not receive his share of his inheritance in a will. For in the lawsuit about the will his brother shows the judge a portrait of Olympikos, who was judged to be an imposter, bearing no resemblance to his own picture. (Lucillius, *Greek Anthology* 11.75, trans. W. E. Sweet)

The timeless tribute to Olympic athletes by Lucian evokes images of superbly trained athletes taking part in a festival of sport that was as noble as it was religious. Lucian and Epictetus were not the only individuals who extolled the heroics of Olympic athletes. The Greek poet Pindar (518–446 B.C.) lived several centuries before Epictetus and Lucian attended the Olympic, Pythian, Nemean, and Isthmian games. Pindar relates the magnificent athletic feats in a series of lyric poems known as "odes." He wrote 14 Olympic Odes, 12 Pythian Odes, 11 Nemean Odes, and 8 Isthmian Odes. As noted earlier, the philosopher Aristotle helped to update the records kept at Olympia. We know that Plato attended the games. He attended to watch the athletes and listen to the orations of philosophers from all over the Greek world who gathered to "match wits" against each other. It is important to understand the significance of the Olympic Games. Although the athletes were in the spotlight, the huge crowds who came to Olympia were eager to see the best that Greece had to offer—the best philosophers, poets, military heros, and artists along with the best athletes. The Olympic Games featured the athletic and intellectual elite of the Greek world.

The Olympics were as much a religious ceremony for Greek citizens as an event in which athletes competed for fortune and fame. As the games grew, it was not unusual for an athlete to hire out to the city that offered him the most money and attendant luxuries, as long as he kept winning. It appears that the practice of athletes becoming "free agents" has a long history!

SUMMARY

Perhaps no other civilization in history embraced athletic competition and intellectual development as did the ancient Greeks. The foundation for the tradition of athletics emblematic of the Hellenes was influenced in part by the Egyptians, the people of Crete, and possibly the Phoenicians. Various athletic contests and games were carried to mainland Greece by merchant sailors from distant lands. We can assume that during the course of military expeditions, the Greeks adopted some of the ways of their conquered enemies, including games and sports that appealed to them.

The Olympic Games enjoyed a great deal of popularity in the ancient Mediterranean world. The athletic festival in Olympia appealed to Greeks and non-Greeks. Josephus, a Jewish philosopher and historian who lived in the first century A.D., wrote that the appeal of Greek institutions was widespread. King Herod was interested in the Olympic Games, and Josepheus notes that "it is not surprising to see some elements of Greek athletics appearing in Judea."

As a general idea, the Greeks believed in the physical development of the body in a way that was aesthetic as well as athletic. Although athletics was a priority, intellectual nourishment and development as we know it was not uniform among the politically diverse Greeks. Athens was emblematic of cultural and political supremacy; Sparta, in contrast, was a cultural desert and politically was ruthless and repressive. It was not unusual for the Greeks to wage war against each other or come to the aid of another Greek city-state when attacked by non-Greeks.

Athletic festivals emerged on the local and national level and ultimately became institutionalized, which afforded a meeting place for all Greek men and, more important, provided an arena in which the city-states and their quasi-nationalistic athletes could compete. The earlier concept of the magnificent athletic festivals of the Panhellenic Games, based on honor to Zeus and ideals of honesty and fair play, gave way to the era of professional athletes who represented the city that was able to pay them the most money. In the early sixth century B.C., the Athenian king Solon offered 500 drachmae to Athenian athletes victorious at Olympia, and he offered smaller amounts of money and prizes to Athenian athletes who won at lesser athletic festivals. Under Roman rule, the athletic festivals continued to operate but no longer served as an agency of physical education or promotion of individual excellence. The Greeks gradually started to place less importance on individual physical development, and by the fourth century A.D., the intellectual and athletic ideal of developing the all-around individual who was an educated citizen, an athlete, and a soldier in the Athenian sense had vanished.

DISCUSSION QUESTIONS

1. Did the Greeks develop games and sports without outside influences, or does it appear that other cultures may have contributed to the development of Greek athletics?

2. What is meant by dualism?

3. Can dualism affect epistemological beliefs?

4. Generally speaking, where did Socrates and Plato place the development of the body in relation to the development of the mind? What was their rationale?

5. What were the two opposing ideas of physical education that existed in ancient Greece according to Fairs?

6. What was the relationship of the military to physical education in ancient Greek culture? Does this same relationship exist today?

7. What role did religion play in ancient Greek sport?

8. What was the role of women in sport in ancient Greece? Were all the city-states the same in this respect? To what extent was athletic competition available to women?

9. How did the Greeks view the body? How, if at all, does their position (view of the body) affect contemporary society today?

10. Were the ancient Greek athletes "amateurs"? Where does this idea of amateurism come from?

11. What were the organizations, training, rules, and events essential to the success and popularity of the ancient Olympic games?

12. Read some of the odes that Pindar devoted to Greek athletes. What are some of the themes that Pindar seems to stress?

13. What similarities can you identify between the way Greek athletes trained thousands of years ago and the way athletes train today?

14. In your opinion, were the athletes of ancient Greece better overall athletes than the athletes of today? Why or why not?

15. How did Athenians feel about the women athletes of Sparta?

16. Were stadiums and athletic competitions confined only to Sparta, Athens, and the Panhellenic Games?

17. How pervasive were the concepts of agon and arete in ancient Greece? Did they seem to apply to women as well as men? Is arete taught or instilled by coaches or physical educators in their athletes/students today?

INTERNET RESOURCES

Perseus Digital Library: Ancient Olympics
www.perseus.tufts.edu/Olympics
Provides information on ancient Greek sports, Olympic games of antiquity, and related topics.

National Geographic News: Ancient Olympics
**http://news.nationalgeographic.com/news/2004/08/
   0809_040809_nakedolympics.html**
Tells an entertaining and informative story about the ancient Olympics.

Ancient Greece: Directory of Online Resources
www.academicinfo.net/histancgreece.html
Provides information about ancient Greek civilization and culture.

Greek Sports: Track and Field
www.hellenism.net/eng/sports_olympics1.htm
Provides information about ancient track-and-field competitions.

Athletes Tunic Up for "Real" Olympics
www.abc.net.au/sport/features/2003/s1166217.htm
Contains an article and links about the Nemean Games.

Archaeology Magazine: Olympic Resources
**www.archaeology.org/online/features/olympics/
   resources.html**
Lists Olympic resources on the Web and in the library.

History and Philosophy: Greece
http://users.bigpond.net.au/bstone/greece.htm
Provides information about the philosophy and culture of ancient Greece.

Ancient Nemea
www.nemea.org
Tells the history of the Nemean athletic competitions.

Visit the *History and Philosophy of Sport and Physical Education* Online Learning Center (www.mhhe.com/mechikoff6e) for additional information and study tools.

SUGGESTIONS FOR FURTHER READING

Balme, M. "Attitudes to Work and Leisure in Ancient Greece." *Greece and Rome* 1, no. 2 (October 1984): 140–52.

Cahn, J. L. "Contributions of Plato to Thought on Physical Education, Health, and Recreation." Doctoral dissertation, New York University, 1942.

Crowther, N. B. "Weightlifting in Antiquity: Achievement and Training." *Greek, Roman, and Byzantine Studies* 24 (1977): 111–20.

———. "Studies in Greek Athletics." *Classical World* 78 (1984): 497–558.

———. "Studies in Greek Athletics." *Classical World* 79 (1985): 73–135.

Dyson, H. G. Geoffery. "The Ancient Olympic Games." *Journal of the Canadian Association for Health, Physical Education, and Recreation* 42, no. 4 (March–April 1976): 3–7.

Fleming, W. *Arts and Ideas.* New York: Holt, Rinehart & Winston, 1963.

Hyde, W. W. "The Pentathalon Jump." *American Journal of Philology* 59, no. 4 (1938): 405–17.

Journal of Sport History 30, no. 2 (2004). Issue devoted to ancient Olympics and Greek society and politics.

Lee, H. M. "Athletic Arete in Pindar." *Ancient World* 7, nos. 1–2 (March 1983): 31–37.

Matz, David. *Greek and Roman Sport: A Dictionary of Athletes and Events from the Eighth Century B.C. to the Third Century A.D.* London: McFarland, 1991.

Miller, Stephen G. ed. *Nemea: A Guide to the Site and Museum.* Berkeley: University of California Press, 1990.

———. *Arete—Greek Sports from Ancient Sources.* Berkeley: University of California Press, 1991.

———. *Ancient Greek Athletics.* New Haven, CT: Yale University Press, 2004.

———. *Plato at Olympia.* Athens: Lucy Braggiotti Editions, 2008.

Mouratidis, J. "Games and Festivals as a Unifying Force in Ancient Greece." *Physical Education Review* 8, no. 1 (1985): 41–49.

Nagy, B. "The Athenian Athlothetai." *Greek, Roman, and Byzantine Studies* 19, no. 4 (1978): 307–13.

Pindar. *The Odes of Pindar. Including the principal fragments, with an introduction and an English translation by Sir John Sandys,* rev. ed. (London: W. Heinemann; Cambridge, MA: Harvard University Press, 1937).

Raubitschek, A. E. "The Agonistic Spirit in Greek Culture." *Ancient World* 7, nos. 1–2 (March 1983): 3–7.

Romano, D. G. "The Ancient Stadium: Athletes and Arete." *Ancient World* 7, nos. 1–2 (March 1983): 9–16.

Scanlon, Thomas Francis. *Greek and Roman Athletics: A Bibliography.* Chicago: Ares, 1984.

Seltman, C. "Life in Ancient Crete II: Atlantis." *History Today* 2, no. 5 (May 1952): 332–43.

Sutts, A. "Our Greek Heritage." *Journal of Physical Education, Recreation, and Dance* 55, no. 1 (January 1984): 27–28.

Swaddling, J. "Olympic Glory." *Natural History* (June 1984): 60–74, 77.

Valavanis, Panos. *Games and Sanctuaries in Ancient Greece: Olympia, Isthmia, Nemea, Athens.* Los Angeles: J. Paul Getty Museum, 2004.

Young, D. C. "Professionalism in Archaic and Classical Greek Athletes." *Ancient World* 7, nos. 1–2 (March 1985): 45–51.

NOTES

1. Labib Boutros, *Phoenician Sport—Its Influence on the Origin of the Olympic Games* (Amsterdam: J. C. Gieben, 1981), 1.

2. Sophia Vakirtzi, "Athletic Activity in Phoenicia" (research paper presented at the International Olympic Academy, Ancient Olympia, Greece. May 10, 2000).

3. Boutros, *Phoenician Sport,* 1–2.

4. John R. Fairs, "The Influence of Plato and Platonism on the Development of Physical Education in Western Culture," *Quest* IX (December 1968): 14–33.

5. Ibid., 14.

6. *Phaedo* and the *Republic.* All references are to B. Jowett, trans., *The Dialogues of Plato* (New York: Washington Square Press, 1966).

7. *Metaphysical dualism* is the philosophical division of existence into two components: mind and body. Dualism is evident in the words *mind* and *body* and is a tradition in the thought and languages of Western civilization.

8. This can be compared with *asceticism,* whereby one rejects the body in favor of the promise of spiritual salvation.

9. William Fleming, *Arts and Ideas* (New York: Holt, Rinehart & Winston, 1966), 43–44.

10. Stephen G. Miller, Plato at Olympia (Athens: 2008), p. 61; Stephen G. Miller, Ancient Greek Athletics (New Haven CT: Yale University Press, 2004), p. 119; Personal correspondence with Stephen G. Miller via email Nov. 21, 2008.

11. B. Jowett, *Phaedo* and the *Republic,* 62.

12. Ibid., 78.

13. *Phaedo,* 80.

14. *Republic,* Book II, 253.

15. Ibid., 258–59.

16. Ibid., 262–64.

17. Jesse Feiring Williams, "Education Through the Physical," *Journal of Higher Education* 1 (May 1930): 279–82.

18. Charles Harold McCloy, *Philosophical Basis for Physical Education* (New York: F. S. Crofts, 1940), 77–78.

19. William S. Sahakian, *History of Philosophy* (New York: Barnes & Noble, 1968), 63.

20. Ibid., 76–78.

21. Stephen G. Miller, *Arete—Greek Sports from Ancient Sources,* 3rd ed. Berkeley: University of California Press, 2004), ix.

22. Ibid.

23. Stephen G. Miller, *Arete—Greek Sports from Ancient Sources,* 2nd ed. (Berkeley: University of California Press, 1991), vii, viii.

24. Pausanius 8.40, 1–5; Miller, *Arete,* 2nd ed., 36.

25. Nurtensevinc, Reyhan Körpe et al. "A New Painted Graeco-Persian Sarcophagus from Can," *Studia Troica* 11 (2001), Verlag Philipp von Zabern–Mainz Am Rhein, 383–420; Reyhan Körpe and Mikhail Treister, "Rescue Excavations in the Necropolis of Lampsacus, 1996," *Studia Troica* 12 (2002), Verlag Philipp von Zabern–Mainz Am Rhein, 429–50; Reyhan Körpe and Funda Körpe, "A New Inscription of Asklepios from the Troad, 2005," *Studia Troica* 15 (2005), Verlag Philipp von Zabern–Mainz Am Rhein, 205–8; Reyhan Körpe and Funda Körpe, "A Lead Medallion from Skepsis in the Troad," *Studia Troica* 11 (2001), Verlag Philipp von Zabern–Mainz Am Rhein, 421–26; C. Brian Rose and Reyhan Körpe, "The Granicus River Valley Survey Project, 2004," research paper presented at the annual meeting of the Archaeological Institute of America, Montreal, Quebec, Canada, January 5–8, 2006.

26. James G. Thompson, "Clues to the Location of Minoan Bull-Jumping from the Palace at Knossos," *Journal of Sport History* 16, no. 1 (Spring 1989): 62–69.

27. H. W. Plecket, "Games, Prizes, Athletes, and Ideology: Some Aspects of the History of Sport in the Greco-Roman World," *Stadion* 1 (1975).

28. David C. Young, *The Olympic Myth of Greek Amateur Athletics* (Chicago: Ares, 1984).

29. Cynthia S. Slowikowski, "Alexander the Great and Sport History: A Commentary on

Scholarship," *Journal of Sport History* 16, no. 1 (Spring 1989): 73.

30. Allen Guttman, *From Ritual to Record: The Nature of Modern Sports* (New York: Columbia University Press, 1978).

31. Variae Historiae Aeliani 14:7, in Clarence Forbes, *Greek Physical Education* (New York: Century, 1929), 33.

32. Deobold B. Van Dalen and Bruce L. Bennett, *A World History of Physical Education,* 2nd ed. (Englewood Cliffs, NJ: Prentice-Hall, 1971), 47.

33. Miller, *Arete,* 3rd ed., ix.

34. Ibid., 139.

35. Rachel Sargent Robinson, *Sources for the History of Greek Athletics* (Cincinnati, OH: Author, 1955), 152.

36. Miller, *Arete,* 2nd ed., 107.

37. Ibid., 107.

38. Ibid., 103.

39. Ibid., 100.

40. Ibid., 102–3.

41. Judith Swaddling, *The Ancient Olympic Games* (London: British Museum, 1987), 43.

42. Miller, *Arete,* 2nd ed., 100; Swaddling, *Ancient Olympic Games,* 42.

43. Biblical Archaeology Review, p. 80, March/April 2010 Vol. 36 No. 2.

44. Kleanthis Palacologos, "The Course of the Evolution of the Ancient Olympic Games" (paper presented at the International Olympic Academy, Twenty-Fourth Session, Ancient Olympia, Greece, July 4–19, 1984), 76.

45. Miller, *Ancient Greek Athletics*, 6 (New Haven, CT: Yale University Press, 2004), 6.

46. *Descriptions of Greece* v. 24.9; Swaddling, *Ancient Olympic Games,* 41.

47. Swaddling, *Ancient Olympic Games,* 35, 41.

48. Ibid., 35–36.

49. Ibid., 36.

50. Ludwig Drees, *Olympia: Gods, Artists, and Athletes* (New York: Drager, 1968).

51. Anacharsis 12; Swaddling, *Ancient Olympic Games,* 79.

52. Swaddling, *Ancient Olympic Games.*

4

Rome

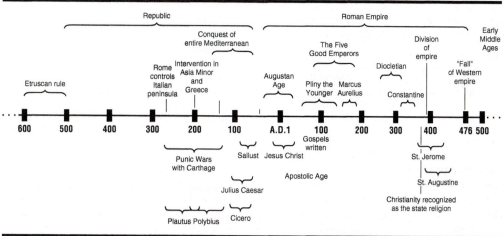

Ancient Rome.

O B J E C T I V E S

Upon completing this chapter, you will be able to:

- Identify the cultural impact that the Etruscans had upon Roman civilization, especially in regard to ritual sacrifice in the arena.
- Identify sporting competitions and physical activities that were significant cultural components of Etruscan civilization.
- Understand the role of women in Etruscan culture and their participation in competitive sport.
- Recognize the pervasiveness of sport in Etruscan culture.
- Discuss the Etruscan philosophical view of the human body.
- Understand the institutional and cultural differences between the Roman Republic and the Roman Empire.

General Events

B.C.
100–44 Julius Caesar
29–19 Virgil writes *The Aeneid*
27–A.D. 14 Augustus reigns
A.D.
c. 16 Maison Carrée at Nimes
c. 50 Pont du Gard at Nimes
  built
54–68 Nero reigns
70 Titus captures Jerusalem;
  temple destroyed
79 Eruption of Vesuvius;
  Pompeii and Herculaneum
  destroyed
81 Arch of Titus, Rome, built

82 Colosseum, Rome, finished

c. 93 Quintilian writes *Institutes of Oratory*

96–180 Antonine Age; Roman Empire reaches pinnacle of power and prosperity

96–98 Nerva, emperor

98–117 Trajan, emperor

c. 100 Suetonius writes *Lives of the Caesars*

100 Pliny the Younger delivers Panegyric to Trajan before Roman Senate

100–102 Trajan's first Dacian campaign

105–106 Trajan's second Dacian campaign

110 Via Iraiana built between Benevento and Brindisi, Baths of Trajan built

113 Forum of Trajan built, Column of Trajan erected

114 Arch of Trajan built at Benevento

117–138 Hadrian, emperor

120–124 Pantheon, Rome, built

138–161 Antoninus Pius, emperor

161–180 Marcus Aurelius, emperor

217 Baths of Caracalla, Rome, built

Philosophers and Literary Figures

80 B.C.–A.D. 14 Golden Age of Literature

106–43 B.C. Cicero

c. 96–55 B.C. Lucretius

84–54 B.C. Catullus

70–19 B.C. Virgil

65–8 B.C. Horace

59 B.C.–A.D. 17 Livy

43 B.C.–A.D. 17 Ovid

A.D. 14–117 Silver Age of Literature

3 B.C.–A.D. 65 Seneca

A.D.

23–79 Pliny the Elder

c. 66 Petronias died

c. 90 Epictetus flourished

35–95 Quintilian

c. 40–102 Martial

c. 46–120 Plutarch

c. 55–117 Tacitus

c. 60–135 Juvenal

62–113 Pliny the Younger

c. 75–150 Suetonius

c. 160 Apulius flourishes

c. 200 Tertulian flourishes

- Appreciate the influence of Greek culture on the Etruscans and Romans.
- Understand how Nero, emperor of Rome, was influenced by Greek culture and his desire to become an Olympic champion.
- Understand the philosophical schools and related beliefs of Romans, as well as their view of the human body.
- Explain the role and scope of sport and physical education during the Republic and during the Empire.
- Explain the role and scope of Roman military training and the Roman distaste for Greek nudity.
- Understand the contributions that Claudius Galen made to exercise and his attitude toward professional athletes.
- Understand the Roman attitude toward Greek athletics.
- Recognize the extent to which Roman women participated in exercise and gladiatorial combats.
- Understand the Roman fascination with viewing and cultural necessity for staging brutal spectacles and mass combats in the Flavian Amphitheater and other venues.
- Identify athletic competitions and exercise programs that were popular with the inhabitants of the Republic and the Empire.
- Recognize the pervasiveness of horse and chariot racing.
- Identify the different types of gladiators and gladiatorial combats that were popular in Rome.
- Understand the "life" of a gladiator.
- Identify some of the huge and elaborate venues that were built for mass public entertainment.
- Appreciate the logistics and costs necessary to mount massive entertainment programs.
- Understand the relationship between sport and Christianity.
- Discuss the extent to which the Greeks embraced Roman gladiatorial combat and similar spectacles.
- Discuss the popularity of chariot racing in Constantinople and the rivalry between the Greens and the Blues.
- Identify the eight main types of gladiators and how specialized and specific gladiator combats became.

INTRODUCTION

No one knows the precise date when Rome was given the status of the Eternal City. This title continues to reflect its geographical location and historical position as the gateway to Mediterranean culture and to civilizations that perished long ago (Figure 4-1). What was to eventually become one of the most legendary and prolific civilizations the world has known grew out of a small community known as Latium, situated near the Tiber River and the much-acclaimed seven hills of Rome. There are two sources that explain the birth of Rome. The first is the legend of Romulus and Remus, twin brothers who were suckled by a she-wolf who found the two infants on a riverbank where they had been abandoned. The twins were raised by a shepherd. Romulus eventually murdered his brother and proclaimed himself the first king of Rome in 753 B.C. The second explanation is the historical record, which says that in 509 B.C. the residents of Latium—the first "Romans"—defeated the

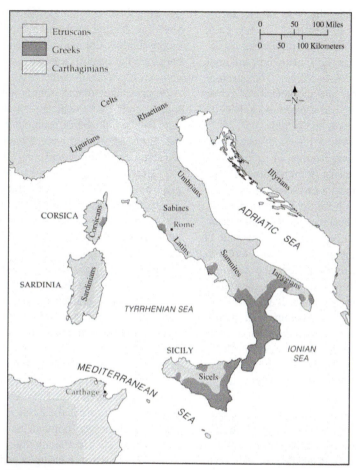

Figure 4-1
Italy, fifth century B.C.

Etruscans and the Roman Republic was born. Who were the Etruscans, and to what extent did they influence Roman culture?

THE ETRUSCANS

Etruria, the region inhabited by the ancient Etruscans, is located in present-day west central Italy. It was bordered to the north by the Arno River, to the east and south by the Tiber River, and to the west by the Tyrrhenian Sea, which is part of the larger Mediterranean Sea. Scholars do not have a precise understanding of the origins of the Etruscans; however, three hypotheses are possible. The first was posited by Herodotus (484–435 B.C.), the famous Greek historian and the "father of history." He concluded that the Etruscans migrated to west central Italy from Lydia, an ancient kingdom in the western part of Asia Minor—a peninsula in western Asia, between the Black Sea and the Mediterranean Sea, that includes Turkey. In approximately 100 B.C., Dionysius of Halicarnassus went on record with the second hypothesis: that the Etruscans were probably indigenous to Italy. The third hypothesis is that the Etruscans migrated to Italy from the north. Evidence for this hypothesis was found in the Alps where Etruscan inscriptions were discovered.[1] In any case, the Etruscans were significantly influenced by the Greeks, the Phoenicians, Egyptians, and the civilizations who occupied Asia Minor.[2] The development of Etruscan games and sport, as well as their philosophy of the body, had a profound impact on the growth of Roman sport and games.

Apart from the written record of Herodotus and others, our primary source of information about the Etruscans consist of archaeological evidence obtained from ancient Etruscan tombs. These underground tombs, built for the Etruscan nobility, were quite large and designed in a circular fashion; they resemble the burial mounds popular in the ancient world. Many of the tombs are well preserved, partly because they were not above ground and subject to vandalism, and partly because their location had long been forgotten. It was not until the early part of the nineteenth century that interest in Etruscan civilization began to develop. Archaeologists and historians began the process of determining the location and subsequent excavation of the tombs. What they discovered was amazing.

The tombs were furnished with utensils and other necessities for everyday life. Perhaps the most revealing source of information is the paintings and murals that adorn the walls of the tombs, some of which are very elaborate and detailed. In addition to the paintings, statues were found that depict activities enjoyed by the Etruscans. The contents of the tombs and artwork in the form of paintings, murals, and statues provide ample evidence that the wealthy Etruscans enjoyed a high standard of living. Beautiful jewels have been found, and artists painted scenes of the deceased enjoying banquets amid lavish surroundings, with plentiful food and libations.

In 1958, a tomb was discovered in which there were elaborate paintings and murals that depicted athletes and various sporting scenes. This tomb is called the Tomb of the Olympic Games. Other tombs contained portrayals of athletes and sport as practiced by the Etruscans. So what did these ancient people do for sport and physical activity? Paintings depict them running footraces, jumping,

throwing the discus, jumping over wooden hurdles, wrestling, boxing, swimming, throwing the javelin, racing chariots, doing gymnastics—especially acrobatics on the back of a horse—and waging armed combat in which, in some cases, both men died.[3] A bronze statue, dating from around the end of the fourth century B.C., depicts men and women wrestlers competing against each other, which suggests that Etruscan women were actively taking part in wrestling competitions and competing against men.[4]

The most popular sport for the Etruscans may have been the chariot races. Many tomb paintings portray this activity in great detail. The Etruscan chariots were, like the Greek chariots, adopted from a design that was widely used in Asia Minor. This lends some credibility to the claim of Herodotus that the Etruscans migrated to Italy from Asia Minor and that the civilizations in Asia Minor influenced the Etruscans as well as the Greeks. In the ancient world, equestrian talent and the ability to train horses and race chariots may have been more advanced in Asia Minor than in Greece or Etruria. Horse racing seems to have been as popular in the ancient world as it is in the modern world.

Music was enjoyed by the Etruscans and played a major role in their culture. Aristotle wrote that flute music was popular (as it was in Greece) and would often accompany ritual ceremonies such as boxing matches, hunting expeditions, dancing, and the beating of slaves.[5]

The Etruscans, like the Greeks and Egyptians, also enjoyed festivals. Various athletic competitions were an important part of the festival. The Etruscans used captured prisoners as sacrifices to honor dead warriors and, later on, used these unfortunate souls as "performers" who entertained the crowds. Etruscan art frequently depicts human sacrifices, and an account by Herodotus mentions that after the battle of Alalia, the victorious Etruscans rounded up a large number of prisoners and stoned them to death. The Etruscans had no qualms about killing prisoners of war or using them and other condemned individuals as public entertainment.

Over time, organized combats were staged that added an exciting and dramatic dimension to the festivals.[6] In these combat sports, the victor lived and the loser paid the ultimate price, dying a horrific and bloody death to honor the deceased during funeral games or during mass executions where The Condemned fought to the death. Paintings show the combatants covered with blood; depict wounds that were inflicted by spears, daggers, swords, and fists; and illustrate the moment when the death blow was delivered. The combats were not limited to humans. The Etruscans enjoyed watching men fight wild animals, especially bulls. What is particularly illuminating is that, according to the Roman architect Vitruvius, the Etruscans paid a great deal of attention to the planning of their cities. He noted that the cities were centered on an open oblong area that served as the place where games and sports were conducted.[7] Grandstands were erected around this area to accommodate the spectators who would gather to watch athletes compete in traditional sports and to watch the spectacles that featured combat to the death.

Etruscan art provides information about how the Etruscans viewed the human body. People of wealth wore "bright colored" clothing that was richly embroidered. Nakedness and artworks depicting the nude body were frowned upon by the ancient Etruscans and, for that matter, most of the ancient cultures of the Near East.[8] In the archaeological museum in Modena, Italy, Etruscan paintings depict nude males performing as athletes and dancers. However, unlike Greek art, Etruscan art does not feature full frontal nudity. The Etruscans were significantly influenced by the Greeks. The Greeks exported their artwork to the Etruscans and other cultures to make money. However, the Etruscans insisted that the amphoras and other Greek "objets d'art" sent to Etruria be adorned with individuals who were not naked. Needless to say, the nude as an object of art and as a symbol of aesthetic and physical beauty was not valued by the Etruscans. If Etruscan art portrayed individuals in the nude, it was people who had low social status or prisoners engaging in combat sports. It should come as no surprise that after the Romans defeated the Etruscans in 509 B.C., the victorious Romans continued to practice many

of the customs and beliefs of their former masters. The "blood sport" of the Etruscans would become one of the hallmarks of Roman civilization.

The Romans were utilitarian; that is, when they conquered an enemy, they determined if various practices and approaches used by their former foes were better than current Roman practices. If the vanquished city had a better method in medicine or a better approach to physical education, the Romans probably adopted the practice. The Romans found a lot to like about the Etruscan approach to sport in the traditional sense. They wrestled, boxed, raced chariots, swam, and competed in footraces. These sports prepared them to be better soldiers and so were popular in the ancient world, just as they remain popular today.

There is no question that the Romans adopted many of the practices of their former masters, especially when it came to contests of brute strength and bloodletting. Roman culture adopted the brutal and gruesome spectacles that pitted man against man and man against beast to entertain the spectators, who enjoyed watching the dramatic and deadly spectacles. Like the Etruscans, the Romans believed that it was necessary to honor their dead with human sacrifices; human immolation can, in a sense, be understood as a source of nutrition for the deceased, as well as various deities that were worshiped in antiquity, especially those that were worshipped by the spilling of blood. As a form of public entertainment, they used captured prisoners and other unfortunate groups that threatened Roman order. The armed combat between men and beasts appeared to be a popular form of Etruscan entertainment. Over time, the Romans would develop a thirst for spectacles that exceeded the Etruscan enjoyment of the dramatic and deadly. However, although the Etruscans appear to have engaged in brutal and bloody exhibitions that resembled latter-day gladiatorial combats, some scholars believe that gladiatorial combats did not originate with the Etruscans but in Campania, an area in southwest Italy near present-day Naples.[9]

In *Blood in the Arena* (Futrell, 1997) support for a Campanian—not Etruscan—origin for gladiatorial combat is discussed. The Campanian Theory was suggested by Georges Ville who believes that in the late fourth century B.C., and early third century B.C., armed men would fight in organized combats. Etruscans refined the Campanian competition to conform with Etruscan cultural and religious beliefs. Futrell notes that the literary evidence to support the companion Theory is limited, relying exclusively on the references provided by Livy (59 B.C.–A.D. 17), Strabo (64/63 B.C.–A.D. 24), and Silius Itlicus (28 A.D. 103 A.D.)[10]

After the Etruscans were defeated, the Roman Republic was formed, creating in effect an aristocratic oligarchy.[11] The Roman Republic lasted until 146 B.C., the year Rome finally conquered Greece by defeating and sacking the city of Corinth. Between 146 and 27 B.C., Rome survived a number of rulers and self-serving politicians until the establishment of the Roman Empire in 27 B.C. The Empire lasted until A.D. 476 when the Teutonic leader Odoacer ousted the last Roman emperor in the West. The Roman Empire was ultimately divided into two geographical regions: the Western Empire, centered in Rome, and the Eastern, or Byzantine, Empire, located in Constantinople (now Istanbul, Turkey). The Byzantine Empire survived the fall of Rome and lasted until 1453. Later in this chapter we will describe the various contests that took place in and around Constantinople. The influence of the Greeks on Roman civilization was significant and, where appropriate, will be discussed to provide an informative cross-cultural comparison. We can illustrate this point by highlighting the Greek influence on the emperor Nero.

NERO

The influence of Greek culture upon the emperor Nero, who reigned from A.D. 54 to 68, was profound. He was more concerned about his achievements in the arts than with his achievements as a ruler. He preferred the company of Greeks to that of his fellow Romans because the Greeks could relate to his exquisite taste in art, literature, theater, music, and poetry. Nero had an enormous ego and

believed that the Greeks alone were worthy of his genius, whereas his fellow Romans were unappreciative of his grandiose visions and cultural refinements. Once, while in Greece, he received word that his presence in Rome was urgently required. He enjoyed the company of Greeks so much that he refused to return immediately, instead completing another one of his concert tours, which, Nero was certain, were enjoyed by all who attended.[12]

The Romans had a fondness for size and spectacle. Nero was no different in this regard. He was in need of a massive house worthy of his stature and position. The young emperor drew up plans and ordered that construction on his Golden House begin as soon as possible. It was to be the largest and most opulent palace yet built by an emperor. Visitors had to pass in front of a statue of Nero that was more than 120 feet high! Once inside, visitors must have been overwhelmed as they wandered among the many rooms adorned in ivory and other expensive accoutrements. Panels could be removed from various rooms to release a perfumed mist or discharge a cascade of freshly gathered roses. The Golden House had a huge pool, artificial lake, gardens, and lawns upon which exotic animals roamed freely.[13]

Nero did not endear himself to his fellow Romans. He fancied himself as a gift to Rome from the gods; however, this feeling was not shared by everybody. Nero was so conceited about his many talents that he demanded that the Greeks hold a special Olympic Games so he could compete. In A.D. 67, he competed in the chariot race and fell! To no one's surprise, he was still declared the winner, adding the title of Olympic champion to his many accomplishments. Nero perceived himself as "larger than life." He died by his own hand when he was 31 years old. After the Greeks learned of his death, they revoked his win at Olympia.

The recipient of one of Nero's appointments was Vespasian. He served Nero as a soldier in Africa and was also sent to Palestine to subdue the Jews, who were causing trouble for Nero. Vespasian eventually became emperor of Rome and began work on the vast Flavian Amphitheater that would later become known the world over as the

Figure 4-2
The Via Sacre (Sacred Way) was the route to the Flavian Amphitheater from the Forum. Today tourists walk the same road used by ancient Romans to go to and from the Colosseum. To get a sense of scale, compare the size of the tourists with the massive exterior of the Colosseum.

Colosseum. This enormous monument was built on the remains of an artificial lake that Nero had constructed to adorn his Golden House (Figure 4.2).

CROSS-CULTURAL ANALYSIS OF THE GREEKS AND ROMANS

The Romans did not display the cultural genius and intellectual acumen of the Greeks, which we know bothered Nero. With the possible exception of Greek music, most Romans were not comfortable with the all-around development of the individual that emphasized the aesthetic and educated aspects of Greek culture. Nor did the Romans make monumental philosophical or scientific contributions. The Romans were great civil engineers, however, and many Roman roads are still in use today.

Roman civilization had instead as its foundation an ordered, pragmatic, utilitarian focus on the practical and purposeful. Romans were results-oriented, deliberate, and methodical in their acceptance of civic responsibilities and duties. As a result, the aesthetic, abstract, and harmonious approach to life advocated by the Greeks did not have universal appeal. Like the Greeks, the Romans were polytheistic. The Roman gods and goddesses were essentially the Greek ones, with a few name changes. For example, Zeus, the chief deity of the Greeks, became Jupiter, the chief god of the Romans; Hera, the wife of Zeus, became Juno; and Ares, the god of war in Greece, became the Roman god Mars (Figure 4-3). During the time of the Empire, however, a substantial number of "blue-collar" Romans rejected the mythological gods of

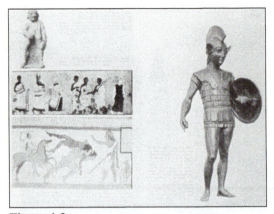

Figure 4-3
Mars, the Roman god of war.

the state and began to embrace Christianity. Some Romans chose life without religion and turned to the post-Aristotelian schools of philosophy for guidance and understanding.

In contrast to the Greeks, most Romans were not profound, speculative, or metaphysical thinkers. Metaphysical questions and speculations about the nature of things were not conducive to the utilitarian and pragmatic Roman thought. Being purposeful and practical people, the Romans were quick to recognize and adopt the cultural, scientific, philosophical, architectural, and engineering achievements of the countries they conquered. Thus, the Romans imported, refined, and added their signatures to science, philosophy, architecture, mathematics, and so on, acquired during their conquests.

PHILOSOPHICAL ORIENTATION

During the fourth and third centuries B.C., the Roman Republic was emblematic of an ordered civilization in which economic and political freedom was prevalent. The influence of religion on education was significant in that moral and military training took precedence over intellectual achievement, which no doubt must have pleased Mars, the Roman war god. Roman religion was relatively spiritless and practical:

> Their religion, both family and state, lacked the beauty and stately ceremonies of the

Greeks, lacked the lofty faith and aspiration after faith that characterized the Hebrew and later Christian faith, was singularly wanting in awe and mystery, and was formal and mechanical in character.[14]

The Republic exhibited military characteristics and promoted the acquisition and development of "*Virtus*"—courage. These early Romans were adamant that character formation was critical to the development of Roman citizens and, ultimately, the survival of the Republic. However, when the ordered Republic collapsed, the Empire emerged, and it became the philosopher's task to provide the individual with a code of conduct that would enable him to "pilot his way through the sea of life . . . based on a certain spiritual and moral independence."[15] As a result, philosopher-directors were asked to serve the same tasks that spiritual directors, or priests, did in the Christian world.

The Roman concept of society was inclusive compared to Greek society. The Greeks believed that the cultures beyond their shores were inhabited by philistines and barbarians who were culturally inferior. The "blended" world advocated by the multicultural Romans was anathema to the harsh eugenics proposed by Socrates, Plato, Aristotle, and their Greek brethren. The cosmopolitan society that evolved under Roman leadership was bound to an ideal of individualism in which philosophy responded by encouraging the individual to provide guidance in life.

This philosophical orientation dispensed by the philosopher-directors was based predominantly on ethical and practical doctrines advocated by the philosophers Zeno (Stoicism) and Epicurus (Epicureanism). These two philosophical schools competed with Christianity during the time of the Empire and are compared with Christianity by Frederick Copleston:

> Insistence on ethics alone leads to an ideal of spiritual independence and self-sufficiency such as we find in both Stoicism and Epicureanism, while insistence on religion tends rather to assert dependence on a Transcendental Principle and to ascribe the purification of the self to the action of the Divine. . . . Both tendencies, the

tendency to insist on the ethical, the self-sufficient perfection of the personality or the acquisition of the true moral personality, and the tendency to insist on the attitude of the worshipper toward the Divine or the need of the non-self-sufficient human to unite himself with God contributed to the same want, the want of the individual in the Greco-Roman world to find a sure basis for his individual life, since the religious attitude brought with it a certain independence vis-à-vis the secular Empire.[16]

Liberally interpreted, the passage states that Romans desired answers to profound questions and a fundamental basis for the meaning of life, and they used both philosophical and religious means to obtain answers to their questions. Both methods were encouraged in the Roman Empire, which *de facto* separated church and state.

The Stoics

Initially, Zeno was influenced by the Cynics, a philosophical school that preceded and influenced Stoicism, but he became uncomfortable with their anarchistic views. Zeno was concerned with the essence of political and social life, which, not surprisingly, were of paramount concern to Plato and Aristotle. In approximately 300 B.C., Zeno established his own philosophical school, called *Stoicism,* derived from the site (*stoa* translated into English means "porch") from which he lectured.

The Stoics, although influenced by Plato and Aristotle, rejected various beliefs put forth by Plato (the transcendental universal) and Aristotle (the concrete universal).[17] Through discussion and contemplation, the Stoics concluded that only the individual exists, and what knowledge we do have is knowledge of specific objects. This belief was based on their epistemology (the study of how we acquire knowledge). Whereas Plato and Socrates did not trust the body and the subsequent acquisition of information and knowledge through sense-perception, the Stoics believed, as did Aristotle, that knowledge is based on sense perception. As a result, the philosophical position of the body in Stoic doctrine was of significant importance,

especially when compared with the position of the body in the *Phaedo,* in which Socrates condemns the body. The Stoics emphasized personal conduct and the attainment of personal happiness in a world that required the Stoic to accept whatever life dealt him and to remain optimistic. The ethical function of the Stoics "consists essentially in submission to the divinely appointed order of the world and no doubt gave rise to the famous Stoic maxim 'Live according to Nature.'"[18]

The appeal of Stoicism to the Romans was grounded in part to the principle of conduct essential to Roman rule and organization. The great Roman Stoic Seneca looked on philosophy as the science of conduct. Self-development and an acceptance of the fate nature has dealt each person reflected Roman ideology as well. Copleston provides an illuminating look at the Stoic conduct: "Character, then, is the chief point stressed in truly virtuous conduct—which is fulfillment of duty (and) is performed only by the wise men. Moreover, he is lord over his own life, and may commit suicide."[19] The Stoic demeanor reflected a lack of emotion and approved of the discipline and acceptance of death displayed by the gladiators fighting in the arena.

The Epicureans

Epicureanism was much like Stoicism in that it rejected metaphysical or religious claims on human behavior. It rejected Plato's idealism by arguing that the body and its senses are "real" and are the best way of coming to "know" reality. Epicureanism, however, also promoted the development of cultured individuals who sought happiness and pleasure through the joys of the mind. The relationship of the mind and the body, then, was that we have greater control over the mind than the body, so we should concentrate on the friendship of gifted and noble men, on the peace and contentment that comes from fair conduct, and on good morals and aesthetic enjoyments to obtain pleasure and happiness.[20] One consequence of this philosophy is that the body and the senses are considered a viable way of knowing pleasure and obtaining happiness. As a result, the philosophical view of the body, as well as its role in the epistemological process, is more important to Epicurean thought than to Platonic thought. However, the ideas of friendship, peace, contentment, nobility, and pleasure are valid objects of knowledge. The sensations of pleasure are not supposed to be the result of Epicureanism; sensations are how we come to know these ideas. Indeed, Epicureanism is often incorrectly associated only with bodily pleasures. So, while the body is definitely more important in this philosophy than in those philosophies that emphasize ideas, it is still ideas that are paramount.

Marcus Tullius Cicero

Marcus Tullius Cicero (106–43 B.C.), the great Roman orator and philosopher, had a stormy career as a politician partly because of his disgust with the unethical politics engaged in by Julius Caesar, Pompey, and Crassus. These three rulers banished Cicero from Rome due to his social and political criticism of their activities. Because of the danger of attacking the rulers directly, Cicero became a social critic of arena sports, in the belief that they were representative of the larger social and political problems of Rome. Cicero was very concerned with ethics and how man could attain the highest moral virtue. In this regard, Cicero was heavily influenced by the Greek philosopher Antiochus of Ascalon.[21]

Antiochus

Antiochus's ethical system sought the achievement of ultimate good, which he interpreted as the ability to live in accordance with nature. To achieve this goal, one concentrated on the total development of all of one's capacities.[22] Antiochus stated that "wisdom's task was to perfect the whole man neglecting no side of him."[23] The optimum development of both mind and body was absolutely essential to Antiochus and his followers. To quote Antiochus, "The full and perfect philosophy was that which investigated the chief goal of man, left no part (of) either mind or body uncared for."[24] The emphasis of the Greek philosopher Antiochus, especially on the development of both mind and body, was attractive to the Romans, especially the Stoics.

Sport and Physical Education

Over the course of a millennium, the Romans went through a number of political and social changes. The Stoic and Epicurean philosophies had a significant impact on the social and political order of Rome during the Republic and the Empire. Eventually, these philosophies gave way to a morally corrupt and hedonistic social and political order that collapsed from within. We shall examine the various forms of sport and physical education while keeping in mind that a number of social historians and sport sociologists suggest that sport tends to reflect society, and society reflects sport. In this framework, the various forms of sport that dominate a society's existence are emblematic of its moral health or illness.

Under the Empire, the sporting activities of the Romans had evolved into massive spectacles of entertainment, debauchery, and carnage. However, this was not always the situation. During the early years of the Republic, physical exercise was enjoyed by the citizens of the fledgling Republic, although not nearly to the extent that it was in Greece.

As a culture, the early Romans enjoyed ball games based on throwing and catching, as well as a form of handball. The baths, or *thermae* as they were called, were popular. Mild exercise, but not the intensely competitive physical regimen of the Greeks, had great appeal to the Romans. It was a common sight to see men, in groups or alone, heading toward the baths after lunch, where they might engage in mild exercise such as ball playing prior to entering the baths. The idea was to work up a sweat before immersing themselves in the waters, not to engage in strenuous physical competition. Prior to the beginning of the Christian era, there were 200 baths available in Rome, and by A.D. 400, there were around 900. Most of the thermae were privately owned, but some of the larger ones were public.[25]

During the time of the Empire, some Romans, especially wealthy ones, came to accept the concept of health gymnastics, because the maintenance of health was a worthwhile and natural goal for them. To this end, Greek physicians were used to instruct Romans in the benefits of health-related exercise.

As in Greece, the Romans paid homage to their gods to ensure a bountiful harvest or curry their favor, offered prayers for prosperity, and made other, similar requests. Physical activities such as footraces, ball playing, equestrian displays, and wrestling contests allowed mere mortals to exhibit their physical skills before the gods thought to be in attendance during religious holidays. Religion was important to the Romans, and like the Greeks, they had numerous gods. The Romans believed they were selected by providence to rule the world. As a result, the divinely inspired and guided Roman rulers became pragmatic and utilitarian where physical training was concerned.

MILITARY TRAINING

The military was extremely important in both social and political terms in Roman life. The legion was the primary unit of the Roman army. Each legion consisted of 3000–6000 foot soldiers and 100–200 mounted soldiers. The Roman legion was legendary in the social fabric of Roman society and was supported by Stoic virtues of honor and duty. In Rome, the training of youths had but one purpose: to make them obedient, disciplined, and ready to be warriors. With this in mind, the Romans developed their own system of physical training and did not borrow much from the Greeks in terms of military training techniques. Greek athletics were considered too individualistic and "soft" for Roman tastes and did not embody the "team unity" that the Romans demanded.

The Campus Martius in Rome was a large, open area with a temple dedicated to Mars, the Roman god of war. It was here that fathers from wealthy families brought their sons to teach them the physical skills required prior to their induction into manhood, signified by wearing the Roman toga, and

then into the military. Skills such as running, jumping, swimming, wrestling, horsemanship, boxing, fencing, and archery, as well as complete obedience to commands, were taught at the Campus Martius and at other locations throughout the realm. These physical activities had a dual purpose: (1) Basic military skills would be learned, and (2) the benefits of healthful exercise could be enjoyed. War was the most prestigious profession of the Romans, which necessitated brutal methods for training the body. For instance, 20-mile forced marches were made about three times per month at four miles per hour, with marchers carrying packs that weighed up to 85 pounds.[26] Over the years, Rome built a professional army that was divided into five classes according to how much property each man held. First-class soldiers were wealthy and had a great deal of land. The soldiers in the fifth class were the poor who had no land and consequently had few weapons to use in battle. Soldiers of the fifth class joined the military to share in the "spoils of war"— if they managed to survive the fight.

CLAUDIUS GALEN

Galen (A.D. 130–200) began the study of medicine when he was 17; he also studied under the Stoics, the Epicureans (whom he rejected), the Academicians, and the Peripatetics. Traveling throughout the Mediterranean, Galen became knowledgeable in the healing arts, the surgical procedures of the day, and the use of drugs. He developed a reputation in Alexandria for his ability to heal gladiators. Due to his success, Galen believed himself to be the most accomplished physician of his time: "No one before me has given the true method of treating disease."[27] He was one of the first to incorporate medicine and biomechanics into the science of exercise.

Galen also was opposed to the idea of professional athletes being worshiped as heroes because, in his way of thinking, they were the antithesis of a healthy citizen. In his work titled "Exhortation on the Choice of a Profession," he stated his opinion about the professional athlete:

In the blessings of the mind athletes have not. . . . Beneath their mass of flesh and blood their souls are stifled as in a sea of mud. . . . Neglecting the old rule of health which prescribes moderation in all things they spend their lives in overexercising, in overeating, and oversleeping like pigs. . . . They have not health nor have they beauty. Even those who are naturally well proportioned become fat and bloated.[28]

Galen's concern is astonishingly similar to a contemporary one shared by parents, coaches, physical educators, and others: that talented youths will follow the often ill-fated road to perceived quick riches and rewards when the prospects of a career in athletics lures them away from completing their education and eschewing "moderation in all things" as Galen had prescribed. These same youths in Galen's day were apparently only too quick to abandon the halls of education and medicine for the shallow and short lives of the arena.

Galen had considerable knowledge about diet, exercise, and the kinship between mind and body, and provided this information to the general populace. Galen believed that

mental exertion, alone, makes a person thin; but if it is combined with some physical exercise and rivalry ending with pleasure, it very greatly assists the body to health and the mind to intelligence. There is no unimportant advantage of an exercise, if it can help both the body and the mind toward the perfection innate in each.[29]

In "Exercise with the Small Ball," Galen stated, "Now I maintain that the best gymnastic exercises of all are those which not only exercise the body but also bring delight to the mind."[30] Galen apparently believed in "education through the physical" long before Jesse F. Williams supported this concept in the twentieth century![31] Galen believed that this type of exercise (with the small ball) required that all of the body be in constant motion to achieve a conditioning effect. Exercises could be violent (strenuous) ball exercises or of a mild type. In "Maintenance of Health," he identified wrestling,

the pancratium (pankration), running, and boxing as forms of gymnastic exercises.[32] Galen believed the Greek athletic and gymnastic system to be more beneficial than the Roman approach to conditioning. He advocated both vigorous (performed with strength, not speed), and violent (combining strength and speed) exercises. For example, the exercise of digging was classified by Galen as a vigorous and strong exercise but one that did not require quick motion. The practice of rope climbing required strength. Jumping continuously without rest was a form of exercise, like hurling the discus, that would develop strength and speed.[33] Galen was the chief fitness expert of his time and one of the first to practice sports medicine. He stressed the development of the body in a harmonious way. Galen discouraged running because it wears a person thin, furnishes no training in bravery, and causes some parts of the body to be overtaxed.[34]

Greek Athletics

Galen continued to embrace the Greek ideals of harmoniously proportioned bodies that made them alert and physically fit for both civil and military duties, in contrast to the Roman approach that demanded a severe and harsh training program to produce a disciplined and obedient warrior. In general, the Romans who lived during the Republic were not interested in the formal athletic competitions of the Greeks, which demanded, in their view, excessive athletic training. The athleticism of the Greeks was not valued militarily by the utilitarian Romans. Another factor in the Roman disfavor for Greek athletics was the Roman prejudice against the nudity of the Greeks. What little appeal for Greek athletics that did exist was found primarily in the wealthy and literate classes. Greek athletics (*athletik*) did enjoy popularity during the era between the late Republic and early Empire. Some of the emperors of this period played a significant role in advancing the benefits of Greek exercise by establishing public facilities such as the Imperial Thermae or baths that also had palaistrai. Roman youths from wealthy families enjoyed Greek gymnastics (*gymnastik*). In contrast to the Roman Republic, Greek athletics fared well during the early Roman Empire, in part because of the changing attitudes of the pragmatic Romans, who appreciated the value of exercise and good health available through the practice of Greek gymnastics.[35]

The Emperor Domitian (A.D. 51–96) built a stadium in central Rome that featured Greek athletic competitions. The stadium of Domitian can still be seen today. The trendy Piazza Novena occupies the site of the stadium. Cafés and shops line the perimeter of the ancient stadium. The center of the ancient stadium—the "infield"—can be easily discerned by standing near the famous fountain by Bernini (A.D. 1598–A.D. 1680) in the middle of the Piazza.

WOMEN AND SPORT

The role of women in athletics—as spectators and athletes—is not nearly as well documented as that of the men. There is no doubt that athletics were the primary occupation of males due in no small part to the social and political system of the Republic and the Empire, based on a system of patriarchy and class stratification. During the first century A.D., the emperor Domitian instituted races during the Capitoline Games in Rome that featured young women; 100 years later, during the "Romanized" Olympic Games at Antioch in Syria, girls attired in shorts participated in wrestling and running.[36] There is general agreement that the participation of women in sport during the time of the Empire and the Republic was for entertainment and not taken seriously.[37] Swimming and dancing, along with tossing balls back and forth, were activities that women engaged in along with visits to the thermae (Figure 4-4). Some evidence suggests that fashionable women of Rome performed weight-training exercises to tone muscles. The account provided by Juvenal of Rome is revealing:

> It is at night that she goes to the baths, at night that she gives orders for her oil-flasks and other impediments to be taken there; she loves to sweat among the noise and bustle. When her arms fall to her sides, worn out by the

heavy weights, the skillful masseur presses his finger into her body, and makes her bottom resound with his loud smack.[38]

Did women compete as gladiators? Yes—the existence of female gladiators has been known for some time. The Roman historian and biographer Suetonius (A.D. 70–A.D. 130) provides us with information about female gladiator. He was Emperor Hadrian's personal secretary and wrote *Lives of the Caesars* in A.D. 121. Suetonius tells us that the Emperor Domitian (A.D. 51–A.D. 96) sponsored a number of "over the top" spectacles and extravagant shows in the Flavian Amphitheater which featured men and women gladiators. Domitian insisted on novelty, he became bored very quickly. As a result he staged one gladiatorial show featuring women gladiators who fought dwarfs.[39]

The number of women gladiators steadily increased over the years, especially during the reign of Emperor Nero (A.D. 37–A.D. 68). The Roman satiric poet Juvenal (circa A.D. 55–circa A.D. 138) heaped scorn and contempt on Roman society because they enjoyed watching women gladiators fight. By the third century the number of women gladiators was so appalling that the Emperor Septims Severus (A.D. 145–A.D. 211) forbid women from competing in the arena. However Alan Baker (2000) notes that "the presence of women in these places of blood and death suggests, curiously enough, a certain equality in the context of the particular *virtus* (or skill) of killing and facing death with courage and dignity. It seems that in ancient Rome, this *virtus* was considered of greater importance than gender."[40]

In 1996, archaeologists discovered an elaborate grave in London, near the river Thames. The deceased was a woman who may have been a gladiator during the time London was a Roman province. She was buried with dishes and other artifacts associated with gladiators. In Italy, an inscription in Pompeii makes reference to women gladiators in the arena. K. Coleman provides additional evidence that female gladiators may have been more prevalent than previously believed. She notes that the British Museum houses a marble relief, found at Halicarnassus, that depicts two female gladiators.[41]

Figure 4-4
Roman women exercising.

To summarize, we can conclude that women competed as gladiators. As their numbers increased over time, the spectacle and carnage became so disgusting that Emperor Septimus Severus outlawed their participation in A.D. 200.[42]

GAMES AND SPECTACLES

Holidays during the era of the Republic evolved from simple religious occasions and agricultural offerings into elaborate games and festivals financed and administered by the government. The government introduced official sporting events during which all businesses were closed, and admission to the games was generally free. Apparently, only during the early period of the Republic did Romans actually participate in games and sports like their counterparts in Greece. Aside from the warriors, the Romans grew into a nation of spectators, not participants, who enjoyed watching slaves and professional athletes perform as competitors while the less fortunate Christians, criminals, and political prisoners were unwilling participants. Roman games and sporting events did not serve as a catalyst for physical education, as happened in Greece. Spectacular gladiatorial fights and combat

 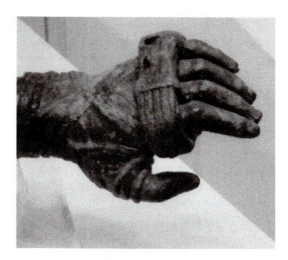

Figure 4-5

Terra cotta statuettes of African boxers, Roman art, circa, second or first century B.C. The older, balding boxer is staggering back from an upper cut. Their gloves are the Roman caestus. Roman boxers as well as some Greek athletes used CAESTUS, an early and very lethal form of what we know as brass kunckles. The CAESTUS was made out of metal and embedded with sharp metal spikes and jagged pieces of glass in order to inflict maximum pain and blood loss on the opponent. Competitions where the CAESTUS was allowed resembled a knife fight. An agonizing death in front of thousands of spectators was not that unusual.

National Archeological Museum; Athens, Greece. R. Mechikoff.

between slaves (Figure 4-5) and prisoners in the Flavian Amphitheater, along with horse and chariot races at the Circus Maximus, provided large-scale, immensely popular entertainment. The individual athletic contests of the Greeks had little appeal for the Romans because these athletic activities were boring by Roman standards and did not prepare men for war as well as the Roman method. To the Greeks, athletic competitions were great religious events in which every man aspired to compete; they were contests between citizens to demonstrate their physical fitness and to honor the gods e.g. Zeus at Olympia, Posidon at Isthmia, Athena at the Panathenaia. The Romans, however, redefined sport as spectator entertainment, with an emphasis on brutality and not much of a connection with religion.

During the time of the Empire as well as the Republic, politicians promoted games and spectacles for blatant political purposes. Politicians sometimes used their own money to produce spectacular and often bloody events to curry favor with their constituents, who often behaved like thrill-hungry mobs. This process of pandering to the masses came to be known as *panem et circenses,* or "bread and circuses," where the people of Rome were fed and entertained in exchange for their support.

J. Carcopino, in *Daily Life in Ancient Rome,* maintains that the Romans were guilty of despicable behavior as a result of the executions that occurred in the Flavian Amphitheater, which was turned into a torture chamber and human slaughterhouse.[43]

There is no question that the bloody "games" and "despicable behavior" that occurred within the confines of the Flavian Amphitheater and other venues around the Roman Empire were popular. Were these cruel spectacles merely a form of entertainment that appealed to the basest instincts of the Roman psyche? Or, as Donald Kyle asks,

Was the cruelty of the arena inconsistent with—or central to—Roman civilization, and why did Romans have such an ambivalent attitude to gladiators, stigmatizing them in society, literature and legislation and yet attending, glorifying, and sometimes even volunteering for combats?[44]

Thomas Wiedemann reports that the killing of beasts and humans as a part of Roman society was a symbolic defense of Roman civilization against nature, barbarism, and criminality. The Flavian Amphitheater and other venues in the Roman world that staged these horrific spectacles enabled Romans to challenge the limits of the human world when confronted with the uncivilized nature of the natural world, where order, in the Roman sense, was nonexistent.[45] Gladiators became a fundamental aspect of Roman culture and, for all time, a symbol of Roman identity.

The term *gladiator* originates from a weapon called a "gladius" that was used by Romans. Every gladiator was a specialist.

There were eight main gladiatorial types:

1. **Samnites** are the oldest. They were beaten by the Romans and their allies, the Campanians. After the battle, the Campanians collected the armor and weapons of the slain Samnites and outfitted their gladiators with these. Initially the Samnites were enemies of Rome but later became their allies. When this happened, Emperor Augustus believed it was a disgrace to feature Samnites as gladiators and replaced them with two new types, the Secutor and the Hoplomachus.
2. **Hoplomachus** gladiators were similar to appearance to Thracian gladiators. His opponent or Nemisis in the arena was the Thracian or Murmillo.
3. **Thracian** gladiators were captured enemies whose homeland was ancient Thrace, modern Bulgaria. The most famous gladiator of antiquity, Spartacus (109 B.C.–71 B.C.) was a Thracian nobleman who was captured by the Romans and sent to Capua (near present day Naples) to train and fight in the massive arena. He would fight the Hoplomachus, Murmillo, or another Thracian.
4. **Secutor** gladiators were also known as Contraretiarius and would fight the Retriarius.
5. **Retriarius** gladiators fought with a net in one hand and a trident in the other and fought the Murmillo.

6. **Murmillo** gladiators were recognized by the fish that was etched on their helmets. He was paired against the Retriarius, possibly because of the association of the fishing net used by the Retriarius and the fish that was etched on the helmet of the Murmillo. As time past, the Murmillo specialized in fighting the Thracian and the Hoplomachus exclusively.
7. **Provocator's** were gladiators who would fight other Provocators.
8. **Eques** gladiators fought on horseback, was armed with a lance and small shield. They exclusively fought other Equites and were often featured in marble reliefs and mosaics without their horse, probably because they had fallen off (no saddles) and finished the fight in hand to hand combat.

There is some disagreement about whether gladiators fought animals as well as other gladiators. There were some who were designated as Bestiarius (beast fighter), special gladiators who were sometimes trained in the Ludus Matutinus school. The Bestiarii were the lowest in status in the gladiator ranks and were often sent "ad bestias" as a form of execution. The gladiators dressed up to resemble Rome's enemies (Figure 4-6), and these "enemies" fought to the death in the arena. The primary reason for making gladiators dress like the enemies of Rome was that, when the bloody and gory gladiator fights were held and men died by the hundreds in front of tens of thousands of screaming Roman fans, nobody felt sorry for the dead because they were seen as the enemy.

Contrary to public opinion, not all gladiator combats ended in death. Most—not all—gladiators were prisoners-of-war and slaves—"select" individuals sent to gladiator schools for expensive training. In the arena, a number of gladiators who fought well were spared so they could live to fight another day. Some freemen also desired to live the life of the gladiator. These individuals, known as *auctorati,* entered into an arrangement of partial servitude to the *lanista,* an entrepreneur

Figure 4-6
Gladiator helmets on display at the museum in Capua, Italy. The great amphiteater at Capua where Spartacus fought and escaped from.

who purchased gladiators and sold them as well. The lanista also rented his gladiators to those who desired to stage a *munrus* (contest) to honor a particular individual. The lanista was considered a butcher, the seller of humans doomed to a life of cruelty, pain, and probable death. He had the same social standing as the pimp who ran prostitutes.[46]

There were a number of gladiator training centers or schools. Two of the best known were located at Pompeii and Capua. The gladiator arenas or venues could be found as far north as England, as far south as North Africa, and as far east as Turkey. The Flavian Amphitheater seated about 50,000 spectators while other venues seated between 5000 and 35,000. Many of these ancient arenas are well preserved and are popular tourist destinations today. In Rome, there were four gladiator training schools, one of which was exclusively devoted to the training of Bestiarii. There were rules for gladiator combats, and each fight was supervised by two judges. It is likely that no rules were followed when the day's events focused on sacrificing the condemned to a horrific death by being torn apart by lions, tigers, and other beasts that devoured the enemies of Rome.

Gladiators were a paradoxical element in Roman society. On one hand, the best-known gladiators were admired by many Romans for their bravery and skill in the arena. On the other hand, as noted by Kyle, Roman society was ambivalent toward them. This ambivalence was likely due in part to the fact that there seemed to be an expectation that gladiators would reflect the bravery and stoic attitudes of Roman society, also found in the code of conduct of the military.[47] The stoic virtues of Roman society, which did not encourage displays of emotion, were reflected in the ambivalent attitude that Romans had toward gladiators who were expected to perform and probably die in the hostile arena; it was their fate. Indeed, gladiators took an oath to be "burnt with fire, shackled with chains, whipped with rods, and killed with steel" (*uri, vinciri, verberari, ferroque necari*).[48]

In Chapter 1, we discussed the definition of "sport" and noted how the term is subject to debate. Clearly, the Greeks practiced a style of sport not at all like the Roman version. Noted historian H. A. Harris, who extensively researched sport in the ancient world, wrestled with the issue of a proper definition of sport. He equated sport with the Hellenic (Greek) athletic activities and limited the concept and scope of Roman sport to those aspects of Greek sport that survived or were adopted by the Romans. The gruesome entertainment spectaculars that took place in the Flavian Amphitheater and other venues throughout Rome to entertain thrill-hungry mobs were not "sport" by his definition. Harris presented a vivid description of the Greek and Roman concept of athletics:

> In Greece, athletics were the traditional sport, hallowed by centuries of experience. It had links with religious observance; it had enjoyed a Golden Age when it had been the leisure occupation of the wealthy. Even before the first impact of the Romans on the Greek world, it had become public entertainment provided by well-paid professional performers. . . . In the Roman world, Greek athletics had no tradition of centuries and no belief in a Golden Age to lend a romantic glow. Athletics meetings were introduced by ambitious politicians as an amusement to gratify the people.[49]

Harris clearly saw more differences than similarities between Greek and Roman sport. Politicians during the time of the Republic instituted games and spectacles on a frequent basis to divert the attention of a nation weary from and depressed by constant warfare. Roman emperors designated one official holiday after another, and by 173 B.C., 53 public holidays existed. This already large number of holidays was added to until A.D. 300, when 200 days were set aside as public holidays, 175 of which were devoted to spectacles and games. Roman games and spectacles served the utilitarian function of pacification, a way for the masses to spend their idle time and to keep from being bored. Roman leaders feared that a bored citizenry could lead to revolution. In addition, the Roman emperors kept the masses entertained to preserve their political fortunes. During the reign of Emperor Marcus Aurelius, 135 days out of the year were devoted to festivals, and at one point, 17 of the 29 days in April were spent at the circus, amphitheater, or theater.[50]

The Circus Maximus in Rome was the premier hippodrome in the Roman Empire (Figure 4-7). Situated in the heart of Rome, the Circus was a 2000-foot-long, 600-foot-wide, three-tiered stadium adorned with statues, obelisks, and elaborate arches. One end of the Circus was rounded to facilitate the chariots and horses that raced before as many as

Figure 4-7
Model of Circus Maximus.

a quarter of a million spectators (Figure 4-8). The Circus Maximus was destroyed by fire on two occasions. Some of the seating was on wooden grandstands that at times became so crowded that they would collapse, and in the process, many spectators lost their lives. The Circus Maximus appealed to men and women of all social classes, as well as some Christians. Deobold Van Dalen and Bruce Bennett provide an illuminating look at the chariot races that took place in the Circus Maximus:

> Hours before the games people placed bets while the poor eagerly waited to see if the sponsor of the games would have presents thrown among the audience. Everyone gradually found a seat, the emperor, magistrate, and Vestal Virgins occupying special places. With much ceremony, the sponsor of the game and a procession of men proceeded to an altar to make sacrifice, paid their respects before the imperial box, and then the games commenced.
>
> In vaulted stalls with barred doors, the charioteers awaited the starting signal. There were usually four chariots in each race and in later days as many as twelve. . . . Each driver controlled as many as seven horses although a team of four was the most common. . . . The charioteers struggled for the lead in the seven-lap race around the SPINA, a distance of about three miles. Speed alone was not the decisive factor in those races, for a driver had to negotiate sharp turns around a sandy track

Figure 4-8
Chariot race. Notice the strewn bodies under the chariots.

and avoid the other driver as well. Charioteers employed every device to keep the lead and upset the carts of their competitor. The intense rivalry often resulted in arguments, riots, and bloodshed.[51]

During the era of the Republic, it was unthinkable for men of class and wealth to take part in chariot races, gladiatorial contests, and Greek athletics. However, during the Imperial era, Nero and Caligula, two infamous emperors, participated in these activities.

Between chariot races, riders on horseback displayed their courage and athletic ability by jumping from one galloping horse to another. However, these equestrian feats and the occasional footraces and wrestling matches were not as popular as the well-timed wrestling/boxing matches. In these latter contests, each pugilist protected his hands by wearing crude leather straps. On the outside of these "gloves" were jagged pieces of metal that would rip the flesh of opponents to shreds, much to the delight of the spectators. The last chariot race held in the Circus Maximus was in A.D. 599.

For sheer carnage, nothing exceeded the gory gladiatorial combats. Spectators also watched the slaughter of Christians and criminals or the staged naval battles made popular by Julius Caesar, Augustus, Claudius, and Nero. In A.D. 52, Emperor Claudius ordered 19,000 slaves onto ships and sent them into battle against each other. Because the slaves were outfitted in armor, more perished by drowning than by bloody combat. The crowds, however, not in a position to see this spectacle up close, soon became bored and lost interest in the slaughter, turning their attention elsewhere.[52]

Construction of the most famous landmark in Rome, the Flavian Amphitheater or Colosseum, was begun under the direction of Emperor Vespasian (A.D. 69–79) and completed during the reign of his son Titus in A.D. 80. Vespasian financed the construction of the Flavian Amphitheater by looting the Temple of Jerusalem of all its gold, silver, precious stones, and priceless religious objects. In addition to sacking the Temple, Vespasian also enslaved 12,000 Jews and brought them back to Rome where they were forced to build the Flavian Amphitheater. The 12,000 Jews were literally worked to death. Titus was so proud of the magnificent structure that the opening ceremonies lasted for 100 days. He issued orders that the mint strike a new coin to commemorate the occasion.[53]

The Flavian Amphitheater, an engineering marvel, is a four-tiered oval with 80 entrances that permitted the giant structure to be emptied in a reasonable amount of time. Retractable awnings protected the approximately 50,000 onlookers from the scorching sun while streams of scented water spewed from numerous fountains to cool them. The floor of the arena was made of wood and covered with sand, and could be flooded to provide yet another venue for deadly naval battles. The massive amphitheater could be lit at night by torches so those attending the events could escape the oppressive heat of the day.

Around the arena, behind the wall that separated the spectators from the participants, were various seating arrangements. Close to the action was an elaborate and beautiful marble terrace where members of the aristocracy sat in regal splendor. Above this section rose tier after tier of marble seats divided into two main sections and several secondary ones. The first section was reserved for wealthy Romans and their guests, and the second section for members of the Roman middle class. Another section was set aside for foreigners and slaves, while a fourth section, high above the floor, was for women and the poor, who sat on wooden benches.

A typical agenda of events in the arena began with animal fights in the morning and included elephants, bulls, tigers, lions, panthers, bears, boars, apes, and crocodiles (Figure 4-9). During the reign of Nero, 400 tigers lashed into bulls and elephants during one day! However, this paled in comparison to the frequent slaughter of men and women, mauled and devoured by lions, tigers, and panthers (Figure 4-10). Criminals condemned to death were dressed in animal skins and thrown to the starved lions, much to the delight of the crowd. In this manner, the pragmatic Romans were able to dispose of criminals and other undesirables, especially Christians, and provide entertainment at the same time.[54] No doubt this practice had an impact on how Christians viewed sport, and as Van Dalen and Bennett note, "Small wonder that the Christians, themselves often thrown to the lions, developed a fanatical antipathy to the cruelty of the games and carried a general aversion to sport well into the Middle Ages."[55]

In addition to citing the carnage that awaited them in the Flavian Amphitheater and other venues, Wiedemann offers another reason why Christians opposed gladiator combats. He notes that Christians opposed such combats because the concept of gladiatorial resurrection competed against the Christian concept of resurrection. Gladiatorial resurrection involved the idea that a gladiator who fought in the arena could escape death by a display of virtue and thereby gain redemption. In addition, Wiedemann claims that the demise of the gladiator shows was not necessarily due to a

Figure 4-9
Moving the animals to the Flavian Amphitheater (Colosseum).

Figure 4-10
Man against beast.

legislative decree but the result of a gradual trend as the Christian definition of resurrection prevailed over the idea of gladiatorial resurrection.[56]

The most popular events in the amphitheater were the gladiatorial fights, generally held in the afternoon after the animal fights (Figures 4-11 and 4-12). The gladiators generally were criminals and slaves, but during the second century A.D., many were volunteers![57] The emperor Hadrian also landscaped the Flavian Amphitheater with bushes, trees, and plants to resemble a jungle. Trapdoors were installed near trees and bushes. While the thousands of spectators watched, individuals made their way from one end to the other. Attendants would spring the hidden trapdoors to release a lion or other wild animal upon the unfortunate souls making their way through Hadrian's jungle. This was a popular and brutal show, but it could not compare with the main attraction—the gladiators.

The gladiators entered and "exited" the arena through one of two tunnels assigned exclusively to them. One of the entry tunnels was given the name Porta Libitinaria after the Roman goddess of death, Libitina. This same tunnel was used to remove the bodies of the slain gladiators from the blood-soaked sands of the arena to unmarked graves. However, gladiators who achieved fame in the arena and died a courageous death were frequently buried in graves marked with impressive tombstones or markers. The second entrance started in Ludus Magnus—the major gladiatorial school in Rome, located directly across from the Flavian Amphitheater. The gladiators would emerge from a subterranean tunnel that linked the two venues. When they emerged from the tunnel and marched stoically into the huge arena, the roar from the crowd was deafening. Today's athletes must experience a similar feeling when they enter huge stadiums, filled with thousands of

Figure 4-11
Gladiators training for combat.

Figure 4-12
Gladiators in action.

fans, to compete—to fight! Potter (2011) has identified 259 gladiator markers and tombstones.[58]

It is important to understand that while mass gladiatorial combats were held, they were not common. Gladiators were expensive to train and house, and their owners were not interested in seeing their entire investment wiped out in a single day. However, from time to time, mass combat did take place. More often, two gladiators were pitted against each other. According to William Baker,

> In the most brutal of all gladiatorial contests, only one of a great number escaped alive at the end of the day. The slaughter began with two men facing each other. When one fell, the other took his place, more often than not slaying the original victor who was now fatigued. On and on, a succession of gory fights filled an entire afternoon. Admittedly, this form of combat was exceptional. Usually it was held when a good number of murderers, robbers, and incendiaries were on hand, having been sentenced, literally, to "death in the games."[59]

Clearly, this was one event where being last in line was a definite advantage! In A.D. 846, the Flavian Amphitheater was severely damaged by an earthquake. Later, it was converted into a medieval fortress and became known by its sobriquet, the Colosseum. When it was abandoned, the local citizens used the Colosseum as a source of building materials. During the Renaissance, Cardinal Farnese used material from the Colosseum to build his palace.

Pompeii, buried during the eruption of Mount Vesuvius in A.D. 79, contains the remnants of the best-preserved gladiatorial training school and amphitheater. The excavation of Pompeii uncovered the skeletons of four gladiators who were in chains and shackles when Vesuvius erupted. Within the same compound, 17 gladiators were uncovered, along with a woman wearing expensive jewels and in all probability engaging in a business or amorous transaction that involved pleasures of the flesh. This might suggest that the gladiators were either pampered slaves or a desirable commodity, or perhaps both.

SPORT AND CHRISTIANITY

The growth of Christianity had a profound impact on sport. In much the same manner as the Jews, the early Christians came into contact with adherents of Greek and Roman sport. Christian writers were knowledgeable about sport. Their literature went from using metaphors from Greek sport to issuing emphatic denunciations of Roman sport. The early church leaders were not opposed to the care of the body or health promotion and were tolerant of some Greek sports; however, Roman sport was condemned.[60] The Christian writers targeted both Christians and non-Christians relative to the immoral and hideous displays of Roman sport because Christians were still attending the games. Richard Franklin DeVoe, in "The Christians and the Games: The Relationship Between Christianity and the Roman Games from the First Through the Fifth Centuries, A.D.," provides insight into the relationship between the Roman games and a "Christianized Rome." His research indicates that the impact and influence of Christianity on Rome was significant both politically and socially. With regard to Christian participation in the games, Christianity was definitely Romanized.[61] The extent and scope of Christians' participation, as spectators and athletes, in Christian Rome has yet to be subjected to extensive research and will no doubt provide the basis for much discussion.

Christians were the dominant force opposing the carnage of the games and spectacles of ancient Rome. The Christians were more often than not the victims of these "entertainments" and had a great deal to gain when the atrocities ended. Ignatius, bishop of Antioch (A.D. 108), stated that the Roman spectacle was one of the most "cruel tortures of the devil" with which Christians had to contend.[62] The triumph of Christianity over the pagan religions of the Romans and Greeks did not immediately put an end to sports. The Greek athletic festivals and the Roman gladiatorial combats and animal slaughters eventually came to an end. However, the real irony is that the Roman tradition of chariot racing was so popular that it was adopted by the Christian (Byzantine) Empire and remained popular for centuries.[63]

SPORT AND JUDAISM: KING HEROD'S GREEK AND ROMAN SPECTACLES IN JERUSALEM

Flavius Josephus (A.D. 37–circa 100) was a Roman historian and son of a Jewish priest. He was well educated and authored extensive writings. Although he fought the Romans and was imprisoned by Vespasian in A.D. 63, he managed to gain favor with the future Emperor and was released from prison. Josephus became a Roman citizen and took a Roman name "Flavius Josephus" after the his name of his patron, the Emperor Titus Flavius.

The Works of Josephus is revered by both Jews and Christians. A superb historical account of the history of the Jews from the reign of Antiochus Epiphanes (175 B.C.–A.D. 163) to the fall of Masada in A.D. 73. In Book 15 / Chapter 8 Josephus provides us with an account of the foreign practices (Greek and Roman sports and spectacles) King Herod (circa 74 B.C.–4 B.C.) introduced to the people of Jerusalem which mortified the Jews and violated their religious laws. According to Josephus:

> . . . Herod revolted from the laws of his country and corrupted their ancient constitution, by the introduction of foreign practices . . . we became guilty of great wickedness afterward while those religious observances which we used to lead the multitude to piety, were now neglected . . . In the first place, he appointed solemn games to be celebrated every fifth year, in honor of Caesar, and built a great theater at Jerusalem . . . also a very great amphitheater in the plain. Both of these were costly works and opposite to Jewish customs for we had no such shows delivered down to us . . . he celebrated these games every five years in the most solemn and splendid manner. He also made proclamations to the neighboring countries and called men to gather out of every nation. The wrestlers and the rest of those that strove for the prizes in such games were

> invited out of every land both by the hopes of rewards and the glory of victory . . . the principal persons [athletes] that were most eminent in these sorts of exercises were gotten together . . . for there were great rewards . . . not only for those who performed their exercises naked . . . but also to musicians. He spared no expense to attract the most famous for these exercises.

> He also proposed . . . rewards for those who ran for the prizes in the chariot race when they were drawn by two, or three, or four pair of horses . . . he also made a great preparation of wild beasts and of lions themselves in great abundance and of such other beasts as were of uncommon strength or . . . rarely seen.

> These were prepared to fight with one another or that men who were condemned to death were to fight with them . . . foreigners were greatly surprised and delighted at the expense . . . and the great dangers that were to be seen; but to natural Jews this was no better than a dissolution of these customs for which they had so great a veneration. It also appeared no better than . . . barefaced impiety to throw men to wild beasts to delight the spectators and it was an act of impiety to change their own laws for such foreign exercises.[64]

The spectacular plays, shows and music displays as well as the chariot races that were instituted by Herod in his theaters offended the Jews who looked at these displays as heathenish sports that would corrupt the Jewish nation and ultimately the dissolution of the law of Moses and were condemned by the sober and pious Jews.

A group of Jews hatched a plot to murder Herod, however, Herod's spies were everywhere. Herod learned of the plot and rounded up the conspirators who did not deny the plot to kill him. They were tortured and executed. It was not long before the Jews learned who the spy was. They captured him and according to Josephus, ". . . was not only slain by them but pulled to pieces, limb from limb and given to the dogs."

Jews and Christians were not generally fans of Roman or Greek sports. However, there were

Jews and Christians who attended the races at the Circus and other sports and spectacles. They were ostracized and banished but there numbers would grow over time much to the dismay of Jewish priests and Christian leaders. To what extent does this exist today?

GREEK REACTION TO THE INTRODUCTION OF ROMAN SPORT

There was some opposition to Roman sport in Greece; however, by the first century A.D., gladiatorial contests were being staged in Athens and Corinth. In Corinth, though, riots broke out when the Roman proconsul attempted to force the Greeks to accept Roman sport on a mass scale. The Greeks had no love for the Romans, who were their masters, and Greek criticism of Roman sport was largely the reaction of people who believed they were watching the demise of their sporting heritage at the hands of the Romans. However, several emperors liked the Olympic Games and from the first to third century A.D. spent vast sums of money to rebuild Olympia and other Greek athletic venues destroyed during the Roman conquest of Greece. The Greeks responded by erecting marble statues of the Roman emperors who restored Greek sport.[65]

THE HIPPODROME OF CONSTANTINOPLE

The Hippodrome in Constantinople (present-day Istanbul) was a huge chariot racing venue. Constantinople's Hippodrome could seat approximately 100,000 screaming fans. The first adaptation of the hippodrome was erected by Emperor Septimius Severus (A.D. 145–211) in the third century A.D. Emperor Constantine the Great enlarged the hippodrome and erected a passage from the Great Palace to the Royal Box, probably to avoid mingling with the masses.

The chariot races at the Constantinople Hippodrome were just as popular as the chariot races throughout the Empire. Eventually two racing syndicates emerged and were known by their colors—the Greens and the Blues. Thousands of people aligned themselves with either the Greens or the Blues. On race day, the Hippodrome was a sea of green and blue as race fans dressed in the colors of their "team." The drivers and chariots were decked out in their respective colors as well; little has changed today relative to fans sporting the colors of their favorite team. Betting was heavy in Constantinople. The ancient fans, like the fans of today, wagered huge sums of money on horse races.

Over time, the Greens and Blues morphed into political parties. As if it wasn't contentious enough, politics became yet another subject to argue about between the Greens and Blues. The political clout of the Greens and Blues was significant. Many Byzantine Emperors were very careful not to offend either faction, but this tactic did not always work. The noted Byzantine historian Mehmet Fatih Yavuz of Canakkale Onsekiz Mart University in Turkey and other prominent scholars note that in A.D. 532 the Hippodrome became the scene of a violent revolt between the Greens and the Blues. The Nika Revolt, as history records it, was a tragic event in which thousands of fans representing the Greens and the Blues slaughtered each other in the Hippodrome. The fighting spilled out of the Hippodrome and lasted for days. Much of Constantinople was destroyed before the Emperor Justinian sent an army of mercenaries to quell the riot. These mercenaries managed to trap over 30,000 supporters of the Greens and Blues in the Hippodrome where they killed them all.

Today this same Hippodrome can be visited in Istanbul. It is in a peaceful park-like setting, directly across from the Blue Mosque (Figure 4-13).Most of the tourists who visit the site are unaware of the horrific slaughter that occurred here in A.D. 532 The road that goes around the infield and the Spina follows the exact course of the track the chariots thundered down over a fifteen hundred years ago (Figure 4-14). Several of the monuments that were used to adorn the Spina are still there. One does not have to walk far to see the huge, ancient walls and vaults that formed the perimeter of the most famous racetrack in Byzantium.

Figure 4-13

The configuration of the ancient Hippodrome, built in Constantinople (present-day Istanbul), can be seen in this photo. To the right and left are roads that follow the original track. In the background are two giant obelisks that were part of the original spina—the barrier that divided the racetrack. Today, the ancient Hippodrome is a park.

Figure 4-14

A four-horse chariot is featured on one of the remaining obelisks at the Hippodrome in Istanbul.

SUMMARY

The conquering Romans, ever utilitarian and pragmatic, were quick to adopt those aspects and practices of their vanquished foes that were compatible with their culture. The Romans incorporated sport from both the Etruscans and the Greeks with varying degrees of success. The events associated with the circus and arenas were derived from the Etruscans, who were preoccupied with death. The displays of brutality and carnage that occurred with monotonous regularity in the Flavian Amphitheater and other arenas differed sharply from the Greek form of athletics, which focused on individual physical excellence and attendant health. Yet the Romans found room for both even though the practitioners of Greek athletics were in the minority. The Romans blended the features of conquered nations to their liking. Sport in Rome was a significant part of Roman life, as it was in Greece and as it is in the United States. When possible, comparisons have been made between Rome and Greece to provide insight into the role, scope, and nature of sport in a cross-cultural context.

The impact and influence of the Greeks on Roman civilization cannot be underestimated. Romans assimilated the philosophy and deities of the Greeks. The ethos of the Romans was characterized by cruelty, slavery, patriarchy, class stratification, obedience to authority, and an educated elite, which is but a mirror image of Greek society except for the cruelty that seemed to personify itself in the arena. Romans and Greeks shared an

enthusiasm for sport. Sport was imbedded in the cultural fabric of Rome as it was in Greece, although their respective views of the body were dichotomous, as were their methods of physical education and training. The scientific exercises advocated by Galen, along with his promotion of health through fitness, did much to help the erudite Romans appreciate the benefits of physical activity and Greek gymnastics. Galen's skill in attending to the injuries of Roman athletes has earned him the distinction of being the "Father of Sports Medicine."

The emperor Constantine, sensing the inevitable collapse of Rome due to both internal and external forces, left Rome in A.D. 330 and moved the capital of the Empire to Byzantium, which he renamed Constantinople (modern-day Istanbul). The massive hippodrome built in Constantinople featured chariot races between the Greens and the Blues. By the fifth century, Rome was in economic chaos, and the once-mighty Roman Empire collapsed in 410. The Circus Maximus was torn down, and the Flavian Amphitheater was abandoned. The Dark Ages soon followed.

DISCUSSION QUESTIONS

1. How did the Romans differ from the Greeks in their feelings about sport?

2. Did the Romans believe in physical education? If so, for what purposes did the Romans use it?

3. How did the Romans use sport as a means of social control?

4. How is Roman sport similar to sport in the United States today?

5. What contributions did Galen make to the health of Romans? According to Galen, what were the benefits of exercise?

6. In general, how did Romans view the body? Was it an asset to be cared for? If so, what were some of the methods used by the Romans to care for their bodies?

7. What influence did the Etruscans have on the development of Roman sport?

8. What were the philosophical views of the body espoused by the Stoics and the Epicureans? How did their beliefs about the body in an

epistemological sense differ from the approach of Platonic thought?

9. How did Cicero use sport as a forum for his views?

10. Why were gladiators the premier athletes of Rome?

11. Were gladiator combats "big business"?

12. To what extent did women compete as gladiators?

13. Who and what put an end to gladiatorial combat and other mass spectacles of the Roman Empire?

14. Do the various activities that took place in the Flavian Amphitheater and other venues throughout the Roman Empire qualify as sport?

15. How many gladiator types competed in the arena? To what extent were gladiators specialized?

16. To what extent were chariot races popular in Constantinople?

17. To what end did King Herod promote Greek and Roman sports? Did the Jews attend the games that Herod sponsored or were they disgusted with them?

INTERNET RESOURCES

Classical History: Roman Sports
http://ancienthistory.about.com/od/romansports/
Provides articles on Roman sports, including gladiators.

**www.ualberta.ca/~csmackay/CLASS_378/
   Gladiators.html**
Offers a university course on sport in ancient Rome.

British Museum: Gladiators and Caesars
www.murphsplace.com/gladiator/museum.html
Gives information about Roman life and sport.

Historical Colosseum
www.eliki.com/ancient/civilizations/roman/content.htm
Is an excellent site with a virtual tour and photos of the
Colosseum.

Gladiatorial Games
www.vroma.org/~bmcmanus/arena.html

Roman Sites
**www.ukans.edu/history/index/europe/
   ancient_rome/E/Roman/RomanSites*/home.html**

Barbara F. McManus Classics Pages
www.cnr.edu/home/bmcmanus/

Lacus Curtius: Into the Roman World
**www.ukans.edu/history/index/europe/ancient_rome/
   E/Roman/home.html**

Roman Gladiatorial Games
**http://depthome.brooklyn.cuny.edu/classics/
   gladiatr/index.htm**

Visit the *History and Philosophy of Sport and Physical
Education* Online Learning Center (www.mhhe.com/
mechikoff6e) for additional information and study
tools.

SUGGESTIONS FOR FURTHER READING

Auguet, Roland. *Cruelty and Civilization.* London:
   Routledge, 1998.

Barton, Carlin. *The Sorrows of the Ancient Romans:
   The Gladiator and the Monster.* Princeton, NJ:
   Princeton University Press, 1993.

Bonfante, L. "Human Sacrifices on an Etruscan
   Funerary Urn." *American Journal of Archaeology*
   88, no. 4 (October 1984): 531–39.

Bury, J. B. *A History of the Roman Empire.* New York:
   American Book, 1927.

Crowther, N. "Nudity and Morality: Athletics in Italy."
   Classical Journal 75 (1980–81): 119–23.

Fowler, W. W. *Roman Festivals of the Period of the
   Republic.* London: Macmillan, 1899.

Freeman, Charles. *Egypt, Greece and Rome:
   Civilisations of the Ancient Mediterranean.* Oxford:
   Oxford University Press, 1996.

Futrell, Alison: *Blood in the Arena: The Spectacle of
   Roman Power.* Austin: University of Texas Press, 1997.

Grant, Michael. *Nero.* London: Weidenfeld & Nicolson,
   1970.

———. *Gladiators.* London: Penguin Books, 2000.

Hopkins, Keith. *Death and Renewal.* Cambridge:
   Cambridge University Press, 1983.

Hornblower, Simon, and Antony Spawforth (eds.).
   Oxford Classical Dictionary, 3rd ed. Oxford:
   Oxford University Press, 1996.

Lee, H. M. "The Sport Fan and Team Loyalty in
   Rome." *Arete: The Journal of Sport Literature* 1,
   no. 1 (Fall 1983): 139–45.

Meier, Christian. *Julius Caesar.* London:
   HarperCollins, 1995.

Norman, N. J. "Excavations at Carthage, 1982."
   American Journal of Archaeology 87, no. 2 (April
   1983): 247.

Pascal, N. "October Horse." *Harvard Studies in
   Classical Philology* 85 (1981): 261–91.

Petronius. *The Satyricon.* London: Penguin Books,
   1986.

Plutarch. *Fall of the Roman Republic.* London: Penguin
   Books, 1972.

Potter, David. The Victor's Crown: A History of
   Ancient Sport from Homer to Byzantium, Oxford
   University Press, USA, 2011.

Seneca. *The Apocolocyntosis.* London: Penguin Books,
   1986.

Suetonius. *The Twelve Caesars.* London: Penguin
   Books, 1989.

Tacitus. *The Annals of Imperial Rome.* London:
   Penguin Books, 1996.

Wiedemann, Thomas. *Emperors and Gladiators.*
   London: Routledge, 1996.

Notes

1. Ellen Macnamara, *The Etruscans* (Italy: British Museum, 1990), 11.

2. Vera Olivova, *Sports and Games in the Ancient World* (New York: St. Martin's Press, 1985), 155.

3. Ibid., 156–57.

4. P. Ducati, *Storia delle'arte Etrusca,* vol. II (Florence, 1927); G. M. Haufmann, *Etruskische Plastik* (Stuttgart, 1956); C. M. Lerici, *Nuove Testimonianze delle'arte e della civilta Etrusca* (Milan, 1960); G. A. Mansuelli, *Etruria and Early Rome* (London, 1960); G. Camporeale, *I Commerci di Vetulonia in eta' Orientalizzante* (Firenze, 1969); Bandinelli R. Bianchi and M. Torelli, *Etruria—Roma* (Torino, 1976); F. Poulsen, *Etruscan Tomb Paintings* (Oxford, 1922); Olivova, *Sports and Games,* 157.

5. Olivova, *Sports and Games,* 156; J. Heurgon, *Daily Life of the Etruscans* (London, 1964); Aristotle, *Politics,* trans. H. Rackham (London: Loeb Classical Library, 1959).

6. Olivova, *Sports and Games,* 158.

7. Vitruvius, *De architectura,* 5, I, 1. Rome, circa 1 B.C.; Olivova, *Sports and Games,* 159.

8. Olivova, *Sports and Games,* 159.

9. Alison Futrell, *Blood in the Arena: The Spectacle of Roman Power* (Austin: University of Texas Press, 1997), 11–19.

10. Ibid., originally put forward by F. Weege, "Oskische Grabmalerei" Jahrbuch des deutschen archäologischen Instituts, 24 (1909): 99–162. See G. Ville, La Gladiature en occident des origines alamort de Domitien (Rome: Ecole francsise de Rome, 1981) first chapter is devoted to this discussion, pp. 1–56. See J. P. Thuillier, Les Jeux athletiques dans la civilisation etrusque (Rome: Ecule francaise de Rome, 1985).

11. An oligarchy is a government in which political power rests in the hands of a few people.

12. Peter Quenell and the Editors of Newsweek Book Division, *The Colosseum* (New York: Newsweek, 1971), 15.

13. Ibid., 15.

14. Ellwood P. Cubberly, *The History of Education* (Boston: Houghton Mifflin, 1920), 58.

15. Frederick Copleston, *A History of Philosophy,* vol. 1 (Westminster: Newman Press, 1966), 380.

16. Ibid., 381.

17. The transcendental universal, according to Plato, is the perfect idea that is poorly imitated in the material world, whereas the concrete universal, according to Aristotle, is the idea predicated on or induced from the material world. In both cases, the material world is secondary to the world that "transcends reality." As a consequence, the body is believed to be less important than the mind.

18. Copleston, *History of Philosophy,* 395.

19. Ibid., 398.

20. P. H. De Lacy, "Epicurus," *The Encyclopedia of Philosophy,* vol. 3 (New York: Macmillan/Free Press, 1972), 3–5.

21. Lawrence W. Fielding, "Marcus Tullius Cicero: A Social Critic of Sport" (University of Louisville).

22. Ibid.

23. Cicero, *De Finibus,* 339–341.

24. Ibid.

25. William J. Baker, *Sports in the Western World* (Totawa, NJ: Rowman & Littlefield, 1982), 29.

26. Deobold B. Van Dalen and Bruce L. Bennett, *A World History of Physical Education,* 2nd ed. (Englewood Cliffs, NJ: Prentice-Hall, 1971), 77.

27. Robert Montraville Green, *A Translation of Galen's Hygiene* (Springfield, IL: Charles C. Thomas, 1951), xxii.

28. Quoted in E. Norman Gardiner, *Athletics of the Ancient World* (Cambridge: Oxford University Press, 1930), 115.

29. Rachel Sargent Robinson, *Sources for the History of Greek Athletics* (Cincinnati: Author, 1955), 187.

30. Ibid., 177.

31. Ibid., 178.

32. Ibid., 188.

33. Ibid., 188.

34. Don Kyle, "Directions in Ancient Sport History," *Journal of Sport History* 10, no. 1 (Spring 1983): 24–25.

35. Harold Arthur Harris, *Sport in Greece and Rome* (London: Thames & Hudson, 1972), 41.

36. Ibid.

37. Ibid., 150.

38. Alan Baker, the Gladiator—The Secrete history of Rome's warrior slaves (Cambridge MA: DA Capo press, A member of the Perseus Books Group, 2000), 27–28.

39. Ibid.

40. K. Coleman, "Missio at Halicarnassus," *Harvard Studies in Classical Philology* 100 (2000), 487–500; M. Vesley, *Echos du Monde Classique* 62, no. 17 (1998): 85–93.

41. B. Levick, "The Senatus Consultum from Larinum," *Journal of Roman Studies* 73 (1983): 97–115; J. F. Gardner, *Women in Roman Law and Society* (Bloomington: Indiana University Press, 1986).

42. J. Carcopino, *Daily Life in Ancient Rome* (Harmondsworth: Penguin Books, 1941), 267.

43. Donald G. Kyle, "Rethinking the Roman Arena: Gladiators, Sorrows, and Games," *The Ancient History Bulletin* 11 (1997): 94–97.

44. Thomas Wiedemann, *Emperors and Gladiators* (London and New York: Routledge, 1992).

45. Luciana Jacobelli, Gladiators at Pompeii (Los Angeles; The J. Paul Getty Museum, 2003), 7–17. Actual artifacts depecting each type of gladiator.

46. L. Jacobelli, *Gladiators at Pompeii* (Los Angeles: Getty, 2003), 19–20.

47. Wiedemann, *Emperors and Gladiators;* see also Carlin Barton, *The Sorrows of the Ancient Romans: The Gladiator and the Monster* (Princeton, NJ: Princeton University Press, 1993); Paul Plass, *The Game of Death in Ancient Rome: Arena Sport and Political Suicide* (Madison: University of Wisconsin Press, 1995); Alison Futrell, *Blood in the Arena: The Spectacle of Roman Power* (Austin: University of Texas Press, 1997).

48. M. Grant, *Gladiators* (New York: Barnes & Noble, 1967), 31; see also E. Kohne and E. Wigleben (eds.), *Gladiators and Caesars: The Power of Spectacle in Ancient Rome* (Berkeley: University of California Press, 2000).

49. Harris, *Sport in Greece and Rome,* 73.

50. Van Dalen and Bennett, *World History of Physical Education,* 78.

51. Ibid., 81.

52. Baker, *Sports in the Western World,* 33.

53. Quenell, *Colosseum,* 36.

54. Ibid., 33–34.

55. Van Dalen and Bennett, *World History of Physical Education,* 82.

56. Wiedemann, *Emperors and Gladiators;* Kyle, *Rethinking the Roman Arena,* 95.

57. Baker, *Sports in the Western World,* 34; personal correspondence, Barbara Rieger, September 2004.

58. David Potter, The Victor's Crown: A History of Ancient Sport from Homer to Byzantium. Oxford University Press USA, 2011, p. 259.

59. Baker, "Sports in the Ancient World," p. 34.

60. Kyle, "Directions in Ancient Sport History," 30.

61. Richard Franklin DeVoe, "The Christians and the Games: The Relationship Between Christianity and the Roman Games from the First Through the Fifth Centuries, A.D." (Ph.D. diss., Texas Tech University, 1987).

62. Ibid., 37.

63. Kyle, "Directions in Ancient Sport History," 30.

64. The works of Josephus. Translated by William Whiston (Peabody MA: Hendrickson Publishers, Inc)" The Antiquities of the Jews," 1987 Book 15/ Chapter 8, pages 415–416.

65. Of particular interest to the student or scholar of sport history is the fact that a significant amount of archaeological excavation has uncovered a treasure trove of artifacts and structures in Roman Corinth. However, the Roman amphitheater that caused the conquered Greeks so much angst has never been excavated. The site of the amphitheater can be visited and is near the only Greek structure that was not destroyed by the Romans in 146 B.C., the Temple of Apollo. With some imagination, you can "see" the arena, and if you listen, it will speak to you.

In Athens, the gladiatorial combats were held in the ancient stadium where today a beautiful marble stadium sits, constructed in 1896 for the first modern Olympics. It is unlikely that many visitors know of the horrific slaughter of humans and animals that drenched the arena floor with blood 19 centuries ago.

SECTION

II From the Spiritual World to the Secular World

Changing Concepts of the Body

CHAPTER 5

Philosophy, Sport, and Physical Education During the Middle Ages: 900–1400

General Events

Dark Ages (A.D. 476–900)

402–476 Ravenna capital of Western Roman Empire

527–565 Justinian, Eastern Roman Emperor

533 *Digest of Laws*

590–604 Gregory the Great, pope; liturgy of Roman Catholic Church codified; Gregorian chant established

768–814 Charlemagne, king of the Franks

800 Charlemagne crowned Holy Roman emperor by pope

841 Vikings invade northern France and colonize French territory

Middle Ages (A.D. 900–1400)

962 Otto the Great (936–973) crowned Holy Roman emperor

ca. 995–1050 Guido of Arezzo, author of musical treatises, inventor of staff notation

ca.1000 Leif Eriksson, Viking navigator, reaches coast of North America

1000–1150 Romanesque Period at height

1050 Holy Roman Empire at height; ascendancy of papal power

OBJECTIVES

Upon completing this chapter, you will be able to:

- Understand the impact of Christian theology on the philosophical beliefs of the Middle Ages, also known as the Medieval Period.
- Understand the view of Christian theology regarding the worth or value of the human body.
- Recognize the influence of Christianity and the philosophies of ancient Greece on the ideas and practices in vogue during the Middle Ages.
- Identify the philosophical views of the body during the Middle Ages and their subsequent impact on the development of sport and physical education.
- Appreciate the contributions of St. Thomas Aquinas, Moses Maimonides, and St. Bonaventure in changing attitudes regarding the human body and the value of exercise.
- Understand the relationship between sport and religion.
- Appreciate the role and scope of holidays, ball games, equestrian competitions, and English football games in society.
- Understand the reaction of the church to sporting competitions.
- Identify the social status enjoyed by knights of the Middle Ages and identify the various competitions they could take part in.
- Discuss the rationale used by the church to support the violent competitions that knights engaged in.
- Identify the medical knowledge of the time and the various means of maintaining and restoring health.
- Identify the combat sports depicted on the Bayeux Tapestry.

INTRODUCTION

The period beginning with the tenth century and ending with the birth of the Italian Renaissance in the fourteenth century has been termed the Medieval Period or, more commonly, the Middle Ages. For the student of physical education, the Middle Ages represent an intriguing time, with events ranging from the athletic feats of knights during the Age of Chivalry, to the use of sport in preparation for the Crusades, to the ascetic views of Christian monks. The latter emphasized self-denial and even bodily mortification—that is, self-inflicted pain and mystical punishment that were designed to inhibit bodily lusts and desires, and in so doing prepare one's soul for heaven.

Generally speaking, the philosophical view of the body during the Middle Ages reflected theological beliefs. Most early Christians, rather than glorify the body, held it in contempt. There were some notable exceptions, however, that will be presented later in this chapter. While the ancient Greeks were tremendous athletes who admired the human form and consequently sought to develop great physiques, they were pagans in the eyes of the early Christians. Greek athletes competed nude in the Olympic Games to honor a pagan god, Zeus. Athletics became a symbol tied to pagan rituals. To the Christians of the Middle Ages, this ancient Greek practice of worshiping pagan gods by way of athletic prowess and the achievement of physical perfection was seen as paying too much attention to secular concerns (the glorification of the human body), and not enough attention to spiritual concerns (the nurturing of the eternal soul). In the *Phaedo,* Socrates voiced similar concerns: that his fellow Athenians spent too much time attending to their secular/material needs and too little time improving the soul.

The majority of Christians believed that to participate in athletics or engage in physical training to glorify the body was to contaminate the body, which "housed" the soul, and make the soul impure. The negative attitude that medieval Christians had toward the body was in no small part the result of a reaction to paganism.

Although the Christians' negative attitude toward the body stemmed from a reaction to paganism, many of the same Christian theologians came to embrace the ideas of Plato and other "pagan" Greeks. Philosophy during the Middle Ages was mixed with religion and many times emerged as a vague collection of ideas that were difficult to grasp and explain. For example, some of the ideas that originated with the Greeks (particularly Plato's and Socrates' metaphysical dualism), were accepted, while others (such as physical education) were to a great extent ignored.

THE IMPACT OF CHRISTIANITY

The Christian Church was one of the few remaining institutions left intact by the barbarian hordes that overran Europe after the fall of Ravenna, the last capital of the Western Roman Empire. In addition to the Christian influence

1056 Westminster Abbey
1063 Pisa Cathedral begun
1066 William, Duke of Normandy, conquers England; reigns as king of England
1078 Tower of London begun by William the Conqueror
1096–1291 Crusades: European Christians fight Muslims and Saracens; extend Christianity and open trade routes
1163–1235 Cathedral of Notre Dame in Paris built
1198–1216 Innocent III, pope; church reaches pinnacle of power

on European civilization, Judaism and Islam also had a profound impact upon the development of European civilization. Europeans were exposed to new ideas and unique cultural aspects that were essential elements in Jewish and Muslim society as a result of expanding trade and military campaigns that brought Europeans to the Middle East. The Crusades provide an example of how Europeans came to the Middle East as soldiers. If they were fortunate enough to survive the bloody battles and return home, they brought back with them "new" foods, weapons, garments, and medicinal cures, and an expanded insight into Middle Eastern philosophy and religion.

The collapse of Rome in A.D. 476 resulted in a state of chaos that drove many people to seek protection from powerful aristocrats who demanded complete allegiance and subjugation. As many people fled Rome, the advances made by the Roman Empire in commerce, trade, and public administration were eventually forgotten. Instead of going forward, Western civilization deteriorated and entered a bleak period known as the Dark Ages (476–900). Europe regressed into kingdoms similar to tribal societies. Society gradually became feudalistic, with castles and walled cities designed by people desperate for protection and self-preservation. Wars and armed conflict between knights and feudal armies, which would often lay siege to the walled cities, were the order of the day in the Dark Ages. Organized sport and physical education during this era was, for the most part, nonexistent.

With the inception of the Middle Ages around 900, people began to emerge from the cultural and intellectual "darkness" that epitomized the Dark Ages. Although it was still dangerous to travel and wars were still common, the Middle Ages were an improvement over the Dark Ages. Trade and commerce revived, and a market economy gradually emerged. Metaphysical questions began to surface once again, and these questions were almost always linked to the religious beliefs of the time. So where did people turn to for guidance and answers during the Middle Ages? In general, it depended upon the religion one practiced. For Christians,

the church was the lone cultural institution that, through intellectual and spiritual leadership, provided a symbol of stability and order amidst fear and chaos. Jews continued to seek spiritual leadership and guidance in their temples, while Muslims found comfort and spiritual leadership by praying in the mosques and following the teachings of Mohammed. Judaism and Islam were practiced in the Middle East and parts of Spain and Northern Africa as part of thriving economies and rich cultures. However, while these religions played significant roles in shaping the thoughts and ideas found in Western civilization, the dominant cultural and religious force in Europe during the Middle Ages was Christianity.

Christianity spread throughout the ruins of the Roman Empire. The Roman Catholic Church in particular felt obligated to convert all those who were not Catholic to Catholicism. It did not matter if you were a Jew, Muslim, or mere pagan; conversion to Catholicism was a prime goal of the Roman Catholic Church. This practice eventually resulted in the Inquisition, a religious movement designed to convert nonbelievers to Christianity—by force if necessary—and to root out the heretics within the Catholic Church. In hindsight, the Inquisition can be seen as a tragic and brutal episode in the history of the Catholic Church.

The Inquisition was a medieval court inspired in part by the beliefs of St. Augustine, who interpreted the biblical passage found in Luke 14:23 as permission to use force against heretics. Heretics were identified as those individuals who held controversial beliefs and were not in agreement with the official teachings of the Roman Catholic Church. In 1231, the papal Inquisition was used by Pope Gregory IX, who issued a papal decree that ordered heretics to be burned at the stake. If an individual was accused of being a heretic, that person could either confess or deny the charge. If a confession was made immediately, the church authorities could issue sentences that ranged from flogging to praying. However, if the charge was denied and there was reason to believe that the person was not telling the truth, it was necessary to "extract" a confession. The church was not supposed to shed blood, so secular authorities were given the task of obtaining the necessary confession through the use of torture. The most severe practice was torture on "the rack," followed by execution. To add insult to injury, the condemned person's property was confiscated. In most cases, death by burning was carried out almost immediately after the sentence was announced.

Among the most infamous of these medieval church tribunals was the Spanish Inquisition. The impetus for this most cruel of inquisitions was Ferdinand II of Aragon and Isabella I of Castile. Under pressure by these two rulers, Pope Sixtus IV authorized the Spanish Inquisition in 1483. The primary targets of the Spanish Inquisition were the Marranos (Jews who converted to Christianity) and the Moriscos (Muslims who also converted to the Christian faith). The Spanish Inquisition was headed by Tomas de Torquemada, who was as sinister as he was cruel. He believed that the Marranos and Moriscos were still secretly practicing their original faiths. The Marranos and Moriscos who denied the charges were subjected to the cruelest of tortures and then burned to death. Clearly, this was a corrupt and violent period in the history of the church.

The church gradually and deliberately became both the source of all spiritual solutions for Christians and an enormous political and economic power. Within the Catholic Church, this control was exercised through various popes. The theology of the church was based on absolute faith and belief in the certainty of *divine revelation*—a way of knowing by which "truth" is obtained through prayer and directly from God. This epistemology, along with scripture, was the philosophical basis of the medieval Christian Church. From a political perspective, all Christians were gradually brought under complete church control through a kind of carrot-and-stick philosophy. Failure to comply with church authority was to risk eternal damnation, which the enemies of the church would most surely suffer.

On the other hand, by obeying church laws, or dogma, one could hope to bask in the infinite glory of God in heaven. Life during the Middle Ages was relatively harsh, so the prospect of an eternity in heaven looked pretty good![1]

CHRISTIANITY AND GREEK PHILOSOPHY

The early medieval philosophers did not have access to a wealth of literary sources. What they did come to possess were works of the ancient Greek philosophers, especially Plato and Aristotle. Both Plato and Aristotle were interested in the metaphysical concepts that form the foundation of Christianity: the existence of the soul, the personification of and belief in God, the nature of being/existence, and the codes by which people should conduct their lives. Early Christian writers were compelled to accept specific beliefs from the philosophy of the ancient Greeks so they could reconcile Greek philosophy with Christian theology.[2]

Not all Christians were eager to embrace the merging of Christianity with Greek philosophy. In the second century A.D., Tertullian, for instance, demanded bodily mortification and was adamant in his opposition to recognizing and accepting the pagan philosophy of the Greeks. Tertullian, however, and those who believed as he did were in the minority. Platonism not only was recognized by Christian theologians but also "was commonly regarded by Christian thinkers as having been an intellectual preparation for Christianity."[3]

Christian theologians attempted to use philosophy to prove their theological Christian dogma. This means that medieval theologians, also men of philosophy, tried to prove the essence and nature of God using philosophical methods. This task, to say the least, is difficult. The Schoolmen, or Scholastics, as they were known, spent their lives formulating philosophical positions that would prove and support the existence of God and divine revelation. To this end, St. Augustine, Boethius, John Scotus Erigena, St. Anselm, Peter Abelard, St. Bonaventure, and the greatest Scholastic of all,

St. Thomas Aquinas, resurrected the philosophical traditions of antiquity and embarked on a metaphysical quest tempered by their beliefs as theologians and Scholastics.

The attempted marriage of theology and philosophy was at best awkward and cumbersome. Although philosophers and theologians both use reasoned inquiry and rational thought, they differ in their presuppositions. Philosophy rejects "blind faith" which is essential to Christian theology. Theologians accept the existence of God on faith alone—not necessarily by philosophical deductions based on reasoned and rational inquiry. Indeed, it is the "leap of faith" that makes religion such a unique and powerful force in life.

PHILOSOPHICAL VIEWS OF THE BODY IN THE MIDDLE AGES

With the exception of the work of Jewish and Islamic philosophers, the home of medieval philosophy was the Catholic Church. As mentioned earlier, Christian theologians recognized and incorporated the works of Plato and Aristotle into a philosophy uniquely Christian in purpose. The Arab world had preserved the works of Plato and Aristotle and passed them on to Christians during the twelfth and first half of the thirteenth centuries.[4] The works of the original Greek writers were translated from Arabic and Greek into Latin, and translations were also made of works by Islamic and Jewish philosophers. All of these works were of considerable importance to the development of theology and philosophy in Western Christendom.[5]

The portrayal of Jesus in these translated works was one of perfection in body, mind, and soul. An interesting dilemma that occurred in the framing of the philosophical views of the body was the idea that when God made heaven and earth and added man and woman, he approved of his work; mankind was made in his image. This certainly implied that both the body and the soul were good, and that God would not purposely create something that was harmful or evil. Logically,

then, the human body was a good thing.[6] This discussion regarding the body of Jesus became quite confused during medieval debates, however, and the metaphysical arguments that ensued were catalysts for the eventual splitting of Christianity in 1054 into Eastern Orthodoxy (centered in the Eastern Roman Empire in Constantinople) and Roman Catholicism. According to William Fleming, during the late fifth and early sixth centuries,

> the main doctrinal battle centered on the nature of the Trinity. . . . The Ostrogoths believed that since Jesus was created by God the Father, he was subordinate and not of one substance with God. . . . The Arians revered Christ as the noblest of created beings, but as human rather than divine. In Byzantium, it was held that Christ as the Incarnated Word was of one single substance with the Father and hence of divine nature only. The Roman Papacy found a middle ground between the two extremes and took the position that since the Word was made flesh, Christ possessed both divine and human natures and was a full member of the Trinity.[7]

Some Orthodox Christians consistently rejected contentions that the body was evil; however, they were in the minority. The minority view was that because God was omnipresent, He was in all things, including the body. The body, filled with God, was good.[8] However, this view was not without controversy. Elements of the early Christian church, along with various powerful and influential "streams" of Roman Catholicism during the early Middle Ages, looked upon the human body as vile and corrupt and beyond redemption.

The subject of the corporeal nature of Christ, the influence of Neoplatonism, and the position of the church combined to create a distinct but inconsistent Christian view of the worth of the body. The beliefs of those Christians who were ascetic dualists represented a combination of Platonic philosophy, early Christian theology, and Islamic and Jewish influences. *Ascetic dualism* is the belief that the human body should be denied any kind of pleasure in order to purify the soul.

This concept is not necessarily the position put forth in the Old and New Testaments. Biblical concepts of the body, soul, and flesh describe man as a whole being, as opposed to having a dualistic existence.[9] Not all scholars are in agreement on this point, however. There were, and continue to be, confusing and contradictory views of scripture, especially on the position and role of the body. Important to our discussion is the understanding that the various interpretations of scripture can have a significant impact on the perceived worth or value of the body, which directly affects the nature, development, and scope of sport and physical education.

One perspective on the body is that "the enfleshment of God" is the cardinal belief of Christianity.[10] By "enfleshment," Frank Bottomley means that human beings are "bodily images" of a perfect God, and therefore the "body" part of our existence is, in some profound way, good. The merging of the corporeal with the divine nature of God as a result of "enfleshment" resulted in a heightened respect for the body. Hebrew writers insisted that man—the only true image of God—was a psychosomatic entity of both body and soul. Had this concept been accepted by the Western world, it could have effectively ended the dualism of body and spirit. However, the bubonic plague swept through Europe during the fourteenth century, leaving in its wake despair, intense physical and emotional suffering, and an obsession with death (Figure 5-1). The eventual result was that the body came to be viewed as the "messenger of sin";[11] God had punished mankind with the plague as a result of human wickedness. Bodily suffering was used to convey God's wrath.

Another perspective on the value of the body during the Middle Ages appears to be a result of the merging of Eastern Orthodox religion and Greek philosophy. This can be seen in the monastic life of early Christian monks, which was "ascetic." The monks sought enlightenment through bodily mortification, vows of silence, prayer, and renunciation of material possessions.

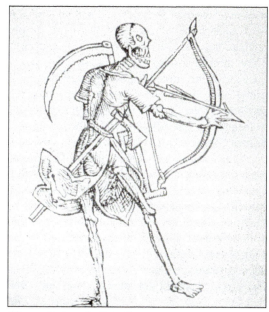

Figure 5-1

Skeletal bowman. The bow and arrow was often used by medieval artists to symbolize death and destruction. This skeletal bowman, in a German woodcut of 1514, reminded the devout of the Middle Ages to reflect on man's mortality.

The consensus among medieval historians is that, with the exception of ritual dancing and manual labor, Christians were encouraged to avoid the pleasures and temptations of the flesh. Deobold Van Dalen and Bruce Bennett explain:

> The Christians eventually came to regard the body as an instrument of sin. The body was mortal and of little consequence to a man seeking eternal salvation. . . . Many men came to accept the premise that life in the world to come could best be secured by rising above all thoughts of the body, even to the extent of ignoring and neglecting essential physical needs. In such an atmosphere, even the most worthy ideals of physical education could not exist.[12]

While physical education could not exist according to adherents of such a perspective, this does not mean that the early Christian monks were not "aware" of the body. Indeed, the monks were *extremely* aware of the body and argued long and hard against the pleasures of the flesh, bodily temptations, and the meaning of these concepts. Their attitude toward the body, and the consequences of this attitude, was a matter of choice: These early monks *chose* to deny themselves the pleasures of the flesh. In so doing, they "proved" to themselves that they were, from the perspective of their Christian faith, worthy of eternal salvation.

From both theological and philosophical positions, then, physical education and sporting activities appear to be all but absent from the Middle Ages, except for the military activities of the time. This, however, was not entirely the case. Although most Christians who lived during the Middle Ages did not glorify the body as did the ancient Greeks, there did exist some individuals and groups that did not abandon the body. The Scholastics saw value in physical activity, and instead of emphasizing the differences between mind and body, they argued for a close relationship between the two.[13]

The Body And Physical Fitness According to St. Thomas Aquinas

The greatest of the medieval Scholastics, St. Thomas Aquinas (1225–1274), embraced the idea of physical fitness and recreation as a positive force in promoting social and moral well-being. In his classic work *Summa Theologiae*, Aquinas argued that

> in order to achieve happiness, perfection in both the soul and body are necessary. Since it is natural for the soul to be united with the body, how is it credible that perfection of the one (soul) should exclude the perfection of the other (body)? Let us declare, then, that happiness completed and entire requires the well-being of the body.[14]

In what was no doubt a bold assertion for his time, Aquinas stated what physical educators have argued for years: Intelligence depends in part on the physical fitness level of the individual. He noted that "because some men have bodies of

better disposition, their souls have a greater power of understanding."[15] He went on to say that

> a man is rendered apt of intelligence by the healthy disposition of the internal powers of the organism, in which the good condition of the body has a part. Consequently intellectual endowments can be in the powers of sense, though primarily they are in the mind.[16]

From an epistemological perspective, Aquinas believed that we can come to know things through our bodies as well as through our minds, although the mind was to remain superior to the body. A healthy mind and a healthy body were desirable qualities for all to have.

Why did Aquinas believe that physical fitness was of benefit to the physical, mental, social, and moral well-being of Christians at a time when most Christians renounced the body? For example, the heretical Manicheans and Albigensians denounced the body, and matter in general, as evil. An evil and perishable body could never be fully integrated with a noble and immortal soul. The body imprisoned the soul and, as a result, did not contribute in a positive way to mental, social, and moral well-being.[17] Plato's view of the body, as stated in the *Phaedo*, was embraced by the Manicheans and Albigensians.

Aristotle, however, did not agree with his teacher (Plato) and put forth a much different view. The Greek philosophers, especially Aristotle, had a profound impact upon the Scholastics. Aquinas and others approved of Aristotle's position—that man is an integral composite of body and soul—and that the soul needs a body to acquire knowledge. This philosophical belief was in direct contrast to the beliefs espoused by Plato in the *Phaedo*—that the nature of man is divided into two parts, body and soul. In addition, Plato believed that the body could corrupt the soul and was not to be trusted when seeking knowledge. As a result of Aristotle's influence, the theory of the unity of man was adopted by the Scholastics of the thirteenth century.[18] Scholasticism also received support from Orthodox Christians who believed that because God was omnipresent, he was in all things, including the body. The body was filled with God, and therefore the body was good; it was not an instrument of sin.[19] Under the tutelage of Aquinas, the Scholastics nurtured a philosophical and religious justification for cherishing the body and valuing physical fitness and recreation for physical, mental, social, and moral well-being.[20] Aquinas clearly saw the relationship between physical well-being and mental and biological health. In any case, Plato and Aristotle had a profound impact on Christian theology. Some factions of Christendom embraced Plato's view of the nature of man, some embraced Aristotle's idea of a composite of body and soul, and some refused to accept any ideas or beliefs espoused by pagan Greeks.

MOSES MAIMONIDES AND ST. BONAVENTURE

Although most intellectuals in the Middle Ages were dualists, Aquinas was not alone in his view that the body was important to the mind and soul. The noted Jewish philosopher and physician Moses Maimonides (1135–1204) observed that "nothing is more useful for the preservation of health than physical exercise."[21] Similarly, at the University of Paris, perhaps the best university of the time, St. Bonaventure (1217–1274) wrote that the body does not imprison the soul but is a friend and companion, and therefore the individual exists as a natural union of body and soul.[22]

Even though Aquinas, Maimonides, and Bonaventure saw the relationship of the mind, body, and spirit as a close one, the understanding of the majority of Catholic clergy was very different. And the views of these monks about the role of the body led to some ambiguous attitudes toward sport and physical education. Generally, the church tolerated "fun and games" because it could not stop them, yet the church never really condoned these types of activities.

LINKING THE SPIRITUAL WITH SECULAR SPORT

Change is a difficult thing to accept, especially if it necessitates that an individual or an institution tolerate a new practice or idea that was at

one time discouraged. This was the situation that the Christian Church had to deal with in relation to sport and games. The negative attitude toward sport and other secular activities evident with the early Christian monks was changing. This change started to take place in the eleventh and twelfth centuries.[23] During this time, many nobles elected to become monks, primarily because of the manner in which property was inherited. Generally, the oldest son inherited the lands of his father, leaving his younger brothers to a life either as a knight or as a member of the priesthood. In the case of the young priest, secular habits such as hunting, falconry, and perhaps even the combat sports used to train knights remained popular. Young nobles who became priests introduced these activities into the ecclesiastical community, and over time, these athletic activities came to be accepted by the church.[24]

Perhaps the best example of the "noble priest" is provided by Bishop Odon of Bayeux (1049–1097), a noble knight who served in the army of his half-brother, William the Conqueror. Bishop Odon was able to blend his spiritual virtues with the secular athletic skills of a knight.[25] Bishop Odon's exploits, as well as various sports and other physical activities in medieval England, both aristocratic and servile, are depicted on the Bayeux Tapestry (Figure 5-2). The tapestry is a multicolored cloth woven around A.D. 1070; it is 19½ inches wide and about 230 feet long. This embroidered work of art was supervised by Bishop Odon of Bayeux (hence the name). The tapestry shows numerous sporting activities such as archery, hunting, hawking, fishing, cockfighting, fencing, jousting, bearbaiting, bullbaiting, riding, and assorted ball games, and is a primary source of information about sporting activities in England during the Middle Ages.

HOLIDAYS AND BALL GAMES

The agrarian life of the peasant-serf was particularly hard. The serf of the Middle Ages was not a slave; he owned his home and worked a plot of land as a tenant (renter). Rent and taxes went to the lord of the estate in the form of crops, other

Figure 5-2
Bayeux Tapestry. In a bloody battle, the Saxons are defeated on October 14, 1066, and William is crowned King of England.

agricultural products, and services in return for protection. Primitive farming techniques (which improved during the tenth century with the invention of the plowshare and the horse collar) meant long, arduous workdays. The only regular opportunity for peasant recreation came on Sundays after church services. With the permission of local church authorities, serfs participated in various types of ball games and amusements such as picnics and leisurely walks (Figure 5-3).

Major holidays such as May Day, Shrove Tuesday, and Whitsuntide celebrations were considered pagan holidays.[26] Such seasonal agricultural holidays extended over several days and were associated with generous amounts of food and alcohol and various entertainments and games. Fine points of etiquette and genteel manners were not required of peasants, and so it was not uncommon for these festivals to degenerate into drunken free-for-alls that resulted in debauchery, property damage, injury, and sometimes death (Figure 5-4).

RUGGED BALL GAMES, EQUESTRIAN EVENTS, AND ENGLISH FOOTBALL

Ball games that had been popular during Roman times continued to be popular in the Middle Ages and often took place on church land if a common area was not available. A ball game called *soule* was popular among the peasantry, and it often contributed to property losses and personal injury.

Figure 5-3
Games and amusements.

Figure 5-4
Free-for-all.

The game resembled the modern game of soccer and was played with an indeterminate number of men on each side. Possession of a stuffed leather ball was the goal, and two teams played the game between two goals. During the heat of competition, the achievement of this goal sometimes left the "playing field" (and often someone's private property) in ruins. Most accounts of the game describe it as a violent affair, and one scholar noted that the players engaged in "a veritable combat for the possession of the ball for which they fought like dogs battling for a bone."[27] King James noted that the game was "meeter for the maiming than making able the (players) thereof."[28] As you can imagine, soule was quite violent, and this contributed to the church's ambivalence about its association with the game. Local customs governed the rules of play, and there were many versions of the game throughout Europe.

There were other ball games as well, some that employed sticks and were precursors to modern field hockey and baseball. Another game, *kegels,* was similar to bowling. Although the legacy of some ball games was distinctly Roman, there is evidence to suggest that ball games were being played by Germanic tribes and by the Irish and Scots before Roman occupation in the first centuries A.D. The Moors of Northern Africa also introduced their own ball games to Spain in the eighth century.

William Fitzstephen, a noted writer and clerk for Thomas Becket, the archbishop of Canterbury, lived in London during the twelfth century. The London described by Fitzstephen was a dynamic city that assimilated immigrants from the continent into the social classes that were the staple of British society. Fitzstephen provided an account of nobles and nonnobles assembling at a smooth field every Friday for the local horse show: "It is pleasant to see the nags, with their sleek and shining coats."[29] He reported that part of the reason for attending was to watch the horses race: "The horses . . . are eager for the race . . . upon the signal being given, they stretch out their limbs, hurry over the course, and are borne along with unremitting speed."[30]

English football was also gaining popularity in London, and the following account written by Fitzstephen in *Descriptio Londoniae* helps us visualize the athletes and spectators who enjoyed the game in medieval London:

> After dinner, all the young men of the city go out into the fields to play at the well known game of football. The scholars belonging to several schools have each their ball; and the city tradesmen, according to their respective crafts, have theirs. The more aged men, the fathers of the players, and the wealthy citizens, come on horseback to see the contests of the young men, with whom, after their manner, they participate, their natural heart seeming to be aroused by the sight of so much agility, and by their participation in the amusements of unrestrained youth.[31]

The apparent universality of ball games, their popularity with the peasant-serfs, the interest of the tradesmen and upper classes, their association with Christian holidays, and the long tradition of quiet acceptance of such games by church authorities made it extremely difficult for the church to end its association with these games. Yet it became increasingly difficult to tolerate the mayhem that surrounded peasant recreations in the last decades of the Middle Ages. Outraged by the number of incidents of damage to property and persons and the openly lewd conduct, the church intervened with prohibitions against games that involved gambling and immoral behavior. Such condemnations were only partially successful, however. Time, traditions, and human nature mitigated against any permanent solution to the church's dilemma—the difficulty of teaching moral introspection and spiritual self-examination to illiterate peasants.

MEDIEVAL SOCIAL STRUCTURE: KNIGHTS, NOBLES, AND WORTHY PURSUITS

As the Middle Ages moved from the early centuries to their close around 1400, a complex hierarchy of aristocratic privilege and power was established. From the beginning, feudal relationships were based on military and political responsibilities. These responsibilities primarily involved military allegiance to the local monarch for his personal protection. The tradition of a personal bodyguard was a customary practice of Germanic and Roman ruling classes. In return for his pledge of personal military service, the lord or vassal was given land (a fief) and servants and peasants sufficient to supply the needs of his family. These vassal lords then had the right of taxation over their serfs. The control of wealth (feudalism) by the upper classes was based on land ownership and the labor of the serfs.

This system provided another essential quality that distinctly separated the nobility from the serfs. The wealth of the aristocracy came from the labor of others, so leisure became the unique commodity of nobles. Even if a peasant could afford the horse and the arms required of a knight, he would not have had the necessary time to practice the skills of war. Leisure became the signature of European aristocracy from the Middle Ages until the twentieth century. It is this consequence of wealth, established during the Middle Ages, that led to many of the differences between the recreational pursuits of upper and lower classes.

By the tenth century, the titles, property, and privileges of the nobility, as well as the feudal subordination of the serfs to an overlord, were considered a hereditary right. This greatly restricted the opportunities of warriors to move into the nobility, opportunities that had been available in the eighth and ninth centuries. Although it happened rarely, from the fifth to the ninth centuries even serfs who could save money and buy additional land had the chance of upward social mobility. The increasing costs of personal armor, weapons, and horses provided another barrier to upward mobility. A horse cost five times as much as an ox, and the most important piece of armor, the cuirass, cost 100 shillings, a considerable amount of money at that time; full armor cost several pounds. To give you an idea of the worth of a pound (100 shillings) in that era, it would sometimes take years for a serf to

save just a few pennies (one-twelfth of a shilling) due to the lack of paying jobs and an economy largely based on the barter system, in which food, chickens, or services were traded for work. By the last centuries of the Middle Ages, wealth, leisure, and hereditary rights had made the warrior class exclusive.

The feudal system was also strengthened by Christian beliefs. Loyalty was viewed as a basic Christian ideal, with Christ being the embodiment of this ideal. Christians believed that God gave his son for the salvation of man because of his loyalty to humanity, and similarly, the lord of the fiefdom was loyal to and protected his vassals. Thus was born the concept of *noblesse oblige,* which required persons of high social rank to be the epitome of honorable and generous conduct. In turn, the vassal had to give his complete loyalty to his overlord for the salvation of both, and he trusted in his lord to protect him from outside forces.

Loyalty within a hierarchy of political power was perfectly in tune with the medieval worldview of social order. The entire concept of heavenly order was based on hierarchical Christian concepts. God, the ultimate overlord, presided over well-defined levels of heavenly grace. Even the angels had nine tiers of importance, with the archangels at the top level and cupids at the lowest level. Entry into heaven involved stages of acquiring grace; only saints went directly to heaven. In this manner, Christian idealism reinforced and perpetuated the existing social structure.

SPORT OF THE ARISTOCRACY

Military service was the main function of the noble classes, so it is not surprising to find that the most popular sporting events were war games and demonstrations of military skills. The most famous of the war games was the medieval tournament, or joust.

Medieval Tournaments

Tournaments were gala affairs that served several important recreational and social functions. Recreationally, the tournament allowed all members of society a break from the duties of everyday life. Peasants enjoyed the gaily colored tents and banners erected for the occasion. They also enjoyed feasts, wine, games, and perhaps a brawl or two! The warriors could display their military prowess and receive kudos from their fellow warriors.

Socially, the tournament represented a celebration of the order of feudal society. The overlord or king presided over festivities in which his vassal lords participated with their warrior knights. Historically, the tournament grew out of the realities of war, where the winner took all—property, armor, horses, and people. These early tournaments were rough free-for-alls on horseback, played on a field bounded by ropes. Chivalry was unknown, and it was not uncommon for several knights to gang up on another knight. After subduing him, they ransomed him back to his family for all they could get. In this way, fortunes were made and lost, all for the thrill of the battle. There was no such danger in the carefully planned tournaments of the late Middle Ages.[32]

Notable events in the tournament were the joust and the melee (Figure 5-5). The joust was between two mounted horsemen who charged at each other wielding long, wooden lances; the object was to knock the opponent from his horse. In the melee, groups of opposing knights engaged in hand-to-hand combat with dull swords. Contestants could fight from horseback or on foot. Although the purpose of these contests was not to kill the opponents, injuries were inevitable,

and deaths occurred as a matter of course. Eventually, social pressures, the dominant force being the church, transformed both the concept of chivalry and the tournament. The church had always frowned on the carnage and brutality of the melee, and during the twelfth century, popes had issued papal bulls, or laws made by the pope, that forbade the tournaments from being held. The participants were threatened with eternal damnation. Caesarius of Heisterbach, a Cistercian monk of the early thirteenth century, warned, "For there is no question but such as are slain in tournaments go down to Hell, if they be not helped by the benefit of contrition."[33] However, for utilitarian reasons, the church did embrace the ideal of chivalry and the knightly sports of the tournament and melee during the era of the Crusades (1096–1291). By the fifteenth century, changes in warfare, the brutality of the events, and the disapproval of the church made the tournament an obsolete curiosity of the nobility.

Hawking, Hunting, and Other Pastimes

Other recreational pastimes of the nobility were longer lived. Hawking and hunting were particularly popular and were exclusively the sports of the nobles. The privilege to hunt and hawk was denied the lower classes by cost considerations and legal restrictions. Ladies often accompanied the men on these outings. Such games as *le jeu de paume* (a form of handball) and royal

Figure 5-5
The melee.

tennis, played within an enclosure (and having only modest resemblance to modern tennis), were widely enjoyed. Shuffleboard, billiards, and board games such as chess imported from India were more sedentary forms of recreation. Board games provided the aristocracy and the clergy with amusement and intellectual challenge. Vikings developed a board game called Tafl, which meant "board." Over time, Tafl became Tabula (Slate) and developed into the popular game of Backgammon.[34]

MEDIEVAL CONCEPTS OF HEALTH AND HYGIENE: GALEN REVISITED

The medical arts of the Middle Ages reflected the classical Greek knowledge of Hippocrates, codified and amplified by Galen (131 A.D.–210), the Greek physician of second century A.D. Galen was born in Pergamum (modern day Bergama) which became one of Asia minor's most powerful and wealthiest small kingdoms. Galen practiced medicine in the Asclepion of Pergamum where he gained widespread fame as a healer. He was a favorite among Pergamum's gladiators and also ran a gymnasium; one of three that existed. Galen's gymnasium and healing expertise was legendary in antiquity. His medical procedures were the basis for Western medicine well into the 16th century (Figure 5-6). Galen's major contribution to the theoretical concepts of medicine was in the area of anatomy. He developed his body of knowledge through the dissection of animals, particularly apes, and, when permitted, humans. Galen's principle work, *De Medicina,* became the "bible" of medical knowledge during the Middle Ages. In it, he presented his understanding of human physiology, which he believed was composed of four essential humors— blood, phlegm, yellow bile, and black bile—which resided in certain primary areas of the body.

Blood was to be found in the veins and arteries, although it was also partially located in the heart and liver. Phlegm was seated in the brain but was also evidenced in the bladder and chest. When these humors blended in certain ways within the body, the person would be in a state of health. The concept of health was seen as a state of balance,

Figure 5-6
Galen's Gymnasium in Ancient Pergamon e.g. modern day Bergama in Turkey.

which was further complicated by the four qualities associated with each humor: moist, dry, cold, and warm. The natural state of blood was warm and moist; yellow bile was warm and dry; black bile was cold and dry; phlegm was cold and moist.

In addition to the four qualities, each humor was associated with characteristics that predominated at different stages of life and during different seasons of the year. Blood was bitter, phlegm salty and sweet, black bile strong, and yellow bile sharp. In this way, there was an explanation for the exuberance of childhood, the strength of youth, the maturity of middle age, and the slowness and weakness of old age.

Human moods, personality, and disease were controlled by the disposition of the humors. Blood could make a person happy, kind, fat, or sleepy, whereas phlegm could move a person to thoughtfulness and prudence. An overabundance of one or more of the humors brought on physical maladies. Too much yellow bile caused worry; too much blood brought on mental disorders identified by laughing and singing. An overabundance of phlegm caused anorexia.

A large part of medical treatment was therefore focused on correcting humoral imbalances. One of the most common treatments was phlebotomy (bloodletting). It was believed that phlebotomy could clear the mind, restore the memory, improve digestion and sleep, cleanse the stomach, and stop tears. The amount of blood taken depended on the age and physical condition of the patient. The removal of any blood, however, was done with the intent of restoring the humors to a state of healthy balance.

Other means to restore the humoral balance of the body included a vast array of plants (herbs), minerals, and animal materials. Many times, the belief in the therapeutic value of these materials commingled with superstition, magic, and astrology. Along with such mundane treatments as herbal teas and poultices, medical prescriptions included some disgusting preparations. Drinking one's own urine or the boiled extract of cow's dung was recommended as a cure for the plague. Hemorrhoids were treated by boiling a particular type of worm in linseed oil and applying the oil to the affected area. A fresh ram's lung placed on the forehead supposedly cured a headache. Apparently, precious metals and jewels were highly therapeutic for almost any ailment.

In addition to classical humoral medicine, Christian faith was a factor in the treatment of disease, viewed as punishment by God or the work of evil forces. Invoking the help of God through the saints became as important a therapy as humoral treatments. Pilgrimages, relics of saints, amulets, and incantations were as popular as other therapies. Certain saints were associated with cures for specific diseases, and the possibility of miracle cures through saintly or heavenly intervention was widely accepted. This was reinforced by the belief that miracles did not have to occur immediately but could be accomplished over time.

SUMMARY

The Christian Church had a significant impact on the nature and purpose of sport in the Middle Ages, and this impact was based on its view of the body. Some factions in the early church were profoundly influenced by the Greek philosophers, and the view of the body in classical Greece, as well as within some segments of the church, occupied a respected position. The Greek gods and the Christian concept of God assumed human form, which in Christianity is expressed as the "enfleshment." The corporeal nature of human existence necessitated proper care of the body and the mind.

Physical fitness and health were advocated by the Scholastics, because perfection in both the soul and the body were necessary to achieve happiness. The early Christian monks, however, sought enlightenment through bodily mortification and denounced all forms of sport and physical activity designed to promote health. This difference in opinion reflected the majority position in the church that the body was vile and corrupt and beyond redemption. The early Christian monks (majority viewpoint) and the Scholastics (minority viewpoint) thus were in disagreement concerning the worth of the body and the value of physical activity.

The church tolerated the games and amusements of the peasants and the aristocracy. There was not much the church could do to suppress the natural instinct for people to play and frolic, but it intervened when the games deteriorated into drunken brawls and lewd behavior. No doubt strong sermons and reminders of proper behavior, along with other appropriate chastisements, were used. The brutality and carnage often present during the medieval tournament and melee were opposed by the church. During the Crusades, the church did permit the contests associated with the tournament and melee to be practiced in preparation for war.

The body was an object of medical research during this era. Galen's principle work, *De Medicina,* was the undisputed authority. Galen was also one of the first physicians to "specialize" in sports medicine and was interested in the training of athletes. He wrote about the necessity of proper exercise and warned against the dangers of jogging.

The treatment of disease was multitherapeutic. Christians believed that bodily diseases were punishment from God, and that the body was a mechanism by which mortal sins were punished by God. This belief was devastating to the earlier views of some Christians, who held the philosophical and theological view of the body as a good and worthy creation of God.

DISCUSSION QUESTIONS

1. What was the prevalent concept of the body during the Middle Ages? Where did this concept come from, and what impact did it have on sport and physical education?

2. What were the main types of sport and physical activity during the Middle Ages? Which social group participated, and what did they gain from their efforts?

3. Who in the church was in favor of physical education? Were there any in the church who were against physical education? Why?

4. What was the connection between the tournaments and the Crusades?

5. Was Aquinas able to reconcile church dogma with philosophy? What was Aquinas's position on the body, and how did it conflict, if at all, with church dogma?

6. What impact did Plato and Aristotle have on Christian theology? Were the beliefs of Plato and Aristotle about the nature of human existence and the acquisition of knowledge the same, or did they differ?

7. Who valued the senses as a means of attaining knowledge, Aristotle or Plato?

8. Explain the types of health cures—for example, humoral medicine—used during the Middle Ages. Are any of these healing methods used today?

9. What impact did Galen have on the development of Western medicine?

10. In general, what type of athlete did Galen attend to? Do you think modern day athletic trainers could treat and rehab both ancient athletes and the athletes of the Middle Ages?

INTERNET RESOURCES

Medieval Sport Photos
www.mgel.com/medieval/photos/medieval-sport
Includes scans of images of medieval sport.

Medieval and Renaissance Games
http://jducoeur.org/game-hist
Includes descriptions of period games and links to related resources.

Center for Reformation and Renaissance Studies
www.crrs.ca/events/conferences/athletes/
   athletes.htm
Reproduces a presentation given at a conference on athletes and athletic competitions, 1000–1650 A.D.; identifies topics and authors.

Internet Medieval Sourcebook
www.fordham.edu/halsall/sbook.html
Identifies Internet sources on medieval history.

The Medieval Review
www.hti.umich.edu/t/tmr
Provides information for students and teachers interested in medieval history.

Medieval Illuminated Manuscripts
www.kb.nl/kb/manuscripts/index.html
Represents a detailed guide to medieval manuscripts, with richly illustrated art.

Visit the *History and Philosophy of Sport and Physical Education* Online Learning Center (www.mhhe.com/mechikoff6e) for additional information and study tools.

SUGGESTIONS FOR FURTHER READING

Ballou, R. "Early Christian Society and Its Relationship to Sport." *National College Physical Education Association for Men 71st Proceedings* (1968): 159–65.

Boulton, W. B. *The Amusements of Old London.* London: J. C. Nimmo, 1901.

Bretano, R., ed. *The Early Middle Ages, 500–1000.* Glencoe, IL: Free Press, 1964.

Carter, J. M. "Sport in the Bayeux Tapestry." *Canadian Journal of History of Sport and Physical Education* 11, no. 1 (May 1980): 36–60.

———. *Ludi Medi Aevi: Studies in the History of Medieval Sport.* Manhattan, KS: Military Affairs/ Aerospace Historian, 1981.

———. *Sports and Pastimes of the Middle Ages.* Columbus, GA: Brentwood Communications, 1984.

———. "A Medieval Sports Commentator: William Fitzstephen and London Sports in the Late Twelfth Century." *American Benedictine Review* 35, no. 2 (June 1984): 146–52.

———. "Muscular Christianity and Its Makers: Sporting Monks and Churchmen in Anglo-Norman Society, 1000–1300." *British Journal of Sport History* 1, no. 2 (September 1984): 109–24.

Cheyette, F. L., ed. *Lordship and Community in Medieval Europe.* New York: Holt, Rinehart & Winston, 1967.

Clepham, T. C. *The Tournament: Its Periods and Phases.* London: Methuen, 1919.

Cripps-Day, F. H. *The History of the Tournament in England and France.* London: Bernard Quartich, 1918; AMS reprint, 1980.

Dahmus, J. *The Middle Ages: A Popular History.* Garden City, NY: Doubleday, 1968.

Davis, R. H. C. *A History of Medieval Europe: From Constantine to Saint Louis.* London: Longmans, Green, 1957.

DeAneslev, M. *A History of Early Medieval Europe, 476 to 911.* London: Methuen, 1956.

Evans, J. *The Flowering of the Middle Ages.* New York: McGraw-Hill, 1966.

Henderson, R. W. *Ball, Bat and Bishop: The Origin of Ball Games.* New York: Rockport, 1947.

Hoskins, C. H. "The Latin Literature of Sport." In *Studies in Medieval Culture.* New York: Rederereick Ungar, 1958.

Hoyt, R. S., ed. *Life and Thought in the Early Middle Ages.* Minneapolis: University of Minnesota Press, 1967.

MacKinney, L. C. *Early Medieval Medicine: With Special Reference to France and Chartres.* Baltimore: Johns Hopkins University Press, 1937.

———. *The Medieval World.* New York: Farrar & Rinehart, 1938.

Morrall, J. B. *The Medieval Imprint: The Foundation of the Western European Tradition.* London: C. A. Watts, 1967.

Painter, S. *French Chivalry.* Baltimore: Johns Hopkins University Press, 1940.

———. *A History of the Middle Ages.* New York: Alfred A. Knopf, 1953.

Pole, A. L. "Recreation." In *Medieval England,* vol. II. Oxford: Clarendon, 1958.

Reynolds, S. *Kingdoms and Communities in Western Europe 900–1300.* Oxford: Clarendon, 1984.

Riesman, D. *The Story of Medicine in the Middle Ages.* New York: Paul B. Hoeber, 1935.

Rubin, S. *Medieval English Medicine.* New York: Barnes & Noble, 1974.

Ruhl, J. K. "German Tournament Regulations of the 15th Century." *Journal of Sport History* 17, no. 2 (Summer 1990): 163–82.

Sandoz, E. "Tourneys in the Arthurian Tradition." *Speculum* 19, no. 4 (October 1944): 389–420.

Savage, H. "Hunting in the Middle Ages." *Speculum* 8, no. 1 (January 1933): 30–41.

Strutt, J. *The Sports and Pastimes of the People of England.* London: Methuen, 1893.

Thiebaux, M. "The Medieval Chase." *Speculum* 27, no. 3 (April 1967): 260–74.

Twietmeyer, Gregg. "A Theology of Inferiority: Is Christianity the Source of Kinesiology's Second-Class Status in the Academy?" *Quest* 60, no. 4 (November 2008): 452–466.

Walsh, J. J. *Medieval Medicine.* London: A & C Black, 1920.

NOTES

1. The "carrot" was the bliss obtained by living in a state of Christian grace; the "stick" was the punishment meted out by the Inquisition and the fear of going to hell. This explanation is a social and political one and stops short of an endorsement of any religious explanation for the rise of the Catholic Church during this period. We do not wish to discount the legitimacy of the Catholic Church from a theological perspective, nor are we qualified to do so. Whether the Catholic Church, or any other church, is the sole repository of the will of God requires a "leap of faith" that we leave to each reader.

2. Frederick C. Copleston, *Medieval Philosophy* (New York: Harper & Row, 1961), 10.

3. Ibid.

4. Ibid., 60.

5. Ibid., 62.

6. David Sanderlin, "Physical Education in the Medieval Universities" (unpublished paper, San Diego), 7.

7. William Fleming, *Arts and Ideas* (New York: Holt, Rinehart & Winston, 1966), 136.

8. Sanderlin, "Physical Education in Medieval Universities," 7.

9. D. R. G. Owen, *Body and Soul* (Philadelphia: Westminster Press, 1956); Wheeler H. Robinson, *The Religious Ideas of the Old Testament* (London: Duckworth, 1913); Daryl Siedentop, "A Historical Note on the Concept of Organismic Unity" (typewritten manuscript, Hope College, 1989).

10. Frank Bottomley, *Attitudes to the Body in Western Christendom* (London: Lepus Books, 1979).

11. Ibid.

12. Deobold B. Van Dalen and Bruce L. Bennett, *A World History of Physical Education* (Englewood Cliffs, NJ: Prentice-Hall, 1971), 90.

13. Sanderlin, "Physical Education in Medieval Universities," 1.

14. St. Thomas Aquinas, *Summa Theologiae,* trans. Blackfriars (New York: McGraw-Hill, vols. 1–60, 1964–66); first part of the second part, question 4, article 6 (abbrev. S. T., I–II, 4, 6).

15. Saint Thomas, I, 85, 7, trans. from the edition by the Fathers of English Dominican Province (New York: Benziger Bros., 1947), I, 439.

16. Thomas Gilby, ed., *St. Thomas Aquinas: Philosophical Texts* (London: Oxford University Press, 1951); S. T., I–II, 50, 4, reply obj. 3. Trans. from Gilby, *Philosophical Texts* 203, no. 548.

17. Sanderlin, "Physical Education in Medieval Universities," 6.

18. Maurice deWulf, *An Introduction to Scholastic Philosophy: Medieval and Modern,* trans. P. Coffey (New York: Dover, 1956), 124–25.

19. Sanderlin, "Physical Education in Medieval Universities," 7.

20. Ibid., 8.

21. Moses Maimonides, "Treatise on Asthma," in *The Medical Writings of Moses Maimonides No. 1,* ed. Suessman Munter (Philadelphia: Lippincott, 1963), 26.

22. Matthew M. de Benedictis, O.F.M., *The Social Thought of Saint Bonaventure: A Study in Social Philosophy* (Washington, DC: Catholic University of America Press, 1946), 46.

23. John Marshall Carter, *Ludi Medi Aevi: Studies in the History of Medieval Sport* (Manhattan, KS: MA/AH Publishing, Eisenhower Hall, Kansas State University, 1981), 62–63.

24. Ibid., 63.

25. Ibid., 63.

26. The pagan nature of these games led the Calvinists/Puritans of the seventeenth century to denounce both the amusements associated with these holidays and the Catholic Church for permitting these pagan celebrations to occur.

27. Allen Guttmann, *Sports Spectators* (New York: Columbia University Press, 1986), 49.

28. Ibid.

29. William Fitzstephens, *Descriptio Londoniae;* see J. M. Carter, *Ludi Medi Aevi,* 1981; F. M. Stenton's Norman London (Historical Association Leaflets, nos. 93, 94, 1934); English Historical Documents, 1042–1189, ed. D. C. Douglas and G. W. Greenaway (New York, 1953); Stow's Survey of London (London, 1965), 500–509.

30. Carter, *Ludi Medi Aevi,* 82.

31. W. Fitzstephens in Stow, *Descriptio Londoniae,* 501.

32. Stephen H. Hardy, "The Medieval Tournament: A Functional Sport of the Upper Class," *Journal of Sport History* 1, no. 2 (1973): 91–105.

33. Hardy, "Medieval Tournament," 102.

34. Martha Bayless, "Tabletop Tactics," in Archaeology, Vol. 58, No. 1, January/February 2005, pp 37–40.

CHAPTER 6

The Renaissance and the Reformation: 1300–1600

OBJECTIVES

Upon completing this chapter, you will be able to:

- Explain the political position of the Catholic Church and describe how the decline in the authority of the church came about.
- Understand the difference between the Renaissance and the Reformation.
- Identify the genesis of the Renaissance and the Reformation.
- Identify selected leaders of the Renaissance.
- Understand the impact of humanist philosophy on attitudes toward the body and physical activity during the Renaissance.
- Understand the view of the body during the Reformation and its impact on physical education and sport during this era.
- Appreciate the cultural impact of the Renaissance and its influence on the value placed on the body and physical activity.
- Identify the philosophers and educators of the Renaissance and describe their contributions to the establishment of physical education in the schools.
- Recognize the impact of Greek philosophy on Renaissance thought.
- Identify selected leaders of the Reformation.
- Discuss the philosophical beliefs that prevailed during the Reformation and the educators who, in addition to reforming the church, set out to reform education according to theological beliefs.
- Understand the concern that leaders of the Reformation had about the body and sport.

General Events

1270–1347 William of Occam, Scholastic philosopher
1309–1376 Popes reside at Avignon, France
1314–1321 Dante Alighieri writes *Divine Comedy*
1338–1453 Hundred Years' War
1348 Black Death sweeps Europe
1370–1444 Petrus Vergerius
1378–1417 Great Schism between rival popes
1378–1446 Vittorino da Feltre
1400–1468 Johann Gutenberg and movable type
1405–1564 Aeneas Silvio Piccolomini
1452–1519 Leonardo da Vinci
1453 Fall of Constantinople to Turks
1462–1525 Pietro Pomponazzi
1469–1517 Desiderius Erasmus
1469–1527 Machiavelli
1475–1564 Michelangelo

INTRODUCTION

The influence of the Catholic Church on European culture in the late Middle Ages cannot be overestimated. It permeated every aspect of culture—scholarship, politics, economics, and even private lives. The eras following the Middle Ages are known as the Renaissance and the Reformation, and these periods stand out as a time of cultural change with respect to the church. The Renaissance was in part caused by the reintroduction of Greek and Roman thought in intellectual circles. As a result, the church had to compete with the philosophies, literature, and paganism of ancient Greece and Rome. The Reformation was an effort to reform the church and return it to the ways of the original Christians. One way to distinguish the Renaissance from the Reformation is to note that the Renaissance was an intellectual reawakening confined primarily to the upper classes and nobility, while the Reformation was a religious reawakening that affected all of Western civilization. In both cases, however, the authority of the Catholic Church was diminished, and this change had a significant impact on how Western civilization viewed the body.

Different theories of how to view the human body were developed during the Renaissance and the Reformation, and as a consequence, the groundwork was laid for different attitudes toward sport and physical education. The Renaissance was heavily influenced by the classics—the great works of literature written during the times of the Greeks and Romans—especially the philosophies of Aristotle and Plato. These arguments were adopted by the *Humanists*—philosophers who believed in the concept of "humanism" and its focus on humans as opposed to the otherworldly or heavenly concerns of earlier philosophies. The ancient Greeks believed that the human body played an important role in everyday life, and their philosophies accounted for this belief. Eventually, Renaissance arguments evolved into the ideal of the "universal" or "Renaissance man": a well-rounded individual who used the body to develop discipline and character. The Reformation was more complex; religious reformers argued that the body "housed" the soul. As such, the body could not be denigrated because it was the temple for the soul, and eventually it was argued that the "quality of the soul" could be determined by observing one's behaviors. Implicitly, then, the body was considered by scholars and leaders of the Renaissance and the Reformation to be more important than it had been in the Middle Ages. How these positions developed is what makes the Renaissance and the Reformation interesting to scholars and students in kinesiology.

CULTURAL CHANGES OF THE RENAISSANCE

The Renaissance, which occurred roughly between 1300 and 1550, was a time of radical change as European culture emerged from the Middle Ages. The word *renaissance* means "rebirth or revival of classics," which was how European culture described the writings of the ancient Greeks and Romans.

Intellectuals during this period considered themselves enlightened because of their return to the classics. The idea that the Middle Ages were "dark" began with the Renaissance scholars who were so critical of that period. The previous chapter discussed how the Middle Ages were characterized by feudalism and an agrarian economy and were dominated politically and intellectually by the Catholic Church. The Renaissance, by comparison, was characterized by secular influences on thought and culture, the development of nations, and urban economies based on trade and commerce. These changes were considered an improvement and occurred for a variety of reasons, such as war, disease, and an influx of new ideas. None of these changes, however, came easily to those who endured them.

Because the Renaissance fostered a rebirth of classical thought, it helped end medieval ways of thought associated with the church. Prior to the Renaissance, the church was the voice of secular authority, which gave the church a significant amount of religious, political, and economic control over the lives of Christians. *Secular* refers to matters of this world—the "here and now"—such as politics and education; it can be contrasted with matters of the church—otherworldly or heavenly concerns. Church leaders from the pope on down told Christians how to live in this world so that they could gain entrance to heaven in the next life. Ignoring the authority of the church could result in excommunication, a threat that implied enduring the fires of hell for eternity. Similarly, the church also promised a life of eternal bliss in the presence of God if one obeyed its ways. This approach facilitated church control over how people lived their everyday lives.

The Renaissance undermined the philosophical basis used by the church to control its members by creating an environment in which competing philosophies were read and discussed, especially those of the Greeks and Romans. In intellectual circles during the Renaissance, the classical philosophies of Plato and Aristotle rivaled Christian theology. While several scholars had previously attempted to reconcile the classics with the dogma of the church (most notably Thomas Aquinas with regard to Aristotle's philosophy), this proved difficult. The classical philosophies emphasized how to live in *this* world, while Christian religion emphasized life in the next. Many intellectuals began to break with the church as to what was "reality," and a consequence of this change was the view that the material world and sensory experiences were "real" and important. These ideas led to important educational changes. As a consequence of its worldly focus, Renaissance philosophy laid the groundwork for the revival of physical education and sport in Western civilization. It is no accident that the leading educators of the Renaissance incorporated physical education into their educational curricula.

The rise of the nation-state also took control away from the church. Kings and the nobility gained political power throughout the Renaissance and developed the idea that a nation could exist separate from the church. This change was made easier by the "schisms," or divisions, that developed within the church (1378–1417). Basically, the schisms resulted from political groups within the Catholic Church competing for power among themselves, power that would give these groups more control over the material wealth of the church. Perhaps the best measure of these divisions was the simultaneous election in 1409 of three popes, all of whom had their own secular goals![1] Ironically, as the popes consolidated their power in the secular, material world, they came under increasing attack for abandoning their role as spiritual guides. These schisms were a major impetus for the Reformation, a movement that sought to "reform" the Catholic Church and return it to its original mission.

Politics and philosophical/religious factors were not the only causes of the development of the nation-state. During this era, Europe experienced several vicious wars, particularly the Hundred Years' War (1338–1453) between England and France. Initiated by the English king Edward III, the war had its roots in economic factors like the struggle for control of the wool industry in Flanders and the centuries of animosity that existed between the French and the English, dating back to the Norman Conquest in 1066. It appeared that the English would win for much of the war, controlling large parts of France including the entire northern half and the southwestern coast in 1429. Eventually, however, the French were able to cast the English from their lands with the development of military technology that included gunpowder and cannons.

Another event that had a significant impact on the Renaissance was the ongoing war between Christian Europe and the "infidel" Turks. Christians banded together throughout the late Middle Ages and the early Renaissance to travel to the East in "Crusades," the purpose of which was to free Constantinople, the Byzantine capital of eastern Christianity, from control by the Islamic Turks. The Turks, however, surrounded Constantinople in the early 1400s. They defeated the crusaders and took control in 1453.

Since the fall of Rome a thousand years earlier, many of the great works of ancient Greece and Rome were housed in Constantinople, and as the Turks came closer to conquering the city, many scholars left for the relative safety of the West. Indeed, while the fall of Constantinople was a disaster from the perspective of Europeans, it caused an infusion of scholars and classical ideas into European intellectual circles that jolted philosophers and educators out of their old ways. In addition, the war caused the trading of goods that supplied the soldiers and the travel of many people to distant lands, which helped break down feudal culture and led Europe into a period of economic and cultural growth. So, while war had obvious devastating consequences, it also had the effect of shaking Europe out of its feudal traditions and providing an opportunity for the exchange of philosophical ideas.

War was not the only destructive force that changed European culture. In the fourteenth century, Europe was ravaged by bubonic plague, known to contemporaries as the "Black Death." An often fatal disease carried by flea-infested rats, it reached a peak in 1348–1350 and is estimated

to have killed almost *one-third* of Europe's population. There were several causes of the plague, among them famine, a poor understanding of hygiene, and a complete misunderstanding of the causes of the plague. By 1300, it was difficult to grow enough food for Europe's increasing population, and most people faced at least one period of famine in their lives. Life during the Renaissance for the average person was difficult. Indeed, the life span of the average European in the late Middle Ages was only thirty-five years! Famines followed the population explosion, hitting newly developed urban areas extremely hard. In addition, Europe experienced an economic depression, making food much harder to obtain. As a result of these factors, Europeans in the early fourteenth century were in generally bad health. This led them to be highly susceptible to the plague.

In sum, there is no one single cause of the end of the Middle Ages and the beginning of the Renaissance and the Reformation. War, intellectual curiosity, plague, religion, overpopulation, famine, and a variety of other factors combined to cause great changes in the fabric of European culture. Every institution was forced to change, and education was no exception.

THE REFORMATION

While the Renaissance was stimulated by the ideals of the classics and the concept of the "universal man," the Reformation was stimulated by religious zeal. As a consequence, at the end of the Middle Ages, things looked quite a bit different in northern Europe than in the south. The Renaissance in Italy was at its height when the ideas it fostered came to northern Europe, and as far as the intellectuals of fifteenth- and sixteenth-century England and northern Europe were concerned, the Reformation was the Renaissance.

The Reformation had as its goal the "reforming" of the Catholic Church. By the time of the Reformation, the church as a political institution was corrupt, and its agents at every level sought money for church accounts. Money seeking had an impact on the truly devout, as monks pestered people in the street with their begging. Because the monks were doing God's work by seeking money to operate the Church and the faithful contributed what they could, both groups had high hopes of gaining entrance into heaven. The clergy were skilled at getting tithes and perquisites from parishioners, who noted that the popes no longer looked like the Apostles when they wore their fine clothes. According to Desiderius Erasmus, a famous critic of the Catholic Church, the popes sought riches, honors, jurisdictions, offices, dispensations, licenses, indulgences, ceremonies and tithes, excommunications, and interdicts![2] Popes lusted for legacies, hoped to be worldly diplomats, and fought bloody wars. It was difficult to argue with Erasmus when he asserted that this was no way to run a church—unless you were the pope!

Religious reform was not the only reason for removing the pope and the church from political power. In 1530, Henry VIII broke with the Catholic Church and formed the Anglican Church because the pope would not, or could not, further the political interests of England. There were three reasons for Henry and the pope to be at odds. First, Henry, who was married to Catherine of Aragon, intensely desired a son. When Catherine did not bear a son, Henry tried to divorce her and sought an annulment from the pope. However, politics intervened. In the early 1500s, Rome was controlled by the troops of Charles V, a Spaniard who was also Catherine's nephew. As long as Charles's troops surrounded the Vatican, the pope would not grant an annulment. Second, Henry resented the pope because he believed that since 1511 England had fought Continental wars for the pope without reward.[3] Third, the Catholic Church owned a considerable amount of real estate in England, all of which was exempt from taxes. It did not take long for Henry to figure out that eliminating the Catholic Church and establishing the Anglican Church—of which he would be the head—would make him incredibly wealthy.

Political interests aside, those who sought to reform the church for religious reasons wanted to go back to the original tenets of Christianity. They claimed for themselves the label of "Christians" and sought to differentiate themselves from "Catholics" (formerly, all believers in Christ were known as "Christians"). The Reformation, from a religious perspective, moved the Catholic Church from the role of "middle man" and placed the authority of one's religiosity in the hands of that individual. From a social and political perspective, the Reformation led to the creation of various Protestant (from "protest") sects and a rebuilt version of the Catholic Church. Furthermore, the Reformation strengthened the newly developed idea of nationalism by undermining the authority of the Catholic Church, and it helped to develop the idea of a middle class. As J. Bronowski and Bruce Mazlish noted,

> The Reformation, at least in its Calvinist version, made religion a thing of this world and achieved the miracle of identifying good works with the accumulation of riches. The shame of profiteering was wiped away and what was formerly the lust for wealth became the fulfillment of God's purposes on earth.[4]

These ideas came together during the Reformation. For our purposes, the combination of changes in culture and Reformation ideas regarding the nature of the human body, the soul, and the mind had a radical impact on education. Indeed, many ideas from the Reformation are alive and well today in our attitudes toward sport and physical education.

THE PHILOSOPHERS AND EDUCATORS OF THE RENAISSANCE

Unlike the Middle Ages, the Renaissance did not produce philosophers who had a lasting impact. The most studied philosophy of the Renaissance was Scholasticism, a highly intellectual school of thought that emphasized the mind and tried to reconcile the theology of the Christian Church with rational thought. In other words, the Scholastics tried to prove that reason and faith were consistent with each other. This effort lasted through the Reformation before waning during the eighteenth century, succumbing to attacks from philosophers like William of Ockham, who argued that the senses and the material world are all we can know. The influence of the Scholastics has lasted to this day, however, and is evident in the emphasis placed on the intellect and mind in our educational institutions. The emphasis on the mind by the Scholastics can be seen in the connotations of the words *scholar* and *scholastic,* two words derived from Scholasticism that even today emphasize intellectual learning.

Philosophers of the Renaissance spent a considerable amount of time resurrecting the philosophies of antiquity, especially those of Plato and Aristotle. These philosophies were compared and contrasted to the teachings of the church. Like Aquinas, these philosophers hoped to show that the classical philosophies went hand in hand with the teachings of the church. Instead, however, Renaissance philosophers paved the way for the philosophical undermining of the church. This occurred because the link that the Renaissance philosophers tried to find between medieval Christian virtues and the classical philosophies did not exist. The church of the Renaissance emphasized the ascetic and monastic virtues of self-denial and even bodily mortification. Those "pleasures of the flesh" that the Christian Church allowed, such as sex, eating, and drinking, were necessary for bodily survival. Furthermore, the church accepted these "vices" as proof that humans were by nature weak. In contrast, the classical philosophies of the Greeks and Romans accepted the human body. Indeed, so different were Scholasticism and the classical philosophies that a new group of Renaissance philosophers developed. This group eventually attacked the monastic virtues as having been falsely imposed on the true structure of Christianity.

This new group of Renaissance philosophers, known as humanists, disagreed with the monastic, ascetic approach to daily life emphasized by the Scholastics and refused to think of the human body

as evil. Indeed, the Humanists rejected the idea of original sin, "the belief that the soul and the body are sharply divided and that, because man cannot express his soul except through his body, he carries an unavoidable sin."[5] Instead, the Humanists believed in the doctrine of original goodness, the Greek belief that "the soul and the body are one, and that the actions of the body naturally and fittingly express the humanity of the soul."[6]

As noted previously, humanism had as its ideal the universal or Renaissance man, also known as *l'uomo universale.* The universal man cultivated interests in the arts, sciences, and languages; was well traveled and well mannered; and was skilled in the martial arts, games, and sports. Ideally, he was able to function in all possible settings of contemporary life, and his ability to do this was to be given to him through schooling. Consequently, education reflected this well-rounded approach and provided the necessary instruction to meet its goals. Certainly, physical education became more valued because of the focus of humanism.

The Italian scholars, in particular, adopted the humanistic approach, emphasizing three main ideas. First, the Humanists admired the ancient Greeks and Romans and sought to understand the philosophy and history of the classics. This approach to education was adopted by the church in the late Middle Ages. Second, the Humanists emphasized the joy of living and sought to enjoy their corporeal lives. *Corporeal,* another word for "bodily" or "material," was used to emphasize an idea that is clearly not "spiritual" in nature. Third, the Humanists argued that the corporeal life was worth contemplating. These three ideas existed in sharp contrast to the view of the church and represent a significant difference between humanism and Scholasticism.

Aeneas Silvio Piccolomini's *De Liberorum Educatione* (*The Liberal Education*), Pietro Pomponazzi's *De immortalitate animae* (*The Immortal Animal*), and Baldassare Castiglione's *The Courtier* are some of the most famous books of the Renaissance and represent the culmination of humanist thought. Inspired by the work of the humanists who preceded them, these writers told the universal man how to live and think. The writings of Piccolomini, Pomponazzi, and Castiglione in turn influenced many of the leading intellectuals of the Renaissance, who helped the philosophy of humanism come to life in the shape of the universal man. And these writings affected women as well. One of the characteristics of these books was an attitude toward women that was, by Renaissance standards, "liberating." While these changes were not accepted by everyone, the fact that there was a debate indicates that the traditional role of women was an important topic. The following passage from Castiglione's *The Courtier* illustrates this discussion:

> And whereas the Lorde Gasper hath said, that the verie same rules that are given for the Courtier serve also for the woman. I am of contrarie opinion. For albeit some qualities are common and necessarie as well for the woman as the man, yet are there some other more meete for the woman than for the man, and some again meete for the man, that she ought in no wise to meddle withall.
>
> The verie same I say of the exercises of the bodie: But principally in her fashions, manners, wordes, gestures and conversation (me think) the woman ought to be much unlike the man. For right as it is seemely for him to shew a certaine manlinesse full and steadie, so doth it well in a woman to have a tendernesse, soft and milde, with a kinde of womanlye sweetenesse in every gesture of hers, that in going, standing, and speaking what ever she lusteth, may alwaies make her appeare a woman without anye likenesse of man.[7]

The universal man valued knowledge for its ability to expand his awareness of the world. He was as interested in knowing about the world as in being an interesting individual, and as a result was well read in many fields of study rather than a specialist in a few narrow fields. Many of the things he studied would never be used, but this generalization helped make him the interested and interesting person of the Renaissance ideal.

Petrus Paulus Vergerius

Petrus Paulus Vergerius (1370–1444), one of the first of the great Italian humanists, was the "true founder of the new education." His *De Ingenuis Moribus,* written for Ubertinus, the son of the lord of Padua, described the basic ideas upon which humanist education was built. Influenced by Plato, Vergerius believed that education was a matter of public interest and should create a good citizen of the state. However, Vergerius's educational program was aimed primarily at the sons of the wealthy, and not just any citizen. He believed that the best way to develop good citizens was to start teaching children at an early age, emphasizing morals along with activities suitable to the age group.

Vergerius's model was Sparta, and he tried to adapt the methods of contemporary warfare to the Spartan model of training young men for war. He believed that the purpose of physical education was to prepare one for the military. Vergerius's attitude toward sport in this respect was not significantly different from that of educators during the Middle Ages, when military matters were of utmost importance. The main difference with Vergerius was that physical education was incorporated into the education of the total individual. Components of Vergerius's program included the Greek pentathlon, swimming, horsemanship, and use of the shield, spear, sword, and club.

Vittorino da Feltre

The most famous of the Italian humanists was Vittorino da Feltre (1378–1446) (Figure 6-1). Like Vergerius, da Feltre was educated at Padua, where he studied grammar, mathematics, and Greek. He became a professor of grammar and mathematics at Padua, and he remained there until 1415 when he resigned, as one scholar put it, because of the undisciplined and decadent life of the university town.[8] Da Feltre was offered the chance to teach the children of the Marquis Gonzaga of Mantua, and the school that he developed, La Giocosa, was the first to blend the spirit of Christianity with both

Figure 6-1
Vittorino da Feltre.

the classics and Greek concepts of physical education for the sons of the wealthy. La Giocosa, or
Pleasant House, was an ideal setting for a school. It
was surrounded by meadows and bordered a river,
so students were able to exercise freely. Indeed, da
Feltre eventually adopted the name Gymnasium
Palatinum, or Palace School, in imitation of the
ancient Greek gymnasia. This was a radical departure from schools of the Middle Ages, where education was only for the mind.

Da Feltre believed in educating the mind, but
he also believed in educating the body and the soul.
So, while Renaissance education was, to a certain
extent, separated from the church compared to
medieval education, da Feltre serves as an example
of how Christian values continued to be taught. Da
Feltre believed that he could create the Renaissance
version of Plato's philosopher-king: educated
princes who would rule with wisdom and justice.
Da Feltre believed that the development of the ideal
citizen required a combination of the classics and
Christian morality. As W. H. Woodward noted,

> He brought with him to Mantua a desire to
> combine the spirit of the Christian life with the
> educational apparatus of classical literature,
> whilst uniting with both something of the
> Greek passion for bodily culture and for
> dignity of the outer life.[9]

It was da Feltre's commitment to this combination
that made him so effective. Starting with only three
students, he soon had as many as 70. His fame as
an educator spread throughout Europe and had an
impact that is felt even today. Woodward called da
Feltre the first "modern schoolmaster."

One reason for his excellence as a teacher was
that he could do everything he taught. Da Feltre
could teach all of the "arts" (grammar, dialectic,
rhetoric, history, and moral philosophy), as well as
mathematics and languages (primarily Latin and
Greek). Together, these areas of study came to be
known as the "liberal arts"; it was argued that studies in these areas literally "liberated" the educated
person from the chains of ignorance and prejudice. Da Feltre believed that these subjects disciplined and educated the mind. Yet he also believed
that the body had to be disciplined and educated,
and he practiced what he preached. Apparently a
small, thin man, he subjected himself to the cold
to endure it better. He exercised regularly and
never ate or drank too much. His regimen must
have been effective, for he was never sick until the
final illness that took his life. He was also deeply
religious, going to Mass and confession regularly.
No wonder his students learned; da Feltre led his
students as much as he instructed.

For our purposes, Vittorino da Feltre was one
of the first, if not the first, to incorporate physical
education as an important part of an educational
curriculum during the Renaissance. He may have
been emulating Plutarch's *Education for Boys,* a
text translated in 1411 and popular in Renaissance
Italy. Da Feltre's goal was to develop the health of
his students, and he did this by having them participate two or more hours daily in physical activities
including games, riding, running, leaping, fencing, and ball games—watched by teachers skilled
in these activities. During the summer, he moved
his school to the Castle of Goito, where the students went hiking and camping for days at a time.
Da Feltre also sought to educate future rulers in the
military skills that might be needed to defend their
lands. To this end, his students practiced archery,
fencing, and riding.

Vittorino da Feltre was the first educator to effectively bring together the humanist ideals of mind, body, and spirit to develop the ideal citizen. He believed that each part of the individual needed cultivation and that education was the means to do this. Clearly influenced by Plato's ideas, he may have gone one step further than Plato by putting these ideas into practice and living by them as well. La Giocosa became the model upon which subsequent physical education programs were based.

Aeneas Silvio Piccolomini

Most humanist philosophers were commissioned by the aristocracy and courts of the Italian princes, and it was for these students that the Renaissance concept of the universal man was established. Aeneas Silvio Piccolomini (1405–1464), also known as Aeneas Sylvius and, later, as Pope Pius II, wrote *De Liberorum Educatione* for Ladislas, king of Bohemiaand Hungary. Like Vergerius and da Feltre, Piccolomini's ideas on education were reserved for the children of the rich. In *De Liberorum Educatione,* Piccolomini argued that children should be taught to use the bow and sling, throw spears, ride horses, and swim to be good soldiers. Yet Piccolomini was also interested in the general well-being of students:

> As regards a boy's physical training, we bear in mind that we aim at implanting habits which will prove beneficial through life. . . . A boy should be taught to hold his head erect, look straight and fearlessly before him and to bear himself with dignity whether walking, standing, or sitting. . . . Games and exercises which develop the muscular activities and the general carriage of the person should be encouraged by every teacher.[10]

Piccolomini, one of the earliest Renaissance writers, emphasized military proficiency because he believed these skills were necessary for Christians to defend themselves against the Turks.

Baldassare Castiglione

Baldassare Castiglione's (1478–1529) *The Courtier* was written to teach young members of the aristocracy how to behave at court. Castiglione did not attach as much importance to military training as Piccolomini, although he still viewed it as important to the universal man. Castiglione did not believe the courtier should be a professional soldier. Indeed, he was as at home at court (hence the name *courtier*) as on the battlefield. This emphasis on the well-rounded individual can be seen when Castiglione makes fun of a man who refused an invitation to dance with a gentlewoman because he did not think it was "professional." In this conversation, the gentlewoman insults the would-be courtier:

> 'What then is your profession?' 'To fight.' Then said the gentlewoman, 'Seeing you are not now at war nor in place to fight I would think it best for you to be well smeared and set up in an armory till time were that you should be occupied, lest you wax more rustier than you are.'[11]

The well-rounded nature of the courtier can be seen in the many types of activities he experienced in school:

> It is fitting also to know how to swim, to leap, to run, to throw stones. . . . Another admirable exercise, and one very befitting a man at court, is the game of tennis, in which are all shown the disposition of the boys, and quickness and suppleness of every member, and all those qualities that are seen in nearly every other exercise. Nor less highly do I esteem vaulting on horse, which, although it be fatiguing and difficult, makes a man very light and dexterous more than any other thing; and besides its utility, if this lightness is accompanied by grace, it is to my thinking a finer show than any of the others.[12]

By the time of Castiglione, a soldier's life was seen by socialites at court as a specialized career. Castiglione encouraged courtiers to be more well rounded. Ironically, the rise of the professional soldier gave the courtier time to practice his social skills, and therefore made the courtier possible. In this sense, Castiglione was criticizing the very profession that made his courtier possible.

The Philosophers and Educators of the Reformation

As stated previously, the theme of the Reformation was that of the reform of the Catholic Church. Many other changes occurred as well during this time: Commerce and industry expanded, people moved from the country to the cities, and an emphasis on education became evident as its benefits were recognized by the upper class. Tying in with our discussion, education came to be seen as a necessity in a changing world where trade and commerce were increasing rapidly. Physical education was part of the total educational package of many philosophers, in both antiquity and the Renaissance, so it became more common in the curriculum than it had been in the Middle Ages. By and large, however, physical education was a small part of the total curriculum, and where it did exist, it was usually associated with the education of the wealthy.

This emphasis on education did not occur without some resistance. In 1391, English feudal landowners petitioned Richard II to enforce a rule that forbade the children of serfs to attend school without their lord's permission. Richard refused, and the next king decreed that any child could go to school. While the move toward public education proceeded slowly, the change from education for only the elite to mass education had begun.

As in the Middle Ages, most teachers were priests. Priests had always been trained in reading and language, but during the Renaissance, and even more so during the Reformation, the curriculum expanded to include the catechism, the Creed, the basic prayers, reading, writing, arithmetic, singing, and flogging.[13] During the Reformation, the body was often seen as a tool that could be used to compel a reluctant mind to learn. Flogging

was often the method of choice, but all methods of corporal punishment relied on the same idea: Use the body to get to the mind. As Will Durant noted,

> Even in secondary schools flogging was the staff of instruction. A divine explained that 'the boys' spirits must be subdued': the parents agreed with him; and perhaps 'tis so. Agnes Paston urged the tutor of her unstudious son to 'belash him' if he did not amend, 'for I had rather he were fairly buried than lost for default.'[14]

The main emphasis on education in secondary school was religious training, but grammar and composition were added during this time, including classic literature from ancient Rome. In 1372, the first of England's "public" schools was formed to provide college preparatory training for a limited selection of boys.[15] In 1440, Henry VI established Eton School to prepare students for King's College, Cambridge. The public schools became famous in the 1800s for their use of sport to teach desirable virtues such as discipline and courage. Eton School, in particular, was famous for this practice, as can be seen in the saying "The Battle of Waterloo was won on the playing fields of Eton." This saying reflects the belief of nineteenth-century Britons, who argued that those traits necessary to winning wars were learned not in the classroom but on the playing fields, where rough-and-tumble athletic competition was a daily ritual that built character and made boys into men.

The education of women continued, for the most part, to be scattered and incomplete by modern-day standards. Many women of the middle class learned to write English, and a few women learned literature and philosophy. After elementary school, however, women were confined largely to the home and were responsible for raising children and keeping house.

The sons of the aristocracy were educated differently from the children of the middle class. Until the age of seven, male children of the nobility were taught by the women of the house. After this, they often served as pages for relatives or for neighboring nobles. At the age of 14, they became squires, a kind of adult assistant to the lord of the manor in which they served. At this stage, their education was primarily physical education: They learned to ride, shoot, hunt, joust, and practice those physical skills necessary to wage war. No doubt this life of sport was more enjoyable than the intellectual exercises practiced by their social lessers, and the sporting life to a certain extent distinguished the nobility from those who worked for them. As Durant noted, "Book learning they left to their inferiors," indicating that the intellectual skills learned by the middle class were to be put to use by the nobility to preserve the social order.[16]

The early part of the Reformation witnessed the development of one of the great institutions of the Western world, the modern university. Oxford and Cambridge both grew significantly, adding "halls," or places of residence for select students. While there was much growth, these colleges were not quite recognizable as such. Most classes were held in schoolrooms or auditoriums scattered throughout the town. Still, some of the great philosophers of the fourteenth century came out of Oxford, including Duns Scotus and William of Ockham.

Sport was not yet part of the life of the college student, indicating that the education of the mind was still the prime task of schooling. Furthermore, the influence of the church curtailed sporting activities for the same reasons as it had for the previous several centuries: The body was meant to be disciplined, not used for pleasure. Durant noted that without sport students were left to other, less wholesome pursuits:

> Forbidden to engage in intramural athletics, they spent their energy in profanity, tippling, and venery; taverns and brothels throve on their patronage. Attendance at Oxford fell from its thirteenth-century peak to as low as a thousand; and after the expulsion of Wyclif academic freedom was rigorously curtailed by episcopal control.[17]

While attendance at Oxford fell, it grew at Cambridge until by the 1400s both colleges were

roughly equal in size and prestige. During this century, classes became more structured, beginning at six in the morning and continuing until five in the afternoon. Courses were strictly intellectual, and physical activities were largely prohibited.

The dominant philosophy of the Reformation was that of Scholasticism. As noted earlier, Scholasticism as a philosophy attempted to show the consistency of reason with religious faith. In such an environment, with the noted exceptions of St. Bonaventure and St. Thomas Aquinas, the use of the body and its senses was not encouraged. However, it is during this time that certain philosophers began to undermine the Scholastics, and in so doing paved the way for the acceptance of the human body and the senses as a way of knowing reality.

Philosophers like William of Ockham developed a philosophical foundation for the use of the body and sensations in the education of children, and therefore anticipated the philosopher John Locke by almost 300 years. It is upon these types of philosophical arguments that the field of physical education is based. However, while the philosophical arguments that justify the existence of physical education became more frequent during the Reformation, the practice of physical education was not evident for several centuries. The theologians of the Reformation argued against sport and physical education as, at best, a waste of time and, at worst, proof that one's soul was doomed to hell! The arguments that developed during the Reformation continue to burden physical educators in that we have to continually justify playful activities as being educational.

The value in understanding these arguments, and knowing how they came about, is that they are in direct contrast to the extreme intellectualism that existed at the time and, to a great extent, still exists in modern-day education. The philosophical arguments used against overintellectualism are as potent now as they were then. Furthermore, understanding the arguments against the value of play enables physical educators and kinesiology professionals to overcome prejudices that are centuries old. Indeed, the bias against play as a valuable educational tool reached new heights during the Reformation, and this bias still exists among educators who do not know the history of the Reformation and its consequences in the modern world. Understanding Luther and Calvin can help modern physical educators and kinesiology professionals justify the existence of their profession in the modern institution of education.

William of Ockham

One of the most famous philosophers of his time was William of Ockham (c. 1285–1349). Ockham was raised in a Franciscan order until the age of 12, when he was sent to study at Oxford. Ockham did not address physical education directly. However, he argued against the layers upon layers of philosophical abstractions that were the hallmark of medieval philosophy. Ockham did not like strictly intellectual arguments over strictly intellectual issues. (How many angels can dance on the head of a pin?) Ockham developed a philosophical method now known as "Ockham's razor," which meant "cut to the quick." Simply stated, it is the argument that the correct answer to any question is the one that is not convoluted; the simplest explanation may be the best or correct answer. He argued for the use of the body and sensations (bodily senses) as a way of knowing reality: "Applying the principle to epistemology, Ockham judged it needless to assume, as the source of material knowledge, anything more than sensations."[18] From sensations arise memory, perception, imagination, anticipation, thought, and experience.

Ockham's philosophy was a controversial one in his day, and it is hard to understand, from the modern worldview, why he created such an uproar in his time. Ockham criticized both the intellectualism of his times and the philosophical foundation upon which the Christian Church rested. Ockham attacked the style of philosophy that had been used to support the Christian Church for centuries, and an attack on the philosophy was seen as an attack on the church. During Ockham's time, the church was associated with a kind of antiphysicalism, so Ockham can be seen as one who made it possible for physical education to be valued in the future even though he was not an advocate for it in his time.

Desiderius Erasmus

Desiderius Erasmus (1469–1517) is a pivotal figure, representative of the humanists of the Renaissance yet central to the Reformation in northern Europe. Indeed, while Erasmus can be considered a figure of the Renaissance, he was famous for his use of humanistic scholarship and literature to criticize the Catholic Church as a political institution, and he helped usher in the Reformation. Many contemporaries of Erasmus believed that he was the cause of much of the religious struggle during the Reformation, that he "laid the eggs which Luther . . . hatched."[19] Erasmus, however, disassociated himself from the reformer Martin Luther because he felt Luther's revolutionary zeal was too extreme. Still, his attitude toward the human body reflects that of many Reformation theorists.

Trained as a priest, Erasmus was fluent in Greek and Latin. He used his knowledge to interpret ancient texts, but he became famous for his satirical portraits of anyone who boasted of their knowledge, power, or piety. Erasmus's *The Praise of Folly,* his most famous work, argued that the human race owed its existence to folly rather than the methods of reason. In 1516, he wrote *Education of a Christian Prince,* in which he argued for lower taxes, less war, fewer monasteries, and more schools. Erasmus's work helped to undermine the absolutist powers of the church and to justify an approach to religion that relied on an individual's interpretation of the Bible rather than the official Catholic Church version. In so doing, he helped make education a part of every person's life, regardless of social class.

While Erasmus was an advocate for education, he appears to have argued against physical education in education curricula. He believed that after age six the intellectual demands on a child were so great that they precluded much time spent on sport and games. This can be seen in his dualistic position on the body, in which he separates mental powers from physical condition:

> We have to meet an argument against early training drawn from the superior importance of health. Personally I venture to regard the mental advantages gained as outweighing some slight risks in the matter of physical vigour.[20]

Erasmus was somewhat ascetic, which can be explained by his strong beliefs regarding the proper role of religion in culture. His ambivalence regarding the virtues of health and physical education in favor of the intellect was manifest in the colleges and universities of northern Europe during the Reformation.

Martin Luther

Perhaps the best known figure of the Reformation was Martin Luther (1483–1546) (Figure 6-2). Luther's famous *95 Theses,* posted on the door of the Wittenberg Church, condemned the selling of indulgences. *Indulgences* were remissions of punishment granted by Catholic priests. Upon hearing confession, a priest would grant a sinner indulgence, which placed the sinner's soul in the state of grace necessary for entrance into heaven. In the Reformation, indulgences were sold by priests, and in many cases, the holy act of confession was perverted into a form of extortion used to enrich the bank accounts of corrupt church officials. Briefly put, Luther argued that the selling of indulgences was wrong, that sinners should be forgiven for their sins through their faith and acceptance of the merits of Christ. This removed the church as "middle man" and put the responsibility for religion directly on the shoulders of the individual. Luther's intention was to remove the Catholic Church from its perceived role of arbiter of heaven and hell. The effect, however, was far more dramatic. Luther helped make practical the ideas of democracy that were to follow in the

Figure 6-2
Martin Luther.

Enlightenment—that each individual, rather than some other power, chooses his or her beliefs. He also paved the way for the idea that all individuals, no matter what their social class, need to be educated.

Luther studied theology and philosophy in the university at Erfurt and, after a brief stint in law school, became a monk. Eventually, he was ordained a priest. Luther believed that people could be "saved" only by complete faith in Christ, and this led him to believe in the power of individual faith. As a consequence of his belief that each individual must interpret the word of God, Luther was a strong advocate of education.

In the time of Luther, however, many parents began to reject the type of education commonly available because it was oriented mainly toward developing priests and nuns. In other words, education was strictly intellectual and primarily taught religious dogma. And because they were not in school, children spent their time as children will—playing. To Luther, the idea that children were playing rather than learning how to read and commune with God was wrong. Instead, Luther argued that boys and girls should spend an hour or two a day in school learning how to read, rather than "spend tenfold as much time in shooting crossbows, playing ball, running, and tumbling about. In like manner, a girl has time to go to school an hour a day . . . for she sleeps, dances, and plays away more than that."[21] As this statement suggests, Luther believed that play could not take the place of education and that playing games was in direct conflict with "real" education.

Having been raised in a family that believed in both superstitions and religion, Luther struggled with matters of the body and the spirit. He attempted to practice the monastic virtue of self-denial as a young man, but he rejected this idea in adulthood and came to believe that complete subjugation of the body was impossible. Consequently, he advocated music, games, and dancing as acceptable pastimes for adults because they were not in themselves evil, and these activities were better than the entirely unwholesome and sacrilegious alternatives that were available at the time. Luther believed that people should be able to engage in

> honorable and useful modes of exercise . . . so that they might not fall into gluttony, lewdness, surfeiting, rioting, and gambling. Accordingly, I pronounce in favor of these two exercises and pastimes, namely, music, and the knightly sports of fencing, wrestling, etc., of which, the one drives care and gloom from the heart, and the other gives a full development to the limbs, and maintains the body in health.[22]

Clearly, Luther believed that the human body should be taken care of, for both spiritual and physical reasons. He argued that Christians should take care of their bodies because, in so doing, it enabled them to be hard workers. This argument was different from the medieval view that the body was to be denied to obtain spiritual purity. Luther helped

change the focus of spirituality from the next world (heaven or hell) to this world, and consequently helped change the attitude of Christians toward the human body. But to say that Luther was an advocate for physical education and sport would be a grave error, for Luther saw these activities as, at worst, a waste of time and, at best, an alternative to the sin of seeking physical pleasure. To summarize, while Luther did not endorse physicality in the same way as did the humanists, he was more favorable toward it than the monks of the Middle Ages.

John Calvin

While Luther helped change attitudes toward the use of our bodies, John Calvin (1509–1564) may have had the greatest impact on modern attitudes toward sport. At the age of only 26, he composed, in the words of one scholar, "the most eloquent, fervent, lucid, logical, influential, and terrible work in all the literature of the religious revolution."[23] *The Principles of the Christian Religion* was a brilliant treatise that rejected the humanist concern with earthly excellence and turned men's thoughts again to the afterworld. As such, Calvin was a dualist who wished to spend time on the spirit and none on the body. Eventually, his ideas were accepted by millions of Protestants in Switzerland, France, Scotland, England, and North America. As a Puritan, Calvin resisted the idea of gentle birth, and like Luther, Calvin helped democratize religion by making each individual more important.

One major difference between Luther and Calvin was that Calvin accepted the idea of *predestination,* the belief that God destined some souls to salvation and the rest to hell. Only God knew where one's soul was bound. This idea, also accepted by many later Protestant reformers, was considered absurd by Luther. Calvin argued that by a simple act of faith one could believe that one was *predestined* to go to heaven, the "divine election." This concept must have been of tremendous relief to those who could not afford to buy indulgences from Catholic priests during the Reformation. Another belief of Calvin's was that most people were destined to burn in hell because God, seen as an angry, vengeful being, created people as sinners. It was left to individuals to elect to believe that they were predestined to go to heaven, and those who elected to believe were members of Calvin's church. If they did not choose, then they would burn in hell.

While it appears that individuals could merely choose to go to heaven, it was not that simple. Behaviors were continually observed, and only those with souls predestined to go to heaven would behave in the proper way. Only God knew for sure where each soul was headed; people could only guess at their destination as measured by their habits and disposition toward prayer and work. Proper behavior included a good work ethic, abstinence from gambling and drinking, and general avoidance of any type of observable, physical pleasure. This avoidance included many of the playful pursuits of Calvin's time, so many of the activities associated with physical education and sport were prohibited by Calvin's theology. Those whose behaviors tended toward drinking, gambling, and the pursuit of physical pleasure through play were seen as destined to go to hell.

Of importance to physical educators are the ways in which belief in predestination affected attitudes toward work and play.[24] If someone believed in Calvin's doctrine of predestination, his or her behaviors were disposed toward work and prayer. Those who enjoyed work were destined for heaven; those disposed toward play were predestined for hell. The logical conclusion of this theological formula is that physical education and sport are the activities of those destined for hell. Clearly, John Calvin was no friend of physical education and sport!

Central to Calvin's argument was a different concept of how people viewed time. Before the Reformation, time was viewed cyclically; each day, season, or year would renew itself. Using this logic, people believed that each day the sun would rise just as it had the day before, each winter was followed by spring, and every year was a copy of the year before. Prior to Calvin, people accepted this view, which historians describe as *cyclic time.* But Calvin argued for a concept historians call *linear time,* the way that people view time in the modern world. Each moment was considered "God given" and not to be wasted. Once a moment was gone, it could never be used as God saw fit. Consequently, to waste this God-given gift was a sin, and those who wasted God's time were sinners. Calvin argued that the best use of God's time was to be productive and to pray. The few people elected by God to go to heaven were disposed toward using God's time well and could be observed as having the necessary character to use time wisely.

Calvin's ideas about time, work, and prayer had a negative effect on participation in sport and physical education that has lasted into the twenty-first century. While his rationale was different from that of the early Christian monks, Calvin's theology had the consequence of working against participation in physical education, sport, and other playful activities. The monks believed that denying the body purified the soul; Calvin believed that work and prayer were a good use of God's time. Both interpretations of the Bible, however, had the same consequence: Sport, play, and physical education were to be avoided. Calvin's ideas eventually evolved into Puritanism, where the way to tell the difference between those saved and those condemned could be seen in individuals' discipline and good deeds. Those destined to be saved were industrious and hardworking; those who were not used their time poorly by, among other things, playing. Besides being forbidden to engage in activities like dancing, playing cards, and singing, people were forbidden to *enjoy* sensual pleasures like sex, drinking, and gambling because these activities eventually would seduce them away from God.[25] In Calvin's words,

> It is clear that this consecration means that licentious abuse is to be curbed, and confirms the rule of St. Paul that we should make no provision for the flesh to fulfill its lusts (Rom. 13:14), which, if they are given too much scope, boil over furiously out of control.[26]

Calvin's argument put an emphasis on the value of the body in that what one did with his or her body determined where one's soul was bound. In so doing, Calvin argued against the ideas of the early monks that the body is evil or to be denied. The only saving virtue of this position is that the body is, at least, good for physical work. This position can be used to argue for concepts such as healthful living, for a healthy person can work harder than one who is not. Yet, at the same time, Calvin sought to remove play and games from the lives of everyday people. If you were not working, you were wasting God's time. A saying that reflects Calvin's theology is "Idle hands are the Devil's workshop." Eventually, Calvin's position evolved into the Protestant work ethic, whereby one's inner moral goodness could be measured by observing his or her work habits. In this situation, if you are playing, you are showing that you are a sinner. Clearly, if one were a follower of Calvin's religious beliefs, one would refrain from any sporting activities.

Thomas Elyot

Like the educators of humanist Italy, many who were involved in education in northern Europe were associated with the monarchy. However, the universities and schools in England were much more influenced by Erasmus, Luther, and Calvin than they were by the humanists of Italy. As a consequence, two "schools" developed in England: (1) those associated with the monarchy and (2) those associated with the public schools and universities. Those who sided with the monarchy and the ways of the court favored a more sporting life. The curriculum of the public schools and universities was similar to that of the monasteries in the Middle Ages in that the body was to be denied to purify the soul.

Thomas Elyot (1490–1546) was much more like the Italian humanists. The ideal of the universal man dominated the English royal court, and to this ideal, the English added the notion of the "governor." Elyot's *Book of the Governor* argued that the Tudor gentleman should be versed in literature, science, and philosophy; he should be educated in both writing and fighting; and he should be able to read Greek and speak modern languages, to dance and to make music, and to read and write poetry. In addition to these humanist skills, the governor should know something of law so that he might serve England in the capacity of a magistrate, officer, or administrator. This concept of citizenship was popular in England and was influenced by a strong tradition of local government.

Unlike his Reformation counterparts, Elyot's concept of education concerned primarily the nobility. Elyot believed that gentle birth was necessary to a gentleman, whereas Puritans argued that one could be made a gentleman. Elyot supported his view by arguing that society was composed of inherited "degrees." A person was born into one of these degrees and, according to Elyot, should stay in this social position throughout life. To alter this system was to shake the order of society. This put Elyot at odds with the Puritans, who disagreed with the idea that those born to the nobility were distinctly different from those who were not.

Elyot devoted several chapters of his book to physical education. In so doing, he tried to educate the sons of the nobility as to how to conduct themselves in contemporary England. The games and sports Elyot recommended came from his own time as well as antiquity; running, swimming, and hunting were easily defended. But not all sports were considered good by Elyot, and in this respect, we can see the influence of Luther and Calvin. Some exercises were more acceptable for English gentlemen than others. Football in particular was frowned upon because it left the body beaten and the spirit inflamed. No doubt Puritan ideas of restraint had some impact on Elyot's thinking. Dancing was acceptable, but not if it was associated with idleness and sexual pleasure. In sum, Elyot's program of physical education supported Calvin's and Luther's ideas that pleasure is not at the heart of physical education and sport. This position eliminated "fun" games like football, which was played because of the pleasure derived from doing so.

Elyot is notable for his efforts to improve physical education because he was familiar with the latest medical teaching of his time. He claimed six physiological benefits that could be derived from exercise: it (1) aided digestion, (2) increased one's appetite, (3) helped one live longer, (4) warmed the body, (5) raised one's metabolism, and (6) cleansed the body of its wastes. By following this physical education program, individuals would be healthier. And, because of improved health, they could do God's work better. In sum, Elyot was concerned with several objectives, the most important of which had to do with health and physiological efficiency needed to do God's work. His book was the first to use the science of his day to achieve his objectives. Were Elyot to be judged by today's standards, however, he would be considered more of a health educator than a physical educator, for he was not concerned with playful skills as much as with doing God's work.

Roger Ascham

Like Elyot, Roger Ascham (1515–1568) was an English humanist. A professor at Cambridge University, Ascham is famous for his book *The Schoolmaster,* in which he advocated the study of Latin and Greek as a means of obtaining a liberal arts education. From these sources, he recognized the importance of physical education. Ascham urged young men to

> engage in all courtly exercises and gentle-manly pastimes. . . . All pastimes joined with labor, used in open place and in daylight, con-taining either some fit exercise for war or some pleasant pastime for peace, be not only comely and decent but also very necessary for a courtly gentleman to use.[27]

Ascham also appreciated the value of exercises as a means of resting the mind so that it may be sharper at a later time. This idea fit nicely with the coming of the first industrial revolution and

became the justification for recreation when it was recognized that people had to rest to work harder. Influenced by the Puritans, Ascham's educational values lent themselves to the work ethic developing in the sixteenth century.

The activities that Ascham believed necessary included the ability to ride and run; "to run fair at the tilt or ring"; to be able to use all weapons and to shoot a bow and gun; to vault, leap, wrestle, swim, dance, sing, and play musical instruments; to hawk and hunt; and to play tennis. Ascham also wrote a treatise, *Toxophilus,* on the art of shooting the bow.[28] In it, Ascham discussed everything from how to choose and care for the bow to how to shoot it properly. It was one of the first how-to books in sport in the Western world.

Leonardo da Vinci and Michelangelo

The Renaissance was a time of dramatic philosophical change. It was also a time when painters and sculptors celebrated the human form. The Italian Renaissance was the epitome of Renaissance achievement on all levels. Leonardo da Vinci (1452–1519) and Michelangelo (1475–1564) are among the most exalted Masters of the Italian Renaissance. Da Vinci was an extraordinary talent. Frequently identified as the quintessential Renaissance Man, he excelled as a painter, sculptor, architect, musician, engineer, mathematician, and scientist. He studied human anatomy by dissecting corpses in Florence, Milan, and Rome. He made more than 200 drawings that are accurate in every detail. His anatomical drawings and attendant notes on physiological function educated Renaissance scientists and others interested in exercise and kinesiology.

Michelangelo, like da Vinci, was a gifted genius. He was an accomplished painter and sculptor and also achieved fame as an architect and poet. Like da Vinci, Michelangelo studied human anatomy. From 1501 to 1504 he worked on a sculpture that would bring him eternal fame. The white marble masterpiece, titled "David," features a young nude male that is a stunning symbol of strength, youth, and beauty. The body is a perfect anatomical and physical specimen. Like Myron's "Discobolus" (sculpture of a nude Greek discus thrower), it illustrates the most beautiful form on earth—the human body—in a way that is so visually appealing, nothing composed in the modern era can compare with it.

SUMMARY

The Renaissance was an intellectual reawakening that helped change medieval attitudes toward the human body. Turning back to the classic Greek and Roman philosophers, scholars began to reexamine all aspects of their lives in classical perspective. Eventually, this led to the discussion of the Catholic Church in terms of the classical philosophers, and this discussion helped lead the Western world out of the Middle Ages. While the Renaissance was primarily an upper-class movement, it laid the groundwork for those who followed.

Like Plato and Aristotle, the intellectuals of the Renaissance focused on living in this world as opposed to living in the next world, or heaven. This philosophy, known as humanism, emphasizes our humanness rather than our spiritual selves. As a direct consequence of this type of thinking, affairs of the human body were considered much more acceptable. Sport and physical education were direct beneficiaries of this philosophy.

While the Reformation was primarily a religious movement, it had a lasting impact on Western civilization in all aspects of life and for every social class. After the Reformation, the Catholic Church no longer had a stranglehold on matters of political, national, or intellectual importance. Indeed, the very nature of how people interacted with religion was different. Because of the Reformation, religion was relegated to people's private or "inner" lives and was to be determined by each individual. So, even though the Reformation focused more on social and religious reform than it did on individual growth, a consequence was that each individual would be expected to read and interpret the Bible for him- or herself. The impact on education was significant. All people, no matter what their social class, needed to learn to read. From this position, it was a short step to the development of an educational system for all, sponsored by the state.

In addition, the Reformation encouraged the rise of the middle class and, in its Calvinist version, made religion a tool with which to judge people's behavior. The Reformation caused people to identify good works and prayer with hard work and industriousness, and as a consequence caused Protestants to concentrate on the affairs of the soul in this world rather than the state of the soul in the next. These changes had a significant impact on how people viewed the activities of play and work.

The Reformation, especially Calvin's version, emphasized what one did with his or her body, because how one used the body was a measure of the quality of one's soul. A good soul was predestined to go to heaven, and a bad soul was predestined to go to hell. To work and to do good deeds clearly represented the best use of one's time and was the mark of a person bound for heaven. Indeed, after the Reformation, Western civilization viewed time in a completely different manner than it did before the Reformation.

For the most part (there were exceptions), Luther's and Calvin's version of the Reformation sought to remove play and games from the lives of everyday people. Eventually, this argument evolved into the Protestant work ethic, whereby one's inner moral goodness could be measured by observing one's work habits; an athlete was a sinner. This attitude toward work and play, in its more modern form, is still evident in America. Luther and Calvin undermined the medieval belief that the body should be denied to purify the soul and replaced it with the idea that the body is here to do God's good work using God-given time in the appropriate manner. But the effect of the Reformation with respect to play and physical education was much the same as that of the philosophy of the early monks: Both theologies worked against play, sport, and physical education. It falls to a later time to justify the activities that we have come to view as acceptable in physical education and sport.

DISCUSSION QUESTIONS

1. To what extent has history repeated itself relative to the crusaders of the twenty-first century once again waging war against Muslims in the Middle East?

2. What was the Renaissance? How did it differ from life in the Middle Ages? Did this difference affect sport and physical education?

3. What was the Reformation? How did it differ from the theology of the Middle Ages? Did this difference affect sport and physical education?

4. What ideas from the Renaissance and the Reformation are with us today in sport and physical education?

5. The theology of the Reformation differed from that of the early Christian monks with respect to the value of the body, yet the consequence for sport and physical education is much the same. Why?

6. Identify the individuals who advocated the promotion of physical education.

7. Identify the types of sports and physical activities that were popular during this period. To what extent are they done today?

8. To what extent do the six physiological benefits identified by Thomas Elyot (1490–1546) reflect the benefits of exercise claimed by exercise scientists in the twenty-first century?

INTERNET RESOURCES

Renaissance: The Elizabethan World
http://renaissance.dm.net
Includes articles and links related to the Renaissance.

Renaissance Magazine
www.renaissancemagazine.com
Is an interesting and informative resource that provides students and teachers with articles about and references to the Middle Ages and Renaissance.

Renascence Editions
http://darkwing.uoregon.edu/~rbear/ren.htm

Contains an online repository of works of Montaigne, Shakespeare, and others printed in English between 1477 and 1799; an excellent source for scholars.

Medieval and Renaissance Fact and Fiction
www.angelfire.com/mi/spanogle/medieval.html
Represents a good source of facts, information, and links about the Renaissance.

Visit the *History and Philosophy of Sport and Physical Education* Online Learning Center (www.mhhe.com/mechikoff6e) for additional information and study tools.

SUGGESTIONS FOR FURTHER READING

Bronowski, J., and B. Mazlish. "The Expanding World: From Leonardo to Galileo, 1500–1630." In *The Western Intellectual Tradition: From Leonardo to Hegel*. New York: Harper & Brothers, 1960.

Calhoun, D. "From Fun to Business: Sport in Modern Society." In *Sports, Culture, and Personality*. Berkeley, CA: Leisure Press, 1981.

Hackensmith, C. W. "The Renaissance" and "Realism in Education." In *History of Physical Education*. New York: Harper & Row, 1966.

Rice, E., J. L. Hutchinson, and M. Lee. "The Renaissance" and "Realism." In *A Brief History of Physical Education*. New York: John Wiley, 1969.

Van Dalen, D., E. Mitchell, and B. Bennett. "Physical Education in the Middle Ages and Early Modern Times." In *A World History of Physical Education*. Englewood Cliffs, NJ: Prentice-Hall, 1953.

NOTES

1. J. Bronowski and Bruce Mazlish, *The Western Intellectual Tradition: From Leonardo to Hegel* (New York: Harper & Brothers, 1960).

2. Ibid.

3. Ibid.

4. Ibid., 106.

5. Ibid., 62

6. Ibid.

7. *Three Renaissance Classics: Machiavelli, The Prince; More, Utopia; Castiglione, The Courtier,* intro. and notes Burton A. Milligan (New York: Scribner, 1953), 455.

8. W. H. Woodward, *Vittorino da Feltre and Humanist Educators* (Cambridge: University Press, 1921).

9. Ibid., 27.

10. Ibid., 137–38.

11. Baldassare Castiglione, *The Book of the Courtier,* trans. Sir Thomas Hoby (New York: Dutton, 1959), 37.

12. Castiglione, *Book of the Courtier,* 29–31.

13. Will Durant, *The Reformation* (New York: Simon & Schuster, 1957).

14. Ibid., 235.

15. England's public schools are different from those that exist in contemporary America. "Public" in fourteenth-century England meant that the school existed outside of the homes of the nobility and that professional teachers who were paid through tuition fees taught the children.

16. Durant, *Reformation,* 236.

17. Ibid., 236.

18. Ibid., 247.

19. Bronowski and Mazlish, *Western Intellectual Tradition,* 74.

20. Desiderius Erasmus, *The Education of a Christian Prince,* trans. Lester K. Born (New York: Columbia University Press, 1936), 27.

21. Martin Luther, "Letters to the Mayors and Aldermen," *Classics in Education,* ed. William Baskin (New York: Philosophical Library, 1966), 376.

22. Frederick Eby, *Early Protestant Educators* (New York: McGraw-Hill, 1942), 176.

23. Durant, *Reformation,* 460.

24. This interpretation is developed by Max Weber, *The Protestant Ethic and the Spirit of Capitalism,* trans. Talcott Parsons (New York: Scribner, 1906). See also Don Calhoun, "From Fun to Business: Sport in Modern Society," *Sports, Culture, and Personality* (Berkeley, CA: Leisure Press, 1981).

25. Ellen Gerber, "John Calvin," *Innovators and Institutions in Physical Education* (Philadelphia: Lea & Febiger, 1971), 36–39.

26. Albere-Marie Schmidt, *John Calvin and the Calvinist Tradition,* trans. Ronald Wallace (New York: Harper & Brothers, 1960), 142.

27. Roger Ascham, "The Schoolmaster," *The Whole Works of Roger Ascham,* ed. Rev. Dr. Giles (New York: AMS Press, 1965), III, 139.

28. Roger Ascham, *Toxophilus, the Schole of Shootinge* (New York: Da Capo Press, 1969).

C H A P T E R

7

The Age of Science and the Enlightenment: 1560–1789

OBJECTIVES

Upon completing the chapter, you will be able to:

- Explain how the transition from the emphasis on the spiritual world to the secular world happened.
- Understand the historical events of this era and how these events contributed to the development of modern culture.
- Explain how religion responded to this transition from spiritual to secular.
- Explain how the Age of Science ushered in a new way of looking at reality that had no basis in theology.
- Explain how humanist philosophy contributed to the Age of Science.
- Explain how the Age of Science and secular interests contributed to interest in all things human, especially the body.
- Understand the beliefs of the philosophers of science.
- Explain how the Age of Science contributed to the development of physical education and sport.
- Understand the genesis of the Enlightenment.
- Understand what it means to be "enlightened."
- Identify selected leaders of the Age of Science and the Enlightenment, and discuss their contributions to physical education and sport.
- Identify the beliefs of the philosophers of the Renaissance.
- Understand the philosophical impact that René Descartes, Thomas Hobbes, and George Berkeley had on the "mind and body" issue.
- Identify the educational philosophy of educators during this era and their contributions to physical education and sport.
- Identify the philosophes (not philosophers)—Jean-Jacques Rousseau, Johann Bernhard Basedow, and Johann Friedrich GutsMuths—and discuss their beliefs about the value of physical education and sport.

General Events

Age of Science

1561–1626 Francis Bacon
1562 and 1594 French
  religious wars
1564–1642 Galileo Galilei
1588–1679 Thomas Hobbes
1596–1650 René Descartes
1618–1648 Thirty Years' War
  in Germany
1619–1622 Great Depression
1630–1632 Plague in France
1642–1727 Isaac Newton
1642–1648 English civil war
1647–1649 Plague in France
1660 Return of English
  monarchy
1665 Plague in England;
  invention of printing press
1685–1753 George Berkeley

Enlightenment

1688 English Revolution
1715 Death of Louis XIV
1715–1723 Period of the
  Regency
1723–1774 Reign of Louis XV
1723–1790 Adam Smith
1748 Hume's *Inquiry
  Concerning Human
  Understanding* and
  Montesquieu's *The Spirit of
  the Laws*

**Sport and Physical
Education**

INTRODUCTION

From the mid-1500s to 1789, the Western world was, philosophically speaking, turned upside down. The orientation toward what was real and how one came to know it changed radically, and the corresponding view of the human body changed as well. In short, the changes argued for by philosophers in the Renaissance and the Reformation became reality during the Age of Science and the Enlightenment. As a consequence of these philosophical changes, many people no longer lived in this world by rules that would get them into heaven. The Ten Commandments, the Bible, and the influence of the various Christian faiths became less important in the Western world, while medicine, science, and technology came to dominate the thoughts and behaviors of all people. People began to live, more and more, according to rules that would serve them well in this world. Consequently, the Age of Science and the Enlightenment are perhaps best known for the change in style of political governance—a movement from the rights of divine governance through kings to the rights of individuals to govern themselves.

Broken down into roughly 100-year increments, the Age of Science (1560–1688) and the Enlightenment (1688–1789) have in common an emphasis on living in the secular world—the "here and now." This change from an emphasis on anticipation of living in the next world to an emphasis on living in this world did not come easily. Indeed, this 230-year period was one of the most conflictual in the history of civilization. Yet, while religion, politics, science, law, and other institutions changed radically, people still enjoyed their recreational and sporting activities. To a certain extent, these activities were legitimized by the actions and arguments of prominent philosophers and educators. While physical education and sport continued to play a larger part in the lives of Europeans and Americans, they still represented a minor part of Western culture even as the arguments for these activities became more substantial and widely accepted. Important to our discussion, the arguments for physical education and sport advanced in the Age of Science and the Enlightenment are still valid today. These arguments justify the use of science to understand human movement as a way of making people healthier.

The Age of Science: 1560–1688

The seventeenth century witnessed explosive changes in Western culture. On the one hand, this period continued the change in thinking, begun in the Renaissance and Reformation, from "otherworldly" concerns to those of the observed, natural world. On the other hand, philosophers sought to understand the natural world in terms that were theoretical and timeless by developing rules and laws that could be used to explain particular experiences. Together, these changes continued the march begun in the Renaissance toward what is now called "modern" culture: the idea that humanity can understand life in terms of scientific laws. This change in thinking led to major advances in science, such as Galileo's astronomical discoveries and Newton's explanations of the physical universe. And the use of science to create new laws led historians to call this period both the Age of Reason and the Age of Science.

These changes did not come easily, nor did they occur at a leisurely pace. In many respects, they were responses to contemporary problems. After a relatively steady economic expansion in the sixteenth century, Europe experienced a large-scale economic downturn in the seventeenth century. By 1600, Spain was losing its political influence, along with its control of the South Atlantic and therefore its silver supply. There was a depression from 1619 to 1622, and as international trade dropped off and unemployment increased, a pool of mercenaries was created to fight the many religious wars that wracked Europe: the Thirty Years' War (1618–1648) in Germany, the civil wars (1642–1648) in England, and the two religious wars in France (1562 and 1594).

The religious wars pitted one religion against another and all religious faiths against nonbelievers. As one scholar noted, the early seventeenth century looked like a scene from the Middle East in our times, where people had a fair chance of having their throats cut and their houses burned down by strangers who merely disliked their religion![1] In Central Europe, the German states were in constant battle, Protestants against Catholics. The Thirty Years' War started due to religious disagreements and concluded with both sides agreeing to tolerate one another's religion. France divided along religious lines between the Huguenots (Protestants) and the Catholics, and England experienced a civil war between Catholics and Anglicans.

Among other factors, the English civil war was precipitated by the Declaration of Sport, an edict issued by King James in 1618 and reissued by his son Charles in 1633.[2] The edict stated that sport could be played on Sunday after church services. The Puritans, however, strongly disagreed with this edict and believed that Sunday should be devoted exclusively to worship. In 1643 the Declaration of Sport was revoked. In its place was an order issued by Parliament that all existing copies of the Declaration of Sport be burned by the Hangman! This position, known as "Sabbatarianism," and various "Blue Laws" remained popular in the United States until the 1930s.[3] *Blue Laws,* or

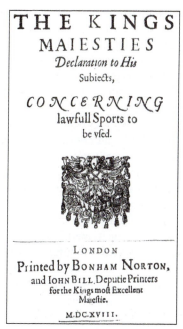

Figure 7-1
Declaration of Sport.

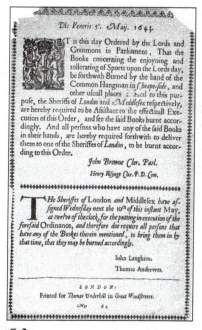

Figure 7-2
Order to burn all existing copies of the Declaration of Sport.

laws that prohibited certain acts, gained their name from having been printed on blue paper. Most frequently, Blue Laws prohibited drinking, gambling, and other playful and "sensory" activities associated with drinking and gambling.

The seventeenth century was marked by increasing religious intolerance manifested in all aspects of life. People were forced to commit to one religion or another, and critical discussion of religious doctrine became increasingly rare. To a great extent, the philosophies developed during the Age of Science were an attempt to avoid the emotional intensity that accompanied religious debate. By being "objective," one could discuss an idea, religious or otherwise, on its merits and come to a solution that was reasoned. From this perspective, the development of reasoned inquiry based on the experienced world was a reaction to religious turmoil.

On top of the economic and religious crises were recurrences of the Black Plague. France suffered from 1630 to 1632 and from 1647 to 1649, while England experienced her final serious outbreak in 1665. In addition, Western Europe experienced a period of lower-than-normal temperatures that we now call the Little Ice Age. Whole rural areas were depopulated, causing city slums to grow. This population shift caused further outbreaks of disease and increases in poverty. The combination of profound religious strife, economic depression, global cooling, plague, rural depopulation, and urban growth had an incredible impact on life in Europe in the seventeenth century. The philosophies developed during this century reflect these historical conditions.

On a more positive note, the seventeenth century witnessed the continued growth of books in print and an increasingly educated group of laypeople. Roughly defined, *laypeople* were educated people who were not explicitly tied to the church in the same way that a monk, nun, or priest would be. As a consequence, a layperson could use his education for means other than those of the church. Eventually, this concept of an educated person not associated with the church became commonplace. Since the invention of the printing press in the 1300s, cheaper books were available, and more people could afford to buy them. This allowed more people to read and led to more schools where people could learn how to read. Some argue that printing led to the Age of Science and paved the way for the Enlightenment, for the American and French revolutions, and for democracy.[4]

As a result of the increased number of laypeople, educated citizens were no longer as strongly influenced by church dogma. It is not an accident, then, that the growth of science occurred at a time when the church was losing its hold on education. One consequence was the move away from the concentration on the afterlife to a focus on one's existence in the present on earth.

The emphasis on science was probably the most explicit measure of this concentration on the present, and tools of science were developed to expand people's observational powers. Microscopes and telescopes, thermometers, barometers, hydrometers, better watches, and finer scales all enhanced humanity's ability to observe the material universe, and these instruments to a great extent affected the manner in which philosophers in the Age of Science explained the nature of reality.

It was during this time that science came to be seen as a separate area of study from philosophy. What we now call "science" was formerly called "experimental philosophy" or "natural philosophy," and those who practiced "science" considered themselves philosophers. These men had a tremendous impact on philosophy. Seeking to overcome the otherworldly concerns of the church, science turned its attention from metaphysics to the natural world. The goal of science was to improve the quality of life on earth, and this goal was in direct contrast to the medieval idea of asceticism or self-denial—that it was our duty to suffer on earth by denying the body.

The Age of Science, then, was a continuation of the philosophies of the Humanists developed during the Renaissance. But the Age of Science was not limited to the use of the classics and "pure reason." Reason and tradition could be balanced by methodical investigation based in the material world. Science accepted as its realm only that which could be measured and quantified, mathematically expressed, and experimentally proved. It was up to the philosophers to explain this radical shift in thinking.

The change from otherworldly concerns to the here and now had a direct impact on education in general and physical education in particular. Sport and physical education were more easily justified as philosophers came to accept the material world and the place our bodies occupy in it. Scientists and philosophers used new ways of thinking to understand our bodies and explain how they function. This approach led to advances in medicine, improved educational techniques, and a variety of ideas believed to better our earthly existence, some of which would eventually include exercise and sporting activities.

The Enlightenment: 1688–1789

What was the Enlightenment? *Enlightenment* literally means "the process of making bright that which is dark." Applied to eighteenth-century Western civilization, the term describes how a relatively large, well-educated public believed that a new way of thinking would "enlighten" the thoughts and behaviors of the civilized world. "Enlightenment" tells us that the old ways of Europe were "dark," while the new, scientific ways of Newton, Galileo, Hobbes, Locke, and Descartes were the "light" that would guide humanity toward a basic harmony of interests. Indeed, much of our attitude toward the "Dark Ages" of medieval Europe, which modern historians have shown were not really so "dark," comes from the attitudes of intellectuals who argued for change during the Enlightenment. Many disagreed with the philosophers and intellectuals who advocated this new way of thinking, but there is no doubt that the Enlightenment had an incredible impact on the modern world.

Many ideas that had their genesis during the Enlightenment are taken for granted in contemporary education, and it is helpful to physical educators and exercise scientists to know how and why these ideas came about. Indeed, modern education is intimately connected to the Enlightenment tradition. Perhaps the most powerful advocates of the Enlightenment were the educators who organized the public schools and had ready access to printing

and publishing. Their views are well represented in books from the eighteenth century and have had a significant impact on subsequent educators. Physical education and sport were similarly affected by the Enlightenment, especially since the many Enlightenment critics had so much to say about the virtues of human movement as a means of creating the ideal individual and community.

THE PHILOSOPHERS OF SCIENCE

Prior to the seventeenth century, science, philosophy, and education were not distinct academic areas as they are in twenty-first-century America. As mentioned previously, scientists during the seventeenth century considered themselves philosophers.[5] Perhaps the most important of these scientist philosophers were Galileo Galilei, Isaac Newton, and Francis Bacon, all of whom had a lasting impact on both science and philosophy. These men had in common the goal of understanding the world in a systematic and reasoned way. They helped move the Western world from a type of thinking that emphasized strictly intellectual processes to a type of thinking that emphasized the examination of the material world. Included in the material world is the human body. Questions from the new perspective included these: How do bodies in motion work? What are the rules that guide all matter? These questions and others like them can be applied to the study of the human body, which explains why we discuss the contributions of Galileo, Bacon, and Newton to the Western mentality. Although they had nothing to say about the study of physical education, the type of thinking about the material world that they initiated is assumed in modern day science. Modern science is one of the cornerstones of contemporary kinesiology and physical education.

Galileo Galilei

Galileo Galilei (1564–1642) was an Italian astronomer and physicist who made famous the Copernican view of the universe. In the *Copernican view* of the solar system, the sun is at the center of the solar system. This is not the first time that a sun-centered (not earth-centered) solar system was proposed. Aristarchus of Samos posited circa 200 B.C. a sun-centered solar system. However, this idea was dismissed by Aristotle and Ptolemy's "common sense" earth-centered universe. Although he created no systematic philosophy, Galileo's influence on modern philosophical thought is considerable. Scholars credit Galileo, along with Descartes, for much of the philosophical foundation on which modern culture operates. To Galileo, we owe much of the drive to separate the physical sciences from philosophy, and his work lent credibility to the idea that what we observe through our senses is both real and important. This approach legitimized the use of the senses (the human body) instead of Catholic dogma as a means of acquiring knowledge. What was so important about Galileo's work was that it removed humanity from the "center of the universe" and elevated the corporeal world in importance. Galileo's influence can be seen especially in the writings of Thomas Hobbes and Isaac Newton.

We can learn much about the spirit of the Age of Science by looking at how well Galileo's ideas were received. While modern culture appreciates his scientific views, his religious contemporaries were dismayed by their religious and political implications. The attitude of the Inquisition is summarized by this historic edict:

> The view that the sun stands motionless at the center of the universe is foolish, philosophically false, and utterly heretical, because [it is] contrary to Holy Scripture. The view that the earth is not the center of the universe and even has a daily rotation is philosophically false, and at least an erroneous belief.[6]

Galileo was convicted of heresy by the Inquisition and forced to repudiate the Copernican theory in 1633. He was sentenced to prison but was allowed to live in his villa near Florence, where he was free to study and teach, write books, and receive visitors. Even his "imprisonment" had an impact. Many scientists sought to avoid the philosophical implications of science on religion, and philosophers were careful to avoid the wrath of the church. It was not until 1835 that the Catholic church withdrew the works of Galileo from its Index of Prohibited Books.

Francis Bacon

Francis Bacon (1561–1626), a contemporary of Galileo's, was a highly versatile man, if not the "universal man" so desired during the Renaissance. He was well read in politics, law, literature, philosophy, and science, and he achieved the office of chancellor in England, where he ruled in the absence of the king. Bacon's most lasting contribution was to the philosophy of science; he used the methods of philosophy to justify and legitimize the use of science. Bacon called for the support of colleges, libraries, laboratories, biological gardens, and museums of science and industry; for better pay for teachers and researchers; and for the funding of scientific experiments.

Most important, though, was that he developed an organizational scheme of what could be learned by science. Denis Diderot, the French encyclopedist, once said of Bacon, "When it was impossible to write a history of what men knew, he drew up the map of what they had to learn."[7] Bacon attempted to classify the sciences in a logical order and to determine their fields of inquiry to obtain answers to major problems awaiting solutions. This type of thinking is evident in physical education and kinesiology today with the division of the discipline into various subdisciplines like exercise physiology, sport history, and motor learning. Bacon believed in the betterment of life through the proper application of knowledge and thereby connected science to the lives of everyday people.

Bacon also believed that this betterment of humanity could be best achieved through the methods of *induction*, the process by which one draws conclusions based on many observations. Put differently, we might describe induction as "finding the common denominator" among a group of situations. According to Bacon, induction is the process by which one moves from particular facts or observations to a more general knowledge of forms, or generalized physical properties.[8] Bacon sought mastery over the human condition through the expansion of what was known, and this goal has had a tremendous impact in all fields that use science as a means of acquiring knowledge. This method of developing general rules and standards from particular experiences is widely used by physical education and exercise science researchers today.

Isaac Newton

Isaac Newton (1642–1727) was an English mathematician and physicist whose work revolutionized the study of the physical world. In short, Newton's mechanical theory was used to support the view that God created the world as a perfect machine. Physicists had only to discover the laws that governed the machine to have the keys to the universe. His most famous work was *Mathematical Principles of Natural Philosophy* or, in short, *Principia,* published in 1687. In it were the three "laws" of motion from which theorems and corollaries are subsequently deduced. These are required reading in any biomechanics class today:

1. According to Newton's First law, an object (body) at rest will remain at rest unless it is impacted by an unbalanced force. An object (body) in motion continues in motion with the same speed and in the same direction unless impacted by an unbalanced force. This law is known as The Law of Inertia.
2. Newton's second law states that acceleration is produced when a force acts upon a mass. The greater the mass (size) of the object (body) being accelerated, the greater the amount of force needed to accelerate the object for example, think of a discus thrower who throws several discus, each discus weighs more than the one thrown previously. Heavier objects (body) require more force (strength) to move the same distance as a lighter body. $F = MA$ or Force = Mass $\times$ Acceleration.
3. Newton's third law states that for every action, there is an equal and opposite reaction. In other words, when we push an object one way, it will push back in the opposite direction equally as hard. When an athlete jumps up and down, he/she pushes down on the ground via energy coming from the body. The subsequent reaction is that lifts up with an equal force of energy similar to a rocket engine that pushes thrust to the ground in order to lift off.

Eventually, Newton's work was used to argue that the universe is guided by timeless and unchanging laws. The *Principia* became the model of scientific knowledge and had a significant impact on all subsequent scientific inquiry in all fields.

THE PHILOSOPHERS

The influence of Galileo, Bacon, and Newton was felt by all in their day, especially the philosophers who tried to explain the impact of these new scientists. The Age of Science coincides with the beginning of "modern" philosophy, when philosophers began to break from the traditional methods of philosophy used in the Middle Ages and during the Renaissance. Most philosophers of this time still considered God to be creator and conserver of the universe. But some philosophers began to argue that nature could be studied and expressed as a dynamic system of bodies in motion without any immediate reference to God and that the intelligible structure of the universe could be expressed mathematically. This was due in large part to the influence of science, particularly the work of Galileo and Newton, who envisioned the mechanistic conception of the world. In addition, many prominent philosophers worked outside the prestigious European universities. As a result, they were able to develop ideas free from the influence of the church and the Greek philosophers who had inspired the Renaissance; they were able to break with the traditions of the church and Scholasticism.

This approach to understanding the world caused a stir among the intellectuals of the seventeenth century. The problem of reconciling the scientific approach, which emphasized the material world, with the traditional approach, which emphasized God and one's spiritual soul, divided many philosophers. The traditional approach argued that each human is a material being who possesses a spiritual soul, is endowed with the power of free choice, and partly transcends the material world and the system of mechanical causes. The scientific approach argued that the material universe includes all that one is, that one's psyche is material, and that there is no free will.[10] Indeed, the Age of

Science was well represented by many philosophical extremes, yet most of them emphasized the development of the individual. The two extremes discussed here, represented by Thomas Hobbes and René Descartes, are evident in many of the philosophical writings of the Age of Science.

The ideas of the Enlightenment were to a great extent influenced by philosophers such as John Locke, George Berkeley, and David Hume.[11] Locke lived in the seventeenth century, and the impact of his writings was felt well into the eighteenth century in the work of Berkeley and Hume. These philosophers contributed theories of knowledge that came to be accepted in their time and are still debated in their contemporary forms. In their most basic sense, these theories hold that people come to know something through their experiences, particularly through their senses. Humans are considered to be "of nature"—that is, they are as much of this world as are the plants, animals, and elements. This idea is important to education, for it means that the body can and should be used as a learning tool. Indeed, if the body is not used, then a person cannot learn in a "natural" way. Clearly, the epistemologies of Locke, Berkeley, and Hume differ from those that say learning occurs only in the mind or soul through reading, rote memorization, and repetition. This is important for our purposes in that these epistemologies do not eliminate physical education from the educational spectrum as do other metaphysical positions.

By understanding the metaphysical positions of Hobbes, Descartes, Locke, Berkeley, and Hume, we can also understand how the philosophers of the Age of Science and the Enlightenment believed humans learned, what their relationship to nature was, and, for our purposes, what they believed the role of physical education was in developing an individual.

Thomas Hobbes

Strongly influenced by Galileo's and Newton's mechanical conception of nature, the English philosopher Thomas Hobbes (1588–1679) applied the basic idea of mechanics to all reality.[12] He argued that the realm of philosophy is only that which can

be observed and that reality is composed solely of matter in motion—for example, bodies in motion and all things material. This removed the idea of God from philosophy, but not from religion or theology. Put differently, Hobbes removed philosophy from religion, and it was this that angered his critics. Hobbes considered humans to be purely material beings and was not concerned with their immortal souls or minds, because these cannot be directly observed or measured. The question can then be asked, "What do we call consciousness?" Hobbes believed that the mind was the product of atoms and chemicals interacting with each other, and nothing more.

Hobbes was severely criticized for this approach because of the implications. Religious critics branded Hobbes a heretic and banned his work, and for a time he lived in France, fearing for his life. This was a practical consideration, to say the least! Philosophically, however, Hobbes's philosophy was revolutionary because it states that humans are composed of only one thing: the body, which is material, not spiritual! There are no confusing concepts of mind or soul to worry about because, if one cannot observe them, they are not the concern of philosophy. Indeed, Hobbes argued that philosophy and science could not be used to prove whether the mind or soul exists. This monistic approach relies on the idea that all there is to nature is matter in motion. If one has enough knowledge about the composition of matter and the forces that act upon it, then one can predict what will happen. This philosophy can be applied to human bodies, with each person considered to be only the sum of the different chemical components that make up his or her physical being.

This is a plausible idea in many respects, and it makes sense in an age of machines (like computers) that can predict to a high degree of certainty how objects will affect each other. However, this philosophy has been criticized on the grounds that it is deterministic. *Determinism* is the doctrine that every fact in the universe is guided entirely by law. Applied to people, determinism holds that all the actions of an individual are determined (or predetermined) by previous causes and not by free will. Indeed, there is no such thing as free will in deterministic philosophy. Put another way, what one has done in the past, combined with one's environment, determines how the individual will behave. According to Hobbes's argument, even though an individual *believes* that he or she chooses to behave as he or she does, there really is no choice in the matter. According to determinism, thoughts are *determined* by one's past actions and environment.

Hobbes's materialism is evident in the field of behavioral psychology, in which concepts of mind are abandoned and the psychologist concentrates only on behavior. Behaviorists argue that this is all a psychologist can observe and that behavior is all that can be influenced. Behaviorism has been an important part of research in physical education and has had some success in shaping behavior both in the physical education classroom and in the sport environment, where one is concerned strictly with performance. Hobbes's philosophy is perhaps most evident in the subdisciplines of sport psychology and pedagogy.

Critics of behaviorism argue that because determinism does not accept the idea of free will, it has difficulty explaining where new ideas and creativity come from. Furthermore, determinism does not explain one's sense of being. So, while Hobbes's philosophy can be used to explain the material world and human behavior in a logical and systematic way, it can be criticized by those who believe in free will. Which side of this argument do you favor? Do you believe there is no such thing as free will?

René Descartes

Unlike Hobbes, the French mathematician and philosopher René Descartes (1596–1650) epitomized the dualistic approach of mind and body. Descartes contributed two important concepts to the modern world. His philosophy argues that knowledge can be created from simple ideas and developed into more complex ideas, and that knowledge is not valid unless we are certain of its authenticity. The process of creating knowledge step-by-step has been

called the "building block theory of knowledge," in which subsequent theories rest on prior, simpler theories. He also argued that what is certain is only that which can be inferred or rationalized because we cannot trust our body or our senses. Descartes believed that the material world could be described in terms of mathematical theories, identified with geometrical extension (Descartes developed "Cartesian coordinates" in geometry), and motion.[13] He believed that all bodies, including living bodies, are in some sense machines.

But Descartes also believed that our being cannot be reduced only to that of a member of a mechanical system. This was due to his belief in a spirit or soul that transcends the material world. Indeed, Descartes believed that the soul is the essence of our being, seen in his famous statement *Cogito, ergo sum:* "I think, therefore I am."[14] Perhaps one of the most influential statements ever made in philosophy, the "Cogito" emerged out of an attempt to prove the existence of God and to develop a way of coming to know reality with absolute certainty. Out of this argument came Descartes' method of rationalism, a way of knowing reality through purely intellectual means.

Descartes, in a powerful argument, claimed to doubt everything, even that he was awake. He eliminated all of his experiences and senses as a means of acquiring absolute knowledge, arguing that they are unreliable sources. As a result, he reduced the state of existence to an act of mind and advocated a way of knowing called *rationalism.* Ironically, Descartes' argument had the result of emphasizing the existence of humanity. By putting the word "I" in the statement "I think, therefore I am," Descartes inadvertently placed humans in a position of importance. Before Descartes, someone might have said, "God thinks, therefore humans are."

Descartes emphasized the use of mathematics to construct new knowledge by starting with simple theorems and moving to the more complex. He viewed the process of constructing new knowledge as being completely the function of reason and argued that this method could be used in any of the sciences to continue to add to the knowledge already developed. Important to education, Descartes' approach implies that the body is less important than the mind as a way of knowing anything.[15] Rationalism argues that absolute knowledge can only be generated through inference or other processes of the mind.

This powerful argument is still prevalent in educational systems today, where matters of the mind are considered more important than matters of the body. One consequence of this position, important to physical educators, is that it becomes difficult to account for the interaction between mind and body. Descartes did not adequately explain how this process occurs, at least to the satisfaction of those involved in the study of human movement.[16] These scholars argue that from Descartes' perspective it is difficult to justify human movement as an educational experience. Do you agree?

While Descartes' approach would seem to reject physical education as education, Hobbes's approach would seem to say that all education is physical education—that is, matter material is all physical and always in motion. Yet we must be careful when drawing this conclusion. It has been noted that the positions of Hobbes and Descartes are *metaphysical positions* attempting to establish the nature of reality.[17] It does not follow that a certain metaphysical position constitutes a specific plan for a physical education program. However, understanding the metaphysical positions of Hobbes and Descartes yields many insights into what types of activities were thought to be of most benefit to people. Understanding these same arguments helps us understand attitudes toward sport and physical education in the twenty-first century. Educators and social critics were significantly affected by these new concepts of mind and body, and these ideas were manifest in their educational philosophies and curriculums.

George Berkeley

George Berkeley (1685–1753), an Irish philosopher and Anglican bishop, is known for his theory of idealism. Unlike many philosophers, Berkeley was not "godless." He sought to reconcile his religious ideals with the empirical basis of science,

and he argued that this could be done if one understood the relationship between perceiver and that which is perceived. Berkeley believed that all that exists is that which either perceives or is perceived. In Berkeley's words, "*esse* is *percipi*."[18] This means that the existence of something depends on its being perceived. Put differently, if you cannot perceive something, it cannot exist. Nothing can exist other than active beings that experience with their senses (perceive) and those things experienced (perceived) by those active beings.

Berkeley's argument has been outlined in the following way:

1. Sensible qualities of objects are nothing but "ideas" in the mind.
2. Physical objects are nothing more than their sensible qualities.
3. Therefore, physical objects are nothing but "ideas" in the mind.[19]

Berkeley used his famous analogy of the tree falling in the forest to illustrate his argument. Berkeley asked a simple question: If a tree falls in the forest, does it make any sound if there is no one there to hear it fall? If we accept Berkeley's philosophy at face value, the answer would be no. No one was around to perceive the noise made by the tree falling, so that sound never existed. However, Berkeley used his argument as part of an attempt to prove the existence of God, and in so doing, he arrived at a different answer. The noise generated by the tree would be perceived by God, the ultimate perceiver. God perceives everything, so the noise exists whether a human hears it or not.

Although this argument may seem silly, it was a necessary one for Berkeley because in his mind it "proved" the existence of both humans and God. In so doing, Berkeley rejected the "godless" approach of Hobbes and his strict materialism in which everything is "body." By arguing for the primacy of perception, Berkeley argued that the existence of the world depends entirely on the perceptive abilities of the mind or soul. Consequently, the body is not necessary to our existence, but the mind is.

Berkeley's metaphysical position was that of a *monist:* Because all of reality depends on perception, there is no division between the mind and the body. Everything is of the mind. Yet Berkeley's argument had one consequence that he could not have foreseen. A result of his chain of reasoning is that our bodily senses are a viable mechanism for perceiving, or knowing, reality. Can you make the argument that kinesiology benefits from any epistemology that places the body in the position of perceiving and dealing with reality?

THE EDUCATORS

Despite the differences between these scientists and philosophers, they shared assumptions about the place of rationality in culture. This consensus is what marks the Age of Science and the Enlightenment as different from the Middle Ages and the Renaissance, and this difference was manifest in the views of educators. These new, or "modern," educators accepted the idea that being human is "natural" and not necessarily evil, and that an individual can change his or her life on earth for the better. These educators are known as "realists" for their advocation of the study of the "real" things of life.

Realism was a radical change from the Middle Ages and the Renaissance, where life on earth was guided by the hope for eternal bliss in heaven. During this time, education consisted of learning to read and write in Latin and Greek, and the texts were those of the Bible and the classical Greek and Roman authors. Methods of instruction were authoritarian and discipline oriented, and students were not necessarily encouraged to concentrate on the present.

Realists seeking to change this situation emphasized three main approaches: (1) humanist realism, (2) social realism, and (3) sense realism. The *humanist realists* used Latin, Greek, and classical literature as a basis for their educational curriculum but rejected the idea that this was the only means of education. They added physical education as a means of creating a well-rounded individual. The *social realists* accepted a modified curriculum of classical literature and added to

this approach instruction in the social graces and political affairs. The *sense realists* were the most radically different from the old style. Sense realists argued that students should be taught in their own language and should learn useful arts and sciences based on scientifically sound principles. All three approaches emphasized the secular, "here-and-now" perspective of their philosophical contemporaries, resulting in an emphasis on skills that can help in everyday life. So, while philosophers paved the way for the modern world to think about nature in a new and "scientific" way and to use more "rational" methods to deal with the problems of life and society, educators put these ideas into practice. Physical activities thus became a means of improving one's life on earth.

Among the three schools of realism, the sense realists were particularly interested in educating girls, although most of the realists were interested as well. Educational opportunities for girls were limited because it was believed that women would never have an opportunity to apply the skills they developed. In addition, even in the Age of Science and the Enlightenment, women were considered inferior to men, and there was some debate as to whether women could be educated. What is important to remember about the realists is that even though some were skeptical about the intellectual prowess of women, they laid the foundation for the public education of women during a time when women were educated only in the home or in the convent for a life of devotion to the church. In so doing, the realists broke away from the traditional treatment of women. Their contemporaries considered them very liberal even though their programs would be considered tentative by today's standards.

François Rabelais

François Rabelais (1483–1553), a French educational theorist, is considered a humanist realist because of his emphasis on the development of the whole person. He published his views in *The Life of Gargantua,* a book that contrasted the style of education of the Renaissance and the Latin grammar school to a new, improved version based on the revolutionary ideas of his times.[20] The former style of education was marked by rote memory drills, reading, and prayer, and concentrated on the spiritual development of the pupil. A critic of this old style of education, Rabelais called for an educational program that would integrate the social, moral, spiritual, and physical aspects of life. While he believed that books were the source of all education and that mastering these texts provided for the education of students, he believed physical activities would help him reach his goal of the well-rounded individual. These activities ranged from horsemanship, martial arts, and hunting to ball playing, running, and swimming. By concentrating on many different types of activities, Rabelais hoped to develop individuals capable of adapting to the many problems in the real world.

Richard Mulcaster

Richard Mulcaster (1530–1611), an English schoolmaster, was one of the sense realists. For Mulcaster, the purpose of education was to develop both the mind and the body, and the senses were the best means of doing so. This meant that experience was more important than studying or reading and that learning one's native language well was as valuable as learning Greek or Latin. Mulcaster also believed that the teaching process should be adapted to the learner, rather than following the formal method of lecture and reading used by the traditional schools.

Mulcaster was among the first educators to emphasize students rather than the subjects being taught. This radical shift reflected the change in philosophy from concentration on the afterlife to concentration on the present. His thoughts on education are described in his book *Positions,* which dealt specifically with physical education.[21] Schoolmasters who proposed an extensive program of physical activities appear to have been rare, and it is this distinction that makes Mulcaster important to the history of physical education. For indoor activities, he recommended reading and speaking out loud, talking, laughing, weeping, holding one's breath, dancing, wrestling, fencing, and climbing. For outdoor activities, he recommended walking, running, leaping, swimming, riding, hunting, shooting, and ball playing. Mulcaster believed that school was better than a tutor, and this facilitated some of the activities he used for physical education. To this end, Mulcaster may be considered the "father" of the modern educational practice of including sport in the curriculum.

Michel de Montaigne

The French essayist Michel de Montaigne (1553–1592) preceded Descartes and Hobbes and was strongly influenced by the humanist movement of the Renaissance that argued for the well-rounded individual. Montaigne, like Hobbes, believed that our experiences are valid and that our senses are an important means by which we learn. And like Descartes, he believed that we have a mind that can be "experienced" when we think. As a monist, Montaigne argued against the dualistic view that the mind and the body were separate, saying that to try to separate the mind from the body was to try something that cannot really be experienced. For Montaigne, the mind

> has such a tight brotherly bond with the body that it abandons me at every turn to follow the body in its need. I take (the mind) aside and flatter it, I work on it, all for nothing. In vain I try to turn (the mind) aside from this bond. . . . There is no sprightliness in (the mind's) productions if there is none in the body at the same time.[22]

Montaigne believed that the two were closely connected and that to separate them was a philosophical convenience: "He who wants to detach his soul, let him do it . . . when his body is ill, to free it from the catagion; at other times, on the contrary, let the soul assist and favor the body and not refuse to take part in its natural pleasures."[23] Montaigne came to this position because he believed that philosophers who advocated dualism were uncomfortable with their bodies and as a result took refuge in the purity of the mind.

Michel de Montaigne is identified as a social realist for his emphasis on the development of character, right habits, manners, morals, and citizenship. A skillful writer, Montaigne described his educational theories in the essays "Of Pedantry," "Of the Education of Children," and "Of the Affection of Fathers to Their Children."[24] Montaigne was trained in the humanist tradition, but he disagreed with the soft lifestyle this sort of education promoted. Instead, he advocated "manly exercise," whereby the child experienced the rougher life in the outdoors. His rejection of the dualistic nature of humans led him to promote physical education as a means of achieving his goals:

> It is not enough to fortify his soul; you must also make his muscles strong. . . . It is not the mind, it is not the body we are training; it is the man and we must not divide him into two parts. Plato says we should not fashion one without the other, but make them draw together like two horses harnessed to a coach. By this saying would it not indicate that he would rather give more care to the body, believing that the mind is benefited at the same time?[25]

The mind and the body should act as one unit, and this could be done by acclimating students to heat and cold, wind and sun. Students should not fear danger and should not have any effeminate characteristics. Montaigne's views were somewhat elitist in that he was trying to develop citizens of the upper classes, which is easily explained given his own upper-class background. However, many of his ideas have been accepted in modern education, which attempts to make them available to everyone.

John Comenius

Czech theologian John Comenius (1592–1671) believed in many of the same ideas as Mulcaster. Comenius differed in that he did not include knightly sports as a means of physical development or even recreation, for he believed that to do so was expensive and useless for the type of students he had. Most people did not need to acquire skills in swordplay, courtly dances, and riding because they could not afford this style of living. Like other sense realists, Comenius believed that exercise served as a respite from other parts of the learning process. Indeed, the argument that physical education exists to refresh the body and enable students to work and study more efficiently can be traced back to Comenius, and this argument is widely used by contemporary physical educators. Sense realists were strongly influenced by Descartes' building-block theory of knowledge and developed a curriculum that moved from the simple to the complex and from present knowledge to the unknown. As a result, classes were taught in a certain logical order, a practice common to contemporary curriculum development; for example, sports skills, foreign languages, and mathematical concepts use this process, moving from beginning to intermediate to advanced knowledge.

John Locke

John Locke (1632–1704), also a social realist, is better known as a philosopher than as an educator. Thomas Jefferson and the framers of the United States Constitution were strongly influenced by his ideas of "life, liberty, and property," adapted in the Constitution to read "life, liberty, and the pursuit of happiness." Trained as a physician, he wrote extensively on philosophy, and his ideas on nature and epistemology strongly influenced the philosophers of the eighteenth century.

In his *Essay Concerning Human Understanding,* Locke developed the philosophical foundation on which many other philosophers and educators based their arguments for reason over revelation.[26] Locke believed that the mind was a *tabula rasa,* or "blank slate," on which the senses of the body acted. Consequently, in Locke's epistemology, the body was of much more importance than in other epistemologies that emphasize the soul or the mind. Locke believed that if you can control a person's experiences, then you can control the formation of the mind, the character, or any other aspect of what a human can become. The result of this chain of reasoning is that the body becomes a means to train all aspects of the person: mind, body, or soul.

He went so far as to argue that physical education was of primary importance in developing an educational foundation. Locke's reasoning influenced the philosophers who followed him. While they may not have agreed with him, they at least had to refute him or risk ridicule for not recognizing the logic of his ideas.

While Locke believed that the body was the vehicle by which the other aspects of the whole person could be educated, he was definitely a dualist. Mind and body were considered to be separate, as the following quote suggests: "A gentleman's more serious employment I look on to be study; and when that demands relaxation and refreshment, it should be in some exercise of the body, which unbends the thought and confirms the health and strength."[27] Our point is not to criticize Locke for his dualistic approach to education as much as it is to show what dualism looks like in practice. Physical activity is used here to *refresh* the individual to pursue more important intellectual pursuits. This understanding of the role of human movement is prevalent in contemporary education, and it can be contrasted with a monistic view of activity that explains movement as a function of the *union* of mind and body. Locke's understanding does not preclude enjoying the activity, however. Locke defined a good recreational activity as one that was inherently enjoyable and that left the participants refreshed and relaxed, an idea in keeping with the Puritan work ethic.

Locke also had an impact as an educator in his time. He wrote "Some Thoughts on Education" for the sons of the wealthy, whom he considered spoiled and soft.[28] Locke argued for the health of students, which could be enhanced through proper diet and exercise. He believed that "a sound mind in a sound body" was essential for maintaining a happy state in the world and a foundation for moral and intellectual training. In so doing, one could develop the knowledge and social skills necessary for a "Man of Business, a Carriage suitable to his Rank and to be eminent and useful to his Country, according to his Station."

THE PHILOSOPHES AND PHYSICAL EDUCATORS

As the eighteenth century progressed, one social class in particular grew not only in size but in hostility to the privileges claimed by the monarchy and the aristocracy. This social class was called the *bourgeoisie* and was composed of the well-educated middle class that was strongly influenced by the new writers of the eighteenth century. The bourgeoisie believed that a free society could be achieved in which each person would be allowed to create life in the manner he saw fit.

These new writers were known as the *philosophes*. It was in an environment of war, social change, and economic growth that the philosophes developed and advocated a new way of thinking to solve age-old problems. The philosophes were French educators, politicians, journalists, and men of letters dedicated to the use of "human reason, science, and education as the best means of building a stable society of free men on earth."[29] They differed from "philosophers" in that they did not develop an entire coherent philosophy as did Plato or Aristotle. Rather, they were much more concerned with practical changes that would occur during their lives. The philosophes were not "separated" from the philosophers. The distinction between the two groups is arbitrary, based on modern scholarship's interpretation of the types of work the two groups did. The philosophes were intellectuals and social critics rather than academic philosophers, and they can be compared with popular social critics of our time, such as newspaper columnists and television pundits.

The Enlightenment was marked by suspicion of any epistemology, or theory of knowledge, based on simple authority, religion, tradition, custom, or faith. It was a secular movement, or one that was divorced from religion, and was subsequently attacked from many quarters because of its "godless" nature. The philosophes rejected much of what the church stood for in education and the development of society and the individual. As one scholar noted,

> The philosophes, could they have been polled in the modern way, would probably have

ranked the Roman Catholic Church—indeed, all Christian churches—as the greatest single corrupting influence of their times. According to the philosophes, priests were selfish, cruel, intolerant. . . . But at bottom the great evil of the church, for the enlightened, was its transcendental and supernatural base, which put faith and revelation above reason.[30]

The position of the philosophes can be contrasted to that of the aristocracy, which relied on tradition, custom, and religion for its authority. The philosophes sought to undermine the "Old Guard" to improve their lot, and they developed arguments for a freer society in order to do so. They offered the first model of how to build a community out of completely "natural" ideas, or those ideas generated by humans through their powers of reason. Out of the ideas of the philosophes, four common principles emerge:

(1) Man is not natively depraved; (2) the end of life is life itself, the good life on earth instead of the beatific life after death; (3) man is capable, guided solely by the light of reason and experience, of perfecting the good life on earth; and (4) the first and essential condition of the good life on earth is the freeing of men's minds from the bonds of ignorance and superstition, and of their bodies from the arbitrary oppression of the constituted authorities.[31]

The philosophes believed that the newly created society based on these principles would then be more responsive to the immediate needs and desires of every individual. The literate classes of Europe, with the exception of those that stood to lose power, like the church and the monarchies, promoted the ideals of the Enlightenment. These groups believed that the realization of Enlightenment ideals could not fail to benefit them in the way that each desired.[32] What made the philosophes so different was that they were effective social and educational critics in their time, and that no such group had existed since the Sophists in ancient Greece. They did not lead the changes in eighteenth-century Europe as much as they represented them. The ideas they articulated were expressed by many intellectuals.

As educators, the philosophes had several positions in common. First was their faith in nature as the guide by which humans should live. Another commonality was their view that children should be allowed childlike activities because the philosophes did not wish to limit play expression. Play was felt to be a natural activity that could be used to develop other human faculties, and so those activities children seemed to inherently enjoy should be encouraged. Eighteenth-century educators accepted Locke's idea of how children should be taught: "They must not be hindered from being children, or from playing, or doing as children; but from doing ill. All other liberty is to be allowed them."[33] The result of this type of thinking was that physical activity was viewed as a matter of primary importance.

Now that we have a basic understanding of the philosophes' ideology, we can turn our attention to perhaps the most famous of them all—an educator who was a champion of exercise, physical education, health, and athletic vigor.

Jean-Jacques Rousseau

Jean-Jacques Rousseau (1712–1788) was born in Switzerland, the child of a Swiss mother and a French father. He had a troubled childhood: His mother died shortly after he was born, and his father neglected him, which may explain his failure to care for his own five children. (Rousseau's family situation was ironic, for while his classic work *Émile* is one of the most famous books on education, Rousseau's children became workers and peasants because of their lack of education.) He held a variety of odd jobs throughout his youth: notary, engraver, lackey, secretary, and tutor. Rousseau even studied for a short time to enter the priesthood. This varied experiential background may explain Rousseau's sympathy for the plight of the peasantry, who worked hard yet had little hope of material gain in eighteenth-century France. These experiences, combined with years of self-study, led Rousseau to write an essay that was one of the single greatest literary influences on the French Revolution: *The Social Contract*.[34]

Rousseau believed that the will of the people constituted a kind of social contract that was the basis of society. Like Locke and Hobbes, Rousseau believed that society was composed of autonomous individuals and that each person needed to be educated in a way that would make him or her a good citizen. Therefore, how each citizen was educated was important to the determination of what society looked like. This was one of Rousseau's great contributions to modern education: his view that the individual and the corresponding relationship to the community are strongly influenced by the educational process. While this idea was not new (Plato understood this relationship and described his corresponding educational ideas in the *Republic*), Rousseau reiterated it in a way that is now taken for granted in modern education.

The educational philosophy of Rousseau can be summarized by the first sentence of *Émile:* "Everything is good as it leaves the hands of the Author of things; everything degenerates in the hands of man."[35] In short, "nature" should determine what constitutes a good education, not the traditional methods used by civilization. Rousseau differed from contemporary educators in his belief that individuals were essentially good and that the corrupting influence on individual character was civilization, not original sin. Consequently, Rousseau argued that the ideal educational curriculum should follow the whims of nature and make the educational process as "natural" as possible.

With his emphasis on nature, Rousseau argued that the mind and the body work in harmony with one another. Yet we should not call him a monist, for he recognized the differences between mind and body and ascribed to each a separate function, with the mind directing the body:

> It is a most pitiable error to imagine that the exercise of the body is harmful to the operations of the mind, as if these two activities ought not to move together in harmony and that the one ought not always to direct the other.[36]

Direction was the function of the mind, yet it was to work in harmony with the body. So close was this bond that the quality of one affected the performance of the other. Indeed, the ability of the mind to direct was closely related to the wellness of the body:

> Thus his body and his mind are exercised together. Acting always according to his own thought and not someone else's, he continually unites two operations: the more he makes himself strong and robust, the more he becomes sensible and judicious. This is the way one day to have what are believed incompatible and what are united in almost all great men: strength of body and strength of soul; a wise man's reason and an athlete's vigor.[37]

In *Émile,* Rousseau described this ideal education process for both boys and girls. The child should be educated continuously from birth through adulthood, an idea we now take for granted but one that was new with Rousseau. Rousseau's first requirement in the education of the child was the development of the child's health. If this could be facilitated, then the child had a strong foundation upon which to build other aspects of his or her being. Rousseau believed, then, that the body was of primary importance in learning, not of secondary importance as argued by many of his contemporaries. It was only after the body was developed and made healthy that one could develop the properties of the mind:

> Do you, then, want to cultivate your pupil's intelligence? Cultivate the strengths it ought to govern. Exercise his body continually; make him robust and healthy in order to make him wise and reasonable. Let him work, be active, run, yell, always be in motion. Let him be a man in his vigor, and soon he will be one in his reason.[38]

The powers of reason were not of secondary importance, however. They were to be developed after the physical aspects of the individual. Rousseau's logic was powerful and persuasive, and he sought to elevate physical education to a position not seen since the time of the ancient Greeks.

Rousseau began with the idea that children should be outdoors and active. In so doing, the child would develop his senses through his experiences. The senses would then provide the background against which ideas took shape. By moving and touching everything, seeing and hearing, tasting and smelling, the child would begin to associate the objects of the external world with the five senses. "It is only by movement that we learn that there are things which are not us."[39] Emotions follow, along with the concepts of extension and motion.

As the child aged, Rousseau wished to develop the senses through specific physical activities:

> There are purely natural and mechanical exercises which serve to make the body robust without giving any occasion for the exercise of judgment. Swimming, running, jumping, spinning a top, throwing stones, all that is quite good. But have we only arms and legs? . . . Do not exercise only strength; exercise all the senses which direct it. Get from each of them all they can do.[40]

And,

> In the morning let Emile run barefoot in all seasons, in his room, on the stairs, in the garden. . . . Let him know how to jump long and high, to climb a tree, to get over a wall. Let him learn to keep his balance; let all his movements and gestures be ordered according to the laws of equilibrium. . . . If I were a dancing master . . . I would take him to the foot of a cliff. There I would show him what attitude he must take, how he must bear his body and his head, what movements he must make, in what way he must place now his foot, now his hand, so as to follow lightly the steep, rough, uneven paths and to bound from peak to peak in climbing up as well as down. I would make him the emulator of a goat rather than of a dancer of the Opera.[41]

It would seem from this quote that Rousseau had the physical educator in mind when he created the ideal teacher! Rousseau hoped that by performing a variety of tasks, the child would develop the skills necessary to perform well in life, and it was the role of the teacher to provide the appropriate experiences:

> When a child plays with the shuttlecock, he practices his eye and arm in accuracy; when he whips a top, he increases his strength by using it but without learning anything. I have sometimes asked why the same games of skill men have not given to children: tennis, croquet, billiards, football, musical instruments. . . . To bound from one end of the room to the other, to judge a ball's bounce while still in the air, to return it with a hand strong and sure—such games are less suitable for a grown man than useful for forming him.[42]

Rousseau was one of the first modern educators to promote the education of women. Yet his model is not what we would use today:

> Men's morals, their passions, their tastes, their pleasures, their very happiness also depend on women. Thus the whole education of women ought to relate to men. To please men, to be useful to them, to make herself loved and honored by them, to raise them when young, to care for them when grown, to counsel them, to console them, to make their lives agreeable and sweet—those are the duties of women at all times, and they ought to be taught from childhood.[43]

To say the least, by contemporary standards, Rousseau was a "chauvinist pig." But by his standards, he was a daring educational revolutionary, arguing that women have been endowed by nature "to think, to judge, to love, to know, to cultivate their minds as well as their looks."[44] And, like boys, girls should develop their bodies first:

> Since the body is born, so to speak, before the soul, the body ought to be cultivated first. This order is common to the two sexes, but the aim of this cultivation is different. For man this aim is the development of strength; for woman it is the development of attractiveness. Not that these qualities ought to exclude one another; their rank order is merely reversed in each sex: women need enough strength to do everything they do with grace; men need enough adroitness to do everything they do with facility.[45]

While we cannot learn much from Rousseau with respect to specific physical education programs for girls, we do know that he was ahead of his time. This implies that his attitude toward the education of women, as "barbaric" as it appears, was still better than that of his peers! And in recognizing this, we know much about that which Rousseau reacted against. Education for girls must have been stifling by today's standards, emphasizing those qualities in women that would make them desirable in marriage. Rousseau argued that women, too, were human beings, and should develop their human qualities in addition to their looks.

Rousseau did not live to see the revolutions he advocated in either politics or education. He died one year before the French Revolution and before his ideas could take root in educational institutions. His impact lived on, however, in the acceptance of his ideas by the most progressive schools of the eighteenth century.

Johann Bernhard Basedow

If Rousseau was the educational innovator in theory, the German Johann Bernhard Basedow (1723–1790) was the educational innovator in practice. More of an educator than a social critic like Rousseau and the philosophes, Basedow was a radical in the implementation of the ideas of the philosophes. Basedow founded his school, the Philanthropinum, in 1774, modeled on the theories of Rousseau. (Ironically, *Émile* was more influential in Germany than it was in France; in Germany, the book was used as a guideline for developing a new "aristocracy of worth" based on the dignity of man and the rightness of nature.[46] Basedow was an intellectual in his own right, having published several books on educational theories and methods. After the publication of *Address to Philanthropists and Men of Property on Schools and Studies and Their Influence on the Public Wealth,* he was able to secure funding for his school from the Duke of Anhalt, Prince Leopold Franz. Basedow opened the Philanthropinum in Dessau, later renamed the Dessau Educational Institute.

Basedow combined the educational ideas of Rousseau with those of Francis Bacon and John Comenius. He emphasized the use of the senses in the learning process and used nature as a guide. This approach led Basedow to treat children as children rather than as small adults, an idea we take for granted in modern education. In Basedow's time, children dressed as adults did: in formal coats, with powdered wigs, rouged cheeks, and small swords. Basedow rejected this practice and instead argued children should "act their age" and engage in activities appropriate for them according to nature. Children at the Philanthropinum dressed in simple uniforms that allowed for the freedom of movement called for in Rousseau's *Émile,* and they were encouraged to act like children instead of adults.

According to the Philanthropinum's prospectus, approximately half of each ten-hour school day was to be spent in intellectual activities, and the other half in bodily activities. For the physical activities, three hours were allotted to recreational activities like fencing, riding, dancing, and music. Two hours were to be spent in manual labor such as carpentry and masonry. Once the children were of the proper age, they were taught the appropriate martial arts, and for two months in the summer, they lived in tents and engaged in hunting, fishing, boating, and swimming activities.[47]

It is not surprising, given the innovative nature of the Philanthropinum, that the teacher responsible for the physical education activities is considered by many to be the first "modern" physical educator. The program was developed by Johann Friedrich Simon, who had students of different ages engage in activities appropriate to their "natural" abilities and desires. Younger students, for instance, engaged in "Greek gymnastics"—contests in running, wrestling, throwing, and jumping, similar to the activities of the ancient Greek games. The older students practiced the "knightly exercises," which included dancing, fencing, riding, and vaulting on live horses. Other activities included shuttlecock, tennis, skittles, and playing with a large, air-filled ball.[48]

While many of the ideas put into action in the Philanthropinum are accepted today, such as specialists in physical education, outdoor activities, and specialized equipment and facilities, these ideas were not nearly as accepted in Basedow's time. At most, the Philanthropinum had 53 students, and it closed in 1793 because it was not financially solvent. In addition, Basedow was a difficult man to work with. He was described as "coarse, arrogant, argumentative, vulgar in his language, and given to drunkenness. It is amazing that a school could be entrusted to such a man."[49] Basedow resigned in 1778, and the school closed 15 years later in 1793. Yet the school had a significant impact on education in Europe because of its innovative nature and the quality of the teachers.

Johann Friedrich GutsMuths

While Simon may be credited with being the first "modern" physical educator, Johann Friedrich GutsMuths (1759–1839) legitimized the profession of physical education with the quality of his work. While he also taught geography, French, and technology, physical education was his favorite. GutsMuths was the second physical education teacher at the Schnepfenthal Educational Institute. The first, Christian Andre, duplicated nearly all of the exercises that he had seen at the Philanthropinum. GutsMuths adopted the program Andre established and continued to develop it for the next 50 years. His teaching techniques and writings became the standard by which subsequent physical educators were judged.

When visitors arrived at the Schnepfenthal Educational Institute, one of the first things they noticed was the physical layout of the school. Situated on an estate near Gotha, Germany, the campus was in an ideal location for outdoor activities, and when weather did not permit, indoor facilities were available. Many of the activities had to be performed outdoors—climbing ropes, masts, and rope ladders, and swinging required the use of trees and other large apparatus. In addition, students balanced rods on their fingers or performed exercises while standing on one foot. Swimming was a highly valued exercise, and GutsMuths wrote a book, *Manual on the Art of Swimming* (1798), on how to perform

and teach the activity. In another book, *Gymnastics for the Young* (1793), GutsMuths classified his exercises according to how they developed the individual: (1) walking and running; (2) jumping, free and with apparatus; (3) lifting and carrying exercises of the back muscles such as pulling, pushing, thrusting, and wrestling; (4) fencing; (5) climbing; (6) exercises to maintain equilibrium, or balancing with the aid of apparatus; (7) throwing and archery; (8) bathing and swimming; (9) exercises of suppleness, to train the aesthetic sense, willpower, and organs of speech; (10) dancing; and (11) exercises to train the senses. GutsMuths led camping expeditions, some of which lasted four days, to help students feel at one with nature. Schnepfenthal became famous for its well-lit and well-ventilated rooms, and the wholesome but simple food gave students a healthy glow that impressed those who came to visit.

GutsMuths used several ideas to develop his physical education programs. He believed that many educational institutions were not aware of the value of gymnastics, or what we call physical education. He argued that a nation should promote the health of its people to become a stronger nation. GutsMuths believed that the best way to develop health was through his gymnastics program. This idea was attractive to Germans, who argued that the separate German states should be united as one strong nation. He also believed that exercises should be fun and should have as their purpose the harmonizing of the mind and the body. This idea of the blending of mind and body was different from the philosophies guiding most other educational institutions, which emphasized the development only of the mind through reading and oral repetition. Like Rousseau, GutsMuths argued that the development of the body should come first, and only after the body was developed could the mind and its processes be developed. And like Rousseau, GutsMuths argued that girls and women should engage in light gymnastics and games, but not in the heavy work of men. In so doing, they would become healthy, refined, and pleasing.[50]

GutsMuths had an immediate impact on physical education in the more progressive schools of his time. Perhaps most significant is that people began to place their children in programs that taught gymnastics. With increased demand, schools began to teach it, and universities began to study gymnastics in a manner we would recognize today.[51] Although he was not the first modern physical educator, GutsMuths is considered the real founder of physical education because of his 50 years of service and the books he wrote. *Gym-* *nastics for the Young* and *Games* (1796) were the first manuals published by an experienced professional in physical education and were based on the accepted medical and physiological principles of his time. GutsMuths also published *Book of Gymnastics for Sons of the Fatherland* (1817) and *Catechism of Gymnastics, a Manual for Teachers and Pupils* (1818).[52]

SUMMARY

The Age of Science and the Enlightenment witnessed the growth of a belief in the powers of human beings to understand and manipulate their environment. This belief was at first limited primarily to small groups of intellectuals, but as time passed these ideas came to represent the dominant belief system in the Western world. The philosophers, scientists, educators, and an increasingly well-read public began to live in the eighteenth century according to the new philosophies developed during the seventeenth century. With the colonization of North America, a new realm was formed whose leaders were well versed in Enlightenment ideas, and these ideas eventually found their home in the Declaration of Independence and the Constitution.

During the Enlightenment, the methods of science were applied to many other aspects of life such as politics, social thought, and philosophy. The new, scientific ways of Newton, Galileo, Hobbes, Locke, and Descartes were the "light" that guided humanity toward the basic harmony of interests that we are comfortable with today. As a consequence, many of our contemporary attitudes stem from the attitudes of intellectuals who argued for change during the Enlightenment.

Significant ideas that had their genesis during the Enlightenment are taken for granted in contemporary education, such as democratic education. Indeed, education is intimately connected to the Enlightenment tradition. Physical education was similarly affected by the Enlightenment, especially because the many Enlightenment critics had so much to say about the virtues of human movement as a means of creating the ideal individual and community, and the role that "nature" had in the development of the whole human being. It is no accident, then, that the first physical educators in "modern times" lived during the Enlightenment, and many of their ideas are still with us.

DISCUSSION QUESTIONS

1. How did the Age of Science influence beliefs about the body?

2. To what extent did the Age of Science and the Enlightenment influence the educational curriculum?

3. What types of physical education programs evolved during the Age of Science and the Enlightenment?

4. How did Hobbes's materialism have an impact on the development of physical education? How did Hobbes view free will and concepts of the mind and spirit?

5. How did Descartes' rationalism have an impact on the development of physical education? How did Descartes view the body?

6. How did Newton have an impact on how we view the body? How are his "Three Laws of Motion" used in physical education today?

7. What is Montaigne's metaphysical position? How is it different from that of Hobbes and Descartes? Does he seem to support physical education?

8. How was Rousseau's *Émile* representative of Enlightenment thinking? How does *Émile* differ from educational philosophies that preceded it? What type of education would Rousseau provide for women?

9. Explain the contributions of the Realists to the education of women.

10. What contribution did Johann F. GutsMuths make to the development of physical education?

11. Who was Johann B. Basedow? What educational and philosophical innovations did he bring to physical education?

INTERNET RESOURCES

The European Enlightenment
www.wsu.edu/~dee/ENLIGHT/ENLIGHT.HTM
Represents a good introduction to the European Enlightenment; contains information on the history, culture, and philosophers of the time, plus a glossary of terms and good links.

University of Evansville: Creative Impulsive
http://history.evansville.net/enlighte.html
Offers good resources on the Enlightenment.

Roots of Consciousness
www.williamjames.com/History/ENLIGHT.htm
Provides discussions related to the ideas of Descartes, Berkeley, and Newton.

Jean-Jacques Rousseau Association
www.wabash.edu/rousseau
Is dedicated to students and scholars of Jean-Jacques Rousseau.

Visit the *History and Philosophy of Sport and Physical Education* Online Learning Center (www.mhhe.com/mechikoff6e) for additional information and study tools.

SUGGESTIONS FOR FURTHER READING

Brailsford, D. "Puritanism and Sport in Seventeenth Century England." *Stadion* I, no. 2: 316–30.

Burke, R. K. "Naturalism and Physical Education." In *The Philosophic Process in Physical Education,* by Elwood Craig Davis. Philadelphia: Lea & Febiger, 1971, 56–80.

Gerber, E. "François Rabelais," "Michel de Montaigne," "Richard Mulcaster," "John Amos Comenius," "John Locke." In *Innovators and Institutions in Physical Education.* Philadelphia: Lea & Febiger, 1971, 54–75.

Kleinman, S. "The Classic Philosophers and Their Metaphysical Positions." In *Physical Education: An*

Interdisciplinary Approach, by Robert Singer, David Lamb, John Loy, Robert Malina, and Seymour Kleinman. New York: Macmillan, 1972.

Ross, S. "Cartesian Dualism and Physical Education: Epistemological Incompatibility." In *Mind and Body: East Meets West,* ed. S. Kleinman. Champaign, IL: Human Kinetics, 1986, 15–25.

Rousseau, J.-J. *Émile.* Trans. Allan Bloom. New York: Basic Books, 1979.

Struna, N. L. "The Declaration of Sport Reconsidered." *Canadian Journal of History of Sport* 14 (December 1983): 44–68.

NOTES

1. Stephen E. Toulmin, *Cosmopolis: The Hidden Agenda of Modernity* (New York: Free Press, 1990).

2. J. Bronowski and Bruce Mazlish, *The Western Intellectual Tradition: From Leonardo to Hegel* (New York: Harper & Brothers, 1960). As Bronowski noted, the economic and social issues that led to the Puritan Revolution were expressed in religious and political terms. This terminology is indicative of how economics, social class, politics, religion, and sport were interwoven in sixteenth-century England.

3. Dennis Brailsford, "Puritanism and Sport in Seventeenth Century England," *Stadion* I, no. 2, 316–30.

4. Will Durant, *The Reformation* (New York: Simon & Schuster, 1957).

5. The association of science and philosophy has survived to this day at the older universities like Oxford, where a chair of Experimental Philosophy still exists. This person is engaged in what we now know as science, not philosophy.

6. Abraham Wolf, *History of Science, Technology, and Philosophy in the Sixteenth and Seventeenth Centuries* (London: Allen & Unwin, 1960), 36.

7. Quoted in Maurice Cranston, "Francis Bacon," *The Encyclopedia of Philosophy,* vol. 1 (New York: Macmillan/Free Press, 1967), 235.

8. Dagobert D. Runes, ed., "Francis Bacon," *The Standard Dictionary of Philosophy* (New York: Philosophical Library, 1983).

9. Dudley Shapere, "Newtonian Mechanics and Mechanical Explanation," *The Encyclopedia of Philosophy,* vol. 5 (New York: Macmillan/Free Press, 1967), 491.

10. Frederick Copleston, *A History of Philosophy,* vol. IV (London: Burns & Oates, 1969).

11. Philosophers differed from the philosophes only in that the philosophers developed more formal, rigorous systems of thought. Some contemporary philosophers no longer differentiate between the two groups. See Crane Brinton, "Enlightenment," *The Encyclopedia of Philosophy,* vol. 3 (New York: Macmillan, 1967), 519–25.

12. Bronowski and Mazlish, *Western Intellectual Tradition.*

13. John Dewey, *Types of Thinking* (New York: Philosophical Library, 1984).

14. René Descartes, *Meditations,* trans. Laurence J. Lafleur (New York: Liberal Arts Press, 1951).

15. Saul Ross, "Cartesian Dualism and Physical Education: Epistemological Incompatibility," in *Mind and Body: East Meets West,* ed. S. Kleinman (Champaign, IL.: Human Kinetics, 1986), 15–25.

16. Ibid.

17. Seymour Kleinman, "The Classic Philosophers and Their Metaphysical Positions," *Physical Education: An Interdisciplinary Approach,* by Robert Singer, David Lamb, John Loy, Robert Malina, and Seymour Kleinman (New York: Macmillan, 1972), 337.

18. George Berkeley, *The Principles of Human Knowledge* (Cleveland, OH: World, 1963), 18.

19. Kleinman, "The Classic Philosophers."

20. François Rabelais, *The Five Books of Gargantua and Pantagruel* (New York: Modern Library, 1936).

21. Richard Mulcaster, *Positions: Wherein Those Primitive Circumstances Be Examined, Which Are Necessary for the Training Up of Children, Either for Skill in Their Booke, or Health in Their Bodies* (London: Thomas Vautrollier, 1581).

22. Michel de Montaigne, quoted in Toulmin, *Cosmopolis,* 37–38.

23. Ibid.

24. Michel de Montaigne, *The Essays of Michael Lord of Montaigne,* vol. I and II, trans. John Florio (New York: E. P. Dutton, 1927).

25. Ibid.

26. John Locke, *Essay Concerning Human Understanding,* 5th ed., ed. J. W. Yolton (London: Cambridge University Press, 1970).

27. John Locke, "Some Thoughts Concerning Education," *Essays by John Locke* (London: Ward Lock, 1883), 153.

28. Robert H. Quick, *Some Thoughts on Education by John Locke* (Cambridge: University Press, 1880).

29. Anchor, *Enlightenment Tradition,* ix.

30. Ibid., 520.

31. Ibid., 7–8.

32. Ibid.

33. Locke is quoted in Deobold Van Dalen, Elmer Mitchell, and Bruce Bennett, *A World History of Physical Education* (Englewood Cliffs, NJ: Prentice-Hall, 1953), 194.

34. Ellen Gerber, "Jean-Jacques Rousseau," *Innovators and Institutions in Physical Education* (Philadelphia: Lea & Febiger, 1971), 76–82.

35. Jean-Jacques Rousseau, *Émile,* trans. Allan Bloom (New York: Basic Books, 1979), 37.

36. Ibid., 118.

37. Ibid., 119.

38. Ibid.

39. Ibid.

40. Ibid., 132.

41. Ibid., 139–40.

42. Ibid., 146–47.

43. Ibid., 365.

44. Ibid., 364.

45. Ibid., 365.

46. Ellen Gerber, "The Philanthropinum," *Innovators and Institutions in Physical Education* (Philadelphia: Lea & Febiger, 1971), 83–86.

47. Ibid.

48. Ibid., 85.

49. Ibid.

50. Emmett A. Rice, John Hutchinson, and Mabel Lee, *A Brief History of Physical Education,* 5th ed. (New York: Ronald Press, 1969).

51. Ibid.

52. C. W. Hackensmith, *History of Physical Education* (New York: Harper & Row, 1966).

CHAPTER **8**

Philosophical Positions of the Body and the Development of Physical Education

Contributions of the Germans, Swedes, and Danes in Nineteenth-Century Europe

O B J E C T I V E S

Upon completing this chapter, you will be able to:

■ Discuss how the philosophy of idealism affected the Western world.

■ Discuss how, as an educational philosophy, idealism influences the development of physical education and sport.

■ Understand the nature of the self as an essential aspect of human existence and how it contributes to idealist thought.

■ Understand the nature of knowledge as an essential aspect of human existence and how it contributes to idealist thought.

■ Identify the contributions of the German idealists—Immanuel Kant, Johann Fichte, and Georg Hegel—to metaphysical and epistemological positions regarding the body, and their impact, via inference, on the historical development of physical education and essence of sport.

■ Identify the historical and philosophical contributions of selected educators to the value placed on a mind-and-body education.

■ Identify the historical and philosophical contributions to the value of play, physical education, and sport made by (1) Johann Heinrich Pestalozzi, (2) Friedrich Wilhelm August Froebel, (3) Friedrich Ludwig Jahn, (4) Charles Follen, (5) Charles Beck, (6) Francis Lieber, (7) Franz Nachtegall, and (8) Per Henrik Ling.

■ Discuss the belief held by Niccolò Machiavelli (1469–1527) that "the end justifies the means" and describe the extent to which this belief prevails today in sport and society.

INTRODUCTION

In the Western world, the philosophy of idealism can be traced back to the beliefs and logic articulated by two sages of ancient Athens, Socrates and Plato. Idealism has competed with naturalism for adherents since ancient times. According to *naturalism,* all events, human and natural, share the same character and can be explained as a process inherent in nature; that is, nature is reliable and dependable. In this chapter, we will discuss the general parameters of idealism with initial concentration on the German idealists of the nineteenth century and their role in developing a philosophical position that had an impact on the body and physical education. Then we will turn our attention to the historical role of education during this era, concentrating on the development of physical education under the watchful eyes of (1) Johann Heinrich Pestalozzi, (2) Friedrich Wilhelm August Froebel, (3) Friedrich Ludwig Jahn, (4) Charles Follen, (5) Charles Beck, (6) Francis Lieber, (7) Franz Nachtegall, and (8) Per Henrik Ling. However, we must first discuss idealism and the proponents of German idealism, namely, Immanuel Kant, Johann Fichte, and Georg Hegel.

The tenets of idealism relative to the body, purpose of education, and corresponding epistemological beliefs are significant to physical education. *Idealism* evolved in ancient Greece, as did other philosophical schools. The ancient Greeks were interested in the "ideal" development of man—the complete development of corporeal, spiritual, and intellectual aspects of human existence. These three areas of personal development have occupied a prominent position in the philosophical beliefs of many physical educators and coaches. The German idealists provided physical education with philosophical underpinnings, which helped to justify physical education as a means to develop the ideal individual. The German idealists relied on the work of the ancient Greek philosophers to support their beliefs. Idealism is interested in ethics: establishing a code of conduct that helps us determine the proper course of action as opposed to an improper or unethical course of action (determining right from wrong). Ethics traditionally has manifested in physical education and sport as sportsmanship.

IDEALISM

Idealists from both ancient Greece and nineteenth-century Germany focused much of their energy and effort on three topics: (1) the existence of God, (2) the self, and (3) knowledge. These issues compose the fabric of the metaphysical (God and self) and epistemological (knowledge—how we come to know things) positions that help form the major components of idealism. These components are not limited to idealism but form the basic tenets of all philosophies. Two other components of idealism are logic and axiology, which address ethical, aesthetic, religious, and social values, and which also are manifest in other philosophical schools.

According to idealism, reality is mind. (If this statement appears to be abstract and somewhat mind-boggling, don't panic!) Idealists believe that the entire universe is that which is conceived by the mind; the world of material objects is secondary. In other words, what the mind or spirit experiences and perceives as real is essentially authentic. For example, idealism holds that the world we actually exist in is an imperfect world. However, we are able to visualize or conceive of a perfect world, which according to idealism also must exist and so be real. The fact that we have an *idea* of a perfect world is evidence that it exists. The use of logic is essential to idealism. Since the idea is conceived by the mind, idealistic logic dictates that in all probability it exists, because according to idealism, reality is what the mind is able to comprehend.

The mind, to the idealist, is composed of a spiritual quality, which logically results in the view that *ultimate reality,* as it exists, is beyond the phenomenal, sensory-perceived secular world. In contrast, the *basic, fundamental nature of reality* to the idealist is mind or reason, which manifests itself in everyday consciousness. At this point it will be helpful to distinguish between two philosophical views inherent in idealism: (1) metaphysical idealism and (2) epistemological idealism.

Metaphysical idealism analyzes the universe as a psychic or mental reality; all "things" in the universe are linked by an ideal element that can be logically deduced. Plato, St. Augustine, and, to a lesser degree, Aristotle were proponents of metaphysical idealism. The difficulty with metaphysical idealism, like most metaphysical inquiries, is that the facts or evidence in support of the position are obtained through deductive and subjective logic, which delights the skeptics who oppose metaphysical inquiry. *Epistemological idealism,* on the other hand, approaches the study, and indeed the actual identification of reality with "mentally knowable" data, which are perceptible truths.[1] Whatever is "out there" beyond our minds, all we can know, is what is in our minds. Epistemological idealism is limited to reality determined by the mind—by the ability to engage in critical thought. Metaphysical idealism is vast because of the belief in an infinite, and therefore incomprehensible, element that links everything together. Metaphysical idealism has its roots in ancient Greek philosophy. Plato and Socrates relied on metaphysical idealism to determine reality. Idealism can use both inductive and deductive reasoning.

In general, what do idealists actually agree on and believe? To reiterate, the three primary subjects that idealism investigates are (1) the existence of God, (2) the personal self, and (3) the acquisition of valid knowledge.

The Self

The reality of our existence, in philosophical terms, rests with the acknowledgment that the *self* is a certainty. This question about self as a certainty is abstract philosophizing. We refer back to René Descartes, discussed in Chapter 7, because he was able to provide insight into the reality of the self. Kleinman analyzed Descartes' beliefs as follows:

> The nature of the body and that of the soul have nothing in common. Thus, these two entities or substances may be regarded as substances distinct in kind. Therefore. . . the soul, or mind, needs no knowledge of, nor must it

have dependence upon the body, in order to exist.[2]

In his *Meditations on First Philosophy,* Descartes decided that if he really was going to "know things" as they truly exist, he must rid himself of all that he had been taught and even doubt his own existence or self.[3] Descartes, as you remember, eventually concluded through deduction that he could not have faith in what his physical senses revealed to him and therefore could not rely on prior experiences to be real or authentic. Descartes continued his logic and inquiry in the *Meditations* to the point where he started to doubt his own existence or self: What am I—body, mind, soul? Do I actually exist? It was the doubt that Descartes had about his existence that actually rescued him from his quandary. Doubt became one of the most direct routes to the discovery of the self. Donald Butler states that "in doubting everything, as Descartes did, even to the point of questioning if the world about us is any more real than our dreams, we can scarcely fail to observe before long that there is someone who is doubting. Doubt is thought and thought involves a thinker."[4] In Descartes' classic statement "I think, therefore I am," Descartes' "self" was mindful activity, thereby confirming the logic of idealism that reality is mind—that which is determined to be real has been figured out by the mind, by rational thought. The senses, according to Descartes, did not assist the mind in determining reality. Descartes did not believe it was important to develop the body. Fortunately, idealists believe it is important to develop the body, and generally are supportive of physical education, just like the ancient Greeks.

Knowledge

Idealists assert that understanding the nature of knowledge will logically clarify the nature of reality. In other words, ideals that are accepted as true and authentic must be derived from evidence. The *evidence* can be established by the process of logic using both inductive and deductive reasoning. Like anything else, the initial data that our sensory experiences provide us must be interpreted and validated as authentic and true or as unreliable and inaccurate. Earle Zeigler describes truth for the idealist:

> Truth for idealists is orderly and systematic. A test for truth is its coherence with knowledge that has been previously established. An individual, therefore, attains truth for himself by examining the wisdom of the past through his own mind. Everything that exists has a relationship to something else and is intertwined. Reality, viewed in this way, is a system of logic and order—a logic and order that has been established by the Universal mind. Experimental testing helps to determine what the truth really is with the chips falling where they may.[5]

THE GERMAN IDEALISTS: KANT, FICHTE, AND HEGEL

The idealist believes that the world and the universe are primarily spiritual (spiritual being part of the perfect ideal). Pure idealists do not accept the theory of evolution, which in part portrays humankind as high-grade monkeys. Humans are composed of more than the corporeal; they each have a soul, and this alone places them in a higher order than any creature inhabiting the earth. The soul is the "link" to the spiritual nature of reality, which to the idealist is the only true reality—ultimate reality is spiritual, which may be manifest in mind. Bishop George Berkeley (1685–1753), one of Ireland's major contributors to philosophy, believed that the world has meaning because our minds are able to discern it. Because worldly experience allows us, through the mind, to assimilate and extract quality and meaning from our existence, "something" must exist that provides the elements of quality and meaning. Berkeley identified this "something" as the universal mind or God that provides quality and meaning as a process. Ever the idealist, Berkeley supported the idealistic concept that reality is mind; in this case, ultimate reality is the universal mind. German idealists did not necessarily identify their belief in ultimate ideals with the traditional Western belief in God.

Having presented some general ideas about idealism, we now turn our attention to the German idealists. Before we begin our discussion of Kant, Fichte, and Hegel, it is historically relevant to provide a brief account of the relationship between these three giants of philosophy. Immanuel Kant is revered as one of the greatest philosophers who ever lived. From an idealistic position, he addressed epistemological and metaphysical questions such as personal freedom, the reality of the self, moral law, God, and immortality. Kant's interest in ethics was of considerable importance. He developed the concept known as the "categorical imperative," which will be presented later in this chapter. Sport philosophy has tied Kant's categorical imperative to the ideal that serves as the foundation of sportsmanship. It is interesting to note that Kant did not identify with any form of organized religious worship during adulthood because of his disgust with the primitive forms of religion he had encountered in his younger days.

Kant received his education at Königsberg University, where he later returned to teach and achieved full professorship after 15 years of service. Johann Gottlieb Fichte was so spellbound by and in awe of the great master that early on he traveled to Königsberg to discuss philosophical issues with Kant. However, Kant dismissed Fichte as yet another student who obviously did not know the first thing about the philosophical process. Fichte was not to be denied. He stayed around long enough to produce an article that examined an area of Kant's philosophy that had eluded and perplexed even the great master himself. Kant was so impressed by the article that he proclaimed Fichte a "philosopher." Fichte later became the chair of the philosophy department at the University of Berlin, a position eventually occupied by Georg Hegel. It was Fichte who was able to link the philosophy of Kant with that of Hegel.[6]

Immanuel Kant

The work of Kant (1724–1804) is difficult to comprehend, and therefore the student of Kant must exercise patience and persistence. As Butler states:

"Because of the great comprehensiveness and caliber of his thought, it often seems that there is no end to the detailed excursions on which he takes the reader."[7] He did not publish his first major book until he was 57 years old. Kant asked one of his friends to read *Critique of Pure Reason,*[8] and the friend replied that he was sure he would lose his ability to reason (along with his mind!) if he read it through to the end.

Kant could be pedantic. In *Critique of Pure Reason,* he made a complete and thorough analysis of the reasoning process and presented his theory of knowledge. He concluded, in part, that conscious reason is the catalyst or genius for all of humankind's experience. It is our conscious experience (mind) that provides unity and order. According to Kant, the world is represented (not presented) to us by way of our physical senses and the sensory input we receive. Sensations are chaotic and therefore unrelated. Kant believed that these sensations we perceive are manufactured and *caused* by "something out there." It is the act or mechanism of conscious thought (mind) that can actually describe and order these sensations into two perceptible components of space and time. Simply put, Kant believed that we can link and therefore unify our sensory input by placing sensations in time and space and categorizing them, which is made possible by mindful activity (consciousness). As a result, we examine and catalogue these sensations as reliable and unreliable. Butler states:

> It is reason. . . that fits perceived objects into their respective classes and thus supplements perception in giving us the perfectly integrated experience we will normally possess. Kant spoke of this aspect of mind as the understanding; the classes in which we group objects according to similarities and differences as conceptions.[9]

Kant believed that there exist only 12 kinds of conceptions, which he called *categories.* What Kant attempted to get across is that knowledge and reason constitute an interactive process that in general has its origin and direction from the mind toward the world (interactive) and not from the world toward the mind (passive). Thus, our ability to understand allows us to categorize and relate/link things logically.[10] Epistemologically speaking, we can come to "know things" in this fashion.

We now return to the "thing out there," as Kant described it, as the source in the external world that manufactures and gives us sense impressions and assigns a quality to them. Kant referred to this "thing" as the "Thing in Itself"— something so great and omnipresent that it defies our knowledge and therefore can never be known. Some scholars believe that the "Thing in Itself" is God or universal reason. Kant, however, based his belief in God on moral grounds and not necessarily on supernatural phenomena. As such, he appears to be agnostic in defining the "Thing in Itself." Perhaps another way to approach the issue is from the following perspective: As humans, we have a finite (limited) existence and finite capacity for knowledge. Logic dictates that because we are indeed finite, we can never comprehend or know something that is infinite. An infinite "thing" can know us; however, we do not have the intellectual capacity or ability to know the infinite "Thing in Itself." This form of logic suggests that God in the Judeo-Christian sense is unknowable beyond what God chooses to reveal to us.

What did Kant actually believe? The following five beliefs are recognized as central to his inquiry into philosophy:

1. *Moral law.* Kant believed that there exist universal moral laws. The only acts/behaviors that we can do are those acts or behaviors that are practiced by all of us. For example, if someone were to murder another person, the actual taking of a life might be indeed justified because of the circumstances. However, if "casual" murder became an accepted and universal practice, it would result in the eventual annihilation of the human race. Thus, there exists a universal moral law that eliminates this possibility from ever happening.

2. *Categorical imperative.* In addition to the existence of moral laws, Kant believed that each and every person has a feeling of obligation to obey these moral laws. Because this obligation and sense of duty to *obey* moral laws are grounded in reason (not in experience), Kant referred to this sense of duty and obligation as a categorical imperative. According to Kant, the categorical imperative is the one duty that everyone must regard as sacred or universal. It acts as a universal ethical mandate that says, "Treat others as an end in themselves rather than using people to serve your own ends." This ethical belief would act as a guide for all decisions. In contrast, an unethical individual who ignored Kant's categorical imperative would use others as a means to an end, as tools to achieve some personal goal.

3. *Freedom.* Kant believed in freedom. That is, it is quite possible for us to do good purely out of the desire to do good (we are free to act in this way) and not because we are motivated by an extrinsic reward. According to Kant, to do good for the sake of doing good for its own sake is the only unqualified (not dependent on ulterior motives) good in the world.

4. *Immortality.* Kant believed in the immortality of the soul.

5. *God.* Kant believed that the categorical imperatives and the lack of moral guarantees in the natural world make the existence of God a certainty: "It is necessary that there be a Supreme Intelligence as the cause of the moral obligation in us."[11]

Kant's philosophy is highly relevant to physical education and sport. Human existence to Kant manifested itself as a unified consciousness that participates (1) in a sensory/corporeal world by which we are defined/determined and (2) in the world of reason in which we are free. As a result, we have both a sensuous (natural) and a rational aspect to our existence.[12] The sensuous aspect compels us to the particularity of idiosyncratic inclination, caprice, and desire. The reasoned and rational aspect impels us to the universality of moral obligation and the acceptance of the categorical imperative, which can be equated with the traditional ideal of "sportsmanship." Kant argued from his categorical imperative position that the moral law, unlike the natural law, which is sensuous and capricious, commands unconditionally or categorically to "act only according to that maxim by which you can, at the same time, insure that it should become a universal law."[13] Kant added clarity to this belief as he continued his line of reasoning: "Act so that you treat humanity, whether in your own person or in that of another, always as an end and never as a means only."[14]

Robert Osterhoudt is an eminent scholar in the field of sport philosophy. He provides a revealing look at Kant's categorical imperative and the significant relationship it has with sport and physical education:

> The imperative commands that we universalize our respect for each person as a free moral agent, and so withhold regarding him as a mere object externally found to, and thereby exploited by our sensuous or egoistic inclinations. This notion entails extending to others what we, as free, self-determining, rational beings, would have extended to ourselves. Kant therefore proposes a union of all rational beings in a realm of common law (a 'realm of ends') in which the general ends of all become the ends of all others. In this the individual and common goods coalesce. Accordingly, it follows that a willful violation of this principle is humanistically self-destructive in a general fashion, let alone in a fashion particular to sport.
>
> The use of the imperative in sport secures an internal relationship with those laws (rules and regulations) which define and govern it, and with those other persons who also freely participate in it. A regard for these laws as self-legislated, and an intrinsic respect for those others is nonetheless presupposed by a free entry into the sporting activity . . . this is what is meant by such an entry; that is the taking on of the laws of sport as one's own, and the cultivation of a divining sympathy for all others who have also made such a choice.

The categorical imperative commands that we abide by the laws for their own sake (for they are expressions of our most fundamental nature), and that we consequently treat others with a regard that we ourselves would prefer—that is, treat others as ends-in-themselves. Only insofar as persons make such a treatment, do they stand in a positive and viable relation to reason, and so to one another.[15]

The categorical imperative of Kant is an ethical belief that remains timely and has tremendous relevance to physical education and sport. Sportsmanship and moral conduct in athletic competition and physical education represent an ideal situation in which to instill and teach the humanistic qualities espoused by Kant.

Niccolò Machiavelli

Niccolò Machiavelli (1469–1527) was an Italian philosopher, statesman, and author. His most famous book, *The Prince,* was written in 1513 and is still widely read today. In *The Prince,* Machiavelli states that "the end justifies the means." He advocates using whatever means are available, including deception and dishonesty, to achieve the desired results. Along these lines, some people claim that the traditional concept of sportsmanship that espouses fair play and positive core values has become obsolete—no longer discussed and practiced in contemporary physical education, and replaced by the philosophy of "win at all costs." What are your thoughts about the way contemporary sport and physical education are practiced? To what extent do Machiavellian coaches, athletes, and athletic organizations exist today?

Johann Fichte

Johann Gottlieb Fichte (1762–1814) devoted most of his writing to the ethical issues that challenge humans. He described reality as a morally purposeful will and believed that the phenomenal world in which we live was actually designed to nurture and develop the "will" of men and women and thus bring their character into being. Fichte and Kant

parted company when the subject of the "Thing in Itself" surfaced. Unlike Kant, Fichte believed that the "Thing in Itself" (Kant's description) was indeed knowable. There are, of course, evils in the world over which people have no control but that are part of the overall plan; that is, evil is necessary. According to Butler, Fichte would say that

these apparent evils in the very texture of the natural world are the prods for awakening the human spirit and spurring it to active achievement. Man's relation to nature could not be altogether soothing and comfortable, or the human spirit would be allowed to sleep on and never awaken to achieve consciousness. . . . Health of the body is essential to vigor of mind and spirit.[16]

The philosophical position of the body and the corresponding association between mind, body, and spirit, which is a fundamental component of idealism, enables physical education to look upon Kant and Fichte as providing a philosophical position (as did Aristotle) that demands a healthy and fit body for each person to reach his or her full potential. Philosophically, the body and physical education are accorded a position of critical importance within the educational scheme advocated by Kant and Fichte. The mind would be at a disadvantage without a healthy and fit body. Also, evil appears to occupy an intentional and purposeful place relative to our existence.

Georg Hegel

Georg Wilhelm Friedrich Hegel (1770–1831) grew up in Stuttgart, attended the University of Tübingen, and went on to the University of Jena, where he was awarded a professorship in 1805. Unfortunately for Hegel, a year later Prussia suffered a crushing defeat defending Jena, and Hegel was ousted from his position at the university. He was not able to obtain another professorship until 1816 when the University of Heidelberg hired him. He stayed at Heidelberg for two years and then left to occupy the chair at the University of Berlin made famous by Fichte. During his tenure at Berlin, where he remained until his death in 1831, Hegel was the preeminent philosopher in Germany.

The metaphysical positions espoused by Kant were the epitome of classic idealism. But, contrary to his predecessors, Hegel believed that war was necessary to develop and fortify the idealist concept of man's spiritual being beyond the position adhered to by Kant. Hegel developed the ideal that ultimate realities that affected humans must be within the realm of their reason to comprehend them. Kant believed that humans did not have the capacity to comprehend ultimate realities. Hegel asserted that reason could fathom all aspects of human experience. Philosophy, therefore, had but to determine all the laws by which reason functions within humans.[17] Hegel assigned a greater value to the ability of humankind to "know things" than did Kant and other idealists.

Arthur Schopenhauer (1788–1860), a pessimist to be sure, and Herbert Spencer (1820–1903), a true independent thinker and nonconformist, took exception to Hegel's philosophy of man having the capacity to reason the nature of ultimate reality. Hegel's idealism states that the parts must always be viewed as they relate to the whole, not as independent entities: The individual (part) must be viewed as he or she relates and interacts with the universal (whole). To extend Hegel's thesis further, he believed that we can indeed "know" ethical and spiritual realities through reason, and as previously stated, this was unthinkable to Kant and his contemporaries. Hegel's philosophical process was a trial of (1) thesis (the idea), (2) antithesis, and (3) synthesis. The thesis and antithesis are opposite and contradictory to each other; the synthesis combines the positive and affirmative elements of both. To illustrate this process, Hegel believed that the history of the human race

> is a story of successive contradictions and conflicts that have been resolved only by successive synthesis that cause new trades to arise in the social process. Progress is made through the long ages by the external pendulum swing of thesis and antithesis in human affairs.[18]

Hegel believed there is unity throughout the universe. Karl Marx later applied Hegel's principles to economic history, arguing that the thesis of capitalism met by the antithesis of revolution would result in a new synthesis of communism. For Hegel, thought operated according to the dialectical process whereby the act of reasoning involves a systematic analysis of concepts that will be in conflict, and the resulting synthesis will result in truth. His Absolute Idea was the grand synthesis, an inclusion of the truths of philosophy into an all-inclusive global conformity. Hegel was the consummate idealist who posited the physical corporeal world as a limited or finite idea, near the bottom of his hierarchy. According to Hegel, the body, although recognized and dealt with, occupies an inferior position to that of mind, spirit, and the infinite idea, which, as you may logically conclude, occupies the top of his hierarchy. Man's finite existence in this temporal, corporeal, and imperfect world is part of the process that will eventually be realized as the Absolute End, which is a reflection of the Absolute Mind.

In general, idealists believe that within the educational process, growth will occur through self-activity. Self-activity facilitates and nourishes mental development and the corresponding mental maturity. The vast majority of physical educators agree with contemporary idealists who believe that the ultimate responsibility to learn is with the student.

THE APPLICATION OF IDEALISM TO PHYSICAL EDUCATION

The self-activity that idealism embraces is not an abstract process that ignores the physical. To develop the self includes the development of the body. Idealism embraces and supports the inclusion of physical education. The physical educator who incorporates the philosophical beliefs of idealism starts from the premise that the educational process is ideal-centered as opposed to child-centered or subject matter–centered.[19] The nature of idealism allows us to arrive at an opinion of what all that is "good" embraces. The "ideal good" may be based on the beliefs contained in scripture or on a profound sense of moral duty and obligation. Additional possibilities that can form the basis for determining the ideal good include the moral basis for classic sportsmanship, or the concept of "muscular Christianity." In concrete terms, the idealist physical educator must attend to issues of (1) students, (2) values, (3) objectives, (4) curriculum, and (5) evaluation criteria.

Students

Idealism will not support an educational process that views existence as purely corporeal, "a biological organism responding to 'natural forces.'"[20] Idealism views existence as one of body and soul; in general, that is reality for the idealist. As a result, if physical educators are indeed dedicated professionals who are committed to doing the greatest good for the students, they must not look on them as simply bodies to be trained and made physically fit; they must do more! They must teach moral values and, where appropriate, spiritual values. The body, to the idealist, is the physical expression of the soul. The weight-training and cardiovascular programs in contemporary physical education must be understood by themselves; according to idealists, they are not end products and therefore have no true significance to the student.[21] This aspect of "education of the physical" ignores the moral and spiritual bases of our existence and therefore has blatantly omitted a significant component of the self. Physical education students must ask whether they aspire to become educators or mere technicians who train and mold the body without regard to the personal, moral, and spiritual development of their students.

Values

Delbert Oberteuffer is without question one of the most prolific scholars in the history of American physical education. Oberteuffer asserted that "idealism believes in only two values which are rooted in existence: persons, and the moral

imperative."[22] Put simply, athletes and students do not represent to the coach or teacher a means to an end. They are not "meat on the hoof" or commercial products that can be exploited by capitalizing on their athletic ability for the benefit of the coach, school, or team. Athletes and students in the care of physical educators represent individual and unique personalities that consist of mind, soul, and body. In this respect, the coach and physical education professional must understand that athletes and students in physical education classes are ends in themselves, not means to an end. The ruthless exploitation of high-school and college athletes by coaches, agents, and some educational concerns is reprehensible to idealists. The shockingly low graduation rates of college athletes at many of our well-known, sports-oriented colleges and universities point to the fact that the system has lost sight of the athlete as a person. The moral imperative that Kant spoke of—"Act so that in your own person as well as in the person of every other you are treating mankind also as an end, never merely as a means"—does not fit with the sports-as-big-business approach so pervasive today. The abysmal graduation rates of athletes, especially minority athletes, from big-time athletic programs offer proof that athletes are often used as means to an end. The ends are money, glory, a perception of power, and the ego gratification that participants in the process appear to live for. Working from the position of idealism, what positive values, ethical progress, and ideal good actually occur as a result of big-time college and high-school athletics? Realistically, does Kant's moral imperative have a place, a future, in highly competitive sports and physical education programs of today?

Objectives

Idealism holds that achievement of a superior life is the objective of students. The idealist does his or her best to ensure that every opportunity is available for students to grow physically, intellectually, morally, and spiritually.[23] The objectives of physical education must benefit the development of the whole person. The development and nurturing of an individual's personality and corresponding character is an important objective of the physical educator who adheres to idealism in the cultivation of health, because "it enhances and makes surer and richer the realization of the social, moral, and spiritual-mental aims."[24]

Curriculum

Instruction in social, moral, and spiritual values occupies a prominent position in the curriculum. The idealist has formed an opinion of the ideal good on the basis of belief in God and/or moral obligations. The idealist believes in the importance and necessity of being a positive role model, which enables him or her not only to articulate social, moral, and spiritual values but also to be emblematic of these values. The curriculum is ideal-centered, with emphasis on the development of the self toward perfection insofar as this is possible. The idealist is suspicious of curricular innovation and fads, and prefers a stable curriculum based on the tried and true. The *ability* and *potential* of students is of primary importance to the idealist when determining how best to provide for each student to realize his or her potential. Self-improvement will manifest itself in opportunities for students to develop self-reliance, self-responsibility, self-direction, self-examination, and other, related personal improvement.[25] Both Plato and contemporary adherents of idealism believe that the unexamined life is not worth living.

Evaluation Criteria

How students changed with regard to the self is what interests the idealist. The outcomes in physical education are analyzed as to the extent they contributed to the development and subsequent enhancement of students in areas of social interaction, self-confidence, social and psychological maturity, physical growth, skills development, and

moral and spiritual growth, which is considered character development in many circles. Because the idealist strongly believes in a developmental process that is indeed subjective with regard to the perspective of the evaluator, subjective grading is quite acceptable. The teacher is interested not only in what each student does but also in "what each student knows, thinks, feels, and is. . . . Students will be evaluated with regard to appropriate behavior, citizenship, and sociomoral conduct."[26] The idealist does not accept purely statistical evaluation, nor does he or she rely completely on objective tests to determine the worth and subsequently the grade assigned to each student. The idealist does not rely on quantitative measures but waits to see (subjectively) what changes are made in the self.[27]

THE EDUCATORS

We have highlighted some fundamental concepts of idealism as they pertain to sport and physical education. We now turn our attention to the educators who incorporated physical education into their curricula.

Johann Heinrich Pestalozzi

Perhaps the greatest educational reformer of all time was Johann Heinrich Pestalozzi (1746–1827). His father was an established surgeon in Zurich but died when Pestalozzi was only five years old. He was raised by his mother and a faithful servant, who were dedicated to shielding the young boy from inappropriate influences. As a consequence, young Pestalozzi had no male role model or association with boys his own age while growing up, and he remained shy, weak, and awkward for the remainder of his life. When he attended school, Johann was a social outcast and avoided by his classmates to the point where he was cruelly nicknamed "Harry Oddity of Foolborough." Although always frail and weak, he advocated mandatory physical education.

Prior to becoming an educator, Pestalozzi tried his hand at a number of professions. He studied theology, practiced law, and eventually became a farmer. Pestalozzi was influenced by the writings of Rousseau and may have become a farmer because of the return-to-nature advocacy espoused by Rousseau. Fortunately for educators everywhere, Pestalozzi was not a success on the farm, so he converted his house into a place where children from poor families and other unfortunates could receive an education and perform manual labor, a form of early vocational and physical training not to be confused with physical education as we know it. Five years later, in 1779, Pestalozzi ran out of money and was forced to abandon his efforts at educating children. The following years found Pestalozzi in wretched conditions of poverty and despair. Although he had written articles and opinions during his student days while attending the Collegium Humanitatis in Zurich, he had abandoned his writing after leaving the Collegium. He started writing again during the 18 years he lived in Neuhof after closing his school, but his early writings were largely ignored.

In 1780, he published "The Evening Hours of a Hermit," which reflected the influence of Rousseau. The article focused on what Pestalozzi perceived to be the natural aptitude of man and the necessity for this natural aptitude to be developed: "The pure and beneficent powers of mankind are not the gifts of art or of accident . . . their development is the fundamental need of mankind . . . nature develops all the powers of mankind through exercise, and their growth results from use."[28] One year later, Pestalozzi published his much-acclaimed *Leonard and Gertrude,* which told the story of a humble peasant woman and her devotion and dedication to her village. *Leonard and Gertrude* made Pestalozzi famous because in this work he wrote about something he was quite knowledgeable about (peasant life and its attendant hardships) and provided a format whereby peasant life could be improved. Pestalozzi believed that education is of value only if the knowledge gained can be put to use.[29]

Even though Pestalozzi was famous, he still lived in poverty. In 1798, France annexed Switzerland, and Pestalozzi embraced the newly arrived French government, which had earlier honored him with the title "Citizen of the French Republic." During the French occupation, Pestalozzi filled a number of celebrated educational positions. In 1800, he established an institute at Burgdorf, where he taught teachers how to teach in addition to providing instruction to his beloved pupils. In 1804, he moved to the Castle of Yverdon near Lake Neuchatel, where he established one of the most celebrated schools in the annals of education.[30]

The school at Yverdon had a fabulous reputation and students and educational reformers from all over the world came there to study and observe the methods of Pestalozzi and his staff. Pestalozzi left Yverdon in 1825 because the school was torn apart by internal dissension. Pestalozzi's theory of education stated that three elements or aspects compose the education of the young: (1) intellectual education, (2) moral education, and (3) practical education. His views on practical education were of great benefit to physical education. Like Fellenberg (with whom he worked briefly in 1804 at Hofwyl), Pestalozzi believed in the necessity of providing vocational training along with intellectual training. This approach necessitates the development of all the identified capacities of students. Pestalozzi developed the physical capacities of his male students through physical work, which was also called manual labor in the educational jargon of the era. He advocated gymnastics and games in addition to physical labor.

Besides the development of strength and dexterity, Pestalozzi believed that physical education could also develop healthy and cheerful children, which in his moral education of children were two very important goals. Gymnastics, he asserted, promoted a spirit of union and brotherly association as well as habits of industry, openness and frankness of character, personal courage, and manly conduct. Slightly ahead of his time, Pestalozzi also was adamant that women, especially mothers, should become knowledgeable in gymnastics so they could direct their children's activities in a way that would be beneficial and helpful.[31] However, education for women, although unusual and therefore seemingly progressive, was intended not to expand women's options but to help them better avail themselves of their restricted options.

The physical education program at Yverdon included gymnastics as part of the daily curriculum. Additional activities included hiking, swimming, sledding, skating, dancing, and fencing. Military drill was also practiced. According to Ellen Gerber,

> The kind of Physical Education done at Yverdon under the direction of Pestalozzi was not particularly well developed or unique. The significance of the work at Yverdon lies in its connection with the great educational reforms. Finding new theories of education which influenced both the new and old world, he included as part of the course of study, gymnastics exercises. Pestalozzi's 'imprimatur' gave an important impetus to the general progress of physical education as a school subject which has a part in the fulfillment of educational goals.[32]

Although both Pestalozzi and his contemporary, Friedrich Froebel, undisputedly had an impact on educational theory in the nineteenth and early twentieth centuries, they were both inept organizers and administrators. Both had great ideas but were hard-pressed to see their schools remain free of internal strife and financial problems. Froebel's greatest contributions to education in general and physical education in particular were the establishment of the kindergarten and his theory of play. Play, according to Froebel, was the highest phase of child development.

Friedrich Wilhelm August Froebel

Friedrich Froebel (1782–1852) was the son of an Orthodox Protestant minister who was a strict and rigid role model. When he was 10 years old, Friedrich left the small German village of Oberweissbach and went to live with his uncle's family at Stadt-Ilm, where life was far more pleasant. He became a forester at age 15 and later enrolled at the University of Jena, where he was profoundly influenced by the works of Kant, Fichte, and Hegel. Unfortunately for Froebel, he could not pay his debts and was sent to debtors' prison. After his release, he held many jobs prior to moving to Frankfurt to study architecture. It was in Frankfurt that Froebel made the acquaintance of Anton Gruner, whose mentor was none other than Pestalozzi. Gruner was using the methods he had learned from Pestalozzi at the Model School of Frankfurt, where he served as director. Gruner urged Froebel to become part of the teaching staff, and Froebel wrote his brother that he had at last found his niche in life. He stayed on at the Model School for approximately one year, during which time he visited Pestalozzi's school at Yverdon.

After leaving the Model School, he hired out as a private tutor to three pupils. He later took his pupils to study at Yverdon for two years. In his autobiography, Froebel stated:

> The boys play... games in the open air, and learned to recognize their mighty power to awake and strengthen the intelligence and the soul as well as the body.... The games, as I am now fervently assured, formed a mental bath of extraordinary strengthening power.[33]

His belief in physical education was further strengthened when he met Friedrich Jahn, discussed later in this chapter, while teaching at Johann Ernst Plamann's school in Berlin. Like Jahn, he fought in the Teutonic War of 1813 against Napoleon. Froebel enlisted in Baron von Lutzow's army and became a member of the Black Hunters led by Jahn.

In 1816, Froebel established the Universal German Institute in Griesheim, and a year later, he moved the school to Keilhau, where he remained for twelve years. During this time, he experienced great difficulty in keeping the school financially solvent and administratively cohesive.[34] Froebel published *The Education of Man,* which provided him with a forum to present his theories on the education of children. According to Gerber, the book "reflected the influence of Kant's 'new' philosophy as applied by Schelling and Hegel."[35] The influence of the German idealists on Froebel was obvious. Froebel stressed that his students appreciate the unity or oneness in all things through self-activity that sought to encourage (1) observation, (2) discovery, and (3) creativity because these three activities would use and benefit those aptitudes and talents humans possess.[36] In *The Education of Man,* Froebel supported the place and purpose of physical education when he established his theory of *play:*

> Play is the highest form of child development— of human development at this period; for it is self-active representation of the inner- representation of the inner necessity and im- pulse. Play is the purest, most spiritual activity of man at this stage, and, at the same time, typical of human life as a whole—of the inner hidden natural life in man and all things. It gives, therefore, joy, freedom, contentment, inner and outer rest, peace with the world. It holds the sources of all that is good. A child that plays thoroughly, with self-active deter- mination, perseveringly until physical fatigue forbids, will surely be a thorough, determined man, capable of self-sacrifice for the promo- tion of the welfare of himself and others.
>
> Play at this time is not trivial, it is highly serious and of deep significance . . . to the calm, keen vision of one who truly knows human nature, the spontaneous play of the child discusses the future inner life of the man.[37]

Froebel believed that play in the form of phys- ical education was a wonderful mechanism for stress reduction and what we would call "character and moral development." He believed that physical education would help nourish the intellectual fac- ulties and developed the idea of giving five specific toys to a child in sequence that would teach the concepts of space and mass and basic movement patterns. The first gift was a ball; the second was a cube and sphere; the third, fourth, and fifth items in progression were "complicated divisions of the cube into a series of rectilinear solids, oblong prisms, and obliquely divided component cubes."[38]

These toys could challenge and help develop the mental and physical components of the child. His work in education was insightful and enlightening and remains with us today in the form of kinder- garten, which is nothing less than an institution in America, and in his belief in the purpose and value of physical education. In his *The Education of Man,* Froebel wrote, "Without such cultivation of the body, education can never attain its object, which is perfect human culture."[39] He believed that when teachers and students participate together in physical education activities such as play and organized games, children come to understand the world of humanity.

Friedrich Ludwig Jahn

After Napoleon was crowned emperor of France in 1804, 16 south and west German princes seceded from the "Holy Roman Empire of the German Nation"[40] to support him. They established the Confederation of the Rhine, which ended the empire and began more than a decade of occupa- tion, wars, and uprisings.[41]

Prussia, which was one of the German states that did not collaborate with the Confederation, was defeated by Napoleon in 1806, at the Battle of Jena and Auexstedt during the Fourth Coalition War. After the resulting Peace of Tilsit in 1807, Prussia lost its western and Polish territories, and Napoleon stationed his Ninth Corps in Berlin. Introduction of several domestic reforms after 1807 established in Prussia a new society that ended the old feudal and legal order. The populist concept of nationalism became the driving force behind the Prussian resistance to French rule and the wars of liberation that began in 1813.[42]

One of the principal patriots behind the growing nationalist movement in Prussia was a Berlin gym- nastics teacher, Friedrich Ludwig Jahn (1778–1852) (Figure 8-1). Jahn was an orthodox monarchist who firmly believed that Prussia was destined to become the leader of all the German states. This belief even- tually led to Jahn's hatred of anything foreign, and his goal was to eliminate foreign influences from

Figure 8-1
Friedrich Ludwig Jahn.

Prussia that "might corrupt the purity of the German Volk."[43]

Jahn was born at Lanz, the son of a Prussian clergyman. He spent his early years studying at various gymnasia throughout Prussia. He attended the university at Göttingen around 1800. Although he never obtained a degree, Jahn pursued an eclectic course of study that included physical education.

Jahn's physical education studies were based on the work of Johann Friedrich GutsMuths, who has been called "the most important philanthropic physical educator and establisher of systematic physical exercise at school."[44] GutsMuths believed that

> body and intellect. . . [exerted] a reciprocal influence on one another and [were] in need therefore of being exercised as a unity. The senses had to be schooled so as to train the intelligence . . . [and] health was the precondition for moral fitness. Reason and strength were united in his educational ideal.[45]

Jahn applied these beliefs to his own work, which would become, ultimately, the pursuit of national unity for Germany and freedom from French rule.

With his formal but incomplete education behind him, Jahn spent several years writing and teaching gymnastics. He observed the Prussian defeat and concluded that it had resulted from the cultural influences of the French occupation. These French impurities, as Jahn perceived them, had caused a loss of German national pride. Jahn felt that the basis for reviving patriotism in Prussia was to be found, in part, in the study of German language and customs. Furthermore, the concept of national democracy, which originated in the French Revolution, resulted in Jahn's belief in the

> [propagation] of a national education devoted to the training of responsible citizens and [he] called for the abolition of aristocratic privileges, development of a People's Army in place of an army of mercenaries, and elimination of bondage and all forms of oppression including the corporal punishment then still usual in the army.[46]

To achieve his objectives of national unity in the German states and the liberation of Prussia, Jahn first moved to Berlin in 1809. There he became an auxiliary teacher at the Friedrich Werdescher Gymnasium and got involved with other Prussian patriots whose goals matched his. Because Prussia had remained resistant to French rule during Napoleon's occupation, it became a haven for German patriots and the center of the "all-German movement for national freedom."[47]

Sometime during the following year, Jahn and two other patriots, Karl Friedrich Friesen and Wilhelm Harnich, established the German League. This secret society was composed mainly of army officers and teachers who sought "the spiritual renovation of Germany at the moment of its deepest humiliation."[48] The constitution of the German League called for a nationwide program of physical education and spiritual renewal in all German universities. According to Heinrich von Treitschke, "The conspirators assembled at night in the woods near Berlin and consecrated themselves to the struggle for the fatherland."[49] This organization provided the patriots with little more than a means of expressing their anger with the French occupation. Its main contribution to the cause of freedom became apparent later, when the Burschenschaft (student societies) were formed in 1815. The constitutions of these societies contained the same basic concepts as those found in the constitution of the German League. In 1813, at the start of the wars of liberation, the German League was dissolved.

Shortly after the formation of the German League, Jahn became a member of the Grauen Kloster Gymnasium in Berlin, where he started teaching at Plamann's school. Twice each week, on Wednesday and Saturday afternoons, he taught gymnastics and general physical exercise to his pupils. They practiced outdoors, in a yard near the school. These afternoons were the precursor of Jahn's *turnen* (gymnastics) programs, which he started the following year.

The spring of 1811 marked the beginning of the German turnverein movement. Coining what he believed to be an extinct Teutonic word—*turnen* (to perform gymnastic exercises)—Jahn established the first *turnplatz* (outdoor gymnastics field) on the Hasenheide just south of Berlin (Figure 8-2). He organized the first *turnfest*

Figure 8-2
Exercising on a turnplatz.

(outdoor gymnastics festival) on June 19, 1811, which was a big success. By Christmas of the same year, Jahn had left Plamann's school to devote his time to the *Turners*—a gymnastics/physical education society with a patriotic/political agenda.[50]

Turnvater (father of gymnastics) Jahn, as his pupils called him, worked hard to instill a sense of national pride in his gymnasts. He reorganized the Hasenheide Turnverein during 1812 and increased the number of exercises offered at the turnplatz. During the summer, Jahn and Friesen set up the Gymnastics Association in an effort to spread their program throughout Prussia. They also won the support of School Inspector Wilhelm Schroder, who called publicly for schools to accept gymnastics as part of their curricula.[51]

The wars of liberation against France started in 1813 and lasted until 1815. Jahn and a group of his gymnasts joined the Lutzow Free Corps, which fought as a unit throughout the war. By the time they returned, assured of France's defeat and confident of the German states' future unity as a nation, the Turners had acquired a sense of nationalistic pride, and Jahn was their acknowledged hero. The Turners' marching song made their feelings abundantly clear:

> When for the people's old and sacred rights
> Bravely the Turnermeister, Friedrich Jahn,
> Strade to the field where man for freedom fights,
> A warlike generation followed on.
> Hey, how the youths leapt after him,
> Fresh and joyful, godly, free!
> Hey, how the youths sang after him:
> Hurrah![52]

The Turners returned from war and Prussia's newly found freedom also served to rejuvenate the popularity of gymnastics.

After the wars of liberation ended in 1815, the goals of the Turners became less clear. Prussia had been liberated from French oppression; domestic reforms since 1807 had brought about a new tolerance for more liberal views; and the gymnastics societies were popular throughout the Germanies. As a result, the Turners concentrated

on the internal nature of their societies, becoming, in effect, a self-contained nation. Jahn refused to acknowledge the possibility that the army or the schools had any part in the development of German youth. Instead, "his gymnastic grounds were to constitute a world apart, a nursery of Germanism, inspired by his spirit alone."[53] Jahn believed that the only true German was a Turner—"virtuous and vigorous, continent and courageous, pure and prepared, manful and truthful"—whereas all others were "false Germans."[54] He exhorted his gymnasts to "immediately report the discovery of anything which friend or foe of the turncraft may say, write, or do for or against the said craft, in order that at the fit time and place all such fellows may be thought of with praise or blame!"[55] The Turners had found a new cause—themselves—and believed that they would bring about the unity of the Germanies by fighting anyone who stood in their path, including their fellow countrymen, if necessary.

In their zeal, the Turners overlooked the fact that the German states had become more unified since the wars of liberation. The French had brought about some positive changes during their various European campaigns. Specifically, their actions had generated a spirit of democracy among many nations in Europe. This spirit provided the foundation for social reform and the establishment of constitutional freedom. In the German states, this foundation took the form of popular demands for certain rights, including "the separation of justice and administration, public and oral court proceedings, trial by jury, freedom of the press, and equality before the law for all citizens."[56]

At the University of Jena in 1815, a group of student patriots, advocating the adoption of these rights, formed the first Burschenschaft (student society). The students adopted the constitution of Jahn's German League, and the societies soon appeared on many German university campuses. The purpose of the Burschenschaft was the pursuit of freedom and constitutionalism, and gymnastics was the symbol and means by which the students would reach their goal. The "student gymnasts at universities would prepare the way for German unity that had not been achieved in the political sphere."[57]

What started out as peaceful protest, however, soon degenerated into chaos and violence. The Burschenschaft, also known as the Patriotic Students, became gradually more involved with the Nationalist Gymnasts, an activist group that Jahn had formed in 1816. These two groups brought the nationalism so typical of the nineteenth century to university lecture halls and influenced what had initially been idealistic endeavors in a way that turned out to be most dangerous.[58]

Alarmed at the vandalism and increasing violence perpetrated by members of the Burschenschaft in Austria and Prussia, King Friedrich Wilhelm III intervened. Two events precipitated his actions. First, the Wartburg Festival of October 31, 1817, which started as "a great festivity of romantic and patriotic uplift and of religious reflection,"[59] turned rapidly into a riot. Second, the Breslau festival, which was based on the objectives of gymnastics, also became a heated political confrontation. The king was forced to close the Breslau gymnastics field, and he directed the universities to more closely supervise their students. The king later found, however, that his tactics were not adequate.

By 1819, the liberal movement had gained strength, and the king was losing control over the situation. He was spurred to more drastic action when a gymnast and theology student named Karl Sand murdered Alexander von Kotzebue, a dramatist who had made the fatal error of writing critically about gymnastics. The king turned reluctantly to Austrian Chancellor Metternich for assistance. Metternich met secretly with Prussian Chancellor Hardenberg to find a solution to the problems caused by the liberals. Together these men drafted a set of decrees that allowed authorities to investigate the universities and impose political censorship throughout the German states.[60]

In July 1814, a conference of German confederation ministers approved the decrees at Carlsbad. Known as the Carlsbad Decrees, they caused the almost immediate disappearance of the liberal movement, especially in Prussia. Their issue brought about the surveillance of student activity at the universities, caused the banning of student organizations, and encouraged the harassment of those suspected of leading the liberal movement.[61]

King Friedrich Wilhelm III was relieved by the suppression of the liberal movement, although he was not fully aware of some of the actions that were taken. Unbeknownst to the king, Chancellor Metternich took matters into his own hands and ordered the arrests, in both Austria and Prussia, of anyone whom he or Chancellor Hardenberg suspected of treasonous acts. On July 13, 1819, Jahn was arrested "on suspicion of secret, treasonable connections"[62] (which were never specified) and sent to Spandau Fortress. He was transferred to Kustrin Prison a short time later. Although he was released on May 22, 1820, Jahn was then forced to live under house arrest in the town of Kolberg until 1825.

The fate of Turner gymnastics appeared bleak between 1820 and 1848. The Prussian government had originally planned to assume control of gymnastics by including it in the schools' curricula. As a result, in March 1819, the government banned gymnastics in Turner societies. On January 20, 1820, however, a Prussian royal decree was issued banning all gymnastics in the state and ordering the closure of more than a hundred gymnastics fields. They would not reopen in any form until 1842, when a younger and more liberal King Friedrich Wilhelm IV assumed the throne.[63]

Jahn was acquitted and released from house arrest in 1825. He moved to Freyberg/Unstrut, where he lived until his death in 1852. As a condition of his release from imprisonment, Jahn was not allowed to live in a town with a university or gymnasium. Because he could not practice his beloved gymnastics, his career appeared to be over. Jahn remarried in 1825 (after the death of his first wife in 1823), and he focused on domestic life for the next several years.[64]

During the period that Jahn was imprisoned and gymnastics was banned in the German states, the lives of Charles Follen, Charles Beck, and

Francis Lieber, three of Jahn's followers, took turns that ultimately led them to the United States as the pioneers of American physical education.

Charles Follen

One of the results of the ban on gymnastics in Prussia was that some of the more patriotic rebels formed secret societies in which they nurtured their political zeal. One of these societies, known as the Blacks,[65] was a particularly subversive group formed in 1816 that worked hard at annoying the Prussian authorities, especially Metternich. The Blacks believed that they were divinely guided to "direct the emancipation of the enslaved peoples,"[66] by which they meant all Germans. Late in 1819, one of the Blacks considered to be most dangerous by Prussian authorities, a lawyer named Charles Follen (1795–1840) and a follower of Jahn, escaped to Strasburg. Earlier that year, he had been found guilty of providing money for the journey taken by Karl Sand to murder Kotzebue. He was not convicted of the act, however, because Prussian laws at the time did not provide any grounds for legal action against him. Follen managed to escape to Strasburg before the Prussian authorities could detain him.

Follen left Strasburg during the summer of 1820, when he moved to Basel, Switzerland, to take up a position teaching jurisprudence at that city's university. For three years, he lived and worked in Basel under the constant fear of being deported back to Germany. He was a political refugee and, like all political refugees, feared for his safety. When the danger became too great, he fled to Paris, where he met Charles Beck. Together they sailed from Le Havre to New York, where they arrived as emigrants on December 19, 1824.

Charles Follen secured a teaching position at Harvard University, where he taught German. Follen requested permission from the Harvard administration to construct a turnplatz on the campus where he could teach German gymnastics to the students on a voluntary basis. He was allocated an area on campus known as the Delta, where he built the turnplatz and taught gymnastics. His efforts were not too successful, and interest died out after a few years. He later taught gymnastics at the Boston Gymnasium.

Charles Beck

Charles Beck (1798–1866), another of Jahn's followers, was a classical scholar who had also trained in theology. He worked for many years to establish a student society based on Christianity, but he found that he could not pursue a career and survive politically in his native country. As a result, Beck moved to Basel in 1823, where he taught classical literature for a year. By late 1824, Beck also found that his proximity to Prussia was too dangerous, and he sailed with Follen to New York. He secured a teaching position at the Round Hill School in Northampton, Massachusetts. The school was founded by Joseph Cogswell and George Bancroft, who had studied in Germany and, while there, became familiar with the gymnastics of the Turners. Upon returning to the United States, Cogswell and Bancroft instituted a required program of daily physical education and hired Charles Beck, who is credited with being the first physical education teacher in America. Round Hill School is historically significant as the first school with mandatory physical education in the form of German gymnastics.

Francis Lieber

The third member of the group of German emigrants who provided the basis for American physical education was Francis Lieber (1800–1872), an ardent follower of Jahn since the early days of the Hasenheide in 1811. Lieber was arrested shortly after Jahn in 1819 but was released after four months. He completed his doctorate in 1820, after which he fled the continued persecution of the Burschenschafts to fight for the Greeks in their attempt to overthrow their Turkish oppressors in 1821. Lieber wanted to return to Prussia in 1823, and he was assured by both the Prussian king and that state's minister of police that it was safe to do so. When he arrived in Berlin in August 1823, however, Lieber was subjected to the beginning of three years of harassment and imprisonment by the state police. In May 1826, Lieber escaped to London, where he lived and taught the German language for a year. In April 1827, Lieber accepted an offer to serve as Follen's successor at the Boston Gymnasium, and he arrived in New York on June 20, 1827.[67]

The turnverein movement served as an important instrument of social change in the German states. The Turners led the drive toward a unified democracy of those states during the period between 1811 and 1819. Encouraged by the ideals of freedom and independence from French rule, the Turners practiced their unique form of physical activity, gymnastics, in order to be physically and mentally ready to liberate their nation.

Another significant contribution of the Turners was the export of their gymnastics methods. In America, the turnverein movement catalyzed the emergence of physical education as an important area of study. Charles Beck succeeded in establishing the first recognized, school-sponsored physical education program in the United States. The Turners were the pioneers of modern physical education in America in the nineteenth century.

Franz Nachtegall

The acknowledged father of physical education in Denmark is Franz Nachtegall (1777–1847). He was born in Copenhagen, the son of an immigrant German tailor, and was educated at a private school and later entered the university to study theology. During his university days, he earned a reputation as a formidable fencer and was skilled in vaulting in the gymnastic sense. But he quit the university when his father passed away, becoming a tutor to support and care for his mother. It was during this time that he read "Gymnastik fur die Jugend," by Johann GutsMuths (1759–1839), whom many historians refer to as the grandfather of physical education.

Nachtegall was so inspired by GutsMuths's gymnastics that he began to teach it in addition to Latin, geography, and history. He is credited with establishing and operating a private gymnasium, which he started on November 5, 1799, and which was "the first institution for physical training to be opened in modern times."[68] The gymnasium was so successful that by 1804 he had an enrollment of 150 children and adults, along with six assistants.

In addition to operating his own gymnasium, Nachtegall provided instruction in gymnastics in public and private schools throughout Copenhagen. The equipment employed by Nachtegall included hanging ladders, climbing poles, balance beams, vaulting horses, and rope ladders (Figure 8-3). As his reputation grew, Nachtegall began to attract notice from a number of influential and powerful people, including none other than the king of Denmark and Per Henrik Ling, the founder of Swedish medical and pedagogical gymnastics, who attended Nachtegall's gymnasium.

In 1804, the king appointed him professor of gymnastics at the University of Copenhagen and director of the Military Gymnastic Institute, which remains in existence to this day. An avid swimmer, Nachtegall launched the Society for Promoting the Art of Swimming, which provided free swimming lessons and organized competitive meets for children from poor families.

Fortune continued to smile on Nachtegall when one of his former students, Prince Frederick, ascended the throne in 1808 and became one of Nachtegall's primary supporters in his efforts to introduce compulsory physical education into the schools. In 1809, a law was passed that required, whenever possible, secondary schools to provide gymnastics; five years later, the law was modified to also include instruction in the elementary schools, albeit only for boys. To ensure that elementary and secondary school teachers were able to provide physical education instruction, a law was passed in 1818 that made gymnastics a required course in the teacher-training colleges (Seminarier) in Denmark.[69] However, despite all the work of Nachtegall and the support of the Danish government, physical education programs ranged from substandard to nonexistent. In spite of the mandatory physical

Figure 8-3
Vaulting the horse.

education requirement in teacher-training colleges, few teachers were actually trained in gymnastics or schooled in the importance of physical education. This situation was mitigated to some degree in 1821, when Nachtegall was appointed gymnastics director with authority over the entire civilian and military gymnastics program. He focused his efforts on ensuring that gymnastics was taught in all the schools in Copenhagen, public as well as private. Although Nachtegall did not create a new system of physical education, he did introduce and champion the system of gymnastics developed by GutsMuths.

Nachtegall emphasized the need to train physical education teachers and provide instruction for students. To this end, he turned to the Military Gymnastic Institute and established a cooperative arrangement between the institute and the public school, which later became the Normalskole (Normal School) for Gymnastikken, where military and civilian teachers could conduct classes. The Normal School opened its door in 1828 with

160 students and 200 teachers, all working to hone their knowledge of and expertise in gymnastics. Women were included in 1838 when Nachtegall helped to establish an experimental school for girls. The girls received instruction in gymnastics three times a week, with the dubious distinction of being subjected to the method of instruction provided by three army sergeants and two women. This suggests that the educational and military orientation for boys was similar for girls. One year after the establishment of the experimental school for girls, the Normal School of Gymnastics for Women (Normalskole for Kvindegymnastik) was established in 1839. The curriculum consisted of teaching methods and exercises that reflected the methods advocated by GutsMuths, which was the curriculum for men.

Danish gymnastics received a boost when Nachtegall and four of his associates wrote a "Manual of Gymnastics for the Village and Town Schools of Denmark" in 1828. The manual was distributed to all the schools in Denmark by authority of the king, who simultaneously decreed that instruction in gymnastics immediately begin in every school in Denmark. By 1839, most of the schools in Denmark were in compliance with the law; however, the need for physical education teachers, to achieve compliance with the law, necessitated that the primary source of teachers was the military. The military presence and influence in Danish physical education was not objectionable to the Danes. As in Germany and Sweden, gymnastics was appreciated more for its military applications than its educational contributions.

As a tireless champion of physical education, Nachtegall was the driving force behind the inclusion of gymnastics in the schools of Denmark. He resigned as director of the Military Gymnastic Institute when he turned 65, but he returned to his position as director of gymnastics for Denmark and visited schools and colleges in Denmark, forever encouraging and promoting gymnastics. However, military gymnastics eventually became the dominant program in Denmark, brought on in part when the Normal School, which trained gymnastics teachers for the schools, closed its doors. Beginning in 1859, the students in the teacher-training college received their instruction in gymnastics from military men assigned to the college or physical education teacher. As a result, Nachtegall's school physical education program, consisting of the gymnastics of GutsMuths, began to disappear and was soon replaced by military gymnastics.

Per Henrik Ling

The originator of Swedish gymnastics was a consummate scholar and athlete. Per Henrik Ling (1776–1839) was born in the south of Sweden in the town of Smaland, where his family had lived for generations (Figure 8-4). Life was not easy for the future member of the Swedish Academy (a distinguished body of 18 of Sweden's most noted leaders) and champion of physical education. His father died when he was 4, and his mother passed away when he was only 13. He attended high school and in 1793 matriculated at the university in Lund, where he stayed for two semesters. He then moved to Stockholm, where he worked as a clerk and

privately tutored students in French and German. From 1799 to 1804, he lived in Copenhagen, where he participated in Nachtegall's gymnastics program and enrolled in the university. While at the university, Ling was introduced to the Danish poet Oehlenschläger and the philosophy of Schelling by one of his countrymen who happened to be teaching at the university. He began to study the literary and ethnic heritage of his ancestry and eventually was profoundly influenced by both the poetry and philosophy of Sweden and Denmark.

Ling also began to take fencing lessons and noticed that fencing and the associated exercises had a wonderfully therapeutic effect on his arthritic arm; thus began his lifelong interest in the medical effects of exercise. In 1804, he returned to Sweden and the university in Lund, where he became fencing master as well as a student of anatomy and physiology.

During this time, Sweden's once mighty empire crumbled, primarily due to the military assaults by the French and Russians. In 1805, Gustavus IV of Sweden attempted to stop Napoleon by entering into a military agreement with England, Russia,

Figure 8-4
Per Henrik Ling.

and Austria. This was a major mistake. By entering into an alliance with England and opening ports to English ships, the king incurred the wrath of the Russian czar, who conquered Finland in 1808 (Finland was part of Sweden); this resulted in a reduction of Sweden's empire by one-third. Napoleon conquered Swedish Pomerania in 1807 along with Stralsund and Rugen, the last Swedish possession south of the Baltic.[70] The citizens of Sweden were outraged. King Gustavus was subsequently dethroned, and eventually, the Swedish Diet appointed the distinguished French general Jean Baptiste Jules Bernadotte as king in 1818 and designated him Charles XIV. After suffering humiliating military defeats at the hands of the French and Russians, the French-general-turned-king-of-Sweden was anxious to proceed with a rapid military buildup and supported Ling's idea to build and administer a physical training institute because of its obvious military applications.

Ling was appointed fencing master in 1813 at the Royal Military Academy, and the king approved and financed his plan to make Stockholm a center for physical training. In 1814, the Royal Gymnastics Central Institute, as it was named, was where Ling developed his system of gymnastics, which was to become known worldwide as the Swedish system. J. G. Thulin describes the basis of Ling's system as follows:

> Physical exercise must be based on the laws of the human system, and influence not only the body but also the mind. The fundamental principles can be briefly comprised in the following four clauses:
>
> 1. The aim is all-around harmonious development of the body.
> 2. The attainment of this is sought by means of biologically and physiologically grounded physical exercises in definite form and, as far as possible, of known effect.
> 3. The exercises must have developmental and corrective values, be easily understood, and satisfy our demand for beauty.
> 4. The exercises must be carried out with a gradually increasing degree of difficulty and exertion.[71]

What Ling did was to ground his system in the science of the day, and as a result, he incorporated (1) aesthetic, (2) military, (3) pedagogical, and (4) medical aspects of exercise. He believed that these four components were linked with each other and in concert enabled his pupils to achieve a unifying relationship of mind, body, and duty to Sweden; health was a harmony between the nervous, circulatory, and respiratory systems. Ling's system was designed to help achieve this end. Ling did not enjoy notoriety because, ironically, his scientific foundation of exercise received criticism because his theory of gymnastics was said to be inconsistent and illogical.

Ling did not accept Jahn's work or approach because he believed German gymnastics was too complicated; Ling wanted exercise to result in a "demonstrated effect." Gymnastic apparatus was designed to revolve around specific exercises that would have certain results. He invented the stall bar, Swedish broom, Swedish box, window ladder, and oblique rope.[72] His gymnastic equipment did not require complicated movements, unlike those used by the Turners under the leadership of Jahn. Ling preferred free exercises without hand-held dumbbells or wands. He concentrated on body position as opposed to movement sequences and was quite exact with regard to actual location/position of the trunk, head, arms, and legs. Gerber states that "Ling gymnastics began to consist of positions retained for the length of time it took the teacher to observe and correct the faults. This meant that an entire class was often held for a long time in the artificial and strained position specified."[73]

The sad truth is that Ling's Swedish gymnastics was a bore and did not achieve popularity, even in Sweden. His system did gain some respect in the northeastern United States, especially the Boston area, but never did catch on in the United States the way that German gymnastics did. Ling's gymnastics was based on the scientific and medical knowledge of the day (albeit at times untenable), which is more than we can say of its chief rival, Jahn's German gymnastics.

SUMMARY

Philosophically, the German idealists reflected the goals of the ancient Greeks. Like the Greeks, the German idealists believed in the development of the self. The body, soul, and intellect as the primary mode of being had to be educated. The overall development of each person was based on the idea of perfection. Moral and ethical development can be found in Kant's categorical imperative, which can provide the moral fabric for sportsmanship and fair play.

The justification for and development of physical education benefited greatly from the philosophy of idealism and the tireless efforts of physical educators in Germany, Sweden, and Denmark. The use of physical education as a political tool was at the foundation of the Turner movement in Germany. The Turners sought to fan the flames of nationalism and patriotism under the direction of Friedrich Jahn, the architect of the turnverein movement. The political situation that resulted from the activities of the Turners was partly responsible for the importation of German gymnastics to America. During their student days in Germany, Joseph Cogswell and George Bancroft were heavily influenced by German gymnastics as practiced by the Turners. Upon their return to the United States, they opened the Round Hill School in Northampton, Massachusetts, and hired Charles Beck, a political refugee due to his activities in support of the Turners, as the first physical education teacher in America.

Franz Nachtegall, the father of Danish gymnastics, is credited with promoting a physical education program based on the work of GutsMuths. He influenced Per Ling during Ling's stay in Copenhagen. Nachtegall saw the need for the inclusion of physical education in the Danish school curricula and was very successful in achieving his goal.

The work of Ling established the basis for grounding physical education in the medical and scientific aspects of exercise. Swedish gymnastics did not enjoy the popularity that German gymnastics did when it was brought to America.

The promotion of physical education in Germany, Sweden, and Denmark was for military purposes rather than for its educational and health value.

DISCUSSION QUESTIONS

1. What three basic topics are fundamental to idealism? How do these three tenets of idealism manifest themselves in contemporary sport and physical education?

2. According to Kant, you should "act so that you treat humanity, whether in your own person or in that of another, always as an end and never as a means only." How could you incorporate this idea into contemporary sport and physical education?

3. Idealism has as a basic tenet the development of the "self." How could this be achieved through participation in sport and physical education?

4. Does the body play a prominent role in the epistemology of idealism? Why or why not?

5. Johann Fichte believed evil was necessary for the individual to reach his or her potential. Do you agree with him? Explain your answer.

6. How did Friedrich Jahn use the gymnastics programs of the Turners to further German nationalism?

7. What was the initial impact of the Turners on the development of American physical education?

8. How can one utilize the philosophy of idealism, especially its metaphysics, and physical education and athletic competition?

9. Potentially, what is the impact of Kant's philosophy on physical education?

10. Compare and contrast Ling's Swedish gymnastics with Jahn's German gymnastics. Which was the better system to promote physical education?

11. If you played on a team coached by an individual who held Machiavelli's belief that "the end justifies the means," what kind of behavior do you think the coach would expect from you and your teammates? Would the team members have a moral obligation to question the tactics advocated by the coach? If you were the athletic director or principal, how would you deal with this Machiavellian coach who has won five state championships in the last seven years? Keep him or fire him?

INTERNET RESOURCES

Idealism Philosophy
**www.spaceandmotion.com/Philosophy-Georg-Hegel
.htm**
Provides information on Hegel; not an easy read.

Internet Encyclopedia of Philosophy: German Idealism
www.iep.utm.edu/g/germidea.htm
Focuses on German idealism.

Free Dictionary: Idealism
www.thefreedictionary.com/idealism
Includes tenets, definitions, and a glossary related to
idealism; offers a good set of links.

German Turnverein
**http://cscwww.cats.ohiou.edu/~chastain/rz/ turnvere
.htm**
Gives a brief overview of the German gymnastics
movement.

Cincinnati Central Turners and Milwaukee Turners
www.gacl.org/turner.html

**www.milwaukeeturners.org/Milwaukee-Turners/
index.shtml**
Provides information on the Turners and the
introduction of physical education into public schools.

Hickok Sports
www.hickoksports.com/history/gymnastics04.shtml

Provides information on the Turners and Swedish
gymnastics, the Czech Sokols, and the Swiss American
Gymnastics Association; offers good links to sport and
physical education history sites in the United States.
The main site (www.hickoksports.com) includes rules
and records.

Visit the *History and Philosophy of Sport and Physical
Education* Online Learning Center (www.mhhe.com/
mechikoff6e) for additional information and study
tools.

SUGGESTIONS FOR FURTHER READING

Bair, D. E. "An Identification of Some Philosophical
Beliefs Held by Influential Leaders in American
Physical Education." Doctoral dissertation,
University of Southern California, 1956.

Clark, M. C. "A Philosophical Interpretation of a
Program of Physical Education in a State Teachers
College." Doctoral dissertation, New York
University, 1943.

Hackensmith, C. W. *History of Physical Education.*
New York: Harper & Row, 1966.

Hocking, W. E. *The Self, Its Body and Freedom.* New
Haven, CT: Yale University Press, 1928.

Hoernle, R. F. A. *Idealism as a Philosophy.* New York:
Doubleday, 1927.

Kleinman, S. "The Nature of Self and Its Relation to an
'Other' in Sport." *Journal of the Philosophy of
Sport* II (1975): 45–50.

Leonard, F. E., and G. B. Affleck. *A Guide to the
History of Physical Education.* Philadelphia: Lea &
Febiger, 1947.

Machiavelli, N. *The Prince* and *The Discourses.* New
York: Modern Library, 1950.

Pfister, G. "The Medical Discourse on Female Physical
Culture in Germany in the 19th and Early 20th
Centuries." *Journal of Sport History* 17, no. 2
(Summer 1990): 183–98.

Royce, J. *Lectures on Modern Idealism.* New Haven,
CT: Yale University Press, 1919.

Savage, H. J., et al. *American College Athletics.* New
York: Carnegie Foundation for the Advancement of
Teaching, 1929.

Schopenhauer, A. "The World as Will and Idea." In
Masterworks of Philosophy. New York: Doubleday,
1946.

Weiss, P. "Some Philosophical Approaches to Sport."
Journal of the Philosophy of Sport IX (1982): 90–93.

Zeigler, E. "In Sport, As in All of Life, Man Should Be
Comprehensible to Man." *Journal of the Philosophy
of Sport* III (1976): 121–26.

Zwarg, L. F. *A Study of the History, Uses, and Values of
Apparatus in Physical Education.* Philadelphia:
Temple University, 1929.

NOTES

1. William S. Shakian, *History of Philosophy* (New York: Barnes & Noble, 1970), 369.

2. Seymour Kleinman, "The Classic Philosophers and Their Metaphysical Positions," in *Physical Education, an Interdisciplinary Approach,* ed. Robert N. Singer (New York: Macmillan, 1972), 331.

3. *Descartes' Philosophical Writings,* sel. and trans. Norman Kemp Smith (London: Macmillan, 1952). See Meditations I, II, and VI.

4. Donald J. Butler, *Four Philosophies and Their Practice in Education and Religion,* 3rd ed. (New York: Harper & Row, 1968), 148.

5. Earle F. Zeigler, *Philosophical Foundation for Physical, Health, and Recreation Education* (Englewood Cliffs, NJ: Prentice-Hall, 1964), 174.

6. Butler, *Four Philosophies,* 132.

7. Ibid., 128.

8. Immanuel Kant, *Kritix der reinen Vernunft, English. Critique of Pure Reason,* abr. ed., trans. with intro., Norman Kemp Smith (New York: Modern Library, 1958).

9. Butler, *Four Philosophies,* 130.

10. Ibid.

11. Ibid., 132.

12. Robert G. Osterhoudt, "In Praise of Harmony: The Kantian Imperative and Hegelian Sittlichkeit as the Principle and Substance of Moral Conduct in Sport," *Journal of the Philosophy of Sport* 3 (September 1976): 65–81.

13. Immanuel Kant, *Foundations of the Metaphysics of Pure Morals,* trans. Lewis W. Beck (Indianapolis, IN: Bobbs-Merrill, 1959), 39.

14. Ibid., 47.

15. Osterhoudt, "In Praise of Harmony," 67–68.

16. Butler, *Four Philosophies,* 161.

17. Zeigler, *Philosophical Foundation,* 37.

18. Butler, *Four Philosophies,* 137.

19. Delbert Oberteuffer, "Idealism and Its Meaning to Physical Education," in Elwood Craig Davis, ed., *Philosophers Fashion Physical Education* (Dubuque, IA: Wm. C. Brown, 1963), 17.

20. Ibid., 18.

21. Ibid.

22. Ibid., 19.

23. William A. Harper et al., *The Philosophic Process in Physical Education* (Philadelphia: Lea & Febiger, 1977), 133.

24. Ibid.

25. Ibid., 135.

26. Ibid., 137.

27. Oberteuffer, "Idealism and Its Meaning," 23.

28. Lewis Flint Anderson, *Pestalozzi* (New York: McGraw-Hill, 1931), 13.

29. Ellen W. Gerber, *Innovation and Institution in Physical Education* (Philadelphia: Lea & Febiger, 1971), 88.

30. Ibid., 89.

31. Ibid., 91–92.

32. Ibid., 92.

33. Friedrich Froebel, *Autobiography,* trans. and annotated by Emile Michaelis and H. Keatley Moore (Syracuse: C. W. Bardeen, 1889), 82.

34. Gerber, *Innovation,* 95.

35. Ibid.

36. Friedrich Froebel, *The Education of Man,* trans. and annotated by W. N. Hailman (New York: D. Appleton, 1896).

37. Ibid., 54–55.

38. Gerber, *Innovation,* 97.

39. Froebel, *Education of Man,* 250.

40. Horst Ueberhorst, *Friedrich Ludwig Jahn and His Time, 1778–1852* (Munich: Heinze Moos Verlag, 1978), 102.

41. The authors are grateful to Alida J. Moonen for permission to quote extensively from her master's thesis, "The German Turnverein Movement in San Diego, 1873–1913," San Diego State University, 1987.

42. Ueberhorst, *Jahn,* 32–35; and Heinrich von Treitschke, *History of Germany in the Nineteenth Century,* 7 vols. (New York: Ams Press, 1968), 1:358.

43. R. R. Palmer and Joel Colton, *A History of the Modern World to 1815* (New York: Alfred A. Knopf,

1978), 403; and Treitschke, *History of Germany,* 1:358.

44. Ueberhorst, *Jahn,* 22.

45. Ibid.

46. Ibid., 36.

47. Palmer and Colton, *History of the Modern World,* 404.

48. Ueberhorst, *Jahn,* 39.

49. Treitschke, *History of Germany,* 1:354.

50. Treitschke, *History of Germany,* 1:359; and Ueberhorst, *Jahn,* 103.

51. Ueberhorst, *Jahn,* 103.

52. Treitschke, *History of Germany,* 3:6.

53. Ibid., 3:8.

54. Ibid., 3:6.

55. Ibid., 3:11.

56. Ueberhorst, *Jahn,* 38.

57. Ibid., 42.

58. Ibid.

59. Ibid., 105.

60. Treitschke, *History of Germany,* 3:168.

61. Treitschke, *History of Germany,* 3:135–233; see also, Ueberhorst, *Jahn,* 44–46.

62. Ueberhorst, *Jahn,* 106.

63. Ibid.

64. Ibid., 106.

65. Treitschke, *History of Germany,* 3:73.

66. Ibid., 4:73.

67. Fred E. Leonard, *Pioneers of Modern Physical Training* (New York: Association Press, 1915), 77–81.

68. Gerber, *Innovation,* 178.

69. Ibid., 179.

70. Ibid., 156–57.

71. J. G. Thulin, "The Application of P. H. Ling's System to Modern Swedish Ling Gymnastics," *Mind and Body* 38 (November 1931): 625–31.

72. Gerber, *Innovation,* 159.

73. Ibid., 161.

III The Historical and Philosophical Development of Sport and Physical Education in America

Sport in the Colonial Period

General Events

O B J E C T I V E S

Upon completing this chapter, you will be able to:

- Identify some of the social and cultural forces that helped shaped the role and scope of sport in Colonial America.
- Discuss the nature and scope of sport as it functioned in England during the colonial period.
- Recognize the link between religion and sport during this time.
- Understand the Puritan view of sport and other "frivolous" pastimes.
- Explain the contributions made by the Puritans to the development of a prosperous New England and how their beliefs affect us to this day.
- Identify physical activities that the Puritans considered appropriate.
- Discuss what religious concerns Puritans and Quakers had relative to the use of time and why sport and amusements were generally considered a waste of precious time.
- Understand why horse racing was so pervasive in Colonial America.
- Identify the types of sporting activities southerners participated in and why they were not encumbered by the religious restrictions present in New England.
- Discuss the role of slaves in southern sporting events.
- Understand why boxing had such wide appeal in the South.
- Recognize the role Benjamin Franklin (1706–1790) played as America's first recorded advocate and promoter of physical education and sport.

INTRODUCTION

When Christopher Columbus sailed from Europe in 1492 to find a new route to India, he instead discovered America. For the next century, Europeans struggled to grasp the significance of this New World, and toward the end of the 1500s, settlements were established on the eastern shores of the continent. As far as the explorers and colonists of this new land were concerned, the

North American continent was empty; the native American "Indians" who already lived there were considered to be uncivilized, primitive, and "lower" than the European colonists.[1] That the land was both empty and inhabited by "savages" was a contradiction the European settlers never really considered. It was left to twentieth-century Americans to come to grips with the manner in which their country was developed in the image of Europe.

The development of America from 1500 to 1700 was marked by the importation of the ideas of Western civilization—from the ancient Greeks and the Catholic Church to philosophers, theologians, and scientists of the Renaissance, Reformation, Age of Science, and Enlightenment. The attitudes of the colonists toward sport and recreation were representative of the regions of Europe from which the settlers came, and during the first two hundred years of colonization, these attitudes were most strongly influenced by religion. This stands to reason in that many of the colonists were motivated to make the perilous journey to the New World because of religious persecution in the Old World.

SPORT IN ENGLAND: A TALE OF TWO CULTURES

To understand the development of sport in Colonial America, it is helpful to begin with the role of sport in England during the same period. Sport in England was influenced significantly by the Reformation, especially John Calvin's brand of religion. During the 1550s, hundreds of English converts fled from the harsh Catholic reaction to Protestantism under Queen Mary Tudor ("Bloody Mary," who ruled from 1554 to 1557).[2] Even as 300 of their brethren were being executed, they studied Calvin's theology in Geneva, eventually returning to England. This story epitomizes the conflict in England during the 1500s: The monarchy, along with the common people and the Catholics, were allied against the Puritans and Parliament. These alliances were about the changing nature of the Western world. The monarchy, Catholics, and common people of England favored a lifestyle that was primarily agrarian, was cyclical with regard to time, was patriarchal and ascriptive in terms of family and position, and generally represented the way that Europeans had lived for centuries. In contrast, the reformers represented the world that was to come; they supported a meritocracy, were bourgeois or business oriented, viewed time in a linear fashion, and sought to change the nature of English culture.

These differences manifested themselves in business, religion, politics, and, for our purposes, sport. The most significant religious group in England was the Puritans, who sought to make God's kingdom come alive on earth. Puritans wanted to use God's time in the most efficient manner possible. Idleness was the most serious of sins, for wasting the gift of time was a sin for which one could never atone. Once time was gone, it could never be brought back and used more efficiently.

We can see how this type of thinking fits with a newly industrialized society. While sixteenth-century England was not "technological" in the sense with which we are familiar today, the advent of water and steam power in the lives

Sport and Physical Education

1647 General Court in New England outlaws shuffleboard, bowling, and gaming

1665 First organized horse race in New York City

1733 Schuylkill Fishing Company, Philadelphia

1734 Students at Harvard play "baseball"

1736 First known admission fee charged for sporting event, a horse race in New York City

1766 First Jockey Club founded, Philadelphia

1768 Horse racing begins on Long Island

of the English revolutionized the manner in which products were refined and brought to market. This new technology could be used twenty-four hours a day, and to fail to use this time was both unprofitable and a sin against God. It is easy to see how industry and religion combined to create a culture that was urban and technological rather than rural and agrarian, and that the new ways of life were radically different from the old and required different ways of looking at the world.

Sport in England was similar to that in other parts of Europe. Football was a popular game, yet city administrators had tried to put an end to the game even before the Puritans came along. Football was a violent affair, usually taking place after church on Sunday and accompanied by drinking and many bumps, bruises, and broken bones. Drunken boys and men chased one another through the fields, towns, and villages, all in pursuit of an inflated pig bladder, in a contest that was more like "king of the hill" than any modern game. In the process, windows were broken, furniture smashed, and bodies incapacitated through drink or injury.

> In the cities, especially, football was considered a disruptive game best prohibited. . . . Urban footballers not only interfered with commerce but also destroyed property. In 1608 the town council of Manchester complained that 'a company of lewd and disordered persons' annually broke 'many men's windows and glass at their pleasures.'[3]

No doubt the participants had a lot of fun, but the next day they were probably not fit to work, to say the least!

While town fathers tried to put an end to the game because of the civic disorder it created, the Puritans hated the game because of the drinking, the wasted time, and general disrespect players and spectators seemed to have for the "Lord's Day," the Sabbath.[4] Any playful activity that removed the chosen few from "Godliness" was considered wicked, especially if it occurred on Sunday. Football, and most other recreational activities, were wicked because they did just this.

Playful activities were considered wicked for a variety of reasons. The keeping of the Sabbath,

or "Sabbatarianism," reflected Puritan ideals about work and rest. Sunday was the Lord's day, a day of rest, and was not to be used for selfish and sinful indulgence in physical pleasure. Other games and recreations were sinful as well: stoolball, quoits, bowling, and dancing; boxing and wrestling; running, jumping, and throwing contests; and blood sports such as cockfighting and bear- and bullbaiting. All of these games had in common the seeking of physical pleasure (an association with the "paganism" of Catholicism) and gambling.

Gambling was associated with winning money without toil and wasting money earned—both viewed as sinful activities. Gambling also was associated with taking delight in carnal pleasures, and the association with drinking, gambling, and sex made traditional pastimes off limits to Englishmen. "In the Puritan equation, the active pursuit of pleasure meant a first step down the path of immorality, away from the portals of heaven."[5] In sum, there were many arguments against the old ways of play and recreation, all of which facilitated profitability and religiosity in the new industrial world as well as mitigated against idling away one's time seeking physical pleasure.

This conflict in cultures came to a head in 1618 when King James was petitioned to support the "common folk" and their traditional dancing and playing after church on Sundays. In a previous chapter, we noted that James issued a royal Declaration on Lawful Sports, ordering that "after the end of divine service our good people be not disturbed . . . or discouraged from any lawful recreation such as dancing, either men or women, archery for men, leaping, vaulting or any other such harmless recreation."[6] James ordered that his Declaration be read from the pulpits in churches all over England, and those who refused were punished. However, this did not stop the Puritans from pressing their views on play, and after James died in 1625, his son Charles had to deal with the same issue. In 1633, Charles had the Declaration expanded and reissued, which led to still more discord between the monarchy and the Puritans. Eventually, the Puritans rose in violent rebellion, initiating the English civil war, which led to the

Puritans executing Charles and taking control of Parliament and the country.

The Puritans were not entirely successful, even though they won the war. Traditional pastimes remained popular, and maypole dances, football games, drinking, and other activities continued, although they were significantly curtailed. In 1660, the monarchy was restored, which allowed for some of the traditional games to be held again. However, the Puritan Sabbath was exported to America, where Puritans sought to create the perfect society in a land untainted by the paganism of old Europe.

SPORT IN NEW ENGLAND: THE PURITANS

New England Puritans were strongly influenced by the Puritan movement in seventeenth-century England and for the most part did not encourage playful activities. The initial generation of Puritans in Massachusetts tried "to establish a society dedicated to the preservation of the visible church and bound by a philosophy which clearly defined man's role and niche in the world."[7] This philosophy valued hierarchy, inequality, mutability, variety, and order.[8] The New England Puritans believed that all men, as descendants of Adam, were corrupted by Original Sin. This meant that all human beings were born "flawed" in the eyes of God, and so it was necessary to build a community that could restrain the evil impulses of the sinner. As Perry Miller noted,

> Without a coercive state to restrain evil impulses and administer punishments, no life will be safe, no property secure, no honor observed. Therefore, upon Adam's apostasy, God Himself instituted governments among men. . . . He enacted that all men should be under some sort of corporate rule, that they should all submit to the sway of their superiors, that no man should live apart from his fellows, that the government should have full power to enforce obedience and to inflict every punishment that the crimes of men deserved.[9]

New England Puritans, like their English ancestors, were extremely concerned with the religious

life, and their interpretation of what was the good religious life determined how they should behave on this earth. Seen this way, Puritanism in New England was a throwback to the Middle Ages and the Reformation, during which eras the way one lived life on this earth played a role in whether one's eternal soul went to heaven.

With this idea in mind, the Puritans sought to develop governments that would fulfill God's will here on earth. Government to the Puritans was quite a bit different from that which we experience today. Indeed, government to the Puritans was an active vehicle to promote the good religious life:

> The state to them was an active instrument of leadership, discipline, and wherever necessary, of coercion; it legislated over any or all aspects of human behavior. . . . The commanders were not to trim their policies by the desires of the people, but to drive ahead upon the predetermined course; the people were all to turn out as they were ordered . . . there was no idea of the equality of all men. There was no questioning that men who would not serve the purposes of the society should be whipped into line. The objectives were clear and unmistakable; any one's disinclination to dedicate himself to them was obviously so much recalcitrancy and depravity.[10]

Salvation could be had only through the control of both one's emotions and behaviors, so the Puritans debated extensively just what the proper emotions and behaviors for the saved soul were. The Puritans were God-fearing people who left their legacy in the form of the Protestant work ethic, which personified the principles of hard work, sobriety, and piety. Although men and women were believed to possess a natural desire for play and recreational activities, the Puritans also believed that play and games could be the "workshop" of the devil. The Puritans were very utilitarian, and the climate in New England required that if people were to survive the harsh winters and short growing seasons, then an enormous amount of hard physical work had to be completed. This efficient use of time left little time for amusements, but it was enormously profitable and undoubtedly led to the success of the early Puritan colonists. Had it not been for their thrifty and hardworking attitude, it is arguable that they would never have survived the harsh New England winters. Consequently, the environment of New England played an important role in confirming the Puritan lifestyle of hard work, thriftiness, and efficient use of time.

Any available free time was, according to leading Puritans, supposed to be spent in church or an appropriate recreational activity. The Puritans adhered to a classical religious dualism that separated soul and body. Puritan dogma argued that spiritual nourishment was provided for the soul while the body was made for work and prayer, and not play. The early Puritan mentality with respect to work and play can be illustrated by the Puritan saying "Idle hands are the devil's playground."

The Puritans recognized, however, that an absolute ban on recreation was impossible, and two extremes in Puritan attitudes eventually evolved. The first extreme was that sport in the right form was beneficial if pursued in the appropriate manner and helpful in maintaining civic order. John Downame, a New England minister, argued that moderate recreation might even be necessary to keep individuals refreshed in order to work and pray. Similarly, John Winthrop, the first governor of the Massachusetts Bay Company, found that abstention from recreation created disorder in his life. Moderate activities were necessary to refresh both the body and the overworked mind. In so doing, order was maintained by achieving the balance between mind and body that was ordained by God. Recreations such as fishing, hunting, and walking became acceptable because it was believed that they improved health and renewed spirits so that people could return to work refreshed.[11]

The other extreme was negative and represented the response of the New England magistrates. The magistrates wrote laws that ensured both the sanctity of the Sabbath and the promotion of the public good, demonstrating the integrated nature of New England government and the Puritan church. In 1630, a man named John Baker was ordered to be whipped for bird hunting on the Sabbath.[12] What concerned the magistrates was Baker's failure to keep the Sabbath, and not his bird hunting.

Still, the primary means of recreation in seventeenth-century New England was sporting, and as a consequence, it was sporting recreation that frequently was condemned. By 1635, all persons absent from church meetings faced fines or imprisonment. Activities that detracted from the economic success of the colony were also condemned, and sport was one means by which colonists could shirk their obligations. But it was not the only one. Inns and taverns were felt to disrupt the orderly arrangement of society, and in 1647, the General Court outlawed shuffleboard and, soon after, bowling and gaming in general. But it was not the games as much as it was the drinking, gambling, and wasteful use of time associated with the games that threatened the magistrates' sense of social order. As one historian notes, "The delay in banning these games, as well as the emphasis on unprofitability and drunkenness, suggest that the magistrates did not intend to denounce the nature of the game, but rather to attack overspending and inebriation."[13]

The influence of Puritanism reached its peak during the mid-1600s, yet even at this time, many colonists ignored the sermons that argued against play and games. Only one in four colonists in New England was a church member, and once the colonies were firmly established, the urgency of the Puritan message was lost.[14] The exceptions to this rule were the "Great Awakening," a period in which Puritan ideas enjoyed a powerful resurgence in the middle of the eighteenth century; the pockets of Puritanism that lasted well into the nineteenth century; and the admonishments against playful activities on Sunday, which persist even today in the form of various Blue Laws.

If an individual who lived in Massachusetts or Pennsylvania wanted to leave the Quaker or Puritan sphere of influence for a mug of ale or other forms of entertainment, he did not have to travel far. Two days or less on horseback heading away from Boston or Philadelphia would put the traveler in an area where taverns and inns were beyond the reach of most religious authorities. It was in the taverns that the playful amusements of the colonial period were held.

AMUSEMENTS IN NEW ENGLAND

The taverns and inns that the magistrates tried to manage were the American version of English pubs, German beer halls, and European inns. People needed a place to stay when traveling, and they also gathered at taverns and inns for amusements, conversation, drink, and friendly competition. Taverns were built about a day's ride by horseback from each other, extending from Canada to Georgia. Frontier taverns provided amusements and lodging for the weary traveler and sports fan alike.

It was not unusual for tavern keepers to arrange contests and promote them by offering prizes, charging fees, and selling food and drink. Darts and cards were popular games, and marksmanship, boxing, cockfighting, and horse racing were among the most popular contests. In shooting contests, a nail was partially driven into a tree, fence, or post, and each contestant attempted to finish driving the nail by shooting at it with his rifle from a preset distance. Turkey shoots were also popular. In this contest, the unsuspecting turkey was tied behind a tree stump so that only its head would pop up. The victor was the marksman who could literally blow the turkey's head off at a distance of 80 yards or more.

Puritan influence in New England gradually eroded with the wave of non-Puritan immigrants who settled in New England. In addition, third- and fourth-generation Puritans began to question the practices of the church. However, rampant recreation did not spring up overnight. The Puritans remained politically powerful in New England, but over time, amusements such as hopscotch, horse racing, ice skating, and sleigh riding became more socially acceptable.

SPORT IN THE MID-ATLANTIC REGION

The Quakers of Pennsylvania influenced sport in much the same way as the Puritans did in New England. Dutch Calvinists in the New York area, in contrast to the Quakers and the Puritans, were somewhat more friendly toward playful activities. In 1743, Benjamin Franklin wrote proposals relating to the education of youth. Franklin's educational philosophy was focused on the building of academies where the youth of Philadelphia would learn how to prepare and face life; this same philosophy remains relevant in the 21st century.

Franklin was very concerned about the educational environment that pupils would be emerged in. He called for a healthful environment that featured a garden, meadows, orchards, and playing fields where students could participate in sports such as running races, wrestling competition, leaping and swimming. In 1749, he opened the doors to his first academy in Philadelphia where physical education and sports competition were part of the curriculum.[15] It seems likely that Franklin, an expert swimmer, gave swimming lessons to his students. Dutch immigrants "smoked their pipes, played at bowls, and skated on the wintry ice."[16] Eating, drinking, and gambling were common activities of the Europeans who settled in what was originally known as New Amsterdam. The Dutch immigrants continued to observe their traditional European customs as much as their lives in the New World permitted, and this included their sporting activities.

Horse racing was popular from the beginning, ostensibly for the improvement of the breed but also because New Yorkers loved to watch the races and gamble on the outcomes. During the 1700s, horses were imported from England to improve the American breed, and as soon as this occurred, rivalries arose. As early as 1768, a race was held between Figure, an English horse, and the American horse Salem. The English horse prevailed, but the interest generated from the race gave birth to intersectional rivalries in America.

New Yorkers also enjoyed bowling, golf, and early versions of croquet, tennis, and cricket. Shooting matches were popular, and in the winter, many New Yorkers enjoyed sleigh rides and skating. The sporting life evident in New York City in the early twenty-first century can trace its origins back to the early days of the city in the seventeenth and eighteenth centuries.

SPORT IN THE SOUTH

The American South was different from the North in many respects. The growth of sport in the South was facilitated by a favorable climate, the absence of Puritan reformers, and the importation and practice of sports, games, and amusements by the various immigrant groups, especially the English. Catholicism was a fixture in the South and was considerably more tolerant of sports activities than Puritanism. Unlike the New England colonists, southern settlers immigrated more for adventure and opportunity than for the pursuit of religious freedom.

The southern gentlemen of Virginia were extremely competitive, individualistic, and materialistic, elements that reflected the economic conditions of the South. As one scholar notes, the wealthy planters enjoyed wagering money and tobacco on horse races because "competitive gaming was for many gentlemen a means of translating a particular set of values into action."[17] Indeed, gambling reflected the core elements of seventeenth- and eighteenth-century gentry values. The great plantations occupied huge tracts of land, and the planters aggressively sought to acquire more land to increase their income. This led the plantation owners to develop attitudes of rugged individualism and competitiveness, and these attitudes manifested themselves in their playful pastime of wagering on horses. "In large part, the goal of the competition within the gentry group was to improve social position by increasing wealth."[18] A number of prominent American politicians, including many of the Founding Fathers, enjoyed horse racing. George Washington, Thomas Jefferson, James Madison, John Marshall, Henry Clay, and Andrew Jackson, among others, loved to wager on the races.

The first horse races were a quarter mile long, a distance that eventually led to the name of the Virginia quarter horse. During the early days of horse racing, it was not unusual for races to be held on town streets. Racetracks were built in Virginia, Maryland, and South Carolina. Wagering was often heavy, and both women and men placed bets. The big races were often followed by elaborate festivities attended by those who could afford to participate. Horse racing, however, was not the only popular sport. Southerners also enjoyed fox hunting, hunting, fishing, rowing, lawn bowling, dancing, cock fighting, boxing, and fencing which were "imported" by English settlers and other European immigrants who settled in the South. Shooting matches were popular throughout Colonial America, and the South was no exception. One story illustrates the meaning of the contests to the participants. The legendary Daniel Boone described an encounter between himself and some of his Indian friends: "I often went hunting with them, and frequently gained their applause for my activity at our shooting matches. I was careful not to exceed many of them in shooting; for no people are more envious than they in this sport."[19]

During the antebellum era, and afterward as well, social class often dictated appropriate sporting behavior. Proper southern gentlemen were expected to exhibit requisite social and athletic skills that included riding, dancing, fencing, and conversation. Southern gentlemen were more often observers and producers of sports than actual participants, especially in boxing and horse racing, where the athletes frequently were slaves (Figure 9-1).

The vast majority of slaves were subject to a hard life of either fieldwork or domestic service. Slaves often endured harsh conditions and punishment and were purposely kept ignorant by their masters. It was illegal in many parts of the South to teach a slave to read and write, although many whites risked their lives to do this. Yet slaves were also participants in southern sport as jockeys and boxers, providing entertainment and betting opportunities for whites.

American boxers, or "pugilists" as they were known, were strongly influenced by the English. Eighteenth-century Elizabethan England is recognized as the birthplace of modern boxing. According to William Lewis,

> With the decline of fencing, boxing became increasingly popular in England. Fighters were called 'bruisers.' They lost a fight only if they failed to come up to 'scratch,' a line drawn in

Figure 9-1
Black jockeys in the South.

the middle of the ring. Since there was no time limit, fighters took a tremendous beating. A round was considered over only when a man went down. Gouging and hair pulling were allowed and since no gloves were worn, broken bones were common. . . . There was no medical supervision and most fighters died young.[20]

America's first well-known pugilist was Tom Molineaux, who gained his freedom from slavery by fighting on the Southern Plantation Circuit (Figure 9-2). After beating the best that the North was able to offer, Molineaux went to England in 1810 to fight the British champion, Tom Cribb. The fight took place in the pouring rain, and after 29 rounds, Molineaux was beating Cribb. When the partisan British fans were able to stop the fight briefly on a technicality, Molineaux caught a chill and was eventually beaten by Cribb in the fortieth round. They fought again later on, but the result was the same.

While this particular fight caught the attention of many Colonial Americans, boxing as a sport did not attract a large following until the latter part of the nineteenth century. Boxing's early years were spent in obscure and questionable surroundings, for boxing was outlawed in most of the states and territories (Figure 9-3). Fights took place in barns, river barges, and other secluded locations.

Figure 9-2
Tom Molineaux, early American boxer.

Figure 9-3
Early American boxing match.

Figure 9-4
Native Americans playing lacrosse.

CONTRIBUTIONS OF NATIVE AMERICANS

The Native American sport of lacrosse, as well as other ball games, exerted a significant influence during sport's formative years, and lacrosse is still popular in many regions of the country. Native Americans originated the game of lacrosse in the Northeast (Figure 9-4). The Iroquois, which was actually an Indian confederacy of the Cayuga, Oneida, Mohawk, Seneca, and Onondaga tribes of New York, were known for their lacrosse skills. With the introduction of horses to North America by the Spanish, the Indians of the Great Plains and Far West soon became expert riders and engaged in horse racing and tribal dances. Stories of courage and athletic prowess of Native Americans and

Figure 9-5
Ball playing among the Choctaw Indians.

slaves soon spread throughout the various regions of North America (Figure 9-5).

SUMMARY

Sport in Colonial America developed largely along regional lines and was influenced by the cultural, political, and religious agendas of the era. Quakers in Pennsylvania, Puritans in New England, Catholics in the South, and Native Americans all exerted a significant influence during sport's formative years.

The link between sport and religion in Colonial America was significant. The Quakers in Pennsylvania and the Puritans in New England believed that the path to salvation was through prayer and hard work. Time was "God given," and what people did with their time on earth determined, to a large degree, their prospects for salvation. Generally, engag-

ing in play, games, and sport did not constitute the wise use of time. While Puritans and Quakers realized that they could not stop people from engaging in play and games, they did their best to discourage it, with some notable exceptions.

As time went by, immigrants began to settle in New England and Pennsylvania who were not Puritans or Quakers. These immigrants, along with second -and third-generation Puritans, were more favorable toward recreational activities. In large part because of the hard work that their ancestors did, third- and fourth-generation Puritans and Quakers were quite prosperous and had the time and resources to enjoy games and sports. With the exception of the Great

Awakening, Puritanism as a theology declined in popularity from the mid-1600s. All that was left were some of the more explicit measures of the religion, such as the keeping of the Sabbath and the Blue Laws.

America's founding fathers, most notably Benjamin Franklin, enjoyed horse racing and other physical activities. The Dutch Calvinists settled in an area they called New Amsterdam, now New York. Like the Quakers and Puritans, the Dutch left Europe for religious freedom and the promise of a better life. However, the Dutch were not opposed to play, games, and sport. They enjoyed horse racing, bowling, golf, and other activities that were frowned upon by the Quakers and Puritans. Religious beliefs did not affect the Dutch in the same way they affected the Quakers and Puritans with regard to sports and related activities.

In the southeastern part of Colonial America, the Catholic Church was the dominant religious institution. Catholics enjoyed games and sports, unlike their counterparts in Pennsylvania and New England. The English who settled in Virginia brought with them their passion for horse racing, which flourished in the South. Boxing was also a popular sport.

The early colonists, then, were influenced by a variety of factors including the attitudes toward sport they brought with them from Europe, the nature of the early American economy, and religion. These attitudes for the most part remained unchanged throughout the colonial period, although each region continued to experience growth through immigration. It was not until the 1800s that American attitudes toward sport experienced any significant change.

DISCUSSION QUESTIONS

1. How did Puritanism have an impact on the development of sport in New England? Are any ideas of the Puritans with us today in contemporary sport?

2. What were the popular sports in Colonial America? Why were many of these sports so violent by today's standards?

3. How did sport in the South differ from sport in New England? What factors contributed to the growth and popularity of sport in the South?

4. Who was Tom Molineaux? Research his journey to England and the boxing match he had in 1810 against the British champion, Tom Cribb.

5. To what extent did Benjamin Franklin believe in the value of physical education and sport? Did he excel as an athlete in any particular sport?

INTERNET RESOURCES

Archiving Early America
http://earlyamerica.com
Includes archival materials such as maps, newspapers, and writings of Colonial America; also provides links related to notable women in Colonial America, a chronological history, and a list of milestone events.

Puritans in Colonial America
http://lonestar.texas.net/~mseifert/puritan.html
Includes interesting information about the Puritans.

International Museum of the Horse: Legacy of the Horse
www.imh.org/imh/kyhpl3a.html
Provides information on horse racing in England and Colonial America.

The Sporting Past in American History
www.oah.org/pubs/magazine/sport/borish.html

Contains an article published by the Organization of American Historians.

African Americans in the Sports Arena
www.liu.edu/cwis/cwp/library/aaitsa.htm
Presents information on African-American athletes and their involvement in basketball, football, baseball, boxing, horse racing, cycling, and track and field.

Slavery in America: Historical Overview
**www.slaveryinamerica.org/history/hs_es_overview
.htm**
Covers the history of slavery in America through the Civil War; includes valuable information on black athletes of the era.

Visit the *History and Philosophy of Sport and Physical Education* Online Learning Center (www.mhhe.com/ mechikoff6e) for additional information and study tools.

SUGGESTIONS FOR FURTHER READING

Baker, W. J. *Sports in the Western World.* Urbana: University of Illinois Press, 1988.

Betts, J. R. "Mind and Body in Early American Thought." In *The American Sporting Experience,* ed. Steven A. Riess. NewYork: Leisure Press, 1984.

Brailsford, Dennis. "Morals and Maulers: The Ethics of Early Pugilism." *Journal of Sport History* 12, no. 2 (Summer 1985): 126–42.

Cone, Carl B. "The Molineaux–Cribb Fight, 1810: Was Tom Molineaux Robbed?" *Journal of Sport History* 9 (Winter 1982): 83–91.

Struna, N. "Puritans and Sport: The Irretrievable Tide of Change." In *The American Sporting Experience,* ed. Steven A. Riess. New York: Leisure Press, 1984.

Swanson, R. A., and Betty Spears. *History of Sport and Physical Education,* 4th ed. Madison, WI: Brown & Benchmark, 1995.

NOTES

1. James Oliver Robertson, *American Myth, American Reality* (New York: Hill & Wang, 1980).

2. W. J. Baker, *Sports in the Western World* (Urbana: University of Illinois Press, 1988).

3. Ibid., 75.

4. Ibid., 75.

5. Ibid., 77.

6. Ibid., 79.

7. Nancy Struna, "Puritans and Sport: The Irretrievable Tide of Change," in *The American Sporting Experience,* ed. Steven A. Riess (New York: Leisure Press, 1984), 16.

8. Ibid.

9. Perry Miller, *Errand into the Wilderness* (New York: Harper & Row, 1956), 142–43.

10. Ibid., 143.

11. Betty Spears and Richard A. Swanson, *History of Sport and Physical Education,* 3rd ed. (Dubuque, IA: Wm. C. Brown, 1983).

12. Ibid.

13. Ibid., 19.

14. Baker, *Sports in the Western World.*

15. Benjamin Franklin, "Proposals Relating to the Education of Youth." Report of U.S. Commissioner of Education, vol. 1, 1902, pp. 182–185. Franklin had a strong belief in the virtues of physical education. He was a superb swimmer and spent time as a swimming instructor. He became so good that as a young man he was invited to give a swimming exhibition in London. Mabel Lee, one of America's great sport and physical education historians claims that Franklin was the first recorded promoter of physical education in America! Mabel Lee. *A History of Physical Education and Sports in the U.S.A.* (New York: John Wiley & Sons, 1983), P. 16.

16. John R. Betts, "Mind and Body in Early American Thought," in *The American Sporting Experience,* ed. Steven A. Riess (New York: Leisure Press, 1984), 62.

17. Thomas Breen, "Horses and Gentlemen: The Cultural Significance of Gambling Among the Gentry of Virginia," *William and Mary Quarterly* 34 (1977): 243.

18. Ibid., 245.

19. Daniel Boone, "The ADVENTURES of Col. Daniel Boone; Containing a NARRATIVE of the WARS of Kentucke, 1798," in *The Discovery, Settlement and Present State of Kentucke,* ed. John Filson (New York: Coring Books, 1962), 65.

20. William A. Lewis, "Man to Man—A History of Boxing," *Mankind* 3, no. 6 (April 1972): 32–41.

CHAPTER 10

Changing Concepts of the Body

An Overview of Sport and Play in Nineteenth-Century America

OBJECTIVES

Upon completing this chapter, you will be able to:

- Recognize some of the social and technological changes that were taking place in America that would have an effect on the philosophical view of the body.
- Recognize some of the social and technological changes that would shape the development of sport and play in nineteenth-century America.
- Discuss the influence of transcendentalism and pragmatism on the philosophical view of the body and the necessity for physical activity.
- Understand the impact of the writings of Ralph Waldo Emerson and Henry David Thoreau on the philosophy of dualism.
- Understand the impact of Charles Darwin's theory of evolution on society, the environment, and the role and scope of physical education.
- Identify the contributions of pragmatists Charles Sanders Peirce and William James to monist thought and the value placed on sport and physical education.
- Recognize how religion, in the form of muscular Christianity, was used to justify sport and manly physical activity.
- Apply modernization theory to the historical development of sport and physical education, especially in nineteenth-century America.
- Identify the individuals and organizations that improved and popularized the following sports in the nineteenth century: horse and harness racing, cricket, baseball, football, rowing, and track and field.
- Explain the appeal of the amateur sports movement in America and its use as a tool of class warfare.
- Discuss the hardships that Marshall "Major" Taylor had to endure during his athletic career.
- Understand the extent of racial segregation in American sport during the nineteenth century.

General Events

1803–1882 Ralph Waldo Emerson
1809–1882 Charles Darwin
1812 War of 1812
1817–1862 Henry David Thoreau
1821 First public high school, in Massachusetts
1833 Oberlin College founded, first coeducational college
1837 Telegraph invented by Samuel Morse
1839–1914 Charles Sanders Peirce
1840 2800 miles of railway tracks in U.S.
1842–1910 William James
1844 First telegraph in regular operation
1846 Sewing machine invented
1859 Darwin publishes *On the Origin of Species*
1860 30,000 miles of railroad tracks in U.S.
1861–1865 Abraham Lincoln president; Civil War
1876 Telephone invented by Alexander Graham Bell

Sport

1819 John Stuart Skinner writes articles on sport in *American Farmer*
1823 Sir Henry v. Eclipse horse race
1825 "The Sporting Olio," first column on sport, deals with horse racing

INTRODUCTION

The nineteenth century was a time of rapid change. Viewed from the perspective of today, it is difficult to say which changes were the most significant. These changes do seem to have one characteristic in common, though: All of them have some basis in an awareness of the material aspects of life. This interest in the "here and now" remains a characteristic of the contemporary American character.

Changes in the United States can be described from a variety of perspectives: demographic, technological, cultural, political, and philosophical. No one view can adequately describe all of the different types of change that occurred, and the use of many perspectives helps the student of history understand the plurality of American culture. In short, America is not only a big "melting pot," as so many historians have put it. Rather, America is also a nation created by a variety of peoples and cultures living through changes upon which each group has a unique perspective. What these peoples and cultures had in common in nineteenth-century America was an understanding that the material, secular world was real and important to their lives. While religion and spiritual matters maintained an important role in the lives of Americans, the emphasis on the material world was manifest in a growing awareness of the use of technology to make life better, the gradual movement from the country to the city to facilitate industry, the use of rationality to understand how to live better, and the use of philosophy to understand the material world. The four perspectives through which we examine these changes are urbanization, industrialization, modernization theory, and the ways in which all of these changes coincided with philosophical changes among intellectuals.

In the 1820s, America began to shift from a farming nation to an urban-industrial nation. Americans simultaneously experienced a technological revolution that radically changed the way they lived. As historian John R. Betts noted,

> Telegraph lines went up all over the landscape, the railroad followed the steamboat from the East to the Midwest and the South, and by 1860 a network of over thirty-thousand miles of track covered the United States. An immigrant tide helped populate midwestern states, and Cincinnati, St. Louis, Chicago, Milwaukee, and Detroit gradually became western metropolises. The reaper and other new tools slowly transformed farm life; agricultural societies sprouted up; journals brought scientific information to the farmer; and the agricultural fair developed into a prominent social institution.[1]

These changes facilitated a shift from an isolated farming lifestyle to a more city-oriented lifestyle. Railroads facilitated the shipping of goods from east to west and made travel much faster, easier, and safer. Telegraphs made the exchange of information much more rapid than anyone had dreamed possible. Through the use of telegraphs by newspapers and magazines, the institution of modern journalism developed. Americans had access to inexpensive information, and this change had an impact on every facet of American life. This ability to assimilate large amounts of information was indicative of the fact that more Americans than ever were able to read and write, and the level of literacy in turn encouraged the development of communication technologies in a kind of snowball effect.

EARLY TECHNOLOGICAL INNOVATIONS AND THEIR IMPACT ON SPORT

Other technological changes affected American society as well, and many of these made possible sport as we know it. Mass production during the nineteenth century enabled the manufacture of cheap athletic equipment like bats and balls. The sewing machine made mass production of team uniforms possible and sports equipment toward the end of the nineteenth century. Vulcanized rubber facilitated the manufacture of bicycle tires, as well as resilient rubber balls for golf and tennis. The incandescent light bulb, developed by Thomas A. Edison in 1879, ushered in a new era in the social life of the cities. Electric lights eventually replaced the smoky, dim gas lamps that had made large indoor events difficult to hold. Electrification allowed for the development of home appliances that made everyday life easier and helped create more leisure time. The replacement of horse-drawn carriages with electric streetcars directly affected the development of sport by transporting large numbers of people who wished to see professional baseball games.[2] As Betts noted,

> Numerous inventions and improvements applied to sport were of varying importance: the stop watch, the percussion cap, the streamlined sulky, barbed wire, the safety cycle, ball bearings, and artificial ice for skating rinks, among others. Improved implements often popularized and revolutionized the style of a sport, as in the invention of the sliding seat of the rowing shell, the introduction

of the rubber-wound gutta-percha ball which necessitated the lengthening of golf courses, and the universal acceptance of the catcher's mask.[3]

After the Civil War, cameras were used to record images of sporting experiences. In 1872, Edward Muybridge made one of the first "moving pictures" of a trotting horse, a technique eventually applied to celluloid film and early research in biomechanics. The telephone, the typewriter, the phonograph, the automobile, and many other inventions were developed in the nineteenth century and in one way or another had an impact on sport. Betts summarized these changes by noting that

> While athletics and outdoor recreation were sought as a release from the confinements of city life, industrialization and the urban movement were the basic causes for the rise of organized sport. And the urban movement was, of course, greatly enhanced by the revolutionary transformation in communication, transportation, agriculture, and industrialization.[4]

As these changes suggest, the patterns of life that we enjoy today took shape in the nineteenth century. It was left to the philosophers and historians to explain these changes—to provide systematic and rational explanations of how to understand a rapidly changing world.

NINETEENTH-CENTURY AMERICAN PHILOSOPHY: TRANSCENDENTALISM AND PRAGMATISM

During this era, two major philosophical movements developed in the United States: transcendentalism and pragmatism. The New England transcendentalists were a very influential group of writers, critics, philosophers, theologians, and social reformers who lived in and around Concord, Massachusetts, from about 1836 to 1860.[5] *Transcendentalism* was more of a literary phenomenon than a philosophical movement, a passionate outcry on the part of a number of brilliant and articulate young Americans who were influenced by European philosophers like Immanuel Kant, Johann Fichte, and Georg Hegel. Basically, this group rejected the narrow rationalism, pietism, and conservatism of eighteenth-century America and developed a "philosophy" that was eclectic, individualistic, and relevant to almost every aspect of nineteenth-century American life.

While transcendentalism was representative of a strain of thought that was developed in Europe, it had its own characteristics that were very attractive to Americans. Transcendentalists believed in the godlike nature of the human spirit and insisted on the authority of the individual. They rejected the idea of metaphysical dualism, arguing that all aspects of being human were somehow connected. This meant that individuals should not be seen as separate from society, that humans were a natural part of the universe, and that the mind and the body were as one. Transcendentalists believed that (1) imagination was better than reason, (2) creativity was more important than theory, (3) the creative artist was the epitome of civilization, and (4) action was more important than contemplation. This last characteristic manifested itself in an awareness of the importance of physicality. Indeed, the transcendentalists were physical in a contemporary sense of the word. They were reformers who sought to change the way nineteenth-century Americans lived and who believed that nature is "real" and that humans are a very important part of nature.

In advancing these arguments, transcendentalists helped make many types of sport and physical education necessary and important. Activities in the outdoors became much more acceptable to Americans, as transcendentalists successfully argued that these activities taught people independence, survival skills, and other desirable virtues.

Ralph Waldo Emerson

Ralph Waldo Emerson (1803–1882) was born, raised, and educated in Boston. Like many philosophers, Emerson initially studied to become a preacher. After completing his studies, he accepted a pastorate in Boston, but he left after the death of his wife from tuberculosis in 1831. He eventually sailed for Europe, a trip crucial to the development of the "philosophy" of transcendentalism.

Emerson was not really a philosopher, however, as much as he was a writer and poet. Like the philosophes of Enlightenment Europe, Emerson was concerned with the nature of the self and the universe. Emerson believed that religion as he had been taught it was inadequate to explain his personal relationship with reality, but he still wanted an explanation that could accommodate his religious beliefs and satisfy his intellectual curiosity. What he developed was an expression of his individuality and the admiration of the hero, traits that fit well with ideas popular with his contemporaries. Emerson was the first of the American transcendentalists, and perhaps the most influential of the group. His optimism infected those who followed him, and his ideas of overcoming, or "transcending," the dichotomies that were used to describe American life were readily accepted by Americans. Those who read Emerson's essays saw themselves as intimately connected, both physically and mentally, with nature and the city. This helped lead Americans out of the dualistic lifestyles advocated by the New England Puritans who preceded Emerson.

Physicality and the desire to live within and around the beauty of the natural world appealed to the transcendentalists. This belief and practice provided philosophical support to the emerging field of physical training.

Henry David Thoreau

While Emerson was the first American transcendentalist, Henry David Thoreau (1817–1862) may be the best known. Born in Concord, Massachusetts, Thoreau was a brilliant student, described by his teachers and friends as a moral and intelligent man. Early in life, Thoreau adopted the ideas of the New England transcendentalists and gave up all plans of having a regular profession in life. As such, he "dropped out" to make pencils and work as a land surveyor, jobs that enabled him to earn a living for the rest of his life. But his best hours were spent trying to understand his relationship to his fellow man and to nature, and many of these hours were spent in the wilderness alone near Concord at Walden Pond.

For two years, Thoreau lived with Emerson in the Massachusetts countryside, absorbing Emerson's ideas and developing his own. Nature, for Thoreau, represented an "absolute freedom and wildness" that was superior to anything that humans could create. Therefore, humans were at their best when they lived as one with nature. This idea fit well with Americans who were moving westward, developing farms, and "carving civilization" out of the wilderness. Thoreau's ideas regarding the human spirit and the wilderness are described in one of his most famous works, *Walden, or Life in the Woods,* an experiment in which Thoreau tried to live in the most "natural" manner he could.[6] Thoreau believed that true freedom was to be found on the western frontier, and this idea was in step with the pervasive American attitude toward the taming of the wilderness.

Thoreau was not concerned only with nature, though. His essay "Civil Disobedience" has been the most influential of his works because of its guidelines on how to conduct a peaceful revolution. Thoreau's belief in individualism led him to argue that on certain occasions resistance, and even active rebellion, against the state was a valid moral choice. Gandhi developed his own doctrine of passive resistance from a reading of Thoreau's essay, and the Rev. Martin Luther King, Jr., was also influenced by his reading of Thoreau. In Thoreau, then, we see the philosophy of American individualism at its peak: Each person has the right and a moral obligation to protect his or her individuality with respect to the state.

In sum, Emerson, Thoreau, and their transendentalist colleagues abandoned dualistic philosophy and, in its place, created a philosophical or social movement that, in part, emphasized the physical character of being human and communion with the nature.

Pragmatism

Another perspective on the way that America changed in the nineteenth century was provided by a group of late nineteenth-century American intellectuals who developed the American philosophy known as *pragmatism.* The philosophy of pragmatism evolved from the desire to do two things: (1) determine the differences between the many philosophies developed in the preceding 2500 years, and (2) develop a practical method for dealing with the social unrest generated by the rapid changes in American society.

Pragmatism was a product of one of the most important scientific advances of all time, the seminal work on genetics by Charles Darwin. The value of Darwin's work to physical education may not be obvious at first, yet his influence on the modern mind is unquestioned in historical and philosophical circles. In short, Darwin revolutionized thinking by arguing that biological systems are the *response* to some change in the environment. Consequently, the moving human body can be seen as a response to a changing environment.

THE INFLUENCE OF CHARLES DARWIN

Charles Darwin (1809–1882) had a profound impact on both scientific investigation and philosophical inquiry, primarily through two works: *On the Origin of Species* (1859) and *The Descent of Man* (1871). Darwin's work is of particular historical importance to physical educators, for it was only after *Origin* was written that our physical selves were studied as a consequence of our environment. To a great extent, this is a goal of physical education and exercise science today.

In *Origin,* Darwin established beyond reasonable doubt that all living things, including humans, developed from a few extremely simple forms. His theory contradicted the prevailing explanation for the origin of each species, known as the "doctrine of special creation," which held that each species was created independently from every other species.[7] Monkeys, for instance, were believed to have always been monkeys and to have no genetic link to any other species. Darwin's scientific explanation of the origin of the species was applied to the disciplines of philosophy, science, and biology. In so doing, the explanations each discipline used for the nature of humanity were turned, literally and figuratively, upside down.[8]

Prior to Darwin, philosophers, theologians, teachers, and many others believed that the capacity to think was a result of a special gift of some type. Most accepted a religious answer for this phenomenon, that God somehow gave the gift of intelligence to humans. Interestingly, Americans living prior to Darwin did not believe that religion and science were incompatible. Rather, they believed that the findings of science would reinforce the revelations of the Bible.[9] For instance, a common class in the colleges of the day was titled "Evidences of Christianity," in which students were taught to view the wonders of the scientific world, and specifically the biological world, as evidence of God's incredible power.

After Darwin, however, popular explanations for the nature of the universe, along with romantic and transcendental explanations, were questioned. Darwin provided a scientifically convincing explanation for the genesis of humans, one that contradicted popular beliefs generally and the Bible specifically. Darwin's work, then, had important consequences for how intellectuals perceived our ability to think. As Cynthia Russett noted, "What was once seen as a unique philosophical faculty for perceiving abstract truths is now seen more simply as an ability to recognize empirically significant possibilities."[10]

What Darwin's work meant is that the ability to think is a product of our biology and not a special gift. This scientific explanation for the ability to think was world shattering, and the debate about whether it is a correct explanation of our intelligence continues to rage today. To understand how this argument must have affected Americans in the nineteenth century, we need only examine the heated contemporary debate between "creationists"

and "evolutionists" over content in school biology curricula. Basically, creationists believe the biblical version, described in the book of Genesis, of how humans were created by an act of God. Evolutionists, in contrast, believe that humans evolved from primates and that the ability to think is a product of adapting to the environment. Each argument is believed to be true by its proponents, and neither side will submit to the authority of the other.

Darwin's research legitimized the theory of evolution in a manner that seriously challenged the biblical story of Genesis. Furthermore, it legitimized the use of our senses and our powers of reason to understand the material world. According to Darwin's doctrine of natural selection, change must be supported by natural forces that can be observed, and extranatural forces, like religious miracles, are simply irrelevant to physical changes. Specifically, his work promoted the idea that our environment—both the material world around us and the social world in which we live—is the cause of the changes we experience, not other forces that we cannot observe. It is no coincidence that physical education in the modern world, which can be described as an attempt to control students' environments to promote skill acquisition and physical, social, spiritual, and psychological growth, began after Darwin's research was published.

THE PRAGMATISTS

Shortly after the publication of *On the Origin of Species,* a group of intellectuals around Harvard University began to talk about the impact of the book on philosophical issues. This group, which called itself the "Metaphysical Club," was composed of what later became the preeminent group of "progressives" in America. Yet, as Philip Smith notes, the name "Metaphysical Club" was selected more as a joke than anything else. None of the members of the club believed in metaphysics as the term was defined by contemporary philosophers. These men had as a goal the undermining of traditional metaphysics as a means of knowing reality.[11] Charles Peirce and William James were the group's most famous members, but men like Oliver Wendell Holmes, Jr., later a well-known Supreme Court justice, also attended the discussions. Out of the meetings of the Metaphysical Club came the ideas known in philosophy as "pragmatism."

Charles Sanders Peirce

Charles Peirce (1839–1914) was the principal organizer of the Metaphysical Club and one of its more notable members. As the founder of pragmatism, he formulated the first tenets of the philosophy. His first step was to reject everything Descartes said about the nature of reality: that all we can know absolutely are ideas. Descartes began by doubting everything, even his own existence, which Peirce said was silly. Peirce asserted that it is rational to accept some things as true even if we are not absolutely certain of their truth.

Peirce argued that there is no reality outside of nature where ideas exist. Rather, he suggested, we come to know ideas by using our senses. In so doing, Peirce unified the physical world and the ideal world, and so was a monist. Peirce argued that by empirically investigating the material world, we could create ideas, and that ideas induced in this manner are "real" in a philosophical sense. In other words, human beings *create* ideas, and the best way to do this is to use the scientific method. Peirce hoped that, for the first time, the ideas used to understand the world would be experimentally developed, tested, and laid to rest.

Peirce's hopes rest easily with most Americans. It makes sense to try to discover the nature of the universe by using the methods of science. One aspect of his philosophy has not been borne out, however. Peirce believed that the rules and generalizations we use to describe the world would be unchanging and universal. Yet, in the history of science, there has not been one law that does not have an exception. Even the law of gravity has been found by physicists to have exceptions. In any event, Peirce's contribution to the development of pragmatism is significant

to physical educators and exercise scientists. For our purposes, Peirce's pragmatism connects the human body with the mind in a way that makes them both one and the same: a unity. If there is no division between mind and body, then there is no placing of one over the other in an educational hierarchy. The education and training of the mind is just as important as the education and training of the body, since mind and body are considered a unified entity. Furthermore, his insistence that the scientific method is at the foundation of research helped to focus the research orientation of physical educators. Exercise physiology began to prosper since it was, at the time, the most scientific area within the physical education curriculum.

William James

William James (1842–1910), the other well-known member of the Metaphysical Club, was formally trained as a scientist. Beginning with physiology and anatomy, James eventually earned an M.D. degree. However, he never practiced medicine, turning instead to psychology and then philosophy. James taught at Harvard (1872–1907) during a time when the methods of science were applied to every field of study, including psychology. James is best known for shifting the interest in psychology from the study of consciousness to the study of behavior. This move was made because James believed that we cannot observe consciousness, but we can infer the states of consciousness by observing behavior.

James approached philosophy from the perspective of a psychologist. Critics of his philosophy argue that James's pragmatism was too subjective, that it was whatever the individual wanted it to be. As Smith said of James, " 'Truth,' he argued, is 'what works' or 'what pays,' or more precisely, that if the results of accepting a particular belief are 'good' or 'satisfactory,' then that belief must be counted as true."[12] Truth, according to James, was relative to the individual. Each individual could create "truth" by applying his or her own experiences, which might differ from anyone else's. Peirce hated this definition of pragmatism because, as previously stated, he believed that there is only one truth for everyone that would be discovered by the methods of science. Another contribution of James and the pragmatists was the assertion that many previous philosophers had debated questions that were essentially unprovable. James said that this was foolish. Rather, he argued, we should use philosophy to improve our daily lives in tangible ways. In so doing, James embodied a characteristic popular with many Americans.

Both Peirce and James were monists in that they rejected the idea that the mind and the body are separate in any way. Both believed that one begins with observations in the creation of knowledge, and in so doing developed a philosophy that was friendly to the human body. Yet they did not reject the concept of mind. Rather, their philosophies tried to unite the ideas of mind and body in an integrated whole. Their philosophies affected popular ideas of sport and physical education in the late nineteenth and early twentieth centuries by influencing the leading educators of the times.

SPORT IN THE NINETEENTH CENTURY

As stated earlier in the chapter, a number of perspectives can be used to explain the rise of sport in America in the nineteenth century. American culture became increasingly urban and industrial, providing both the necessary numbers of people as athletes and spectators and the technology necessary for sports as we know them today. During the nineteenth century, Americans became less resistant to the idea that adults could use their spare time for recreational activities, and among their leisure pursuits were playing and spectating. American culture underwent a period of modernization in which the roles of individuals and institutions with respect to all types of activities came to be viewed in radically different ways. In short, America experienced a cultural revolution, and sport changed along with everything else.

JUSTIFYING SPORT IN THE NINETEENTH CENTURY

Attitudes toward sport in America changed along with attitudes toward religion. Nineteenth-century Puritans generally opposed sport involvement. Certain activities were acceptable that "re-created" an individual, but for the most part physical activity was frowned upon. What is interesting about the nineteenth century is how religion was used to *justify* participating in sport. This phenomenon had it roots in England, where a movement known as "Muscular Christianity" developed.

Other arguments were used as well. The idea that competitiveness is a desirable virtue developed during this time. In addition, health issues associated with living in the city justified participation. Sport was seen as a "man builder," an activity that would turn boys raised by mothers into men while their fathers worked in the factories. All of these arguments were used by the newly developed media with great effectiveness, and at the end of the nineteenth century, attitudes toward participation had turned around completely from where they had been early in the nineteenth century.

Religion as an Argument for Sport

According to the doctrine of *Muscular Christianity,* there was something innately good and godly about brute strength and power. Physical weakness was considered to be unnatural because it was a reflection of moral and spiritual weakness. Consequently, an effort to overcome physical weakness could also be construed as an effort to be Christian, to be moral and good. Sport activities came to be seen as representing an effort to be a good Christian. In addition, Muscular Christians believed that the body was the temple, that housed the soul which demanded their attention and pledge to keep their bodies in shape and to be strong and physically fit!

Developed by Bishop Fraser, Thomas Hughes, Charles Kingsley, and Charles Wordsworth, Muscular Christianity associated godliness with manliness. Perhaps the most influential argument for Muscular Christianity was made in *Tom Brown's Schooldays* by Thomas Hughes.[13] Published in 1857, the book was incredibly popular among English and American students and went through six editions in its first year of printing. Many of the teachers and students who read the book were associated with the English public schools (which Americans would call elite private schools), and the ideas of Muscular Christianity permeated these educational institutions.

The particular effect of Muscular Christianity on education has been described by Gerald Redmond as follows:

> The sentiments of the Muscular Christian gospel [held] that physical activity and sports (especially team games like cricket and football) contributed significantly towards the development of moral character, fostered a desirable patriotism, and that such participation and its ensuing virtues were transferable to other situations and/or to later life (such as from the schoolboy playing-field to the military battlefield).[14]

These ideas were readily accepted by Americans who were developing education in the late 1800s. In addition, Baron de Coubertin (1863–1937), the French man credited with establishing of the modern Olympic Games, was influenced by the ideas of Muscular Christianity. Some of the cherished ideals of Muscular Christianity have not lost their appeal among religious and sports leaders in the new millennium. On October 28, 2000, the leader of the Catholic Church, Pope John Paul II (1920–2005), officiated at the opening of a weeklong celebration of sport called the Sports Jubilee. He urged athletes and officials to abide by the inherent benefits of sport, especially "the spiritual and human ideals." Among the thousands in attendance at this historic occasion in St. Peter's Square was the president of the International Olympic Committee, Juan Antonio Samaranch (1920–2010). Pope John Paul II remarked that "sport is not an end but a means. It can become a vehicle of civility and genuine fun, pushing people to give the best of themselves on the field, shunning that which can be of danger or serious damage to themselves and others."[15]

His belief in the potential benefits of sport reflects some of the attitudes and goals of the Muscular Christians. Ideas about appropriate decorum and sportsmanship are rooted in the tenets of Muscular Christianity. The pope apparently subscribed to this concept because, prior to his Sports Jubilee address, he condemned the behavior of fans and athletes who engage in the violence and racism that have become a fixture at soccer games in Europe and Latin America (see the Online Learning Center for more information on fan violence).

The pope's interest in sport was rooted in his youth when he was an accomplished goalkeeper for his soccer team in Poland. He also enjoyed hiking and skiing. The attention to sport paid by Pope John Paul II is important because it clearly establishes that some of the ideals that define the nature of sport and religion remain closely linked. This contemporary example demonstrates how modernization theory, discussed later, can help us understand how sport and physical education changed over time. The current state of affairs between sport, physical education, and the Catholic Church is far removed from the Middle Ages, when the Catholic Church held the corporeal nature of humans in contempt and generally scorned those who engaged in sports and games. As the church moved from premodern to modern ways of thinking (modernization theory), its beliefs changed, including its beliefs about sport. For example, what is the University of Notre Dame known for?

Other Arguments That Justified Sport Participation

The ideas of Muscular Christianity meshed nicely with other philosophies. Transcendentalists sought a return to nature and promoted ideas of rugged individualism. Physicality became a desirable image during the 1850s, and as one scholar noted, "Winning in athletics gave colleges visibility in a physical form. The physical nature of the individual and of American society appeared to be a desired quality in the age of Darwin."[16] Specifically, after Darwin, the idea of being competitive was important, and sport was seen as the tool with which to teach young children the necessary virtue of how to physically adapt to the environment, to become stronger. The goal of "social Darwinism"— to eliminate the weak so that only the best would survive or "win"—was and still is embedded in the ethos of athletic competition and in the classroom when students compete for grades and academic honors.

Another argument that justified physical activity was the idea that manliness was a necessary characteristic in the "modern" world.[17] Families moved from the country to the city so that fathers could work in factories and offices. Fathers became concerned that, with their sons no longer working with them in the fields, extensive contact with mothers would cause their sons to grow up to be feminine. The physicality associated with sports was seen as a desirable counterbalance to the influence of women in the lives of young boys.

All of these justifications were used at one time or another in the nineteenth century, and all served to overcome the Puritanism that had mitigated against playful activities for over 200 years. While this strategy was successful, it was not without its drawbacks. For every argument put forward to justify sport, a limitation has been found. For instance, as the logic goes, if sport builds men, then women who play sport must be . . . *manly!* In the twentieth century, women had to fight to overcome this stereotype, and it has not been easy for women. Similarly, not all agree with the idea that competitiveness is a virtue. Could cooperation be as much of a virtue as competitiveness?

DEVELOPMENT OF SPORT IN THE NINETEENTH CENTURY

In general, playful recreation in the early 1800s tended toward games and less competitive activities, while the concept of competitive sport as we know it became more prevalent in the late 1800s. This does not mean, however, that Americans

were not competitive in the early 1800s and that less competitive games were nonexistent in the late 1800s. Americans had both characteristics throughout the nineteenth century; the difference is one of degree.

Sport as we know it today began in the early 1800s, where "sport" can be distinguished from the activity of "games" and "play."[18] Most definitions of *play* describe it as a free or voluntary activity, one that stands outside ordinary life and is not "serious."[19] *Games* add the element of competition and always involve a struggle to win.[20] *Sport* can be both play and game, and is also characterized by a demonstration of skill, often within an institutional framework. For example, a group of friends can "play" a "game" of football on a Sunday afternoon, where they enjoy themselves immensely by involving themselves in a playful activity and where the recreational activity is "not necessarily oriented to outcome or production as (the) primary objective."[21] They can then watch a "game" of football on television. The game they watch represents "sport," where the teams are members of the institution that organizes professional sport: the National Football League. The rules are highly organized, the level of play is very high, the players are highly skilled, and the purpose is to win. The first game of football, as we have defined it, is more a "game" than "sport," while the second is more "sport" than "game." This distinction does not devalue either activity; on the contrary, a large body of literature argues that both activities are valuable. Rather, the purpose of the distinction is to describe how sport, as we know it now, has many characteristics.

A perspective that describes how play and games evolved into sport is provided by *modernization theory*—an organizational scheme used by historians to describe how a culture changes from a set of "premodern" characteristics to "modern" characteristics.[22] Applied to sport, modernization theory argues that sport tends to change from a set of premodern sporting characteristics to a set of modern sports characteristics. To understand how sport changed in the United States in the nineteenth century, we need to understand how American society changed in the nineteenth century. Sport "mirrored" this change. In fact, sport may have been a tool in teaching Americans how to make the transition from traditional beliefs and practices to more contemporary or "modern" ways.

Traditional society is stable and local, is governed by men at both the family and political level, has little specialization of roles, and depends on muscle power. Historian Mel Adelman notes:

> The past, present and future are the same, and time moves in endless cycles. Traditional society is further characterized by the weaving together of family and community in labor, leisure, and religion. Ritual flows through the entire experience of traditional society, and no precise boundaries exist between the secular and religious life, or between work and leisure. The prevailing outlook is one of actual acceptance or of resignation toward life as it is;

the repetition of past ways rather than innovative action is encouraged. By contrast, modern society is dynamic, cosmopolitan, technological, and marked by a functional social structure that conforms to shifting political and economic structures; most of all, it is rational. The desire for change and the belief that it can be achieved through the application of rational analysis is central to modern society.[23]

Adelman concludes that the assumptions of modern life, especially the belief that we can use rational methods to manipulate objects, the environment, people, and ideas, undergird the way that we see the world today. Sport changed in a similar manner, and the characteristics of premodern and modern sport can be described and applied to all sorts of sporting situations. The characteristics of premodern and modern ideal sporting types can be seen in Table 10-1.

TABLE 10-1	Characteristics of Premodern and Modern Ideal Sporting Types	
	Premodern Sport	**Modern Sport**
Organization	Either nonexistent or at best informal and sporadic; contests are arranged by individuals directly or indirectly (e.g., tavern owners, bettors) involved.	Formal; institutionally differentiated at the local, regional, and national levels.
Rules	Simple, unwritten, and based on local customs and traditions; variations exist from one locale to another.	Formal, standardized, and written; rationally and pragmatically worked out and legitimized by organizational means.
Competition	Locally meaningful only; no chance for national reputation.	National and international, superimposed on local contests; chance to establish national and international reputations.
Role Differentiation	Low among participants; loose distinction between playing and spectating.	High; emergence of specialists (professionals) and strict distinctions between playing and spectating.
Public Information	Limited, local, and oral.	Reported on a regular basis in local newspapers, as well as national sports journals; appearance of specialized magazines, guidebooks, etc.
Statistics and Records	Nonexistent.	Kept and published on a regular basis; considered important measures of achievement; records sanctioned by national associations.

Source: Melvin Adelman, *A Sporting Time: New York City and the Rise of Modern Athletics, 1820–70* (Urbana: University of Illinois Press, 1986), 6.

Modernization theory is useful because, applied properly, it can explain many changes in American culture, including the manner in which sport and physical education changed. For example, over time, exercise physiology became the foundation of exercise science which, while complementary to physical education, is now a separate academic discipline. However, modernization is not a *cause* of change. Americans did not want to become "modern" in the nineteenth century any more than we want to be "traditional" right now; indeed, Americans then did not know what "modern" was. This theory merely explains, from an artificially convenient perspective, the types of changes that took place over 100 years ago.

How sport developed from play and games can be explained within the framework of modernization theory; examples of modernization are the development of horse and harness racing, baseball, and some of the supposedly "amateur" sports. Modern is not necessarily better than premodern. Those who raced horses or trotters before those sports were modernized no doubt enjoyed themselves just as much as those who raced after those sports were modernized. Yet the settings in which these participants raced were very different, and modernization theory describes what these differences were.

Sport and Play in Nineteenth-Century America

The forces that changed the manner in which nineteenth-century Americans participated in sport are evident in the sports themselves. The sports that we enjoy in the twenty-first century developed in the nineteenth century, and the story of how these sports evolved helps explain why they look the way they do. Sports such as horse and harness racing, baseball, rowing, boxing, and track and field evolved into sporting institutions that shaped the organization of all subsequent sports. In the twenty-first century, a sport *must* look like these nineteenth-century activities in terms of organizations, written rules, and easy availability of public information and statistics; otherwise, we do not

even recognize the activity as a sport. So the story of the development of certain sports provides a model for the development of any sport in our time.

Horse and Harness Racing

One of the most popular American pastimes during the nineteenth century was horse racing (Figure 10-1). While the North tried, with limited success, to ban horse racing (in 1802, New York State passed an antiracing law), Americans of all social classes would gather to see which of two horses was the faster. Southern Americans, particularly the wealthy, enjoyed horse racing as far back as the mid-1600s. Horse racing served both to amuse audiences and to distinguish the upper classes from other social groups. As one scholar noted,

> By promoting these public displays the great planters legitimized the cultural values which racing symbolized—materialism, individualism, and competitiveness. These colorful, exclusive contests helped persuade subordinate white groups that gentry culture was desirable, something worth emulating. . . . The wild sprint down a dirt track served the interests of Virginia's gentlemen better than they imagined.[24]

This activity was more "game" than "sport" as we have defined it. Southern planters wagered on the contests and no doubt enjoyed them as playful diversions, but the contests were unorganized, informal, and sporadic. The justification for racing horses was to "improve the breed," to find out which horses were faster and stronger and had more endurance, and then to breed them to one another. In so doing, the main means of transportation during the early nineteenth century would be improved.

Legalized horse racing resumed in New York in 1821 when the antiracing law was modified. Racing was deemed acceptable for two days each year on Long Island, as long as the public was safeguarded by the sheriff and attempts were made to eliminate gambling and the accompanying undesirable

Figure 10-1
Maryland Jockey Club, Pimlico, 1802.

elements. Races ranged from 1 to 4 miles in distance, usually between only a few horses. Wagering was common, and prizes by the jockey club New York Association for the Improvement of the Breed (NYAIB) varied from $1000 to $1900.

While horse racing was legal, then, it did not capture the hearts of Americans until the famous 1823 race between Eclipse and Sir Henry, in which Eclipse represented the North and Sir Henry the South (Figures 10-2 and 10-3). Eclipse

Figure 10-2
Eclipse.

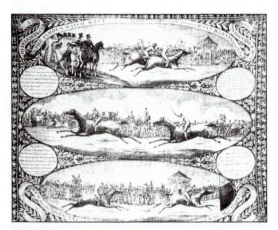

Figure 10-3
The great North–South horse race. The race took place in 1823 on the Union Course on Long Island. A crowd of 60,000 turned out to watch the northern horse, Eclipse, defeat the pride of the South, Sir Henry. Eclipse won two out of three 4-mile heats.

defeated Sir Henry two out of three races over 4 miles to the delight of tens of thousands of spectators. The following passage describes what it must have been like to be part of one of the first major sporting events in America:

> Those who had not attended the contest waited anxiously for the results. The *Post* came out with a special edition, probably the first sporting extra in American journalism, while the *American* did not go to press until informed of the winner. The coverage of the race in subsequent days was extraordinary, especially given the four-sheet format of local newspapers and the limited space allocated to news. The picture drawn by the New York newspapers was generally favorable. They noted that numerous men of wealth and taste were present and that the ladies' stands were nicely filled. Although the match attracted a large crowd, perfect decorum was evident among a gathering of good losers and subdued winners.[25]

The race between Eclipse and Sir Henry served as a model throughout the 1820s. In the 1830s, more horses raced in each event, and tracks were built throughout America. Jockey clubs such as the NYAIB were formed to facilitate the social desires of owners and the logistical needs of races by standardizing the rules that governed the sport. Magazines like the *American Turf Register* and *Sporting Magazine* provided summaries of races and documented the history and breeding of American horses. These changes are characteristic of modern sport.

Harness racing, or trotting, began in the cities (Figure 10-4). Early on it consisted of impromptu contests between individuals who merely wanted to race their carriages. More formal matches were a natural outgrowth and were conducted on tracks and city streets, with the prize being the wager between the two contestants. In 1824, interested racers formed a trotting club, with the NYAIB as the model. They built a racecourse on Long Island, met twice a year, and used the same argument (improvement of the breed) to justify their interest

(Figure 10-5). As horse racing declined in popularity in the late 1830s, trotting became more popular, perhaps because many people owned trotters while only the wealthy could afford thoroughbred racehorses. Furthermore, the egalitarian bent of harness racing overcame the aristocratic trappings of horse racing. This difference manifested itself in the commercialization of trotting, making it available to almost everyone. Harness racing was the leading American spectator sport by the early 1850s. As Melvin Adelman noted,

> The founding of the National Trotting Association in 1870 symbolized the transformation

Figure 10-4
Trotting.

of harness racing from a premodern sport to a modern sport. In contrast to the informal road contests that took place in the Northeast half a century earlier, harness racing had evolved into a highly organized, national sport with relatively uniform rules. The emergence of a trotting literature . . . and developments in the breeding industry . . . in the 1870s further demonstrated the centralizing and modernizing forces at work in the sport.[26]

In sum, horse racing and harness racing changed significantly between 1820 and 1870. Initially contests between a few participants and of local interest, horse and harness races came to meet all of the criteria that describe modern sport. For better or for worse, a pattern was established that was emulated in many other sports.

Cycling: The Story of Marshall W. "Major" Taylor

In the latter part of the nineteenth century, cycling was both a popular pastime and a serious competitive sport. The bicycle provided a means of transportation as well as a mode of racing by the serious speed-seeking athlete. In Europe, Australia, and America, cycling clubs and cycling stars were venerated by fans from all walks of life.

Figure 10-5
Opening day on the Fashion Course.

Before the Tour de France (which started in 1903) became cycling's premier event and long before Lance Armstrong became a household name, there was Marshall W. "Major" Taylor, the first superstar of cycling. He was born on November 26, 1878, in rural Indiana. His parents were descended from slaves, and although Indiana was a "free state," racism was so entrenched that he was not permitted to join the local YMCA. The family moved to Indianapolis. Taylor's father was employed by a very wealthy and prominent white family as their coachman. His son, the future superstar of cycling, had the good fortune of being raised and educated in their home. He soon became fast friends with their son who had what every kid wants: toys and bikes. It was the bike that called out to young Marshall, and before too long, he was performing cycling stunts that became legendary.

In 1892, at the age of 14, Taylor was hired by the owner of an Indianapolis bicycle store to perform cycling tricks and stunts to attract customers. He was outfitted in a soldier's uniform and before too long, became known as Major Taylor. Later that year he started racing and won a number of cycling races. There were few African American cyclists at that time so the vast majority of the time, Major raced against white cyclists. Once again, racism reared its ugly head. Major was not safe racing in Indiana, which drew the attention of promoter and cycling aficionado Louis "Birdie" Munger.

Munger convinced Major to move to Worcester, Massachusetts, where cycling was extremely popular and the racial climate was more accepting than that of Indiana. Although Worcester was far removed from Indianapolis, racism would once again haunt Major Taylor. Since he had been raised and educated in privileged white society, he was quite comfortable in the presence of whites. He had a regal presence and was socially polished, which infuriated the bigots and racists, especially those who were cyclists. At the age of 17, Major Taylor, because of his success as an athlete—an athlete who almost always beat his white competitors—became a target of the racists and bigots who were involved in cycling.

The League of American Wheelmen (LAW) was the organization that granted official sanction to bicycle racing in America. If you earned a living as a cyclist or raced as a cyclist in the "big events," it was necessary to hold membership in the LAW. In 1894, the LAW held its annual meeting in Kentucky, where a group of cyclists managed to enact a "Whites Only" rule relative to who could hold membership. The LAW representatives from Massachusetts worked to defeat the rule, but their efforts failed. However, Major's manager and friend, Birdie Munger, was not to be deterred. He convinced the New York chapter of LAW to issue Major a professional racing license. Once again, the race was on, but not for long.

In 1896, Major returned to Indianapolis where he unofficially broke two world records for paced and un-paced one-mile races. As a result, he was banned from the Capital City track in Indianapolis. Once again, his success as an African-American athlete offended whites. A few months later, Taylor entered his first professional race, which was held in New York's Madison Square Garden. It was a six-day endurance race. He finished in sixth place. In 1897 and 1898, he was prevented from competing in the American Sprint Championship series because he had not raced in the Southern Circuit. He no doubt would have had cause to fear for his life if he had done so. Although the Civil War was over, African Americans were still frequently lynched at that time in the American South. By the end of 1898, Major Taylor held seven world records. In 1899, at the age of 20, he won the world cycling championship in Montreal, Canada. In 1900, he finally was allowed to enter the American Sprint Championship series, and he won.

From 1902 to 1904, Major Taylor raced overseas and continued to win. He made a comfortable income and in 1902, married Daisy V. Morris. He "retired" from cycling in 1905 and 1906 and attempted a comeback in 1907. It did not turn out well. In 1910 the greatest cycling superstar of the era retired for good. He made one bad business decision after another and by 1930, he was alone, living at the YMCA in Chicago, where he sold his self-published 1928 biography, *The Fastest Bicycle Rider in the World*. In 1932, at the age of 53, Major Taylor died in the charity ward of Cook County Hospital in Chicago. He was buried in an unmarked grave until 1948 when a group of former professional cyclists, with the assistance of Frank Schwinn, exhumed his body and reburied the great cyclist in Mount Glenwood Cemetery. This time he had a headstone.

Ball Games: Cricket, Baseball, and Football

Modern baseball is the culmination of a variety of simple bat, base, and ball games played as early as the colonial period. However, these games did not capture the hearts of Americans until the early to mid-1800s. Several bat, base, and ball games, among them rounders, town ball, and "base-ball" (as it was known in its early forms), evolved into the modern game of baseball between 1840 and 1870. Many have argued that baseball is the "national pastime," yet the status of baseball as any kind of American game was, during the early and mid-1800s, problematic. How and why baseball developed the way it did is the subject of American mythology and historical study.

It has been argued that for ball games to be attractive to Americans, a tradition of spring and summer rituals that involved bats and balls was needed.[27] However, Americans did not have this tradition, and as a consequence, it took longer to develop ball games than it had taken in England. In addition, Americans were much more individualistic than their English counterparts. Americans enjoyed "solo" sports such as hunting, racing, and boxing. Furthermore, ritualistic games were considered "pagan" by Puritans, who associated ball games with the rituals of the Catholic Church. Finally, ball games were not considered "manly" activities because those who played were usually children and did not have well-developed skills.

As a consequence, the quality of play was low and the games did not attract much attention.

Cricket

The various ball games in the early 1800s included English cricket, a slightly older and more formalized game than baseball. Interestingly, cricket was more popular than baseball between 1840 and 1855.[28] Cricket received more attention in the press than any sport other than horse and harness racing. However, it was a sport played primarily by English immigrants and was not easily accepted by Americans for a variety of reasons.

Cricket had been popular in England for nearly a century, and it benefited from an English tradition of playing ball games. As Adelman notes,

> Unlike other sports which sprang from day-to-day activities, ball games originated in religious and magical functions and were closely associated with fertility rites. The Church adopted these ritualistic ball games and used them for Christian purposes, with some modification in their meaning. In Europe various ball games became part of the Easter observance and other springtime customs. . . . (T)he subsequent development of the bat and ball games so familiar to us hinged on the adoption of the pagan ball rites into the Easter Christian ceremonies.[29]

Cricket was the first sport to try to overcome these obstacles to popularity in America, but it had several "strikes" against it.[30] First, cricket in England was a highly evolved, competitive sport relative to the simple ball games played by American children. It was too hard for Americans to play and so had a difficult time catching on. Second, it was highly organized and had the basic characteristics of a modern sport with standardized rules and a central governing authority, the Marleybone Cricket Club in England. For cricket to be played properly it had to be played the Marleybone way, and this was difficult to do in an America that was, for the most part in the early and mid-1800s, rural and decentralized. Third, cricket was closely associated with gambling, an association that was distasteful to many Americans who had the time to play. Fourth, cricket in England had a tradition of allowing the lower social classes to play with the upper classes. But this tradition did not exist in America, where those with time to recreate would not associate with those of the lower classes. But perhaps the most important reason that cricket did not catch on was that it had no "manly" virtues, and so men would not spend the time to develop the skills necessary to play it. Instead they would play the game of their youth: baseball.

Around 1855, the popularity of baseball began to overtake that of cricket. One reason was that cricket was associated with its English origins, while baseball was the "American" game familiar to schoolboys. In addition, the outbreak of the Civil War in 1861 had a dramatic and immediate impact on baseball. Baseball was a much easier game to play than cricket and was taught to fellow soldiers in both the North and the South. After the war, soldiers returned home and continued to play baseball. Finally, baseball was a much faster game. Cricket matches could last days, while baseball could be played in a matter of hours. Eventually these characteristics of the game came to be associated with nationalistic claims. Baseball became the "American" game, while cricket was the "English" game.

Perhaps most important, however, was that Americans were playing any kind of ball game at all. As stated, games were associated with children and were not considered a good way for adult men to spend their time. Cricket and baseball did much to undermine this argument, and the arguments used to promote these two sports still resonate with Americans today:

> The character value argument had profound importance for the development of ball games in general, and it was especially critical to the acceptance of ball playing as a manly activity. Claims that ball playing promoted healthful exercise were important but did little if anything to overcome the charge that ball playing was for children; hence, statements

that cricket and baseball were manly often accompanied claims that they were healthy activities. . . . The argument concluded that if ball games called these virtues into play—and in fact they were critical to doing well at such sports—then ball playing was obviously one way of demonstrating manhood.[31]

If one played ball, then, one either was manly or could become so. It should not be surprising, then, that women had such a difficult time breaking into sport in the twentieth century. The very argument that justified the inclusion of sport in American culture precluded women, because it meant that sport would make men out of them!

Baseball

Many myths surround baseball, and to the extent that they capture and enhance the flavor of the game, they do much good. One of them has to do with baseball's origin. As the myth goes, Abner Doubleday created baseball in 1839 in Cooperstown, New York. In reality, this story was created by Albert Spalding, the former major league pitcher and sporting goods magnate, who had formed a commission to investigate the origins of the American game. Spalding was trying to promote baseball, and believed that the acceptance of this story was critical to popular acceptance of baseball; baseball must have an American pedigree!

Baseball evolved from the games of rounders and town ball and was known to be played in various forms as early as 1734 at Harvard.[32] A dozen or so clubs sprang up in New York City between 1845 and 1855, composed of middle-class, white-collar workers. One of the most popular of these clubs was the Knickerbocker Base Ball Club, and one of its members, Alexander Cartwright, helped develop the rules that we use today. By 1860, there were over 100 clubs in the New York area alone, and contemporary newspaper reporters were stunned by the popularity and the growth of the sport.

This sudden growth and the competition between the teams pointed to the need for consistent rules. It was difficult to play a game when the two teams involved used different rules.

Figure 10-6
1869 Cincinnati Red Stockings became the first professional baseball team because each player received a salary to "play ball"!

Some of the rules debated were the adoption of the nine-inning game over the twenty-first run rule, treatment of caught fly balls as outs, and the elimination of throwing the ball at the runner to get him out. In 1858, 26 clubs banded together to form the National Association of Base Ball Players, an organization that would govern baseball for 13 years (Figure 10-6). This organization was weak and ineffective, but it marked the beginning of an era in which players would meet to revise the rules, settle disputes, and try to control the game.

In 1871, the National Association of Professional Base Ball Players (NAPBBP) was formed—a reflection of a variety of changes in America relative to sport in general and baseball in particular. Prior to 1871, professional athletes existed, but their status was problematic because of American attitudes regarding wagering, play, and sport. With the exception of the Cincinnati Red Stockings, most "professionals" prior to 1871 were paid under the table. Also, professional athletes could not exist unless spectators were willing to pay them, indirectly at least, to compete. Finally, the fact that men were paid to play baseball meant that Americans no longer believed sport to be the domain of children. "More than any other sport in America baseball came to sym-

bolize the increasing tendency of Americans to watch athletic contests. . . . The rise of spectator sports permitted onlookers to enjoy 'vicariously' what they would have liked to do themselves."[33] In the end, the emergence of baseball as a professional sport legitimized participation in sport generally. Sport advocates argued that (1) it had health and recreational benefits; (2) it served as a counterbalance to the evils of the city; (3) it developed character through the exercise of discipline, self-control, and teamwork; and (4) it was a valuable educational tool. In 1876, the National League was formed and in 1901, the American League was born.

Baseball was a popular sport within the African-American community during the nineteenth century. Popular amateur teams such as the Colored Union Club which called Brooklyn, New York home would compete against other African-American teams such as the Pythian Club of Philadelphia.

African-American professional teams started to take shape in the later part of the nineteenth century. Two of the more successful teams were the St. Louis Black Stockings and the Cuban Giants who called New York City home. Racial segregation in America during this time was found most everywhere, including athletic teams. It was rare for a white baseball team to include athletes of color but it did happen.

Moses Fleetwood "Fleet" Walker was an African-American who played for the Toledo Blue Stockings in the minor leagues. When the Blue Stockings were set to play the all, white Chicago White Stockings in 1883, Adrian "Cap" Anson, who was the best player on the White Stockings team, refused to play the game if Walker played. Eventually Anson relented and the game was played.

In 1884 the Blue Stockings joined the "Major Leagues" when it became a member of the American Association. Walker was still playing for the Blue Stockings and some historians believe that it was Walker not Jackie Robinson, who should be credited as the first African-American to play in the Major Leagues.

In July of 1887 the stench of racism became a dominant feature of the International League as it banned teams from signing African-American ball players. However, the league agreed to allow African-American ball players who were already on a team to remain—BUT NO MORE! The "color line" in Major League Baseball had been established and would not be broken until the great Jackie Robinson (1919–1972) took the field in a Brooklyn Dodgers uniform on April 15, 1947.

At the close of the nineteenth century, African American professional ball players began to slowly integrate baseball. Colored teams, as they were called, would play white teams and there were colored teams that played in mostly all-white leagues. But this was rare.

The United States Navy promoted baseball during this era and just about every ship in the Navy had a baseball team. The baseball team from the USS Maine was integrated with one African-American player, William Lambert, who was their star pitcher. In December of 1897, the team from the USS Maine played the team from the USS Marblehead and won 18 to 3, winning the Navy baseball championship. Sadly, a few months later, on February 15, 1898, the USS Maine blew up in Havana Harbor in Cuba, which ignited the Spanish American War (April 25–August 12, 1898). With

the exception of John Bonner, all of the baseball team perished in the inferno along with hundreds of sailors who were on the ship.

Football

Long before the first collegiate football game between Rutgers and Princeton on November 6, 1869, men had made a contest of moving an object between two goals by brute force. For centuries, the English had played rugby, primarily an upper-class sport, and other ball games somewhat similar to American football. English ball games were often a contest between two towns or villages, with the abled-bodied men of the towns squaring off on the adjoining green or commons. Massive brawls often occurred that caused many an injury among the commoners of seventeenth- and eighteenth-century England. American football primarily evolved from soccer and rugby, with the rules gradually modified until the modern game of football emerged in the early twentieth century.

Early American football was characterized by its violent nature, a characteristic emblematic of the sport today. The first games represented adaptations of the format established by the London Football Association. The ball was round, and the athletes wore no protective clothing or equipment. Players worked the ball toward their opponent's goal by a series of short punts, relying on the team's ability to keep the opposing players from gaining control of the ball. This was usually accomplished by using mass formations, which proved to be brutal. Carrying the ball was not allowed, and the forward pass was also prohibited. Goals were scored by kicking the ball into the opponent's goal.

Football in the early 1800s resembled soccer more than rugby. The students at Harvard modified the game, and by 1871, the modified rules permitted picking up the ball at any time, much like in rugby. In 1873, Princeton, Yale, Columbia, and Rutgers formed the Intercollegiate Association for Football, which allowed the members to refine and codify the rules of the game. Perhaps no one person gave more to the game of football than Walter Camp. While coaching at Yale in 1879, he began to change the game from rugby to American football. He was a member of every football rules convention in college football's early years, and many consider Walter Camp the "father" of American football. Contributions by Camp include (1) replacing the rugby "scrummage" with the line of scrimmage, (2) using a system of downs tied to yards gained as a means to retain possession of the ball, (3) assigning eleven players to a team, with specific positions, (4) allowing tackling below the waist, and (5) prohibiting use of the arms while blocking.[34]

The evolution of football from a kind of rugby to a distinctly American game, using the basic rules outlined, was not a smooth transition. The rule changes were debated extensively, yet as Michael Oriard argues, these changes were necessary to develop the American game:

> First the creation of the scrimmage, as a substitute for the rugby scrummage (players from both teams massed about the ball, all trying to kick it out to a teammate), gave the ball to one team at a time; then the five-yard rule guaranteed that the team possessing the ball either advanced it or gave it up. Later revisions—rules on scoring, on blocking and tackling, on movement before the ball was snapped, on the number of offensive players allowed behind the line of scrimmage, most crucially on forward passing—were necessary before American football assumed a form in 1912 that we would recognize today as our game. Nonetheless, in the evolution of American football from English rugby, the distance from 1882 to 1993 is less significant than that from 1876 to 1882.[35]

The study of football reveals much about how Americans feel about rules. It was necessary in America to have referees to enforce the rules that were developed, for American coaches and players continually sought to use the rules to win the game rather than to penalize ungentlemanly conduct, as was the case in Victorian England. The "American character" differed from its English counterpart in that, since the beginning of modern sport, Americans valued the *outcome* of the game more than *how* the game is played. In contrast, English sportsmen valued the *style* of play and the way the games supported the British social class system. The two approaches to sport are made explicit by the following quotes. Oriard notes that an English gentleman objected to the imposition of rules because of the assumptions that support their need:

> It is a standing insult to sportsmen to have to play under a rule which assumes that players intend to trip, hack and push their opponents and to behave like cads of the most unscrupulous kind. I say that the lines marking the penalty area are a disgrace to the playing field of a public school.[36]

In contrast was the American attitude that applauded tripping, hacking, and pushing opponents if it served to win the game. This strategy was evident in early baseball, where rules were regularly circumvented to give one team an advantage and included such situations as

> a manager substituting himself as a foul ball sails toward the dugout, just in time to catch it; a catcher throwing his mask a few feet down the first-base line to trip the runner; an outfielder juggling the ball as he trots toward the infield, preventing a runner from advancing on a sacrifice fly. Buck Ewing, a baseball manager early in the twentieth century, summed up this spirit: 'Boys . . . you've heard the rules read. Now the question is: What can we do to beat them?'[37]

Football was similar in this respect, and many applauded the "brainy" nature of the college athlete who could figure out a way around the rules to take advantage of them. The scrimmage line was continually redefined because players used tricks to interfere with the center snap. Rules on blocking, mass plays, scoring, holding, and so on were developed through the late nineteenth century. "Until a rule made it impossible, a clever team discovered that it could score repeated touchdowns simply by bunting the after-touchdown goal kick to its own man, who then touched the ball down behind the goal line."[38] In sum, Americans will do anything to win, and they needed rules to limit behavior so that all could play the "game."

Another characteristic of American sport is revealed in the role of the modern coach. English tradition limited the role of the coach to that of an active "team captain," but Americans sought the help of more seasoned leaders who, because of their knowledge of the game, could lead a team to victory with more frequency. Initially, sideline coaches were banned, as team captains led their squads on the field, but attempts to circumvent this rule were made as soon as the rule was in place. The next step toward the professional coach was the unpaid graduate student who had played the game. Paid professional coaches originated at midwestern colleges such as Minnesota and Chicago, and eventually they held positions at all colleges that had football. Professional coaching was considered a "shady practice," however, and was only grudgingly accepted. By the beginning of the twentieth century, paid professional coaches were here to stay. But the debate over the role of professionals in sport had only begun.

"Amateur" Sports

One of the movements that developed in American sport during the 1800s was amateurism. The popular definition of an *amateur* is someone who competes for the love of the sport and as a consequence receives no money for his or her athletic efforts.[39] Nineteenth-century historians, primarily English but also American, sought to identify contemporary athletic efforts with ancient Greek practices. Their interpretation (an inaccurate one) of the ancient Greek Olympic athletes, who competed only for the "wreath" that symbolized victory, called for them to disassociate with those who would earn money through athletic pursuits. More recent scholarship, however, shows that amateurism developed in the 1860s and 1870s, when upper-class athletes refused to compete against their middle- and lower-class counterparts, primarily on the track and on the water (in rowing).[40] The social clubs formed around these two sports

remain to this day, although the concept of amateurism is no longer accepted as a valid distinction between athletes. For over 100 years, however, the idea of who and what an amateur is has dominated many American sports.

Rowing

Rowing was one of the most popular sports in the early to mid-1800s (Figure 10-7). Rowing races began as simple, unorganized contests between working-class "watermen," rowers who lived in port cities and made a living by rowing. In the 1800s, rowers were needed to quickly reach incoming sailing ships with news and supplies, and they also made a living by ferrying customers across rivers and bays where there were no bridges. In both cases, the speed of the rowers was critical to their making a living, and racing was a natural by-product of their desire to prove they were the fastest (not to mention that racing was fun!). Rowers would race for bets, and occasionally outsiders would also bet for the fun of it. In the early 1820s, several races were held in New York that drew large crowds and large wagers. One race, between a crew from the English frigate *Hussar* and a New York rowing club called the Whitehallers, drew between 20,000 and 50,000 spectators. The Whitehallers' victory was a source of national pride and elevated the popularity of rowing for several years after the race.

In contrast to the watermen were the young men from prominent families who rowed for social

Figure 10-7
Single sculler.

diversion rather than for a living or for competition. The first clubs were formed in the 1830s and 1840s in New York, Boston, and Philadelphia, and as far back as 1837, they had rules against competing for money. The Undine Barge Club, formed in 1856, had a rule stating that any member who raced against another boat for a wager would be fined 25 dollars, and furthermore, for "tyrranical or ungentlemanly conduct (one) was liable to a fine of five dollars."[41]

Rowing clubs became more numerous following the Civil War and continued to try to distinguish themselves from their lower-class counterparts. The reason for this distinction is fairly clear in retrospect: Members of the upper class did not want to look bad by losing to members of the lower classes in sporting contests, which in the case of rowing were highly visible. At the same time, however, rowing races were becoming increasingly popular, and members of the exclusive rowing clubs wanted to be a part of these races. Between 1845 and 1865, professional rowers dominated rowing, and crowds of up to 10,000 people watched the biggest races. By 1870, over 200 rowing clubs had been formed, and there was a corresponding increase in the number of regattas.

In 1872, an event was held that marked the beginning of amateurism.[42] In June of that year, the Schuylkill Navy Rowing Association held the National Amateur Regatta, and among its "Special Rules" was the following: "Amateur Oarsmen only, will be admitted. We define an Amateur Oarsman to be one who has never rowed for money, and who has never depended upon rowing for his livelihood."[43] For the first time, an athletic event excluded those who were not "amateur." The problem with this definition was that it could not be fairly applied, and in hindsight, scholars have called amateur rules a "weapon of class warfare."[44]

The National Amateur Regatta was considered a success, and in August of that year, 27 clubs formed the National Association of Amateur Oarsmen (NAAO). This association, like the NAPBBP in baseball, was formed to develop uniform rules and to govern the sport. Unlike the NAPBBP, however, one of the rules was to exclude professionals, and in taking this step, rowers were the first to clearly separate amateurs from professionals. This separation, widely criticized at the time, reinforces the contention that no accepted view of amateurism or professionalism had emerged by the 1870s.[45]

Amateurism during this period was, by modern standards, a type of social discrimination. It was a rule that separated athletes by social class—specifically, working men from "gentlemen." Begun in England as an effort to separate noblemen in sport from the common man on the basis of right of birth, amateurism looked much different in America, where there was no acknowledged "nobility." Therefore, instead of using nobility as a means of distinguishing social class, the leaders of the amateur movement in the United States used racing for money. This idea eventually became intertwined with the concept of "sport for the love of sport" and was used to separate those who did physical work for a living from those of the higher social classes.

While rowing was one of the most popular sports in the mid-1800s, by the late 1800s, it was limited to the amateur clubs and elite universities in the East. It no longer attracted large crowds, and betting was limited to college oarsmen racing for the shirts of their opponents. The reason for the decline in popularity of professional rowing is subject to debate. One theory has it that rowing was difficult to commercialize because rowing races do not lend themselves to spectating. Another is that spectators became disgruntled after several races were "thrown" by the contestants to collect on their wagers. At any rate, by 1870, amateur rowing was a "modern" sport, with "a higher level of modern structure than any other sport in America, with the exception of harness racing and baseball."[46]

Track and Field

Much like rowing, track-and-field competition was affected by the amateur movement. Sometimes called "pedestrianism" in its early days (from the walking contests that were part of early track-and-field contests), track-and-field athletics were stimulated by the initiation of the Caledonian Games.[47] Organized by Scottish immigrants to the United States, the Caledonian Games continued a tradition of informal annual gatherings that included athletic competition. The first games were held in 1853, and Caledonian Clubs were organized in Boston, New York, and Philadelphia in the next few years.

The games included throwing the heavy hammer and light hammer, putting the light stone and the heavy stone (precursors to the shot put and the hammer throw of modern athletic competition), and tossing the caber, wheelbarrow races (conducted blindfolded), as well as sack races, the standing high jump, the running long jump, a short running race, and dancing.[48] These initial contests sometimes offered cash prizes and quickly became highly organized and popular events.

While the Caledonian Games were popular, they were clearly not amateur in their intent. Track and field took on these characteristics through the influence of the New York Athletic Club (NYAC), formed in 1868. Three men—William Buckingham Curtis, John Babcock, and Henry Buermeyer—were involved in sports in the New York City area and were attracted to the English model of track

and field to which they had been exposed when traveling in that country. Curtis, a noted sport enthusiast, was especially influential in the formation of the NYAC. A successful weightlifter, a track-and-field enthusiast, and also a champion rower, Curtis was also influential in the formation of the National Association of Amateur Oarsmen. In 1868, the NYAC sponsored its first indoor meet in the Empire Skating Rink, and among the innovations Curtis introduced were spiked running shoes, imported from England.

By 1879, there were over 100 athletic clubs in New York City, and many other cities followed the amateur model. Influenced by the success of the NAAO and the NYAC, these clubs promoted athletics in conjunction with the concept of amateurism. In 1879, an organization was formed that everyone hoped would settle all disputes regarding amateurism and help organize national championships in amateur sports. The National Association of Amateur Athletes of America (NAAAA) attempted to do this but was largely ineffective. In 1888, 15 clubs, led by the NYAC, joined to form the Amateur Athletic Union (AAU). The AAU, a much stricter organization, banned athletes from their competitions if they competed in any open race they did not sanction. By the 1890s, the AAU had control of all amateur competition in the United States.

SUMMARY

Horse and harness racing, cricket and baseball, and rowing and track and field were not the only sports played in the 1800s. Boxing and golf developed as professional sports during this time, while football, yachting, tennis, bicycling, and many other sports began on an amateur basis. Sporting competitions were held between the colleges as early as 1852 with the Harvard–Yale crew race. Furthermore, not all sport activities were competitive. Americans continued to practice traditional recreations such as hunting, fishing, dancing, and bowling.

The 1800s mark the time when Americans came to be more comfortable with physical activity for its own sake, and this can be associated with a significantly

more favorable view of the human body. They were much more health-conscious with the change from the "healthy" agrarian lifestyle to the "unhealthy" urban lifestyle, and sports were one of the means to overcome this change. Furthermore, the development of desirable social and personal skills came to be associated with sport. Manliness, character building, discipline, and many other virtues were associated with sport to legitimize it as an activity worthy of adults. The association of sport with educational institutions meant that Americans believed these activities were in some way educational. During this time segregation, especially in the South, was part of the social fabric of America. As such, most but not all, sports reflected this policy.

Almost every organized sport underwent a process of modernization that helped it develop governing institutions, organize rules, and keep statistics. Organized sports were exposed to the various media, and their competitions became meaningful on a national level.

Athletes developed the specialized skills necessary to be competitive. Clearly, the 1800s were a time of rapid change for sport, and many of the changes that occurred during this century are still with us.

DISCUSSION QUESTIONS

1. What is modernization theory? How does modernization theory explain the changes in sport in the nineteenth century?

2. What was the metaphysical position of Charles Peirce and William James? How did their views of the mind-body relationship reflect the changes in American sport?

3. What impact did the evolutionary theory of Charles Darwin have on the significance of athletic competition?

4. How pervasive is social Darwinism in our society today? How does athletic competition perpetuate social Darwinism?

5. How did the emphasis on manliness affect the evolution of baseball in America?

6. How influential were English sporting traditions on the development of sport in America?

7. If Major Taylor were alive today, what changes, if any, would he see?

8. How extensive was racial segregation in America? Was American sport immune to racism or did American sport reflect American society?

INTERNET RESOURCES

Transcendentalists
www.transcendentalists.com
Provides information about transcendentalism and the contributions of Emerson and Thoreau.

The Pragmatism Cybrary
www.pragmatism.org
Is an excellent source of information on pragmatism and the contributions of Charles Sanders Peirce and William James.

Westmont College
**http://library.westmont.edu/bibinst/SearchAids/
   KNSreligion.html**
Includes links to databases, sites, and books that focus on or include information about sport and religion.

Horse Racing History and Museums
http://horseracing.miningco.com/od/history1/
Includes information about and links to the history of horse racing, museums devoted to horse racing, statistics, famous jockeys, and other resources.

Major Taylor Association, Inc.
www.majortaylorassociation.org
Describes the accomplishments of Marshall W. "Major" Taylor and is dedicated to recognizing sportsmanship, promoting nonviolence, and caring for those who are less fortunate.

Professional Football Researchers Association
www.footballresearch.com
Provides information on football and links to related sites.

Baseball Almanac
www.baseball-almanac.com
Is a good source for information on the history of baseball.

History: The Baseball Archive
www.baseball1.com/c-history.html
Contains information on the history of baseball, team histories, and league histories.

Negro Baseball Leagues
www.blackbaseball.com
Is a terrific source of historical information.

Baseball Links
www.baseball-links.com
Contains over 11,000 links to baseball information.

Cricket
http://sportsvl.com/ball/cricket/cricket.htm
Is an excellent site for everything related to the sport of cricket, including rules, history, and cricket for beginners.

USA Track and Field
www.usatf.org
Provides information about track and field events, including competition rules.

Friends of Rowing History
www.rowinghistory.net
Tells the history of rowing.

Visit the *History and Philosophy of Sport and Physical Education* Online Learning Center (www.mhhe.com/mechikoff6e) for additional information and study tools.

SUGGESTIONS FOR FURTHER READING

Betts, J. R. *America's Sporting Heritage: 1850–1950.* Reading, MA: Addison-Wesley, 1974.

Betts, J. R. "Mind and Body in Early American Thought." In *The American Sporting Experience,* ed. Steven A. Riess. New York: Leisure Press, 1984, 61–79.

Bissinger, B. *3 Nights in August: Strategy, Heartbreak, and Joy Inside the Mind of a Manager.* Story takes place over the course of three days in August 2003 when Tony La Russa managed the St. Louis Cardinals. St. Louis was playing the Chicago Cubs and the story details the preparation, angst, elation, and sorrow of La Russa and the Cardinals.

Deford, F. *The Old Ball Game.* New York: Atlantic Monthly Press, 2005, 240 pgs. One of the best sportswriters in America, Frank Deford provides a great story and interesting anecdotal history of how baseball became America's pastime. He credits New York Giants pitcher Christy Mathweson as baseball's first superstar and manager John "Mugsey" McGraw with making baseball a huge success.

Eig, J. *Luckiest Man.* New York: Simon & Schuster, 2005, 420 pgs. Story of Lou Gehrig of the New York Yankees, who played in 2,130 consecutive games before amyotrophic lateral sclerosis, the disease that is commonly known today as Lou Gehrig's disease, ended his life.

Gutmann, A. *From Ritual to Record: The Nature of Modern Sports.* New York: Columbia University Press, 1978.

Henderson, R. W. Ball, Bat and Bishop: The Origin of Ball Games. Urbana: University of Illinois Press, 2001, 220 pgs. First published in 1947, Henderson provides readers with a historical account of the development and evolution of ball games from ancient times to the nineteenth century. Henderson believes that all ball games can be traced back to ancient fertility rituals used by the Egyptians.

Oriard, M. *Reading Football: How the Popular Press Created an American Spectacle.* Chapel Hill: University of North Carolina Press, 1993.

Ritchie, A. *Major Taylor: The Extraordinary Career of a Champion Bicycle Racer.* Baltimore: Johns Hopkins University Press, 1996.

Stone, E. *Wrong Side of the Wall.* The Lyons Press, 2005, 309 pgs. In 1948, St. Louis Browns' pitcher Ralph "Blackie" Schwamb went from the Big Leagues to prison in California for life, San Quentin and Folsom, after he murdered a man. This is the story about the greatest pitcher in the history of prison baseball.

Struna, N. "Puritans and Sport: The Irretrievable Tide of Change." In *The American Sporting Experience,* ed. Steven A. Riess. New York: Leisure Press, 1984, 15–33.

Vaccaro, M. *Emperors and Idiots.* New York: Doubleday, 2005, 384 pgs. Great story of the 100-year rivalry between the New York Yankees and the Boston Red Sox. Presents the reader with the story of "Curse of the Bambino," which happened because the owner of the Red Sox, Harry Frazee, sold Babe Ruth to the Yankees. After Ruth was sold to the Yankees, New York won the World Series. Vaccaro notes that Frazee simply made a very bad business decision. Frazee has plenty of money and didn't need to "sell" Ruth to the Yankees. However, history will forever identify Frazee with the "Curse of the Bambino"! It should be noted that in 2004, the Red Sox won their first World Series since 1918!

Wojciechowski, G. *Cubs Nation.* New York: Doubleday, 2005, 432 pgs. The last time the Chicago Cubs played in a World Series was in 1945.

The last time they won the series was in 1908! Long-suffering Cubs fans will enjoy this book as the author follows his beloved Cubs throughout the 2004 season.

Young, D. C. *The Olympic Myth of Greek Amateur Athletics.* Chicago: Ares, 1984.

NOTES

1. John R. Betts, *America's Sporting Heritage: 1850–1950* (Reading, MA: Addison-Wesley, 1974).
2. Stephen Riess, *Touching Base: Professional Baseball and American Culture in the Progressive Era* (Westport, CT: Greenwood Press, 1980).
3. Betts, *America's Sporting Heritage,* 78.
4. Ibid., 84.
5. Michael Moran, "New England Transcendentalism," in *The Encyclopedia of Philosophy,* vol. 7, ed. Paul Edwards (New York: Macmillan/Free Press, 1967), 479–80.
6. Henry David Thoreau, *Walden, or Life in the Woods* (Boston: Houghton Mifflin, 1906).
7. Cynthia Eagle Russett, *Darwin in America: The Intellectual Response, 1865–1912* (San Francisco: W. E. Freeman, 1976).
8. Goudge describes the impact of Darwin in intellectual circles as being "more far reaching than that ushered in by Copernicus." T. A. Goudge, "Charles Robert Darwin," in *The Encyclopedia of Philosophy,* vol. 2, ed. Paul Edwards (New York: Macmillan/Free Press, 1967), 294.
9. Ibid.
10. Russett, *Darwin in America,* 18.
11. Philip Smith, *Sources of Progressive Thought in American Education* (Lanham, MD: University Press of America, 1981), 21–22.
12. Ibid., 108.
13. Gerald Redmond, "The First Tom Brown's Schooldays: Origins and Evolution of 'Muscular Christianity' in Children's Literature, 1762–1857," *Quest* 30 (1978): 4–18.
14. Ibid., 7.
15. *San Diego Union Tribune,* 29 October 2000, C7.
16. Ronald A. Smith, *Sport and Freedom: The Rise of Big Time College Athletics* (New York: Oxford University Press, 1988), viii.
17. Melvin Adelman, *A Sporting Time: New York City and the Rise of Modern Athletics, 1820–70* (Urbana: University of Illinois Press, 1986).
18. The definition we use is arbitrary, but it does serve to distinguish between types of activities in a manner that serves the purposes of this book.
19. Allen L. Sack, "Sport: Play or Work?" in *Studies in the Anthropology of Play: Papers in Memory of Allan Tindall,* ed. Phillip Stevens (West Point, NY: Leisure Press, 1977), 186–95.
20. John Loy, "The Nature of Sport," in *Sport, Culture, and Society,* ed. John W. Loy and Gerald Kenyon (London: Macmillan, 1969), 43–61.
21. Adelman, *A Sporting Time,* 11.
22. Ibid.
23. Ibid., 5.
24. T. H. Breen, "Horses and Gentlemen: The Cultural Significance of Gambling Among the Gentry of Virginia," *William and Mary Quarterly* 34 (April 1977): 329–47.
25. Adelman, *A Sporting Time,* 36.
26. Ibid., 73.
27. Ibid.
28. Ibid.
29. Ibid.
30. Ibid.
31. Ibid., 106.
32. Smith, *Sport and Freedom.*
33. Ibid., 149.
34. Ibid., 140.
35. Michael Oriard, *Reading Football* (Chapel Hill: University of North Carolina Press, 1993), 26–27.
36. Quoted in Oriard, *Reading Football,* 27.
37. Oriard, *Reading Football,* 29.
38. Ibid., 29.

39. Steven G. Estes. "The 1872 National Amateur Regatta: The Definition of an Amateur Oarsman" (master's thesis, San Diego State University, 1985).

40. David C. Young, *The Olympic Myth of Greek Amateur Athletics* (Chicago: Ares, 1984).

41. Louis Heiland, *The Undine Barge Club of Philadelphia: 1856–1924* (Philadelphia: Drake Press, 1923), 14–15.

42. Estes, "The 1872 National Amateur Regatta."

43. Ibid., 67.

44. Allen Gutmann, *From Ritual to Record: The Nature of Modern Sports* (New York: Columbia University Press, 1978).

45. Adelman, *A Sporting Time.* Even today there is no agreed-upon definition of an amateur. This is one of the reasons that amateurism has been removed from the Olympic Charter and that professional athletes will be allowed to compete in the Olympics based on eligibility requirements of the national governing body of their sport.

46. Adelman, *A Sporting Time,* 197.

47. Gerald Redmond, *The Caledonian Games in Nineteenth-Century America* (Cranbury, NJ: Associated University Press, 1971).

48. Betty Spears and Richard Swanson, *History of Sport and Physical Education in the United States,* 3rd ed. (Dubuque, IA: Wm. C. Brown, 1983).

11

The Impact of Science and the Concept of Health on the Theoretical and Professional Development of Physical Education: 1885–1930

O B J E C T I V E S

Upon completing this chapter, you will be able to:

- Understand the importance of health maintenance and health promotion in the nineteenth century.
- Identify selected cures used to restore health during this era.
- Discuss social and institutional changes that were taking place in America during this era.
- Understand how important it was for physical educators to develop professional standards, ensure professional competence, and establish a discipline and occupation that gained the public's trust.
- Understand how the criteria for establishing that which is true and accurate changed from classical absoluteness to scientific evidence.
- Explain the process by which physical education established itself as a profession.
- Identify the early leaders of the profession and their contributions to the growth of physical education.
- Recognize the necessity of developing a sound theoretical base as the foundation of a profession.
- Identify the various ideas and beliefs that physical education professionals used to create a theoretical base for the new profession.
- Recognize the need for a sound scientific basis in the construction of a credible theory of physical education and the extent to which early professionals incorporated sound science in the theoretical development of physical education.
- Identify the problems that physical educators sought to overcome in their attempt to construct a credible theory.
- Explain the philosophical ideas and beliefs used by physical educators to build a credible theory.
- Discuss the impact of evolutionary theory on the development of physical education.
- Understand the problems that quacks and charlatans presented to the emerging profession of physical education.

General Events

1886 Haymarket riot and bombing in Chicago; Geronimo surrenders; American Federation of Labor (AFL) organized
1889 Johnstown, Pennsylvania, flood, 2200 people perish
1890 Battle of Wounded Knee; Ellis Island opened as immigration depot; Sherman Antitrust Act enacted
1893 Nationwide financial depression
1896 Supreme Court rules in *Plessy v. Ferguson* to allow "separate but equal" treatment of people
1898 U.S. battleship *Maine* blown up in Cuba; U.S. declares war on Spain; U.S. annexes Hawaii
1899 John Dewey publishes *School and Society*
1900 Boxer Rebellion in China, U.S. sends troops
1901 President William McKinley assassinated by Leon Czolgosz
1903 Panama Canal agreement signed; first airplane flight by Orville Wright
1906 Great San Francisco earthquake and fire
1907 Nationwide financial depression

1908 First automobile race from New York to Paris. Six autos from four countries begin the race. Five months later, the Thomas Flyer from the United States reaches Paris and is declared the winner

1909 Admiral Robert E. Peary reaches North Pole; National Conference on the Negro held, leads to establishment of National Association for the Advancement of Colored People (NAACP)

1910 Boy Scouts of America founded

1911 First transcontinental plane flight

1912 U.S. sends Marines to Nicaragua

1913 U.S. blockades Mexico

1914 President Wilson declares neutrality re: war in Europe

1915 First telephone conversation coast to coast; *Lusitania* sunk by Germans, 128 American passengers perish

1916 Jeanette Rankin is first female member of Congress, from Montana; John Dewey publishes *Democracy and Education*

1917 U.S. enters World War I

1920 19th Amendment ratified, giving women right to vote

1924 Law approved by Congress making all American Indians citizens of U.S.

1925 Scopes trial in Tennessee addresses teaching evolution in schools

1927 Charles A. Lindbergh flies nonstop from New York to Paris

1928 Amelia Earhart is first woman aviator to cross Atlantic

1929 St. Valentine's Day massacre in Chicago; stock market crashes, Depression begins

1931 Empire State Building opens

1933 Prohibition ended; U.S. abandons gold standard

- Recognize that during the early days physical education was actually a "specialty" of medicine and many of the early leaders in physical education were physicians.
- Understand how exercise was conducted and what benefits it was supposed to provide.
- Understand how physical education was conducted for women and why physical education was considered essential for them.
- Discuss the impact of anthropometric measurement on the development of physical education.
- Recognize the significant contributions of women educators to the growth and development of the profession of physical education.
- Understand the nature of a professional and academic discipline and why it is essential that physical education and kinesiology define the scope of the discipline.
- Recognize the contributions to the growth and development of physical education made by German physical educators who immigrated to America.
- Discuss the impact that Catherine Beecher and Dio Lewis had on the development of physical education for women.
- Understand the differing approaches of the Swedish system and the German system relative to their respective physical education programs and training of physical education teachers.
- Identify the contributions of Dudley Sargent and Edward Hitchcock in the creation of a physical education program that was unique to America.
- Understand how professional physical education teachers were trained and what training programs were available during this period.

INTRODUCTION

One of the major concerns of nineteenth-century Americans and Europeans alike was health. Health was the subject of books, lectures, articles, and pamphlets, all of which extolled the virtues, and pitfalls, of an endless variety of health enhancement techniques. It should not be surprising that health was considered so important to Americans in the early half of that century when we consider the routine occurrence of disease. American cities were ravaged by epidemics of cholera, typhus, typhoid, scarlet fever, influenza, diphtheria, smallpox, measles, and whooping cough. Illnesses such as tuberculosis, or consumption, were common. The state of medical knowledge during the nineteenth century was poor. As a result, physicians and other "healers" were not very effective in treating disease.

In the twenty-first century, physicians, physical educators, and other allied health professionals continue to investigate the link between health and the mind and body. This dualistic relationship and its impact on health and well-being has been an area of interest for centuries. This concept is especially significant in the history and philosophy of physical education. It was during the nineteenth century that a dialogue between physicians and physical educators began over the relationship between mind and body with regard to health. This common interest remains very strong today as health promotion and disease prevention remain essential philosophical components of physical education, exercise science, and medicine.

Although Louis Pasteur's germ theory of disease was proposed in 1860, it was not widely accepted by the medical profession until the end of the nineteenth century. Instead, medical knowledge was based on the dualistic idea that health consisted of a balanced constitution (the body) and temperament (the mind and spirit). Known as *humoral medicine,* the medical diagnosis and treatment of illness consisted of "heroic" procedures, which many times resulted in tragic consequences for the patient. Treatments included bleeding, leeching, and cupping. Large doses of medicine were administered that contained toxic substances such as arsenic, strychnine, emetics, and mercurial compounds.[1]

In addition to these invasive methods of purging the body to restore it to a state of "health," which meant a balanced constitution, medical experts believed that the state of one's mind could predispose the body to disease. Health was believed to be a matter of moral character. Such characteristics as diligence, integrity, honesty, hard work, and right action were demonstrable traits of a mind and spirit operating in a state of harmony. The belief that "A healthy mind resides in a healthy body"—the translation of the old Roman saying *"Mens sana en corpore sano"*—was the foundation of attitudes toward health.[2]

SOCIAL AND INSTITUTIONAL CHANGE IN NINETEENTH-CENTURY AMERICA

The nineteenth century was one of radical change in the United States. Seemingly, all aspects of American society were in flux. One of the consequences of this change was the development of a middle-class, bureaucratic society based on specialization and expertise. The field of physical education experienced this change in a way that reflected the more general social and institutional changes that occurred in every other aspect of American culture. Specifically, specialists and organizations were developed to determine the needs and direction of the emerging profession.

The development of the "professional" is a phenomenon of the nineteenth century. In the early part of that century, practitioners of law, medicine, and religion served as mediators between the public and their fields of expertise. Schooled in classical absoluteness (the belief that their knowledge was the absolute, unchanging "truth"), these self-designated experts explained and interpreted both the mysteries of the world and classical knowledge to the everyday person.

However, the epistemological belief in an immutable truth eroded late in the nineteenth century because of the expansion of knowledge. The experimental sciences and the emerging urban society advocated the idea that a new epistemology focused on new "truths" could develop as new knowledge was gained. By the end of the nineteenth century, the exclusive professional authority once given to experts in law, medicine, and religion was gone, and new disciplines were developed to house the evolving bodies of

1935 Will Rogers killed in plane crash; Senator Huey Long (LA) assassinated

Sport and Physical Education

1885 American Association for the Advancement of Physical Education founded
1887 First National Women's Singles Tennis Championship
1888 Amateur Athletic Union founded
1889 Boston Conference in the Interest of Physical Training established
1891 Basketball invented by James A. Naismith
1899 Committee on Women's Basketball; American Association for the Advancement of Physical Education (AAAPE) formed
1900 Davis Cup tennis competition begins; American League of Professional Baseball Clubs formed
1903 First baseball "World Series" played
1905 Intercollegiate Athletic Association of the United States founded, would later evolve into National Collegiate Athletic Association (NCAA)
1906 Playground Association of America founded
1910 Jack Johnson–James J. Jeffries boxing match
1916 American Tennis Association founded by black tennis players
1919 Chicago Black Sox baseball scandal
1919–20 Man O' War wins 20 of 21 horse races
1922 Paris track meet sponsored by Federation Sportive Feminine Internationale (FSFI)
1923 White House Conference on Women's Athletics
1929 Carnegie Foundation's investigation of men's college athletics
1930 Bobby Jones wins Grand Slam in golf

1931 Mabel Lee first woman president of American Physical Education Association (APEA)
1932 Babe Didrikson stars in Olympics
1934 Madison Square Garden hosts Men's Collegiate Basketball Tournament

Sport and Physical Education time line from Betty Spears and Richard A. Swanson, *History of Sport and Physical Education in the United States* (Dubuque, IA: Wm. C. Brown, 1988), 150, 206.

knowledge. These new disciplines created new epistemologies that provided additional "ways of knowing" that would augment and sometimes replace older epistemologies.

Some of these new disciplines found a home in American higher education. Prior to the nineteenth century, colleges and universities focused primarily on the liberal arts (literature, language, history, and philosophy). During the nineteenth century, this changed as the American university began to cater to pragmatic, career-oriented students through an elective system centered on specific disciplinary departments. For those fields wishing to achieve professional status, acceptance into the academic community was essential. College degrees came to be valued by the middle class—equated with social status and material success.

Colleges and universities became increasingly "professional," and during the 1880s and 1890s, the new, young professionals sought to create communities of academic interest through professional associations. Examples of these were the American Historical Association (1884), the American Economic Association (1885), the National Statistical Society (1888), and the American Political Science Association (1889). Medicine, closely allied at this time with physical education, was represented by the American Medical Association (1847), as well as subdisciplinary groups such as the American Neurological Association (1875).

One such subdisciplinary group focused on physical education. On November 27, 1885, 49 people came together at the invitation of William G. Anderson, M.D., to discuss their common interest in physical education. An important issue involved the "Battle of the Systems," a debate that centered on the advantages and disadvantages of German gymnastics and Swedish gymnastics. The growth of physical education was reflected in the fact that by 1885 there were already teacher-training institutions, gymnasia, and physical education programs in nonschool settings such as the YMCA. These early physical education programs used, in general, the Swedish system, the German system, or a combination of both. In addition, physical educators were incorporating exercises that were not identified with either system, such as the system of calisthenics developed by Catherine Beecher (1800–1878) (Figure 11-1), and the gymnastics system favored by Dioclesian Lewis (1823–1886). Both Beecher and Lewis devoted their efforts to promoting health and exercise for women. They were not advocates of the German system primarily because German gymnastics was considered too physically demanding for the women of this era.

Of particular interest is Beecher's system of calisthenics. Her system was based on a physical education program structured around 26 lessons in physiology and two courses in calisthenics, one designed for schools and the other for exercise halls. Her system used "light exercises," sometimes performed with the use of light weights.[3] She wanted her students to develop beautiful, strong bodies and believed her calisthenics would serve "as a mode of curing distortions, particularly all tendencies to curvature of the spine,

Figure 11-1
Catherine Beecher.

while at the same time, it tends to promote grace of movement, and easy manners."[4]

The composition of those who attended the 1885 meeting called by Anderson reflected the medical orientation of these early physical educators: 25 were medical doctors, most of whom were associated with a university. The large proportion of doctors provided a beginning point for the development of a body of knowledge in physical education. Becoming a legitimate and recognized profession was essential for physical education to be accepted by the public and other learned professionals. One of the outcomes of the meeting was the formation of the American Association for the Advancement of Physical Education (AAAPE). In 1903, the AAAPE was renamed the American Physical Education Association (APEA). The formation of the AAAPE was an important step in developing professional standards and identifying

the theoretical basis for the emerging profession of physical education.

THE THEORETICAL BASIS OF AMERICAN PHYSICAL EDUCATION

Interest in health, hygiene, exercise, and physical education had been growing unevenly in America since the 1830s. New programs emerged between 1830 and 1860 that became much more focused and formalized from 1870 to 1900. Terms such as *gymnastics, physical culture, physical training,* and *physical education* were used more or less synonymously to describe the systematic exercise programs that emerged during this time. Of these, *physical education* survived as the name that became most closely identified with the professional field and the academic discipline. When the AAAPE was formed in 1885, any of the four terms might have been used to describe an organized system of physical exercise. All of these terms supposedly reflected some type of theoretical understanding of the nature and operations of the human body.

Just what this theoretical base was, however, was the subject of a good deal of disagreement. The new profession of physical education accommodated many different ideas that were advanced as its theory. However, this same flexibility caused much concern among the leaders of the field. Basically, they felt that it would be difficult, if not impossible, to achieve harmonious relationships among members who held radically different ideas as to what physical education was.[5] The term *theory* is not used here in a strict, scientific sense. For our purpose, the term refers to both tested and untested assumptions used to explain physical activity.

The mixture of ideas, opinions, and verified facts that composed the theoretical base of early physical education was derived from a variety of sources. Findings in experimental science, particularly anatomy and physiology, were especially important. Physical education drew heavily on medicine to establish its body of knowledge. It is not surprising, therefore, that a large percentage of the founders of the AAAPE, as well as directors of college gymnasia at the turn of the century, were holders of an M.D. degree. Being strongly influenced by medicine, however, posed its own problems. Physical educators often had a hard time deciding on their own unique focus or territory of research. This "identity crisis" complicated the establishment of physical education's theory base.

Cultural values, especially those of the middle class, also played an important role in influencing physical education theory. Physical educators demonstrated a high degree of sensitivity to ideologies and attitudes that defined the nature of health and hygiene, the development of character, and the improvement of society. Physical education was also deeply influenced by the nineteenth-century social reform movements that connected physical and moral perfection, and the movements that connected the individual to society.

A strong social reformist attitude was one of the hallmarks of professional physical educators in the late nineteenth century. Simply put, many physical education professionals believed that physical education should be used to enhance the health and moral and intellectual development of individuals in much the same manner espoused by the philosophy of idealism. However, not all members of the AAAPE agreed on how this should happen. For example, Dioclesian Lewis blended ideas about physical exercise and hygiene to promote temperance and women's rights.[6] Lewis tied his work in physical education to a social justice agenda that sought to advance the rights of women as well as to ban the sale and consumption of alcoholic beverages.

In 1864, he hired Catherine Beecher (his system was actually an adaptation of Beecher's) to teach at his school for girls in Lexington, Massachusetts. His school attracted "mostly girls of delicate constitution sent there for their health." Lewis was a self-promoter and charlatan; he presented himself as a physician even though the title was an honorary one from Cleveland Homeopathic College, which underscores the dubiousness of the medical profession during this era. Lewis was an advocate of social reform and a health crusader who helped organize the Women's Crusade, which later evolved into the Women's Christian Temperance Union. Others, such as Dr. Edward Mussey Hartwell, America's first historian of physical education demanded a cautious, measured, and objective approach.[7] However, even the scientific and objective Hartwell became convinced that a proper program of physical education could make a boy into a better man and enable him to transmit to his children an aptitude for better thoughts and actions. Character development would soon become an essential part of the emerging profession of physical education.

Still others expressed the opinion that physical education should not be limited strictly to training the body. The U.S. commissioner of education, William T. Harris, declared, "We wish to discuss physical training in view of hygiene, and to avoid . . . all narrow interpretations of our subject." In observing that "the old physical education had thought that muscular education was all that was necessary to the training of the body," Harris argued that the new physical education was much broader in scope.[8] In so doing, Harris touched on a debate that would become central to twentieth-century physical education.

The conviction that physical education was good both for the individual and the community was a major component of physical education's theory base. For many practitioners, this conviction was the entire basis for physical education, yet there was no scientific grounding for this belief. Such was the case with William Blaikie, a prominent New York attorney. Blaikie wrote a popular book on physical exercise titled *How to Get Strong and Stay So*.[9] This book perpetuated the myth that exercise was a cure for tuberculosis, even though the findings of Louis Pasteur, German physician Robert Koch's work in bacteriology, and the germ theory of disease showed that exercise had nothing to do with the cure. Still, Blaikie was influential in popularizing physical training and was an active member and officer of the AAAPE. Blaikie also provides a good example of how educated men were concerned with matters of health and physical activity.

Three Distinct Periods

Three rather distinct periods occurred between 1885 and 1939 during which the theoretical framework of physical education was developed and modified. The first period was characterized by the nineteenth-century belief that health was a balance or harmony between the mind, body, and spirit. Science was seen to be the provider of knowledge and truth, and the tools of science (experimentation, observation, measurement) were the symbols of learned authority. The second period was a transitional one occurring between 1900 and 1917. During this period, physical education was engaged in a debate regarding the appropriate methods and goals of the field. In addition, in this period, physical education began to accommodate sport as a significant component of its theoretical and philosophical base. (The accommodation of sport by physical education will be discussed in the next chapter.) The third period occurred from 1917 to 1930 and was characterized by the acceptance by physical education of psychosocial and behavioral principles as a major part of its theoretical foundation.[10] This is not to say that these new developments were unopposed. However, physical education accepted these new trends and ideologies while also adopting popular notions regarding the virtues of physical activity. In so doing, it tried to legitimize itself in the eyes of both the public and other professionals.

During the post–Civil War years, interest in exercise increased for a variety of reasons: (1) changing concepts of work and leisure, (2) the desire of individuals to improve themselves, (3) popular literature that stressed the relationship between health and exercise, (4) an expanding body of knowledge about human physiology, and (5) the influence of evolutionary theory on concepts of race regeneration. Interest in exercise and health was also influenced by the athletic craze

that swept the country between 1870 and 1900.[11] In addition, some medical doctors treated physical deformities and chronic conditions with exercise, a treatment known as the Swedish Movement Cure[12] (not to be confused with Swedish gymnastics).

One reason for the increased interest in health was an intensified sense of personal anxiety. Americans continued to move to the cities in the late 1800s, and with this urban growth, there emerged a need to reaffirm a sense of physical, social, and psychological community. The loss of the traditional rural lifestyle left many Americans struggling to adapt to a new urban way of life. Consequently, many Americans favored an energetic style of living that would minimize the negative impact of their urban environment.[13] Americans pragmatically sought a connection between ideas and action, and in this social and psychological environment, the body became the means by which this connection could take place.[14]

All of this turmoil occurred at the same time that a significant number of Americans were beginning to lose faith in the ability of religion to solve social and moral problems. Sin was no longer seen as the single root cause of moral, social, and health problems. Instead, many Americans now believed that individuals were at the mercy of a possibly amoral social environment. Yet, although many felt powerless to control this environment, they still wanted control over their own bodies. Whether the search was for personal order, social order, or communal identity, it was believed that exercise and the corresponding enhancement of health were necessary to ensure total wellness and equilibrium of the whole person—mind, spirit, and body.

Biological and Philosophical Issues

The approach that identified the whole as the sum of its parts was influenced by the rapidly expanding body of knowledge in the biological sciences. This type of thinking related easily to the concept of the "social organism," which made each individual a "cell" in the "body" of society. With the discoveries in the biological sciences, influenced by

Charles Darwin, humans were increasingly viewed as an organismic part of the social body. Health was seen as a balance between the organic systems of the body and those systems that set humans apart from other creatures. People were part of the biological world; however, they were also unique.

What made humans unique were those qualities associated with the human mind. Will, volition, cognition, emotion, and character were unique to humans, yet these characteristics were increasingly studied as physiological phenomena. One example of this is William James, who turned psychology from the study of mind to the study of behavior. Scholars studied how the mind and body were related and functioned. The success of the biological sciences influenced the manner in which the unique qualities described previously were studied.

The relationship between mind and body has occupied the agendas of scientists and philosophers alike. The identification of the neural pathways leading from the brain and spinal cord to the muscles and organs of the body, and back to the spinal cord and brain, lent evidence to the possibility that mental processes were biological functions. This idea was not new. If you recall, Thomas Hobbes posited similar materialistic notions of reality.

Biological concepts, however, could not completely accommodate notions of the will. The concept of biological determinism called for the will to be a product of the body. In application, this meant that willpower was genetically predetermined and was therefore a product of one's parentage rather than other mental factors. To many nineteenth-century Americans, this idea was preposterous, almost sacrilegious! Most believed that will was one aspect of being human that separated humans from the lower animals. As the foundation of character, will separated the superior individual from the inferior one. If will was a product of biology, then individuals had little control over who was superior.

The nature of the will and its relationship to the body was the focus of much scholarly work. For example, in *Principles of Mental Physiology,* William B. Carpenter wrote that he could explain will strictly in terms of physiology.[15] Wilhelm

Wundt also gave considerable thought to the subject of will. He investigated the physiological basis of sensory perceptions, instinctive and involuntary actions, and sense feelings. Wundt believed that these aspects of our bodies were necessary to the development of higher mental processes. Yet Wundt also recognized that certain psychic processes could never be fully understood and that these processes lie outside individual consciousness.[16] For Wundt, will was related to character in that it was both physically inherited and socially acquired. This was significant to physical education, which would develop strong and healthy people and contribute to the formation of character and will. These desired traits would then be passed on to subsequent generations through heredity. Not surprisingly, the work of Wundt was popular in physical education during this time.

There were two rationales for the development of physical education in the latter part of the nineteenth century: (1) that the mind is in part a product of biology, and (2) that character can be acquired through the exercise of the will. The identification of neural pathways was used to build a strong case for exercise as essential to the healthy, integrated self.[17] For instance, Edward Hartwell, a leading nineteenth-century physical educator at Johns Hopkins University, stated that a single muscle is not a simple organ. Rather, it is made up of two clearly distinguishable, yet intimately related, parts: (1) the contracting muscle and (2) the stimulating nerve. If the two parts were to disassociate, or if either part atrophied for any reason, the dual organ was "thrown out of gear" and ceased to function as a muscle. This process was felt to be similar to the human body when it was treated as two parts and trained to function separately as "fractions"—in other words, mind and body.[18]

The impact of science on nineteenth-century thought was profound. The epistemology of dualism was increasingly challenged by the epistemologies of science. However, this is not to say that dualism was abandoned. The nature of human existence and the role of physical education in enhancing life were popular topics then and remain so today. Is human existence divided into two separate but interrelated parts: mind and body? Or can our existence as humans be explained in terms of a unified biological organism as opposed to one part body and one part mind?

Contemporary physical educators seem to identify with the unity of mind and body as opposed to a dualistic approach. However, this choice or belief is not as clear-cut as science would like. Although scientific inquiry provides the basis for research and teaching in physical education, the philosophy of idealism, which strives to improve the "self," remains very popular with physical educators and coaches. This attention to "self" involves physical improvement, cognitive improvement, moral and character development, and, in many cases, spiritual development. More importantly, idealism lends itself to dualism more than to a unified approach. Most physical educators and coaches use an eclectic approach that incorporates several epistemologies. Do you use more than one epistemology—more than one way of knowing? Do you identify more with dualism or monism?

Evolution

Evolutionary theory was combined with physiological assumptions about the relationship between mind and body to justify physical education.[19] However, much of the early theory base of physical education was rooted in assumptions about its virtues and not on scientific evidence. This a priori approach to physical education was therefore the cause of both the successes and the failures of the discipline.

Exercise was thought to be one of the measures of biological improvement of the species. Anthropomorphic measurement revealed that changes in the body could occur in as little time as a few weeks, and according to the logic of the day, improvements in physical stature were symbolic of mental and moral improvement as well. As the theory went, individual improvements would enhance the evolutionary process of the entire human race, and therefore physical education was of benefit to the race.[20] This strong statement enabled physical education to work in a direction that would continue to link its theoretical base with established scientific theory—in this case, evolution.

Exercise was felt to be critical to the normal evolutionary development of humans. Early physical education theory dictated that exercise not only improved the human form but also was essential to building nerve centers and sound minds. The often repeated *"Mens sana in corpore sano"* was truly part of physical education's belief system. Jay Seaver, a physical educator at Yale University, reiterated the dependence of the functioning of the mind on the health of the body:

> We may have fine intellectual powers and attainment in persons whose condition is like 'sweet bells jangled out of tune and harsh' whose central nerve power may be grand, but whose peripheral ganglia may be so morbidly out of tune as to make every process pathological.[21]

Seaver's statement represented the antidualistic view of intellectuals who felt that proper physical exercise facilitated the functional unity of the individual. As such, exercise promoted harmony within the individual.

Evolutionary theory provided a strong scientific basis for the emerging theoretical basis of physical education. In the normal development of the species, evolution demonstrated that the ability to adapt and change was the key to survival. The species that did survive were stronger than those that became extinct. Exercise and its attendant health benefits helped to ensure that men and women would continue to grow stronger and thus increase their ability to adapt to change and to survive. Strength was also equated with health, which could be handed down from one generation to the next. Women were identified by physical educators as being especially helped by evolutionary theory, as we shall see later in this chapter. It is certain that nineteenth-century physical education benefited from evolutionary beliefs.

THE DISEASE—NEURASTHENIA; THE CURE—EXERCISE!

Even as physical educators argued for the unity of mind and body as opposed to a dualistic separation, they continued to wage a campaign against nervous disorders. Known as neurasthenic disease, this kind of dysfunction was thought to be of epidemic proportions in the late nineteenth century. For instance, George M. Beard published a book, *American Nervousness,* that contributed to the belief that nervous disorder was widespread.[22] It was felt that the urban environment, which cloistered workers in offices and factories, made everyone susceptible. The emphasis on brain work and on fine motor movements such as writing placed stress on the brain and nerve centers, and exercise would restore the balance. Randolph Fairies, a medical doctor and physical educator, argued that exercise was therapeutic with respect to the "brain overwork" brought about by too much studying, overanxiety, and the many moral decisions and responsibilities with which nineteenth-century Americans were faced.[23] Fairies felt that the organs of "thought" (the brain, spinal cord, and nerves) were stimulated through exercise, with new blood sent to the nervous system and the old blood carried away.

Students were regarded as especially susceptible to mental overstrain because young scholars were still developing physically. Exercise for students was therefore viewed as a therapeutic and a developmental agent. The preoccupation with neurasthenia and the influence of Fairies may have been among the impetuses for offering physical education to students during the nineteenth century.

EXERCISING TO BUILD BRAIN POWER

In the late nineteenth century, questions arose regarding how intelligence developed, how it could be improved, and how it could be measured. Randolph Fairies reported to the AAAPE in 1894 that men who exercised their limbs had well developed convolutions of the cerebral mass. His research indicated that intelligent men have highly convoluted brains, whereas the cerebral mass of "idiots" was almost smooth. The conclusion reached by Fairies was startling: Intelligence could be physiologically observed and controlled through exercise. Apparently, Fairies missed the obvious conclusion: If his theory were true, all great athletes would be Phi Beta Kappas!

If, as Fairies argued, exercise actually stimulated willpower, character, and other mental attributes, then it had tremendous potential for the rehabilitation of deviant classes. Hamilton D. Wey, a doctor from a state reformatory in New York, believed exercise could rehabilitate "criminals and dullards." Wey reported to the AAAPE the astonishing benefits of exercise with his patients: gains made in weight, posture, and general vigor. With these gains came an improvement in their mental capacities never before manifested in their prison life.[24] Furthermore, Wey concluded that social deviants could be "exercised" into an acceptable level of moral behavior.[25] This concept remains popular and can be observed in prison camps and other correctional institutions that use physical training in the form of boot camps as a means of establishing "correct" moral behavior.

WOMEN: MOTHERS OF THE RACE

The evolutionary principles popular in the latter part of the nineteenth century affected attitudes toward exercise, health, and the bodily development of women, especially white women since this group was the focus of attention (Figure 11-2). Health was important for everyone, but it was particularly important for women in their role as progenitors and nurturers of new life. As the argument went, defective women produced defective children, whereas healthy women strengthened the race through their offspring. The procreative function of women gave them a special need for physical education.

The prevailing attitude toward women was that their unique biological functions required exercises that catered to their special physiology. This type of thinking implied that exercise for men and women should not be the same. Dr. Angelo Mosso, a professor of physiology in Italy, stated that the muscles used in respiration and those of the abdomen were much more important for women than for men because those were the muscles used in giving birth.[26] He also believed that exercise for men and women should not be the same.

Exercise for women, viewed within the parameters of nineteenth-century thinking, was

Figure 11-2
Mount Holyoke Seminary students in the early 1860s at exercise.

enthusiastically endorsed by both male and female physical educators. However, Victorian attitudes of the late nineteenth century did not permit women to dress in a fashion that allowed the freedom of movement necessary to do calisthenics and exercises as intended. On the contrary, women could often be seen "layered" in undergarments, blouses, and skirts that no doubt made any sudden movement difficult, to say the least! This style of dress carried over into the gymnasium and compounded the problem. Clearly, the workout attire of the nineteenth century did not permit for a vigorous program of physical education for women when compared with the high-intensity fitness programs of today.

An additional justification for women's physical education was that it made women more attractive. For instance, in 1894, physical educators argued over the virtues of heavy apparatus in exercise programs for women. Many believed that heavy apparatus could detract from the womanly form by making the shoulders too wide and the hips too narrow. Most physical educators believed that "heavy work" was permissible if it was used

for the overall development of health, but it should not be used for increasing strength. The object of physical education was to perfect the female body, both in its outward contours and in its ability to resist lifelong wear and tear. Physical education prepared women for motherhood, and health was essential to that role.

In 1894, Mary E. Allen, owner of the Allen Gymnasium in Boston, summarized the benefits of exercise for late nineteenth-century women. She argued that healthy women could maintain their equilibrium, sick women could restore their health, depressed women could be cheered, fat women could reduce, thin women could build up, mature mothers could maintain their youth to meet the needs of growing children, young mothers could make their bodies "the sound and holy temple it should be" for the creation of life, and all young women could increase their vigor and make their figures supple.[27] Although gender differences were recognized and maintained, many nineteenth-century physical educators actively supported physical education opportunities for women, and women benefited from the social and biological imperative toward good health during this period. Many of the attitudes and justifications regarding physical education articulated by Mary Allen are still manifest in contemporary physical education.

WOMEN, HIGHER EDUCATION, AND PHYSICAL EDUCATION

Physical educators supported higher education for women, and nowhere was the health of women more of an issue than in women's colleges. The growth of higher education for women was a phenomenon of the post–Civil War years, and dissenters to the experiment believed that women were too frail to withstand the rigors of academic study. The physical constitution of women was not something administrators could dismiss easily. Nervous disorders were believed to be particular to American culture, and American women were believed to be the most susceptible.

The female nervous system received much attention from the medical community in the last half of the nineteenth century and was a major argument against higher education for women. Dr. Edward Clarke suggested that intellectual education would unduly tax the nervous system of women by redirecting the nervous energy necessary for reproduction toward intellectual development.[28] Many of Clarke's contemporaries who supported higher education for women strongly disagreed. The inclusion of physical education programs in college curricula was the response in many cases.

Historians have generally overlooked the contributions of women to the field of physical education. Most physical education textbooks that present information about the contributions of women state that Delphine Hanna was the first woman to achieve the status of full professor (the highest professorial rank) in physical education; in fact, it was Clelia Mosher who could claim this achievement. Historian Alison Wrynn observes that physical educators and sport historians seem to be narrowly focused and hindered by selective memory relative to the contributions of outstanding women. Wrynn asks, "Why then is the reality of Mosher's experiences pushed to the margins of our history?"[29] Good question!

THE GOLDEN AGE OF ANTHROPOMETRIC MEASUREMENT: 1885–1900

The emphasis on form was manifest in the new academic area of *anthropometry*—the study of the measurements of body segments, girths, and lengths. Anthropometry was used by many different disciplines, particularly anthropology, to prove or disprove all kinds of theories on the nature of humans. For instance, Charles Roberts, an English M.D., measured the heights and weights of men of the artisan class and compared these measurements with those of the "most favored," or upper, class. Roberts's study showed the artisan class to be inferior in height, weight, and chest girth, and he concluded that height differences were probably due to inherited characteristics whereas weight was influenced more by the conditions of life.[30]

This kind of work had a significant impact on physical educators in the late nineteenth century. Roberts's *Manual of Anthropometry* was cited by Dudley A. Sargent in his address on anthropometry before the AAAPE in 1890.[31] Dr. Henry P. Bowditch studied the growth of Boston schoolchildren, and William T. Porter initiated an anthropometric study of 33,000 schoolchildren in St. Louis. Porter concluded that children with less-than-average mental ability were lighter, shorter, and smaller in the chest than children of average or better mental ability.[32] Such physical measurement was tremendously important in the minds of physical educators in the latter part of the nineteenth century. In 1891, Roberts and Bowditch were made honorary members of the AAAPE; Porter was already an active member of the association.

Anthropometry was an especially popular research tool during this period and was particularly well suited to the research needs of physical educators who sought to both quantify their scientific status and legitimize their claim to professional status. Anthropometry suited research, pedagogical, and status needs, lending an aura of scientific validity to physical education.

As were all academic questions, those generated by physical educators were influenced by post-Darwinian thought. Darwinism emphasized inheritance and health as the mechanisms of social progress. One sign of health was the attainment of the ideal form for humans—a shape that had symmetry and harmony of proportion. Physical educators used anthropometry to determine the ideal proportions of man and woman. However, "ideal" to nineteenth-century physical educators did not mean what it does today: the concept of ultimate bodily development. Interestingly, physical educators defined "ideal" as an average, or a norm, of the measurements of large numbers of people.

This norm, according to scientists, could be improved by changing the environment, and one of the best ways to change the environment was to provide students with the opportunity to exercise. Influenced by the studies of contemporary anthropometrists on the inheritance of mental and physical traits, Dudley Sargent stated his conclusions regarding the improvement of the human race through exercise in an address to the AAAPE in 1890:

> Both the intellectual and physical supremacy of a people are dependent upon the intellectual and physical condition of the masses. In other words, the only way to produce the highest specimens of the individual, improve the condition of the race and better the quality of future humanity, is to raise the normal or mean standard of mental and physical development.[33]

Clearly, according to physical educators, the means to improve the physical, mental, and moral aspects of the race was through exercise. By associating themselves with the goal of race improvement through the mechanism of science, primarily anthropometry, physical educators attempted to establish themselves as the new arbiters of racial supremacy. The physical educators of this era who were engaged in research focused their attention on white males and females; there was little, if any, interest on the part of physical educators in studying people of color during this period.

During the late nineteenth century, the most highly honored physical education researchers were those men and women who directed programs at the college level. Edward Hitchcock, M.D., professor of physical education and hygiene at Amherst College, was the epitome of what physical education professionals aspired to be. Anthropometry was at the cutting edge of physical education research, and Hitchcock collected anthropometric measurements from 1861 to 1901 as part of the mandatory physical examinations of all students. Dudley Sargent was professor of physical training and director of the gymnasium at Harvard, and in a similar manner, he collected measurements from which he devised his anthropometric chart of the ideal: a graph that plotted the norms of symmetrical development of predominantly white, college-age men. Sargent concluded that the closer a student was to the fiftieth percentile, the more symmetrical the individual.[34] Men were not the only subjects for anthropometric research. Delphine Hanna, M.D., at Oberlin College; Lucile E. Hill and Mary Anna Wood at Wellesley; Carolyn C. Ladd, M.D., at Bryn Mawr; and others routinely collected anthropometric measurements of white female students as a part of scientific gymnasium work.[35]

Social prejudice and the homogeneous nature of college student populations of both genders acted as parameters for physical education research. The thousands of measurements collected were of a generally homogeneous socioeconomic group of upper- or middle-class Anglo-Saxon college students. These students routinely were shown to be taller, heavier, and larger in girth than those whose economic and social status made attending college difficult. Unfortunately, and contrary to the methods we now use in the scientific world, the information gathered from anthropometric studies was erroneously used to validate nineteenth-century racial prejudices. It was not until the twentieth century that many of the misuses of anthropometry were understood and discounted.

Although some anthropometrists claimed to offer proof of racial superiority, this was not really the point of anthropometric research. The purpose of these studies, according to Hitchcock, was to understand the physical data of the typical or ideal college student. By observing every student possible with the most modern of anthropometric measuring devices, Hitchcock hoped to compute the "average" student and then to instruct students to achieve the average. What needed to be determined and agreed on, then, was what constituted "perfection," or the average.[36]

DEFINING THE SCOPE OF THE DISCIPLINE

The assumptions, theories, and scientific evidence that made up the theoretical base of physical education supported the conviction that exercise was good for the individual and good for society. The arguments and rationales drawn from the related disciplines of physiology, psychology, and medicine combined ideas about individual health, public hygiene, race improvement, physical and moral rehabilitation, and educational reform through the science of physical education.

Founded on these beliefs, physical education had both strengths and weaknesses. The blend of theory, assumption, and knowledge congruent with contemporary beliefs provided the enthusiasm and reformist zeal during the initial growth period of physical education. However, this same blend also provided the basis for possible contradictions within the theoretical foundation of the field. Physical education attempted to gain acceptance with groups that had different views on the nature of "truth." If, for instance, physical educators catered to the needs of the public and condoned popular ideas not based on scientific evidence, then the academic world would not respect the work done in the discipline. If, however, physical education attempted to define itself solely in terms of scientific empiricism, it might not have the base needed to attract a popular following.

Dr. George Fitz, a research physiologist at Harvard's Lawrence Scientific School, was one of the first to understand the paradigmatic problems of the new discipline. Admonishing his colleagues on the lack of high-quality research, Fitz cautioned the AAAPE that physical education must not rely on general assumptions lacking a basis in the findings of science. He felt that many theories were valueless as working hypotheses because they were not based on experiments or experience, but instead were accepted a priori (on assumptions).[37]

Although he continued to press his fellow physical educators to test the assumptions that they promoted and perpetuated, Fitz was in the minority. His promptings went largely unheeded for several reasons. One was that other physical education leaders disagreed with Fitz on the scope of physical education. For instance, Dr. Edward Hartwell had a larger vision of physical education, one that accepted the integrated person as the legitimate sphere of physical education. He believed that almost all human actions could be understood as the union of the body moving under the control of the mind. He also asserted that bodily actions warranted first consideration because without them mental power, artistic feeling, and spiritual insight could not occur. His definition covered almost all facets of human existence and therefore made physical education central to being human.[38] Fitz eventually became exasperated with these lofty characterizations of the field of physical education and left it to study physiology.

Most physical educators, however, continued to concentrate on anatomical and anthropometric studies. Unlike today, few physical educators paid attention to physiological research, mainly because the science of physiology was changing during this period. Most physiologists were interested in cellular function, whereas physical educators were interested in the functioning of the human body as a whole. Strength was seen as both a dynamic indicator of functional efficiency and a measurement of bodily integration, and measuring strength became a part of anthropometric testing. Physical educators such as Dudley Sargent, Jay Seaver, and Watson L. Savage agreed that one of the principal objects of physical training was the development of muscular power leading to physical strength, and as a consequence, anthropometry remained the dominant research topic through the 1890s.

The desire to be the professional standard bearer of anthropometric research led the AAAPE to create the Committee of Anthropometry and Vital Statistics at its first meeting in 1885. A major task of this committee was to establish a chart of anthropometric measures that would become the recommended standards of the organization. Before such a standard was achieved, however, the annual AAAPE meetings evolved into a political battle over procedural protocol, measurement sites, and equipment. For example, the matter of whether to measure height with shoes on or off was of considerable concern at the 1891 AAAPE annual meeting. Both Hitchcock and Sargent had developed their own anthropometric charts that they had used in their college work, and each felt that his method was superior. Sargent vigorously campaigned for the adoption of his system.[39] Eventually, a standard of fifty measures were agreed on as the recommendations of the AAAPE.[40]

THE CONTRIBUTIONS OF GERMAN GYMNASTICS, DIO LEWIS, AND THE SWEDISH SYSTEM TO TEACHER TRAINING

The theories discussed by physical educators in colleges and universities were supposed to be applied in primary and secondary schools, and during the late nineteenth century, the primary pedagogical methods of physical education were gymnastics, calisthenics, and exercise programs. The best known of the various systems was the German system of Friedrich Jahn, which, as you remember, was introduced in the United States in the 1820s. The most notable feature of the German system was the use of heavy apparatus, including jumping horses and horizontal bars, and light equipment such as dumbbells and wands. German gymnastics was popular in Massachusetts between 1830 and 1860. It was not unusual to see devotees of German gymnastics marching in formation or doing calisthenics and other similar drills on command.

The civil unrest in Germany in 1848–1849 caused a large number of Germans to immigrate to the United States. This infusion of Germans led to the formation of several Turner societies, and in 1850, a turnerbund was created in New York.

Modeled after Turner societies in Germany, these groups offered gymnastics work in addition to serving as social societies for the German-American community. The Turners believed in the value of physical education in the form of German gymnastics, and actively campaigned for mandatory physical education instruction in the schools. They volunteered to provide instruction free of charge and were especially successful in the Midwest, where there was a large concentration of German immigrants. By 1867, there were 148 Turner societies consisting of 10,200 members.[41] Their influence was considerable in Ohio, where, in 1892, a law was passed stipulating that physical culture be taught in the larger schools; in 1904, the law was amended to include all schools. Anton Leibold and John Molter, both Turners, introduced the law in the Ohio state legislature.[42]

The Turners of the New York City turnerbund began a seminary in 1866 for training teachers of German gymnastics. Nineteen men enrolled in 1866 and attended class primarily during the evening hours and on Saturday, which enabled them to hold jobs. Only Turners could enroll, and a per capita tax of 10 cents a year was levied on the membership to support the teacher-training program. The one-year curriculum included classes in history, anatomy, first aid, aesthetic dancing, theory of physical education systems, terminology, and the practice of gymnastics with emphasis on teaching methods. Five faculty members taught the courses; nine men finished the coursework and took the final exam, but only five were awarded diplomas.[43] Three more classes were offered, two in New York in 1869 and 1872, and one in Chicago in 1871. Each class was six months long, but results were very discouraging.

The Turners decided that attempts to train teachers would be more successful in the West. The North American Gymnastic Union, the formal name for the Turner society, voted in 1874 to move the Normal School for the teaching of gymnastics to Milwaukee, where it operated under the direction of George Brosius from 1875 to 1888 and awarded 103 diplomas.[44]

In 1860, Dioclesian Lewis introduced his own system of light gymnastics to men, women, and children in the Boston area. He opened a private gymnasium and offered teacher training for those who wished to teach gymnastics. Another system of gymnastics was the Swedish system of Per Ling. This system was first introduced to the United States at the Swedish Health Institute in Washington, D.C., by Baron Nils Posse, the leading proponent of making Swedish gymnastics the program of physical education in American schools. By 1887, Swedish gymnastics was being used at Johns Hopkins University. The Swedish system used light equipment such as dumbbells and chest weights, but to a lesser extent than the German program (Figure 11-3).

During the nineteenth century, physical training was associated with some form of systematic exercise regimen and was no doubt influenced by the European style of calisthenics, primarily German or Swedish. These systems reflected contemporary thinking, which sought to develop bodily symmetry through disciplined, well-ordered, and progressively graded exercises. In the first 15 years of the AAAPE, physical educators debated the most appropriate exercise system, the one that would best serve the needs of the American people. The German system and the Swedish system were often promoted by their respective adherents as the "correct" system of physical education, and the controversy surrounding the two approaches is known as the "Battle of the Systems." Meanwhile, physical educators called for an American system tailored to American needs, needs that could not be met by foreign systems.

PHYSICAL EDUCATION THE AMERICAN WAY

A conference on physical training was held in Boston in 1889 to develop an American system of gymnastics. Influential educators and the leading physical educators of the day attended the meeting, chaired by William T. Harris, United States commissioner of education. The purpose of the meeting was to discuss the various systems of training in an effort to decide what method of exercise would be most suitable for American educational institutions. Spokesmen for the German system and the Swedish system presented what they felt were the unique contributions of each. Both systems graded their programs according to the age, sex, and physical condition of the individual and proceeded to more difficult work as physical conditioning improved. Dudley Sargent provided information about his programs at Cambridge, as did Edward Hitchcock about his program at Amherst. Sargent's program, which prescribed an individualized regimen of exercises for each student, differed from the Swedish and German systems, which emphasized class groups. Hitchcock conducted his program in class groups, although he did examine each student and suggest further work to correct deficiencies.[45] Also in attendance at this conference was Baron Pierre de Coubertin, sent from France as an observer. In 1894, at a conference he organized at the Sorbonne in Paris,

Figure 11-3

Baron Nils Posse, the leading proponent of Swedish gymnastics in the United States.

Coubertin would proclaim the revival of the Olympic Games. It should be noted that Coubertin was not impressed with American physical education.

The notable feature of this conference was the participants' openness to new ideas and willingness to develop a system of gymnastic exercise based on the best available knowledge and methods. The desire to understand the underlying principles of movement and how they related to hygienic and educational issues was very much in evidence in the discussions that followed the formal presentations.

CHANGING CONCEPTS OF HEALTH

While physical educators conducted research in anthropometry and debated the various gymnastic systems, the very concepts on which their work was based began to change. The nineteenth-century concept of health, as a balance among mind, body, and will, became impossible to sustain in the face of new biological and medical evidence. Specifically, the understanding of germs and their connection to disease undermined the idea that health was a balance of mind, body, and will. New medical techniques such as inoculation, purification of water and milk, new surgical techniques, and asepsis (infection prevention) led to a new faith in invasive medicine's ability to control, cure, and restore health. It became increasingly difficult to blame moral indiscretions on the lack of physical capacity, and vice versa. By 1900, the conceptual foundation of health began to shift away from the old paradigm, and the constitution of a healthy human being was beginning to be defined in terms of social interaction and behavioral action.[46]

A CHANGING PROFESSION

During this period, an emphasis on reform manifested itself in almost every aspect of American culture including physical education. The reform movement and the desire for professional status and recognition were very important to the nature and development of American education. Physical education found itself adjusting its focus

and purpose in the light of these changes, and although some welcomed the changes, others did not. The latter included those who continued to promote gymnastic exercise as the pedagogical heart of physical education and anthropometry as its research core. Those who sought change promoted the adoption of play theory as the rationale for physical education and the pedagogical use of play, games, and sport as the methodology of physical education.[47] To complicate matters, a number of self proclaimed experts emerged on the scene. These individuals had little, if any, formal training. However, they knew how to market themselves as professionals. Many of them identified with physical culture while some claimed expertise in physical education, much to the detriment and embarassment of the new profession. These quacks and charlatans frequently injured their clients, or worse. On November 11, 1903 Dr. Ernst H. Spooner, M.D. addressed his peers and other interested parties and said in part "I am a strong advocate of physical culture and the higher development of brawn and brain . . . but not as we see it set forth in the flaming advertisements in the public press of today. Instruction in physical culture is to important a thing to be left to charlatan and quacks, but should be in the hands of only those who are competent . . ."[47A] How do you think Dr. Spooner would react to the Internet certifications of personal trainers?

One of the major products of the health-reform movement of the nineteenth century was the creation of career opportunities. Jobs in physical education became available for both men and women in the form of gymnasium directors, physical training instructors, playground leaders, and hygiene teachers. Before 1885, most of those who were employed in these jobs did not have the benefits of formal training in college or university programs. When William G. Anderson founded the Association for the Advancement of Physical Education (AAPE) in 1885, one of the most important goals of the organization was to improve and professionalize the teaching of physical education. The 1885 meeting was the beginning of a systematic attempt to train physical education instructors. At the second meeting of the AAPE of the organization in 1886, the name was changed to the American Association for the Advancement of Physical Education (AAPE).

THE PROFESSIONAL PREPARATION OF TEACHERS

The debate between the promoters of gymnastics and the play theorists was not the only one important to the direction of teacher preparation. In a debate that would be very familiar to physical educators today, a difference in opinion as to how teachers should be trained existed between administrators of the AAAPE and the teachers who worked in the schools. The national executive council, made up entirely of college men and women, state superintendents of physical education, city directors of physical education, and other administrators, judged teacher behavior by standards that were more applicable to higher education (colleges and universities). The problem with their goals was that what was professionally necessary to enhance the authority of people in administrative and college-level positions was quite different from the needs of teachers in elementary and secondary education.

The majority of men and women in leadership positions in the AAAPE held medical degrees. Medical training continued to be seen as necessary for college physical educators, as well as for those men and women who sought administrative positions.[48] This makes sense in light of the strong health orientation that existed in physical education at this time. In opposition to this group were the practitioners who were the frontline workers in playgrounds, summer camps, and physical education programs. The preparation programs that developed to provide trained workers for these positions were limited by the desire to put qualified teachers into the marketplace as quickly as possible.

One institution that facilitated the needs of the teacher/practitioner was the "normal school."

During the nineteenth century, private normal schools offered certificates of completion for one- or two year courses under the direction of well-known physical educators. Normal schools were well respected before World War I; the Sargent Normal School of Physical Education is a good example of this. Until the 1890s, these private normal schools were the only programs available for training physical educators. Sargent's proposed curriculum was an ambitious one that emphasized anatomy and physiology along with practical gymnasium experiences. In 1891, the program was lengthened to two years, and in 1902, the school merged with Boston University to become the Sargent College of Physical Education.

The YMCA International Training School, later named Springfield College, was established in 1887 in Springfield, Massachusetts. The school offered a two-year course in professional physical education, which enabled the YMCA to staff its gymnasia with qualified teachers. Luther Halsey Gulick, M.D., was appointed as an instructor in the Department of Physical Training. One of the great leaders of physical education, Gulick remained at the YMCA Training School from 1887 to 1902. In 1889, after the resignation of Robert J. Roberts, Gulick was appointed superintendent. He remained superintendent until 1900. From 1887 to 1902, he served as the YMCA's first secretary of the Physical Training Department of the International Committee of the YMCA of North America.[49] His contributions to the field of physical education were of such magnitude that the American Alliance for Health, Physical Education, Recreation and Dance (AAHPERD) has made the Gulick Award the highest honor to be given a member.

Gulick started a summer school course for the training of physical education teachers who were already in the field. The first graduate coursework in physical education was started in 1891. Courses were offered in (1) physiological psychology, (2) the history and philosophy of physical education, (3) anthropometry, and (4) the literature of physical education. Coursework culminated in a thesis of 3000 words. Upon successful completion of the graduate program of study, a graduate diploma in physical education (not a graduate degree) was awarded. Three men completed the work necessary for a diploma between 1891 and 1900.[50] The first graduate degree program in physical education was established at Teachers College, Columbia University in 1901; it led to a master's degree.

The Chautauqua Summer School was operated by William G. Anderson, M.D., who later turned administrative duties over to Jay Seaver, M.D. Founded in 1888, the school offered a teacher preparation (normal school) program in gymnastics, playground supervision and management, first aid, sports skills, and aquatics instruction. Completion of the normal course required attending three six-week terms. Classroom instruction was given in anatomy, physiology, anthropometry, psychology, medical gymnastics, orthopedics, Swedish and German gymnastics, and storytelling.[51]

Dudley Sargent operated the Harvard Summer School of Physical Education, which he opened in 1887 (Figure 11-4). The school "was probably the most important source of professional training in the United States during the early part of the twentieth century."[52] The alumni totaled 5086 students from the United States and abroad. Coursework

consisted of classes in anatomy, physiology, hygiene, anthropometry, applied anatomy, and lectures on the various gymnastic systems, including their history and philosophy. Course offerings were later expanded to cover calisthenics, first aid, physical diagnosis, testing for normal vision and hearing, and treatment of spinal curvature. Sports were added in 1900 for men and women.[53] The school closed in 1932 because a bachelor's degree was required by the state to teach physical education, which forced potential educators into a four-year program.

In 1866, California passed a state law requiring physical education in the schools. John Swett was superintendent of public instruction for the state of California and the person responsible for implementing the law requiring mandatory exercise (Figure 11-5). Signed on March 24, 1866, by Governor Lou, the law stated:

> Instruction shall be given in all grades of schools, and in all classes, during the entire school course, in manners and morals, and the

Figure 11-4
Dudley Sargent's laboratory: Hemenway Gymnasium, Harvard University, 1885.

Figure 11-5
John Swett.

laws of health; and due attention shall be given to such physical exercises for the pupils as may be conducive to health and vigor of body, as well as mind; and to the ventilation and temperature of school rooms.[54]

There are two important points relevant to the California legislation. First, the 1860s was a period in the history of America that evoked concern about the nation's young men relative to their physical condition and ability to bear arms in defense of the country. California made physical education mandatory in an effort to promote health and vigor. Second, the concern over the physical readiness of the nation's youth to provide the means for the military defense of America's interests abroad and at home resulted in most educators favoring mandatory military drill, not gymnastics, in the schools. In 1863, the Teacher's Institute urged the teaching of military drill in the public schools.[55] But John Swett successfully argued on behalf of mandatory gymnastics rather than military drill. As a result, Swett enabled California to lead the nation in requiring mandatory physical education in the public schools at a time when many people were concerned about the health and physical ability of the nation's youth—concerns that continue to be voiced today. However, not enough is being done today to ensure the health and physical well-being of the nation's youth. Enhancing health and preventing disease, especially obesity, is a national issue that constitutes the foundation of effective physical education programs.

As discussed earlier, Ohio passed a law in 1892 requiring that physical culture be taught in the state's larger schools. This law was a big victory for the large population of German Turners living in Ohio, advocates of mandatory physical education in the schools. The state legislature modified the law in 1904 to require that all schools, not just the larger ones, teach physical education. Louisiana in 1894, Wisconsin in 1897, and North Dakota in 1899 were other states that passed laws requiring physical education. With state legislation mandating physical education,

the professional preparation of physical education teachers was at the top of the political and professional agenda.

Concern over the training of new practitioners was typical in the professionalization process. It had to be addressed successfully if the profession was to grow in stature, prestige, and authority. From the beginning of the AAAPE, there was constant pressure to improve training, and in 1896, Jakob Bolin argued for the improvement of teacher preparation programs:

> It is deplorable that, in matters pertaining to physical education, the gymnastic teacher, who, from the nature of the avocation ought to be considered as experts, have far less influence than the pedagogue [regular teacher] . . . the insufficient general and special education of our gymnastic teacher, I see [as] the cause of the lost state of physical education in our land. Our teachers are not thoroughly acquainted with the fundamental principles of their work.[56]

Although professional preparation programs were steadily improving, professionals were concerned with the quality of instruction and sought to improve it to legitimize their positions.

Four-year major programs were introduced between 1892 and 1911 at Stanford (1892), Harvard (1892), the University of California (1898), the University of Nebraska (1899), Oberlin (1900), Teachers College, Columbia University (1901), and the University of Wisconsin (1911). Yet there was considerable diversity among these degree programs. The blend of personalities involved in the development of each school and the place that new physical education departments assumed within the structural organization of the college affected the manner in which the programs developed. The program at Stanford reflected the interests of Thomas D. Wood, the first chairperson of the Department of Physical Training and Hygiene. Health and hygiene were the strength at Stanford, whereas Harvard, under the leadership of George Welk Fitz, emphasized physiology.[57]

As teacher preparation courses developed in other colleges and universities, many departments were placed within schools of education. One reason for this was that many states legislated mandatory physical education, and colleges and universities responded to the increased need to prepare physical educators. Michigan, for example, passed mandatory physical education laws in 1911 and 1919, and the University of Michigan added a four-year teacher-training course in physical education to the curricula of its School of Education in 1921.

Despite these improvements, some physical educators felt that standards within the profession remained weak. In 1914, it was noted that "professional standards should be established which would elevate the profession. In time the license to practice gymnastics will be as thoroughly regulated by state laws as the license to practice medicine."[58] Until 1919, however, there were no state licensure laws for a teaching specialty in physical education. Although certain similarities in program content existed in both private and public college curricula, standards and emphases depended on the personalities, motivations, and interests of those involved. Without state licensure, teachers could claim a specialty in physical education by taking a summer school course, a normal course that varied from one to three years, or a four-year degree program at a college or university that offered such a specialty. Until standards could be developed and agreed on, practitioners of physical education were able to certify themselves with little, if any, professional instruction.

Due to World War I and the poor physical condition of many of the nation's young men, interest in physical education increased during the 1920s. The sense of urgency regarding health and conditioning after the war created a sympathetic attitude toward physical education, and by 1921, 28 states had compulsory public school physical education.[59] By 1930, some type of certification was required for teaching in 38 states.[60] A four-year course leading to a bachelor's degree became the standard of training in the 1920s, and as this trend continued, private institutions such as the Sargent School of Physical Education began to merge with degree-granting colleges.

Despite increases in the number of schools offering physical education curricula in an effort to license practitioners, physical educators continued to express feelings of professional inadequacy over what constituted a trained physical educator. Two factors contributed to this problem. First, some felt that physical education was unable to attract competent recruits, particularly men.[61] The quality of recruits was not as high as in other disciplines, and a corresponding loss of professional prestige was the result. Second, physical educators were seen as those who merely organized play activities. Even though teacher-training curricula were based on natural sciences such as anthropometry, physiology, anatomy, kinesiology, biology, and hygiene, the actual practice of physical education teaching did not demonstrate the body of knowledge gained through the training process. Physical education teachers did not teach physiology or kinesiology; they taught games. They may well have called on their knowledge of these sciences to organize activities and evaluate student progress, but this was not a daily, demonstrable element of their work.[62] Sadly, this same argument, first offered in the early 1900s, continues today in physical education.

The tremendous need for teachers in the wake of state legislation made it possible to teach physical education courses with a minimum of training. This may have been the most devastating blow to the prestige of the profession. Also, the qualifications of physical education practitioners already in the field undermined the claims by the AAAPE and other professional organizations of a need for improvements. In the end, it was probably a combination of all these factors that led to feelings of professional inadequacy on the part of physical education practitioners.

SUMMARY

During the nineteenth century, one of the major concerns of Americans and Europeans was health. In this era, disease was a routine occurrence, and the ability of medical science to cure the sick and prevent disease was poor. The nature of health, according to the medical authorities, was manifest in a balanced constitution (the body) and temperament (the mind and spirit). The relationship between mind and body with regard to health continued to be an area of interest. Although physicians attempted to treat disease and restore health, their methods frequently did more damage to the patient than good. As a result, Americans began to search for alternative medical treatments that would not only cure whatever ailed them but also prevent disease. Science focused on the organic development of the individual, which provided a great deal of impetus in defining the role and scope of physical education.

The nineteenth century was a period of radical change. One of the most notable developments was the establishment of a middle-class, bureaucratic society based on specialization and expertise. The field of physical education experienced this change in that it reflected the more general social and institutional changes that occurred in society. As a result, specialists and organizations were developed to determine the needs and direction of the emerging profession. On November 27, 1885, 49 people came together at the invitation of William G. Anderson, M.D., to discuss their common interest in physical education. The majority of those in attendance were trained as physicians. Out of this meeting came the first serious effort to develop physical education as a legitimate profession. The large proportion of doctors who attended this meeting provided a beginning point for the body of knowledge in physical education based on health and the prevention of disease. The new professional organization was called the American Association for the Advancement of Physical Education.

Physical education was concerned with health promotion and the prevention of disease. Its methods were based primarily on exercise in the form of gymnastics and calisthenics. But the concept of health changed. The understanding of germs and their connection to disease undermined the idea that health is a balance of mind, body, and will. Medical science redeemed itself by developing sound scientific methods that earned the public's trust in its ability to control and cure illness and restore health. As a result, it became increasingly difficult to blame moral indiscretions on an individual's physical capacity or lack thereof. The concept of health now included social interaction and behavioral outcomes as significant components in the development and promotion of health for all Americans. Physical education adjusted to these changes and sought to reflect social interaction and behavioral objectives through the expansion of the curriculum to include play, games, and sports. However, not all physical educators supported this change. These people continued to promote gymnastic exercises and anthropometry as the core of physical education.

The development of the theoretical base of nineteenth-century physical education was grounded in the medical and scientific knowledge of the day. The trend in contemporary physical education is once again toward medicine. It is not unusual to have physicians on the faculty of physical education departments today, as was the custom during the nineteenth century. The professional preparation of teachers continues to stimulate debate in the twenty-first century as it did during the nineteenth century, when the Battle of the Systems was raging. The content of programs taken by physical education majors in the nineteenth century was similar to that of today. Anatomy, physiology, health, first aid, history and philosophy, educational psychology, and sports skills were essential parts of the fledgling physical education curriculum during the era when colleges were introducing the bachelor's degree in physical education. Prior to the four-year college major, normal schools were the primary source of physical education teachers; they offered a similar, but shorter, curriculum. Physical education programs for women focused on matters of health, beauty, posture, and movement. The Swedish system was better suited for women when measured against the content and methods of German gymnastics. Dio Lewis and Catherine Beecher were the leaders in promoting the benefits of exercise for women and advocating women's political and social rights. This was an era in which science was at the cutting edge of research efforts in physical education, and pioneers such as Dudley Sargent, George Fitz, Luther Gulick, Mary Allen, Delphine Hanna, and Catherine Beecher shaped the future of American physical education.

DISCUSSION QUESTIONS

1. What influence did science have on the emerging profession of physical education?

2. To what extent did the nineteenth-century definition of health influence the development of physical education?

3. What was the Battle of the Systems about?

4. What role did physical education play in enhancing the health of women?

5. What impact did anthropometry have on the theoretical development of physical education?

6. What were the main features of the teacher-training programs from 1885 to 1930?

7. What individuals and social forces had a profound influence on the direction of physical education?

8. How did the work of Charles Darwin influence physical education?

9. To what extent did physical education's use of anthropometric measurement inadvertently promote racism?

10. To what extent were physical educators concerned with quacks and charlatans who claimed knowledge and provided "cures" via exercise and health promotion?

INTERNET RESOURCES

History of Health Sciences
www.mla-hhss.org/histlink.htm
Provides links to the history of health and health sciences.

Medical Messiahs
www.quackwatch.org/13Hx/MM/00.html
Focuses on the history of health quackery in twentieth-century America.

MedHist
http://medhist.ac.uk
Offers a guide to the history of medicine resources on the Internet.

American Association for the History of Medicine
www.histmed.org
Includes online articles and links related to the history of medicine.

History and Physical Education
http://members3.boardhost.com/pehistory
Serves as a physical education message board focused on history of physical education.

American Academy of Kinesiology and Physical Education
www.aakpe.org/aakpe1.htm
Provides a historical overview, with information on leaders in the profession.

Canadian Association for Health, Physical Education, Recreation, and Dance
www.cahperd.ca/e/cahperd
Provides information on the Canadian approach to physical education.

American Alliance for Health, Physical Education, Recreation, and Dance
www.aahperd.org
Is an important resource for physical educators and coaches teaching in K–12.

American College of Sports Medicine
www.acsm.org
Provides information on careers and professional certifications in exercise science.

North American Society for Sport History
www.nassh.org/index1.html
Is a good source for information on the early history of American physical education.

Visit the *History and Philosophy of Sport and Physical Education* Online Learning Center (www.mhhe.com/mechikoff6e) for additional information and study tools.

SUGGESTIONS FOR FURTHER READING

Ainsworth, D. *History of Physical Education in Colleges for Women.* New York: A. S. Barnes, 1930.

Aller, A. S. "The Rise of State Provisions for Physical Education in the Public Secondary Schools of the United States." Doctoral dissertation, University of California, 1935.

Eastman, M. F., and C. C. Lewis. *The Biography of Dio Lewis.* New York: Fowler & Wells, 1891.

Haverson, M. E. *Catherine Esther Beecher, Pioneer Educator.* Lancaster, PA.: Science Press, 1932.

Kindervater, A. G. "Early History of Physical Education in the Public Schools of America." *Mind and Body* 33 (June 1926): 97–103.

Leonard, F. *Pioneers of Modern Physical Training.* New York: Association Press, 1919.

Lewis, D. *New Gymnastics.* Boston: Ticknor & Fields, 1862.

Rice, E., J. Hutchinson, and M. Lee. *A Brief History of Physical Education.* New York: Ronald Press, 1969.

Schwendener, N. *History of Physical Education in the United States.* New York: A. S. Barnes, 1942.

Stecher, W. A., ed. *Gymnastics, A Textbook of the German-American System of Gymnastics.* Boston: Lee & Shepard, 1895.

Wacker, H. M. "The History of the Private Single Purpose Institutions Which Prepared Teachers of Physical Education in the United States of America from 1861–1958." Doctoral dissertation, New York University, 1959.

NOTES

1. John S. Haller, Jr., *American Medicine in Transition, 1840–1910* (Urbana: University of Illinois Press, 1981). See also John Duffy, *The Healers: A History of American Medicine* (Urbana: University of Illinois Press, 1979).

2. Paula Rogers Lupcho, "The Professionalization of American Physical Education, 1885–1930" (doctoral dissertation, University of California, Berkeley, 1986).

3. Catherine Beecher, *Educational Reminiscences and Suggestion* (New York: J. B. Ford, 1874).

4. Catherine E. Beecher, *Treatise on Domestic Economy,* rev. ed. (New York: Harper & Brothers, 1870), 56. See also Ellen W. Gerber, *Innovators and Institutions in Physical Education* (Philadelphia: Lea & Febiger, 1971), 252–58; Mabel Lee, *A History of Physical Education and Sports in the USA* (New York: John Wiley, 1983), 46.

5. Lupcho, "Professionalization," 28.

6. Ibid., 29.

7. Ibid., 30. See also Mabel Lee. A History of Physical Education and Sports in the U.S.A. (New York: John Wiley & Sons, 1983) p, III.

8. William T. Harris, "Physical Training," in *Physical Training: A Full Report of the Papers and Discussions of the Conference Held in Boston in November, 1889* (Boston: Press of George H. Ellis, 1890), 1.

9. William Blaikie, *How to Get Strong and Stay So* (New York: Harper & Brothers, 1884).

10. Lupcho, "Professionalization," 32.

11. John A. Lucas and Ronald A. Smith, *Saga of American Sport* (Philadelphia: Lea & Febiger, 1978), 123–66.

12. George H. Taylor, *An Exposition on the Swedish Movement Cure* (New York: Fowler & Wells, 1860); Charles F. Taylor, *Theory and Practice of the Movement Cure* (Philadelphia: Lindsay & Blakiston, 1861).

13. William B. Carpenter, *Principles of Mental Physiology* (London: Henry S. King, 1875).

14. For a more detailed analysis of this view, see Anita Clair Fellman and Michael Fellman, *Making Sense of Self: Medical Advice Literature in Late Nineteenth Century America* (Philadelphia: University of Pennsylvania Press, 1981).

15. Carpenter, *Mental Physiology.*

16. Wilhelm Wundt, *Lectures on Human and Animal Psychology,* trans. J. E. Creighton and E. B. Titchener (New York: Macmillan, 1901).

17. Lupcho, "Professionalization," 38.

18. Edward M. Hartwell, *On the Philosophy of Exercise* (Boston: Cupples, Upham, 1887), 22.

19. Lupcho, "Professionalization," 40.

20. Ibid., 40–41.

21. Jay Seaver, "Military Training as an Exercise," in *Proceedings of the American Association for the Advancement of Physical Education, Third Annual Meeting* (Brooklyn: Rome Brothers, 1887), 18.

22. George M. Beard, *American Nervousness* (New York: G. P. Putnam, 1881).

23. Randolph Fairies, "The Therapeutic Value of Exercise," in *Proceedings of the American Association for the Advancement of Physical Education, Eighth Annual Meeting* (New Haven, CT: Press of Clarence H. Ryder, 1894), 30–37.

24. Hamilton D. Wey, "Physical Training for Youthful Criminals," in *Proceedings for the American Association for the Advancement of Physical Education, Fourth Annual Meeting* (New Haven, CT: L. S. Punderson, 1889), 17–35.

25. Lupcho, "Professionalization," 47.

26. Angelo Mosso, "Training of the Human Body," in *Proceedings of the American Association for the Advancement of Physical Education, Eighth Annual Meeting* (New Haven, CT: Press of Clarence H. Ryder, 1894), 39.

27. Harriet I. Ballentine, "Should Physical Education in Colleges Be Compulsory," in *Proceedings of the American Association for the Advancement of Physical Education, Ninth Annual Meeting* (New Haven, CT: Press of Clarence H. Ryder, 1894), 114.

28. Edward Clarke, *Sex and Education: Or a Fair Chance for the Girls* (Boston: Osgood, 1873).

29. Patricia Vertinsky, "Roberta J. Park and 'The Impossible Dream': Keeping It Together for Physical Education and the Academy," *Journal of Sport History* 20, no. 1 (Spring 2003): 90; Alison Wrynn, "Contesting the Canon: Understanding the History of the Evolving Discipline of Kinesiology," *Quest* 55 (2003): 245; Alison Wrynn, "The Contributions of Women Researchers to the Development of a Science of Physical Education in the United States" (doctoral dissertation, University of California, Berkeley, 1996).

30. Hartwell, *Philosophy of Exercise,* 17.

31. Dudley A. Sargent, "The Physical Test of Man," in *Proceedings of the American Association for the Advancement of Physical Education, Fifth Annual Meeting* (Ithaca, NY: Andrus & Church, 1890), 44; Charles Roberts, *A Manual of Anthropometry: Or, A Guide to the Physical Examination and Measurement of the Human Body* (London: J. & A. Churchill, 1878).

32. Roberta J. Park, "Science, Service, and the Professionalization of Physical Education: 1885–1905," *Research Quarterly for Exercise and Sport Centennial Issue* (April 1985): 13.

33. Sargent, "Physical Test," 50–51.

34. John F. Bovard and Frederick W. Cozens, *Tests and Measurements in Physical Education, 1861–1925: A Treatment of their Original Sources with Critical Comment* (University of Oregon Publications, Physical Education Series, 1926), 15.

35. Edward Hitchcock, "A Comparative Study of Average Measurements," in *Proceedings of the American Association for the Advancement of Physical Education, Sixth Annual Meeting* (Ithaca, NY: Andrus & Church, 1891); Delphine Hanna and Nellie A. Spore, "Effects of College Work upon the Health of Women," *American Physical Education Review* (APER) 4, no. 3 (September 1899): 279–80; Gerber, *Innovators and Institutions,* 329.

36. Hitchcock, "A Comparative Study," 40.

37. George W. Fitz, "Psychological Aspects of Exercise with and without Apparatus," in *Proceedings of the American Association for the Advancement of Physical Education, Eighth Annual Meeting* (New Haven, CT: Press of Clarence H. Ryder, 1894), 14–15.

38. Hartwell, *Philosophy of Exercise,* 3.

39. Sargent, "Physical Test," and idem, "The System of Physical Training at the Hemenway Gymnasium," in *Boston Physical Training Conference* (Boston: Press of George H. Ellis, 1890), 62–76.

40. Bovard and Cozens, *Tests and Measurements,* 6.

41. Henry Metzner, *History of the American Turners* (Rochester, NY: National Council of American Turners, 1974), 25.

42. Emil Rinsch, *The History of the Normal College of the American Gymnastic Union of Indiana University, 1866–1966* (Bloomington: Indiana University, 1966), 139.

43. W. K. Streit, "Normal College of the American Gymnastic Union," *The Physical Educator* 20 (May 1963): 51–55.

44. Gerber, *Innovators and Institutions,* 268–69.

45. Lupcho, "Professionalization," 69.

46. George Herbert Mead, *Mind, Self, and Society,* ed. Charles W. Morris (Chicago: University of Chicago Press, 1974); John Dewey, *Democracy and Education* (New York: Free Press, 1966); Donald J. Mrozek, *Sport and American Mentality, 1880–1910* (Knoxville: University of Tennessee Press, 1983).

47. Dominick Cavallo, *Muscles and Morals: Organized Playgrounds and Urban Reform* (Philadelphia: University of Pennsylvania Press, 1981).

47A. Presentation to Dr. Loeb and the Medical Review Oct. 3, 1903 by Dr. Ernst H. Spooner, M.D. Physician and Surgeon, St. Louis Missouri. Copy provided to author by Edward Franz, Associate Professor Emeritus, San Diego State University.

48. Carl Ziegler, "The Preparation of the Director of Physical Education," *APER* 21, no. 8 (November 1916): 462–71.

49. Gerber, *Innovators and Institutions,* 349.

50. Ibid., 349.

51. Lupcho, "Professionalization," 276.

52. Gerber, *Innovators and Institutions,* 298.

53. Ibid., 299.

54. John Swett, ed., *Second Biennial Report of the Superintendent of Public Instruction of the State of California, 1866–1867* (Sacramento: D. W. Gelincks, State Printer, 1867), 265.

55. Gerber, *Innovators and Institutions,* 101.

56. Jakob Bolin, "Presidential Address at the Annual Meeting of the Physical Education Society of New York and Vicinity, December 4, 1896," *APER* 2:1 (March 1897): 6–7.

57. Lupcho, "Professionalization," 278.

58. "Editorial," *APER* 19, no. 6 (June 1914): 479–80.

59. S. Lyman Hillby, "Statutory Provisions for Physical Education in the United States from 1899–1930" (master's thesis, Stanford University, 1930).

60. K. M. Cook, "State Laws and Regulations Governing Teachers Certificates," *Bulletin No. 19* (Bureau of Education, 1927): 280–85.

61. Elmer Berry, "Problems in the Recruiting of Teachers of Physical Education," *APER* 25, no. 6 (June 1920): 233–39.

62. Frank A. North, "Working Conditions of Teachers of Physical Training," *APER* 28, no. 10 (December 1923): 469.

CHAPTER 12

The Transformation of Physical Education: 1900–1939

OBJECTIVES

Upon completing this chapter, you will be able to:

- Understand the impetus and rationale behind the transformation of traditional physical education activities based on gymnastics and calisthenics to a program that emphasized sports.
- Explain why the transition from physical activity to sports was not embraced by everybody within the profession of physical education.
- Understand how competitive athletics, physical education, and social reform provided the catalyst for this transformation.
- Explain why the "marriage of convenience" between physical education departments and athletic departments occurred, and what the result of this marriage was.
- Understand the status of physical education in higher education during this era.
- Understand the American public's support of athletic competition and the corresponding degree of support accorded to physical education.
- Discuss the rationale and purpose behind the development of play theory and its impact on physical education.
- Identify the contributions made by the following to the promotion of play theory: (1) Herbert Spencer, (2) Karl Groos, (3) G. Stanley Hall, (4) Luther Halsey Gulick, and (5) John Dewey.
- Discuss the reasons why play theory did not enjoy universal support among physical education professionals.
- Discuss the reasons for the decline of gymnastics as a core component of the physical education curriculum.
- Explain the magnitude and impact of the New Physical Education program, developed by Rosalind Cassidy, Clark Hetherington and Thomas D. Wood, as the new paradigm of physical education.
- Identify the components and goals of the New Physical Education.
- Understand how physical education was promoted.
- Discuss how physical education utilized tests and measurements to support the need for physical education.
- Discuss why women were discouraged from serious athletic competition.

General Events

1900 Boxer Rebellion in China, U.S. sends troops
1901 President William McKinley assassinated by Leon Czolgosz
1903 Panama Canal agreement signed; first airplane flight by Orville Wright
1906 Great San Francisco earthquake and fire
1907 Nationwide financial depression
1909 Admiral Robert E. Peary reaches North Pole; National Conference on Negro held, leads to establishment of National Association for the Advancement of Colored People (NAACP)
1910 Boy Scouts of America founded
1911 First transcontinental plane flight
1912 U.S. sends marines to Nicaragua
1913 U.S. blockades Mexico
1914 President Wilson declares neutrality re: war in Europe
1915 First telephone conversation coast to coast; *Lusitania* sunk by Germans, 128 American passengers perish
1916 Jeanette Rankin, first woman member of Congress, from Montana; John Dewey

publishes *Democracy and Education*

1917 U.S. enters World War I

1920 19th Amendment ratified, giving women right to vote

1924 Law approved by Congress making all American Indians citizens of U.S.

1925 Scopes trial in Tennessee regarding teaching evolution in schools

1927 Charles A. Lindbergh flies nonstop from New York to Paris

1928 Amelia Earhart first woman aviator to cross Atlantic

1929 St. Valentine's Day massacre in Chicago; stock market crashes, Depression begins

1931 Empire State Building opens

1933 Prohibition ends; U.S. abandons gold standard

1935 Will Rogers dies in plane crash; Senator Huey Long (LA) assassinated

Sport and Physical Education

1885 American Association for the Advancement of Physical Education founded

1887 First National Women's Singles Tennis Championship

1888 Amateur Athletic Union founded

1889 Boston Conference in the Interest of Physical Training

1891 Basketball invented by James A. Naismith

1899 Committee on Women's Basketball; American Association for the Advancement of Physical Education (AAAPE) formed

1900 Davis Cup tennis competition begins; American League of Professional Baseball Clubs formed

1903 First baseball "World Series" played

1905 Intercollegiate Athletic Association of the United States founded, would later evolve into NCAA

1906 Playground Association of America founded

INTRODUCTION

Significant changes in physical education took place in the early twentieth century. Among the more important reforms were the move toward social development objectives, the adoption of sports by physical education, the new physical education, and the development of play theory.

For almost a century, physical education was focused on making the greatest possible contribution to the health of students. Early pioneers in physical education were doctors and educators who provided students with information and lifestyle orientations that were supposed to contribute to their personal health and well-being. The medium they used to deliver the message revolved around coursework in hygiene, physiology, and instruction in fitness activities. For the most part, the fitness activities used prior to 1900 were gymnastics and calisthenics. But things were about to change.

THE TRANSFORMATION OF PHYSICAL EDUCATION AND THE ADOPTION OF SPORTS PROGRAMS

American education was undergoing reform. In the new educational philosophy, the education of students included social development objectives. To articulate these new ideas, physical education adopted new activities and introduced additional objectives. According to Guy Lewis, the transformation of physical education began with the "athletics are educational" movement, from 1906 to 1916, and was consummated during the age of "sports for all," which began in 1917 and ended in 1939. The result of this transformation was that the traditional health and fitness objectives of physical education were subjugated to the social development objectives. Physical fitness exercises were relegated to a position that was secondary to providing instruction in sports.[1] The important question is whether this change in the focus and scope of physical education was the result of a philosophical reorientation by members of the profession or was due to external forces over which physical educators had little or no control.[2] Lewis observes:

> In response to outside forces and developments within education between 1906 and 1916, physical educators began seriously to consider the place of sports instruction in the basic curriculum and gave some thought to extending the program to include supervised competition for highly skilled students.[3]

In the early twentieth century, the American public was very interested in athletic competition. The sports pages of the daily newspapers were just as popular then as they are now. Physical educators capitalized on this high interest in sports by reforming their philosophy to accommodate sports in the curriculum. According to Bruce Bennett and Mabel Lee, the addition of sports was the result of a determined effort by the American Physical Education Association to put athletics into education and education into athletics.[4] Apparently, what these physical educators failed to realize was that serious athletic competition and intramural sports soon would challenge traditional physical education activities like gymnastics and calisthenics. By 1930, almost all of the instructional activities in physical education were devoted to sports and intramural programs. Lewis notes that several developments led to the adoption of sports programs in physical education. These developments occurred in three areas: (1) competitive athletics, (2) physical education, and (3) social reform.[5]

Prior to 1906, physical education programs in the nation's colleges and universities were administered by the faculty, but this was not the case with athletic competition. Athletic competition was governed by athletic associations controlled by students and alumni. This created many problems. There was no national governing body that effectively oversaw intercollegiate athletic competition. Students of questionable character appear to have enrolled in colleges and universities simply to play football, baseball, basketball, and other sports. Faculty became outraged at the practices of some of these athletic associations that would field teams in the name of the school. Unfortunately, it was not unusual for physical education departments in some universities to become "partners in crime" with the athletic departments to protect gifted athletes who depended on coursework in physical education to retain their eligibility. It did not help the profession of physical education when coaches of dubious character were hired to teach physical education and coach the university sports teams. Many athletes depended on their coaches to find ways to keep them eligible. Eventually, the faculty achieved a modicum of control over athletic competition at both the high-school and college levels.

At the secondary level, this control was enhanced by the merging of athletics and physical education into a single entity. Both public and private secondary schools hired more athletic directors and coaches (not necessarily physical educators) to teach physical education and provide instruction in sports. During this time, interest in physical education grew. There was a significant increase in the number of physical education programs, along with changes in how physical educators were academically prepared. This was seen in the philosophical shift away from the medical orientation that was emblematic of the early professional preparation in physical education. Physical educators no longer received their professional preparation in schools of medicine. Instead, they were trained as educators and soon began to replace doctors in positions of leadership within the field.

Women dominated the ranks of physical educators, and while there were male physical educators, most men preferred to become coaches. From 1900 to about 1920, most physical education programs did not offer coursework in coaching. However, there was a need to train coaches, and many coaching schools were created to do this. In 1919, George Huff developed the first degree program in coaching at the University of Illinois. Other established universities soon developed similar programs to train coaches. While these expanded curricular offerings that focused on coaching were needed, it was not necessary to have a college degree to coach in the high schools or colleges. Things have not

1910 Jack Johnson–James J. Jeffries boxing match
1916 American Tennis Association founded by black tennis players
1919 Chicago Black Sox baseball scandal
1919–20 Man O' War wins 20 of 21 horse races
1922 Paris track meet sponsored by Federation Sportive Feminine Internationale (FSFI)
1923 White House Conference on Women's Athletics
1929 Carnegie Foundation's investigation of men's college athletics
1930 Bobby Jones wins Grand Slam in golf
1931 Mabel Lee first woman president of American Physical Education Association (APEA)
1932 Babe Didrikson stars in 1932 Olympics
1934 Madison Square Garden hosts Men's Collegiate Basketball Tournament

Sport and Physical Education time line from Betty Spears and Richard A. Swanson, *History of Sport and Physical Education in the United States* (Dubuque, IA: Wm. C. Brown, 1988), 150, 206.

changed much. In 2013 there are states that do not require coaches to have a college degree to coach at the high school or college level; California is one example. Unfortunately, as we will see, the practice of hiring coaches not properly trained would serve to undermine the profession of physical education.

Recreation was a new area of study, and this emerging profession promoted the adoption of directed play as an answer to the problems created by the impact of economic forces upon society and attendant social structures. It appeared that the emerging profession of physical education was undergoing constructive reform and would soon become a respected member of the professional educational establishment. But this did not happen. Lewis believes that the most important factor in the transformation of physical education was the existence of highly organized, well-established, and popular varsity athletic competition.[6] Although physical education and athletics share a common history and a common interest, there are distinctive differences. These differences were what concerned physical educators in the early part of the twentieth century. Would their professional identity be compromised by including serious athletic competition and coaches within the domain of physical education? To what extent would the profession of physical education be embarassed by scandals related to coaches and athletes? Was the transformation of physical education in the best interests of the profession?

From 1906 to 1916, the theme "athletics are educational" was a dominant factor in physical education. To build upon this concept, college presidents and administrators in the nation's public and private schools assumed responsibility for intercollegiate and interscholastic athletic programs. From 1917 to 1939, the theme changed from "athletics are educational" to "sports for all," which Lewis calls the final stage in the transformation of physical education.[7]

Athletic competition was heavily promoted. The National Committee on Physical Education and the National Amateur Athletic Federation (NAAF) were charged with increasing sports participation throughout the land.[8] In 1918, the National Collegiate Athletic Association (NCAA) authorized a resolution that called for colleges and universities to make adequate provisions in their schedule of classes for students to participate in physical training and sports. The NCAA worked closely with the National Committee on Physical Education to promote athletic participation in the nation's schools and colleges.[9]

By this time, most states had passed legislation mandating that physical education be taught in the schools. The nation's public schools were in need of qualified physical educators to fill teaching positions, but there was a shortage of teachers. In response to the demand for qualified physical educators, colleges and universities soon established physical education departments where students could earn a degree in the field and become employed in the schools. However, another significant problem arose: There was a dearth of physical educators qualified for academic rank. In their zeal to meet the demand for physical educators, unqualified individuals were given administrative appointments by colleges and universities as directors of physical education programs. In 1929, a survey revealed that out of 177 physical education directors surveyed, only 23 had majored in physical education, and only 4 had earned master's degrees in the field of education. Success as a football coach was the lone requirement for many of these "directors."[10] One observer remarked that "of all the fields of higher education, physical education shows the largest number of members with the rank of professor who have only a bachelor's degree or no degree whatever."[11]

This did not bode well for a profession that had worked so hard to establish a credible theory base and to create high professional standards. However, there was no doubt that sports were becoming the dominant focus in the curricula of most physical education departments. This is understandable. The American public was excited about athletic competition, more so than they were about physical education. In addition, many coaches without a degree in physical education (or any other subject, for that matter) were offered jobs in physical education departments because of their background as an athlete or coach. These individuals could provide instruction in sports skills and little else. By the 1930s, coaching courses had become the primary focus of many physical education departments that offered an undergraduate degree. The Carnegie Foundation released the results of a study in 1929 that said physical education had been used to turn colleges and universities into giant athletic agencies.[12] Lewis provides additional insight into the Carnegie study:

> Opinion favoring sports so pervaded society that few saw the need to question the value system which supported it, but there was evidence that physical education had been reconstructed not for the purpose of fulfilling the ideal of education for all through sports and athletics but to serve the interests of intercollegiate athletics.[13]

Many physical educators were very concerned with the erosion of the profession caused by the hiring of unqualified coaches to provide instruction in physical education. This situation has not changed.

As athletic competition and related interests assumed a dominant role in most physical education programs at both the interscholastic and intercollegiate levels from 1906 to 1939, it became necessary for the profession to modify its philosophy and accommodate these interests. Jesse F. Williams managed to convince those physical educators opposed to accommodating sports that it was the responsibility of the profession to make participation in competitive athletics an educational experience for students. Williams was so successful in this effort that the author of the 1929 Carnegie study that identified physical education as the servant of athletics remarked that education as mind and body "gave currency to a definition of physical education that includes all bodily activity—even sport itself."[14] The legacy of Williams—the accommodation of sport by physical education—is alive and well in the twenty-first century.

Today, physical education programs at the K–12 level incorporate "all bodily activity": sports, lifetime health and fitness activities, developmentally directed play, and appropriate games. Physical

education teachers in the public schools are highly trained professionals who usually wear two hats: (1) physical education teacher and (2) coach. Small colleges and universities continue to employ faculty who both teach physical education and coach intercollegiate athletic teams. Within institutions of higher learning, there continues to be a chasm between coaches and physical educators. In the larger colleges and universities, faculty in physical education, kinesiology, and exercise science departments rarely coach. They devote their professional efforts to teaching, research, and community service. Big-time athletic programs in the nation's colleges and universities hire coaches, and the expectation is that these coaches will devote their time and energy to developing strong athletic teams. These coaches rarely teach courses in other departments. While many of these coaches have degrees in physical education, it is not unusual to find coaches with degrees in other fields such as English or history or no degree at all.

Physical education, like all professions, undergoes periodic reform. The reform that physical education underwent in the early part of the twentieth century did result in a number of significant outcomes. We have already seen how physical education was transformed by sport. We now turn our attention to the development of play theory, one of the more profound changes that shaped the development of physical education in the twentieth century.

THE DEVELOPMENT OF PLAY THEORY: 1900–1915

Between 1900 and 1930, physical educators debated appropriate methods and goals for research and teaching. This debate was a result of changing beliefs and trends in science, broad social changes in American life, and developments in education. Perhaps the most powerful change was the acceptance of play, games, dance, and sport as methods for imparting educational goals, a trend that reflected a growing interest in the phenomenon of play that was evident even before the turn of the century.

Herbert Spencer and William James

One of the earliest champions of play was English philosopher Herbert Spencer (1820–1903). As early as 1855, Spencer conceived of play as an instinctual, natural, and enjoyable activity essential for physical welfare and development.[15] An advocate of Darwin's theory of evolution, Spencer believed that play could be used to expend excess energy. This aspect interested Spencer because he believed that excess energy was that which was not necessary for survival.[16] In *Principles of Psychology* (1890), American psychologist and philosopher William James (1842–1910) agreed that play behavior was instinctual, but he did not believe, as Spencer did, that instinctual behavior was simply a reflex in more complex animals. Instead, James argued that habits and impulses combined with the capacity to reason and therefore helped determine human behavior.[17]

Karl Groos

One of the more influential play theorists was Karl Groos (1861–1946). In 1898, Groos hypothesized that humans played as preparation for life by imitating others. He believed that play behavior was instinctual, but it was an imperfect instinct and needed to be augmented by life experiences. His logic was that if, for some reason, certain kinds of instincts were needed for more serious acts of survival, then humans would have these specific instincts at birth. Play would provide the necessary experiences and prepare individuals for the coming tasks of life.[18] Groos's theory of play as an educational vehicle that could lead to improved adult behavior was important to physical educators because play was considered the exclusive domain of physical education. Play eventually became a critical component of educational theory, and consequently Groos's theory was used to promote physical education as essential to individual development.

G. Stanley Hall

Another important contributor to play theory was psychologist and educator G. Stanley Hall (1844–1924), who taught at Clark University in Worcester, Massachusetts, and was a leader in the child study movement. Hall popularized the saying "Ontogeny recapitulates phylogeny," by which he meant that childhood serves as a rehearsal for the evolutionary process.[19] In Hall's theory, each individual must replay the prehistory of the species. Each stage of human hereditary development is recorded in the phyla of nerve cells of the individual. From birth, an individual mimics the development of the species by assuming a type of behavior required in the development of the species.[20] Play was felt to be a fundamental form of the history of the human species, unlike gymnastics, which was not fundamental but only recently invented by humans. According to the theory, each stage of development promoted the acquisition of the necessary motor skills and psychosocial growth to move on to the next stage of development.

In Hall's view, play and its natural extensions—games and sport—were the ideal mechanisms for development.

> This is why, unlike gymnastics, play has as much soul as body, and also why it so makes for unity of body and soul that the proverb 'man is whole only when he plays' suggests that the purest plays are those that enlist both alike. . . . Thus understood, play is the ideal type of exercise for the young, most favorable for the growth, and most self-regulating in both kind and amount.[21]

This quote expresses Hall's belief that play had as much "soul as body" and helped provide for the unity of the soul and body. His belief in the proverb "Man is whole only when he plays" implies that the purest play was that which used both soul and body equally. This saying reflected the nineteenth-century belief in the unity of the mind and body, yet it helped bring physical education into the twentieth century because it reflected theories of evolution and science. Hall believed that 811 human characteristics could be learned in the developmental play activities of children. He further believed that muscles were the organs of expression and the vehicles of imitation, obedience, character, and even manners and customs.[22] Hall envisioned physical education as the educational process that could connect matters of the body and the mind.

Hall's educational philosophy provided enthusiastic support for play as an essential component of education, and thus offered a theoretical basis to physical educators who desired to incorporate play, games, and sport in physical education classes.

Luther Halsey Gulick

As discussed previously, Luther Halsey Gulick (1865–1918) was one of the most important physical educators of the nineteenth and twentieth centuries. An early adherent of play as a major component of physical education, Gulick made significant contributions to the growing literature on play theory. In *A Philosophy of Play,* published posthumously in 1920, Gulick emphasized the benefits of play for the development of both the private (sense of self) and public (social self) aspects of the individual.[23] Play developed the social consciousness on which democratic civilization was dependent.

John Dewey

Preeminent among educators and philosophers, and important to play theory and physical education, was John Dewey (1859–1952). Dewey saw education as a necessity for democratic citizenship, social efficiency, and social experience. Dewey considered mind and body to be integrated parts of the human whole, and he believed that the physical aspect (body) of humans served as the conductor of experience. Once again, the philosophical position of the body relative to epistemological considerations and the nature of human existence becomes an important issue. Dewey's philosophy was in contrast to the tradition of classical realists and dualists, who believed that the world of the mind was more important than the world of experience. Dewey believed that the socialized mind shared with others a sense of similar experiences and that the agreement among people based on their common experiences produced a better, more efficient society.[24] Dewey also believed that humans should learn how to think and act based on their experiences rather than on some predetermined set of rules. A collection of experiences that were shared could be used to create "consensual" knowledge, and the human condition

would therefore be improved. Dewey's pragmatic philosophy, based on the work of Charles Peirce, William James, and other pragmatist philosophers, was a radical departure from traditional philosophies, and it had a profound impact on the theory of play.

Dewey believed play to be a purposeful activity that directed interest through physical means. Play was not a physical act that had no meaning; rather, it was an activity that integrated mind and body. This approach gave the play act meaning, and therefore it became an argument for play as an important educational tool. Play became a "quality" experience valuable for its educational possibilities rather than an activity in and of itself. The ultimate product of Dewey's educational process would be individuals who participated fully as members of a democratic society.

These kinds of discussions might seem irrelevant to an understanding of physical education, yet they were important in the early twentieth century because they justified entirely new activities in physical education. Before Dewey, playful group activities such as football and baseball were considered poor choices to develop health and community. The philosophy of Dewey and his colleagues was used to justify team sports in physical education because they promoted democratic activities and social interaction. The societal benefits derived from participation in physical education were significant and did much to ensure strong support for physical education and athletic programs.

ADVOCATES AND ADVERSARIES: THE PROMOTION OF PLAY

Play as a natural developmental tool was increasingly recognized by physical educators, yet it was accepted with varying amounts of enthusiasm. Physical educators, like many Americans, viewed the usefulness of play with some ambivalence. As early as 1887, Jay Seaver spoke against the use of military drill in physical education programs, arguing that the lack of play in such exercises was not beneficial to students.[25] The rationale for his program was that the young of every species are fond of play and that play fosters the muscular development necessary for self-preservation.[26]

Yet most physical educators believed that play, games, and sport should play a secondary role in physical education rather than a primary role. In 1889, Edward M. Hartwell, a superb scholar and eminent historian of physical education, presented the consensus viewpoint of the profession. Hartwell recognized the usefulness of play but upheld the educational superiority of gymnastics. As a proponent of gymnastic activities, Hartwell believed that the essential difference between sporting activities and gymnastics was the nature of the products of the activities. The goal of sporting activities was one of recreation, whereas the goal of gymnastics was discipline, training for pleasure, health, and skill. Hartwell believed that gymnastics was more comprehensive in its aims and more formal, elaborate, and systematic in its methods; in addition, gymnastics produced more significant, or measurable, results. Sporting activities during this era were marked by their "childish" origins and so were considered inadequate for physical education.[27]

PLAY AND POPULAR CULTURE

The general public began to take an interest in play between 1890 and 1900, and this phenomenon was noted by physical educators. In 1886, sand gardens (piles of sand or sandboxes) were built in Boston to provide a place for wholesome play for children who lived in crowded urban neighborhoods. In 1889, the Charlesbank Outdoor Gymnasium opened in Boston as part of a large park system initiated 10 years earlier. Similarly, New York City opened several school playgrounds for recreational use in 1889, and Chicago opened the South Park Playgrounds in 1903. Luther Gulick organized the Public School Athletic League in New York City in 1903, and in 1906, the Playground Association of America was founded. Play captured the interest of the public, municipal government, foundations, and reform groups, and as a consequence, the interest in play education grew.[28]

PLAY VERSUS GYMNASTICS

The growing popularity of play with the public at large and among the ranks of physical education professionals between 1900 and 1915 increasingly put advocates of gymnastics exercise on the defensive. Gymnastics advocates found it necessary to acknowledge the perceived benefits of play, games, and sport while at the same time trying to make a case for gymnastic programs. William Skarstrom, M.D., of Teachers College, Columbia University, wrote a series of articles arguing for the use of gymnastics to correct improper posture and development.[29] Skarstrom believed that the function of physical education was to promote community, social success, efficiency, management of self, physical efficiency, and business success.[30] Accomplishment of these goals required a variety of physical activities, among them gymnastics exercise. Skarstrom also acknowledged the usefulness of sporting activities in developing quick perception and judgment.

Despite the efforts of men like Skarstrom, gymnastics continued to diminish in popularity as the primary component in physical education programs. By 1915, those who favored gymnastics programs sought equal time with sporting activities in physical education programs. By this time, play was the primary method of physical education, and gymnastics was used primarily to correct posture problems. In 1912, in an editorial, the *American Physical Education Review* stated that "athletics, properly conducted, are one of the strongest social and moral forces we can use in the development of manhood."[31] In the same year, Paul Phillips wrote:

> [The] importance of play in the physical development and education of the individual has become better recognized and appreciated year by year. . . . It has been shown that normal play is not only important but also absolutely necessary to the normal development of boys or girls both physically and mentally, and morally as well. Play and the play spirit constitute perhaps the most important single element in growth and education: in fact, looked at broadly, play is the most serious thing in life.[32]

Although enthusiasts like Skarstrom kept the gymnastics issue in print, by 1915, the number of educators who believed in the virtues of play was overwhelming. New members to the field of physical education such as Clark Hetherington and playground leaders such as Joseph Lee and Henry Curtis took up the cause of play and influenced their colleagues through their writing, lectures, and association work.[33] These men pressed for the general acceptance of play with the same fervor and intensity with which early nineteenth-century physical educators promoted gymnastics. Play became the dominant method of physical education, replacing gymnastics by 1915. The spirit of sportsmanship, which originated in England and was characterized by fair play, proper conduct, noble virtues, and decorum, also occupied a position of importance when the objectives of American physical education were discussed.

PLAY IN PHYSICAL EDUCATION: 1900–1915

According to leading physical educators in the early 1900s, play had several distinct advantages over gymnastics. Henry Curtis stated that a team game was one in which individual players substituted team goals for individual goals and blended their individual identities into a new unity. Individuals played as a team because the game required group consciousness, loyalty, and leadership. Curtis felt that team games were the highest form of play and one of the highest forms of human activity.[34] We can see the influence of John Dewey on the thinking of Curtis regarding the advantages of play over gymnastics. The inability of the proponents of gymnastics to put up a unified front to defend their interests contributed to the demise of gymnastics. In addition, the visibility and popularity of intercollegiate and professional sports helped propel play, games, and sport to the forefront of physical education, much to the detriment of gymnastics.

Luther Gulick, another strong supporter of play activity, used the biological rationale of recapitulation in his explanation of the play instinct. Gulick believed that sport activities played a critical role in the development of boys, because sports were an inherited activity from a bygone era. Humans survived through the skills of running, throwing, and striking, and sport activities arose because of a need to practice these skills.

Gulick concluded that the humans of his day were the descendants of those whose lives depended on their ability to run, strike, and throw.[35]

In addition to physical skills, however, humans valued the mental and moral qualities of endurance, pluck, teamwork, and fair play. These qualities were developed in connection with play, and because these qualities were the same as those that defined manhood, athletics became both a measure of manhood and a rite of passage for many.

One of the most important and far-reaching effects of the early twentieth-century debate regarding play in physical education was its association with arguments of manliness. Most believed that if athletics, especially team games, were a measure of manliness, then there was little rationale for the use of athletics for the development of women. Gulick used the manliness argument to show that athletics were gender-defined activities and were therefore inappropriate as a means of developing femininity. However, Gulick did approve of basketball for girls.[36] Drawing from the idea that form follows function, Gulick stated that prepubescent girls could be very athletic because they had not yet begun the maturing process into womanhood.[37] Sport activities supervised by school officials provided women with the exercise and recreation necessary in the urban environment. Of great concern to parents and school officials, however, was that women who participated in sport activities might assume masculine qualities. This same faulty logic still exists today, although it is not as pervasive.

In sum, advocates of play were in general agreement about the desired outcomes of play, games, and sport. Play developed health and vigor; it promoted character and the associated habits of loyalty, sportsmanship, friendliness, honesty, and leadership; it fostered ideals such as democracy through group cooperation; it developed moral and ethical values; and it promoted worthy group membership. Finally, because play was instinctive and natural, it was educational. These were the primary concepts in the minds of physical educators and formed the theoretical base of twentieth-century physical education. The evolutionary scope and content of physical education would be shaped by the efforts of a new generation of physical educators, resulting in a paradigmatic basis that incorporated new ideas from education, psychology, and sociology. The results of their effort and commitment became manifest in the form and content of twentieth-century concepts of physical education.

THE PARADIGMATIC BASIS OF THE NEW PHYSICAL EDUCATION: 1916–1930

The Architects of the New Physical Education: Clark Hetherington, Thomas D. Wood, and Rosalind Cassidy

The period from World War I to 1930 was characterized by the acceptance of the social development objectives in the form of psychosocial and behavioral principles as a major part of the theoretical foundation of physical education. These changes in theory were similar to those that occurred in other disciplines such as education, psychology, and sociology, and also to changes in society. The three architects of the "new physical education" were Clark Hetherington, Thomas D. Wood, and Rosalind Cassidy. Hetherington, who studied with G. Stanley Hall, successfully integrated into written form the new theoretical position of physical education. His seminal work, *School Program in Physical Education,* provided the direction for the discipline early in the twentieth century.[38] Although there have been semantic changes over the years, the conceptual structure remains nearly unchanged.

Components and Goals of Physical Education

Hetherington divided physical education into four separate but related areas: organic, psychomotor, character, and intellect. These four areas were blended together in varying degrees to produce five stated objectives of physical education. The first objective was the "organization of child life as expressed in big-muscle or physical training activities."[39] This organization required adult leadership. Only through adult leadership could a child's natural play instinct be guided to its full and complete end, and the necessity of adult supervision meant that play was a legitimate function of education. The adult role was to make the play act efficient and to aid in the democratic organization of play.[40] Reflecting the thinking of Dewey, Hetherington considered physical education an excellent vehicle for imparting democratic skills because of the ability of the teacher to observe students in action and to provide appropriate guidance.

The second objective of physical education was the development of social adjustment skills based on the customs of society. Hetherington viewed play activities as economic, defensive, domestic, communicative, civic, interpretive, artistic, and recreative.[41] Although big-muscle activities did not directly teach adult adjustment skills, play activities provided the proper developmental foundation for acquiring such skills in later life. This objective reflected the thinking of Luther Gulick and his recapitulation theory: Proper use of play created the foundation for the development of skills necessary in adult life.

The third objective was the development of latent powers and capacities, using the theories of psychologist Edward L. Thorndike. Thorndike's stimulus-response theory stated that learning was the result of repeated positive responses to specific stimuli. Each student would either try to gain satisfaction from the stimulus or try to remove the annoying stimulus altogether.[42] Physical education could be used to create certain kinds of stimuli in play so that children could practice those skills that would aid them as adults.

The fourth objective was the development of character, and this objective remains one of the justifications for the inclusion of physical education in school curricula. *Character* was the appropriate and desirable combination of desires, impulses, habits, ideas, and ideals. Sport activities were particularly important to this objective, yet Hetherington objected to the idea that sport activities automatically instilled in students a series of virtues. Leadership provided the crucial element in meeting the objective of building desirable character traits, and so, without proper leadership, the desirable character traits could not be developed. This is where properly conducted physical education became necessary. The idea that sport builds character remains popular in the twenty-first century.

Hetherington's fifth and final objective was the use of big-muscle and fine motor movements to improve thinking. Big-muscle activity was superior because it developed what he called "strategic judgments," defined as alertness, quick response, and rapidity of movement. Hetherington believed that team games were filled with opportunities to learn these skills, and the proof of learning was in the "safety first motor efficiency" of athletes, who, as Hetherington noted, "are not run down by automobiles and street cars."[43] To Hetherington, the abilities acquired by athletes clearly had utility in the urban life of the early twentieth century. He contended that the strategic judgment that physical education could develop was essential for industrial productivity and adult recreation. If physical education could impart big-muscle skills into children and these skills had social benefits, then physical education should be an important component of the educational curriculum.

PROMOTION OF PHYSICAL EDUCATION

Hetherington championed the educational and socially oriented objectives of physical education over the health objectives that were used to justify physical education in the nineteenth century by arguing (1) that physical education required special faculties and leadership, (2) that physical education was the only vehicle to condition self-directed health habits, and (3) that exercise was necessary for adult health maintenance. Children needed four to five hours of physical activity daily, adolescents needed two to three hours daily, and adults needed only twenty minutes. The differences between these groups were due to the differences between the requirements of big-muscle activity. Children and adolescents needed big-muscle activity for physical development, whereas adults needed it for health maintenance.[44] Development was an outcome of physical activity and was differentiated

from the idea of *growth,* which was the outcome of heredity. This line of thought identified development as the fundamental process of education, first built on the quality of play and work experience.[45]

The evolutionary, biological, and psychological influences on physical education thinking were extensive. They imparted a credibility and worthiness to physical education that demanded the attention of educated people. Play was very serious business. Gymnastics had only limited health benefits and, to Hetherington, was useful only as a rainy-day activity. Hetherington used such words as *irksome, artificial, fatiguing,* and *uninteresting* to describe gymnastic exercise. Play, on the other hand, could be systematically developed to achieve the objectives Hetherington outlined.[46] According to Hetherington,

> The natural physical-training (big-muscle) activities are educationally more valuable than gymnastic drills. They give a certain development of intellectual, emotional, nervous, and organic powers not given in the same degree by any other kind of activity in child life, and it is impossible to gain the broad and more significant phases of these values through drills. A comparison of values makes apparent the greater importance of these natural activities.[47]

Hetherington's program provided the basis for the argument that physical education is an essential component of education. Eventually, almost all physical educators came to enthusiastically embrace play, games, dance, and sport as the primary modes of physical education. Hetherington's rationale justifies the use of sport activities in the educational realm. Athletic teams exist in the United States at a level not seen anywhere else in the world. And the justification for this system is best articulated by Hetherington.

PHYSICAL EDUCATION LITERATURE IN THE EARLY TWENTIETH CENTURY

The publication of Hetherington's work marked the beginning of a time when views about the nature and methodology of physical education crystallized. During the 1920s, many textbooks and manuals were written for physical education teachers and teacher-training programs. These publications reflected the directional scope that committed physical education to the physical, social, emotional, and intellectual development of individuals. In 1927, Thomas Wood and Rosalind Cassidy published an influential text representative of this trend. Titled *The New Physical Education: A Program of Naturalized Activities of Education Toward Citizenship,* this book became one of the leading texts in physical education training programs.[48] *The New Physical Education* was an extension of Hetherington's aims and objectives of education, accepting intact that the concerns of physical education were organic, psychomotor, intellectual, and character building.

SCIENCE AND THE QUANTIFICATION OF PHYSICAL EDUCATION

Tests and Measurements

From 1916 to 1930, physical education reflected the work done in psychology and also the establishment of the science of teaching, or pedagogy. These trends were part of the progressive movement in American education, and they had a monumental effect. One example was the intelligence scale devised by Alfred Binet and Theodore Simon. The concept behind this particular scale led to the general conception of scale indexing for characteristics other than intelligence. It was a small step to develop indexed standards of performance in physical education.

The measurement of ability became the focus of much research in education, a movement that is rekindled every few decades.[49] Between 1908 and 1916, Thorndike and his fellow researchers at Columbia University developed ability tests for arithmetic, spelling, reading, drawing, language ability, and handwriting. By 1918, hundreds of ability tests had been devised. This enthusiasm for measurement and quantification, which had been largely a professional matter within psychology and education, gained in popularity.[50]

The quantification offered by intelligence and ability testing became a means toward a science of education. The goal was efficient education that would teach those essential skills that would enable students to perform in and contribute to society. This type of thinking stimulated a sweeping reexamination of curricula in physical education, which sought to define minimum competencies known as essentials. Measurement of essential skills (and defining what those skills were) became a major part of the science of education.

Physical educators engaged in defining motor ability and physical efficiency. Cardiac function was only one criteria. Tests that evaluated strength were pioneered by Dudley Allen Sargent. Motor ability and physical efficiency testing began around 1914 with efficiency testing in Michigan, New Jersey, and New York. The California Decathlon Test was implemented in 1918 under the supervision of Clark Hetherington, the first state superintendent of physical education. Other work on physical ability testing came out of university departments of physical education such as the University of California, Berkeley (1917), the University of Oregon (1924), the University of Illinois (1919), Ohio State University (1920), and Oberlin College (1922). Most of these tests addressed skills such as running, jumping, throwing, and climbing. Some included proficiency in gymnastic skills such as marching, juggling Indian clubs, vaulting, and rope climbing. And some measured swimming proficiency. The science of physical education, reflected by anthropometric work in the nineteenth century, now manifested itself in tests of physical efficiency.

The Relationship Between Physical Ability and Mental Ability

Another major concern of physical education during the 1920s was the idea that physical ability is correlated to mental ability. Many physical educators of the late nineteenth century believed that physical activity promoted cognitive development. Yet this long-held belief was not widely accepted outside the physical education field, so in 1923, M. H. Landis and his colleagues tested the idea "that physical prowess, especially as manifested in athletic achievement, implies inferior intellect."[51] Put differently, they tested the idea that athletes are "dumb jocks." Their correlation study used four physical tests to measure physical ability: (1) the 100-yard dash, (2) the running broad jump, (3) the baseball throw, and (4) the fence climb. The Ohio State University intelligence test was used to determine mental capacity. Not surprisingly, no significant correlation was found between mental ability and physical ability, and other researchers validated their findings.[52]

Interest in these subjects remained high throughout the decade, yet several problems were noted in the studies that tried to correlate physical efficiency with mental capacity. Problems ranged from the lack of clearly defined criteria as to what constituted physical efficiency to the different populations used in the studies.[53] Perhaps the most serious problem with this type of research, however, was the desire on the part of physical educators to obtain the answers they wanted regardless of their measurements. This type of error in research is known as an *artifact*, which means the researcher commits a fundamental error in his or her research that invalidates the study.

Physical educators have long desired to demonstrate that a positive relationship exists between physical and mental ability. The persistence of this belief despite evidence to the contrary reflects the bias of physical educators. A conclusion by Vern S. Ruble in 1928 shows his desire to achieve specific results and serves as an example of a research artifact:

> In no instance do we have a sufficient number of cases to establish norms, and, as has been suggested, it is impossible to draw any definite conclusions from a single test, but the foregoing data are very significant and indicate strongly that there is an important relationship between athletic ability and mental strength as measured by standardized psychological or intelligence tests.[54]

Frederick Cozens's work also contained this bias. He was certain that the physically well-developed child was brighter than the poorly developed child, and he believed that the level of physical ability of bright children was distinctly superior to that of dull

and retarded children. He then asked why a correlation between intelligence and physical ability could not be found. Cozens concluded that the fault lay not with the premise but with the tests—specifically, the physical efficiency tests.[55] In short, Cozens looked for a test that would prove his theory, rather than induce theories that were supported by the data. Both Cozens's and Ruble's work are examples of poor science in that their research findings did not change their opinions. However, the quality of their research was much improved in one respect over that of the scientists who preceded them.

Despite the desires of physical educators to prove that physical education improved intellectual performance, the quality of their research prevented them from doing so. So, even though Cozens and Ruble tried to prove their pet theories, they honestly reported that they could not positively correlate intelligence and physicality. This admission represented a significant change from the pseudoscience of the late nineteenth century, which allowed physical educators to connect physical education to any theory deemed desirable.

Physical Fitness Assessment

The purpose of physical ability testing was twofold: (1) to create a measurement tool that could classify students according to ability and (2) to predict future achievement. Two of the leaders in the area of testing and measurement in physical education were Frederick Rand Rogers and David Kingsley Brace, both trained at Teachers College, Columbia University. Teachers College was at the center of the educational testing movement during the 1920s.[56]

Rogers's book *Test and Measurement Programs in the Redirection of Physical Education* was one of the most interesting texts published during the 1920s.[57] Rogers resurrected strength testing as a major variable in measuring physical ability. From strength testing, he derived a Strength Index represented by a single numerical value. Rogers's assumption was that strength was the major component of physical ability, especially in adolescent boys engaged in team games. From the Strength Index score, individuals could be classified into groups with like ability. This homogeneity of groups was a necessary condition for Rogers's "redirection" of physical education. It was his opinion that inequality in competitive team games "misdirected" individuals from the goals that could be achieved in those types of activities. Social efficiency—defined as courage, perseverance, self-respect, self-confidence, fair play, cooperation, courtesy, and sympathy—could only be achieved when equality of competition was maintained. Unequal or mismatched teams served neither the loser (whose unabashed failure produced frustration) nor the winner (whose victory was too easily acquired). Using statistical procedures, Rogers converted the strength test score into an Athletic Index, which was a numerical expression representing the total athletic ability of a subject.[58]

Rogers also used the Strength Index to determine students' health and progress. Although Rogers believed that the functions of the cardiovascular and digestive systems could not be accurately measured, he assumed an indirect correlation between muscle strength and vital functions. The Physical Fitness Index was therefore a quotient that the physical educator could use to determine individual fitness needs.

The final index presented by Rogers was a refined statistical quotient for use by coaches of competitive athletic teams. Rogers explained the need for the index, along with its uses and limita-tions, when he said that it was a highly valid test of general athletic ability. Rogers noted that although it was adequate for most physical education situations, it was not an accurate measure of endurance and had no correlation with intelligence, two essential attributes of the competitive athlete. It could also be used to discover potential physical educators. To determine the Athletic Index, Rogers provided the following formula:[59]

$$\text{Strength Index divided by } 10$$
$$\text{plus}$$
$$\text{Physical Fitness Index}$$
$$\text{plus}$$
$$\text{Intelligence Quotient}$$
$$\text{equals}$$
$$\text{Athletic Index}$$

The more complex Athletic Index was designed to determine outstanding athletic potential. Intelligence represented by the Intelligence Quotient (IQ) score was added to the statistical analysis.

Much to the chagrin of many physical educators, Rogers cited literature that revealed a negative correlation between mental and physical ability. As for the athletic program, which Rogers viewed as a separate program, the purpose of athletics at any level was not to win the contest but to make athletes live morally.[60]

SUMMARY

Physical education underwent significant reform during this era. According to Lewis, physical education was transformed by several developments. Among the most important was the existence of a highly organized, well-established, and very popular varsity athletic competition. Sports soon challenged traditional physical education activities. Social development objectives, which could be taught through the medium of sports, overshadowed physical education's traditional focus on health-related activities. Physical education expanded its scope and content to provide instruction in varsity athletic competition and to promote intramural sports. However, it appeared that physical education had been used to justify and create "giant athletic agencies" in the nation's colleges and universities. Many physical educators felt that their profession was being undermined by coaches who had little or no training in physical education but were employed in schools and colleges to both coach and teach physical education.

During the 1920s, physical educators were significantly influenced by general trends in education. These trends blended considerations of child interest and motivation with desired social outcomes such as good citizenship. Play, games, and sport were the natural activities of childhood, and if properly organized and directed, they would foster desirable character traits and qualities that could be defined in physical, social, and psychological terms.

The development of physical education from 1900 to 1930 reflected the belief system of the larger society and the major trends in other academic disciplines. The nineteenth-century concept of health as a balance of mind, body, and will gave way to a more physical integration of mind and body that could be expressed in social and behavioral terms. Play theory provided the theoretical vehicle that enabled physical education to redefine itself in these social and behavioral terms.

Three elements of the theory remained unchanged. First, physical education contributed to the health of the individual. Second, physical activity was a major component of character development. Third, physical education was committed to the development of research theory and methodology. Play theory reinforced the idea that gross motor exercise through play developed those positive qualities called character.

In philosophical and theoretical terms, physical education focused on the development of the entire being. This was the objective of early nineteenth-century educators who wished to build body and will (character) through regulated exercise. Physical educators throughout the 1920s reinforced this same view. By 1930, the holistic view of physical education championed by Hetherington had become the standard concept in physical education. The development of health, civic-mindedness, moral conduct, and social growth was most important, and research increasingly focused on pedagogical methods that could facilitate this development. Physical education was committed to the whole being, yet had to separate and fragment the various aspects of the individual for analysis and measurement. The problem then became how to achieve reintegration of the whole person.

DISCUSSION QUESTIONS

1. What arguments did the concept of "play" have to overcome before being taken seriously as a method of physical education?

2. Who were the major play theorists? What were their positions?

3. What influence did John Dewey have on the development of physical education?

4. How were athletics supposed to contribute to character formation, and what types of games supposedly did this the best?

5. What were the cooperative areas of Hetherington's physical education program? How did they work?

6. How was physical education promoted between 1900 and 1930? What were the outcomes of physical education?

7. What impact did tests and measurements have on physical education? What was the relationship between physical ability and mental ability?

8. Why were the advocates of gymnastics as the focus of physical education so opposed to including athletic competition within physical education programs?

9. To what extent do you believe that sport has educational value? Justify your answer.

10. What did Luther Gulick have to say regarding the inclusion of women in athletics?

INTERNET RESOURCES

International Institute for Sport and Olympic History
www.harveyabramsbooks.com/501c3.html
Is a good source for historical studies of American sport and the modern Olympic Games.

American History Education Resources on the Internet
www.ibiblio.org/cisco/tour2.html
Lists American history and educational resources available via the Internet.

International Journal of the History of Sport
www.tandf.co.uk/Journals/titles/09523367.asp
Focuses on the historical study of sport.

International Paralympic Committee
www.paralympic.org
Provides information on sport for the disabled.

YMCA (Young Men's Christian Association)
www.ymca.net
Includes a history of YMCA sport and physical education programs.

History of Women in Sports Timeline
www.northnet.org/stlawrenceaauw/timeline.htm
Gives an excellent chronology of women's involvement in physical activity, exercise, and sport.

Amateur Athletic Foundation of Los Angeles
www.aafla.org
Provides access to holdings in their excellent library.

Visit the *History and Philosophy of Sport and Physical Education* Online Learning Center (www.mhhe.com/mechikoff6e) for additional information and study tools.

SUGGESTIONS FOR FURTHER READING

Betts, J. "Organized Sport in Industrial America." Doctoral dissertation, Columbia University, 1951.

Boyle, R. *Sport—Mirror of American Life.* Boston: Little, Brown, 1963.

Cozens, F. W., and F. S. Stumpf. *Sports in American Life.* Chicago: University of Chicago Press, 1953.

Dean, C. F. "A Historical Study of Physical Fitness in the United States, 1790–1961." Doctoral dissertation, George Peabody College for Teachers, 1964.

Lee, M., and B. L. Bennett. "This Is Our Heritage." *Journal of Health, Physical Education,*

and Recreation 31 (April 1960): 25–33, 38–47, 52–58, 62–73, 76–85.

Petroskey, H. "A History of Measurement in Health and Physical Education." Doctoral dissertation, University of Iowa, 1946.

Rainwater, C. E. *The Play Movement in the United States.* Chicago: University of Chicago Press, 1922.

Zeigler, E. F. "History of Professional Preparation for Physical Education in the United States, 1861–1948." Doctoral dissertation, Yale University, 1950.

NOTES

1. Guy M. Lewis, "Adoption of the Sports Program, 1906–39: The Role of Accommodation in the Transformation of Physical Education," *Quest* 12 (1969): 34.

2. Ibid., 34.

3. Ibid., 36.

4. Bruce Bennett and Mabel Lee, "This Is Our Heritage," *Journal of Health, Physical Education, and Recreation* XXXI (April 1960); Lewis, *Adoption of the Sports Program,* 35.

5. Lewis, *Adoption of the Sports Program,* 35.

6. Ibid., 35.

7. Ibid., 38.

8. Ibid., 38.

9. Ibid., 38.

10. Harry A. Scott, "A Personal Study of Directors . . . ," in *Athletics in Education* by Jesse Williams and William Hughes (Philadelphia: Bureau of Publications, Teachers College, Columbia University, 1930), 119–25.

11. Howard J. Savage, *American College Athletics* (New York: Carnegie Foundation, Bulletin #23), 1929; Lewis, *Adoption of the Sports Program,* 39.

12. Ibid.

13. Lewis, *Adoption of the Sports Program,* 40.

14. Lewis, *Adoption of the Sports Program,* 42; Savage, *American College Athletics.*

15. Herbert Spencer, "Thoughts on Education," *American Journal of Education* 11, no. 27 (June 1862): 491.

16. Herbert Spencer, *Principles of Psychology,* vol. 2, 3rd ed. (New York: Appleton, 1896; first published in 1855).

17. William James, *Principles of Psychology,* vol. 2 (New York: Holt, 1890).

18. Karl Groos, *The Play of Animals,* trans. E. L. Baldwin (New York: Appleton, 1898).

19. Ontogeny recapitulates phylogeny was not an original discovery by Hall; it emerged from work being done by nineteenth-century embryologists who noted remarkable similarities between developing embryos of different animal species. Hall's contribution was the emphasis he placed on postnatal development. Paula Rogers Lupcho, "The Professionalization of American Physical Education, 1885–1930" (doctoral dissertation, University of California, Berkeley, 1986), 117.

20. G. Stanley Hall, *Adolescence: Its Psychology and Its Relation to Physiology, Anthropology, Sociology, Sex, Crime, Religion and Education,* vol. 1 (New York: Appleton, 1907).

21. Ibid., 203.

22. Ibid., 113.

23. Luther H. Gulick, *A Philosophy of Play* (New York: Association Press, 1920), 11, 32–33.

24. John Dewey, *Democracy and Education* (New York: Free Press, 1966).

25. Jay Seaver, "Military Training as an Exercise," in *Proceedings of the American Association for the Advancement of Physical Education, Third Annual Meeting* (Brooklyn: Rome Brothers, 1887).

26. Ibid.

27. Edward Hartwell, "The Nature of Physical Training, and the Best Means of Securing Its Ends," in *Boston Physical Training Conference* (Boston: Press of George H. Ellis, 1890), 112–15.

28. Stephen Hardy, *How Boston Played* (Boston: Northeastern University Press, 1982), 65–123; Allen V. Sapora and Elmer D. Mitchell, *The Theory of Play and Recreation* (New York: Ronald Press, 1961), 57–63; and Foster Rhea Dulles, *A History of Recreation: America Learns to Play* (Englewood Cliffs, NJ: Prentice-Hall, 1965).

29. William Skarstrom, "Kinesiology of the Trunk, Shoulders, and Hip Applied to Gymnastics," *American Physical Education Review (APER)* 13, no. 2 (February 1908): 69.

30. Ibid.

31. "Editorial Note and Comment," *APER* 17, no. 5 (May 1912): 187.

32. Paul C. Phillips, "The Extension of Athletic Sports to the Whole Student Body of Amherst," *APER* 17, no. 5 (May 1912): 339.

33. See Gulick, *Philosophy of Play;* Clark Hetherington, *Normal Course in Play* (New York: A. S. Barnes, 1925); idem, *School Program in Physical Education* (New York: World Book, 1922); Joseph Lee, *Play in Education* (New York: Macmillan, 1917); Thomas D. Wood and Rosalind F. Cassidy, *The New Physical Education* (New York: Macmillan, 1927); Henry S. Curtis, *The Practical Conduct of Play* (New York: Macmillan, 1915); and idem, *Education Through Play* (New York: Macmillan, 1917).

34. Curtis, *Practical Conduct of Play.*

35. Luther H. Gulick, "Athletics Do Not Test Womanliness," *APER* 11, no. 3 (September 1906): 158–59.

36. Lupcho, "Professionalization," 82.

37. Gulick, "Athletics," 139.

38. Hetherington, *School Program.*

39. Ibid., 22.

40. Ibid., 24.

41. Ibid.

42. Ibid., 26.

43. Ibid., 31.

44. Ibid., 39.

45. Lupcho, "Professionalization," 91.

46. Ibid., 93.

47. Hetherington, *School Program,* 43–44.

48. Wood and Cassidy, *New Physical Education.* See also Thomas D. Wood and Clifford L. Brownell, *Source Book in Health and Physical Education* (New York: Macmillan, 1925).

49. The debate about "indexing" and intelligence rages, especially surrounding the reliability of the Scholastic Aptitude Test (SAT).

50. Lupcho, "Professionalization," 95.

51. M. H. Landis, H. E. Burtt, and J. H. Nichols, "The Relation Between Physical Efficiency and Intelligence," *APER* 28, no. 5 (May 1923): 220.

52. R. A. Schwegler and J. L. Engleshardt, "A Test of Physical Efficiency: The Correlation Between Results from Tests of Mental Efficiency," *APER* 29, no. 9 (November 1924): 501–05.

53. Frederick W. Cozens, "Status of the Problem of the Relation of Physical to Mental Activity," *APER* 31, no. 3 (March 1927): 147–55.

54. Vern S. Ruble, "A Psychological Study of Athletes," *APER* 33, no. 4 (April 1928): 221–22.

55. Cozens, "Status of the Problem," 154–55.

56. Frederick Rand Rogers, *Test and Measurement Programs in the Redirection of Physical Education* (New York: Teachers College, Columbia University Bureau of Publications, 1927); David K. Brace, *Measuring Motor Ability: A Scale of Motor Ability Tests* (New York: A. S. Barnes, 1927).

57. Rogers, *Test and Measurement.*

58. Ibid., 27.

59. Ibid., 128.

60. Ibid., 131.

SECTION

IV The American Approach to Sport and Physical Education in the Twentieth Century

CHAPTER **13**

The Evolution of Physical Education: 1940 and Beyond

Time Line

History

1945 United Nations founded
1947 Beginning of "Cold War"
1948 State of Israel proclaimed
1950 Korean War started
1954 Supreme Court overturned
Plessy v. Ferguson;
segregated schools banned
1957 USSR orbited Sputnik;
subsequent U.S. pressure for
more science in schools
1963 President Kennedy
assassinated
Student riots at Berkeley;
then on other campuses
1965 U.S. intervention in
Vietnam escalated
1969 U.S. astronauts landed on
moon
1974 Watergate scandal;
President Nixon resigned
1979–81 Hostages held in Iran
1979–87 Terrorism spread

Sport and Physical Education

1946 All-American Football
Conference formed
1947 Jackie Robinson joined
Brooklyn Dodgers
1949 Ladies Professional Golf
Association formed
National Basketball
Association formed
1951 College basketball
gambling scandal

OBJECTIVES

Upon completing this chapter, you will be able to:

- Understand the impact wars have on physical education programs.
- Explain the idea behind promoting combat sports as opposed to typical physical education classes during times of war.
- Understand the role that men and women physical educators played during World War II.
- Explain why Tom Brokaw called the generation that fought World War II, The Greatest Generation.
- Discuss the situation of baseball during World War II.
- Explain why physical fitness can contribute to national security.
- Discuss the status of physical education at the University of California, Berkeley during World War II.
- Explain the contribution that James B. Conant made to physical education.
- Discuss why the integrity of physical education was called into question.
- Explain the impact that Franklin Henry had on the evolution of physical education.

PROLOG: WORLD WAR II

In 1939, Europe was embroiled in another devastating war. The Axis Alliance of Germany, Italy, and Japan were on the march. Most of Europe was under the control of Germany and Italy by 1941, while Japan was waging war in the Pacific and Southeast Asia. Great Britain and her European allies withstood the unrelenting attacks of the German *Luftwaffe* (air force) by day and night. The United States sent massive amounts of aid and military supplies to Great

280

Britain and others who were fighting the Nazis and Fascists but for the most part, had no desire to become militarily involved.

Many Americans believed it was only a matter of time before "something happened" that would compel the United States to declare war on the Axis alliance. The war was close and getting closer. America did not ignore this fact and began to prepare. In 1940, the Selective Service was organized and millions of American men were ordered to their local draft boards for examination and tests. Those who passed were subsequently drafted into the Army while many others volunteered for the Navy and Marines. Women volunteered for service in the Navy, Army, Marines and Coast Guard. Fifteen million men and women served their country during World War II; 10 million in the Army, 4 million in the Navy and Coast Guard, and 600,000 in the Marine Corps. In excess of 216,000 women served as nurses.[1]

On December 7, 1941, Japan attacked Pearl Harbor. The next day, U.S. President Franklin D. Roosevelt called the day "a date which will live in infamy" when he addressed a joint session of Congress. Shortly after President Roosevelt's address, Congress declared war on Japan, Germany, and Italy on December 8, 1941.

SPORT AND PHYSICAL EDUCATION DURING WORLD WAR II

While the military applauded physically fit Americans, what mattered most was the mental and physical toughness that personified "head-to-head" sports competition. Combat sports such as wrestling, boxing, football, track, and other "winner-take-all" challenges would develop, according to the War Department, men who are tough, hard-nose fighters. Calisthenics and sports competition for men was the order of the day on high school and college campuses; no more "fun and games," a "winner-take-all" athletic competition could be the difference between life and death on the battlefield. Women's physical education programs featured both physical fitness and sports. While millions of men served in the military, millions of women manned the assembly lines making airplanes and military equipment. Women were the backbone of industry during World War II.

Men and women physical education teachers volunteered or were drafted into the service. Many became physical training (PT) instructors, while others supervised athletic competition and fitness facilities. Because of their competitive ethos and leadership abilities, many were sent to officer candidate school and became combat officers and aviators. Women were trained as pilots and flew new airplanes from the factory to military bases worldwide.

It should be noted that Tom Brokaw, one of the preeminent television news anchors and journalists in the United States, wrote *The Greatest Generation,* a book that told the story of those who fought in World War II.

Baseball was still America's favorite pastime during the war years. In 1942, President Roosevelt expressed his belief that professional baseball players

1960 Wilma Rudolph won three gold medals in Rome Olympics

1964 Muhammad Ali won world heavyweight boxing title

1965 Houston "Astrodome" opened

1966 Professional football's first "Superbowl"

Major League Baseball Players' Association formed

1969 Diane Crump first woman jockey on major track

1971 Association for Intercollegiate Athletics for Women (AIAW) established

1972 Title IX of Educational Amendments

1973 Secretariat first horse in twenty-five years to win Triple Crown

Billie Jean King defeated Bobby Riggs in challenge match

1981 Major League baseball strike NCAA sponsored women's intercollegiate sport AIAW suspended operation

1982 NFL on strike

should enlist in the military and serve their country. Many did so, including Jackie Robinson and Joe DiMaggio; however, this act of patriotism was cause for concern. What if there were not enough professional ball players left to play major league baseball? The owner of the Chicago Cubs, Philip K. Wrigley, came to the rescue by organizing the All-American Girls Baseball League to keep Wrigley Field open during the war. Others followed and the popularity of women's baseball soared. Women's teams played modified softball rules that, as time went by, were almost the same rules as major league baseball used.[2] In 1992, actor Tom Hanks, along with Madonna, starred in the movie *A League of Their Own,* which was a fictionalized account of life and competition in the league.

World War II ended in 1945. The United States and its allies combined old countries into new ones and in essence, redrew the world map. The Soviet Union (present day Russia) was an American ally and, as they say, to the victor goes the spoils of war. In return for the Soviet Union's brutal war against Nazi Germany, Europe was divided into two parts. Eastern Europe was governed by the Soviets, led by Joseph Stalin who was a ruthless communist and ruled with an iron fist. Western Europe was controlled by the Western democracies. Less than two years after the end of World War II, a new and potentially more lethal war ensued. The Cold War pitted a nuclear armed West against a nuclear armed and ruthless East. It was communism versus democracy and in 1956, Soviet premier Nikita Khrushchev announced, "We will bury you!" to a group of Western ambassadors.

POST WORLD WAR II

In the aftermath of World War II, and with the start of the Cold War, national security was paramount. The number of men who failed their draft physicals was not acceptable. Physical fitness became a matter of national security, especially with the threat of another war looming on the horizon.

Physical fitness became every American's patriotic duty according to President Eisenhower and many of the nation's leaders. Physical educators

were ecstatic, to say the least. Physical education was mandatory in just about every school in America between 1950 and 1975 (the end of the Vietnam War). From middle school through high school, students completed mandatory physical education classes or, in lieu of this, competed on sports teams. Those with physical disabilities also enrolled in adaptive or corrective physical education programs in the nation's schools. Most colleges had a mandatory physical education requirement regardless of major. Yes, it appeared that Americans everywhere were more concerned about their health and physical fitness than ever before. But would it last?

Most high school and college physical education programs were separated by gender; the men had their own distinct program while the women had theirs. There were also significant philosophical differences. While the program for women was very organized and reflected nationally agreed upon common goals and outcomes, the men's physical education programs were not as complementary and rarely reflect a unified philosophy.

Men focused on "serious" sports competition and as a result, became very specialized over time. At first, coaches coached a number of sports. However, as time went by, the demands on winning teams at the high school and college level became a year around job as opposed to a seasonal job. At one point, physical education and athletics were the same department. With sports specialization, the necessity of having two separate departments became apparent, especially at high schools and colleges with big-time programs and big-time budgets. The culture changed and physical education and athletics soon began drifting apart, each with their separate agenda. Physical education was all about education and research while the athletic department was all about winning. Fortunately, small colleges did not have these aspirations and many physical educators in these fine institutions still wear both hats; physical education teacher and coach.

Co-ed physical education classes emerged in the 1950s. Not everyone looked favorably upon this "progressive" development. In 1950, noted physiologist Arthur H. Steinhaus of George Williams College gave a speech at the 55th Annual Convention of the

American Association for Health, Physical Education, and Recreation (AAHPER) titled "Lessons from Physiology for Coaches and Athletes." In this speech, Dr. Steinhaus articulated his observations about research on overloading muscles as well as some philosophical concerns about co-ed physical education, a subject that really troubled him:

> If we should delve into philosophy for a moment I think you could see how our physical education programs have lost their way sometimes when we have emphasized only the lighter activity, particularly for boys and men. That is the argument I have against coeducational activities. I think they are wonderful for developing social graces and things connected with that. But if you want strength in a boy you don't get it when you match him against a person who is much weaker than he is and to whom he has to show a certain politeness to boot.[3]

Change does not come easily, so it would take some time as well as a new generation of physical education teachers and progressive thinkers before coeducational physical education classes were the rule and not the exception.

PHYSICAL EDUCATION ON LIFE SUPPORT

Colleges and universities must maintain the academic integrity of their course offerings and majors. As a result, courses and degree programs are under constant scrutiny and review in order to ensure quality control. Physical education degree programs during this time prepared students to become physical education teachers. High school teachers and college professors in academic areas such as the sciences and the liberal arts did not view physical education very favorably and frequently questioned the academic quality of its degree programs. To make matters worse, the public and academia saw physical educators, especially men, as teachers of games and sports who merely "played."

Shortly before the beginning of World War II, the University of California, Berkeley, one of the premier universities in the world, decided to review the Group Major in Physical Education and Hygiene. This review was the direct result of an attack on the physical education department by faculty in the College of Letters and Science; Physical Education was a department within this college. The college's executive committee completed their review and determined that the curriculum in physical education lacked the necessary academic content. The academic integrity of the professional program offered by the physical education department was found to be so marginal that the administration decreed that the College of Letters and Sciences would initiate oversight and micromanage the physical education department until it met the academic criteria of the university. If this did not happen, physical education would be nothing but a memory. The handwriting was on the wall—reform or else!

In 1945, the physical education faculty at Berkeley proposed a new plan for the degree, which was approved. The academic discipline of physical education was in its infancy but over time would become the model at most colleges and universities. The physical education faculty at Berkeley sounded the alarm and did their best to convince their colleagues around the country that their future was the academic model and that the "old school" professional teacher-training program was not going to meet academic expectations. While some listened, many ignored the warning for reform.

THE CONANT REPORT

In 1961, the Carnegie Corporation of New York hired James B. Conant, former president of Harvard University to undertake a study of the education of America's teachers. Conant's findings were published in his book, *The Education of America's Teachers* and soon became the metric by which teacher-training programs were evaluated.[4] Physical educators braced for another attack. Dr. Conant stated that:

> The American public and the professional educators, then, are still a bit uncertain as to why instruction should be provided in art, music, foreign language, and physical education . . . Physical education as a required subject one

period a day five days a week obviously takes time away from music and art, as do the academic subjects. Therefore, a certain tension exists, to put it mildly, among the proponents of these fields.[5]

Conant concluded that physical educators suffered from an academic inferiority complex, and in their attempt to gain academic respectability began using terms and language associated with the more intellectual areas found in the arts and sciences. Conant wrote that "The consequences are most ridiculous in their [physical education] graduate programs."[6] Can you just imagine the faculty at Berkeley saying "we warned you this was going to happen but you wouldn't listen!"

Conant supported an undergraduate degree in physical education but did not believe graduate physical education programs were credible. He was also strongly opposed to allowing physical education teachers to teach other subjects. He observed that "Teachers of physical education are today suspect because superintendents and principals of high schools have far too often required them to teach academic subjects that they have hardly studied in college. . . ."[7]

Conant had harsh words for physical education. Although he did not believe that an undergraduate degree in physical education should share the same academic stature that a degree in the liberal arts and sciences has, he did believe that there was room for physical education in the schools.

THE RESPONSE

Shortly after Conant's findings were made public, AAHPER convened a panel that would study Conant's findings and work to upgrade the professional preparation of physical educators. In addition, AAHPER organized a conference to study and assess graduate physical education programs.[8]

The Conant Report as well as peer and public perception made it crystal clear that physical education must establish itself as an academic discipline or face the consequences. We know that the physical education faculty at Berkeley had

designed and implemented this model years before and Berkeley came to the rescue.

Franklin Henry was a professor of physical education at Berkeley. Educated as an experimental psychologist, he authored one of the most important position papers in the history of physical education, "Physical Education—An Academic Discipline" presented to the National College Physical Education Association for Men in 1964. So profound was Henry's presentation that the *Journal of Health, Physical Education and Recreation* featured it in their September 1964 issue. Fourteen years later, in 1978, *QUEST* published it again as a reminder of how far we have come and how far we still have to go in our quest for academic parity.[9]

Because Henry was not trained as a physical educator per se, he saw things differently than the rank and file physical education professionals who did not like what they heard. Henry insisted that physical education must become a bona fide academic discipline and must reign supreme and lord over the profession of physical education which was the cause of all this trouble in the first place. While the professional of physical education program is based on practical application and trains physical education teachers, in contrast, the academic discipline of physical education is grounded in theoretical constructs and a body of knowledge that exists for the purpose of generating research and expanding the frontiers of science.

Franklin Henry provided physical education with a road map to the future; however, the ride did not appeal to everybody. Exercise physiology and the sciences embraced Henry's model, but most professional physical education faculty found little comfort in the "ride" because they would be second class citizens while the scientists reigned supreme.

A NEW ERA

Over time, the profession of physical education (teacher education) reinvented itself and began to utilize established psychological theories in order to teach students how to be effective teachers. Behavior modification, based on the work of

B.F. Skinner, found a home at The Ohio State University. Professor Daryl Siedentop, one of the preeminent behaviorists in teacher education, developed the pedagogy curriculum at Ohio State that trained future physical educators and coaches. Extensive and credible research in physical activity and physical education was soon published in leading national and international educational journals.

Over time, many physical education departments in both high schools and colleges started to identify more with exercise, health, and fitness than traditional physical education activities tied to games and sports.

In the early 1980's, Exercise Physiology began to identify itself with a new focus called Exercise Science and soon after biomechanics, motor control and motor behavior followed suite. The academic discipline of physical education that Franklin Henry proposed was now a reality. Exercise science, sports medicine—athletic training and rehabilitation of sports injuries via physical therapy and kinesiotherapy have to a large extent replaced the physical education programs that Franklin Henry knew "back in the day." Multi million dollar grants that fund intensive research agendas are the norm in many research intensive Exercise Science departments. Collaboration between medical school faculty and exercise science faculty are quite common now a days.

The evolution of physical education continues to this day. Many contemporary physical education departments feature a hybrid curriculum which includes teacher training and exercise science while some have abandon teacher training in favor of exercise science. In your crystal ball, does traditional physical education have a future or has it already been replaced by exercise science and the preparation of fitness industry professionals?

EPILOG

As we continue our march into the 21st Century, we face the same issues as those who proceeded us. America has serious health and fitness concerns. Childhood obesity and diabetes have increased dramatically while physical education and fitness opportunities in the nation's schools have declined significantly primarily due to budget cuts; physical education, music and art are generally the first programs to be reduced or eliminated in times of severe economic downturn.

Has technology in the form of video games created a generation of couch potatoes who have little if any desire to exercise? America has been at war since 2001. Our national security is threatened on a daily basis and the next generation of American Presidents will be fighting wars against insurgents who, like the old Soviet Union, want to destroy democratic nations. What percentage of men between the ages of 18 and 25 would pass the draft physical today? Based on history, do you think physical education and exercise science programs are needed more than ever in the nation's schools to combat disease and for the purpose of national security? If so, what would your curriculum look like?

DISCUSSION QUESTIONS

1. Why was Dr. Arthur Steinhaus concerned about co-ed physical education classes?
2. To what extent was male chauvinism entrenched in the American mind set during the post World War II era? Is this way of thinking and behaving eradicated in the 21st Century or does it still exist?
3. Why did sports competition become more popular than physical education during World War II?
4. If James B. Conant initiated a follow-up study today, what do you think he would say about the status of physical education?
5. From a national security perspective, is America at risk because of an overall lack of physical fitness among our youth?
6. What would you propose to increase the academic integrity of our field?

INTERNET RESOURCES

Baseball in Wartime
Baseballinwartime.com

Women's Baseball During World War II
www.lib.niu.edu.1955/ihy950452.html

African American Trailblazers
www.museumca.org/picturethis/timeline/world-war-ii/sports/info

SUGGESTIONS FOR FURTHER READING

Betty Spears and Richard Swanson. History of Sport and Physical Education in the United States (3 Ed) (Dubuque: Championship Books —A Division of Wm. C. Brown Publishers, 1988) 432 ppg.

Brokaw, T. *The Greatest Generation* (New York: Random House, 1998).

Festle, M. J. *Playing Nice: Politics and Apologies in Women's Sports* (New York: Columbia University Press, 1996) 379 ppg.

Lee, M. *A History of Physical Education and Sports in the U.S.A.* (New York: John Wiley & Sons, 1983) 399 pgs.

Van Dalen, D. B. and Bruce L. Bennett. *A World History of Physical Education* (2 Ed) (Englewood Cliffs: Prentice Hall, Inc. 1971) 694 ppg.

NOTES

1. Samuel Eliot Morison. The Oxford History of American People (New York: Oxford University Press, 1965), 1007—1008; Betty Spears and Richard Swanson, History of Sport and Physical Education in the United States (3 ed) (Dubuque: Championship Books—A Division of Wm. C. Brown Publishers, 1988), 249

2. Spears and Swanson, 250.

3. Arthur A. Steinhaus, "Lessons from Physiology for Coaches and Athletes," proceedings 55th Annual Convention of the American Alliance for Health, Physical Education, and Recreation, Dallas, April 18–22, 1950 Compiled and Edited by Southern District Association, p. 118.

4. James B. Conant. The Education of America's Teachers (New York: McGraw-Hill Publishers, 1963), p. 181.

5. Ibid.

6. Ibid.

7. Ibid., 185.

8. Snyder, R. "Work of the Professional Preparation Panel," in the Journal of Health, Physical Education and Recreation, 1968, p. 39.

9. Franklin Henry. "Physical Education: An Academic Discipline" Proceedings of the 67th Annual Conference of the National College Physical Education Association for Men, January 8–11, 1964, pp. 6–9; Reprinted in the Journal of Health, Physical Education, and Recreation, 1964, Vol. 39 No. 69, pp. 32–33; Franklin Henry. "The Academic Discipline of Physical Education," in QUEST No. 29 (Winter) pp. 13–29.

CHAPTER 14

Sport in the Twentieth Century

OBJECTIVES

Upon completing this chapter, you will be able to:

- Discuss the significance and scope of sport in twentieth-century America.
- Recognize that sport in America is utilized for a variety of reasons.
- Understand how college football evolved, and discuss the problems that were manifest in the sport.
- Identify some of the leading figures and institutions in the history of college football.
- Explain the interest that President Theodore Roosevelt had in reforming the rules of football.
- Understand how the National Collegiate Athletic Association (NCAA) came into being.
- Understand how professional football developed, and discuss the individuals and organizations that contributed to its growth and popularity.
- Understand how race became a factor in football.
- Explain why professional football was not as widely accepted as college football in its early years.
- Explain why the sport of basketball was invented, and identify where it was invented and who invented it.
- Identify some of the leading figures and institutions involved in basketball's early history.
- Recognize the difficulty of developing a uniform set of rules for basketball.
- Discuss the appeal that basketball had as a sport for women.
- Discuss the popularity of basketball in the nation's high schools.
- Explain why the sport of volleyball was invented, and explain where it was created and who is credited with its invention.
- Discuss the types of sports and physical activities that were offered to women in the early twentieth century and the rationale behind them.
- Identify some of the leaders of women's sport and physical education during this era, and discuss their beliefs concerning competitive sports for women.
- Discuss the women's basketball at Wayland Baptist University.
- Identify the greatest women's basketball coach in America.

Sports and Physical Education Time Line

1891 James Naismith invents basketball
1892 Biddle University versus Livingston College: first intercollegiate football game between black colleges
1895 William Morgan invents volleyball
1899 Uniform rules for women's basketball developed
1902 First Rose Bowl
1905 Football crisis, mediated by President Roosevelt; Intercollegiate Athletic Association of the United States founded
1910 National Collegiate Athletic Association founded
1915 Joint Basketball Committee makes uniform basketball rules
1917–1918 U.S. in World War I
1917 Athletic Conference of American College Women formed; National Committee on Women's Sports established
1920 American Professional Football Association formed in Canton, Ohio
1922 Chicago Bears formed
1925 New York Giants formed; Red Grange signs with Chicago
1928 Coast-to-coast football
1941–1945 World War II

287

1946 NBA formed from Basketball Association of America

1948 Fanny Blankers-Koen (Netherlands) wins four gold medals at London Olympics

1952 American Dick Button performs first triple jump on ice skates

1953 Maureen Connolly is first woman to win Grand Slam in tennis

1954 Roger Bannister of Great Britain runs first sub-four-minute mile: 3:59.4

1958 Brooklyn Dodgers move to Los Angeles

1960 American Football League formed

1964 Cassius Clay, later known as Muhammad Ali, wins his first World Heavyweight Boxing title

1966 First Super Bowl

1967 New York Jets defeat Baltimore Colts in Super Bowl, marking the first win by an American Football League (AFL) team over an NFL team

1970 NFL and AFL merge; Marshall University Football team killed in plane crash

1971–1983 Association for Intercollegiate Athletics for Women active

1974 Hank Aaron breaks Babe Ruth's career home run record

1978 First Iron Man Triathlon competition held in Hawaii

1979 Sugar Ray Leonard wins his first world boxing title

1980 "Miracle on Ice" unfolds as the American Ice Hockey team beats the Soviet Union at the Lake Placid Winter Olympics

1982 American Mary Decker sets six world records in track and field; first NCAA women's basketball tournament

1985 Sergi Bubka of the Soviet Union pole vaults over 6 meters and sets a world record; Pete Rose breaks Ty Cobb's baseball record for career hits

- Recognize the impact of societal norms on the lack of opportunities afforded girls and women interested in athletic competition.
- Understand how women's athletics were regulated, and identify some of the organizations involved and their rationales.
- Discuss the influence of Mildred "Babe" Didrikson Zaharias on societal beliefs relative to the level of competition that women could successfully engage in.
- Recognize the historical significance of the Association for Intercollegiate Athletics for Women (AIAW) and the subsequent impact of Title IX of the Educational Amendments Act of 1972.
- Explain why the National Collegiate Athletic Association (NCAA) was vehemently opposed to Title IX and why the NCAA eventually co-opted member schools from the AIAW, leading to its demise.
- Understand and appreciate the appeal of endurance sports in the twentieth century.

INTRODUCTION

The model for sport as we know it in contemporary America was firmly in place by the late 1800s. The demographic, technological, and philosophical changes that occurred in American culture in the nineteenth century were reflected in the ways Americans viewed sport and play. America continued to become more urbanized and industrialized. The trend of Americans moving to the cities led to a continued push for sport and recreational activities that could accommodate urban lifestyles and mitigate against the unhealthy effects of city living. Technological innovation continued at an increasing rate, and these innovations were used in the sports world as much as in any other cultural arena. Sports information was increasingly available via telegraph, then radio, then television. Sports journalism, developed in the nineteenth century, became more than ever a part of American life.

Americans continued to become more comfortable with the human body throughout the twentieth century. One consequence of this was that sport and playful activities, which were associated with the body, were seen as increasingly acceptable. Religion came to be seen as more of a personal guide than a public one and was no longer used as a reason for participating, or not participating, in public activities.[1] Consequently, sport and play, for better or worse, became increasingly free of religious restrictions. By the mid-1900s, religion and sport were rarely associated in conversation in America. Religion was related to the spiritual aspects of a person; sport was related to the physical.

Yet in a country as large as the United States, many different attitudes toward and behaviors about sport can be found. Indeed, the nation is as pluralistic and multicultural as it has ever been, and this applies to sport and play as well. This is so much the case that, although there are trends that can be studied, making any generalizations regarding the current status of sport in any part of America is difficult. Sport and play are practiced in rural as well as urban areas, exist in premodern as well as modern form, and are seen both as the exercise of only the body and as a means of achieving the integration of one's being. Sport and play, as we know these activities, are the summation of how an individual has experienced these activities in his or her own past.

Given the plurality of sport and the conditions surrounding American sport and play, a short discussion of some of the more significant changes in the twentieth century is in order. We have chosen to address endurance sports, football, basketball, volleyball, and women's sports to illustrate some of the trends evident in the twentieth century.

ENDURANCE SPORTS

After the end of World War I, America reinvented itself. The nation was no longer a second-rate world power. It was the country that had rescued Europe from the Germans. It was a land where innovation and invention would be encouraged, where capital markets would finance the world and plunge it into depression in 1929. In the first few years after the Great War, Americans celebrated and engaged in activities that necessitated great bravado and panache. Among the most interesting was the quest for physical endurance titles. As it would turn out, the endurance sports of the early twentieth century would morph into the extreme sports of the late twentieth century. Dance marathons and marathon footraces swept the country. And across the Atlantic in France, the triathlon was born in 1920.

Dancing has been a popular pastime as well as a "rite of passage" in cultural and religious activities for thousands of years. From the 1920s until the end of the Great Depression, endurance dance contests were very popular. If a couple could outlast their competition on the dance floor in what became known as marathon dancing, there was prize money to be won. These marathon dances would last for many hours or even for days. It tested every competing couple's physical and psychological limits. In 1935, Horace McCoy wrote his best-selling book *They Shoot Horses, Don't They?* It was a dark and sad story about the exploitation of marathon dancers by promoters. The book depicts the personal physical and emotional exhaustion that these athletes had to endure in order to make a living during the Great Depression. In 1969, Hollywood made the book into a movie with the same title. Actress Jane Fonda, who later would become queen of the aerobic dance craze in the 1970s and 1980s, starred in the movie. The point is that dance marathons flourished for several decades; endurance competitions would grow until it seemed that the limits of human performance had been reached and athletes could no longer endure. And then the bar would be raised again and again.

In 1928, a sports promoter known as C. C. Pyle (the C. C. stood for "Cash and Carry") organized the Bunion Derby. The derby was a foot race that started in Los Angeles and finished in downtown New York's Madison Square Garden. One hundred and ninety-nine men started the race. Some were athletic; many were not. They raced (ran, walked, limped) every day. Sometimes they would cover as many as 75 miles in a day. They endured desert heat, snow, rain, humidity, and a host of pests (and pets) that would send any sane man to the hospital. Still, they persisted and persevered until 84 days later and 3,421 miles from Los Angeles, 50 endurance athletes arrived at Madison Square Garden.

1986 Mike Tyson becomes youngest world heavyweight boxing champion

1990 Tennis star Martina Navratilova wins record ninth straight Wimbledon singles title

1991 NBA star Magic Johnson retires from basketball

1992 Toronto Blue Jays become first non-American team to win baseball's World Series; top 22 soccer teams in England resign from the Football League and form the English Premier League

1993 Tennis star Monica Seles is stabbed while competing in Hamburg, Germany

1995 Cyclist Miguel Indurain wins fifth straight Tour de France

1997 Women's National Basketball Association (WNBA) debuts

1998 Bowl Championship Series (BCS) formed to promote college football in United States

2001 NASCAR driver Dale Earnhardt killed in crash at Daytona Speedway; Tiger Woods becomes first golfer to hold four major titles at once

2002 Sisters Serena and Venus Williams win three major tennis tournaments

2004 Boston Red Sox win first World Series since 1918

The University of Virginia hires Dave Leitao as their first African-American head coach (basketball)

2005 National Hockey League (NHL) cancels season because of a strike by players

2006 Japan wins first World Baseball Classic in San Diego

2006 Effa Manley is first woman elected to Baseball Hall of Fame

2007 Doping scandals devastate Tour de France, Major League baseball, and Olympics

2008 American Olympian Michael Phelps wins 8 gold medals in Beijing. He becomes the most decorated Olympian in history

Scott Tinley, one of the premier triathletes of the late twentieth century and triathlon historian, identifies a race held in France in 1920 as quite possibly the first triathlon. In 1920, the French newspaper *L'Auto* ran a story about an athletic competition that featured a 3-kilometer run, a 12-kilometer bike race, and a swim across the Marne Channel. The event was called "Les Trois Sports"—The Three Sports. Athletes were not afforded a break; they endured all three events back-to-back. Tinley also identifies French newspaper stories written in 1927 and 1934 about three sport competitions held in Marseille and La Rochelle.

The first American triathlon was held at San Diego's Mission Bay on September 25, 1974. Forty-six athletes competed. Before long, San Diego was the place where endurance athletes from all over the world came to train and to compete. The legendary Hawaiian Ironman Triathlon was, according to Scott Tinley and Dr. Bill Phillips, born during the awards ceremony for the 1977 Oahu Perimeter Relay. The athletes in the relay were drawn from the ranks of swimmers and runners. They would argue about who were was the fittest athletes, swimmers or runners.

In the crowd was a Navy commander, John Collins, who got everyone's attention when he announced that, according to *Sports Illustrated,* a Belgian cyclist had the highest oxygen uptake of any athlete ever researched, so cyclists might be more physically fit than any other athlete. Mon Dieu! The issue must be settled as quickly as possible. Pride was on the line, and history was about to be made.

Commander Collins said the argument could be solved by utilizing the three endurance competitions that were already established on Hawaii: the Waikiki Rough Water Swim, which covered 2.4 miles; the Around Oahu Bike Race, which covered 115 miles; and the Honolulu Marathon, which was 26.219 miles in length.

Planning for the inaugural event began. Commander Collins observed that the start of the bike race could begin at the site of the Waikiki Rough Water Swim (where the swimming competition ended) and end at the Aloha Tower, which was the traditional start of the Honolulu Marathon. All that needed to be done was to cut three miles from the bike race and race counterclockwise around the island. No problem.

On February 18, 1978, each of the 15 men entered was handed three sheets of paper that listed the rules for the first-ever endurance race of this magnitude. Handwritten on the last page was a very motivating message from Commander Collins: "Swim 2.4 miles! Bike 112 miles! Run 26.2 miles! Brag for the rest of your life!"

At the start of the race, Commander Collins announced to the assembled athletes, "Whoever finishes first, we'll call him the Ironman." The rest, as they say, was history. Twelve athletes completed the race, but it was Gordon Haller, who finished in 11 hours, 46 minutes, and 58 seconds, that history records as the First Ironman! Twenty-two years later, in the 2000 Sydney Olympic Games, the triathlon competition made its debut. The Olympic Triathlon uses the following distances: 1500-meter swim, 40-kilometer bike race, and 10-kilometer run. In 1983, the Ironman was moved from Oahu to Kona, on the island of Hawaii. It remains the most grueling of the Ironman competitions.

For insights into the personal philosophy of one of the best endurance athletes of all time, read *Triathlon: A Personal History* (1998) by Scott Tinley. Tinley won the Ironman in 1982 and 1985 and is in the Ironman Hall of Fame.

In addition to marathon dancing and triathlon competitions, other endurance competitions that were popular from time to time in the early twentieth century were flagpole sitting contests and long-distance swims. The flagpole sitters would perch on top of a flagpole and stay there as long as they could. Curious birds could be very hazardous to the competitive flagpole sitter. Long-distance swimmers made their reputation by swimming across the open ocean. Sometimes called channel swimmers, these athletes would race across the English Channel between Britain and France. In America, channel swimmers would swim the Catalina Channel, a treacherous stretch of water 26 miles wide between Long Beach and Catalina Island off the coast of Southern California.

Surmounting seemingly insurmountable obstacles, testing the physical limitations of the human psyche and body, and conquering the elements seem to be the quest of the endurance athlete. History has recorded the epic accomplishments of endurance athletes. Philosophically, these extraordinary men and women find personal meaning and self-reflection in harsh physical activities that would overwhelm most of us. And yet, we, like the ancients, are absolutely captivated by their ability to exceed and excel where most of us would falter and fail. This will never change.

COLLEGE FOOTBALL

By the turn of the century, football had become the most popular sport on American college campuses. Many "big games" emerged during the early part of the twentieth century—for instance, Stanford–California, Army–Navy, and the Rose Bowl, first played in 1902. Football was clearly the "King of Intercollegiate Athletics," with eastern teams dominating teams from the South, Midwest, and West. Coaches became legends and national heroes (Figure 14-1). Among the greatest was

Figure 14-1
Clockwise from top left: Fielding Yost, Glenn "Pop" Warner, Amos Alonzo Stagg, and John Heisman—famous early football coaches.

Figure 14-2
Legendary community college football coach Dick Tucker of Orange Coast College won several national championships, coached countless All Americans and won more conference championships, than most coaches ever dreamed of.

Figure 14-3
Jim Thorpe, All-American.

Amos Alonzo Stagg, who was hired to coach at the University of Chicago in 1892 and who coached there for the next 49 years. Othersincluded Glenn "Pop" Warner, who coached Jim Thorpe at Carlisle Indian School and then coached at Stanford (Figures 14-2 and 14-3); John Heisman,for whom the Heisman Trophy is named, who coached at Georgia Institute of Technology; Fielding Yost, who coached at the University of Michigan; and the immortal Knute Rockne at Notre Dame (Figure 14-4).

The first reported game between two black colleges involved Biddle University, currently known as Johnson C. Smith, and Livingston College. The game was played on Thanksgiving Day in 1892. By 1894, Tuskegee Institute, Lincoln University of Pennsylvania, Atlanta University, and Howard University were playing intercollegiate football. College football programs began to integrate in the late 1800s. In 1890, Amherst's football team had two black players, William H. Lewis and William Tecumseh Sherman Jackson.

The growth of intercollegiate football did not go smoothly. In 1905, 18 football players were killed, and many others were seriously injured. The brutality of the game caused Columbia and

Figure 14-4
Knute Rockne, legendary football coach at Notre Dame.

Northwestern to drop the sport, and Stanford and California reverted to rugby. Mass formation plays,

the most infamous being the "flying wedge," made the game into a devastating contact sport that could maim and even kill.

Safety was not the only issue in college football, however, and many of the problems that developed as a consequence of football's popularity remain with us today. Beginning in the early 1900s, huge stadiums were constructed on college campuses, and football rapidly became a big business. Alumni and fans began demanding winning seasons from their schools, and because of the demand for victories and the large amounts of money involved, football became a victim of its own success. The recruiting of players included promises of money, cars, and other gifts. One result was "tramp" athletes who would play for one school and then attend another under an assumed name as long as the "price was right." Eligibility rules were nonexistent in some colleges and loosely enforced in others. Players began to miss classes due to road games and injuries, and faculty control was minimal. For instance, in 1905, Yale's outstanding athlete, James D. Hogan, was accused of accepting a suite in Vanderbilt Hall, free meals at the University Club, and an all-expenses-paid 10-day vacation to Cuba courtesy of the Yale Athletic Association. In addition, he held a job as a cigarette agent for the American Tobacco Company.[2] Scandals were familiar to college football fans a century ago, just as they are today. The accusations of the early 1900s, like most accusations made today, came from educators who believed that college football perverted the goals of higher education. In 1918, Shailer Mathews, dean of the Divinity School at the University of Chicago, stated:

> Football today is a social obsession—a boy killing, education-prostituting gladiatorial sport. It teaches virility and courage, but so does war. I do not know what should take its place, but the new game should not require the services of a physician, the maintenance of a hospital, and the celebration of funerals.[3]

As a result of the deaths and injuries that occurred in 1905, President Theodore Roosevelt met with administrators and coaches from the leading football universities to reform the game to make it safer. Walter Camp and other coaches who sought to change the game for the better attempted to control events, but it was Roosevelt, an avid football fan, who exerted enough pressure on the administrators to take the necessary steps for reform. Roosevelt's son had been injured while playing football, and so the president took a personal interest in this issue. Also in 1905, Henry McCracken, chancellor of New York University, called a meeting of college presidents and other interested parties to discuss whether college football should be allowed to exist.[4] Thirteen colleges were represented at the first December meeting; they agreed to keep football and to meet several weeks later to form a governing agency for the sport.

The second December meeting was attended by 62 colleges, and the result was the formation of the Intercollegiate Athletic Association of the United States, composed of 38 colleges. This organization was renamed the National Collegiate Athletic Association (NCAA) in 1910. The NCAA saw its role as an educational one, not taking responsibility for enforcement or administration as is the case today. Minimum eligibility rules were adopted by the 38 charter members, but there was no mechanism to enforce the rules. It was during this meeting that the new organization adopted a new rule that was to revolutionize the game of football: the forward pass.

Football grew at a slower rate during World War I. College officials were invited to attend a meeting in Washington convened by the NCAA to discuss the effect of the war on intercollegiate athletics. The secretary of war (today, defense) encouraged students to participate in college athletics, and the NCAA passed resolutions that encouraged colleges to continue to offer athletic programs for all men. In spite of the efforts of the NCAA and the secretary of war, however, sports were dropped by a number of colleges. In their place, colleges offered physical education programs that emphasized military drills and instructional programs such as the Reserve Officer Training Corps (ROTC).

Although intercollegiate athletic programs were dropped by some schools, the war had a generally positive effect on athletics and physical education. Men were strongly encouraged, even required, to participate in the programs offered

to prepare them for military service. Thus began a pattern that continued through the 1980s: During periods of war in which the United States was involved, athletic participation in the schools increased. The competitive atmosphere of athletics coupled with the physical and mental demands of training and competition were believed to prepare young men for the military. Football and wrestling in particular were believed to be of benefit to those who would be called upon to fight in a war.

PROFESSIONAL FOOTBALL

Professional football was played as far back as 1894, when the teams consisted of blue-collar workers and former college players from the mill towns of Ohio and Pennsylvania. During the mid-1890s and early 1900s, teams practiced a few times a week and played primarily on weekends. These games were not held in high regard, however, and professional football struggled to gain the legitimacy of professional baseball. Connie Mack, the legendary baseball manager, also managed the Philadelphia Athletics football team. Philadelphia's two major league baseball teams sponsored two professional football teams as rivals to the powerful Pittsburgh football team, and these three teams were the most financially sound. If an athlete was fortunate enough to sign with one of these teams, he could expect to earn between $400 and $1200 per season. Smaller teams usually paid less.

The popularity of college football and the lure of thousands of paying spectators ushered in the era of organized professional football in 1920. At Ralph Hays's Hupmobile automobile dealership in Canton, Ohio, representatives from 11 football clubs gathered on September 17, 1920, to form the American Professional Football Association (APFA).[5] The APFA's charter teams in 1920 paid $100 for a franchise and agreed not to recruit college athletes who still had eligibility remaining or to attempt to induce players who were bound by contract to other teams in the APFA. The APFA's first president was Jim Thorpe, at that time America's greatest all-around athlete (Figure 14-5). He oversaw the teams that were the first of modern

Figure 14-5
Jim Thorpe signing contract with the New York Giants, 1913.

professional football: The Chicago Cardinals, Massillon Tigers, Dayton Triangles, Cleveland Indians, Rock Island Independents, Akron Pros, Canton Bulldogs, and Rochester Kodaks, as well as teams from Decatur, Illinois, and Muncie, Indiana.

In Jim Thorpe, the APFA had a "big name" and public recognition, but Thorpe's administrative ability was minimal at best.[6] Several of the clubs that started the APFA were in financial difficulty and eventually folded. Joe F. Carr of Columbus, Ohio, became the new president; he changed the name of the APFA to the National Football League (NFL) and lowered the franchise fee to $50. Teams from Muncie, Massillon, and Hammond withdrew, replaced with franchises in Green Bay, Detroit, Buffalo, Cincinnati, and Columbus. The Decatur team was sold to a young man by the name of George E. Halas, who changed the name of Staley Athletic Club to the Chicago Bears in 1922.

Interestingly, in the 1920s, most college coaches discouraged their players from turning pro after graduation. During its formative years, professional football struggled to gain the respect of the public; college football remained much more popular. Two events occurred in 1925 that helped professional football gain the same respect as college football. First, Tim Mara formed the New York Giants and publicized the team in the newspapers of New York City. Football fans were treated to exciting accounts of professional football teams in the biggest media center in the country. Second, and perhaps more important, Harold "Red" Grange, the Galloping Ghost from the University of Illinois, signed with the Chicago Bears. His status was such that it gave the NFL an aura of legitimacy, and fans turned out by the tens of thousands to see him run.

Professional baseball and college football remained more popular than professional football through the end of World War II. After the war, however, professional football enjoyed enormous growth, with the establishment of the American Football League (AFL) in 1960, the inception of the Super Bowl in 1966, and the eventual merger of the AFL and NFL in 1970. The World Football League (WFL) and the United States Football League (USFL) attempted to compete with the NFL for fans and money, but both efforts were short-lived. The WFL played one season, 1974, and the USFL lasted three seasons, from 1983 to 1985. Most recently, football has moved indoors, with arena football, and to Europe, with the World League of American Football (WLAF) in 1991.

The WLAF had 10 teams. In 1993 and 1994 the WLAF shut down, but in 1995 the WLAF reinvented itself and resumed play as NFL Europa. The new league had six teams, five of which were German. Football in Europe never attracted much of a following, and in 2007 the NFL shut down the league.

The Pro Football Hall of Fame in Canton, Ohio, identifies Rube Marshall (1880–1958) and Fritz Pollard (1894–1896) as the first African-Americans to play in the NFL. Marshall was an end with the Rock Island Independents, and Pollard was a halfback with the Akron Pros. In 1922, Akron and Rock

Island joined the newly formed NFL. Less publicized than Jackie Robinson, the first black player in Major League Baseball, these men faced the same discrimination that Robinson endured during his professional career. That these two athletes are not as well known as Robinson for breaking a color barrier in sports tells us much about the popularity of football relative to baseball. Clearly, football was not the national game it would become years later.

BASEBALL

America's "pastime," otherwise known as baseball, was in full swing during the twentieth century. Professional baseball became hugely popular. In fact, baseball's popularity was so extensive that highly organized teams and leagues were available for just about every young male who wanted to play. There were teams for youngsters as young as eight years old. Almost every community park, grammar school, middle school, and high school had baseball diamonds. Colleges and universities fielded teams, as did various businesses, which provided uniforms and equipment for their employees. However, baseball was not without its problems and, in general, reflected societal trends.

Racism was a significant social issue in twentieth-century America, and baseball was hardly immune to the problem. There was baseball for the white population of America and baseball for African-Americans. Major League Baseball was represented by the American League and the National League, which, prior to 1947, were exclusively white. African-Americans played in the Negro Leagues until 1947 when a phenomenal athlete from Pasadena, California, named Jackie Roosevelt Robinson, was signed to a major league contract by Branch Rickey and the "color line" in baseball was broken at last. Rickey owned the Brooklyn Dodgers, who would later relocate to Los Angeles. He had worked hard to integrate Major League Baseball and had been on the lookout for an African-American athlete who would lead the way for baseball's integration. Robinson, a stellar football and baseball player from UCLA, was

up to the task. He was a man of character and integrity who endured racial taunting and threats to his life after he signed to play for the Dodgers. In 1949, he was named the Dodgers' "most valuable player," and he later starred in a film about his life. He paved the way for thousands of black and Hispanic athletes to play professional sports. Perhaps more importantly, Jackie Robinson's exploits on the baseball diamond provided a catalyst to integrate sports.

In contrast to the story of Jackie Robinson breaking the color line in Major League Baseball, historians seldom mention Eddie Kelp, a white man who signed with the Cleveland Buckeyes of the Negro League. Kelp grew up in Erie, Pennsylvania, where he played baseball on integrated teams and enjoyed the experience. He was not a good enough pitcher to play in the major leagues or the minor leagues. However, Ernest P. Wright, owner of the Buckeyes, signed Kelp in 1946 after Kelp played against the Buckeyes as a member of an opposing all-star team. Like Robinson, Kelp became the object of racial taunting. In Birmingham, Alabama, in 1946, police told Kelp that white men were not allowed to play baseball with Negroes. He was ordered to change his clothes and sit in the section reserved for whites. Kelp did not play very long in the Negro Leagues. He became an alcoholic and a petty criminal, and spent time in jail, where he pitched for the prison team.

BASKETBALL

Springfield College, originally established as the Young Men's Christian Association (YMCA) Training School, enjoys a proud tradition of physical education excellence and athletic success. Perhaps the most noteworthy achievement to have occurred at Springfield was the invention of basketball by Dr. James A. Naismith (Figure 14-6). In 1891, the director of the gymnasium, Dr. Luther Gulick, asked Naismith to develop a game that could be played indoors during the winter. At this time, winter athletic activities mainly involved formal gymnastics and calisthenics, pursuits that were considered by the participants to be very boring.

Figure 14-6
Dr. James Naismith, inventor of basketball.

Gulick hoped to develop a game that would be more fun and therefore increase participation.

It is difficult to say for certain where Naismith came up with the concept of basketball, although he may have been aware of the early games played by American Indians and Central Americans between A.D. 1000 and 1500. Naismith tried modified versions of lacrosse, water polo, field hockey, soccer, rugby, and football, but he was apparently unsuccessful. He finally devised a game incorporating a soccer ball and two goals, often described as peach baskets, placed ten feet high at opposite ends of the gym floor. Participants were supposed to pass the ball back and forth and ultimately to "score" by tossing the ball into one of the baskets.

On December 21, 1891, Naismith and future football legend Amos Alonzo Stagg faced each other in what was probably the first basketball game, no doubt wondering how successful the new game would be. Naismith need not have worried. The game was an instant success, and news spread

quickly. As the traveling ambassador for basketball, Naismith introduced the game in northeastern cities, and soon the YMCAs became the "hotbed" of basketball. High schools and colleges adopted the sport, and women played the game as well. Senda Berenson, a physical education teacher at Smith College, modified the game for her students (Figure 14-7). She reconfigured the rules and other aspects of the game to conform with the prevailing nineteenth-century medical, psychological, and social concepts of women's physical capabilities.[7] Basketball played by men was a rough-and-tumble sport, not at all consistent with the appropriate behavior of women athletes of that era. As a result, basketball rules for women varied from place to place and tended to be much more cooperative than competitive. For instance, often women's rules did not allow players to travel the full length of the court. Consequently, passing was emphasized over dribbling.

Leading women physical educators and coaches convened in 1899 at Springfield, Massachusetts, to develop a uniform set of basketball rules, 16 years before the men had a similar meeting. It was decided that the women would use the current YMCA rules for men's basketball with several modifications: (1) The court was divided into three equal zones; (2) stealing the ball from an opposing player was prohibited; and (3) teams were to consist of no fewer than six players and no more than nine. This last rule was based on the belief that women could not play at the pace or intensity of their male counterparts, and it also allowed more athletes to play the game. In 1928, ten states held state basketball tournaments for high-school girls. These tournaments, however, operated outside the control of women physical educators. Most women were opposed to interscholastic competition for girls and instead favored large-scale participation in intramurals.

The men were no better off with regard to rules. By 1900, the only rule that leading men's coaches could agree on was that each team should consist of five players. Beyond that, colleges had one set of rules, the YMCA had another, and the

Figure 14-7
Senda Berenson tossing up ball to start a game, 1904.

Amateur Athletic Union (AAU) had still another. In 1915, the Joint Basketball Committee was established with representatives from the NCAA, AAU, and YMCA to reach agreement on uniform rules. However, the professional teams that appeared during the early part of the twentieth century had their own rules, and still do.

High schools in Denver formed the first basketball league in 1896, and five years later, in 1901, eastern colleges formed the Intercollegiate League. By the start of World War I, basketball was second only to football in popularity in the high schools and colleges where the game was played. The American military introduced the game around the world, and missionaries such as Robert Gailey introduced the game to China in 1898. In Indiana, Kentucky, Kansas, and New York City, basketball enjoyed enormous popularity in the schools and on the playgrounds. However, only in the era of World War I did basketball begin to receive widespread public attention.[8]

BOXING

In the early twentieth century, boxing was outlawed in many states. Still, boxing was a very popular sport. When particular states passed laws that made boxing illegal, it was moved to remote locations, beyond the reach of the law. Large sums were bet, and fortunes were made and lost. In those states where boxing was legal, it drew huge crowds. Boxing was a "manly" sport that required courage, brute strength, athletic skill, and an ability to withstand physical punishment and the accompanying pain.

America has been home to some of the world's greatest professional pugilists—Jack Dempsey, Rocky Marciano, Sugar Ray Leonard, Mike Tyson, Oscar De La Hoya, Joe Frazier, George Foreman, and Cassius Clay (who later changed his name to Muhammad Ali), to name a few. However, as good as these boxers were, they would not have been able to go "toe to toe" and beat perhaps the greatest boxer ever, Jack Johnson, born in 1879 in Galveston, Texas.

Johnson was barred from fighting the white champion boxers for a number of years. However, when he was permitted to fight whites, he pummeled them! Johnson became the first African-American heavyweight champion, reigning from 1908 to 1914. He also lived quite a memorable life, pretending for the most part that racism simply did not apply to him. His personal life was the stuff of tabloid journalism. He was fond of fine clothes, good liquor, fast cars, and white women. He married three times; all three women were white. In the early twentieth century, this kind of behavior from a black man was unthinkable for white Americans. Johnson didn't care. He was smart, handsome, athletic, and perhaps the best prizefighter in history.

White America longed for a white champion, a boxer who could beat the unbeatable Jack Johnson. The former champion, "Gentleman" Jim Jeffries, was persuaded to come out of retirement in 1910 and fight Johnson. It took 15 rounds before Johnson knocked Jeffries out. Shortly thereafter, race riots broke out across America. Meanwhile, white America could not accept that Jack Johnson had defeated the Great White Hope. Something had to be done to put this man in his place. In 1912, Congress passed the Mann Act, which was aimed at stopping the transportation of women across state lines for purposes of prostitution. The U.S. Justice Department charged Johnson with violating the Mann Act in 1913. The jury deliberated for approximately two hours and found Johnson guilty. The jurors ignored the fact that the transgression that Johnson was accused of took place *before* the Mann Act became law and the fact that the woman he took across state lines was his wife! No matter, she was white, and that was the issue, the only issue.

Johnson fled to Canada and then went to live in Europe. In 1915, after 26 rounds, Johnson lost the heavyweight title to American Jess Willard in Havana, Cuba. By 1920, Johnson was homesick and wanted to come back home to America. He agreed to surrender. After crossing back into the United States from Tijuana, Mexico, he was met by federal authorities, who promptly put him on a train headed to the federal prison at Leavenworth, Kansas. A crowd of over 500 fans met Johnson's train at Leavenworth. He served nine months in prison. After his release, he fought in a few small towns and made appearances in traveling carnival shows for a living. He died in 1946, at the age of 67, in an automobile accident.

VOLLEYBALL

During a lunch hour in 1895, a group of businessmen gathered at the Holyoke, Massachusetts, YMCA under the watchful eye of William Morgan. Perhaps sensing a need to provide a recreational activity less demanding than basketball, he developed the game of volleyball (originally called "minonette"). Morgan believed that volleyball would fulfill the needs of his clientele. Initially, the game incorporated the entire gymnasium and used a basketball bladder that was hit over a 6-foot, 6-inch tennis net. Each game was composed of nine innings, and the size of each team depended on who showed up to play. According to the first published account of the game, in July 1896,

> The ball was volleyed back and forth without hitting the floor or the net. A player could dribble by bouncing the ball on the hand while moving but could not go within four feet of the net. A serve had to go at least ten feet and could be helped over the net by a player of the same side.[9]

Volleyball, although popular with the YMCA members, had a difficult time gaining acceptance in school physical education curricula because, as with basketball, it was believed that the sport did little to develop the upper body. In addition, participation in volleyball did not lend itself to a scientific knowledge base in the way that formal gymnastics did. The result was that volleyball was opposed by those physical educators who advocated the regulated and "scientifically established benefits" of gymnastics.

Volleyball was promoted by the YMCA and, like basketball, was adopted by the American military. Although women's volleyball currently is one of the most popular sports in high schools and on college campuses, the game was not embraced by women in its early stages. Volleyball was initially promoted as a men's game, and it was not until later that the YWCA and college women played the game.

WOMEN AND SPORT

Athletic activities for girls and women during the latter part of the nineteenth century and much of the twentieth century reflected the beliefs and biases of many Americans regarding play and sport. One of the arguments used by early sport advocates was that sport built manliness—which meant that women should have nothing to do with it! Additionally, the early twentieth century witnessed a transition from gymnastics to athletics and dance, with dance becoming a popular and integral component of women's physical education programs, especially in the colleges. The efforts of Melvin Ballou Gilbert, Luther Gulick, Elizabeth Burchenal, Isadora Duncan, and others led to dance being a part of the physical education curriculum. Clog, tap, aesthetic, folk, natural, modern, social, and square dancing became important offerings in physical education departments.

Several women's colleges provided athletic programs for their students. In 1901, Vassar College began playing field hockey, and Wellesley College played lacrosse. Smith College promoted volleyball in 1907, and at Bryn Mawr, students played cricket, soccer, and water polo.[10] Coeducational colleges were slow to provide athletic opportunities for women, and high schools were slower still in providing conventional physical education and athletic programs. Much of the problem had to do with the shortage of qualified teachers.

Illinois became a leader in the promotion of girls' athletics when it established the State League of Girls' Athletic Associations in the early 1920s. The association's purpose was to "promote programs of athletics for all girls to offset the undesirable program of interschool athletics maintained in many schools by male coaches for the highly skilled few."[11] Colorado and Nebraska, following the lead of Illinois, formed similar associations. These early organizations promoted and sponsored intramural programs, encouraging mass participation as opposed to participation by a few highly skilled athletes. Awards were given for achievement and participation.

Despite the efforts by women physical educators to discourage the competitive environment of interscholastic athletics, men promoted championships for girls' high-school basketball teams that were highly successful. In 1928, the Ohio tournament had 5500 girls entered, 4000 girls entered in Texas, and 2000 girls participated in the Oklahoma tournament.

Blanche M. Trilling (1876–1964) and Mabel Lee both graduated from the Boston Normal School of Athletics operated by Dr. Dudley Sargent. These two women, along with Agnes Wayman, charted the initial course of physical education and athletic competition for women. However, it was Trilling who provided much of the leadership for women's athletics during its formative years (Figure 14-8). In her position as director of physical education for women at the University of Wisconsin, she was able to convene a meeting in 1917 to discuss athletic participation for women. It was during this meeting that the Athletic Conference of American College Women was formed. From the beginning, the organization denounced intercollegiate athletics for women and vigorously promoted intramural programs in the high schools and colleges.

As women became more interested and involved in sports, William H. Burdick, president of the American Physical Education Association, established the National Committee on Women's Sports in 1917 to determine rules and standards for athletic participation for women and girls. The general philosophy of women's athletics during the early twentieth century was "a sport for every girl and every girl in a sport." During the 1920 meeting of the Conference of College Directors of Physical Education, members justified their

Figure 14-8
Mabel Lee, Blanche Trilling, and Agnes Wayman.

opposition to intercollegiate athletics for women for the following reasons: (1) it led to professionalism; (2) it emphasized the training of the few at the expense of many; (3) it was unsocial; (4) it required professional coaches; (5) physical educators, both men and women, found the results undesirable; (6) it was expensive; and (7) it led to "nerve fatigue."[12]

The control of women's athletics was fought over by the AAU, the National Amateur Athletic Federation (NAAF), the National Federation of High School Athletic Associations (NFHSAA), and the State Leagues of High School Girls' Athletic Association. Eventually, the AAU became the most influential organization for girls' and women's sports. Women physical educators, however, resisted AAU efforts to control and coordinate women's athletics. In 1922, the first Women's Olympic Games were to take place in Paris, and the AAU had every intention of sending a track-and-field team. However, the AAU did not have jurisdiction over track and field and was opposed by many women physical educators. The AAU ignored pleas from women physical education professionals and sent the team to Paris under the direction of Dr. Harry Stewart.

During this time, members of the NAAF asked the wife of President Herbert Hoover to assist them in organizing and promoting women's participation in competitive athletics. Mrs. Hoover convened a conference in 1923 to discuss the proposal and invited leading men and women to participate. Sixteen resolutions were adopted, among them Resolution IV, indicative of the NAAF position on women in athletics:

> IV. Resolved, in order to develop these qualities which shall fit girls and women to perform their functions as citizens:
>
> (a) that their athletics be conducted with that end definitely in view and be protected from exploitation for the enjoyment of the spectator, the athletic reputation, or the commercial advantage of any school or other organization.
>
> (b) that schools and other organizations shall stress enjoyment of the sport and the development of sportsmanship and minimize the emphasis which is at present laid upon individual accomplishment and the winning of championships.[13]

It was not until the 1932 Olympic Games in Los Angeles, when the legendary Mildred "Babe" Didrikson Zaharias won two gold medals and one silver in track and field, that the critics of women's athletics were silenced (Figure 14-9). Didrikson later went on to become a stellar golfer who won every major golf tournament she competed in between 1940 and 1950. She was honored once again in 1950 as the greatest woman athlete in the first half of the twentieth century.

Most of the critics of competitive sports for women, among them women physical educators,

Figure 14-9
Mildred "Babe" Didrikson on her way to victory in the 80-meter hurdle at the 1932 Olympic Games.

believed that women were frail and physiologically unsuited for intense athletic competition. The opinions of these educators, however, were based on the best evidence available at the time. It was only after the basis for these opinions was undermined by the continued success of women athletes like Didrikson that women began to enjoy more opportunities for participation. Still, women physical educators opposed the participation of women in the 1928 and 1932 Olympics.

The NAAF Women's Division and Committee on Women's Athletics adhered to a philosophy that guarded against exploitation and stressed the availability of a broad sports program, medical supervision, and women coaches. They continued to oppose intercollegiate athletics competition for women and collected data and published articles to support their position. Approved and appropriate athletics for college women took the form of play days or sports days, popular with women students who attended Stanford and the university of California, Berkeley

during the 1920s. Informal games such as archery, swimming and running relays, and ball games were the norm, and the more participants, the better! The event was more a social affair than a competitive experience. More often than not, invitations were sent out to potential spectators, and men were discouraged from attending.

The decade preceding World War II was a significant era for women's athletics. The Committee on Women's Athletics reorganized in 1932 into the National Section on Women's Athletics (NSWA), which consisted of a number of sports committees that oversaw rule changes, rated officials, provided educational information, and published the results of athletic contests. In 1936, women's basketball was modified from the three-court configuration to the current two-court (meaning frontcourt and backcourt) configuration. Four major trends in women's physical education and sport occurred during this time: (1) an increase in opportunities in sport for women and an increase in the number of participants, (2) a growing use of research as a basis for planning and improving sport and athletic programs, (3) a greater acceptance in society of the concept of women in sport, and (4) a reexamination of the position limiting intercollegiate athletics for women.[14]

The gradual acceptance of high-level athletic competition for women was facilitated by the performances of Babe Didrikson Zaharias, but compared with the opportunities available to their male counterparts, opportunities for competitive athletics for girls and women were limited. The prevailing attitude of the era continued to be influenced by conservative thinking, which held that sports developed character and helped turn boys into men. Consequently, girls and women were expected to refrain from participating in sports that might detract from their femininity. Interest in women's athletics rose during the Olympic Games, but women continued to take a backseat to men regarding financial support, training opportunities, and press coverage.

During the 1950s, high schools provided opportunities for participation through the efforts of the Girls' Athletic Association (GAA). Colleges continued to offer play days and began to schedule contests against other institutions in field hockey, fencing, basketball, volleyball, softball, gymnastics, swimming, and track and field. The atmosphere was as much social as competitive, and practice and preparation for these athletic competitions were not at the same level of intensity as for men's teams, with one exception.

The Flying Queens of Wayland Baptist University

Long before Baylor, UConn, Tennessee, and Stanford played in front of sold out arenas and national television audiences, Wayland Baptist University in Plainview, Texas featured a women's basketball team that at one point won 131 straight games!

Dwight Eisenhower was President and women's basketball on some college campuses played under the auspices of the AAU. Rules required six women on each team. Players could dribble the ball but only three times before they had to pass or shoot. Teams employed "rovers" who would have been called forwards in the men's game. Only rovers could cross mid court, the other four could not. Rules were very restrictive because it was thought that women were not capable of the up tempo, high-intensity play that was the staple for men.

As a strict conservative university, women could not wear shorts on campus. However, the university encouraged women to play sports and more importantly, to be competitive and successful. Wayland Baptist was very progressive in this respect and one other; the president of the university, J .W. Marshall, integrated the university in 1951, three years before the U.S. Supreme Court ruled in the matter of Brown vs. Board of Education.

During this era, AAU rules were very lenient. In 1948, Wayland's president approached Claude Hutcherson, a rancher and successful businessman, and asked him to provide transportation to Mexico for the women's basketball team where the team had games scheduled. It just so happened that Mr. Hutcherson owned a flying service consisting of a fleet of Beecheraft Bonanzas. He flew the team down to Mexico and immediately became the team's biggest booster. While the men's teams traveled in buses the Flying Queens traveled in private planes, were on athletic scholarships, had their own hair stylists, stayed at the best hotels, dined in fine restaurants, and were attired in matching traveling and playing uniforms that put the men's team to shame.

While in Nashville for a tournament, the Flying Queens met the legendary Harlem Globetrotters who taught the women how to spin the basketball on the tip of their fingers and to dribble behind their legs and behind their backs. Upon their return to the university the women choreographed a new warm-up routine that they learned from the Globetrotters. It was a huge hit and fans starting showing up for the warm-ups as well as the games.

Decades before the AIAW and NCAA sponsored national championships for women's basketball, the women's basketball team from tiny Wayland Baptist won 10 AAU Championships and from 1953 to 1958, won 131 straight games. Sports dynasties come and go and after a while, Wayland Baptist no longer ruled the world of women's basketball, but they sure had a sweet ride while it lasted![15]

TITLE IX, AIAW AND THE NCAA

In 1957, there was enough interest in women's intercollegiate sports to establish a committee to investigate athletic competition. The National Section on Girls' and Women's Sports (NSGWS) was formed under the auspices of the American Alliance for Health, Physical Education, and Recreation (AAHPER). This organization, after several name changes, evolved into the Association for Intercollegiate Athletics for Women (AIAW) in 1971.

The AIAW was administered by women for women athletes, and from the beginning, it pledged to avoid the "evils" of men's athletics. Initially, the AIAW was opposed to awarding athletic scholarships, recruiting gifted athletes, and the win-at-all-costs philosophy that seemed to dominate men's intercollegiate athletics. The AIAW sponsored championships in gymnastics (1969), track and field (1969), volleyball (1970), badminton (1970), and basketball (1972). For a team to qualify for the AIAW tournament or championship, the college was required to hold AIAW membership and abide by organization rules. Membership in the AIAW grew steadily and by the late 1970s had reached 970 colleges and universities.[16] On July 1, 1979, the AIAW broke away from the auspices of the NSGWS and the AAHPER.

If there was one thing that changed the nature of women's athletics forever, it was Title IX of the Educational Amendments Act of 1972. Title IX was an antidiscrimination provision of a federal statute of the Civil Rights Act of 1964. Brought about by the efforts of the Department of Health, Education, and Welfare (HEW), Title IX contained language that specifically addressed physical education and athletics. All physical education and athletic teams in high schools and colleges were open to members of both sexes, with the exception of contact sports. Equal opportunity had to be provided for facilities, coaching, and financial support. If an institution that received federal money failed to provide equal opportunity, then those monies would be withheld.

The NCAA filed suit against the provisions of Title IX as they related to athletics because of the belief that the money required to fund women's athletic programs on par with the men's would threaten the financial stability of intercollegiate athletics. The NCAA's suit was not successful, and athletic departments in colleges and universities across the nation were forced to fund women's athletic programs at the same level as men's relative to coaching, facilities access, travel, scholarships, and so on. In retrospect, Title IX has had a greater impact on sport in the educational arena than any other federal legislation.

After losing its suit, the NCAA decided that it would be in its best interests to control women's athletics. The NCAA and the AIAW entered into discussions about the governance of women's athletics but met with little success. The NCAA decided to hold championships for women and enticed membership in the NCAA with financial support and incentives that the AIAW was unable to match. In 1975, the NCAA proposed national championships for women and did so again in 1978 and 1979. The AIAW filed an antitrust suit against the NCAA over the control of women's intercollegiate athletics in 1981, the same year that the NCAA began offering women's championships. The NCAA prevailed in court, and the AIAW disbanded in 1983. It is ironic that in 1964, the NCAA had gone on record stating, "Acting upon the request of female college sports leaders, the NCAA Executive Committee amended the executive regulation to limit participation in NCAA championships to undergraduate male students."[17]

Women in the twenty-first century enjoy many more opportunities in sport than their counterparts prior to 1970. Many women's programs in today's high schools and colleges are similar to those for men. Indeed, the similarities are striking in that the problems found in men's sports are also manifest in women's sports. The next battles to be fought would seem to deal less with discrimination than with individual athlete abuse, but this remains to be seen.

The Legacy of the Greatest Woman's Basketball Coach of All Time: Pat Summitt

On Wednesday, April 18, 2012, the greatest women's basketball coach of all time, Pat Summitt of the University of Tennessee (UT), announced her retirement eight months after she was diagnosed with early onset dementia. to become head coach emeritus.

For thirty eight years, Coach Summitt was the Head Coach of the Lady Vols where she won more NCAA games than anyone in history. She was initially hired as a graduate assistant at UT in 1974 where she would serve as the assistant women's basketball coach, work on her Masters Degree in Physical Education and taught classes. A few weeks later, the head of the Women's physical education, Department, Dr. Helen B. Watson, called Summitt to announce that the head coach was taking a sabbatical and Assistant Coach Summitt became Head Coach Summitt. In 1974, she was a 22 year old Head Coach who up to that point, had never written a practice plan, run a practice, or made up a schedule. To make matters more interesting, she was the same age as some of the seniors on the team!

During her first season, the Lady Vols won 16 games while loosing 8. The second season her team posted a 16 and 11 record which is the last time the Lady Vols won fewer than 20 games per season. And yes, Coach Summitt completed her Masters Degree while coaching the Lady Vols.

In 1976, Coach Summitt was named Co-captain of the 1976 United States Olympic team where she helped the American women win a silver medal in Montreal. In 1982, she was named head coach of the women's Olympic Team and she led the American women to a gold medal finish in Los Angeles.

A fantastic teacher, recruiter, and mom, Coach Summitt won 8 NCAA national championships, made 18 Final Four appearances and in 2000 was named Naismith Coach of the Century. Her overall record is 1,098 wins and 208 losses. It must be noted that her teams won 32 combine Southeastern Conference championships. She was the first women's coach to earn over a million dollars a year. She has a history of philanthropy. In 2008 she made a $600,000 gift split between UT, Knoxville and UT, Martin where she was an undergraduate physical education major and star basketball player.

She trails UCLA's legendary basketball coach, John Wooden, in the number of NCAA Championships. Wooden had 10 NCAA championships, Summitt has 8. However, Summitt has more Final Four appearances (18) than Wooden who had 11.

In her new capacity as head coach emeritus, Coach Summitt will stay very busy. She will assist in recruiting, evaluate practices, sit in on staff meetings, and advise the Southeastern Conference on all things pertaining to women's basketball. Coach Summitt's replacement is her long-time assistant of 27 years, Holly Warlick.

On April 19, 2012 President Barak Obama (a huge basketball fan and former player) announced that Pat Summitt would be awarded the Presidential Medal of Freedom. Pat Summitt is the personification of *arete* and an inspiration to us all.

SUMMARY

Most of the sports that developed in the nineteenth century continue to do well in the twenty-first century. The process of modernization can explain many of the changes that occurred in each sport as it was developed, and this pattern of change helps us understand, and even predict, how these sports will be organized. Yet not all activities follow this pattern, and no one can say whether sport is better because of these changes.

For instance, the new sport of triathlons, developed in San Diego in the 1970s, began as a premodern sport. Races were informal, there was no organizational structure, race distances and rules varied between races, and the sport was unheard of outside of San Diego. By the early 1980s, triathlons were fully modern, with the United States Triathlon Federation sanctioning and organizing races. Standard distances had evolved, athletes were specialized as to distance, the races were highly competitive, statistics and records were kept, and results were nationally and internationally communicated. Yet there are those who long for the simpler days of triathlons, when they could organize a race and not worry about insurance or traffic control. They knew all the competitors, and winning and losing were not as important as having fun swimming, riding, and running. Which is better? Who can say?

One pattern does seem to be evident, however. There are more opportunities to participate in a wider variety of sports and playful activities than ever before, and there is no indication that this trend will stop. Americans seem to be more comfortable with their bodies with respect to sport and play than at any time since the 1500s. One even hears arguments that too much time is spent on these types of activities. Whether this is true depends on one's perspective. What seems clear is that in one form or another, Americans will continue to participate in sport and play for the foreseeable future.

DISCUSSION QUESTIONS

1. How is sport in the twenty-first century different from that in the nineteenth century? Is the difference one of degree or one of type?

2. During World War I, when a number of colleges dropped sports, what replaced sports? Was this a good idea?

3. To what do you attribute the popularity of basketball for both men and women?

4. Why were women traditionally discouraged from serious athletic competition?

5. To what extent did Title IX influence the evolution of athletic competition at the high-school and college level? Did male coaches and athletic directors initially support Title IX? Why or why not?

6. To what extent twenty-first century women basketball players at the college level have access to the same benefits that the flyings queens of Wayland Baptist enjoyed in the 1950's?

7. What are some examples of the modernization of sport in the twenty-first century? What are some activities that represent premodern sport? Which is better?

8. How did women's sports evolve in the twentieth century? Will these changes continue, and if so, what will sport look like for women in the years to come?

9. What contributions did the YMCA make to sport?

10. What impact did Babe Didrikson Zaharias have on women's athletic participation?

11. What role did Jim Thorpe play with regard to the development of professional football?

12. Will extreme sports become more "extreme" in the twenty-first century?

13. Is there a twenty-first century version of Wayland Baptist in women's basketball?

14. Research coach Pat Summitt. Why do you think she is such a successful coach and role model?

INTERNET RESOURCES

Native Americans: Jim Thorpe
www.nativeamericans.com/JimThorpe.htm
Gives a brief biographical sketch of Jim Thorpe.

America's Library: Jim Thorpe
www.americaslibrary.gov/cgi-bin/page.cgi/jb/gilded/thorpe_1
Includes photos and information about Jim Thorpe.

Negro Leagues Baseball Museum
www.nlbm.com
Provides expert research and is an excellent resource for all information essential to learning about the athletes and social climate during the era of the Negro Leagues.

Hoop Hall: History
www.hoophall.com/history/history.htm
Is a good source of information on the history of basketball, James Naismith, and statistics for NBA and NCAA championships.

USA Basketball History
www.usabasketball.com/history/usab_history.html
Recounts the history of basketball, tells how the U.S. Olympic team is selected, lists rules, and discusses men's and women's basketball programs.

Women's National Basketball Association
www.WNBA.com

National Basketball Association
www.NBA.com

African Americans in the Sports Arena
www.liu.edu/cwis/cwp/library/aaitsa.htm
Good source of historical information as well as current information about African-American athletes.

History of Women's Basketball
www.womensbasketballmuseum.com
Gives information about the history of women's basketball.

Volleyball Worldwide: History of Volleyball
www.volleyball.org/history.html
Gives an excellent chronological history of volleyball.

Women's Sports History Resources
www.northnet.org/stlawrenceaauw/sports.htm
Provides information on women's historical
involvement in sports, with great links.

Women's Sports Foundation
www.womenssportsfoundation.org
Is the home page for the Women's Sports Foundation;
includes historical articles.

Babe Didrikson Zaharias
www.famoustexans.com/babedidrikson.htm
Gives a biographical sketch of Mildred "Babe"
Didrikson Zaharias.

Black Athlete Sports Network
www.blackathlete.com
Includes stories, histories, articles, and related
information about African-American male and female
athletes and coaches.

Visit the *History and Philosophy of Sport and Physical
Education* Online Learning Center (www.mhhe.com/
mechikoff6e) for additional information and study tools.

Suggestions for Further Reading

Betts, J. R. *America's Sporting Heritage: 1850–1950.* Reading, MA: Addison-Wesley, 1974.

Lewis, G. "Theodore Roosevelt's Role in the 1905 Football Controversy." *Research Quarterly* 40 (1969): 717–24.

Miller, P. B., and D. K. Wiggins. *Sport and the Color Line: Black Athletes and Race Relations in Twentieth-Century America.* New York: Routledge, 2004.

Smith, R. A. "Harvard and Columbia and a Reconsideration of the 1905–1906 Football Crisis." *Journal of Sport History* 8 (Winter 1981): 5–19.

Spears, B., and R. A. Swanson. *History of Sport and Physical Education,* 3rd ed. Dubuque, IA: Wm. C. Brown, 1983.

Ward, Geoffrey C. *Unforgivable Blackness: The Rise and Fall of Jack Johnson.* New York: Knopf, 2005.

Notes

1. Michael Harrington, The Politics at God's Funeral (New York: Holt, Rinehart & Winston, 1983).
2. John R. Betts, America's Sporting Heritage: 1850–1950 (Reading, MA: Addison-Wesley, 1974), 127.
3. Shailer Mathews, The Nation XCV (August 24, 1918): 198.
4. Guy Lewis, "Theodore Roosevelt's Role in the 1905 Football Controversy," Research Quarterly 40 (1969): 717–24. See also Ronald A. Smith, "Harvard and Columbia and a Reconsideration of the 1905–1906 Football Crisis," Journal of Sport History 8 (Winter 1981): 5–19.
5. Betty Spears and Richard A. Swanson, History of Sport and Physical Education, 3rd ed. (Dubuque, IA: Wm. C. Brown, 1983).
6. Ibid.
7. Ibid., 176.
8. Betts, America's Sporting Heritage, 132.
9. Deobold Van Dalen, Elmer Mitchell, and Bruce Bennett, "Physical Education in the Middle Ages and Early Modern Times," in A World History of Physical Education (Englewood Cliffs, NJ: Prentice-Hall, 1953), 421.
10. Mabel Lee, A History of Physical Education and Sports in the USA (New York: John Wiley, 1983), 58.
11. Ibid., 146.
12. Bulletin (1920–21), Mary Hemenway Alumnae Association, Department of Hygiene, 48. Wellesley College Archives, Wellesley, Mass.
13. Alice A. Sefton, The Women's Division, National Amateur Athletic Foundation (Stanford, CA: Stanford University Press, 1941), 77–79.
14. Ibid., 245.
15. Jere' Longman, "Before Uconn there was Wayland," The New York Times, December 19, 2010, Sports Sunday, pgs. 1–60.
16. Lee, History of Physical Education and Sports, 313.
17. Ibid., 312.

SECTION

V A Social and Political History of the Modern Olympic Games

C H A P T E R # 15

Pioneers and Progress: 1896–1936

O B J E C T I V E S

Upon completing this chapter, you will be able to:

- Understand the principles of Olympism as an agent of social change.
- Identify some of the goals that the Olympic Games hope to achieve.
- Discuss the international impact of the Olympic Games.
- Recognize the International Olympic Committee as the governing body of all things Olympic as it relates to sport.
- Understand that prior to the first modern Olympic Games in Athens in 1896, the Greeks, as a result of the patronage of the Zappas family, held several "Olympic Games" for residents of Greece.
- Discuss the contributions of Dr. William Penny Brookes to physical education in England and to the revival of the Olympic Games of antiquity.
- Recognize the lifelong devotion of Baron Pierre de Coubertin of France to making the modern Olympic Games a reality.
- Appreciate the dedication of Coubertin to his work and the enormous obstacles he had to overcome to establish the credibility and purpose of the Olympics.
- Identify the actual reasons that drove Coubertin to establish the Olympics.
- Explain the influence that certain social and educational reform movements had on Coubertin and his subsequent inclusion of some radical ideas as part of Olympism.
- Understand how the defeat of France by the Prussians in 1871 affected Coubertin's sense of patriotism and devotion to educational reform.
- Understand the issue of amateurism and how Coubertin used it to his advantage.
- Discuss the impact of the English public schools on Coubertin in developing his educational philosophy and his interest in physical education and rough-and-tumble athletic competition.
- Recognize the relationship Coubertin had with Dr. William Brookes of England and Professor William M. Sloane of Princeton University.

■ Identify and discuss the impact of the following political and social issues on the Summer and Winter Olympic Games:

   a. Coubertin's attitude toward women's athletic competition

   b. Coubertin's efforts to ensure success for the first modern Olympic Games

   c. Coubertin's failure to get the support of his countrymen during the 1900 Olympics in Paris and the subsequent failure of the Paris Olympiad

   d. The political maneuvering that moved the 1904 Olympics from Chicago to St. Louis

   e. The political and social issues that affected the 1908 London Games

   f. The success of the 1912 Olympic Games at Stockholm

   g. The postponement of the 1916 Olympic Games due to World War I

   h. The 1920 Olympic Games in Antwerp, from which Germany, Austria, Hungary, Bulgaria, and Turkey were barred because of their role as aggressor nations in World War I

   i. The establishment of the Federation Feminine Sportive Internationale by Mme. Milliat of France to promote track-and-field competition for women

   j. Track-and-field events for women in the 1928 Amsterdam Olympics

   k. The first Winter Olympics, held in 1924 in Chamonix

   l. The 1932 Olympics in Los Angeles, where Babe Didrikson dominated women's track and field

   m. The 1936 Berlin Olympic Games, which Hitler used as a tool of Nazi propaganda regarding racial superiority

INTRODUCTION

From their humble origins in Athens in the spring of 1896 to the media and athletic extravaganza that spellbinds a global audience for several weeks during designated Olympic years, the Olympic Games have evolved into one of the most significant social forces of modernity. The concept of an international athletic festival designed to act as a social force enables several things:

1. Athletes from all over the world can meet and compete against others representing all colors, races, creeds, and political beliefs.

2. Athletes can travel to other countries to establish communication and dialogue with fellow athletes that will foster and promote international understanding and appreciation of cultural diversity.

3. Athletes can test themselves against the best in the world, in a supreme physical and mental challenge.

4. The ideals of fair play and character formation through athletic participation are promoted throughout the world, for the youths of the world to enjoy and ideally, to emulate.

5. The ideals of peace, harmony, and cooperation transcend political barriers, which allows the Olympics to act as a force for world peace and cooperation.

The Olympic Games are a timeless legacy. Under the auspices of the International Olympic Committee (IOC), the spirit of *Olympism* transcends borders and serves as a viable social force for positive change. Within the modern Olympic movement,

> Olympism seeks to create a way of life based on the joy of effort and on mutual respect. Its aim is to place sport at the service . . . to bring about a world of peace in respect for human dignity. This ideal was proclaimed with fervour at the festivals celebrated every four years by the ancient Greeks at the Olympic Games, in which they devoted themselves to the pursuit of harmonious development, not only of the body and moral sense, but also of . . . cultural and artistic qualities.[1]

The Olympic Games are unlike any of the existing "mega sports" that flourished in the twentieth century. The Super Bowl is one of the most watched and followed sporting events in modern history, broadcast all over the world. However, participation in the Super Bowl is exclusively limited to American professional football teams that belong to the National Football League (NFL). The World Series is another phenomenon of the twentieth century. It is closely followed in North America and around the world, especially in Latin America and Japan. However, this great sporting championship is exclusively limited to professional baseball teams in the United States and Canada that belong to Major League Baseball (MLB). The same situation exists with the National Hockey League (NHL) and the National Basketball Association (NBA) championships. The Super Bowl, World Series, Stanley Cup, and NBA championship are *exclusive* events currently limited to teams from North America. However, the Olympic Games are *inclusive,* in that they belong to the world. This is of enormous benefit. Thousands of athletes, male *and* female, participate in the Olympics, where they have the opportunity to promote peace and understanding throughout the global community.

As the world's premier international sporting event, the Olympic Games are a multicultural athletic festival that captivates millions of fans around the world. Men and women representing different political and social systems and worshiping different religious deities gather in a glorious atmosphere of athletic competition. The inclusive nature of the Olympic Games lends itself to a multiplicity of faces. While the spirit of Olympism embodies the essence of athletic competition, significant political and social events have also left their mark on the Olympics. Athletes who represent their country are understandably patriotic and proud. However, one of the more pervasive problems that has surfaced is how to balance patriotism with the ideal of internationalism, of establishing a global community.

Along with the accomplishments of selected individuals and athletic performances, we have chosen to highlight selected political and social events that have had an impact on the Olympic Games. The Olympics are complex, inspiring, disappointing, and exhausting. Partly because of their intent to include rather than exclude participants, the Olympic Games frequently become embroiled in turmoil. Differences of opinion and disagreements are to be expected when such a monumental event unfolds. As a result, the modern Olympic Games (as were the ancient Olympic Games) are from time to time subject to significant problems. However, what is truly inspiring is that with all the controversy that has surrounded the games, the IOC has remained steadfast to the spirit of Olympism, although some scholars and observers would argue that the IOC is more interested in making money than in promoting Olympic values.

THE ARCHITECTS OF THE MODERN OLYMPIC GAMES: DR. WILLIAM PENNY BROOKES AND BARON PIERRE DE COUBERTIN

The modern Olympic Games were established in England in 1850 by Dr. William Penny Brookes (1809–1895), a physician and member of the Royal College of Surgeons. He is recognized in England as the "Father of British Physical Education." Brookes lived in the small village of Much Wenlock where he practiced medicine and advanced the cause of physical education. He wrote members of the British Parliament demanding that physical education be included in the curriculum of the nation's schools. He was still alive when this goal was achieved.

In addition to being a superb physician, Brookes was an accomplished scholar, well schooled in Latin and Hebrew. He was very knowledgeable about the development of physical education and sport in Europe and in the United States. However, it was the athletes of ancient Greece and their devotion to the development of mind, body, and spirit that really captivated Brookes. In 1850, he formed the Wenlock Olympian Class, an organization that promoted the moral, physical, and intellectual development of area residents. In 1850, Brookes and the Wenlock Olympic Class held the first Wenlock Olympics, which consisted of some track-and-field events and traditional country sports such as cricket and quoits. From the beginning, pageantry and related ceremony were an essential element of the Wenlock Olympics. Bands led the procession of officials and athletes as they paraded through the town, decorated for the games. In 1860, this organization became known as the Wenlock Olympian Society. Initially, the Wenlock Olympics attracted local athletes. It was not long, however, before athletes from London and elsewhere in Britain began making the journey to Much Wenlock to compete in the games.

At about the same time, a prominent family— the Zappas family—living in Greece and Romania wanted to revive the Olympic Games. The Zappas family had a great deal of money and set aside a significant amount to hold Olympic Games in Greece. In 1859, Brookes was in contact with the Zappas family, alerting them that his Wenlock Olympic Society was holding Olympic Games in England. He encouraged and supported the efforts of the Greek Olympic Games by the Zappas family, but the Greek games were not very successful. Participation was limited to the residents of Greece, and the games were held on an intermittent basis. However, Brookes realized that an incredible opportunity had presented itself. Perhaps he could

persuade the Greeks to claim their heritage and once again inspire the world by holding the Olympic Games. Brookes had an ally in J. Gennadius, the chargé d'affaires for the Greek government in London. Both men wanted to see the Olympic Games revived and held in Greece. In 1881, Brookes began writing to government officials in Greece in an effort to convince the Greeks to revive the Olympic Games on an international scale. Unfortunately, the Greek government was not in a financial position to support Brookes's request and politely declined. Brookes was disappointed but not discouraged. He continued to believe that someday the Olympic Games would be revived. In fact, he would live just long enough to meet and inspire a young French aristocrat who would eventually be responsible for making the modern Olympic Games a reality.

The Wenlock Olympics were firmly established by the time Pierre de Coubertin, the French aristocrat who is the acknowledged renovator of the modern Olympics, was born on January 1, 1863 (Figure 15-1). The Coubertin family lived in Paris where they mingled with other members of the aristocracy. The father, Charles Louis Baron Fredy de Coubertin, was an accomplished painter who specialized in religious figures. The mother, Agathe Gabrielle de Crisenoy, was devoted to her children and, like her husband, was a devout Roman Catholic. She would frequently take Pierre and his brothers and sister on walks through the many beautiful parks in Paris. She was also engaged in charity work on behalf of the church and would involve the children as well.

The Coubertins were proud, patriotic, and nationalistic, and the family, like the entire nation, was devastated by France's defeat in the Franco-Prussian War. This event was significant in the early years of the young baron's life.[2] The Prussians achieved an overwhelming victory, which did not inspire confidence in the character and manly ability of French youths. This fact greatly disturbed the young Coubertin, who decided to devote his life to bringing about pedagogical change and improving the national character of the youth of France. He

Figure 15-1
Baron de Coubertin.

was not about to sit idly by and watch his beloved France being trampled by the dreaded Prussians, or the English for that matter.

Young French aristocrats of this era had several occupational paths available to them; the clergy, political office, and finance were among the more popular options. Baron de Coubertin chose pedagogy. Pedagogy, although a noble and honorable profession, was not the first choice of most young men of the aristocracy. England was the world power during this historical period, and after completing his formal schooling in France, Coubertin traveled to Great Britain. The economic and political success emblematic of Great Britain attracted the attention of the young baron. Since he made the decision to devote his life to educational and social reform, Coubertin looked across the English Channel and the Atlantic Ocean for guidance. Over the years, he made numerous trips to England and became quite the Anglophile.

The educational authorities in France, with encouragement from Coubertin, decided to send the baron to the United States where he attended the 1889 Boston Conference on Physical Training. The purpose of the Boston Conference was to identify an appropriate physical education system for use in America. Coubertin believed that he could learn a great deal about the various methods of physical education used in America and, perhaps, select the best one for use in France. While in America, Coubertin visited a number of universities. During his stay, Coubertin also developed a close friendship with Dr. William M. Sloane, a professor of history and politics at Princeton University and a lover of the classics—especially the sports and athletes of ancient Greece.

When Coubertin returned to Europe, he began work on organizing a physical education conference. He enlisted the aid of his friends in England to run announcements of his proposed conference in the British press. Dr. William Penny Brookes responded to Coubertin's announcement. Brookes informed Coubertin about the Wenlock Olympics and invited him to attend the games. In October 1890, the baron arrived in Much Wenlock to discuss physical education and sport with Brookes and to watch the Wenlock Olympic Games held in his honor. The 81-year-old physician explained his dream of reviving the Olympic Games to the 27-year-old French baron. By the conclusion of the Wenlock Olympics, Coubertin knew it was his destiny to revive the Olympic Games.

When Coubertin returned to France, he praised the work of Brookes and made reference to reviving the Olympic Games. In an article he published in the *Athletic Review* (*Revue Athletique*) in December 1890, Coubertin wrote, "If the Olympic Games that Modern Greece has not yet been able to revive still survives today, it is due, not to a Greek, but to Dr. W. P. Brookes." Coubertin referred to Brookes as his oldest friend.

There has been, and will continue to be, debate about the moment of inspiration that caused Coubertin to dedicate his life to reviving the Olympics. Coubertin was educated at the finest universities in France. He spoke several languages fluently and received a classical education that, among other subjects, included the study of ancient Greece. Coubertin was well aware of the contributions that the ancient Greeks made to Western civilization, and he understood the significance of the ancient Olympic Games. There is no doubt that Brookes had a profound influence on Coubertin's idea to reestablish the Olympic Games. Then again, Professor Sloane was a superb scholar and an expert on the sports and athletes of ancient Greece. Who should be given credit for reviving the Olympic Games in modern times? The impetus may have originated in Much Wenlock, but the man who made the premier international sports festival a reality was Baron de Coubertin.

Coubertin's motivation for developing physical education and sport programs was a desire to reform the youths of France. Coubertin and many others believed that French males had become "too soft," lacked "character," and were no longer "manly." As a consequence, the defeat of France by the Prussians was inevitable. How could Coubertin restore the character traits of pride, stoicism, courage, honor, and duty in French youths? He turned to the English model of education.

As a boy, Coubertin had read *Tom Brown's School Days.*[3] He was impressed by the system of sport and games that formed a large part of the social and educational fabric at Rugby School under the direction of Dr. Thomas Arnold, one of the foremost advocates of muscular Christianity of the era. The family's impeccable social connections enabled the baron to be wined and dined in the best supper clubs in London, as well as to have access to the English leadership, which he questioned and studied. All the while, Coubertin was looking for that elusive factor that developed the manly character and stoic courage for which the English leadership was famous and of which the youths of France were in desperate need.

While touring the English public schools, which in reality are private and elite institutions that have educated many of Britain's leaders,

Coubertin found the elusive but obvious catalyst for character development that he had been searching for: athletic competition.

During the afternoons, the students at Rugby School, Eton, Winchester, and other elite institutions engaged in rough-and-tumble games such as rugby, soccer, boxing, and races. Pride and honor were on the line during these sporting competitions, and the result was the character formation that was emblematic of the English and so admired by Coubertin. Coubertin had to "sell" the idea of character development through athletic participation to his countrymen, who historically did not covet or embrace anything that the island nation across the English Channel held dear.

When he returned to France, Coubertin used his political and social connections to gain control over amateur sport in France, although he was strongly opposed by the Gymnastic Union. He invited politically powerful and socially well-connected people to his villa, where he entertained them by showcasing the talents of athletes, both national and international. The majority of the spectators came for the lavish spreads of food and drink and were only mildly interested in the athletic competition. However, Coubertin was able to enlist their support for his efforts to promote athletics throughout France, especially in the schools. The baron believed that by inviting foreign teams in for athletic competitions and exhibitions, much could be learned that would benefit French athletes and his pedagogical goal of securing a place for athletics in the schools. In addition, the gathering of athletes from other nations would promote goodwill and foster understanding; it would thus provide an activity that would promote peaceful cooperation among the youths of the world through fair sporting behavior. Coubertin was an idealist; he truly loved sports, and to him the Olympic ideals of fair play and competition were symbolic of all that was good and honorable. His goals could be achieved by carrying on the work of Dr. Brookes. The Olympic Games must be revived to inspire the youths of France and the world!

During the meeting of the Unions des Sports Athletiques held at the Sorbonne in November 1892, he proposed to renew the Olympic Games almost 1500 years after the Byzantine Emperor Theodosius II terminated pagan festivals. The assembled delegates were indifferent to Coubertin's proposal. Although discouraged, he would try again. The second opportunity arose in June 1894, when Coubertin organized the International Congress of Paris for the study and propagation of the principles of amateurism, again held at the Sorbonne. He planned his second proposal very carefully and enlisted the support of the British and Americans. Invitations were sent to sports associations the world over, and Olympic discussion was placed as the last agenda item of the Congress, which lasted one week. Coubertin used the week of meetings to politic, lobby, and nurture his proposal for reestablishment of the Olympic Games. To Coubertin's delight, the Congress voted to reestablish the Olympics.

Many historians believe that Coubertin had planned to hold the first Olympics in Paris; this may not be accurate. In a letter to Coubertin from Demetrius Vikelas dated June 19, 1894 (the first day of the Paris Olympic organizing Congress) Vikelas expressed his regret in not supporting Coubertin's motion to select Athens as the host city. To make matters more complicated, the majority of the delegates wanted London to host the first Olympics. Coubertin, a skilled politician, did not want London to be considered and had this particular motion tabled. Upon reflection, Vikelas decided that Athens would indeed be the ideal city to host the first Olympic Games of the modern era. Four days later, on the last day of the Congress, Vikelas proposed that Athens be selected to host the Olympics. Accordingly, June 23, 1894, Athens was selected as host city.[4]

The Greek delegate to the Congress, Mr. Vikelas, was selected as president of the newly formed International Olympic Committee (IOC); Coubertin was appointed secretary. Coubertin then selected the 14 charter members of the IOC and began preparation for the first modern Olympiad. Dr. Brookes was an honorary member of the IOC.

It must be noted that Coubertin was not in favor of allowing women to compete in the Olympic Games, due as much to the cultural beliefs of the time as anything else. The IOC traditionally has been primarily a body of elected aristocrats from member nations. It was not until 1982 that the IOC admitted women to membership, when Dame Mary Alison Glen-Haig of Great Britain became the first woman member.

THE IST OLYMPIAD: ATHENS, 1896

Baron de Coubertin had an enormous task ahead of him once support for the Olympic Games was obtained. The games were only two years away, and much had to be done to prepare for them. In general, the Greeks were enthusiastic about Athens hosting the first modern Olympiad. However, the Greek government was financially ill prepared to contribute to the effort. Construction of the stadium was the major hurdle, and it was only after Prince Constantine, honorary president of the organizing committee, contacted George Averoff, a wealthy Greek who lived in Alexandria, Egypt, that the construction of the stadium could begin (Figure 15-2). Averoff donated over a million drachmas, and additional funds were raised by selling stamps, tickets, and commemorative medals.[5]

Another task, equally difficult, was convincing the world and major sporting associations that the Athens Olympiad was indeed legitimate.

OLYMPIC SNAPSHOT

1896 Athens Olympiad:

Opening Day April 6; Closing Day April 15

- 14 countries sent teams
- 241 male athletes—no women
- 9 sports, 43 events: Aquatics, Athletics (Track and Field), Cycling, Fencing, Gymnastics, Shooting, Tennis, Weight Lifting, and Wrestling

Figure 15-2
The beautiful stadium built for the first modern Olympic Games, in Athens, 1896.

The New York Athletic Club, the premier athletic club of the era, scoffed at the suggestion to send a team to represent the United States. However, the Boston Athletic Association accepted the challenge, and along with athletes from Princeton University, traveled to Athens. The American team was organized by Professor Sloane and consisted of five members of the Boston Athletic Association and four Princeton students.

The events at the first modern Olympiad were exclusively for male athletes. There were 12 events in track and field, two in weight lifting, one in Greco-Roman wrestling, four in swimming, six in cycling, two in tennis, five in target shooting, three in fencing, and eight in gymnastics. Competitions in rowing and yachting were scheduled but were canceled due to bad weather. David Wallechinsky reports that 241 athletes representing 14 nations competed.[6] Only first- and second-place finishers were officially recognized. First-place finishers received a silver medal, a crown of olives, and a diploma; second-place finishers were rewarded with a bronze medal, a crown of laurel, and a diploma.

James Connolly, an American, was the first athlete to win a medal in the Athens Olympiad; he won the triple jump. The American team won a total of 18 medals—11 first-place finishes and 7 second-place finishes. The host nation led all

nations in the number of medals won, with 10 silver and 16 bronze, for a total of 26 medals.[7]

Perhaps the most interesting story of the 1896 Olympics involved the marathon. It must be understood that the legend of the origin of the marathon—Philippides running from the battle site of Marathon to Athens (a distance of 26 miles and 385 yards) to announce the stunning victory by the Greeks over the mighty Persian army and navy in 499 B.C.—is a myth! It never happened. Herodotus, the "father of history," wrote about this epic battle and never mentioned the "victory run" by Philippides. The first time the story about Philippides' run from Marathon to Athens surfaced was in A.D., 200, 700 years after it was supposed to have taken place. True, there were professional runners in ancient Greece, and there was even a professional runner named Philippides during this time. However, there is no credible evidence that Philippides, or any other man, made the "Marathon run" in 499 B.C. Nevertheless, during the planning meetings for the 1896 Olympics, Michel Brèal, a trained historian and member of the planning committee, proposed that the marathon race be added to the program to commemorate the myth of Philippides in 499 B.C. The proposal was accepted, and on Thursday, April 9, 1896, 17 "marathoners" were taken to Marathon from Athens, and history of the marathon was born!

One of the competitors in the first marathon was Edwin "Teddy" Flack from Australia. He attended school in England and was a superb runner. The British tried to convince Flack to run for England, not Australia. Flack turned down their offer and proudly competed for Australia. A few hours before the start of the race, Flack had captured first place in the 800-meter race. He would become an Olympic champion in the 1500-meters as well. However, he had never run 26 miles and 385 yards (42,195 meters) before! Albin Lermusiaux was in the lead at the halfway mark, followed by Flack. Not long after, Lermusiaux began to tire and Flack took the lead, but not for long. Flack, who had never run more than 10 miles, became exhausted, and at the 34-kilometer mark, the eventual champion,

Spiridon Louis, who was from a small village in Greece, caught up with Flack. The Australian made a courageous attempt to keep up with the Greek, but at the 37-kilometer mark, Flack became disoriented and stumbled. A Greek spectator rushed over to assist him. However, the confused Flack believed that the Greek was attacking him and proceeded to pummel the would-be Good Samaritan! Flack was placed in a carriage and driven back to Athens. Spiridon Louis won the first marathon with a time of 2 hours, 58 minutes, 50 seconds. Another Greek athlete, Kharilaos Vasilakos, finished second with a time of 3 hours, 6 minutes, 3 seconds.

The first Olympic Games of the modern era were such a success that the Greeks wanted to keep the games in Greece and not award them to other world cities! Fortunately, Coubertin was a superb diplomat and reached an agreement with the Greeks to hold "Olympics" in off years. The first off-year Olympic Games were held in Athens in 1906 but did not enjoy the degree of success of the 1896 Olympics. After the 1906 games in Athens, the Greeks would not host the Olympics again until 2004.

THE IIND OLYMPIAD: PARIS, 1900

The games grew in scope and popularity over the years, but they were not without problems. The success of the 1896 Athens Olympiad, as the Greeks perceived it, demanded that all successive Olympiads be held at Athens and not awarded to a new city as envisioned by Coubertin. He prevailed over the Greeks, however, and the second Olympiad was held in Paris.[8] These games were full of promise, but they fell apart from an organizational standpoint. The Union des Sports Athletiques of France, the governing body of French sport, had no desire to cooperate or share power with the newly created IOC. Nor did they have much confidence in the Olympic movement. The management of the Paris Exposition, where the 1900 Olympic Games were to be held, did not share Coubertin's enthusiasm, nor did they attribute much significance to the Olympic movement.[9] The French were indifferent,

at best, to the 1900 Olympiad and preferred to marvel at the Eiffel Tower and the customary amusements and entertainment available at the exposition. Baron de Coubertin was thoroughly frustrated and discouraged. Facilities were difficult to obtain, and his beloved Olympics were relegated to sideshow status, which pleased the organizers of the Paris Exposition and the Union des Sports Athletiques of France.

In a situation that must have been humiliating, Coubertin reluctantly agreed to include motorcar races, competitions between firemen, balloon races, and trials of carrier pigeons.[10] Tug-of-war turned out to be the highlight of the games, whereas track-and-field meets were the low points; the American team defeated the French in the tug-of-war. The problem was that there were official and unofficial Olympic events. Promoters would claim to be staging Olympic competitions not sanctioned or supported by the IOC. Golf was included as a new Olympic sport. Polo, rugby, and cricket were added as well. Also during the Paris Olympiad, women athletes made their first appearance. Madame Filleaul Brohy and Mademoiselle Ohnier of France competed in croquet, while Charlotte Cooper of England became the first women's Olympic champion in the sport of tennis.[11] Some 997 athletes representing 24 National Olympic Committees (NOCs) participated in the Paris Olympiad.

OLYMPIC SNAPSHOT

1900 Paris Olympiad:

Opening Day May 14; Closing Day October 28

- 24 countries sent teams
- 997 athletes: 22 women and 975 men
- 18 sports, 95 events: Aquatics, Archery, Athletics, Basque Pelota, Cricket, Croquet, Cycling, Equestrian, Fencing, Football, Golf, Gymnastics, Polo, Rowing, Rugby, Sailing, Shooting, Tennis, and Tug of War

Although Coubertin was deeply grieved at the second-class status of his beloved Olympics, there were some noteworthy athletic achievements. Alvin Kraezlein, an American athlete, won four events: the 60-meter sprint, the 110-meter hurdles, the 200-meter hurdles, and the broad jump. American Ray Ewry also was one of the few high points. As a child he had contracted polio and was told he would spend the rest of his life in a wheelchair, paralyzed. He began rehabilitation exercises on his own and became a great athlete. In Paris, he won three events: standing high jump, standing long jump, and standing triple jump. He repeated as Olympic champion in these three events in 1904 and won again in 1908 in the standing high jump and standing long jump. The standing triple jump was eliminated in 1908, and after 1912 all standing jumps were dropped from the Olympic Games. As was the case in 1896, only first- and second-place finishes were recognized in the official records for the 1900 Olympics. It was not until the 1904 St. Louis Olympics that first-, second-, and third-place finishes were recognized with gold, silver, and bronze medals. It is interesting to note that most of the victors in the 1900 Olympics received not medals but cups and trophies. In addition, professionals were allowed to compete in fencing. Albert Ayat from France won the épée competition for amateurs and masters and was awarded a prize of 3000 francs. The Olympics ended on October 28; there were no closing ceremonies. The Paris Olympiad was a major disappointment to Baron de Coubertin; however, it paled in comparison to the politics and program of the 1904 St. Louis Olympiad.

THE IIIRD OLYMPIAD: ST. LOUIS, 1904

The IOC had received proposals to host the games from Chicago and St. Louis. When the IOC met in Paris in May of 1901, Chicago sent a representative to secure the 1904 Olympic Games. St. Louis failed to send a representative, and under the circumstances, the IOC was left with a seemingly simple

decision: award the 1904 Olympic Games to Chicago, which they did. The IOC then offered the presidency of the 1904 Olympiad to President Theodore Roosevelt, who accepted on May 28, 1901.[12]

The city of Chicago celebrated the announcement from the IOC and began preparations for the games. However, what appeared to be a "done deal" was far from over as St. Louis continued its efforts to secure the games. The Louisiana Purchase Exposition, commemorating the purchase of the Louisiana Territory by the United States from France in 1803, was scheduled to open in 1904 in St. Louis. The promoters of the exposition were eager to add the Olympic Games to the exposition program and, when confronted with the fact that Chicago had been awarded the Olympic Games, threatened to organize a rival athletic exhibition.[13] James Sullivan, secretary of the Amateur Athletic Union (AAU), was appointed chief of the Department of Physical Culture of the Louisiana Purchase Exposition by D. R. Francis, president of the St. Louis Exposition. Sullivan was politically powerful and well connected with the nation's leader. If there was a person capable of organizing a rival athletic festival that would overshadow the 1904 Chicago Olympiad, it was James Sullivan. As secretary of the AAU, he would have enormous influence on whether America's best athletes competed in St. Louis or Chicago.

OLYMPIC SNAPSHOT

1904 St. Louis Olympiad:

Opening Day July 1; Closing Day November 23

- 12 countries sent teams
- 651 athletes: 6 women and 645 men
- 17 sports, 91 events: Aquatics, Archery, Athletics, Basketball, Boxing, Cycling, Fencing, American Football, Golf, Gymnastics, Lacrosse, Roque, Rowing, Tennis, Tug of War, Weight Lifting, and Wrestling

The Chicago Organizing Committee realized their fate and proposed to postpone the Olympic Games until 1905, after the St. Louis Exposition was over. Besides having James Sullivan to contend with, Chicago did not have the financial resources to upstage St. Louis.

President Roosevelt let it be known to the IOC that it was his desire that the Olympic Games be held in conjunction with the St. Louis Exposition. On February 10, 1903, the IOC met and voted 14 to 2 to transfer the games to St. Louis. The political character of subsequent Olympiads was all but assured.

The St. Louis organizers assigned the term *Olympic* to all phases of competition, which caused considerable confusion as to exactly which events were truly Olympic. The following "Program of Olympic Events" was published by the *St. Louis Post-Dispatch*:

May 14	Interscholastic meet, for St. Louis only
May 21	Open handicap athletic meeting
May 28	Interscholastic meet for schools of Louisiana Purchase Territory
May 30	Western college championships
June 2	AAU handicap meeting
June 3	AAU Jr. championship
June 4	AAU Sr. championship
June 11	Olympic college championships, open to colleges of the world
June 13	Central Assoc. AAU championships
June 18	Turners mass exhibitions
June 20–25	College baseball
June 29, 30	Interscholastic championships
July 1, 2	Turners international and individual team contest
July 4	AAU all-around championships
July 5, 6, 7	Lacrosse
July 8, 9	Swimming and water polo championships

July 11, 12	Interscholastic basketball
July 13, 14	YMCA basketball championships
July 18, 19	College basketball
July 20–23	Irish sports
July 29	Open athletic club handicap meeting of the Western Association AAU
Aug. 1–6	Bicycling
Aug. 8–13	Tennis
Aug. 18	YMCA gymnastic championships
Aug. 19	YMCA handicap meeting
Aug. 20	YMCA championship meeting
Aug. 29–Sept. 3	Olympic Games
Sept. 8–10	World's fencing championships
Sept. 12–15	Olympic cricket championships
Sept. 19–24	Golf
Sept. 26–Oct. 1	Military athletic carnival
Oct. 14, 15	AAU wrestling championships
Oct. 27	Turners mass exhibition
Oct. 28, 29	AAU gymnastic championships
Nov. 10, 11	Relay racing, open to athletic clubs, colleges, schools, and YMCAs
Nov. 12	College football
Nov. 15–17	Association football
Nov. 17	Cross-country championships
Nov. 24	College football and local cross-country championships: East vs. West[14]

The Olympic Games in 1904 sank to their lowest point. The U.S. team competed primarily against itself because there was little representation from around the world. Germany, Canada, Britain, Greece, Hungary, and Cuba sent athletes, but it was purely an American event. The "Olympic" designation was awarded to everything from a track-and-field meet between 13-year-old schoolboys to "Anthropology Days," in which a collection of aboriginal freaks, rumored to have been drafted from sideshows of the concurrent St. Louis Exposition, performed in athletic competition, much to the amusement of a handful of gawking spectators. When informed of Anthropology Days as an official Olympic event, Coubertin wrote several years later, "In no place but America would one have dared place such events on the program."[15]

In spite of the carnival atmosphere that surrounded the 1904 Olympics, there were some athletic feats of note. Boxing and freestyle wrestling made their first appearance as Olympic sports. American Oliver Kirk won two boxing titles in two separate weight classes: featherweight and bantam weight. Ramon Fonst, a fencer from Cuba, won three times and was celebrated as Cuba's first Olympic champion. Two of the marathoners, Len Tau and Jan Mashiani, from Botswana (Bechuanaland), are recognized as the first Africans to compete in the Olympics. These two men were part of an exhibit about the Boer War in Africa and simply decided to enter the marathon. Tau finished in ninth place and Mashiani finished twelfth.

The 1904 marathon was a low point in the annals of Olympic history. Poorly organized from the start, the race was run in the afternoon in 90-degree weather, over hills and along dry, dusty roads. Automobiles both paced and followed the runners, subjecting them to choking dust and fumes. And then there was the problem of water—one source located at the 12-mile mark. Only 14 of the 32 starters reached the finish, with the "casualties" littering the racecourse. William Garcia from San Francisco was found unconscious by the roadside. One of the African runners lost valuable time when he was chased off the course into the surrounding fields by two vicious dogs. Time went by and there was still no runner in sight of the finish line. Finally, after 3 hours, 13 minutes, Fred Lorz of New York appeared looking extraordinarily fresh and energetic. Just a few minutes before he was to receive his gold medal, it was discovered that he had ridden in a car for 11 miles, gotten out, and again begun to run.

It seems that supplements to supposedly enhance athletic performance are not a recent

phenomenon. Thomas Hicks, who was born in England and immigrated to America, was another marathoner. About 10 miles from the finish, an exhausted Hicks pleaded with his "coaches" for a rest. They refused because he was in the lead! Instead, they provided him with a concoction that consisted of the poison strychnine sulfate and raw egg white, ostensibly to increase his energy level. Hicks did not die, and after a few more miles, his coaches gave him more strychnine laced with brandy! Eventually, he managed to cross the finish line in 3 hours, 28 minutes, 53 seconds to win the marathon, albeit in a stupor!

In the 400-meter hurdles, Americans finished first, second, and third; the third-place finisher, George Poage, was the first African-American to win an Olympic medal. Perhaps the most amazing athlete at the 1904 Olympics was George Eyser. He won six medals in gymnastics: three gold, two silver, and a bronze—all with a wooden leg![16]

American football was on the program for the first and last time. The Americans entered two teams, USA 1 and USA 2. The Canadians entered a team as well. In a stunning upset, the Canadian team beat USA 1 for the gold medal while USA 1 defeated USA 2 for the silver.

Six women athletes from the United States competed in archery and won all of the events. The Olympics, for the second time in a row, had been reduced to a mere sideshow, overshadowed by the more prominent and prestigious international exposition. The obvious had been demonstrated: Coubertin and his beloved Olympic Games had to establish their autonomy before they would be accepted on their merit.

THE IVTH OLYMPIAD: LONDON, 1908

During the 1904 meeting in London, the IOC awarded the 1908 Olympiad to Rome. In 1906, Mount Vesuvius erupted and caused considerable damage and hardship. The financial burden of attending to the needs of the victims of Vesuvius and staging the Olympic Games was too much for Rome to bear. The Italians asked the IOC to relieve them of the responsibility of holding the games. Great Britain was asked by the IOC to host the 1908 games, and promptly accepted. However, once again, the Olympic Games would have to share the spotlight. The 1908 London Olympiad was held in conjunction with the Franco-British Exhibition. The arrangement was purely economic, as the exhibition organizers would pay for the construction of the stadium and other facilities that the games required, and the British Olympic Association would receive one-half of the gross receipts.[17]

OLYMPIC SNAPSHOT

1908 London Olympiad:

Opening Day April 27; Closing Day October 31

- 22 countries sent teams
- 2008 athletes: 37 women and 1971 men
- 21 sports, 110 events: Aquatics, Archery, Athletics, Boxing, Cycling, Fencing, Soccer, Gymnastics, Field Hockey, Jeu de Paume, Lacrosse, Polo, Rackets, Rowing, Rugby, Sailing, Shooting, Tennis, Tug of War, Water Motorsports, and Wrestling

The American team was preoccupied with winning and assumed the posture that "international cooperation was a worthwhile objective as long as America could claim an athletic victory."[18] An enormous athletic rivalry existed between the British and the Americans, as was underscored by headlines in *The New York Times:* "American Athletes Sure of Success," "Britishers Fear Yankee Athletes," and "We Will Knock the Spots Off the Britishers."[19] The English, ever the custodians of the creed of fair play, held to the Olympic ideal of competition. As reported by the *London Times,*

> It is commonly said, and, indeed is put forward as a conclusive argument in favor of the modern Olympic movement, that international

athletics encourage international amity. This is only the case if they are organized in so orderly and impartial a manner that every competitor, whether he has won or lost, goes away satisfied and feeling that every opportunity has been given and every courtesy shown to him. That this will be the case at the Olympic Games of London, no Briton, and we feel sure, none of our foreign visitors can doubt; and, if that be so, the games cannot fail to be an immense value both to those who take part in them and to the nations to which they belong.[20]

Unfortunately, the London games became embroiled in political turmoil and nationalism. The athletes from Finland did not display any national flag or banner because the Russians, politically and militarily powerful at this time, were diplomatically able to mandate that if the Finns carried a flag or banner, it would be a Russian one. Likewise, the Irish were told that they had to display and compete under the flag of Great Britain and that all medals won by Irish athletes would add to the prestige of England.[21] The American team was also beset by "flag issues." The individual selected to carry the American flag in the opening ceremonies was an Irishman, Ralph Rose, a shot putter who had immigrated to the United States. It was the custom for all nations competing to "dip" their flags when their team marched in front of the reviewing stand where the government dignitaries and IOC officials sat. When the American team was in front of the reviewing stand, Rose and fellow Olympian Martin Sheridan, also from Ireland and a discus thrower, stopped, looked King Edward VII of England in the eye, and proudly proclaimed, "This flag dips before no earthly king!" To this day, American Olympic teams do not "dip" the flag. To make matters worse, the British elected to not display the American flag during opening ceremonies in the newly constructed 70,000-seat stadium located in Shepherd's Bush. All of the other participating nations saw their flags flying around the stadium, but no "Stars and Stripes." As noted previously, there was no love lost between the American and British athletes in what became known as the Battle of Shepherd's Bush. In addition, the American team did not like the British scoring system used to determine Olympic victories. American athletes were entered almost entirely in the track-and-field competition and wanted the "Games Trophy" to be awarded based on track-and-field victories only. But the British insisted that all competitive events be included in the determination of the overall Olympic championship. The Americans, ever resourceful, devised their own system of scoring that was more favorable to their efforts and in so doing enabled the specter of nationalism to overshadow athletic competition.

The British and Americans also were at odds concerning the tug-of-war competition. The British won the event; however, the Americans complained that the British used "illegal footwear." As reported by the *London Times,*

> In the tug-of-war a team of light stalwart policemen easily pulled the great hammer, and discus and weight-thrower of the U.S. over the line. The Americans protested against the results of the first bout on the grounds that their conquerors wore boots, but this objection was, of course, overruled.[22]
>
> The British press labeled the American team, as well as the French team, poor sports. The ill feelings between the British and the American teams came to a head over the marathon. Prior to the event the Americans logged a protest against Tom Longboat, the Canadian entry, because the American AAU had declared Longboat a professional. Much to the dismay of the Americans, the British Olympic Council pointed out that the country of nationality, in this case Canada, was the only authority empowered to determine amateur status. Canada certified Tom Longboat as an amateur, and the American protest was disallowed.

Meanwhile, in the marathon, the Italian entrant, Dorando Pietri, reached the stadium first but was so exhausted and disoriented that well-meaning officials helped him across the finish line. The Americans protested the race on the grounds that Pietri had received assistance. The protest was upheld, and an American, Johnny Hayes of New York City, was declared the winner. The games ended on July 25, 1908, amid turmoil and bickering among contestants and between nations. Serious doubts were expressed on both sides of the Atlantic concerning the continuation of the Olympics. The British admitted that there had been problems. The American viewpoint was more direct; changes had to be made or all American participation would end.[23] In the end, the Americans scored more victories in the stadium events (track and field), while the British were the victors in the overall competition. The London Olympiad ended with ill feelings between the British and American teams, between Irish athletes and their British counterparts, and between the Finns and the Russians, much to the disappointment of Coubertin and the IOC. However, on a more positive and progressive note, 37 women representing four countries competed in three sports—tennis, archery, and figure skating. Women athletes also demonstrated their athletic expertise in exhibitions of swimming, diving, and gymnastics.

THE VTH OLYMPIAD: STOCKHOLM, 1912

The Stockholm Olympiad is significant for a number of reasons. First, it would be the last Olympiad in which Russia would compete until 1952, when the Soviet Union sent a team to the Helsinki Olympiad. Second, Jim Thorpe, perhaps America's most gifted athlete ever, was a member of the U.S. team, which also included George S. Patton, Jr., who later became a famous general in World War II; Douglas MacArthur, who would become an army general and World War II hero; and Avery Brundage, who later became president of the IOC (1952–1972). James E. Sullivan would later strip Jim Thorpe of his two gold Olympic medals because of Thorpe's brief career as a semipro baseball player. Third, the American AAU threatened to boycott the games unless American representation in the management of the games was assured. The Americans were still seething from the blatantly biased officiating and scoring by the British Olympic officials during the London Games and demanded to be included in managing the Stockholm Games. Fourth, Finnish athletes demanded to participate as an autonomous team in 1912 and flatly refused to march under the Russian flag. The Russians immediately protested. In addition, Bohemia requested that it be allowed to compete as an independent nation, which did not sit too well with the Austro-Hungarian Empire, which included Bohemia. Finally, women's swimming was recognized as an official event, equestrian competition was held for the first time, and the modern pentathlon began.

Ever the diplomat, Baron de Coubertin was able to assuage political interests so that serious confrontations were avoided. After some political maneuvering, Swedish Olympic officials allowed foreign Olympic commissioners to be appointed to assist the Swedes. President William Howard Taft appointed none other than James E. Sullivan as American commissioner to the games. As the head of the AAU, Sullivan assembled the first truly

OLYMPIC SNAPSHOT

1912 Stockholm Olympiad:

Opening Day May 5; Closing Day July 27

- 28 countries sent teams
- 2407 athletes: 48 women and 2359 men
- 14 sports, 102 events: Aquatics, Athletics, Cycling, Equestrian, Fencing, Soccer, Gymnastics, Modern Pentathlon, Rowing, Sailing, Shooting, Tennis, Tug of War, and Wrestling

representative American Olympic team. Olympic trials were held around the country to ensure that the best American athletes would be in Stockholm in 1912 (Figure 15-3).[24]

According to George Matthews, there were 111 American track-and-field athletes on the American team. Of these, 31 were undergraduate college students, three were American Indians (James Thorpe, Louis Tewanima, and Alfred Sockalexis),

Figure 15-3
Members of the 1912 U.S. Olympic squad. Jim Thorpe is wearing a turtleneck warm-up sweater.

one was Hawaiian (Duke Kahanamoku), and one was African-American (Howard P. Drew).[25]

For the first time, women were able to compete in the Olympic Games as swimmers. On April 23, 1912, the decision was made by the Americans not to send a team of women swimmers to Stockholm; no reason was given.[26]

The Americans and British were eventually able to put the bad blood of the 1908 games behind them. Both the British and the American delegations made sincere efforts to prevent conflict from occurring. The Swedish Olympic Committee did a fabulous job in preparing the facilities and making the necessary arrangements for the hordes of athletes and fans. The games were a rousing success, and Coubertin's hopes and dreams were finally realized. In all, the Stockholm Olympiad hosted 2407 athletes from 28 nations.[27]

H. P. Drew, the lone African-American on the American team, won his qualifying heat in the 100-meter dash. He was accorded much media coverage by *The New York Times* in part because he had a wife and two children to support and was still attending high school! The students at his high school raised funds to provide for his family while he was in Stockholm competing for his country. In a later heat of the 100-meter dash, Drew pulled a tendon in his right leg, but he still managed to win the heat and qualify for the finals the next day. His teammates and America hoped and prayed that he would be able to run in the finals, but it was not to be. The high-school student who had equaled the world's record in the 100-meter dash watched as his teammate, R. C. Craig, won the race in 10.8 seconds and earned the gold medal.[28]

Jim Thorpe won both the pentathlon and decathlon in Stockholm. In the pentathlon, Thorpe won four of the five events and finished third in the javelin competition. One of Thorpe's opponents in the pentathlon was none other than Avery Brundage, who finished fifth. Brundage later became president of the IOC, where he championed the Olympic ideal of purely amateur competition. Brundage was strongly opposed to allowing professional athletes to compete in the Olympic Games.

Less than a year after Thorpe won his Olympic medals, he was accused of playing semipro baseball one summer prior to the 1912 Olympic Games. Thorpe, whom the king of Sweden immortalized as the world's greatest living athlete after his Olympic victories, admitted to the allegation and was stripped of his medals and trophies by James E. Sullivan. What is revealing is that the IOC did not initiate the investigation of Thorpe; it was the American Olympic Committee. Time heals all wounds, and in 1983 Thorpe's medals were restored posthumously. His children dedicated his newly restored Olympic medals to a new youth center in the hope of inspiring the thousands of young people who used this facility. Sadly, less than six months after the medals were displayed, they were stolen and never recovered. In death, as in life, Jim Thorpe's medals were stolen from him.

It was also during the 1912 Stockholm Olympiad that the legend of the "Flying Finns" was born. Hannes Kolehmainen of Finland won three gold medals in the distance races. He won the 10,000-meter race, set a world record in the 5000-meter race two days later, three days later broke the world record in a heat of the 3000-meter race, and on July 15, 1912, finally won the gold medal in the 12,000-meter cross-country race. In doing so, he put Finland on the Olympic track-and-field map.

There were 48 women athletes who represented 11 countries in Stockholm.[29] As noted previously, in addition to women's swimming, equestrian events were held for the first time and the modern pentathlon was inaugurated. The modern pentathlon consisted of running, riding, swimming, fencing, and shooting, and it became popular with military athletes because the skills of the pentathlon were those required of a soldier. The Stockholm Olympic Games were an outstanding success; however, World War I precluded the 1916 Olympic Games. The next Olympics took place in Antwerp, Belgium, in 1920.

1916 Olympics postponed because of World War I.

1920 Antwerp Olympiad:

Opening Day April 20; Closing Day September 12

- 29 countries sent teams
- 2626 athletes: 65 women and 2561 men
- 22 sports, 154 events: Aquatics, Archery, Athletics, Boxing, Cycling, Equestrian, Fencing, Soccer, Gymnastics, Field Hockey, Modern Pentathlon, Polo, Rowing, Rugby, Sailing, Shooting, Tennis, Tug of War, Weight Lifting, and Wrestling

THE VIITH OLYMPIAD: ANTWERP, 1920

Eight years after the last Olympiad, amid the debris of World War I, the Olympic spirit prevailed as the city of Antwerp prepared to host the VIIth Olympic Games. In the aftermath of World War I, the decision to award the games to Antwerp was not made until 1919 and was done so to honor the people of Belgium, who had suffered greatly during World War I. Because Germany, Austria, Hungary, Bulgaria, and Turkey were aggressor nations during World War I, they were excluded from the Antwerp Olympiad. Coubertin wanted to include them to demonstrate that sport provided a means to heal, a means to peace, but he was overruled.

The Antwerp Olympiad initiated two Olympic traditions: (1) the athletes took the Olympic oath before the general public, and (2) the five-ring Olympic flag was unveiled at the games. Victor Boin was the first athlete to take the Olympic oath on behalf of all the Olympians at Antwerp. The Olympic flag had been displayed in Paris during the 1914 celebration of the twentieth anniversary of the revival of the modern Olympics. The flag featured five interlocked rings colored blue, yellow, black, green, and red. Baron de Coubertin examined all the known flags of the world and noticed that every flag had at least one color that was displayed on the Olympic flag. The rings symbolized the linking of athletes from around the world, who would compete and form friendship under the Olympic flag.

Paavo Nurmi, the fabulous distance runner from Finland, made his debut at the Antwerp Games and went down in the annals of Olympic history as one of the greatest distance runners of all time. He captured the silver medal in

the 5000-meter race and the gold medal in the 10,000-meter race. American sprinters were successful, winning both gold and silver medals in the 100- and 200-meter races. The American Olympic team included women swimmers for the first time, and the American women captured the gold, silver, and bronze medals in the 100-meter and 300-meter freestyle, and the gold medal in the 400-meter relay. The U.S. women's diving team swept the fancy diving event by capturing the first four places. Nedo Nadi of Italy won five of the six gold medals in fencing; his brother Aldo was also an Olympic champion, winning three golds and a silver. And Oscar Swahn made Olympic history when, at 72 years of age, he won the silver medal in team fencing. He became the oldest person to win an Olympic medal.[30] American Edward Eagan won the light heavyweight championship of the Antwerp Olympics. In 1932 he was on the four-man bobsled team from the United States that won the gold medal at the Lake Placid Winter Olympics. He is the only athlete to win a gold medal in both the summer and winter Olympic Games.

The Antwerp Games came to a close, and the IOC began preparations for the next Olympiad, to be held in Paris in 1924. Baron de Coubertin focused his energy on an issue that he was not comfortable with: the inclusion of more women in the Olympic Games.

The gradual inclusion of women in the Olympic Games is a significant social event that deserves comment. Anita Defrantz is a former Olympic rower who since 1986 has been a member of the IOC. Among her many duties is her involvement in the IOC working group on sport and women. According to Defrantz,

> The first Olympic Games of the modern era in Athens in 1896 were not open to [women]. The reviver of the Games, Baron Pierre de Coubertin, was a man steeped in the culture of his time, who thought that the Games should traditionally remain "the exaltation of male sport."[31]

Although the IOC was slow to increase the participation of women in the games, it did happen. The example set by the IOC relative to including more and more women's events served as a catalyst to advance the cause of women's rights and enabled women around the world to experience the joy of sport. As students of history, we can reflect on the early twentieth century, when women were not accorded equal rights, let alone the right to vote. It was during this era that significant growth within the Olympic movement occurred. Baron de Coubertin and the all-male membership of the IOC reflected the social and cultural beliefs of this era. As a result, the process of expanding opportunities for women to participate in sport was slow; nonetheless, it continued to move forward.

The post–World War I era ushered in many social and political changes in Europe. European women became interested in track and field, and Alice Milliat of France established the Federation Feminine Sportive Internationale (FFSI) to promote sport for women. Prior to the 1920 Antwerp Olympics, the FFSI had conducted international competition in 15 events with distances up to 1500 meters. Coubertin was intransigent when Milliat requested that the Antwerp Olympics include track-and-field events for women. He

could support women's swimming, but not track and field.

What Coubertin ignored was that a few women actually participated in tennis, croquet, and golf during the 1900 Paris Olympiad, but their participation may have been due to accident, oversight, or apathy.[32] The Paris Games were a fiasco, to say the least, especially with regard to organization and administration, and some competition may have been slipped in without the knowledge of Coubertin. According to sport historian Mary Leigh, Coubertin had no particular objection to women's participation in tennis and swimming. However,

> he drew attention to the fact that fencers, horsewomen, and rowers also existed, and that soon, perhaps, there would be women soccer players and runners who would also wish to be included in the Olympics program. Such sports practiced by women, he felt, would not constitute an edifying sight before assembled crowds for Olympic contests.[33]

The baron was indeed a chauvinist.

Because Baron de Coubertin would not cooperate, Milliat organized the first Women's Olympic Games in 1922. The event was a success, and plans were made for a second Women's Olympics when negotiations with the International Amateur Athletic Federation led to a plan to control women's athletics and to recommend an Olympic program of five events for women. Milliat wanted more events but was rebuffed. To protest the sparse program, the British women athletes stated that they would not compete in the 1928 Amsterdam Olympics. Negotiations continued, and a five-event program for women began in the 1928 Olympics.

Baron de Coubertin was disappointed; however, he was able to prevent track-and-field competition for women in the 1924 Paris Olympiad. Upon retiring as president of the IOC in 1925, he did not miss an opportunity to voice his objections to the inclusion of women as Olympic competitors in some sporting events.[34] Some of the baron's allies were physical educators in the United States. They did not want to lavish money and attention on a few highly skilled Olympic athletes at the expense of ignoring physical education instruction for a great many women. The United States Women's Physical Education Association protested the inclusion of women athletes in the 1928 and 1932 Olympic Games.[35]

In any event, the Olympic Games continued to grow. In 1920, 2626 athletes representing 29 countries took part in the games. Of these, 65 were women, representing 13 countries.[36]

THE VIIITH OLYMPIAD: PARIS, 1924

The 1924 Paris Games were a far cry from the debacle that had occurred when Paris hosted the games in 1900. Remembering the 1900 fiasco, the Paris Organizing Committee worked night and day to ensure the success of the games. Women competed in swimming (seven events), fencing (one event), and lawn tennis (two events).[37] In men's swimming, the American team proved to be a powerful force. In the 100-meter freestyle, Johnny Weissmuller won the gold, and his teammates Duke Kahanamoku and Sam Kahanamoku won silver and bronze, respectively. Weissmuller won another gold in the 400-meter freestyle and yet another gold as a member of the 800-meter relay. Dr. Benjamin Spock, who would become

one of the most famous American pediatricians of all time, won a gold medal as a rower.

The United States won the gold medal in rugby when it beat France 17–3. The only other country to enter a team in rugby competition was Romania, and the Romanian team was terrible! France beat the Romanians 61–3, and the Americans "edged" the Romanians by a score of 37–0. The championship match was played in front of 40,000 fans who watched the American team take the French entirely by surprise with its rough, but legal, tactics learned from playing American football.[38]

The athlete who basked in the limelight in Paris was Paavo Nurmi, the magnificent distance runner from Finland who displayed little emotion or joy during the games. The sullen Finn won four gold medals: 1500-meters, the 5000-meter flat race, the 3000-meter team race, and the 10,000-meter cross-country run. Bill Henry said that "without any question Nurmi's performance was the greatest exhibition of distance running ever seen."[39] Grantland Rice, one of America's greatest sportswriters, called Paavo Nurmi "Superman."[40] Between Nurmi and his teammate, Willie Ritola, the two athletes won nine gold and silver medals. The sports world and the press were circulating numerous theories as to how the Finn had become so successful. According to John Lucas,

> Reams of newspaper and periodical essays were written about the Finnish "secrets" of athletic superiority. Fascinating claims were made for native foods: raw, dried fish; rye bread "hard as biscuit"; and sour milk. The magnificent introvert, Nurmi, added mystery by refusing to discuss anything about his private life and training regimen.[41]

The Paris Olympiad was the last time that tennis was on the program for more than half a century. It would not return until 1988.

Hollywood enjoys making movies about sport, including Olympic sports. The 1981 Oscar-winning *Chariots of Fire* took audiences to the

OLYMPIC SNAPSHOT

1924 Paris Olympiad:

Opening Day May 4; Closing Day July 27

- 44 countries sent teams
- 3089 athletes: 135 women and 2954 men
- 16 sports, 126 events: Aquatics, Athletics, Boxing, Cycling, Equestrian, Fencing, Soccer, Gymnastics, Modern Pentathlon, Polo, Rowing, Rugby, Sailing, Shooting, Tennis, Weight Lifting, and Wrestling

Europe of 1924, especially Great Britain, to tell the story of the legendary British track-and-field athletes Harold Abrahams and muscular Christian Eric Liddell. Abrahams used the services of a professional coach, which was not considered proper during this era. He won the 100-meter sprint, upsetting the Americans who were supposed to sweep this event. Liddell was also supposed to run the 100-meters, but as the race was held on Sunday, he refused to compete even though under enormous pressure to do so. It ended well for Liddell when he entered the 400-meters and won in record time! He also won the bronze medal in the 200-meters. Sadly, Liddell was killed in China where he was doing missionary work. Abrahams became a successful radio sportscaster. It must also be noted that, as with most Hollywood films that "remake" history, there the movie contains historical inaccuracies. For example, Harold Abrahams is depicted as the first person to run the Great Court of Trinity College within the time the Great Clock struck 12 times. The fact is that Lord David George Burghley is the athlete who achieved this feat, which took place in 1927. Lord Burghley was so disgusted at this historical misinterpretation that he refused to watch *Chariots of Fire*. He won the gold medal in the 400-meter hurdles in the 1928 Amsterdam Games.

The Paris Olympiad, like Olympic Games before and after, had problems. The Paris organizers took in 6 million francs at the gate but still ran a deficit of 2 million francs. The French spectators, much to the chagrin of Coubertin, displayed a general lack of sports knowledge and frequently behaved in a discourteous manner. There were fights in the stands, booing by the crowd during national anthems, and a brawl between the French and Americans during the rugby match. There also remained friction between the British and American teams. Several members of the British Olympic delegation demanded that their team withdraw from the Paris Games rather than endure the unfair treatment of the "American Professionals."[42] The issue of professionalism was a topic that the IOC would have to deal with, and soon!

THE 1ST WINTER OLYMPICS: CHAMONIX, 1924

The first Winter Olympic Games were held in Chamonix, France, from January 25 to February 5, 1924. The Winter Olympics were initially opposed by Baron de Coubertin because he believed that they would detract from the Summer Games. Once he became convinced that winter sports were popular, however, he changed his position and joined with the IOC in approving the Winter Games—with certain conditions. The name "Olympiad" would not be used for the Winter Games, and although the country that hosted the Summer Games could also host the Winter Games, the host cities could not be close to each other.

The program at Chamonix consisted of six sports: speed skating for men, individual figure skating for men and women, pairs figure skating, cross-country skiing, bobsledding, and ice hockey. The demonstration sports of military ski race and shooting and curling were also offered. Eleven-year-old Sonja Henie from Norway made her figure-skating debut. She did not medal in 1924 but would capture the gold medal in the 1928 and 1932 Olympic Games. The United States won the gold medal in men's 500-meter speed skating, finished second to Canada in ice hockey, and captured the silver medal in women's figure skating. The first Winter Olympics drew 258 athletes, representing 16 countries. Eleven of these athletes were women, representing 16 countries.[43]

OLYMPIC SNAPSHOT

1924 Chamonix Winter Olympics:

Opening Day January 25; Closing Day February 5

- 16 countries sent teams
- 258 athletes: 11 women and 247 men
- 6 sports, 16 events: Biathlon, Bobsleigh, Curling, Ice Hockey, Skating, and Skiing

THE IXTH OLYMPIAD: AMSTERDAM, 1928

The Dutch had campaigned to host the Olympics on more than one occasion, making proposals to the IOC in 1912, 1921, and 1924. But the Dutch withdrew their proposals in 1919 in favor of Antwerp and again in 1921 when Coubertin expressed his desire that Paris be awarded the games. The Dutch had a long and difficult road ahead. The financial burden that the host city and national government must contend with in producing the Olympic Games is enormous, and the officials of the organizing committees have many sleepless nights. Amsterdam was no exception, and even though it was awarded the 1928 Olympic Games in 1921, the financing of the games remained problematic.

A new stadium was absolutely necessary, as was the construction of much-needed venues and support facilities. The Dutch officials' first attempt at financing the Olympic Games was through a lottery, but that was not successful. Other creative attempts to finance the games failed, and the mood of the Dutch Olympic Committee was glum when loyal people of Holland came to the rescue. Citizens living in the remote Dutch East Indies pledged money, and communities throughout Holland rallied around the Olympic standard with pledges.

OLYMPIC SNAPSHOT

1928 Amsterdam Olympiad:

Opening Day May 17; Closing Day August 12

- 46 countries sent teams
- 2883 athletes: 277 women and 2606 men
- 14 sports, 109 events: Aquatics, Athletics, Boxing, Cycling, Equestrian, Fencing, Soccer, Gymnastics, Field Hockey, Modern Pentathlon, Rowing, Sailing, Weight Lifting, and Wrestling

The press called for support and encouraged every means of raising money. At last, the Dutch Olympic Committee had the financing to ensure the success of the Amsterdam Olympiad.[44] The public and financial support of the Amsterdam Olympiad by myriad people and groups once again illustrates the social significance that people attach to sport, especially the Olympic Games.

There were 2883 Olympic athletes representing 46 nations in Amsterdam; 277 Olympians were women.[45] German athletes participated for the first time since 1912, having been excluded from the Olympic Games because of Germany's involvement in World War I. The Germans quickly asserted their athletic prowess by winning 37 Olympic medals; the United States, led by USOC President Douglas MacArthur, won 56. MacArthur, who would later lead the American military in World War II, said, "We are here to represent the greatest country on earth. We did not come here to lose gracefully. We came here to win, and win decisively."

Field hockey was played for the first time, and nine teams entered the competition. British India, known now as India, beat Holland 3–0 before 42,000 fans to win the gold medal.[46] The American dominance in track and field declined in 1928. With the exception of Ray Barbuti's first-place finish in the 400-meters, U.S. athletes failed to achieve a single first-place finish in the sprints, middle-distance, or distance races. The American 400-meter relay team won the gold medal and followed that with a first-place finish in the 1600-meter relay. Both American relay teams set new Olympic records. The indomitable Johnny Weissmuller once again won the gold medal in the 100-meter freestyle, in record time! Not one to rest, he once again anchored the American 800-meter relay and not only won the gold medal but set an Olympic record in the process.

The equally indomitable Paavo Nurmi, now 32 years old, won the silver medal in the 5000-meter event and the gold medal in the 10,000-meters, where he set a new Olympic record, and he captured another silver medal in the 3000-meter steeplechase.

Women's track and field made its appearance for the first time in Amsterdam. The American women won four medals: E. Robinson won the gold in the 100-meter race, and in so doing set the world record; Mildred Wiley captured the bronze in the high jump; Lillian Copeland took second place in the discus throw; and the American 400-meter relay team won the silver as well.

The 1928 Olympiad was a high mark in Olympic competition. More countries competed than ever before, countries that were regarded as "athletically suspect" performed well, and there was a minimum of difficulty.[47]

THE IIND WINTER OLYMPICS: ST. MORITZ, 1928

The popularity of the Winter Games continued to increase as evidenced by the 464 athletes who competed in 1928 in St. Moritz, Switzerland. Twenty-five countries were represented, and the number of women athletes doubled from 13 in 1924 to 26 in 1928.[48] Norway continued to dominate the Winter Olympics, winning 14 medals; the United States won six. The Americans won both the gold and silver medals in the two-man and four-man bobsled competition. The other two medals were won by J. O'Neil Farrell, who tied for third place in the 500-meter speed-skating competition, and Beatrix Loughran, who finished third in women's figure skating. The United States did not

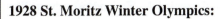

OLYMPIC SNAPSHOT

1928 St. Moritz Winter Olympics:

Opening Day February 11; Closing Day February 19

- 25 countries sent teams
- 464 athletes: 26 women and 438 men
- 4 sports, 14 events: Bobsleigh, Ice Hockey, Skating, and Skiing

send an ice hockey team to St. Moritz. However, Canada continued to be the undisputed champion in ice hockey, capturing its second consecutive gold medal. Sweden followed in second place, and Switzerland won the bronze.

THE ISSUE OF AMATEURISM

During the 1924 Paris Olympiad, several members of the British Olympic team had demanded that the British withdraw from the games because the American team was using professional athletes. The issue of amateurism became such an important topic that after the 1928 Winter and Summer Olympics were concluded, the IOC turned its attention to the question "What is an amateur?" The issue of who should be allowed to compete in the Olympic Games became one of the most volatile issues of the twentieth century. The Olympic ideal of amateurism was a noble concept. However, the concept of amateur participation as measured by traditional standards soon became antiquated. The IOC was steeped in the traditions of Olympism, and the amateur ethic was at the foundation of Olympic eligibility.

The IOC first addressed the question of amateurism in Prague in 1925. During the Prague meeting, the question of "broken time" was also vigorously debated. Broken time involved a situation in which athletes were reimbursed for time lost from work when they were traveling and competing. The prevalent thinking among the IOC was that money given to athletes under the broken-time practice compromised the amateur ethic, so it adamantly opposed the practice of paying athletes via broken-time reimbursement.[49]

In 1930, the IOC convened in Berlin to again discuss the amateurism and broken-time issues. Broken-time payment was supported by the International Football Federation, which controlled soccer. The IOC again opposed outright payments to athletes but ducked the issue of defining the phrase "compensation for loss of salary," leaving the door open for abuse of the amateurism ideal and payments to athletes in one form or another.

THE XTH OLYMPIAD:
LOS ANGELES, 1932

Southern California welcomed Olympic athletes with ideal weather conditions and enthusiastic fans. Los Angeles was decked out with Olympic banners, and enthusiasm for the games was unprecedented. The Los Angeles Organizing Committee was well prepared and well financed. The Los Angeles Coliseum was designed to hold more than 100,000 spectators and was filled to capacity during the opening ceremonies. The male athletes were housed in a newly constructed Olympic Village, while the female athletes were housed in the Chapman Park Hotel to protect their "virtue." The Los Angeles Organizing Committee erected the Olympic Village 10 minutes from the Coliseum. Bill Henry describes the village as consisting of

> miles of flower bordered streets, vast expanses of lawn, cozy cottages of the Mexican ranch-house type were hidden behind a huge white plaster and red tile administration building, and there, secluded from the public but free to follow their own desires, the athletes mingled in their pleasant fellowship.[50]

The games featured the most intense competition to date, and nearly every existing record in track and field was broken.

OLYMPIC SNAPSHOT

1932 Los Angeles Olympiad:

Opening Day July 30; Closing Day August 14

- 37 countries sent teams
- 1332 athletes: 126 women and 1206 men
- 14 sports, 117 events: Aquatics, Athletics, Boxing, Cycling, Equestrian, Fencing, Gymnastics, Field Hockey, Modern Pentathlon, Rowing, Sailing, Shooting, Weight Lifting, and Wrestling

Mildred "Babe" Didrikson of the United States dominated the women's track-and-field competition, winning gold medals in the 80-meter hurdles and the javelin throw and a silver medal in the high jump. Her efforts in the 80-meter hurdles and javelin throw resulted in world records. The Japanese men dominated the swimming events, although the American Clarence "Buster" Crabbe won the 400-meter freestyle. Of the five gold medals awarded to the victors in men's swimming, the Japanese won four, plus the gold in the 800-meter relay. The American men, still the "toast of the world" in diving, swept the competition, finishing first, second, and third in springboard and high diving.

Eddie Tolan, an American, dominated the 100- and 200-meter sprints, setting a new Olympic record in the 100-meters and a world record in the 200-meters. The American men performed well in track and field, but no male American athlete had the "star power" accorded Babe Didrikson. It should be noted that the Americans were humbled on more than one occasion during the 1932 games. Perhaps the most humiliating loss was when the field hockey team from India crushed the Americans 24–1.

The American women dominated the swimming events. Helene Madison won the gold medal in both the 100-meter and 400-meter freestyle in addition to anchoring the gold-medal-winning 400-meter relay team, which set a world record. Madison set two Olympic records as well.

China sent one athlete to compete. Liu Chang-chun competed in the 100- and 200-meter sprints. He did not medal. It would be another 52 years before China won its first Olympic gold medal.

The games did have their problems. Paavo Nurmi, still running for Finland, was disqualified from competing in the marathon because it was determined that he was a professional athlete. In the Parade of Nations, Great Britain, alphabetically supposed to follow behind Germany, was mistakenly placed ahead of the Germans, which resulted in a mild protest. There was confusion in the 3000-meter steeplechase that caused the athletes to run an extra lap. Babe Didrikson was penalized in the high jump because she "dived" over the bar (not jumped), which was illegal in 1932. In all probability, she would have won the gold medal in the high jump but had to be content with the silver. The no-diving rule was eliminated the next year.

The spirit of Olympism and the cooperation among athletes, officials, and fans during the Los Angeles Olympiad could not have been better. However, the Olympics were soon destined to embark on a journey that would forever cast a dark shadow on Coubertin's dream.

THE IIIRD WINTER OLYMPICS: LAKE PLACID, 1932

Seventeen nations sent 252 athletes to compete in the first Winter Olympics held in the United States. There were 21 women, representing 17 countries, who made the trip to upstate New York. A major problem arose, however, when the athletes learned that they would have to compete under American rules, with which the Europeans were not familiar. The Americans benefited from the home-field advantage and won gold medals in the men's 500-meter, 1500-meter, and 10,000-meter speed skating. The American team won both the two-man and four-man bobsled races and finished second to the Canadians in ice hockey. Sonja Henie of Norway, who had won the women's figure skating for the first time at age 15 in St. Moritz, won the gold medal again in Lake Placid. The

demonstration sports featured women's 500-, 1000-, and 1500-meter speed skating along with curling and a 25-mile cross-country dogsled race won by Emile St. Goddard of Canada.

THE POLITICAL NATURE OF THE OLYMPIC GAMES

In the 1930s, the world was undergoing radical change motivated largely by political ideology. Several leaders who emerged during this time would use any and all means to advance specific political and social agendas. The Olympic Games were not immune to such manipulation from forces outside the IOC. Beginning with the 1936 Olympiad in Berlin, unsavory politicians exploited the games for blatant political purposes. Obtrusive politics of regional, national, and international dimensions reflected attempts to undermine the ideals of the Olympics, turning the games from a venue for pure athletic competition to a political vehicle designed to transmit propaganda and ideology.

Global politics and institutional struggles against social and economic inequality became an unwanted part of the Olympic agenda. Indeed, politics became as much a part of the Olympic Games as athletes and sweat. In addition to peace and cooperation, blatant nationalism became a symbol of the Olympics. Despite all this, the members of the IOC dedicated themselves to work even harder to ensure that the Olympic Games would persevere. During decades of global strife and tragedy, the Olympic Games came under attack by the press, self-serving politicians, and terrorists. Thanks to the efforts of the IOC, today the Olympic flame burns more brightly than ever as a symbol of peace, unity, and internationalism. However, the struggle to keep both the flame and the spirit of Olympism alive has been an arduous one, as the ensuing chronicles of the Olympic Games will demonstrate.

Up to this point, the Summer Olympiads and Winter Olympics have been presented as a series of chronological events that reflect selected athletic, social, and political events. The following discussion of the 1936 Berlin Olympiad is

OLYMPIC SNAPSHOT

1932 Lake Placid Winter Olympics:

Opening Day February 4; Closing Day February 15

- 17 countries sent teams
- 252 athletes: 21 women and 231 men
- 4 sports, 14 events: Bobsleigh, Ice Hockey, Skating, and Skiing

significantly more detailed. The reason for this is that the Berlin Olympics involved a number of significant social, political, racial, and religious issues that became part of the Olympic Games. The Olympic Games have come to involve issues that the Baron de Coubertin never intended to include, and as a student of physical education and kinesiology, you should be aware of this. In addition, you should understand that the joy of sport can be taken away from athletes. This was the case in Nazi Germany, when Hitler deliberately set about to persecute Jews and people of color by removing their access to sport—a first step on the road to the Holocaust, in which 6 million Jews and others perished. In addition, you may ask why the United States sent an Olympic team to participate in the 1936 Games, which historian Richard Mandell refers to as the "Nazi Olympics." Although the Nazis tried to undermine the ideal of Olympism, the IOC refused to let this happen.

The XIth Olympiad: Berlin, 1936

Discussion of the 1936 Olympics begins with one of the most ruthless politicians the world has ever known. The reign of terror initiated by Adolf Hitler was among the most heinous and hideous imaginable. As repulsive as Hitler and the Nazis were, it can be argued that Joseph Stalin was just as evil. He murdered millions of Russians and Slavs at about the same time that Hitler and the Nazis were engaged in their despicable acts. They were bitter enemies, Hitler and Stalin. However, Stalin didn't care about the Olympics. In contrast, Hitler saw the games as a political-social platform and fashioned a political agenda that used the Olympics to send his message of Aryan (Nazi) superiority.

Sport and Physical Education in Nazi Germany

Mandell describes Hitler's perspective on sport and physical activity:

> While writing *Mein Kampf* in prison in 1924, Hitler had included some theoretical statements about the value of purposeful physical

OLYMPIC SNAPSHOT

1936 Berlin Olympiad:

Opening Day August 1; Closing Day August 16

- 49 countries sent teams
- 3963 athletes: 331 women and 3632 men
- 19 sports, 129 events: Aquatics, Athletics, Basketball, Boxing, Canoe/Kayak, Cycling, Equestrian, Fencing, Soccer, Gymnastics, Handball, Field Hockey, Modern Pentathlon, Polo, Rowing, Sailing, Shooting, Weight Lifting, and Wrestling

activity. The views on physical training, however, do not bulk large in *Mein Kampf* and are only adjuncts of his reforming schemes for all German education. Characteristically, Hitler viewed the failures of Germany in the past as attributable to a pedagogical regime that was too intellectual, too "unnatural."

Hitler states: "in a race-nationalist state the school itself must set aside infinitely more time for physical conditioning. Not a day should pass in which the young person's body is not schooled at least one hour every morning and evening, and this in every sort of sport and gymnastics."[51]

Hitler's favorite sport was boxing: "No other sport is its equal in building up aggressiveness, in demanding lightning-like decision, and in toughening up the body in steely agility."[52]

Hitler's consistent seeking of grandeur became apparent in his plans for German sport. In the 1930s, Hitler and his compatriots established National Socialist (Nazi) sporting meets, which, like the original Olympiads of the ancient Greeks, were to be racially exclusive. These athletic festivals were the occasion for expansion of the athletic facilities at Nuremberg, where Hitler staged massive Nazi spectacles. The führer felt confident that after 1940 the Olympic Games would, for all time, take place in Germany.

Anti-Jewish legislation was enacted shortly after Hitler became chancellor in 1933 and was an integral part of Nazi terror. The Nazi master-race ethic permeated all aspects of German life, and sport and physical education were no exception. If an occupant of Nazi Germany was a non-Aryan, that person had nearly all aspects of physical activity cut off. On April 1, 1933, when the national boycott of Jewish business went into effect, the German boxing federation announced that it would no longer tolerate Jewish fighters or referees.[53] During that same year, the new Nazi minister of education proclaimed on June 2 that Jews were to be excluded from youth, welfare, and gymnastic organizations and that the facilities of all clubs would be closed to Jews. Jewish athletic teams were first forbidden to compete with Aryan teams and later forbidden to go abroad to compete. A police sports association was forced to expel all the members of its ladies' auxiliary who had competed against a team of Jewish women. By 1935, all private and public practice fields were denied to Jews.[54]

People of color occupied the same category as Jews in Nazi thought; however, there were few blacks in Nazi Germany. Hitler expressed his view on blacks when he said to fellow Nazi Baldur von Schirach, "The Americans ought to be ashamed of themselves for letting their medals be won by Negroes. I myself would never even shake hands with one of them."[55] Hitler apparently thought that the German track athletes would overwhelm the American Olympic team, which had two of the finest sprinters the world had ever seen, Jesse Owens and Ralph Metcalfe, who happened to be African-Americans. Not one male or female German athlete won a gold medal in any running event during the 1936 Berlin Olympiad. However, German athletes did dominate the 1936 Olympics as a team, winning more medals than any other country. German athletes were superb in a number of events. Konrad Frey won five medals in gymnastics (three gold, two silver, and one bronze). Long jumper Luz Long befriended Jesse Owens and helped him determine his start mark in the long jump. In the end, Owens won the gold medal in this event and Long won the silver.

Preparation for the Berlin Olympiad began during the 1932 Olympic Games in Los Angeles. Two Germans were the principal figures in developing, organizing, and staging the Berlin Olympics: Dr. Theodor Lewald, president of the German Olympic Committee, and Dr. Carl Diem, at the time the world's most distinguished sport historian.[56] Lewald and Diem were apparently blind to the Nazi dogma. They were so caught up in staging the Olympic Games that it was too late to stop once they realized what was taking place. In any event, these two men were possibly the closest observers of the 1932 Olympic Games in Los Angeles. Both men had been instrumental in organizing the 1916 Olympics in Berlin and were devastated when their preparatory work was destroyed by World War I. They were not going to be denied a second time.

Both men were tireless workers and digested every detail of the 1932 Olympic Games. Mandell notes:

> As Lewald filled ceremonial functions in Los Angeles, Diem was behind the scenes, seeking masses of material: sketches, models, addresses, flags, programs, tickets, etc., that had been collected for them. . . . Diem took notes as he chatted with designers of the elevator and telephone system. He photographed garages and workshops and stooped and stretched calibrated tapes to take metric measurements of the cottages in Olympic Village. He recorded in his files the statement of the cooks as to the dietary preferences of the participating nationalities.[57]

The two Germans were compiling an extraordinary volume of information about every conceivable aspect of the Olympic production. It was their task to create the ultimate Olympics. The 1932 games at Los Angeles were the most lavish games in modern times. All the facilities were superb. The stadium held 104,000 spectators, and the technical and logistical expertise was the finest available at the time. It was in Los Angeles that the Olympic Village concept became a reality. The living quarters for the Olympic athletes were modern and comfortable. Everything about the 1932 Olympic Games was first class, and it was the responsibility of Diem and Lewald to make those games a second-rate event when compared with the 1936 Berlin Games.

The athletic complex in Berlin was the most complete sporting facility ever built. Construction of the facility progressed rapidly under the direction of Diem, Lewald, and Werner March, the architect. There existed a vast complex of arenas, playing and practice fields, schools, offices, parking lots, and subway stations. The main stadium, the largest ever constructed at the time, occupied only one-twentieth of the entire athletic complex, or Reichssportfeld.[58] The Berlin Olympics had indeed surpassed the spectacle in Los Angeles four years earlier.

Lewald commissioned a German sculptor to construct a giant Olympic bell, which was designed as a major symbol of Nazi pageantry. While the 16-ton bell was en route to Berlin, each town through which it passed held solemn, quasi-religious ceremonies in its honor. Physical education director Dunkelberg extolled the bell as a symbol of the staunch will that characterized the German nation.[59]

The Nazis attempted to play down their anti-Semitic campaign by directing the activities of the visiting journalists to the Olympic Games. The Germans provided almost every imaginable convenience for the visiting press to help them "forget" Nazi racial policies. However, American newspaper readers in 1933 were able to read about the anti-Semitism of the Nazis. And American sports executives were shocked at the removal of Lewald from his post as president of the German Olympic Committee because of his partial Jewish ancestry. During the IOC's meeting in Vienna on June 6, 1933, American Olympic officials demanded that the games be removed from Germany if the Nazis did not cease to discriminate against Jewish athletes. This demand was aired before passage of the Nuremberg Laws in 1935.[60]

The Amateur Athletic Union (AAU) of the United States on November 21, 1933, with but one dissenter, voted to boycott the 1936 games unless the position of Nazi Germany regarding Jewish athletes "changed in fact as well as theory." Gustavus T. Kirby of the USOC had proposed the resolution, and he was vigorously supported by Avery Brundage, then president of the American Olympic Committee.

After the anti-Nazi resolution of the AAU, the USOC continued to postpone acceptance of the German invitation. The facilities for the games in Berlin became another prime public works project of the Nazis. Even as Germany and other nations selected and trained their teams, well-publicized appeals appeared suggesting that the Americans boycott the Berlin Olympics. Strong national sentiment supported this. Nervously, and with yet another fanfare of international publicity, the German Olympic Committee finally announced in June 1934 that 21 Jewish athletes had been nominated for the German training camps. Brundage was suspicious, as were the vast majority of Americans, so the USOC sent Brundage to Germany to investigate.

When Brundage returned to America, he revealed himself to be yet one more important personage dazzled by the order, relative prosperity, and apparent happiness that most travelers observed in Germany at that time. On the basis of interviews with Jewish leaders (who, as one hostile journalist noted, were always met in cafés and were always chaperoned by Nazi officials), Brundage concluded that the Germans were observing the letter and spirit of Olympism.[61] On the basis of Brundage's recommendation, the USOC voted to participate in the Berlin Games. However, the AAU still opposed American participation. Despite Brundage's claims to the contrary, trustworthy accounts of religious and racial persecutions continued to leak out of Germany. For example, it was learned that although 21 Jews were "nominated" for the German Olympic training camp, none was "invited" to attend.[62]

By the summer of 1935, most American Olympic officials had accepted Baron de Coubertin's commandment that, whatever the obstacles, the regular march of the modern Olympiads must take place.

The Berlin Olympics held opening ceremonies on August 1, 1936, with the magnificent new stadium filled to capacity. The German Organizing Committee organized a torch run that originated in Olympia, Greece. Thanks to the efforts of over 3000 relay runners, the sacred flame was transported from Greece across Europe to arrive in Berlin during opening ceremonies. Athletes from 49 countries arrived in Berlin to take part in the games, of whom 331 were women, representing 26 countries.[63] The athletes, coaches, IOC officials, and spectators were treated to a spectacular Olympiad. The Olympic atmosphere was festive, and the enthusiasm of the fans was contagious. The opening ceremonies featured the release of thousands of doves against the backdrop of the massive Olympic flame that burned at the open end of the stadium. The evening ceremonies featured 10,000 dancers and wonderful choreography. They were joined by a chorus of 1500 singers who performed

Schiller's "Ode to Joy," specifically requested by Coubertin.

The superstar of the 1936 Olympics was not a member of the Aryan race from Germany, as Hitler had hoped, but an African-American. Jesse Owens, the son of a sharecropper and grandson of a slave, was born on September 12, 1913, in Alabama. By the time he was seven years old, Owens was working in the cotton fields of Alabama, picking up to 100 pounds of cotton a day. When he was nine, the family moved to Ohio where he set national high-school records in track and field. He was recruited by 28 colleges and selected Ohio State University, much to the dismay of the black leaders in the community (Figure 15-4). At that time, Ohio State University had a reputation as a racist institution.[64]

In 1935, Owens was competing in California and was photographed with a white women named Quincella Nikerson. This was not the kind of attention Jesse Owens needed, especially in an

Figure 15-4
Jesse Owens setting one of four world records at the Big Ten Meet, May 25, 1935, in Ann Arbor, Michigan.

era when interracial dating was taboo. This was the tip of the proverbial iceberg for Owens. In July 1935, a Cleveland journalist confronted Owens with information that he was the father of a young girl and the newspaper would publish a photo of the little girl if Owens did not marry the mother right away. Jesse Owens married Ruth Bolomon the next day. A month later, another report surfaced that as an athlete at Ohio State, he had been provided with jobs where he never had to work but was paid. Jesse Owens paid back the sum of $159, the salary he received, and the matter was settled.[65] All in all, 1935 was not the best year for this sensational athlete; 1936 would be better.

Owens was one of the most phenomenal track-and-field athletes in Olympic history. He won gold medals in the 100- and 200-meter races, running broad jump, and 400-meter relay. He also set world records in the 200-meter race and the 400-meter relay and an Olympic record in the running broad jump. During the 1936 Berlin Olympics, a myth was started about Hitler's refusal to congratulate Owens after a victory. This account is fiction. What did conceivably happen was that Hitler refused to congratulate Cornelius Johnson and David Albritton, two African-Americans who won the gold and silver medals in the high jump the previous day.[66] What is truly appalling is that when Owens returned to the United States as the hero of the 1936 games, President Franklin D. Roosevelt never invited him to the White House for a well-deserved ceremony. In addition, Roosevelt did not bother to write him a letter congratulating him on his incredible accomplishments in Berlin. Fortunately, the good people of New York City and Cleveland held ticker tape parades to honor Owens.[67]

We are not sure why Roosevelt snubbed Jesse Owens. However, it was not the last time that the hero of Berlin would be snubbed. The AAU suspended Owens for his failure to participate in a track-and-field meet in Sweden, a meet in which Owens had never agreed to participate. After this calculated insult, in 1936, the AAU also ignored Owens for the Sullivan Award, given to the country's best amateur athlete. So, whom did the AAU select to receive the Sullivan Award in 1936? The award was given to Glenn Morris, who won the Olympic decathlon in Berlin.[68] Was Owens a victim of racism?

After the Olympics of 1936, Owens held a number of jobs over the years. He was able to secure his financial future by opening a successful public relations firm and soon serving as spokesperson for several corporations. When militant African-American athletes from the United States raised black-gloved fists during the medal ceremony at the 1968 Mexico City Olympics, Owens took the side of the USOC. In 1970, he wrote a book titled *Blackthink,* critical of racial militancy. However, in 1972, he wrote another book titled *I Have Changed,* which retracted his earlier positions.[69] Jesse Owens died from lung cancer on March 31, 1980. In 1984, a street in Berlin was named in his honor.

In addition to racist sentiments, anti-Semitism was not limited to Berlin. Marty Glickman (1917–2001) was 18 when he was selected as a member of the American 400-meter relay. The day before the relay, the assistant track coach, Dean Cromwell from the University of Southern California, dropped Glickman and Sam Stoller from the relay team. Glickman and Stoller were the only Jews on the track-and-field team. Glickman later went on to a stellar career as the preeminent radio voice of sports in New York. He was convinced that Cromwell and Avery Brundage were members of the America First committee and were Nazi sympathizers.[70]

The winner in the men's marathon in 1936 is listed in the official Olympic records as Kitei Son from Japan. However, he was from Korea, which in 1936 was under the control of Japan. The Japanese told the Korean he could run the marathon but would represent Japan and would do so with a Japanese name. The third-place finisher in the men's marathon was Shorya Nan, another Korean running for Japan with a new name. German athletes dominated the equestrian events as well as competitions in men's and women's gymnastics. However, in the decathlon, the event to determine the best athlete in the world, the American team of Glenn E. Morris, Robert Clark, and Jack Parker won the gold, silver, and bronze medals, respectively. In all, the American team collected 56 medals and, as usual, were strong in men's track and field; the host Germans amassed 99.

The Berlin Games were technically the best in history, and nothing had approached the massive scale of the XIth Olympiad. And why not? Hitler was convinced that his Third Reich would last for a thousand years and therefore spared no expense or effort in building the most lavish Olympic facilities history had known. He was positive that all future Olympiads would take place in Berlin. The Winter Olympics were also held in Germany, and, as you might expect, the games at Garmisch-Partenkirchen were a success.

THE IVTH WINTER OLYMPICS: GARMISCH–PARTENKIRCHEN, 1936

At Garmisch-Partenkirchen in 1936, Adolf Hitler was on hand to welcome athletes from all over the world, and 15,000 fans swarmed into the stadium to join the führer during the opening ceremonies. Close to 75,000 people came to Garmisch-Partenkirchen every day to watch the competition.[71] Twenty-eight nations sent teams; 15 countries sent ice hockey

OLYMPIC SNAPSHOT

1936 Garmisch-Partenkirchen Winter Olympics:

Opening Day February 6; Closing Day February 16

- 28 countries sent teams
- 646 athletes: 80 women and 566 men
- 4 sports, 17 events: Bobsleigh, Ice Hockey, Skating, and Skiing

teams, 13 countries were entered in the bobsledding competition, 16 nations were entered in speed skating, and 27 nations sent ski teams. There were 143 athletes from Germany alone![72] In addition, 80 women from 28 countries competed in figure skating and skiing.[73]

The American team won both the gold and the silver medals in the two-man bobsled. The bronze medal in ice hockey and in the 500-meter speed skating were the best the American team could do. The host Germans did not do much better, earning but six medals, as Austria, Norway, Finland, and Sweden dominated the competition.

SUMMARY

The Olympics slowly emerged as one of the most important social and athletic movements in the early twentieth century. Dr. William Penny Brookes of Great Britain and Baron Pierre de Coubertin of France are largely responsible for establishing the modern Olympic Games. Coubertin was inspired by the work of Brookes and the success of the Wenlock Olympian Society in staging the Wenlock Olympic Games. It was Coubertin, assisted by Dr. William M. Sloane of Princeton University, who would elevate Brookes's concept from a regional athletic festival to the all-encompassing international athletic festival that the Olympic Games represent.

From the altruistic beliefs of Brookes to the idealism of Coubertin and the blatant political ideology and propaganda of the Nazis, the Olympics experienced both exhilaration and despair. Coubertin believed that the impact of national governments on the tone and purpose of the Olympics could be minimized if the games were awarded to cities instead of countries. Sadly, the noble ideals of Olympism would give way to the political agendas of nationalism and blatant propaganda. Although Coubertin recognized that politics could undermine the spirit of Olympism, he never envisioned what Hitler and the Nazis would do to his beloved Olympics.

It was not until 1948 that the Olympic flame would burn again, in London during the games of the XIVth Olympiad. The Olympic games had been precluded in

1940 and 1944 as the world plunged into yet another world war. The 1940 Olympics had been awarded to Tokyo and then belatedly to Helsinki, which did not give up hope of holding the games until the Russians invaded Finland in 1939.

The international Olympic community mourned the death of Baron Pierre de Coubertin who, at age 74, died a few weeks after the close of the Berlin Olympiad. His successor, Count Henri de Baillet Latour, an accomplished diplomat, assumed the duties as president of the IOC in a particularly difficult time. Baillet Latour died unexpectedly in January of 1942, his death in all probability hastened by the grief he felt over the death of his son, killed in a wartime plane crash. The IOC honored J. Sigfried Edstrom as the next president of the IOC during the 1946 London meeting. It was during the London meeting of the IOC that Avery Brundage of the United States was elected vice-president of the organization.

DISCUSSION QUESTIONS

1. Was there a political, educational, or social agenda for the establishment of the modern Olympic Games? If so, who were the individuals involved, and how did these political, educational, or social issues manifest themselves?

2. What role did the IOC play with regard to the inclusion of women athletes in the Olympic Games? What were some of the cultural barriers that served to limit the participation of women in sport during the early part of the twentieth century? How would you contrast the participation of women Olympians in the era between 1896 and 1936 with that of the new millennium?

3. What were the ideals that Baron de Coubertin wanted to further through the Olympic Games?

4. How would you balance patriotism with internationalism in the games?

5. Did Hitler use the Olympic Games of 1936 as political propaganda? What political and moral issues were associated with the Berlin Games? Did the USOC have concerns about sending a team to the Berlin Games? What were they? What contributions were made by Owens? To what extent was Owens a victim of racism in the United States?

6. How effective was Baron de Coubertin in promoting the Olympic Games? What were his major victories? What were his major defeats and disappointments?

7. Do you think the Olympic Games encourage nationalism? If so, what examples come to mind?

8. Baron de Coubertin envisioned the Olympic Games as a catalyst for world peace—"peace through sport." To what extent, if any, have the Olympic games achieved this goal?

INTERNET RESOURCES

International Olympic Committee (IOC)
www.olympic.org
Includes links and information about all aspects of the Olympic Games.

International Olympic Academy
www.ioa.org.gr
Is the home page of the International Olympic Academy.

United States Olympic Committee
www.usoc.org
Is the home page of the U.S. Olympic Committee; includes information on Olympic events and athletes.

Olympic Studies Center
http://olympicstudies.uab.es/eng/yellow/dir/om.html

Provides historical and philosophical information about the modern Olympic Games.

Pierre de Coubertin Committee
www.decoubertin.org
Is the home page of the de Coubertin Committee.

International Center for Olympic Studies
www.uwo.ca/olympic/
Provides links for scholars interested in Olympic history and philosophy; also presents lectures and publishes the *International Journal of Olympic Studies—Olympika.*

Visit the *History and Philosophy of Sport and Physical Education* Online Learning Center (www.mhhe.com/mechikoff6e) for additional information and study tools.

SUGGESTIONS FOR FURTHER READING

Books

Brownell, S. *1904 St. Louis Olympic Games and Anthropology Days.* London: Taylor and Francis, 2007.

Coubertin, P. *Olympic Memoirs.* Lausanne: International Olympic Committee, 1997, 236 pgs. Coubertin's *Olympic Memoirs* was first published in 1931 by the Bureau International de Pedagogie Sportive, an organization founded by Coubertin. The International Olympic Committee has published *Olympic Memoirs* since 1976. It is available in English and French.

Kidd, B. *The Struggle for Canadian Sport.* Toronto: University of Toronto Press, 1999, 323 pgs. Written by Olympian and social historian Dr. Bruce Kidd, this engaging book has as its focus Canadian sport history. However, it also contains revealing information and thought-provoking commentary on the Olympic Games.

Large, D. C. *Nazi Games: The Olympics of 1936.* New York: W. W. Norton, 2007.

Lucas, J. A. *Future of the Olympic Games.* Champaign: Human Kinetics Books, 1992, 231 pgs. Professor Emeritus Lucas provides the reader with an illuminating and objective view of the future of the Olympics. Although the book was written more than a decade ago, the prophetic Lucas appears to have a "crystal ball" that is very accurate in the new millennium. Dr. Lucas is an internationally renowned authority on the Olympic Games and was selected by the International Olympic Committee as its "Official Lecturer."

Mandell, R. D. *The Nazi Olympics.* New York: Macmillan, 1971.

Miller, D. *Athens to Athens: The Official History of the Olympic Games and the IOC, 1894–2004.* London: Mainstream Press, 2004.

The Olympic Movement. Lausanne: 1993, 111 pgs. Provides a basic overview of the ideals of Olympism, Olympic Movement, and the organizational structure of the International Olympic Committee. In addition, this handy reference includes information on the international sports federations who govern specific sports worldwide, past IOC presidents, and related Olympic programs. Excellent photos. Ask for the latest edition.

Journal Articles

Lucas, J. A. "Coubertin One Hundred Years Ago: His Second American Visit." *OLYMPIKA—The International Journal of Olympic Studies, Notes and Commentary,* Vol. II, 1993, pp. 103–08.

Pitsula, J. M. "The Nazi Olympics: A Reinterpretation." *OLYMPIKA—The International Journal of Olympic Studies,* Vol. XIII, 2004, pp. 1–25.

Quanz, D. "Civic Pacifism and Sports-based Internationalism: Framework for the Founding of the International Olympic Committee." *OLYMPIKA—The International Journal of Olympic Studies,* Vol. II, 1993, pp. 1–23.

Sullivan, S. P. and R. A. Mechikoff. "A Man of His Time: Pierre de Coubertin's Olympic Ideology and the Via Media." *OLYMPIKA—The International Journal of Olympic Studies,* Vol. XIII, 2004, pp. 27–52.

NOTES

1. *The Olympic Movement* (Chateau de Vidy, Lausanne, Switzerland: International Olympic Committee, 1993), 8.

2. See John Lucas, *The Modern Olympic Games* (South Brunswick and New York: A. S. Barnes, 1980); Mary Leigh, "Pierre de Coubertin: A Man of His Time," *Quest* XXII (June 1974): 19–24.

3. Thomas Hughes, *Tom Brown's School Days* (Boston: A. W. Elson, 1890).

4. David C. Young, "Demetrios Vikelas and Pierre de Coubertin: A Partnership of Destiny," *Journal of Olympic History,* Vol. 15, No. 2, July 2007, pp. 24–25.

5. Betty Spears and Richard Swanson, *History of Sport and Physical Education in the United States,* 3rd ed. (Dubuque, IA: Wm. C. Brown, 1988), 363.

6. David Wallechinsky, *The Complete Book of the Summer Olympics,* Sydney 2000 ed. (New York: Overlook Press, 2000), xx.

7. Ibid.

8. George R. Matthews, "The Modern Olympic Games, 1896–1912" (master's thesis, San Diego State University, 1977), 30–31.

9. Ibid., 37.

10. Pierre de Coubertin, "The Mystery of the Olympian Games," *North American Review* (June 1900): 806.

11. Wallechinsky, *Complete Book of the Summer Olympics,* xx.

12. Matthews, "Modern Olympic Games," 61.

13. Bill Henry, *An Approved History of the Olympic Games* (Los Angeles: Southern California Committee for the Olympic Games, 1981), 52.

14. *St. Louis Post-Dispatch,* 7 April 1904.

15. Henry, *Approved History,* 57.

16. Wallechinsky, *Complete Book of the Summer Olympics,* 70, 71, 90.

17. Matthews, "Modern Olympic Games," 83.

18. Ibid., 84.

19. *The New York Times,* 12 July 1908, 10.

20. *London Times,* 11 July 1908, 17.

21. John Kieran and Arthur Daley, *The Story of the Olympic Games, 776 b.c. to 1948 a.d.* (Philadelphia: J. B. Lippincott, 1948), 86.

22. *London Times,* 18 July 1908, 9.

23. *The New York Times,* 29 July 1908, 9.

24. Matthews, "Modern Olympic Games," 117.

25. Ibid., 118.

26. *The New York Times,* 23 April 1912, 11.

27. *Olympic Movement,* 62.

28. Henry, *Approved History,* 86.

29. Anita Defrantz, "The Olympic Games and Women," *Olympic Review,* XXV, no. 5 (October–November 1995), 56.

30. Wallechinsky, *Complete Book of the Summer Olympics,* xxii.

31. Ibid., 56.

32. *Olympicism* (Lausanne, Switzerland: International Olympic Committee, 1972).

33. Henry, *Approved History,* 98.

34. Leigh, "Pierre de Coubertin," 21.

35. Ibid., 21–22.

36. *Olympic Movement,* 62; Defrantz, "The Olympic Games and Women," 58.

37. Henry, *Approved History,* 125–26; Defrantz, "The Olympic Games and Women," 58.

38. Ibid., 22.

39. Henry, *Approved History,* 369.

40. Ibid., 115.

41. Lucas, *Modern Olympic Games,* 101.

42. Henry, *Approved History,* 116.

43. *Olympic Movement,* 62 and 74; Defrantz, "The Olympic Games and Women," 58.

44. Ibid., 104.

45. Ibid.

46. Ibid., 105–06.

47. Henry, *Approved History,* 133–34.

48. Ibid.

49. Ibid., 134–35.

50. Ibid., 138.

51. Richard D. Mandell, *The Nazi Olympics* (New York: Macmillan, 1971), 234.

52. Ibid.

53. Ibid., 58.

54. Ibid., 59.

55. Ibid., 236.

56. Ibid., 44.

57. Ibid.

58. Ibid., 125.

59. Ibid., 127.

60. Ibid., 70.

61. Ibid., 73.

62. Ibid., 73–74.

63. Ibid.

64. Wallechinsky, *Complete Book of the Summer Olympics,* 6.

65. Ibid.

66. Ibid.

67. Ibid.

68. Ibid.

69. Ibid., 7.

70. *The New York Times,* 4 January 2001, A23.

71. Henry, *Approved History,* 176.

72. Ibid.

73. Ibid.

C H A P T E R **16**

The Cold War Olympics: 1948–1988

O B J E C T I V E S

Upon completing this chapter, you will be able to:

- Explain the impact of World War II on the Olympic Games.
- Appreciate the attempt by the IOC to advance the goal of world peace through international athletic competition.
- Discuss the financial, political, and social impact of World War II on the 1948 London Olympiad.
- Recognize the significance of the Cold War and its impact on international relations.
- Explain how the Olympic Games were used during the Cold War as a weapon in the political propaganda war waged between the United States and the Soviet Union.
- Understand how the conflict in the Middle East between Arab nations and Israel affected the Olympic Games in 1948 and in 1972.
- Recognize that boycotts are a part of Olympic history.
- Understand how the Cold War and the subsequent geopolitical goals of the Communist Eastern Bloc nations led by the Soviet Union and the Western Bloc nations led by the United States were manifest during the 1952 Helsinki Olympiad.
- Understand the impact of South Africa's apartheid policy on the 1952 Olympic Games and subsequent Olympiads.
- Explain why the IOC forced the Olympic teams from East Germany and West Germany to form one team, and discuss the results of the merger.
- Understand how the IOC handled the delicate political situation relative to recognizing Olympic teams from Nationalist China (Taiwan) and the People's Republic of China.
- Discuss the impact of the Cold War on the 1956 Melbourne Olympiad.
- Understand how athletes from Eastern Bloc nations and other nations ruled by Communists used the Olympic Games as a means to defect to the West.
- Trace how the Suez Canal crisis evolved into another war in the Middle East, and discuss its impact on international relations and the Olympic movement.

- Discuss the effects of political tensions and global conflicts on the 1960 Rome Olympiad.
- Understand how extensively the Olympics are used as a tool for political and social propaganda.
- Explain why Olympic judges would award points on the basis of political ideology and not athletic superiority.
- Discuss the geopolitical climate of the world during the 1964 Tokyo Olympics, and describe its impact on the games.
- Identify Olympic teams that were expelled from the Tokyo Olympiad.
- Recognize the effects of political and social protests on the staging of the 1968 Mexico City Olympiad.
- Discuss the impact of the Vietnam War on the United States relative to the widespread political and social protests that took place.
- Understand how the Mexico City Olympiad was used as a means of calling attention to the plight of people of color in the United States.
- Explain the reasoning that led to rioting in Mexico City shortly before the start of the Olympic Games, and describe how the federal government of Mexico responded.
- Understand the response by the IOC to the student demonstrations and rioting that took place in Mexico City.
- Understand how regional conflicts surfaced during the Olympic Games, and discuss the resulting consequences.
- Recognize that the use of the Olympics for political ends increased from 1972 until the end of the Cold War.
- Recognize that, apart from Olympic politics, the major concern of the IOC and most national Olympic committees was the pervasive use of performance-enhancing drugs by Olympic athletes.
- Explain why the practice of racial discrimination in the form of apartheid and its attendant social and political ramifications were of such concern to the IOC.
- Understand how political ideology and religious differences devastated the 1972 Munich Olympiad.
- Understand how other African nations responded to the demand by Rhodesia that its Olympic team be allowed to compete in Munich.
- Recognize the political and economic differences that caused an international crisis between the United States and Canada during the 1976 Montreal Olympiad.
- Discuss the social and political issues that led to the African boycott of the Montreal Olympiad.
- Recognize the need for the intensive security preparations that, in the wake of the 1972 Munich massacre, have become part of the Olympic Games.
- Recognize the propaganda value of Olympic success.
- Appreciate the significant increase in the number of women Olympians and the expansion of the Olympic program that enabled women athletes to compete in many different events that at one time were reserved exclusively for men.
- Understand the Cold War mentality that existed in 1980 and the reasons stated by President Jimmy Carter to boycott the 1980 Moscow Olympiad.
- Discuss the reaction of the U.S. Olympic Committee and American Olympians to the boycott.
- Discuss the reaction of the IOC and the rest of the world to the American boycott.

- Recognize how Olympic athletes can be used as political pawns by their governments.

- Understand the Cold War mentality that existed in 1984 and the reasons given by the Soviet Union for boycotting the 1984 Los Angeles Olympiad.

- Discuss the security measures, and their costs, with regard to potential terrorist attacks during the 1984 Los Angeles Olympiad.

- Understand the political and social propaganda that the United States capitalized on as a result of the American success in the 1984 Olympics.

- Understand the concerns of South Korea regarding the threat of a terrorist attack from neighboring North Korea during the 1988 Seoul Olympiad, and describe the security measures taken to prevent such an attack during the Olympics.

- Identify the political relationship between Japan and Korea, and discuss how this relationship manifested itself during the Seoul Olympiad.

- Recognize the controversy that the National Broadcasting Company (NBC) created as a result of its telecast, repeated a number of times, of a boxing match featuring a South Korean athlete.

INTRODUCTION

The 1936 Berlin Olympiad and the 1936 Winter Games at Garmisch-Partenkirchen would be the last for more than a decade. The IOC, as did everybody else, endured hardship during World War II. However, the spirit of Olympism prevailed against incredible odds. In 1936, the IOC selected Tokyo as the host city for the 1940 Olympiad. However, Japan later began a military adventure that plunged the United States into World War II. The Tokyo organizing committee worked hard to bring the games to fruition but was eventually instructed by the Japanese government to halt preparations because Japan was at war with China. The other city that bid for the 1940 Olympic Games was Helsinki. When Tokyo relinquished the games, the IOC turned to Helsinki. The valiant Finns faced unprecedented difficulties but persisted in the face of a mounting military threat from the Soviet Union. Unfortunately, Finland was invaded by the Soviet Union in 1939, and the Olympic Games were postponed. In a symbolic gesture, the flame that burned brightly above the Los Angeles Coliseum, site of the 1932 Olympiad, was lit once again during the time when the 1940 Olympiad was to have taken place. As was the case during World War I, the Olympic Games were postponed because of war.

Baron de Coubertin and all IOC presidents to follow believed that the Olympics could promote peace and thus help prevent wars. Count Henri de Baillet Latour, president of the IOC from 1925 to 1942, said,

> May there be an overwhelming response of athletes to this call [to the Olympics]. It can be taken for granted that magnificent contests will result when they measure their strength and suppleness of their bodies against each other; but it is my most earnest desire that from this encounter of their ideals there may grow a more profound understanding of their varying points of view, so that these peaceful combats will give birth to enduring

friendships that will usefully serve the cause of peace.[1]

The IOC had been presided over by two presidents who had seen firsthand the horrors of two world wars—Baron de Coubertin and Count Latour. The wisdom of these two former IOC presidents and their goal of promoting peace and friendship through an international athletic festival ought to have been welcomed by all. However, history shows us that their Olympic ideal was ignored on more than one occasion. We can only speculate what may have happened if the Olympic ideal had prevailed in the years surrounding World War I and World War II; where politicians failed, athletes may have prevailed.

THE XIVTH OLYMPIAD: LONDON, 1948

World War II prevented the Olympic Games from being held in 1940 and 1944. The IOC had awarded the 1944 games to London, which provided justification for the British to host the 1948 games. "Hardly had the last shot gone echoing down the halls of time before the International Olympic Committee met in bomb-scarred London in August 1945 to make it official."[2]

The German blitzkrieg had all but devastated London. In addition to rebuilding England, the

---

OLYMPIC SNAPSHOT

1948 London Olympiad:

Opening Day July 29; Closing Day August 14

- 59 countries sent teams
- 4104 athletes: 390 women and 3714 men
- 17 sports, 136 events: Aquatics, Athletics, Basketball, Boxing, Canoe/Kayak, Cycling, Equestrian, Fencing, Gymnastics, Field Hockey, Modern Pentathlon, Rowing, Sailing, Shooting, Soccer, Weight Lifting, and Wrestling

---

British agreed to host the 1948 games. Severe austerity measures were enacted by the government to cope with shortages in food, housing, medical care, and other necessities, so it is understandable that the citizens of London did not embrace the 1948 London Olympiad. Many questioned the decision of the IOC and the British to hold the games in London. In the aftermath of World War II, they argued, there were much more important problems that needed attention than allocating resources for the Olympic Games.

The Political Atmosphere

The political atmosphere in post–World War II England revolved around several critical issues that affected the entire global community. Considerable attention by the *London Times* during July 1948 was focused on the Berlin blockade by the Soviets and the formulation and implementation of the state of West Germany. International relations were strained almost to the breaking point between the four nations that governed Berlin; Britain, France, and the United States were not about to turn West Berlin over to the Communists. According to the *London Times,*

> Mr. Bevin, speaking in the House of Commons yesterday of the events in Berlin, said it was recognized that a grave situation might arise. "Should such a situation arise," he said, "we shall have to ask the House to face it. The British Government and our western allies can see no alternative between that and surrender, and none of us can accept surrender."[3]

Strong criticisms of the action taken by the Soviets in Berlin were reiterated on a daily basis. The Berlin airlift was in progress, and the risk of yet another world war was a real concern.

Britain's evacuation of Palestine, which led to the creation of the new state of Israel, added to the already tense political climate. As the Jews and the Arabs struggled for control of Palestine, both factions engaged in acts of sabotage against the British during their withdrawal.[4] On the same day that the British evacuated Haifa, Arab kings held a conference in Cairo, Egypt, and "reached complete agreement on national and patriotic objectives." The essence of the meeting was agreement to consolidate forces to gain control of Palestine and eventually make the state of Israel Arab territory.

Furthermore, reports from behind the Iron Curtain regarding elimination of freedom and human rights received considerable attention. The fear of communism encompassed the West. Chinese Communists had crossed the Yalu River, and Communist insurgents were causing havoc in the British territories of Malaya and Singapore. The situation was so threatening that Britain outlawed the Communist Party in its troubled territories.[5]

In short, global political issues were at center stage. As a result, press coverage of the London Games was minimal. The American Olympic contingent was shocked at the lack of media coverage of and unconcern for the games by Londoners. John Kieran and Arthur Daley describe the situation as follows:

> The Americans had just left a country where the newspapers were jam-packed with Olympic news, some 3,000 miles from the spot where they were to be held. The skimpy and threadbare London papers mentioned the Olympics to be sure, but that mention was buried away with the classified ads while their sports columns were filled to overflowing with the real important stuff such as dog race results, hoss [sic] race results and a glowing account of the cricket test match with Australia.[6]

Apart from the devastating attack by the Japanese on Pearl Harbor on December 7, 1941, American cities had been untouched by World War II. The United States had a 3000-mile "buffer zone"—the Atlantic Ocean—that separated it from the turmoil that postwar Europe was experiencing. Americans did not have to dig out from the rubble created by the German blitzkrieg as did the people of London. Londoners were far more preoccupied with the events unfolding close by in Europe than most Americans. There was the distinct possibility that Europe would once again be at war with the

newly formed countries behind the Iron Curtain. This accounts for the perceived lack of interest in the London Games by Europeans.

By 1948, the global political alignment was clear: East versus West. Two political camps had been created, and a power struggle was under way. Fortunately, political strife during the London games was minimal, though one interesting political incident did occur.

The new country of Israel sent a delegation to London with the intent of competing in the Olympics. The delegation from Israel was represented by one athlete, a woman who hoped to compete in track and field. On learning of the wishes of the Israelis, the Arab countries made it clear to IOC officials that if the team from Israel was allowed to compete, the Arabs would boycott the games. The IOC denied permission to Israel. The idea of boycotting the Olympic Games was not new. The United States had considered boycotting the 1936 Berlin Olympics. However, the Cold War that ensued after World War II gradually embroiled the Olympic movement in political and social issues. Some of these issues revolved around blatant attempts by both East and West to advance their political agendas. Social issues such as apartheid eventually isolated South Africa from the Olympic community for decades.

The 1948 Olympiad is notable for several reasons. After many people had prematurely proclaimed the end of the Olympic Games as a result of the events of World War II, the IOC once again displayed its indomitable spirit, and the games took place as scheduled. There were more countries participating in the London Olympiad (59) than in any previous Olympiad. The second largest number of athletes ever took part in the games; of these, 390 were women—the largest number of women athletes ever to take part in the Olympics.[7]

In what would become an almost routine occurrence during the Summer Olympics, the London Olympiad was marked by the threat of a boycott. The irony is that Baron de Coubertin had envisioned the Olympic Games as transcending political and social boundaries and actually bringing people together. Instead, some countries threatened to withdraw from or boycott the Olympics if certain other countries were allowed to participate. This attitude reflects political and social differences that could be resolved if the opposing countries were able to enhance their communication and understanding through a common medium that cuts across most political and social barriers. Sports are this medium, and the Olympics represent an international ideal and opportunity that fosters such communication and understanding. The IOC and many others continue to believe in the message of Coubertin: that the Olympic Games provide a great opportunity to promote international understanding and thus contribute to world peace. However, the Cold War and subsequent international disputes have, from time to time, manifested themselves within the Olympics, as the London Games demonstrated. Global politics and related tensions could be removed from the Olympic Games if the individuals and groups that represent various political and social interests would heed Coubertin's message. However, these same individuals and groups apparently have identified the Olympics as a "political resource" and not necessarily as an instrument or means for promoting the spirit of Olympism. The IOC has done a remarkable job considering the circumstances. True, some questionable decisions have been made by the IOC. For example, the IOC awarded the 2008 Summer Olympics to Beijing, China, which has a history of little, if any, respect for human rights. The 2014 Winter Olympics were awarded to the city of Sochi, a resort in Russia. It should be noted that Russia invaded Georgia, a former Soviet Bloc country, on the opening day of the Beijing Olympics.

The Russians did not compete in the London Games; however, Communist attempts to sabotage the games were reported by the media. A reporter from the *London Times* assigned to cover the progress of the Olympic torch run from Olympia, Greece, to London, filed the following account:

> Special precautions in the form of troops, armored cars, and aircraft were taken at Olympia and along the runner's route [Olympic torch bearer] to Katakolon to prevent any interference in yesterday's proceedings by communist forces. General Markos, the rebel leader, is reported to have broadcast orders for the Olympic ceremony to be wrecked. On Friday a small band attacked Katakolon and killed with machine gun fire a policeman who was defending our party.[8]

Sadly, violence and death occurred during the first Olympiad held during the Cold War era, and it would not be the last such incident. Two decades later in Mexico City, the 1968 games were disrupted by student protesters, and many were killed by Mexican authorities. The Munich Olympiad of 1972 saw the massacre of Israeli Olympians by Arab terrorists.

Political defections from East to West occurred during the London Games, as some Czech and Hungarian athletes flatly refused to return home. The repressive political and social systems that reflected Soviet "values" were not to their liking. In future Olympiads, more athletes from Eastern Bloc countries would use the Olympic Games as a means to defect to the West. In 1948, the *London Times* offered prophetic insight prior to the opening ceremonies:

> The Olympic oath, taken on behalf of all competitors, speaks of the honour of a country and the glory of sport—not the other way round as some would have it. Probably only two things now could wreck the Games—one, a political-racial use of them by overambitious states, and two, the virtual subsidizing of the athletes which would be bound to follow.[9]

This prediction was to became a reality.

Notables

The American athletes may have been pleasantly surprised when they participated in the opening ceremonies. Over 80,000 spectators at Wembley Stadium greeted athletes from 59 nations. However, the influence of international politics had already been felt: German and Japanese athletes were excluded from the games because of their actions in World War II.

Bob Mathias, a 17-year-old high-school student from Tulare, California, was the talk of the games as he won the gold medal in the decathlon. Dubbed the "flying Dutchwoman," Fanny Blankers-Koen won four gold medals in women's track. Women's track and field added three new events: the 200-meter run, the broad jump, and the eight-pound shot put. The only American gold medal winner in women's track and field was Alice Coachman, who won the high jump with an effort of 5 feet 6¼ inches, a new Olympic record. The American men dominated track and field, winning 25 medals including 11 gold. Without competition from the traditionally strong Japanese team, the American men also won 16 medals in swimming and diving. In fact, the Americans came in first place in every swimming and diving event. The American team was not "threatened" athletically by the teams assembled for the London Olympiad. However, the level of athletic competition significantly increased during the 1952 Helsinki Olympiad with the return of the Japanese, Germans, and Russians.

THE VTH WINTER OLYMPICS: ST. MORITZ, 1948

Some 669 athletes from 28 nations arrived in St. Moritz to compete in the first postwar Winter Games, including 77 women athletes.[10] The amateurism issue was in the spotlight, and an ensuing scandal involved the International Ice Hockey Federation (IIHF), the United States Olympic Committee (USOC), and the IOC. The amateur standing of the American ice hockey team was in grave doubt, and the IOC was called on to resolve the issue. It seems that the St. Moritz Organizing Committee and the International Ice Hockey Federation declared that the American team was not eligible. The American team did not meet the eligibility requirements at all, even though the IIHF certified them to compete. The IOC was furious with both the St. Moritz Organizing Committee and the IIHF, not to mention the American ice hockey team. The IOC almost decided to ban the ice hockey competition but instead banned the IIHF from any participation

OLYMPIC SNAPSHOT

1948 St. Moritz Winter Olympics:

Opening Day January 30; Closing Day February 8

- 28 countries sent teams
- 669 athletes: 77 women and 592 men
- 4 Sports, 22 events: Bobsleigh, Ice Hockey, Skating, and Skiing

with the St. Moritz Organizing Committee.[11] The U.S. team was also barred from competing.

The American men failed to win a single medal in the skiing competition, although Gretchen Fraser won the gold in the special slalom and the silver in the downhill and slalom for the women's team. Richard "Dick" Button, just 18 years old, won the gold medal for the United States in men's figure skating. J. Heaton from the United States won the silver medal in the skeleton bobsledding competition. In the four-man bobsled, the Americans won both the gold and bronze medals. In men's speed skating, K. Bartholomew and R. Fitzgerald from the United States tied with T. Byberg of Norway for second place. The Canadian team performed well, too. In women's figure skating, B. A. Scott won the gold medal, and in pairs figure skating, the team of Suzanne Morrow and W. Distelmyer won the bronze. The Canadian ice hockey team once again demonstrated its superiority by winning the gold medal. The next Winter Olympics would be in Oslo, and the American teams would enjoy the success that had eluded them in St. Moritz, where the Scandinavian countries were once again overpowering.

THE XVTH OLYMPIAD: HELSINKI, 1952

The Political Atmosphere

In 1952, the global political situation continued to revolve around ideological differences between East and West. The world was in a precarious situation. The Soviet Union and the United States were embroiled in the Cold War, which on several occasions threatened to escalate into actual war and even nuclear war.

The dust had hardly settled from the destruction of World War II when the international community was plunged into yet another war. Korea became the focal point of world attention as the scene of the first volatile confrontation between Communist nations and the free world. United Nations troops, with the Americans at the helm, waged war against the North Koreans and Chinese Communists, who were trained, equipped, and backed by the Russians.

A sense of fear pervaded the West in 1952. The threat of world domination by the "Reds" was evident in the stories published by *The New York Times*. Refugees from East Germany were fleeing to West Germany at every possible opportunity. The horror stories of Communist brutality and repression added fuel to the fire in the psychological warfare tactics used by the Soviets.[12] In addition to the defections and escapes by the East Germans, North Korean soldiers and peasants sought political asylum in the West, echoing the accounts of their East German counterparts.[13] Communists were also causing problems in India and Southeast Asia. In Vietnam, the French were engaged in a war with Communist insurgents, which was to entrap the United States in the coming decade.

OLYMPIC SNAPSHOT

1952 Helsinki Olympiad:

Opening Day July 19; Closing Day August 3

- 69 countries sent teams
- 4955 athletes: 519 women and 4436 men
- 17 sports, 149 events: Aquatics, Athletics, Basketball, Boxing, Canoe/Kayak, Cycling, Equestrian, Fencing, Soccer, Gymnastics, Field Hockey, Modern Pentathlon, Rowing, Sailing, Shooting, Weight Lifting, and Wrestling

---

In retrospect, the Finns managed to produce an extraordinary XVth Olympiad in the midst of a seemingly explosive climate. With the exception of the sequestered athletes representing the Soviet Union and its satellite countries, who rarely if ever mingled with athletes from the West, the Helsinki Olympiad was a success. This is not to suggest that it was completely free from political or social issues.

To illustrate why certain social and political issues became a part of the Olympic fabric, it is helpful to review the major political and social events that were taking place at the time of the Helsinki Olympiad, as well as successive Summer and Winter Games. In this way, you can identify with the times and see that a pattern emerges. We already know that regional and global political and social entanglements have long concerned the IOC and have caused some significant problems. This fact was noted by J. Sigfrid Edstrom, president of the IOC, who, when speaking about the Helsinki Olympics, said:

> International relations improve much too slowly, travel is difficult due to monetary restrictions and other red tape. But nothing can stop young athletes from crossing frontiers to challenge their opponent and get ready for the games.... Preparations are developing actively to see that the games are a brilliant success. Lets [sic] hope that peace will reign when these games take place.
>
> I invite the youth all over the world to the competition and peaceful combats of the 1952 Olympiad, which can and must prepare the earth so that relations among people may be more friendly and understanding. Because the youth of today will be the leaders of tomorrow their experience in the mastery of international sports may become the ideal ferment that will one day transform into trust the stubborn animosities that nowadays separate nations.[14]

The IOC leadership recognizes that the Olympic Games can be undermined by events beyond its control. As best they can, the IOC and associated entities surmount these difficult problems to keep the Olympic ideal alive. The social and political climate is of interest to the IOC and each national Olympic committee because some of these social and political issues may find their way out of the political arena and into the arena of sport. When looked at in this context, the words of Edstrom have special meaning. He was keenly aware that although most of the world's countries field Olympic teams, there still exists animosity and mistrust among the participants.

Today, the IOC and the host cities continue to work as hard as they can to ensure that the games are successful, but in the end, the words of Edstrom echo the sentiments of all when he says he "hope[s] that peace will reign when these games take place."

South Africa's apartheid policy garnered media attention in July 1952 and was eventually cause for the country's banishment from the Olympic Games. Headlines in *The New York Times* read: "Negroes Step Up Their Campaign Against South African Race Laws, Original Violators Refuse Bail or to Pay Fines as 88 More Are Arrested—Leaders Say They Hope to Fill Country's Prisons."[15] The account of civil disobedience reflected a major social issue that divided the people of South Africa according to race. In this particular instance, the civil disobedience resulted in the arrest and detention of about 450 nonwhites, most of them in Johannesburg and Port Elizabeth, where the campaign was well organized. Demonstrators marched through an entrance reserved for whites at a railway station and were arrested by waiting police officers on charges of defying the apartheid laws.

On the home front, the United States entered the era of McCarthyism. Senator Joseph McCarthy had much of the populace convinced that the Communist "Red Menace" was lurking everywhere, and the ensuing Communist "witch hunt" strained the nation. Many people were falsely accused of being Communists or Communist sympathizers. Although McCarthyism did "catch" and identify Communists and their supporters in various levels of government, many innocent people were also labeled as "red." After the McCarthy Senate hearings were completed and the hysteria subsided, historians and pundits began speculating

that McCarthy and his colleagues had created a "tempest in a teapot." However, in the early 1990s, long after McCarthy had died, declassified Soviet cables, known as the Verona Project, proved that there was a lot of truth in what McCarthy had said!

Americans also felt that the possibility of a military attack by the Russians was so probable that drastic precautions were undertaken. For example, the New York City Office of Civil Defense sought 900 recruits to act as aircraft spotters. The mistrust and animosity between the United States and the Soviet Union spilled over into the Olympic Games as each nation attempted to demonstrate the superiority of its social and political ideology through victory in athletics.

A Cold War of Sports

The media made reference to the 1952 games as a "Cold War of Sports." Helsinki marked the first time since the Stockholm Games in 1912 that the Russians had fielded an Olympic team.

The USOC and the public were all for assembling the strongest Olympic team possible to ensure defeat of the Russians. But economic factors almost ruined the American Olympic team. Two weeks prior to departure, the USOC was short $500,000. However, American ingenuity prevailed: Bob Hope and Bing Crosby staged an around-the-clock Olympic telethon and raised over $1 million.[16]

Helsinki was supposed to feature an environment of friendship and cooperation among athletes, but the Soviets brought the Iron Curtain to the XVth Olympiad. Instead of mingling with other athletes at the regular Olympic Village, the athletes from the Soviet Union and its satellites were quartered in their own private Olympic Village at Otaniemi on the far side of town, enclosed by barbed wire and near the big Porkkala Naval Base that the Russians had seized from the Finns in their peace settlement.

The Russians were unapproachable. They spoke to no one and wouldn't even admit the Finns, their hosts, to their camp. Newspapermen, regardless of their nationality, were turned away at the gates.[17] The Russians were doing all they could to discourage political defections by Soviet athletes. When entries were formally filed for the Olympic events, Heino Lipp, the Estonian shotputter who was among the world's best, as well as several Soviet women, were not among the Soviet contingent. "The rumor was that they were considered 'politically unreliable,' something new and unprecedented in Olympic history."[18]

Since the ancient Olympics, a traditional Olympic truce has been declared during the games. The ancient truce allowed the athletes safe passage to Olympia, and wars were suspended. Finland proclaimed an Olympic truce in the hope that the 1952 games would proceed without interruption. However, the Associated Press reported that "the games of the fifteenth Olympiad . . . bring together Russia and the United States in direct sports conflict."[19]

Prior to the opening ceremonies, political disputes marred the games. Gun Son-ho, Olympic representative from Nationalist China (now known as Taiwan), flew to Helsinki from Formosa and insisted that Nationalist China be allowed to compete in the games. The IOC ruled that neither Nationalist China nor the People's Republic of China would be allowed to enter teams. After learning of the attempt by Nationalist China to enter the games, East Germany demanded inclusion as well. According to the United Press International,

> The International Olympic Committee received another hot issue in sport's cold war today [July 12, 1952] when it was asked to decide whether both East and West Germany should be admitted to the 1952 Olympic Games.
>
> The executive Olympic Committee had decided last winter that only West Germany should be admitted after efforts failed to organize a combined East-West entry. There was no protest from the East. . . . Thus the IOC will be asked Wednesday to do something the United Nations has been unable to do—reconcile the East and the West. The IOC reversed its decision and extended an invitation to Nationalist China to compete in the 1952 Olympics. However, the IOC extended the same invitation to the People's Republic of China. The governing

body of the Olympics voted 33 to 20 in favor of a resolution authorizing the athletes of both nations to compete.[20]

In response to the authorization by the IOC to allow the two Chinas to compete, the Nationalist Chinese boycotted the games.

East Germany was not allowed to compete. Not until 1968 would East Germany field an independent team. However, a new twist developed on the Olympic scene. Rolf Marffly, a Hungarian representing political refugee groups, proposed to the IOC that refugees be permitted to compete in the games. The refugees could compete under a Red Cross flag, a special Olympic flag, or the national flag of Switzerland or Greece. But no action was taken on the matter.

A Propaganda War

Avery Brundage, newly elected president of the IOC, was not overlooked by the Soviet press. According to a newspaper account in Moscow,

> *The Young Bolshevik,* the magazine of the youth organization Komsomols, to which most of the Soviet athletes belong, called on athletes everywhere to transform the Helsinki games into a vast demonstration for peace and friendship of peoples.
>
> The journal described United States Olympic leader, Avery Brundage, as "a Chicago business man and an adventurist," and accused him of utilizing every possible means of force and pressure at the 1948 games in London to assure "first places for representatives of the Anglo-Saxon race." Brundage was charged with having bribed referees and Olympic Committee members in an effort to achieve the desired results. . . .
>
> The Helsinki games, it said, had the greatest significance in the world peace struggle and claimed they would be "an arena of the struggle of progressive-minded athletes for peace against the rotten propaganda of Warmongers."[21]

The Russian media called for Russian Olympians to demonstrate superiority over athletes from bourgeois nations. *Pravda, Izvestia,* and other Soviet newspapers were quick to attack the United States. According to *Izvestia,*

> Sport in bourgeois countries, and especially in the United States, was utilized as a means of 'preparing cannon fodder for a new, aggressive war.' In contrast, in the Soviet Union . . . sports played a role in the 'struggle for friendship and security of the people—of peace of the whole world.' . . . Soviet athletes, said *Izvestia,* provide shining examples of the superiority of Soviet culture over that of bourgeois countries.[22]

According to unofficial Olympic scoring being kept by the world press, the Russians had a commanding lead over the Americans. The point total was displayed daily in the Soviet Olympic Village, and the Soviet press used the Russian lead as a viable and visible propaganda weapon. It appeared that the Soviets would be the "unofficial" victors at Helsinki. The IOC does not recognize "scoring," but that did not deter the Russians. The Soviets formally proposed to the Congress of the International Athletic Federation that team scoring be recognized. It was quickly voted down.[23]

The Russians were so certain of victory that Radio Moscow announced, "We are certain to win." But the games ended with America as the victor. The Americans captured the most gold medals: 41 to Russia's 23. The unofficial score showed the Americans triumphing over the Russians, 614–553. The Russian explanation to the Soviet Union was creative.

After the Olympics ended, *Pravda,* the Soviet's media mouthpiece, hailed the "world superiority" of the Russian athletes and proudly asserted that they had won more medals than anyone else. They offered no figures or substantiation. Then, after two more days of point juggling, Moscow announced that the two countries had ended in a dead heat, each with 494 points.[24]

Notables

The propaganda war engaged in by the United States and the Soviet Union had no boundaries. Both countries continued to use the Olympic Games to promote their respective political and social agendas in the name of nationalism. The IOC was appalled by such attempts to undermine the Olympic ideal and did its best to suppress them. Despite the feud between the Americans and the Russians, the Helsinki Olympiad was among the best. Participating in the games were 4955 athletes representing 69 countries. For the first time, over five hundred women (519 to be exact) competed in the games.[25] The great distance runner from Czechoslovakia, Emil Zatopek, became Olympic champion in three events: the 5000-meter and 10,000-meter races and the marathon. His wife, Dana, won the gold medal in the javelin.

The American men made a respectable showing in track and field, winning 30 medals, 14 of them gold. Bob Mathias once again won the decathlon. The American women won but one medal in track and field—a gold in the 400-meter relay—and in doing so set a new Olympic record. American swimmers earned 17 medals—the men ten and the women seven. The Russians dominated both men's and women's gymnastics and made their presence felt in weight lifting (seven medals), freestyle wrestling (three medals), and Greco-Roman wrestling (seven medals).

The superiority of American athletes clearly was being put to the test by athletes from the Iron Curtain countries, especially the Soviet Union and East Germany. The rivalry between the British and American teams now paled in comparison with the intense competition between the Americans and the Russians. However, even as politicians attempted to manipulate the Olympic Games for self-serving ends, some athletes from the United States and the Soviet Union formed lasting friendships that would have made the Baron de Coubertin smile.

THE VITH WINTER OLYMPICS: OSLO, 1952

The Norwegians staged the best-run and best-attended Winter Olympics to date. Although the Soviet Union did not participate, approximately 700,000 people witnessed the displays of athletic prowess by athletes from 30 nations. Once again, the Norwegians demonstrated their superiority in winter sports by capturing 16 medals, followed by the United States with 11. The athletes from Germany, after an absence of 16 years, won both bobsled races.[26]

OLYMPIC SNAPSHOT

1952 Oslo Winter Olympics:

Opening Day February 14; Closing Day February 25

- 30 countries sent teams
- 694 athletes: 109 women and 585 men
- 4 sports, 22 events: Bobsleigh, Ice Hockey, Skating, and Skiing

Richard "Dick" Button again won the gold medal in men's figure skating, and fellow American Andrea Mead Lawrence won the gold medal in the women's giant slalom. Americans Kenneth Henry and D. McDermott won the gold and silver medals, respectively, in the men's 500-meter speed-skating competition. The American ice hockey team, returning to Olympic competition after being barred in St. Moritz, finished second behind—who else—the Canadians!

THE XVITH OLYMPIAD: MELBOURNE, 1956

The Political Atmosphere

The Cold War between the United States and its allies and the Soviet Union and its allies continued unabated in 1956. *Crisis* would be the appropriate term to describe the state of world affairs during the XVIth Olympiad. The Suez Canal crisis brought the world to the brink of yet another war. Rebellion against the Soviet Union, in the form of the Poznan riots in Poland and the short but valiant Hungarian uprising resulted in enormous destruction of persons and property. The nuclear arms race between the Americans and the Russians terrified the world.

In the Middle East, President Gamal Nasser of Egypt instigated a war by nationalizing the Suez Canal. Nasser had been "walking the fence" between Moscow and Washington, receiving economic aid and supplies from both nations. However, the turning point occurred when Nasser asked the United States to construct the Aswan High Dam. Washington agreed, but certain conditions had to be met, the primary ones being (1) ending the border war with Israel and (2) breaking off ties with the Russians.

Instead of agreeing to these terms, Nasser closed the canal. The United Nations responded by proposing that the Suez Canal be placed under the control of an international governing agency. The plan was rejected by Nasser with the support of Syria and Saudi Arabia. During this same time, Arab guerrillas were conducting military operations in Morocco, Algeria, and Tunisia to oust the French. The Arab world was very anti–Anglo-French. However, the Arab states were being equipped and trained by the Russians, and Nasser apparently felt he had the necessary tools at his disposal for such an operation as the closing of the Suez Canal. In response, the British, French, and Israelis launched an offensive against Egypt. Israel attacked on October 29, followed by British and French assaults on October 31. President Dwight D. Eisenhower

OLYMPIC SNAPSHOT

1956 Melbourne Olympiad:

Opening Day November 22; Closing Day December 8

- 72 countries sent teams
- 6 countries boycotted
- 3314 athletes: 376 women and 2938 men
- 17 Sports, 145 events: Aquatics, Athletics, Basketball, Boxing, Canoe/Kayak, Cycling, Equestrian, Fencing, Soccer, Gymnastics, Field Hockey, Modern Pentathlon, Rowing, Sailing, Shooting, Weight Lifting, and Wrestling

pledged no direct American involvement. The Melbourne Games were to open 22 days later.

The purpose of the military attack on Egypt was twofold. Britain and France needed access to the Suez Canal and therefore needed to seize it to keep it open. Israel sought to prevent Nasser from achieving mastery of the Arab world through a series of palace revolutions in other Middle Eastern states and forming a united Arab crusade against Israel.[27] The rebellions in Hungary and Poland kept the Russians occupied militarily, and so the plan was to attack Egypt while the Soviets dealt with problems on the home front.

Perhaps the most disheartening event of the year was the tragedy in Hungary. Hungarians were staggering under the yoke of Moscow and sought independence from Soviet control. Premier Imre Nagy asked Moscow to let Hungary withdraw from the Warsaw Pact. The Hungarians, according to reports, wanted to become a neutral state belonging to neither the Eastern nor the Western camp. Nagy's appeal was made on November 1.

On November 3, Soviet troops invaded the country. By November 5, the Hungarian freedom fighters realized they could not hold out against the Russians without intervention by the United Nations or the West, help that never came. The rape of Hungary was a brutal warning to Soviet satellites and the rest of the world not to interfere with Communist policy. Stalinism was not dead; Hungary was.

Before the Hungarian uprising, the Hungarian Olympic soccer team withdrew from Olympic competition. *Newsweek* gave this account:

> Hungary's withdrawal from Olympic soccer competition was officially blamed on "lack of funds" by Moscow following Hungary's victory over the Soviet Olympic team. With Hungary out of the way, Russia expects to win the gold medal.[28]

When the Russians had "control" over the uprisings in Eastern Europe, they turned their attention to the Middle East. Moscow threatened direct military intervention in the Suez Canal crisis on the side of the Arabs. President Eisenhower suggested that the possibility of nuclear war

existed in Egypt.[29] The announcement by the Russians caused France, Israel, and England to stop short of achieving their military objectives.

Peking and Moscow were ready to send volunteer military units to fight alongside the Arabs against the British, French, and Israelis. The Soviets pledged to send several thousand, and Communist China would respond with 380,000 troops.[30] However, the United Nations was able to invoke a cease-fire order.

Elsewhere, the Indochina war was still raging, and South Africa continued to suppress its black population. Johannes Gerhardus Strijdom, prime minister of the Union of South Africa, demanded complete white supremacy. He planned to herd South Africa's 12 million blacks onto "reservations" comprising no more than 14 percent of the nation's territory.[31] Apartheid was not restricted to South Africa. The Mau Mau Rebellion in Kenya was a race war between blacks and whites in which 15,000 blacks were killed by British forces and 70,000 blacks were placed in concentration camps.[32]

The United States reelected the incumbent White House administration, Dwight D. Eisenhower and Richard M. Nixon. A young Massachusetts senator named John F. Kennedy was starting his climb up the political ladder. A landmark decision by the United States Supreme Court abolished the separate-but-equal-schools policy and ordered school integration. Racial integration of the nation's schools was not accomplished easily; violence rocked the southern states, and the National Guard was mobilized to protect the peace. The United States, like South Africa, had serious social problems that eventually manifested in the Olympic Games.

The Aussie Olympics

Despite a tense world situation, Melbourne was in a festive mood for the XVIth Olympiad. It has often been said that Australia is a sports-loving nation, and the Aussies did not disappoint anyone on that count. Even though the Australians were in a festive mood, the atmosphere among the Olympic Organizing Committee, and others, remained guarded.

Sir William Bridgeford, chief executive officer of the IOC, was quoted as saying, "The Games will definitely go on unless there is a general world war."[33] Bridgeford was saddened by the world political situation but said "we still hope to keep politics and international hatreds out of the games."[34] The Associated Press supplied a brief "political" forecast for the games:

> The Olympic Games walked a tightrope today in an atmosphere of outward calm but growing concern over the fighting in Hungary and Egypt. . . . Other tensions marked this amateur sports spectacle scheduled to open Nov. 22 and end Dec. 8. These included:
> A. The bitter wrangling between Communist and Nationalist Chinese [Taiwanese] groups.
> B. Hungarian immigrants in Australia have made one demonstration against Russian participation in the games and plan another tomorrow.
> C. There is a strong fear of reaction against the British and French for moving into the Suez Canal area in the Egypt-Israel clash, a move supported by the Australian Government.[35]

Avery Brundage decreed that nations at war were eligible to compete in the Olympic Games. This was a difficult decision for Brundage and the IOC. The hope was that the athletes from these warring countries could put aside their differences for the duration of the games and compete athletically and not as combat soldiers. Perhaps the athletes could establish a dialogue that would foster international goodwill and assist the peace process. It was clear that the politicians were not succeeding.

It was first reported on November 5 by Radio Budapest that there would be no Hungarian Olympic team due to "interruptions." Reported killed in fighting against Russian troops in Hungary were three of Hungary's top athletes: Jozsef Csermak, 1952 Olympic hammer-throwing champion; Major Ferene Puskas, captain of Hungary's soccer team; and Gabor Bencdek, runner-up in the 1952 Olympic pentathlon.[36]

The question of South Africa's apartheid policy was brought before the IOC by the Norwegians. Their Olympic committee requested that the IOC consider banning South Africa from Olympic participation because of its social policy of discriminating against blacks in sports organizations. Olay Ditlev-Simmonsen of the Norwegian Olympic Committee believed South Africa should not be recognized by the IOC if it continued practicing apartheid.[37]

Olympic Boycott

Once again, nations engaged in an Olympic boycott for political reasons. The Associated Press reported:

> The Netherlands, Spain, and Communist China withdrew from the 1956 Olympic Games today [November 6]. The Netherlands and Spain decided to withdraw as a protest against Russia's military action in Hungary.
>   Instead of sending athletes to Melbourne, . . . the Netherlands donated 100,000 guilders ($25,000) to Hungarian relief.
>   Dr. Homan [president of the Dutch Olympic Committee] criticized Otto Mayer [chancellor of the IOC] for his recent comment that the Olympic Ideal should prevail over what has happened in Hungary. "How would we like it if our people were atrociously murdered and someone said that sports should prevail?" Dr. Homan asked.[38]

Five nations, as of November 6, had withdrawn from the Games: Egypt, Spain, the Netherlands, Communist China, and Iraq. Once again, Communist China withdrew because of the inclusion of Nationalist China (Taiwan), and Iraq quit in protest over the actions by France, Britain, and Israel against Egypt. Two days later, Switzerland became the sixth nation to quit the Olympics, in response to the Russian actions in Hungary.

Brundage and other members of the IOC appealed to the departed nations to reconsider their position and join the XVIth Olympiad. Brundage maintained that

> every civilized person recoils in horror at the savage slaughter in Hungary, but that is no

reason for destroying the nucleus of international cooperation [Olympic Games]. . . . In
an imperfect world, if participation in sports is
to be stopped every time the politicians violate
the laws of humanity, there will never be any
international contests.[39]

Brundage, like his predecessors, was an idealist
and a champion of the Olympic ideal. He saw the
games as an opportunity to bring people together
regardless of their ideological beliefs. Pulling
teams from competition to protest despicable
social and political events prevented the Olympic
Games from achieving their primary goals of fos-
tering international goodwill and promoting peace.
How was the IOC supposed to nurture and extend
these ideals if athletes were ordered to return
home? These were frustrating and disappointing
times for the IOC, which did its best to keep the
Olympic Games above politics.

Russia captured the "unofficial" team championship at the XVIth Olympiad amid accusations
of prejudicial Olympic judging by Eastern officials
against Western nations. The United States protested
the judging by Russian and Hungarian officials,
claiming that they discriminated against American
divers. The American complaint was rejected.

Athletes from Eastern Bloc countries continued to use the Olympic Games as a means to
defect to the West and seek a better life. For example, *Newsweek* reported that

forty-five Hungarian athletes who had come
out from behind the Iron Curtain to compete
in the Olympics were not going back to their
ravaged country. Some said they would settle
in Australia. Thirty-four asked to enter the
U.S. A few, vague about the future, wept.

Among the defectors was Lavzlo Nadori,
Assistant Chairman of the Hungarian Olym-
pic Committee, who had been a leader in
Budapest's anti-Soviet revolt last month.
Friday, Nadori quietly slipped away from his
Olympic Village quarters leaving a terse mes-
sage. "God bless you," it said, "Farewell."[40]

The Soviet Union, unlike the United States,
allocated significant amounts of money to athletes

in both major and minor Olympic sports. The
American Olympic effort was in support of athletes
who were training for major Olympic competition:
swimming, track and field, and, later, basketball
and boxing. As a result of the decision by Soviet
Olympic authorities to spend money and time
developing both major and minor Olympic athletes,
their ability to win more Olympic medals was significantly better than that of the United States. Still,
the American athletes fared well in the Melbourne
Olympics. The men's track-and-field team won 28
medals, compared with 14 for the Soviet team. The
American women won three medals in track and
field but did much better in the swimming competition, winning 11 medals, including three gold.

Notables

The Melbourne Olympics hosted athletes who
established 36 new Olympic records and 11 world
records. Although six nations did boycott the Olympic Games, the remaining countries enjoyed a spectacular international athletic festival. The Australian
Olympic Committee and the Melbourne Organizing
Committee provided a warm reception for athletes
and spectators. It was the first time that the Olympics
had been held in the southern hemisphere. Since the
seasons are reversed, and the Melbourne Olympiad
was held from November 22 to December 8, it was
summer in Australia! The Olympic Stadium was
filled with 104,000 spectators to watch the opening
ceremonies. The Melbourne Organizing Committee
had planned a program that featured 145 sporting
events and two demonstration sports, Australian
football and American baseball. Over 80,000 fans
turned out to watch American baseball.[41] In the
decathlon, two Americans, Milt Campbell and
Rafer Johnson, captured the gold and silver medals,
respectively, while Vasily Kouznetsoff of the Soviet
Union was a close third. In the marathon, Alain
Mimoun of France, who had finished second to the
great Emil Zatopek in three previous Olympics,
finally won the gold medal. His friend and competitor Zatopek finished in sixth place.

Willye White (1939–2007) was a 16-year-old
high school sophomore from Money, Mississippi,

when she won the silver medal in the long jump. She would compete in five consecutive Olympic Games between 1956 and 1972. White was the only American to compete on five Olympic track-and-field teams. She said that her experience as an athlete enabled her to see beyond the racism and hatred that she experienced as an African-American woman. She said that before her first Olympics, the world seemed to consist of cross burnings and lynchings. Sadly, cross burnings and lynchings were not unusual in the American South during her childhood. The Olympic Games taught her not to judge people by the color of their skin but by what was in their hearts.

Equestrian events had increased in popularity with each Olympiad. But the costs associated with mounting a serious equestrian campaign in the Olympics were high. The horses, facilities, transportation, and riders required significant monetary expenditures. For this reason, the equestrian events of the XVIth Olympiad were held in Stockholm, Sweden, in June.

The Olympic Games were not without romance. Olga Fitokova from Czechoslovakia, who won the gold medal in the discus, wed the American hammer thrower Harold Connolly, who won the gold medal. They later divorced.

THE VIITH WINTER OLYMPICS: CORTINA, 1956

Thirty-two nations sent 821 athletes to compete in the Winter Olympics, held in Cortina in the beautiful Italian Alps. Of these, 134 were women athletes, who proudly represented 32 nations and competed in 24 events.[42] The Soviet team won six gold medals: three in men's speed skating and one each in ice hockey, the 4×10-kilometer relay, and the 10-kilometer women's ski race. The American team had a disastrous showing in men's skiing, managing only a fourth-place finish in the slalom. The U.S. women's skiing team could garner no better than a fourth-place finish in the giant slalom. However, the American men swept the first three places in figure skating (ordinals), finished second in ice hockey to the Russians (the Canadians finished third), and

captured the bronze medal in the four-man bobsledding competition. The American women won both the gold and the silver in figure skating. The Italians were wonderful hosts, as well as proficient in the bobsled, finishing first and second in the two-man event and second in the four-man competition

OLYMPIC SNAPSHOT

1956 Cortina D'Ampezzo Winter Olympics:

Opening Day January 26; Closing Day February 5

- 32 countries sent teams
- 821 athletes: 134 women and 687 men
- 4 sports, 24 events: Bobsleigh, Ice Hockey, Skating, and Skiing

THE XVIITH OLYMPIAD: ROME, 1960

The Political Atmosphere

The Cold War between the United States and the Soviet Union "heated up" in 1960 and significantly affected the global political situation. Political ideology in the form of propaganda was distributed by both the United States and the Soviet Union. The two superpowers had learned to use every available tool at their disposal in the propaganda war, including sport.

Southeast Asia was in political turmoil. Violence in South Korea over election scandals painted a discouraging picture of a "democratic" nation that was economically and militarily supported by the United States. Ten thousand demonstrators in the North Cholla Province of South Korea destroyed county offices and burned ballot boxes to express their feelings about the election scandals. Elsewhere in Southeast Asia, fighting in Vietnam by American troops against Communists was starting to receive attention. President Eisenhower had stationed military advisors there, and also provided military and economic assistance. The war in Vietnam would be the political hot spot in the world during the Mexico City Games in 1968.

The Cuban Revolution and the takeover by Fidel Castro caused concern among members of the Organization of American States (OAS). A Communist regime was now in power less than 100 miles from the United States, and the Soviet Union was pouring technical, economic, and military aid into the island nation. In Washington, the view was that the Russian military installations on Cuba posed a serious military threat to the United States. Mutual animosity between Cuba and the United States led to accusations and threats by both nations—actions that were to result in the Bay of Pigs debacle and the Cuban missile crisis.

Political tensions between the United States and the Soviet Union reached a peak on May 1, 1960. Francis Gary Powers, a pilot for the Central Intelligence Agency, was shot down in his U-2 spy plane while on a mission over the Soviet Union. Powers was charged as a spy, and the Soviet media used every possible avenue of propaganda to condemn the U.S. action. To make matters worse, the Russians shot down an American RB 47 reconnaissance plane that, claimed the Soviets, had violated Soviet airspace over the Arctic waters. Powers was found guilty. After the U-2 incident, the Soviets started expelling American students and businessmen from the country as spies. The United States reciprocated by expelling selected Soviet diplomats as suspected secret agents. The Cold War would not become any "hotter" until the Cuban missile crisis.

A noticeable difference in relations between the two Communist giants emerged as ideological rifts between Moscow and Peking began to surface. Russian technicians in China were being called home to Moscow, and Chinese "students" were leaving the Soviet Union. The Chinese were challenging the leadership role of Moscow; divergent views of how to achieve world Marxism increased the split between the two nations. This situation was especially significant to Chinese athletes and coaches because they were being helped by Russian coaches who were also told to return home.

In the United States, John F. Kennedy and Lyndon Johnson defeated Richard Nixon and Henry C. Lodge for president and vice president, respectively. Kennedy, possibly the most popular U.S.

president since Lincoln or Roosevelt, was ushered into the White House as the leader of the free world.

A Roman Holiday

It has been said that "all roads lead to Rome," and for several weeks, the world focused on the splendor of the XVIIth Olympiad. This is not to imply that the Cold War was forgotten. Men, medals, and Marxism had an impact on the 1960 games. The rivalry between the Americans and the Russians drew the most attention. The victors in the Eternal City would reap the coveted rewards of the Cold War: gold medals and new sources of propaganda.

Italy left nothing to chance when construction of the Olympic complex began. A nine-mile "Olympic Road" was built on the western edge of Rome. The Olympic stadium and supporting facilities were located in the western sector of the city to enable easy access and promote commercial expansion. The venues were fantastic, and many athletes from different parts of the world came together in the festive atmosphere.

East Versus West

Although the express purpose of the Olympic Games is to promote peace and international understanding, the political entities that held power in the East and West attempted to undermine the Olympic ideal in order to serve their own

OLYMPIC SNAPSHOT

1960 Rome Olympiad:

Opening Day August 25; Closing Day September 11

- 83 countries sent teams
- 5338 athletes: 611 women and 4727 men
- 17 sports, 150 events: Aquatics, Athletics, Basketball, Boxing, Canoe/Kayak, Cycling, Equestrian, Fencing, Soccer, Gymnastics, Field Hockey, Modern Pentathlon, Rowing, Sailing, Shooting, Weight Lifting, and Wrestling

political interests. For example, the announced aim of the Russians was twofold: (1) to win as many medals as possible and (2) to demonstrate that the Kremlin's system of mass approach to athletics was superior to all others. Explaining the prowess of Russian athletes, Nikolai Romanov, chairman of the Soviet Sports League, was quoted as saying:

> The first reason is the mass character of the Soviet athletic movement. On August 13 the whole country will be celebrating Athletes Day. The fact that this is celebrated as a national day testifies to the importance to the physical training by the Soviet people, the Communist party, and the Soviet government. . . . 24,000,000 persons in the Soviet Union participate in organized athletics and in the activities of 190,000 physical culture organizations under the direction of 65,000 specialists.[43]

The Soviet Union certainly took athletic competition, both national and international, seriously.

The Italian Olympic Committee was not blind to the animosity that existed between athletes from the West and athletes from Eastern Bloc nations. They constructed the Olympic Village on a segregated plan. The Russians and their Eastern Bloc comrades lived, appropriately, in the eastern section of the Olympic Village. Western Bloc nations, particularly the Americans and British, lived near the western edge of the village. Between the Russians and the Americans were the Olympic teams from Switzerland and Liechtenstein, to act as a buffer. To take it one step further, the Italian Olympic Committee assigned the Russians to eat at restaurant Number V and the Americans at Number III, and again "sandwiched" the Swiss between them at restaurant Number IV.[44] Much to the delight of the IOC and everybody else, when the Soviet athletes arrived in Rome, the majority immediately began to fraternize with athletes from other countries. This was precisely what the Olympic Games were supposed to help foster—international understanding and goodwill.

Whether the Olympic athletes liked it or not, they were pawns in an athletic war that was part of a larger political war, with nationalism running rampant once again. The emphasis on Americans beating Russians and Russians beating Americans was the primary "theme" in the media. This is not surprising since the Cold War co-opted the Olympic Games as a form of propaganda, depending on who won or lost. Nationalism has always been an integral part of the games, but incitement of inherent political nationalism is nurtured by the mass media and self-serving political organizations. A few days before the American track-and-field team departed for Rome, Larry Snyder, the head coach, appeared on a television program. "Will we beat the Russians?" asked Bennett Cerf, the publisher and host. "We'll kill 'em," replied Snyder.[45]

East Germany and West Germany marched under a common Olympic flag and competed as one nation during the XVIIth Olympiad. However,

> political squabbling . . . exists strongly on one team—the German squad, combining 200 West Germans with 140 East Germans. . . . "One team?" Heinz Maegerlein, the leading sportscaster in West Germany, said recently. "Actually, it is two. They live apart, eat apart, hardly speak to each other. It is no good at all."[46]

Nationalist China and Communist China continued to display their political differences. The People's Republic of China refused to participate in the 1960 Games as long as the Republic of China (Taiwan) competed. Therefore, the Communist Chinese did not send an Olympic team. However, the Republic of China was ordered to parade not as China but as Formosa. During the opening ceremonies, the Nationalist Chinese Olympic team followed the decree of the IOC. However, the leader of the delegation displayed a placard just before reaching the reviewing stand that said, "Under Protest." The executives of the IOC maintained that Taiwan did not represent all of China and had to carry the banner of its geographical location. This same sensitive political issue surfaced 16 years later during the Montreal Olympics.

Avery Brundage was up for reelection in Rome as president of the IOC, and it was no secret that the

Russians wanted to replace the Chicago business-man with their own Constantin Andrianov or another Iron Curtain official. "The Soviet Union is mounting a big propaganda campaign," stated the Associated Press, "among satellites and the smaller nations in an effort to wrest control of the IOC from the West."[47] But the Russians were not as successful during the executive meetings as they were in athletic competition. Brundage was reelected for another term.

American Olympic teams have not dipped the flag before the dignitaries of the host nation since 1908, although most other nations do. In 1960, however, the United States was not the only nation keeping its flag erect; Russia also chose not to dip its flag.

Political disputes over judging continued, and the Americans were the most disgusted. Dr. Sammy Lee, the diving coach for the U.S. women's team, said that judges had been prejudiced against American athletes for years. The Olympic officials must have taken note; the judging during the boxing competition was so inferior that the International Federation dismissed 15 judges for incompetence.[48]

Communist nations were also involved in a judging dispute among themselves. John Kieran and Arthur Daley described the situation:

> Also hitting the headlines was a charge by the International Wrestling Federation that the Communist brothers had been playing a bit of hanky-panky. . . . The villain was a Bulgarian who was accused of letting himself get pinned by a Russian in order to prevent a Yugoslav from winning the gold medal in the light-weight division. Only by getting a fall could the Soviet grappler slide past the Yugoslav, and any adherent of [Yugoslavian leader Josip] Tito is anathema to a true-blue—or true Red—Communist.
>
> The Russian got his fall and was given the gold medal. The Federation investigated the dive, disqualified the Bulgarian, but weakly permitted the Soviet performer to keep his medal.[49]

Perhaps the most bizarre claim of the games was when Taiwan accused the Soviet Union of having a Red Chinese on its team. Peng Chuan-Kai, chief of the Formosa team, said,

"We know the Russians have a man on their team who is really a Chinese. . . . We should know a Chinese face when we see one." "This man (Peng) is an out and out liar," said Romanov.[50]

However, reporters covering the games recalled seeing a "Chinese-appearing" athlete in a Russian uniform several weeks ago. He has not been seen since.[51]

The games were over on September 11, but many Americans could not accept that the "unofficial" team standings had the Soviets in front of the United States for a second consecutive Olympiad. Most Americans did not understand how important sports in general, and the Olympics in particular, were to the Soviet Union. In keeping with Communist economic policy, the Soviet Union did not allow any professional sports teams. Instead, they focused their efforts and resources on amateur sports, and the most important athletic event in the minds of the Russians was the Olympic Games. In contrast, then and now, Americans prefer professional sports over amateur sports and do not shower their Olympic teams with the attention and resources that other countries do. As a result, it becomes more difficult to emerge victorious in the Olympics, as many athletes struggle financially to prepare for Olympic competition. Nonetheless, Americans continue to be very nationalistic and expect their Olympic athletes to prevail over everyone. In any event, the Russians beat the Americans in medals and points—unofficially, of course. The stage had been set for Tokyo. Would the American Olympic team perform better four years later and "beat the Russians"?

Notables

The Italian Organizing Committee did a splendid job producing the games. They used both ancient ruins and modern architecture, which provided an Olympic setting that the athletes would not soon forget. The number of women athletes continued to increase, with 134 women athletes competing in 27 events.[52] Americans set two world records and nine Olympic records.

For the first time since 1928, Americans failed to win the 100- and 200-meter sprints. A. Hary from Germany won the 100-meters and set a new Olympic record, and L. Berruti from Italy won the 200-meters and set a new world record. To make matters worse, the American men's 4 × 400 relay team was disqualified when Ray Norton took the baton from Frank Budd past the legal exchange zone.[53] The U.S. women's track-and-field team was led by Wilma Rudolph, who won the gold medal in the 100-meter and 200-meter dashes and anchored the winning 4 × 100 relay team. Perhaps the most popular athlete at the Rome Olympics was Abebe Bikila from Ethiopia. He ran the marathon through the streets of Rome amid the heat of summer barefoot! In doing so, he established a new Olympic record. In the 3-meter springboard diving competition, American Gary Tobian won the gold while his teammate Samuel Hall won the silver. Hall later served in the Ohio House of Representatives. When he traveled to Nicaragua, he was arrested as a "freelance spy." Hall described himself as a "self-employed military advisor and counterterrorist." However, the Nicaraguan government came to the conclusion that this freelance spy did not constitute a threat to their national security. Instead, they decided he was mentally ill and released him.[54]

Perhaps the most heartwarming story of the Rome Olympiad was the battle in the decathlon between Rafer Johnson of the United States and C. K. Yang of Taiwan. Both were students at UCLA and best friends. The decathlon came down to the last event, the 1500-meters. Rafer Johnson had to stay within ten seconds of his friend to win. Johnson finished two seconds behind Yang and, in doing so, accumulated enough points to capture the gold medal and beat his rival and friend.

THE VIIITH WINTER OLYMPICS: SQUAW VALLEY, 1960

California hosted the 1960 Winter Olympics, and the California Olympic Organizing Committee left nothing to chance. Over $8.9 million was spent to build ice-skating rinks, ski runs, dormitories,

OLYMPIC SNAPSHOT

1960 Squaw Valley Winter Olympics:

Opening Day February 18; Closing Day February 28

- 30 countries sent teams
- 665 athletes: 144 women and 521 men
- 4 sports, 27 events: Bobsleigh, Ice Hockey, Skating, and Skiing

and housing for athletes and the large crowds of people expected to attend the games. In keeping with the Southern Californian flair for the big and bold, the ceremonial activities were left to Walt Disney. The Disney production thrilled the fans and the 665 athletes. Thirty countries sent athletes to the VIIIth Winter Games, including 144 women athletes who participated in Nordic skiing, speed skating, figure skating, and Alpine skiing.

The high point for the partisan crowd was the victory by the American ice hockey team over the heavily favored Soviet and Canadian teams. At the end of the championship game between the Russian and American teams, the 8500 fans in attendance gave both teams a standing ovation.[55] The spirit of Olympism had come alive at Squaw Valley. The American men captured a silver medal in the 500-meter speed-skating event, and the American women won the bronze in the same event. The U.S. team continued to dominate the figure-skating events, as both the men and women won the gold medal. In Alpine skiing, the American women won silver medals in the downhill, giant slalom, and slalom. The American men did not win a single medal in Alpine skiing.

THE XVIIITH OLYMPIAD: TOKYO, 1964

The growing military involvement of the United States in Southeast Asia began to receive front-page coverage in *The New York Times* in 1964. Prior to

OLYMPIC SNAPSHOT

1964 Tokyo Olympiad:

Opening Day October 10; Closing Day October 24

- 93 countries sent teams
- 5151 athletes: 678 women and 4473 men
- 19 sports, 163 events: Aquatics, Athletics, Basketball, Boxing, Canoe/Kayak, Cycling, Equestrian, Fencing, Soccer, Gymnastics, Field Hockey, Judo, Modern Pentathlon, Rowing, Sailing, Shooting, Volleyball, Weightlifting, and Wrestling

September 1964, the Gulf of Tonkin in Vietnam was unknown to most Americans and, for that matter, the world populace. There, U.S. warships engaged in a battle with North Vietnamese patrol boats. American naval vessels had been attacked by hostile craft the previous month. The incidents in the Gulf of Tonkin were only the beginning. In 1964, there were some 18,000 American troops in Vietnam. American casualties were mounting in the wake of an escalating war labeled a police action by President Lyndon Johnson. The Southeast Asian "police action" soon became the Vietnam War.

Meanwhile, Nikita Khrushchev was removed from the leadership role in the Soviet Union and replaced by Leonid Brezhnev. In addition, two other major changes in global leadership took place: Harold Wilson was elected as prime minister of Britain, and across the Atlantic, Lyndon B. Johnson was elected president of the United States. Also in 1964, Communist China detonated its first atomic bomb. The Peking government issued a statement declaring that "the purpose of developing nuclear weapons was to protect the Chinese people from the danger of the United States launching a nuclear war."[56]

The Perfect Olympiad

In Japan, the rising sun may have appeared bright and promising to the inhabitants of Nippon, but such was not the case for the remainder of the global community. Although situated in Asia, Japan was far removed from the Vietnam War that was to engulf the United States. The Japanese were hard at work on the games of the XVIIIth Olympiad. Tokyo spent $2 billion in producing the 1964 Games, determined to make their games overshadow all preceding Olympiads.

In planning the Tokyo Games, the Japanese left nothing to chance. Hundreds of observers had been dispatched to Rome for the 1960 Olympics, with every detail of the games scrutinized. Perfection was the objective of the Japanese; to this end, efforts included an analysis of the grass in the infield of the Olympic stadium in Rome.[57] Practice makes perfect, and exactly one year prior to the opening of the Tokyo Olympiad, Tokyo staged an International Sports Week. "It was a dry run Olympics of sorts and attracted some 4000 athletes from 35 countries."[58] The only issues that could draw attention away from the Tokyo Olympiad were political.

Olympic Politics

The major political row that erupted during the Tokyo Olympiad had its roots in the 1962 Asian Games, a regional Olympiad. Jakarta, Indonesia, was the site of the 1962 games. President Sukarno of Indonesia was considered a "political leftist" and had close ties with the Arab bloc and with Communist China. For political reasons, the Arabs and Communist Chinese pressured Sukarno to exclude Israel and Nationalist China (Taiwan) from the Asian Games. The Asian Games received the sanction of the IOC, provided the games were conducted under the terms of the Olympic charter, which opens them to all certified amateurs regardless of race, creed, color, and so on.

However, when the IOC received word of the expulsion of Nationalist China and Israel for political reasons, they declared the Asian Games null and void and expelled Indonesia from the Olympics.[59] In response, Sukarno organized the Games of the New Emerging Forces (GANEFO). He tried to pass the games off as the underdeveloped and "socialist" world's answer to the "imperialist"

Olympics.[60] The International Amateur Athletic Federation, the world governing body in track and field, and the Federation Internationale de Nation Amateur, the world governing body in swimming, deplored the actions of Sukarno. The two international bodies warned Indonesia and all other nations that planned to compete in GANEFO that it was an "outlaw" meet that would result in the automatic suspension and barring of each participant from the Tokyo Olympics.[61]

Arthur Daley, a prominent sportswriter from *The New York Times,* stated:

> For political reasons, the Soviet Union didn't dare refuse to participate [in GANEFO]. But the smart Russians were so fully aware of both the rules and the penalties that they sent only clowns to Indonesia. Not one had even the remotest chance of making the team to Tokyo.[62]

Two nations endeavored to enter athletes in the Tokyo Olympiad who had competed in GANEFO. Indonesia tried to enter 11 athletes, and North Korea six. "The International Federations in both swimming and track bluntly refused to accept the contaminated seventeen, although they did certify all other entries from Indonesia and North Korea."[63] Once again, the IOC deplored the political manipulation of the games and issued a strong condemnation of political interference in sports.

As the IOC was discussing the issue, a delegation of 80 persons presented a petition to Avery Brundage demanding the reinstatement of the ousted athletes of Indonesia and North Korea. A public rally was attended by several thousand Korean residents of Japan who sympathized with the North Korean government and protested the expulsion of the Indonesian and North Korean athletes. Brundage, who was elected to his third term as president of the IOC at a Tokyo meeting, responded:

> It was the disposition of the Committee to be even more firm, if possible, in opposing any political domination or political interference in sports. . . . The organization had acted reluctantly in taking action that penalized "innocent athletes for the decisions of others. But when there is open defiance of our rules, we have no other course to take."[64]

Government officials from Indonesia and North Korea pleaded with the Japanese government to intervene in their behalf and demand that the IOC reverse its decision regarding the suspended athletes.[65] The government of Japan remained true to the ideals of the IOC and refused to add this dimension to the games. In retaliation against the decision of the IOC, Indonesia and North Korea withdrew from the 1964 games. Ecuador was also forced to withdraw due to internal quarreling among the members of its National Olympic Committee. The Indonesian government warned that other nations would follow the course taken by North Korea and the Jakarta government; none did.[66] The Soviet Union attempted to persuade the IOC to lift the ban on the suspended athletes, but it appeared to be a feeble gesture.

President Sukarno was so infuriated at the decision of the IOC that a boycott of all news related to the Tokyo Olympics was instituted throughout Indonesia.[67] Indonesians threatened "all sorts of dire consequences to both a peaceful Olympics and world peace" as they departed Tokyo.[68]

The departure of North Korea from the 1964 games must have been a bitter pill for the North Koreans. They had not competed in an Olympiad since 1952; South Korea had been acting as the "only" Korean representative in the games. The two Koreas had attempted to unify into one team for the Tokyo Olympiad in the same manner as the unified East and West German contingent. However, negotiations broke off after accusations of "treachery and obstructionism." The major difference of opinion revolved around a team name, flag, and anthem. In addition, it was rumored that the South Koreans believed that the North Koreans were better athletes.

United Olympic teams are difficult to produce, as was the case with East and West Germany. The effort to construct the combined German Olympic team was marred by bitter controversy and recriminations by both nations. On more than one occasion, the IOC had to step in to resolve differences of opinion between the two sides. During the flag-raising ceremony at the Olympic Village, a dispute erupted between the East and West Germans. The controversy revolved around who would carry the black, red, and gold banner with the five Olympic rings on it, which was to symbolize the united German team. Agreement could not be reached, so the German Olympic team planned to march to the flag-raising ceremony without a flag. However, the united German team, represented by 199 athletes from the East and 177 from the West, settled their differences, and an East German carried the flag during the opening ceremonies. The East Germans also demanded that they be allowed to enter their own team in future Olympics. Their demand would be met.

The unofficial point scores and medal tabulation has always been a vehicle for inciting nationalism. As in the past, the IOC opposed these numerical statistics. Avery Brundage, in addition to acting as president of the IOC, was president of IBM, which ran the Olympic results service. Brundage did his best to discourage the "record race" by discontinuing the compilation and publication of the medals list.

Even though the medal count was discouraged by the powers that be, all eyes were on the "duel meet" between the Americans and Russians. The Russians boasted that they had assembled their best team in history and would destroy the Americans—athletically, that is. They had accomplished this task in Melbourne and Rome, and most observers felt Tokyo would be no different. "To the victor go the spoils of war," and during the 1964 Olympiad, the spoils were the propaganda value that the two superpowers obtained as a result of Olympic victories. The Russians were bragging before the games were under way that they would once again emerge victorious over the Americans by a wide margin.

Tokyo witnessed the awakening of American athletic prowess as the U.S. Olympic team came out on top of the Russians 36 to 30 in the gold medal race. The American sector in the Olympic Village was referred to as "Fort Knox." *Pravda*, the Communist Party organ, chastised the Soviet athletes and criticized track-and-field coaches who "guaranteed" victory but managed to produce only five gold medals compared with the American total of 14.

Defections

Three Hungarians used the Olympics as a means to a political end. Andras Toro, Denes Kovas,

and Karoly Meinar defected to the United States during the Tokyo Olympiad. However, political defections were not a one-way street at Tokyo. "A Chinese Nationalist Olympic pistol marksman, Ma Ching San, 38, . . . defected to the east to join his parents in Mainland [Communist] China."[69]

A radical departure, in terms of violence and political protest, lay ahead in Mexico City for the 1968 Olympic Games. Sadly, the use of the Mexico City Olympiad as a political platform would be larger than ever before.

Notables

Bob Hayes, who would later star in the National Football League with the Dallas Cowboys, set the world record in the 100-meter dash. Peter Snell, the great distance runner from New Zealand, won the 800-meter event for the second time in a row. He followed his victory in the 800-meters with a gold medal in the 1500-meters as well. Abebe Bikila won yet another marathon title and once again set a new Olympic record; this time, he wore shoes. The Russian and Polish athletes dominated in boxing with one exception—the American Joe Frazier won the gold medal in the heavyweight division. He would later become the world champion. The American men made a strong showing in swimming, winning 19 medals; the U.S. women swimmers won 18 medals, including seven gold. In the 10,000-meter race, Billy Mills, a 26-year-old former U.S. Marine and a Lakota Sioux, pulled off one of the most stunning upsets in modern Olympic history when he came from way behind to win the gold medal. His time of 28 minutes, 24.4 seconds set a new Olympic record. The second-place finisher, Mohamed Gammoudi of Tunisia, came within inches of beating Mills with a time of 28 minutes, 24.8 seconds. Ron Clarke of Australia, the holder of many world records, finished third with a time of 28 minutes, 25.8 seconds. Can you imagine how spectacular the last lap of the 10,000-meters was? The unknown Mills had not even been interviewed by any sports reporters before the race. Mills also qualified to run the marathon. The 1983 movie *Running Brave* is based on his incredible life.

THE IXTH WINTER OLYMPICS: INNSBRUCK, 1964

The only major problem with the Winter Games was a lack of snow. The ever pragmatic Austrians brought in 3000 soldiers who were assigned the task of "snow acquisition," which they did in excellent fashion. The number of athletes increased significantly, from 665 in 1960 to 1091 in 1964! And 199 women athletes representing 36 nations competed in the IXth Winter Olympics.[70] The Soviet Union's athletes won 11 gold medals, more than any other country.[71] Lydia Skoblikova from the Soviet Union won all the women's speed-skating events. In ice hockey, the Soviet team won seven games in a row to win the gold medal; the Canadians finished fourth, followed by the Americans.

America's Olympic successes at Innsbruck were modest in comparison with the Soviet Union's. The United States did not win any medals in men's Nordic skiing; in fact, American men did not place in the top six of any Nordic skiing event (eight events). The American women also failed to win a medal or to place in Nordic skiing (three events). The American women won two medals in Alpine skiing—the silver in the giant slalom and the bronze in the slalom—both by J. Saubert. The United States won the bronze medal in men's figure skating. And Richard "Terry" McDermott earned a rare gold medal for the United States in the men's 500-meter speed-skating competition; in doing so, he established a new Olympic record.

OLYMPIC SNAPSHOT

1964 Innsbruck Winter Olympics:

Opening Day January 29; Closing Day February 9

- 36 countries sent teams
- 1091 athletes: 199 women and 892 men
- 6 sports, 34 events: Biathlon, Bobsleigh, Ice Hockey, Luge, Skating, and Skiing

THE XIXTH OLYMPIAD: MEXICO CITY, 1968

Political activism, especially among college students, was evident throughout the world in 1968. Regional warfare continued to take its toll on life and property in Southeast Asia, Africa, and the Middle East. Student activism surfaced on the campuses of America, France, Mexico, South Vietnam, England, and West Germany. Moscow's Red Army crushed a rebellion in Czechoslovakia, and death and destruction were widespread. Senator Robert Kennedy, running for the Democratic presidential nomination, was assassinated by an Arab immigrant. Thus, the Kennedy family's death toll was two: a president, John F. Kennedy, assassinated November 22, 1963, and his brother Robert, a U.S. senator. Militant political activism in the United States was endorsed and used by groups such as the Black Panthers and Students for a Democratic Society (SDS). Richard M. Nixon defeated Hubert Humphrey for the presidency but resigned six years later as the result of an administration rocked with scandal. American involvement in Vietnam and race relations in the United States were political and social issues that had a significant impact on American society during 1968.

OLYMPIC SNAPSHOT

1968 Mexico City Olympiad:

Opening Day October 12; Closing Day October 27

- 112 countries sent teams
- 5516 athletes: 781 women and 4735 men
- 19 sports, 172 events: Aquatics, Athletics, Basketball, Boxing, Canoe/Kayak, Cycling, Equestrian, Fencing, Soccer, Gymnastics, Field Hockey, Judo, Modern Pentathlon, Rowing, Sailing, Shooting, Volleyball, Weightlifting, and Wrestling
- 1 demonstration sport: Basque Pelota

Demonstrations against the Vietnam War were organized by college students and other interested parties, as America became divided into "hawks" and "doves." The Vietnam War was not the only reason for demonstrations. Major social issues such as education and human rights were championed in America and throughout the world. Colleges were used as a platform to protest "violations."

African-American students demonstrated against alleged human rights offenses and were, at times, joined by antiwar demonstrators. Ohio State University experienced such a situation. According to *The New York Times,*

> Indictments were returned today [May 31] by the Franklin County Grand Jury against 34 Ohio State University students in the takeover April 26 of the school's administration building. Members of the Black Student Union had taken charge of the administration building and held top university officials under restraint for hours while presenting a list of grievances involving alleged racial prejudice. The Negroes were later followed by white anti-war demonstrators.[72]

The racial problems that were part of the social fabric in the United States during this era would manifest themselves on the victory platform during the 1968 Olympiad.

When Mexico City was awarded the games, a number of people questioned the decision. Mexico City is approximately 7500 feet above sea level. It was believed that the altitude would detract from Olympians' performances and might even cause serious health problems. None of these dire predictions came to pass. Olympic teams trained at altitude to prepare for the conditions in Mexico City. Another issue of concern was economic. Mexico was a poor country. Why would the IOC award the games to Mexico City? Would this not be an unfair and unreasonable financial burden? Would there be enough money to complete the venues? What benefits would Mexico City derive from hosting the games? IOC President Avery Brundage responded to these questions by saying:

> There was adverse criticism when the 1956 games were awarded to Melbourne. . . . Prime

Minister Menzies told me that they constituted one of the most important events in the history of Australia. Four years of international Olympic publicity, a record of accomplishment and not of disorder, crime, violence, or warfare, brought not only Australia, but also the entire South Seas area . . . tremendous economic, touristic, and social benefits. . . . What was done will now be repeated all over Latin America and Spanish-speaking countries. The games belong to the world, hot and cold, dry and humid, high and low, east and west, north and south.[73]

Student Demonstrations

The IOC and the Mexico City Organizing Committee invested enormous human capital and resources to help ensure a wonderful experience for the 5516 athletes and thousands of spectators in attendance. However, the XIXth Olympiad was among the most controversial and difficult. The Olympic stadium was built across the street from the National University of Mexico, which enrolls close to 100,000 students. Many of these students questioned President Luis Echeverria as to why so much money was being spent on a sports festival when social programs to help the poor were underfunded. There were severe clashes between students and police, which threatened the staging of the games. Six days of rioting involving 150,000 students seeking more "autonomy" for the university scarred the city. According to *The New York Times,*

> Federal troops fired on a student rally with rifles and machine guns tonight [October 2], killing at least 20 people and wounding more than 100. . . . In an inferno of firing that lasted an hour, the army strafed the area with machine guns mounted on jeeps and tanks. The Mexican government was not about to let student activists take anything away from the games. The nation had become so obsessed by the Olympics and so fearful of anything endangering their success that the crackdown was swift and violent.[74]

It is important to note that on June 30, 2006, 38 years after the Mexico City Olympiad, a Mexican court ordered the arrest of former president Echeverria for his role in the massacre.

Fearful of student activists using the games as a political platform, the government stationed rifle-carrying troops along the main entrance to the Olympic stadium and circulated 5000 military plainclothesmen inside.[75] As it turned out, the Mexican government's precautions were not needed; the students were quiet. Instead, the political demonstrations came from the Olympic athletes themselves.

Olympic Politics

Past Olympiads had been embroiled in politics from the standpoint of East versus West; political propaganda was the main prize, as was the building of nationalism. Political defections and Olympic judges basing their decisions on politics and not athletic achievement were among the issues that injected politics into the games. However, the XIXth Olympiad marked a radical departure from past games in terms of politics.

During the XIXth and XXth Olympiads, it was sometimes difficult to differentiate between activities in the political arena and those in the Olympic arena. Political activists and their activities during the games received as much media coverage as the accomplishments of the Olympic athletes. Militant groups employed the Olympic Games of 1968 and 1972 as political platforms to crusade against injustice, and the cost was astronomical. Once again, the IOC deplored the actions of a few athletes and outsiders that served to undermine the Olympic spirit; however, there was little they could do.

Aside from the student riots, the major political act of the games occurred when U.S. Olympians John Carlos and Tommie Smith staged a demonstration on the victory stand. The demonstration represented the culmination of a long process and added to the political nature of the Olympics.

The planned action undertaken by America's black Olympians during the 1968 games was organized at the 1967 Black Power Conference in Newark, New Jersey.[76] The initial plan called for all black athletes on the U.S. team to boycott the Olympic Games as "a protest against all

forms of American racism and a retaliation for the lifting of Muhammad Ali's heavyweight boxing crown."[77] However, the rules of order during the Black Power Conference mandated that a 75 percent vote was required to carry a particular action; the Olympic boycott received 65 percent. Thus, the boycott was called off. Of the 26 black athletes on the American Olympic team, 12 or 13 "were not willing to boycott under some circumstances," according to Dr. Harry Edwards.[78] Among the best-known black athletes to boycott the 1968 games were three basketball players from UCLA—Lew Alcindor (who later changed his name to Kareem Abdul-Jabbar), Mike Warren, and Lucius Allen.

The majority of America's black athletes would compete, but two months prior to the opening of the games, Edwards declared:

> Negro Olympians will not participate in victory stand ceremonies or victory marches; some athletes have decided to boycott the Games and lesser forms of protest shall be carried out by others.... Protests would also include a sizable contingent of white athletes.[79]

The black athletes who appeared at the XIXth Olympiad agreed to wear black armbands "and demonstrate their support of the black power movement in some manner during the course of the Olympic Games."[80] Sprinters Tommie Smith and John Carlos did not disappoint Dr. Edwards. Edwards sought to use the Olympics as a political platform, and according to Gerald Fraser,

> Other Edwards resolutions asked for support of further disruption "where deemed necessary" and the use of athletics "for greater political leverage in all phases of the black liberation struggle...." "This phase [political demonstrations during the Olympics] of our political movement originating out of the 1967 Black Power Conference has been a success," Edwards said.[81]

Out of the Black Power Conference emerged the Olympic Project for Human Rights, directed by Edwards. Edwards cited the following goals of the project:

1. Exposure of white nationalism and racism instituted in the sports industry
2. Exposure of the Olympic Games as a white nationalistic racist political tool of exploiting oppressive governments
3. The banning of Rhodesia and South Africa from the 1968 Olympic Games
4. Education of black people as to the degree of racism in the United States[82]

At the end of the 200-meter dash, a protest occurred that was unprecedented. Smith finished first, in a record-setting time of 19.8 seconds, and Carlos was third. Smith and Carlos arrived for the awards ceremony "shoeless, wearing knee length black stockings and a black glove on one hand (the right for Tommie, the left for John)."[83] As the American flag was raised and the national anthem played, Smith and Carlos looked at the ground and raised their gloved hands in a black power salute. One reporter called the demonstration "painfully petty." Observers noted that even the Russians, East Germans, and Cubans stood at attention when the American national anthem was played.

Embarrassed and angry, the USOC met for several hours behind closed doors in an effort to decide on a course of action. The USOC "issued a strong reprimand to Smith and Carlos, and apologies to the International Olympic Committee, the Mexican Organizing Committee, and the Mexican people."[84] It was not enough. Avery Brundage, perennial chairman of the IOC, would not tolerate any political or social protests and had warned all competitors that no political demonstrations would be permitted. According to *Time,*

> That challenge helped guarantee the trouble that came, and the I.O.C. bullheadedly proceeded to make a bad scene worse. Unless U.S. officials actually punished Smith and Carlos, the I.O.C. threatened to expel the whole U.S. team from the Olympics. Reluctantly, the U.S. Committee suspended the two athletes from the team and ordered them to leave the American quarters at the Olympic Village.[85]

The social and political issues that surfaced during the games were the most pronounced since the end of World War II. South Africa and Rhodesia originally were barred from the Mexico City Games because of their apartheid policies. South Africa and Rhodesia responded to the IOC by saying that they would integrate blacks into their Olympic teams. The IOC was satisfied that South Africa and Rhodesia would honor their commitments and ordered their reinstatement. However, close to 40 African nations and the Soviet Union immediately announced a boycott of the Mexico City Games unless South Africa and Rhodesia were expelled. The Mexican Organizing Committee, already embroiled in student riots and threatened with demonstrations by black American Olympians, envisioned total devastation of the XIXth Olympiad.[86]

Pedro Ramirez Vasquez, head of the Mexican Organizing Committee, immediately flew to Chicago to plead with Brundage for reconsideration of South Africa's (and Rhodesia's) readmission. Brundage would not budge. As the games drew nearer, the "Olympic fathers" realized that the survival of the Olympic Games was at stake. What if the Russians "persuaded" their East European satellites to boycott the games? Chances were excellent they could. Facing disaster, the nine-man executive committee of the IOC met at Lausanne, Switzerland, and changed their minds: South Africa and Rhodesia were expelled from the Olympic community. South Africa would not compete in the Olympic Games again until the 1992 Barcelona Olympiad.

The 1968 invasion of Czechoslovakia by the Soviet Union also concerned the Mexican Organizing Committee: Would the rape of Czechoslovakia spark a wave of revulsion that would affect the games? In reference to the opening ceremonies of the XIXth Olympiad, Kieran and Daley state:

> In between they streamed into the arena and marched around the brick-red Tartan track in all sizes, shapes, and colors. No country, not even the Mexicans, received the ovation that the Czechs did, born part of sympathy and part of admiration for the way they had stood up against the bullying tactics of the Soviet Union.[87]

Perhaps taking a cue from Smith and Carlos, Vera Caslavska, a Czech gymnast, lowered her head during the Soviet anthem to protest the invasion of her country by the Soviet Union.

The 1968 games served as a point of demarcation from past political actions associated with the games. Political events had sometimes overshadowed athletic events, and now violence and political protests had become a visible part of the Mexico City Olympiad. Sadly, four years later in Munich, the bitter conflict between Arabs and Jews would add a similar chapter to the Olympic Games. These appalling events inflicted serious damage upon the spirit of Olympism; however, the indomitable ideal emblematic of the Olympic Games would ultimately prevail.

THE XTH WINTER OLYMPICS: GRENOBLE, 1968

The Winter Games opened on February 6, 1968, as over 70,000 fans bundled up to ward off icy temperatures. Grenoble greeted 1158 athletes from 37 countries, including 211 women athletes, who participated in 35 events.[88] President Charles de Gaulle of France presided over the opening ceremonies along with Avery Brundage, the 81-year-old president of the IOC.[89]

Jean-Claude Killy of France occupied center stage as he won all the Alpine skiing events: the downhill, giant slalom, and slalom. Peggy Fleming of the United States won the gold medal in women's

figure skating, and T. Wood of the United States won the silver medal in men's figure skating. In men's speed skating, Terry McDermott tied for second place. Overall, however, the Grenoble Olympics were a disappointment for the American team, which managed to win only six medals. The Russians, on the other hand, took home 13, including five gold. The East German team won five medals. The Canadian ice hockey team won the bronze medal, finishing behind the team from Czechoslovakia and the mighty Soviet Union team, which won the gold.

THE XXTH OLYMPIAD: MUNICH, 1972

In 1972, the Cold War mentality that permeated East–West relations was largely responsible for the political and social climate throughout much of the world. A brief review of the global political situation in 1972 will enable you to understand some of the political and social issues that manifested themselves at the Munich Olympiad. One notable change in the political and social scene was that student activism had declined while political terrorism, especially in the Middle East, had increased. Sadly, the XXth Olympiad would not be spared from political terrorism.

OLYMPIC SNAPSHOT

1968 Grenoble Winter Olympics:

Opening Day February 6; Closing Day February 18

- 37 countries sent teams
- 1158 athletes: 211 women and 947 men
- 6 sports, 35 events: Biathlon, Bobsleigh, Ice Hockey, Luge, Skating, and Skiing

OLYMPIC SNAPSHOT

1972 Munich Olympiad:

Opening Day August 26; Closing Day September 11

- 121 countries sent teams
- 7134 athletes: 1059 women and 6075 men
- 22 sports, 195 events: Aquatics, Archery, Athletics, Basketball, Boxing, Canoe/Kayak, Cycling, Equestrian, Fencing, Soccer, Gymnastics, Field Hockey, Handball, Judo, Modern Pentathlon, Rowing, Sailing, Shooting, Volleyball, Weight Lifting, and Wrestling
- 1 demonstration sport: Waterskiing

World Overview

In 1972, the United States was still very much embroiled in the Vietnam War, which had spread to Cambodia and Thailand. The White House believed that American military power was the only way to ensure the existence of the South Vietnamese government. The People's Republic of China and the Soviet Union supplied military assistance to the North Vietnamese, which prompted the United States to mine Haiphong Harbor to prevent Chinese and Soviet ships from delivering needed materials. The Russians already had vessels in the harbor with more due to arrive, so mining the harbor had the potential to foster an explosive confrontation between the two superpowers.

The United Kingdom was plagued with the political terrorism of the Irish Republican Army (IRA) and the Ulster Defense League (UDL). The situation in Ireland involved a combination of social and political issues that evolved into a religious war between Catholics and Protestants. Violence between the two was so severe that British troops were called in to restore order. Terrorists were active in Ireland, and the bombing of public areas resulted in the deaths of many innocent men, women, and children. The IRA, considered the most militant of the terrorist groups, planted explosives in London and carried out attacks against British government officials to force Parliament to recall British troops from Northern Ireland. The axiom "Politics and religion don't mix" was the central theme in the hostilities in Northern Ireland.

This same theme applied in the Middle East, where Jews and Arabs engaged in a political war with religious overtones. In June 1972, the Israeli military launched assaults against Arab terrorist strongholds in southern Lebanon. But Lebanon and Syria continued to equip Palestinian guerrillas with arms, as well as provide sanctuary for them. The worst was yet to come.

Guerrilla attacks by black nationalist groups in Rhodesia (Zimbabwe) and South Africa against the two white minority governments were increasing. The governments of South Africa and Rhodesia and their racist attitudes generated sympathy for the black populations of these countries. And racism was not confined to Rhodesia and South Africa. Idi Amin, president of Uganda, expelled all the Asians in Uganda.

Olympic Politics

Before the games of the XXth Olympiad opened, political turmoil had already begun in Olympic circles. Rhodesia sought to participate in the Munich Olympics, but its social policy of apartheid created problems. If Rhodesia were allowed to compete, the nations in the Supreme African Sports Council and other sympathetic countries threatened to boycott the games. Rhodesia announced to the IOC that the Rhodesian Olympic team would be integrated and pleaded for reinstatement in the Olympic family. The IOC, with the support of the Supreme African Sports Council, agreed to allow the Rhodesians to compete in Munich if the government of Rhodesia agreed to certain conditions. As reported by United Press International,

> The International Olympic Committee solved the problem of Rhodesia's participation in the Olympic Games today [August 9] by guaranteeing to the Supreme African Sports Council that the Rhodesians would compete as British subjects.
>
> Jean-Claude Ganga, general secretary of the sports council, said his organization had accepted the IOC's guarantee that Rhodesia would participate in the Olympics as "Southern Rhodesia" and its athletes as "British subjects."[90]

Rhodesia also agreed to replace its national anthem with "God Save the Queen," the anthem of Great Britain. The conditions imposed on Rhodesia would be the equivalent of having the United States participate in the games as a colony of Great Britain, with America's Olympic athletes relegated to the status of British subjects marching to "God Save the Queen."

The Rhodesian issue was a political charade. *The New York Times* stated: "The Supreme Council for Sport in Africa, the sports governing body for the black African bloc, had approved the conditions ... with the expectation that Prime Minister Ian Smith's government ... would refuse such conditions."[91] To the astonishment of the black African bloc, the Rhodesian government accepted the conditions. The plan had failed. If Olympic politics, instigated by the Supreme Council for Sport in Africa, was designed to make Rhodesia the "goat," the reverse happened. The Rhodesian Olympic contingent, complete with seven black team members, arrived in Munich wearing blazers identifying the team as Rhodesia, not Southern Rhodesia. The leader of the Rhodesian Olympic squad "sneered at the Union Jack and said that they'd march under any flag including the flag of the Boy Scouts or the flag of Moscow."[92]

Rhodesia was not a popular nation in the global community. Rhodesia declared independence from Britain in 1965. However, because the country was white-controlled and adhered to a policy of apartheid, it had been outlawed by a United Nations resolution since 1968. On August 21, a few weeks prior to the opening ceremonies, the United Nations issued a decree to the effect that there was the "possibility that issuance of Olympic identity cards to the Rhodesians violates Security Council sanctions."[93] The prospect of meddling by the United Nations in the affairs of the IOC potentially served to fuel the political aspects of the Munich Olympiad.

Upon arrival of the Rhodesian team in Munich, token opposition began to surface from the smaller African nations whose athletes did not figure prominently in the games. This was the calm before the storm. Ethiopia and Kenya, the two most prominent African nations to compete in international athletic competition, announced that they would withdraw from the Munich Games unless Rhodesia was expelled. Events snowballed from there. Avery Brundage, IOC president, and Willi Daume, head of the German Organizing Committee, issued strong statements of support for Rhodesia. The lines had been drawn; Rhodesia, with its social policy of apartheid, became a focal point of political unity among black African nations.

An unidentified group of black Olympians from the United States also denounced Rhodesia's participation in the Olympics. A statement was issued by the group that read in part:

> In the light of the Rhodesian acceptance into the games, the United States black athletes now in Olympic Park believe it imperative to take a stand concerning the issue. We denounce Rhodesia's participation and if they are allowed to compete, we will take a united stand with our African brothers.[94]

The statement contained no signatures and no direct threats of boycott, but the implications were clear. Demonstrations similar to that of John Carlos and Tommie Smith in Mexico City were a possibility if Rhodesia was allowed to compete. The true Olympic spirit envisioned by the IOC was somewhat upheld when Nigeria declined to quit the games if Rhodesia stayed; however, 11 other nations eventually boycotted.

The issue was resolved on August 22 when the IOC withdrew its invitation to Rhodesia to compete. The final vote after two days of deliberation was 36 in favor of withdrawal, 31 opposed, and three abstentions. "'Political blackmail,' replied Brundage."[95] After the announcement was made, Brundage agreed that political pressure on the Olympics had become intolerable. In any event, the political climate of the XXth Olympiad had been set.

For the first time in Olympic history, the American men's basketball team did not win the gold medal. They were defeated by the Soviet Union 51-50 after the referees put time back on the clock twice in order to give the Soviet Union a second and than a third chance to beat the Americans. It was among the most dispicable acts by politically motivated referees in modern Olympic history. The American team was so outraged that they protested (who wouldn't) the game only to be denied. As a result, they refused to accept their silver medals for finishing second.

Thirty-six years earlier, the 1936 Berlin Olympiad had been cloaked in German nationalism, as the Nazis took significant steps to preclude athletic participation by Jews and people of color. In the

XXth Olympiad, Jews were once again political targets on German soil.

Israel and its Arab neighbors had operated in a climate of hostility and terror since the creation of the Jewish state in 1948. A peace settlement in the Middle East in 1972 was highly unlikely. Egypt, the leader of the Arab bloc, had a deep conviction that it could defeat Israel militarily if they (Arabs) were unable to do so politically. The victory of Israel in the 1967 Arab–Israeli war had proved otherwise. By 1972, the Arab nations had not again attacked Israel. However, Arab guerrilla units continued to operate against Israel, inflicting death and destruction. In response, Israel used the "eye for an eye" approach and attacked the Arab terrorists and their bases in Syria and Lebanon. The Black September Arab terrorist organization would escalate the scope of terrorism by launching an attack on Israeli Olympians in Munich that shocked the world.

The Munich Massacre

In the early morning hours of September 5, eight Arab guerrillas equipped with machine guns and hand grenades made their way into the Olympic Village complex occupied by the Israelis and "reenacted the darkest ritual in German history— the sharp ominous knock on the Jews' door."[96] Nineteen hours later, 17 people were dead: 11 Israelis, five terrorists, and one German policeman. The Arab guerrillas had brought their war with Israel to the XXth Olympiad. The Munich massacre darkened the pages of Olympic history and was the event responsible for the military reprisals carried out by Israel against Arab terrorists.

By dawn on September 5, the terrorists had murdered two Israeli Olympians and captured nine others "as the world watched in horrified fascination on live television."[97] The Arabs secured the remaining nine hostages together in one room and issued demands, an ultimatum, and a deadline. According to *Newsweek,*

> The initial demands included the release of 200 Palestinian guerrillas . . . imprisoned in Israel and safe passage to the Arab world. If the demands were not met by noon, . . . they would begin methodically executing their prisoners— "to show what is what," the terrorist leader said. But in Israel, the government refused to consider the blackmail; and in Munich the Arabs allowed the noon deadline to pass.[98]

German officials worked frantically to secure the release of the Israelis. German chancellor Willy Brandt arrived in Munich to launch rescue efforts through diplomatic channels. However, the Arab guerrillas refused an offer of an unlimited ransom and "summarily turned down German officials who said they would take the place of the captive Israelis."[99] Brandt appealed to Egyptian president Anwar Sadat to intervene but could not reach Sadat. Brandt then contacted Egyptian premier Aziz Sidky, who told the chancellor curtly, "I cannot pre-empt a decision of the guerrillas. We do not want to get involved in this," and hung up.[100]

In a desperate bid for escape, the terrorists and their hostages boarded two helicopters that transported them to Furstenfeldbruck Airport, where a plane was waiting for them. With the plane were five German sharpshooters who ambushed the eight Arabs; the Germans were outnumbered by the terrorists who in turn murdered the remaining Israeli athletes. Three of the terrorists were captured alive, and three others escaped and went into hiding.[101]

The IOC, along with the rest of the world, was shocked and outraged. Israel and *The New York Times* called for an end to the Munich Olympiad. The executive committee of the IOC met to discuss the tragic series of events and to make a decision about continuing with the games. Avery Brundage wanted to continue, but only after a proper suspension and memorial ceremony was conducted. The IOC conducted a memorial ceremony for the slain Israeli athletes and decided to resume the games. However, for many athletes and Olympic teams, the atmosphere of the Olympic Games changed from one of celebration to one of anxiety and apprehension.

Fearing reprisals, the Olympic teams from Egypt, Kuwait, and Syria left Munich for their homelands. Mark Spitz, the American Jewish swimmer who was the talk of Olympic swimming circles, left Munich for safety reasons. Six Arab nations elected to remain for the duration of the games: Lebanon, Morocco, Tunisia, Algeria, Saudi Arabia, and Iran. Norway's Olympic handball team attempted to boycott the remainder of the games to protest the terrorist attack on the Israeli team. However, Norwegian government officials pressured the team into continuing play, because the International Handball Federation threatened to hold Norway responsible for lost gate receipts if their team boycotted. Several thousand deutschemarks were said to be involved.

A few days after the Munich massacre, scores of Israeli planes struck 10 guerrilla bases in reprisal. The guerrilla organization of Al Fatah was the target as the Israeli war planes made their deepest penetration into Syria and Lebanon since the Six Days' War in 1967.[102] Meanwhile, the Israeli secret service, the Mossad, tracked down two of the three terrorists who escaped and killed them. The third terrorist, Hassan Salameh, still lives in hiding and, to this day, the Mossad continues to search for him.

In the summer of 1973, the Mossad was convinced that Salameh was in Lillehammer, Norway. On July 21, 15 Mossad agents arrived in Lillehammer and identified a man they were certain was Salameh. They shot him 10 times as he and his pregnant wife left the cinema. They killed an innocent man. The man they thought was Salameh was actually Ahmed Bouchiki, a waiter from Morocco. The Mossad realized they had killed the wrong man and fled. Six Mossad agents were arrested by Norwegian authorities. Another terrorist, Abu Daoud, was a key player in the attack, although he did not participate. He is still alive; however, he claims that the Mossad tried to kill him in Warsaw, Poland, in 1981. He was sitting in a hotel café when bullets struck his left wrist, chest, stomach, and jaw. He has said that he has no regrets about his role in the killing and would do it again.

The IOC and the entire Olympic community remained stunned by the attack on the athletes from Israel. The reprisal by Israel to avenge the slain athletes brought more pain to the Olympic movement, and the hope for peace in the Middle East dimmed. Then, just when it seemed that the Munich Games would once again resume, two other noteworthy incidents occurred. First, the "troubles" in Northern Ireland spilled over into the Olympic arena when seven Irish Republican Army (IRA) cyclists deliberately crashed into the pack and caused a pileup of 15 competitors. Irish Olympic officials accused the IRA riders of causing the pileup to knock Noel Taggart, the official Irish entry, out of the race. Second, Vince Matthews and Wayne Collett, two African-American Olympians who finished first and second in the 400-meter run, were barred from the Olympic Games for life by the IOC for "disgusting behavior" during the victory ceremonies. The USOC objected, saying that no black power protest of any sort was displayed; both athletes were relaxed and were seen talking informally during The Star Spangled Banner. Both athletes also insisted that no protest gestures were involved. Clifford H. Buck, president of the USOC said he did not believe the athletes had done anything wrong. However, Avery Brundage and the IOC were unmoved. The USOC asked the IOC to rescind its action against Matthews and Collett, but to no avail.

The Munich Olympics went on despite terrorism, boycotts, and protests. This is not to suggest that the IOC, the Olympic athletes, and the Munich Organizing Committee were unfazed by these events. It did not matter what political or social beliefs were represented; millions of people around the world mourned the slain Olympians. However, in the Olympic Village and in Israel, the pain was especially evident. Once again, though, the Olympic spirit was able to transcend political and social differences as millions of television viewers around the world tuned in to watch the world's most anticipated and most celebrated sports festival, albeit with tears.

Notables

The Munich Olympiad hosted the largest contingent of Olympic athletes ever. There were 7134 athletes representing 121 countries, including 1059 women athletes.[103] The Munich Organizing Committee had done a splendid job. The facilities were first-class and the citizens of Munich could not have been more helpful.

Valeri Borzov of the Soviet Union won the gold medal in both the 100- and 200-meter dashes, erasing the supremacy long enjoyed by America's black athletes. Frank Shorter of the United States won the marathon. In women's track and field, the East German sprinters won the gold medal in the 100-meter, 200-meter, and 400-meter events. The West Germans won the 4 × 100 relay, and their sisters from East Germany won the 4 × 400 relay and set a world record. The American women managed three medals in track and field. American swimmers had a sensational meet, with the men taking 27 medals (nine gold). The American women won 30 medals (nine gold). The women's team set six world records and one Olympic record in swimming competition. Twenty-four-year-old Nikolai Aviloff from the Soviet Union set a new record in the decathlon of 8454, eclipsing the mark set by American Bill Toomey by 261 points.

In the pole vault, a problem arose because of the introduction of the fiberglass pole. The 1968 Olympic champion, Bob Seagren, had been practicing with a fiberglass pole and set a world record of 18 feet 5¼ inches in the U.S. Olympic trials. However, a month before the Munich Olympiad, officials decided to ban the use of fiberglass poles because the rest of the world's pole-vaulters had not had an opportunity to use these new poles. Bob Seagren finished second in the pole vault in Munich.

In other events, American swimming sensation Mark Spitz won an incredible seven gold medals. Russian teenager Olga Korbut became the fan favorite in women's gymnastics with her dazzling moves on the balance beam and floor exercises. Although she eventually placed seventh in the all-around competition, the 4-foot 11-inch, 85-pound Korbut gave Lyudmila Turisheva of the Soviet Union all she could handle before a mistake on the balance beam toppled her from first place. Turisheva won the gold.

The gold medal performances by Lasse Viren of Finland in the 5000- and 10,000-meter races were an especially proud moment for Finland, as the Finns had not won this event in more than 36 years. You may recall that for some time, Finnish athletes had "owned" this event with the likes of Gunnar Heckert (1936, 5000-meters champion), Ilmari Salminen (1936, 10,000-meters champion), and the indomitable Paavo Nurmi, who in 1920 won the silver medal in the 5000-meters and the gold medal in the 10,000-meters. In the Paris Olympiad of 1924, Paavo Nurmi won two gold medals in the 1500-meters and the 5000-meters, where he set world records in both events. In the Amsterdam Olympiad of 1928, Paavo Nurmi won the silver medal in the 5000-meters and the gold medal in the 10,000-meters, where he set yet another world record.[104]

THE XITH WINTER OLYMPICS: SAPPORO, 1972

The success of the 1964 Tokyo Olympiad had so favorably impressed the IOC that the XIth Winter Games were awarded to Sapporo. This was the second time the IOC had selected Sapporo to host the Winter Olympics; Sapporo had been scheduled to hold the games in 1940 before the war led to their cancellation.

The issue of amateurism again quickly gained the attention of the press and public. The Austrian skier Karl Schranz was disqualified from the Olympics because he had too openly endorsed a

---

OLYMPIC SNAPSHOT

1972 Sapporo Winter Olympics:

Opening Day February 3; Closing Day February 13

- 35 countries sent teams
- 1006 athletes: 205 women and 801 men
- 6 sports, 35 events: Biathlon, Bobsleigh, Ice Hockey, Luge, Skating, and Skiing

ski manufacturer. The Olympic skiers charged that the IOC had unfairly singled him out. The athletes in the Alpine skiing events threatened to withdraw from the games and hold their own championships, although this never happened.

Thirty-five nations sent 1006 athletes to compete in the games, including 205 women.[105] Seven new Olympic records were set. The best the American men could do in the Nordic events, which consist of nine competitions, was a sixth-place finish in the biathlon relay. The American women, like the men, did not fare well in the Nordic events. Although the men failed to place in Alpine skiing, the American women took the gold medal in the slalom and the silver medal in the women's downhill. The men did not win a single medal in speed skating; however, the U.S. women performed well, capturing the gold in the 500-meters, the bronze in the 1000-meters, another gold in the 1500-meters, and the silver in the 3000-meters. Dianne Holum, who was on the team at the Grenoble Winter Olympics, was a double medal winner. She won the 1500-meters and placed second in the 3000-meters. The American ice hockey team won the silver medal, finishing behind the Russians. The U.S. women collected a total of seven medals during the Sapporo Winter Olympics. The Canadian ice hockey team did not finish among the top six.

THE XXIST OLYMPIAD: MONTREAL, 1976

The politicization of the Olympic Games continued to manifest itself in Montreal. Avery Brundage had resigned as president of the IOC during the Munich Olympiad. Lord Killanin of Ireland replaced Brundage as president of IOC. His first Olympiad as president of the IOC was truly memorable, but for the wrong reasons. The political events surrounding the 1976 games strained diplomatic relations between countries and almost destroyed the games. International relations, economic considerations, race relations, and political defections were the major factors that embroiled the Montreal

OLYMPIC SNAPSHOT

1976 Montreal Olympiad:

Opening Day July 17; Closing Day August 1

- 92 countries sent teams
- 6084 athletes: 1260 women and 4824 men
- 21 sports, 198 events: Aquatics, Archery, Athletics, Basketball, Boxing, Canoe/Kayak, Cycling, Equestrian, Fencing, Soccer, Gymnastics, Field Hockey, Handball, Judo, Modern Pentathlon, Rowing, Sailing, Shooting, Volleyball, Weight Lifting, and Wrestling

Games in turmoil. The initial political crisis evolved several weeks before the opening ceremonies.

The Taiwan Issue

The problem of Taiwan had been simmering for decades. In previous Olympiads, the bitter conflict between China and Taiwan had surfaced more than once. In June 1976, the Canadian government notified the IOC that it would refuse to permit a Taiwanese team that identified itself as the "Republic of China" to participate in Montreal. Relations between Peking and Ottawa were the main reason for the action against Taiwan by the Canadian government. In 1970, the Canadian government had granted diplomatic recognition to the People's Republic of China and severed diplomatic relations with the Republic of China—Taiwan.

Although the government of Canada did not diplomatically recognize Taiwan, it appeared as though the government of Prime Minister Pierre Trudeau was going to allow the Republic of China to compete until Peking intervened. The IOC produced a series of letters in which Peking directly requested that Ottawa bar the Olympic delegation from Taiwan from competing in the Montreal Games.[106] The IOC once again had to deal with international politics and their potential for disrupting the games. The Peking government was able to apply considerable economic leverage against the Canadian government. In 1976, the biggest overseas trading partner Canada had was Communist China. During 1976, the two nations entered into a wheat-exporting agreement that provided new prosperity to farmers in western Canada.[107] Peking flexed its economic muscle to force the removal of Taiwan from the Montreal Olympiad.

The Canadian government did not capitulate completely to Peking. However, the terms imposed on Taiwan were extreme. The initial stipulations were that the Taiwanese Olympic team (1) could not march under the name of the Republic of China, (2) could not display its national flag, and (3) would not be permitted to play the national anthem of the Republic of China if it won a gold medal. Lord Killanin, the new president of the IOC, correctly noted that "Canada's decision was in complete conflict with Olympic rules and principles forbidding discrimination on grounds of race, religion or political affiliation."[108] According to a report by the Associated Press, "During the period of the Games, he said, the International Olympic Committee is the supreme authority."[109]

As a result of the actions against Taiwan, the IOC considered withdrawing its sanction of the Montreal Games, which in effect would have canceled the Olympics.[110] The USOC and other national Olympic committees indicated that they would withdraw their teams if the IOC did not sanction the games. The United States exerted political pressure on Canada by threatening to withdraw from the XXIst Olympiad in protest over the Canadian government's refusal to allow Taiwan to compete as the Republic of China. Other countries were expected to follow suit. President Gerald Ford of the United States phoned Phillip Krumm, president of the USOC, to express his concern over the Taiwan issue and to deplore the actions of the Canadian government.[111]

In an effort to resolve the problem, the IOC and the Canadian government engaged in a series of meetings. The IOC and the USOC tried to force

Canada into a compromise. The irony of the situation was that the IOC had recognized the Taiwan government as the Republic of China, but political squabbles had forced the country to represent itself in the Olympics as something other than the Republic of China.

After five days of nonstop negotiations not directly involving Taiwan, an accord was reached. Pat Putnam describes the compromise:

> Canadian Prime Minister Pierre Trudeau had relented enough to allow the Taiwanese to use their flag. And if they won a gold medal, he agreed, they could play their anthem. But they still could not participate under the forbidden name. "They can play whatever tune they want and they can wave whatever flag they want," he said, "but they can't use a name that isn't theirs." A relieved Lord Killanin, President of the IOC, felt that Canada had made important concessions. "Good show," he said. Phillip Krumm, head of the U.S. delegation said ... "We feel that our loyalty to the Republic of China and our pledge to it has been fulfilled even with this restriction. We took a tough stand—without those concessions from Canada we could have gone home."
>
> The compromise was acceptable to all concerned parties except Taiwan. Said Victor Yuen, secretary of the Taiwan delegation, "Either we are the Republic of China or we go home."[112]

They went home.

Once again the IOC found itself in a difficult position. The Olympic Games were yet again being manipulated by politicians whose only interest was to gain the political upper hand. These politicians did not appear to be concerned with the future of the Olympic movement. The credibility of the IOC was called into question by Robert Trumbull of *The New York Times,* who recalled an "earlier" statement by the IOC:

> Olympic officials declared today [July 9], in a formal statement, that the International Olympic Committee "would have no alternative" but to cancel the 1976 Games, scheduled to

open on July 17, unless Canada relented in its decision to prevent Taiwanese athletes from participating as representatives of the Republic of China.[113]

The games were not canceled even though the government of Canada refused to allow Taiwan to represent itself as the Republic of China. The IOC maintained its commitment to ensure that the Olympic Games remained one of the few opportunities left to bring thousands of athletes from around the world to one place where they could not only compete against the best but also engage each other in conversation and, it was hoped, enhance the prospects for peace. The IOC has had no other recourse than to compromise from time to time to achieve its goals. After all, it is the end result that is important—that the Olympics continue. To this end, the IOC historically has done a splendid job in ensuring that the youths of the world are afforded an opportunity to interact with each other and, in doing so, to break down the political and social barriers that politicians are so fond of erecting.

Diplomatic relations between Washington and Ottawa were strained as a result of the Taiwan issue. The United States was critical of the Canadian government's action toward the Republic of China. Canada was upset over the remarks made by President Ford and the criticism leveled against the Trudeau government by the American press. According to a report by Trumbull,

> In an unusually sharp statement, the Canadian Secretary of State for External Affairs, Allan J. MacEachen, accused the United States of intervening in the Taiwan issue in order to further American foreign policy.
>
>   . . . "The position we have taken does not affect American interests in any way whatsoever," he declared. . . . "Our position is a reflection of our foreign policy, and I believe it ought to be respected as such. . . ."
>
>   "We respect a quite different foreign policy on China than is followed in the United States, and which obviously is the basis of the opposition to our position at the Olympics."[114]

Olympic politics even managed to strain relations between the United States and perhaps its friendliest, closest ally.

The Boycott

On July 16, the Republic of China withdrew from the Montreal Games. Several hours after the Taiwan team had given notice of its departure, Nigeria, Uganda, and Zambia announced that they would boycott the XXIst Olympiad if New Zealand was allowed to compete. The three black African nations joined the boycott movement initiated by Tanzania and Mauritius, which had withdrawn earlier.

The black African nations were angry with the New Zealand government because it had permitted one of its rugby union football teams to tour South Africa. Sixteen black nations demanded that the IOC ban New Zealand from the XXIst Olympiad, "but the IOC refused even to consider it because rugby is not an Olympic sport."[115] The issue was clarified by Abrihim Ordea, head of Nigeria's Olympic Committee: "We are not talking about rugby. . . . As far as we are concerned, it could have been table tennis, football or cycling. We are talking about relationships with countries which support apartheid sports."[116]

New Zealand was singled out as the "goat" by the black African bloc to call attention to the racist policies of South Africa. The same situation had surfaced during the 1968 and 1972 Olympiads. Once again, the black African bloc would use the Olympic Games as a political tool to attack the government of South Africa. On being informed of the developing African boycott, Lord Killanin, IOC president, stated, "This is a tragedy. . . . This is the toughest week I have experienced. The athletes must be sick to their back teeth with all the politics."[117] The government of Tanzania, a prime instigator of the boycott movement, issued the following statement:

> Tanzania has always maintained that political, commercial, and sporting links with the South African apartheid regime strengthen and give

respectability to the fascist state. . . . New Zealand's participation in sporting events in South Africa at a time when the whole world was mourning and condemning the barbaric incidents in the apartheid state was an open approval by New Zealand of the murderous acts.[118]

The statement referred to the fact that the New Zealand rugby team had toured South Africa right after race riots in Soweto "in which more than 170 Africans were killed by the South African police."[119]

An organization was formed with the sole purpose of isolating South Africa from international athletic competition. Known as SAN-ROC (South African Non-Racial Olympic Committee), the organization was based in London and headed by Dennis Brutus. Brutus, a black, had been raised in South Africa, where he spent time in six different jails. According to Brutus, SAN-ROC acted as the force that organized the African boycott and would work to keep governments that believed in the social policy of apartheid, like Rhodesia and South Africa, out of international athletic competition. He maintained that he wanted the Olympic Games to be free of politics but that "it is the first article of the Olympic Charter that discrimination cannot be permitted. Discrimination is the only issue."[120]

Perhaps New Zealand was singled out as the scapegoat for engaging in a rugby game with South Africa while the memory of the Soweto riots was still strong. However, a week before the opening ceremonies of the XXIst Olympiad, Canada was entertaining a South African cricket team in Toronto; and France sold military arms to South Africa. Why did the African bloc not boycott the games in response to the actions of Canada and France? Brutus responded by saying that "New Zealand plays South Africa more; its government appears to tacitly approve. It's an enormously complicated world."[121]

The black African bloc, consisting of Kenya, Nigeria, Ethiopia, Uganda, Chad, Ghana, Upper Volta, Ivory Coast, Togo, Mali, Morocco, Senegal, Niger, Zambia, and the Congo, signed a pledge to follow Tanzania's lead and boycott the games if New Zealand was allowed to compete. Nigeria was not optimistic; before the pledge was delivered to Lord Killanin, the Nigerian team chartered a plane to return home.

And go home they did. The IOC did not force New Zealand out, nor did New Zealand volunteer to withdraw from the games. As a result of the political boycott, 648 athletes representing 25 nations withdrew from the Montreal Games.[122] Social issues and politics had once again disrupted the games.

Security Concerns

As a result of the terrorism during the XXth Olympiad, the Olympic Village at Montreal took on the appearance of a military fortress. To prevent any terrorist activities during the games and ensure the safety of the athletes and spectators, the Canadian government took all necessary precautions. They deployed a force of 16,000 police and military personnel at a cost of $100 million. Five hundred plainclothes officers and assorted undercover agents operated in and around the Olympic complex.[123] Trained police dogs capable of sniffing out explosives were stationed at airports and throughout the Olympic Village. Sharpshooters were placed on rooftops of the Olympic complex. Additional "observers" peered through binoculars as they patrolled the housing areas. Canadian combat troops were highly visible.[124]

Political Defections and Propaganda

The differences in political ideology continued to reflect the tensions between East and West. The first political defection during the XXIst Olympiad was a Romanian rower, Walter Lambertus. He reportedly told an Olympic hostess that he wished to defect to the West. Lambertus was put on a bus for Niagara Falls, where he applied for permanent residence in Canada.[125] The most celebrated political defection was by Sergi Nemtsanov, a 17-year-old Russian diver. The Soviet Union claimed that he had been kidnapped and demanded that Canada return the young diver; "the Canadian government immediately replied that it wouldn't return him."[126] Russian officials issued an ultimatum: Either Nemtsanov be returned to Soviet officials immediately or the Russian Olympic team would withdraw from the last two days of competition.[127]

The next night, Canadian immigration officials and representatives of Nemtsanov met with Soviet officials. In a monitored phone call, Nemtsanov told the Russian officials that he was defecting to the West on his own free will and that he did not want to live in the Soviet Union anymore. The Soviet officials immediately replied that he was still immature and was unable to judge life properly. However, so as not to jeopardize the 1980 games in Moscow, the Russians backed off from their insistence that the diver be returned and agreed to remain in competition.[128]

Alberto Juantorena, a track sensation from Cuba, won the 400- and 800-meter races. He dedicated his gold medals to Premier Fidel Castro and the Cuban revolution. But Cuba's friend and ally across the ocean was not having an easy time during the games. Sergei Pavlov, head of the Soviet Olympic team, claimed that the Russians were "persecuted right from the start of the Games."[129] According to Pavlov, "It is not easy for sportsmen from the USSR to perform on the American continent. Our athletes were persecuted from the very first day by forces for whom Olympic ideals are foreign."[130]

The "persecutions" are interesting to note. The IOC censured the Soviet water polo team after it tried to pull out of the competition when it appeared it could not win. The reason given for the pullout was "sickness and injuries to team members." Dr. Harold Henning, president of the Federation Internationale de Nation Amateur, which governs aquatic sports, said a Soviet representative inquired "about the feasibility of its team withdrawing from competition inasmuch as they would not be able to finish in the top six teams." To make matters worse for the Russians, the IOC expelled pentathlete Boris Onishchenko from the games because he was caught using an illegally wired foil in fencing that would score "hits" when he actually missed.[131]

Besides the defection of Nemtsanov, additional embarrassing political incidents plagued the Russians. The Soviets were the target of anti-Soviet literature and of demonstrations by Ukrainians living in Canada and seeking separation of the Ukraine from the Soviet Union. Pavlov complained that piles of anti-Soviet material "were moved into the Olympic Village almost every day. . . . How it got there was unknown because a lot of police guard the area."[132]

As expected, the Soviet Union captured the unofficial Olympic title, and East Germany came in second, followed by the United States. Pavlov said the results were no surprise to him: "This was predetermined by the social policy of these countries."[133] Moscow would be the host city for the next Summer Olympics in 1980. The Soviets were warned by Lord Killanin that "any attempt at political interference with the 1980 Olympics will not be tolerated."[134] Lord Killanin's mistake was issuing the warning to the Soviets; he should have issued the warning to the United States because it would not be the Russians who mixed sport and politics. Instead, President Jimmy Carter's administration engineered the boycott of the 1980 Moscow Olympiad.

Notables

The Montreal organizers spent over $1 billion on the Olympic Games. The Olympic venues were first-class all the way, much to the delight of both athletes and fans. Queen Elizabeth II of England opened the games before a capacity crowd of 72,000 and a worldwide television audience. The number of women athletes continued to increase, as 1260 women entered the games; these women represented 66 countries and competed in 49 athletic events.[135]

Edwin Moses of the United States won the 400-meter hurdles and set a new world record. Teammate Bruce Jenner, after his tenth-place finish in Munich, won the decathlon, in the process setting a new world record. Nadia Comaneci, a

14-year-old gymnast from Romania, scored seven perfect 10s in gymnastics, which had never before been done in the Olympics, and won five medals, including three gold. Once again, Lasse Viren of Finland was the Olympic champion in the 5000- and 10,000-meter races, while the East German women swept the pentathlon.

The American track-and-field team faced stiff competition in both the men's and women's events. The men won 19 medals, six of them gold. The women's team won three medals but were no match for the powerful East German team, which won 19 medals, 12 more than the Soviet women. In men's swimming, the Americans dominated, winning 27 of 35 possible medals. The East German women demonstrated their aquatic superiority by winning 11 of 13 events, setting eight world records in the process. Sugar Ray Leonard's leadership and prowess helped the U.S. boxing team to win five gold medals. The American men returned to dominance in basketball by defeating the Yugoslav team to win the gold medal. They were not going to repeat the fiasco of Munich, where they had lost the gold medal to the Russians for the first time in Olympic history.

THE XIITH WINTER OLYMPICS: INNSBRUCK, 1976

Innsbruck, Austria, had hosted the Winter Olympics in 1964 and agreed to stage the games once again when Denver, Colorado, had to withdraw.

OLYMPIC SNAPSHOT

1976 Innsbruck Winter Olympics:
Opening Day February 4; Closing Day February 15

- 37 countries sent teams
- 1123 athletes: 231 women and 892 men
- 6 sports, 37 events: Biathlon, Bobsleigh, Ice Hockey, Luge, Skating, and Skiing

The citizens of Denver decided that they did not want to pay enormous sums of money to host the games even though the IOC originally had awarded the Winter Olympics to Denver. Less than a year before the start of the 1976 Winter Olympics, one of the most prominent figures in the world of sport, Avery Brundage, died at the age of 87. He had assumed the presidency of the IOC at a time when geopolitics threatened to undermine the spirit of Olympism. He resisted these attempts and steered the Olympic movement through difficult times.

To ensure the security of athletes and spectators, Austrian security forces blanketed the area. The athletes had to accept the unfortunate necessity of having armed guards protect them.[136] In fact, the number of Austrian police on patrol was double the number of athletes! This would not be the last time the number of security personnel exceeded the number of Olympians. There were 1123 athletes from 37 countries participating in the Winter Olympics, including 231 women athletes, who competed in 37 events.[137] The American Broadcasting Corporation (ABC) televised almost every event during the Innsbruck Games, which were quite popular with the American viewing audience.

Twenty-five percent of the athletes caught the flu or fell victim to the common, but miserable, cold. Strict drug testing was in place, and more than 300 drugs were on the restricted list. The hockey team from Czechoslovakia came down with the flu and innocently took one of the restricted drugs, unbeknownst to them, to fight off the symptoms. They were forced to forfeit a game and settle for the silver medal.[138]

Dorothy Hamill won the gold medal for the United States in women's figure skating. Ice dancing was included on the Olympic program for the first time, and the American team of Colleen O'Connor and Jim Millins won the bronze medal. Bill Koch of Vermont was the first American to win a medal in Nordic skiing, nabbing the silver in the 30-kilometer race. His fellow Vermonters had raised money to enable his mother to attend the Winter Olympics to watch her son compete.[139] The U.S. team came away from Innsbruck with ten medals (four bronze, three silver, and three gold). The Soviet Union ice hockey team did not lose a single game on their way to the gold medal. The U.S. ice hockey team finished in fifth place, while the Canadian team did not finish in the top six for the second time in as many Winter Olympics.

THE XXIIND OLYMPIAD: MOSCOW, 1980

The Moscow Olympiad evolved into a microcosm of East–West relations. The animosity between the United States and the Soviet Union, and the clash of their respective political ideologies, severely affected the XXIInd Olympiad. However, it was not the Soviet Union that undermined the spirit of Olympism but the United States. For the third time since the rebirth of the modern Olympics in 1896, the United States did not send a team to the Olympiad. For the first time in Olympic history, the United States called for and led a boycott of the Olympics. It was not a boycott initiated by the USOC, but rather a calculated political move by President Jimmy Carter that eventually sabotaged the efforts of the USOC to send a team to Moscow. The political arena would once again spill over

OLYMPIC SNAPSHOT

1980 Moscow Olympiad:

Opening Day July 19; Closing Day August 3

- 80 countries sent teams
- 65 countries boycotted
- 5179 athletes: 1115 women and 4064 men
- 21 sports, 203 events: Aquatics, Archery, Athletics, Basketball, Boxing, Canoe/Kayak, Cycling, Equestrian, Fencing, Soccer, Gymnastics, Field Hockey, Handball, Judo, Modern Pentathlon, Rowing, Sailing, Shooting, Volleyball, Weight Lifting, and Wrestling
- 5,615 media / press credentials issued

into the Olympic arena, much to the resentment of America's Olympic athletes and the bitter disappointment of the IOC.

What Led to the U.S. Boycott? The Soviet Invasion of Afghanistan

In April 1978, a Soviet Union-backed coup in neighboring Afghanistan resulted in a puppet government. However, there was continuous rebellion from the Muslim tribesmen who declared a holy war, or jihad, on the Communists. "Executions, imprisonments, and bitter political rivalries had so undermined the Soviet-backed Kabul government that it was unable to function."[140] On Christmas morning 1979, backed by 50,000 troops, the Soviets imposed a military dictatorship, hoping to restore stability and put Russia in a stronger position to capitalize on unpredictable events in Iran and further long-range Soviet goals in the Middle East. President Hafizullah Amin was murdered and Babrak Karmal installed, an Afghan who had been in exile in Czechoslovakia and who swore allegiance to the Soviet Union. The move by the Soviet Union was denounced by the United States, Muslim countries, and others throughout the West. It was the first time since 1945 that the Soviet Union had imposed its will on a nation not formerly under its control.[141] Of major concern to the United States was the danger of Soviet meddling in Pakistan, which shared a long and explosive border with Afghanistan. The United States, by treaty, was committed to defend Pakistan in the event of an invasion.

On January 4, 1980, in his address to the nation, President Carter said, "A Soviet-occupied Afghanistan threatens both Iran and Pakistan and is a stepping-stone to possible control over much of the world's oil supplies, the United States, our allies and our friends."[142] In response to the Soviet invasion, Carter first proposed a worldwide boycott of the 1980 Moscow Olympiad. The United States also sought to have the games moved, postponed, or canceled during the spring of 1980 as tensions mounted between the two superpowers. In their ongoing propaganda war, the object was to embarrass and discredit each other. If Carter could influence the decision-making process of the IOC and have the Moscow Olympiad postponed, canceled, or moved to another location, he could punish the Soviet Union and achieve a major victory in the propaganda war. Unfortunately, the athletes became mere pawns in a political chess game between the White House, the USOC, and the IOC. To the Carter administration, the opportunity to bring American and Soviet athletes together in Moscow to compete, discuss their differences, and foster international understanding and goodwill was not as important as making a political statement. The actions of the White House and the U.S. Congress would end up debasing the spirit of Olympism in 1980.

Laurel Brassy-Inversen provides the following chronology of events from January to April 1980:

On January 20, 1980, President Carter set a deadline of February 20 for the withdrawal of troops from Afghanistan as a condition for the U.S. sending its athletes to the Olympics. Two days later, the President issued letters to 100 nations asking for their support of a boycott.

January 24, the House of Representatives voted to support the President 386 to 12. Then on January 26, USOC Executive Board passed unanimously a resolution to support the President's request that the USOC make a presentation to the IOC; the recommendation was that the games be moved or canceled. The USOC added a third option of postponement.

By February 4, the National Olympic Committees had met in Mexico City and rejected the boycott proposal of the Carter Administration.

On February 10, the International Olympic Congresses began at Lake Placid, New York, prior to the start of the 1980 Winter Olympics. Executive Director of the USOC, F. Don Miller, and USOC President, Robert Kane, addressed the IOC General Assembly on February 11 and presented President Carter's proposal to move or cancel the games. The IOC responded with a unanimous rejection of the proposal and confirmed that the games would go on as scheduled in Moscow.

The February 20 deadline arrived. The situation in Afghanistan remained the same. Hodding Carter, the President's Press Secretary, announced that the boycott was "final" and "irrevocable." However, President Carter said the government had made its position very clear and that the question then would address itself to the USOC.[143]

According to the White House, 50 governments were in favor of a boycott, including some African Islamic nations, some European nations, and Canada, New Zealand, and Australia. However, the choice of accepting the Olympic invitation lies in the hands of each country's own Olympic committee (NOC). Just as the USOC governs Olympic sports in the United States, all other countries have similar governing associations. Technically, it would seem that these committees would make up the IOC, but that is not how it works.

The IOC is an autonomous body whose members are not elected by the national committees. The IOC selects its own members, thereby ensuring that each IOC member's first duty is to the ideal of Olympism; IOC members do not represent their countries, they uphold the spirit of Olympism. The IOC prides itself in having no national or political connections. Nobody is supposed to be able to tell it what to do. The IOC's only allegiance is to the Olympic ideal.

When President Carter set the February 20 deadline, he stated in a letter to Robert Kane, "If Soviet troops do not fully withdraw from Afghanistan within the next month, Moscow will become an unsuitable site for a festival meant to celebrate peace and good will."[144] The government wanted a quick and supportive decision from the USOC, but the USOC postponed it until the House of Delegates was to meet in April.

What ultimately resulted was a clash between the desires of various Olympic teams around the world (go to Moscow) and the political agenda of their respective governments (support the U.S.-led boycott of the Moscow Olympiad). For example, Britain's Olympic Committee stated that not one person from Britain who wanted to go to the games would fail to go to Moscow; they would find a way. However, initially, the British government said Britain would not send a team to Moscow.

On March 12, Carter asked U.S. business interests associated with the Moscow Games to voluntarily stop trade of anything that would support the games. On March 29, he imposed a ban on Olympic-oriented business with the Soviet Union.

On March 23, members of the Athlete's Advisory-Council, an advisory and liaison group to the USOC, met in Washington with the president and submitted a proposal. The United States should send a team to compete in Moscow. However, to show the Americans' feelings about Afghanistan and let the Soviet people know that something was wrong, no athletes would participate in the opening or closing ceremonies. Athletes would stay in the village and leave only for their competitions.

Athletes as Political Pawns

By this point, there was no turning back for the Carter administration. It had taken a hard-line stand and was determined to see it through, right or wrong. For seven months, the administration tried desperately to drum up support for its boycott.[145]

April 1980 was a dark month for the USOC. Early in the month, Sears, the giant retail department store, withdrew its financial support of the USOC, as did Southland Corporation, the parent company of the 7-Eleven convenience stores, which was to commence building the new field-house at the Olympic training center. President Carter was killing not only the hope of the United States sending a team to Moscow but also the hopes and dreams of America's athletes. The USOC is solely supported by donations from private citizens and corporations, and the government's campaign against the Olympics successfully turned millions of Americans against the USOC. But the government told only its side. Almost all donations to the USOC dried up or were withdrawn. The USOC not only sends a team to the Olympics but also develops and helps fund grassroots and development programs, trains athletes, maintains

an Olympic training center, and sends athletes to numerous competitions every year.[146]

The Carter administration's campaign to squelch American support for the Olympics was widespread, reaching into almost every facet of American life. It began as early as January. The Postal Service had issued a series of Olympic stamps for the Summer Games, but for the first time in the history of the Postal Service, a stamp was recalled and taken out of circulation. Corporation after corporation withdrew support for the USOC. The administration also campaigned for votes of the USOC House of Delegates members. Meetings were held at the White House, and mailgrams and briefings were sent to USOC members stating the government's position.[147]

The president dealt the USOC a major setback in April. USOC executives had said that if American participation in Moscow became a threat to national security, they would not send a team. The administration knew this was a touchy topic because if this was true, much stricter actions against the Soviet Union than a boycott of the Olympics would be needed. There was a growing desire among amateur athletes and organizations to send a team to Moscow in defiance of the president's wishes. In a telephone conversation in which the administration tried to stifle this desire, the president's White House counsel, Lloyd Cutler, said,

> The President has stated it will damage American security. The President has insisted that the United States will not send an Olympic team to Moscow to protest and punish the Soviet invasion and military presence of Afghanistan.[148]

At the White House meeting of the National Governing Bodies (NGB), Warren Christopher, deputy secretary of state, explained the administration's position: "The President will take strong measures to see that we are not represented at the Games." However, no threats were made to sports officials because "we haven't reached that point yet." It was revealed that Carter ordered NBC not to make any more payments to the Soviet Union for television rights and to put a halt to the sale of U.S. equipment to be used during the games. "We have not exhausted the measures we can take," said Christopher.[149] NBC was forced to leave in excess of $10 million worth of equipment in Moscow as a result of Carter's decision.

Michael Scott, an attorney for the NCAA, said the administration made it clear it would prefer the USOC House of Delegates to voluntarily vote not to go. Cutler added that the bottom line was, "If you vote not to support the President, you are doing the worst thing you can possibly do."[150] A week before the USOC House of Delegates meeting, Carter threatened legal action, if necessary, to prevent American athletes from participating in Moscow.

On April 12, the meeting was held in Colorado Springs. After intimidating speeches by Vice President Walter Mondale and former secretary of the treasury William Simon, a long-standing USOC member, the assembly voted 1604–797 against sending a team to Moscow. They voted in violation of their own constitution, but considering the monumental pressures of the government, it was not a surprise. In contrast, the NGBs, the backbone of the USOC, voted almost unanimously to go. It was the other member organizations that caved in to the political pressure.[151]

Presidential Pressure and Promises

At one point, the USOC's tax-exempt status was threatened. On the other hand, a quick decision by the USOC not to send a team brought promised rewards of tax-exempt status for NGBs, federal funding to make up the $8 million USOC debt, and a push from the administration to allocate the $16 million promised the USOC by law when the Amateur Sports Act of 1978 was passed.[152]

The Carter administration also promised to take a major role in Operation Gold, a post-Olympic fund-raising program, to enable the USOC to get back on its feet. Operation Gold was planned as a series of luncheons all over the country featuring a White House representative to drum up support for the USOC. It was to be a matching-funds program in which the government would match dollar for dollar any amount raised by Operation Gold.[153]

Many Olympians looking forward to Moscow were angry at Carter for boycotting the games. Athletes at the Olympic Training Center in Colorado Springs called a press conference to express their feelings to the nation. Other athletes all over the country spoke out as well. One young woman, rower Anita Defrantz, a lawyer from Philadelphia, was responsible for organizing many of the athletes. She became such a thorn in the president's side that the Carter administration offered her a job to keep her quiet. She made herself heard and exploited every weakness in the government's position. Public opinion, once estimated as high as 80 percent in favor of the boycott, was evening out but to no avail.[154] She later became a member of the IOC.

The Carter administration held firm to its position, and on July 21, the XXIInd Olympiad in Moscow opened as scheduled. Although 16 countries chose not to participate in the opening ceremonies as a protest to the Soviet presence in Afghanistan, 5179 athletes representing 80 nations attended. The number of women athletes declined because of the boycott, numbering 1115.[155] Thirty-one nations were part of the U.S. boycott, including Canada, China, Japan, Kenya, and West Germany; 26 other nations chose not to compete for their own reasons.

Meanwhile, back in Washington, the members of the U.S. 1980 Olympic team were honored in a special ceremony. It was the first time in U.S. Olympic history that an entire Olympic team was honored by Congress and allowed to gather together outside of the Olympics. Each athlete received a special gold medal struck by Congress and a medal from the USOC. The athletes also received their Olympic apparel from Levi Strauss, one of the only U.S. corporations to continue its support of the team. Washington, D.C., opened its heart to the Olympians and their guests (two each) with parties, dinners, receptions, and tours. To add insult to injury, the USOC was required to organize and pay for the celebration, orchestrated by the Carter administration for purely political reasons.

It was during those few days that the USOC received a check from the Department of the Treasury for $4 million, the first installment of the $16 million granted in 1978 by the Amateur Sports Act. Prior to the Washington gathering, the White House had been drumming up support for alternate games or international competitions. Almost all the NGBs stated that alternate competitions would be meaningless for the athletes, and most athletes did not want to participate. The administration ignored the wishes of the athletes and began making commitments to foreign countries that the United States would compete. It was dictating who would attend these games at the expense of the USOC. The USOC had expressly told the White House that if any alternate competitions took place, they would be organized and agreed on by the NGBs and the USOC. The Carter administration then abandoned its plans.[156] In December 2007, 27 years after the Moscow Olympiad, the United States Congress decided the time was right to award Congressional Gold Medals to the members of the 1980 Olympic team.

Epilogue

By late August, the USOC was $9–11 million in debt due to corporate withdrawal of sponsorships. USOC funding dried up, so there was no money for development programs, the Olympic Training Center, the sports medicine program, world championships, and other programs. Many NGBs felt the heat at the meetings of the Olympic Congress in Moscow during the Moscow Games. For their role in the boycott, U.S. officials and NGB leaders once again became political victims and lost some voting positions on various international federations.

American citizens and the broadcast and news media were allowed to go to the games. Although discouraged by the government, they did not come under the great political pressure placed on the USOC. The media and some spectators still went, but in greatly reduced numbers. The government

realized that it could not win the legal battles that would have ensued had it tried to forcibly keep people from going to the Soviet Union.

To make matters worse, in 1981, the USOC was involved in a lawsuit when the Russian Travel Bureau, which had made all travel arrangements for Americans going to Moscow, refused to refund deposits to thousands of Americans who had planned on attending the Olympics. Many of these Americans sued, holding the USOC responsible for making the decision not to send a team to Moscow. The USOC opted to settle out of court for $450,000 rather than fight the lawsuits in court and pay for lengthy court proceedings. Meanwhile, lawsuits filed by various athletes against the USOC for violating its own charter were thrown out of court.[157] American athletes lost a chance—for many, a once-in-a-lifetime chance—to win a medal doing what they were best at. For many, the chance to participate in the Olympic Games, the greatest peaceful gathering of nations on earth, had passed forever, all in the name of politics.

Lord Killanin, president of the IOC, resigned in 1980. Juan Antonio Samaranch, from Spain and a member of the IOC since 1966, was named the new IOC president.

Notables

President Leonid Brezhnev of the Soviet Union opened the games of the XXIInd Olympiad. The Soviet Union had spared no expense, and the facilities were once again first-rate. Interestingly, Britain did send Olympic athletes to Moscow. The competition was fierce, and 36 world records were broken. The Soviet Union won 80 gold medals, 30 more than in Munich. The East German team won 47 gold medals. Bulgaria, Cuba, and Italy were the next closest to the Russians and East Germans, capturing eight gold medals apiece.[158] Sebastian Coe and Steve Ovett, world record holders from Britain, engaged in a spectacular duel in the 800-meter and 1500-meter races. In the 800-meter, Ovett won the gold medal with a time of 1 minute, 45.4 seconds, edging out Coe by a half second. In the 1500-meter, Coe won the gold with a time of 3:38.4; Jürgen

Straub from East Germany finished second in 3:38.8, followed by Ovett, who captured the bronze with a time of 3 minutes, 39 seconds. Another Englishman, Allan Wells, won the gold medal in the 100-meters with a time of 10.25 seconds.

In the men's 5000-meter race, Miruts Yifter from Ethiopia won the gold medal and set a new world record with a time of 13 minutes, 21 seconds, followed by S. Nyambui from Tanzania. Yifter won yet another gold medal in the 10,000-meter race. The pride of Finland, Lasse Viren, finished fifth in the 10,000-meter. In the women's track-and-field events, it was a dual meet between the Russians and the East Germans. However, the East German women did win the "glamour event," the 4 × 400 relay, setting a new world record.

THE XIIITH WINTER OLYMPICS: LAKE PLACID, 1980

Since the Winter Olympics occur prior to the Summer Olympiads, the American-led boycott of the Moscow Olympics was several months down the road. Had the Russians known that the boycott of their Olympic Games by the United States was a foregone conclusion, it is highly doubtful they would have sent their Olympic team to Lake Placid. But send the team they did.

The "medal count" was essentially a contest between two Communist sports superpowers— East Germany and the Soviet Union. By the time

1980 Lake Placid Winter Olympics:

Opening Day February 13; Closing Day February 24

- 37 countries sent teams
- 1072 athletes: 232 women and 840 men
- 6 sports, 38 events: Biathlon, Bobsleigh, Ice Hockey, Luge, Skating, and Skiing
- 6,703 volunteers

the Lake Placid Games were over, the East German team had for the first time won more medals than the Russians, 23–22. The Russians, however, edged the East Germans in gold medals, 10–9. The United States had its most productive Winter Olympics since 1932, perhaps due to the home-field advantage of upstate New York. The American team won 12 medals, six of them gold. Five of the six gold medals were courtesy of speed skater Eric Heiden, who won the 500-, 1000-, 1500-, 5000-, and 10,000-meter races. He set the world record in the 10,000-meter race.

Eric's sister, Beth Heiden, won the bronze medal in the 3000-meter speed-skating competition. Leah Poulos-Mueller from the United States won silver medals in the 500-meter and 1000-meter speed-skating competitions.

"Miracle on Ice" is what the media called the stunning upset of the Soviet ice hockey team by the American team, which was quite young and had not been given much of a chance by the "experts" to advance into the medal rounds. The victory by the Americans was a true Cinderella story because the Russians were considered virtually unbeatable. After the final period, the Soviet ice hockey team was in shock as the final score read United States 4, Soviet Union 3. The American team went on to beat Finland 4–2 to win the gold medal.

The Lake Placid Organizing Committee did a superb job in coordinating the Winter Games with one exception: transportation. Tiny Lake Placid could not accommodate the tens of thousands of fans who descended on the area. Spectators were bused in from small towns and large cities on a daily basis, which caused massive traffic jams and long delays. It was not unusual for spectators to miss competitions because they were stuck in traffic. Still, the Lake Placid Winter Olympics were a success, even amid the grumbling of some of the athletes, who were housed in a newly constructed prison because of the lack of customary lodging. Corporate sponsorships went into uncharted territory as one of the American bobsled teams was sponsored by a pub, which had painted the establishment name on the sled, which enabled the pub to get free advertising when the television cameras broadcast the race. Another condition of this sponsorship agreement was that after each day of the games, the sled, driver, and brakemen had to appear at the sponsoring pub to cash in on their celebrity status.

THE XXIIIRD OLYMPIAD: LOS ANGELES, 1984

The Los Angeles Olympic Organizing Committee (LAOOC), under the leadership of Peter Ueberroth, produced the first corporate Olympiad in history, sometimes referred to as the "Spartan Olympics." For the first time in Olympic history, the Olympic Games showed a profit, which the IOC prefers to call a surplus, of over $200 million. It was the astronomical cost of the Olympics and the political nature of the games that deterred prospective cities from submitting proposals to the IOC, which continued to demand complete authority over the financial aspects of the games. Recognizing the difficulties faced by the IOC in attracting bids from prospective host cities, the LAOOC drove a

OLYMPIC SNAPSHOT

1984 Los Angeles Olympiad:

Opening Day July 28; Closing Day August 12

- 140 countries sent teams
- 14 countries boycotted
- 6829 athletes: 1566 women and 5263 men
- 21 sports, 221 events: Aquatics, Archery, Athletics, Basketball, Boxing, Canoe/Kayak, Cycling, Equestrian, Fencing, Soccer, Gymnastics, Field Hockey, Handball, Judo, Modern Pentathlon, Rowing, Sailing, Shooting, Volleyball, Weight Lifting, and Wrestling
- 28,742 volunteers and 9,190 media/press credentials issued

hard bargain and, as a result, gained major concessions from the IOC that no one had obtained ever before. Two main concessions were received by the LAOOC:

1. A clause that expressly protected the city of Los Angeles from any financial liability. This allowed the LAOOC to sell corporate sponsorships and corporate advertising to finance major capital improvements. Traditionally, the IOC abhorred the commercialization of the Olympics but had no choice under the agreement with the LAOOC.

2. The right to negotiate the lucrative Olympic television contracts, which account for millions of dollars in revenue.

Historically, the IOC had retained all rights and authority where money was involved. However, almost every city that had hosted the Olympic Games acquired enormous debt, which the IOC expected the host city to incur. The LAOOC was not about to incur any debt; it was not even interested in breaking even. Negotiations between the LAOOC and IOC were long and arduous, but in the end the IOC agreed to the demands and subsequent commercialization of the XXIIIrd Olympiad. The only other host city that was serious about hosting the games was Tehran, Iran. What would the 1984 Olympiad have been like if Tehran had been awarded the games instead of Los Angeles?

The Political Atmosphere

Niccolò Machiavelli, the Italian intellectual who taught the world to think in terms of wielding pure political power ("The end justifies the means"), stated that

> whoever considers the past and the present will readily observe that all cities and all peoples are and ever animated by the same desires and the same passions; so that it is easy, by diligent study of the past, to foresee what is likely to happen in the future.[159]

Even a cursory study of the Olympics could lead us to predict what was likely to happen in

Los Angeles. In 1984, Ronald Reagan was president of the United States and was known as the "consummate Cold War warrior." He managed to fan the flames of the Cold War by referring to the Soviet Union as the "evil empire"—a comment that did little to engender goodwill between the two superpowers or increase the prospects of athletic competition between them.

What Goes Around, Comes Around: The Soviet Boycott of the XXIIIrd Olympiad

The Russians remained angry at the Americans for leading the boycott of their Olympic Games. Reports circulating around the LAOOC suggested that the Russians had spent 9 billion rubles in producing the Moscow Olympiad and were outraged at the boycott. Still, most people believed the Russians would come to Los Angeles.

Peter Ueberroth and his staff undertook extensive lobbying and diplomatic efforts to assuage whatever concerns the Russians had. Numerous trips were made to Moscow to solicit the cooperation of the Soviets and pave the way for their Olympic team. Not surprisingly, the Russians were very difficult to deal with and would not commit themselves one way or another. Some days, it appeared that they would come; other days, the opposite was true.

During one of Ueberroth's trips to Moscow, he encountered a hostile Russian press and Soviet officials. Ueberroth was asked to explain the "fact" that the United States had, in the past, assisted in the defection of Soviet athletes. Once more, the Russians claimed that Ueberroth knew that the CIA had made plans to encourage and assist in the defection of Soviet athletes in Los Angeles. The propaganda war between the Soviet Union and the United States, as in past years, once again spilled over into the Olympic arena. Although the Russians always seemed to win the "unofficial" Olympic team title, the propaganda they derived from their athletic success paled in comparison to the political propaganda the United States was able to marshal due to the defection of Soviet and other East European athletes who risked life and limb to live in the West. The Russians were anguished by the potential propaganda bonanza that the United States would reap in Los Angeles on account of defections.

Visibly angered at the hostile line of questioning he was receiving, Ueberroth responded by saying that if they really believed all those things they were saying about Los Angeles, perhaps they should consider not coming.[160] At that point, a member of the Soviet delegation quickly intervened and, in an attempt to placate Ueberroth, stated that he was anxious to come and that the Soviets did not believe in boycotts; it was only if conditions were not right that they would not participate in the 1984 Olympics.[161]

The Russians could play the cat-and-mouse game relative to attending the Los Angeles Olympiad because it was not until May 24, 1984—only eight weeks before the games were scheduled to begin—that a country had to announce its decision whether to attend or stay home. It is not difficult to imagine the nightmare the LAOOC had relative to logistics. Should it plan for 6000 athletes or 10,000?

Eventually, the Soviet Union announced that it would be unable to compete in the 1984 Olympics because of the "lack of compliance with the Olympic ideals by the USA."[162] The Russians were still outraged at the U.S.-led boycott of the 1980 Moscow Olympics, and their boycott of the Los Angeles Olympiad was in retaliation. Once again, Olympic athletes had been used as political pawns. Last time it was the American athletes; this time the Soviet athletes suffered. With the exception of Romania and Yugoslavia, which sent teams to Los Angeles, the athletes from the Eastern Bloc nations stayed home.

Although most of the Soviet Bloc countries stayed home, Peter Ueberroth scored yet another coup when the People's Republic of China announced they would send their Olympic team to compete in Los Angeles. Chinese Olympians won 15 gold medals, eight silver, and nine bronze. China's decision to send their Olympic team to Los Angeles in all probability saved the Olympic Games. If China had not competed, the 1984 Olympics would have probably been the last one.

Security Concerns

The LAOOC hired a former agent from the Federal Bureau of Investigation (FBI) to head security. The LAOOC building on the campus of UCLA was a fortress. Visitors were thoroughly screened, and nobody was allowed inside the building without proper authorization. The People's Republic of China, sometimes referred to as Red China during the Cold War, sent an Olympic team to Los Angeles. The People's Republic of China had not sent a team to the Olympic Games for decades because of the inclusion of the Republic of China (Taiwan) in the Olympics. President Carter had severed diplomatic relations with Taiwan and formally recognized the People's Republic of China, and in so doing formulated a one-China diplomatic policy. The Chinese were pleased at the action of Carter, but in 1984, it was not Carter in the White House but staunch anti-Communist Ronald Reagan.

To the Chinese, Carter was a more sympathetic figure than Reagan; however, George Bush, Reagan's vice president, had been the U.S. ambassador to China, and the Chinese liked Bush. The Chinese were assured of a warm reception in Los Angeles and politely accepted the invitation to compete. California has a large Chinese-American population that, for the most part, is anti-Communist. There was concern that demonstrations and terrorist activities might be directed against the Chinese team, but fortunately, none surfaced.

In addition, elaborate security precautions were in place to protect spectators and athletes. In the end, the LAOOC did a spectacular job in staging the most secure and successful Olympiad in history. The Los Angeles Memorial Coliseum, home to the 1932 Olympiad, was refurbished as a magnificent symbol of Olympic pomp and pageantry. All the talents of Hollywood went into producing a stunning if not moving opening ceremony. The showmanship of the opening and closing ceremonies was magnificent, as were the performances of the athletes. President Reagan was on hand for the opening ceremonies.

Notables

Marching in the most spectacular opening ceremony in Olympic history were 6829 athletes from 140 nations. The number of women athletes continued to increase, with 1566 competing.[163] Without the participation of athletes from the Eastern Bloc nations, U.S. athletes dominated the games.

The U.S. men's volleyball team won its first gold medal while the American women won the silver medal in volleyball, losing to perennial power Japan. The U.S. men's basketball team, led by Michael Jordan, won the gold medal, as did the U.S. women's team. American sprinter Carl Lewis was clearly the star of the games, winning four gold medals. In an unexpected turn, the U.S. men's gymnastics team beat the Chinese to win the gold medal. Mary Lou Retton from the United States beat Ecaterina Szabo from Romania for the gold medal in the all-around competition. Marathoner Joan Benoit from the United States won the first women's Olympic marathon. Nawal El Moutawakel Bennis from Morocco won the gold medal in the women's 400-meter hurdles—the first Arab woman ever to win Olympic gold. In 1998, after a stellar career as a sports administrator in Morocco and a member of the International Amateur Athletic Federation Executive Bureau, Bennis was selected by the IOC as a member. A tireless champion of Olympic ideals, she has done much to create opportunities for women to participate in the Olympics and to hold key posts in the Olympic movement.

For the first time in decades, the U.S. Olympic team won the "unofficial" team title; however, the gold medals shone less brightly because many of the world's best athletes were forced to stay home and could not compete in the Los Angeles Olympics. If Machiavelli had been alive in 1984, he might have given Olympic athletes the title of "Soldiers of Sport" because, in the name of Cold War politics, the end justified the means.

THE XIVTH WINTER OLYMPICS: SARAJEVO, 1984

The Winter Olympics were held in Yugoslavia in weather conditions that made the competition extremely difficult. Athletes and spectators had to put up with fog, snow, ice, and wind. Some 1272 athletes competed, representing 49 countries. The number of women athletes who participated in the games reached a new high of 274. These women competed in 49 events, surpassing the 38 events of the 1980 Lake Placid Winter Games.[164]

Southern Californian Bill Johnson ignored the adverse conditions and won the gold medal in the men's downhill. Johnson's teammate Phil Mahre, who won the silver medal in the men's slalom in Lake Placid, rebounded and won the gold in Sarajevo. The victories by Johnson and Mahre marked the first time in history that the American men had won both the slalom and the downhill. Steve Mahre won the silver medal in the slalom, finishing second to brother Phil.

Sensational Katarina Witt from East Germany won the gold medal in women's figure skating, and Scott Hamilton from the United States won the gold in men's figure skating. The U.S. ice hockey team, unable to make a second Cinderella showing, was eliminated in pool play. The Soviet Union returned to form and won the gold medal in ice hockey.

OLYMPIC SNAPSHOT

1984 Sarajevo Winter Olympics:

Opening Day February 8; Closing Day February 19

- 49 countries sent teams
- 1272 athletes: 274 women and 998 men
- 6 sports, 49 events: Biathlon, Bobsleigh, Ice Hockey, Luge, Skating, and Skiing
- 10,450 volunteers and 7,393 media/press credentials issued

Debbie Armstrong and Christin Cooper from the United States won the gold and silver medals, respectively, in the giant slalom. In pairs figure skating, the U.S. team of Kitty and Peter Carruthers captured the silver medal. When the Sarajevo Games finished, the United States seemed to be on a comeback trail that would once again enable America's Olympians to compete against the formidable athletes from the Soviet Union and East Germany. Unfortunately, the Americans would not perform as well in the 1988 Calgary Winter Olympics as they had in Sarajevo.

THE XXIVTH OLYMPIAD: SEOUL, 1988

South Korea has been described as the economic miracle of Asia. When South Korea began digging out of the devastation of the Korean War, nobody could have predicted that it would become the fifteenth most technologically advanced country in the world less than 35 years after the war.[165] In 1945, Korea was divided into two countries: (1) the militant North, armed by the Russians, and (2) the South, backed by the United States.

OLYMPIC SNAPSHOT

1988 Seoul Olympiad:

Opening Day September 17; Closing Day October 2

- 159 countries sent teams
- 8391 athletes: 2194 women and 6197 men
- 23 sports, 237 events: Aquatics, Archery, Athletics, Basketball, Boxing, Canoe/Kayak, Cycling, Equestrian, Fencing, Soccer, Gymnastics, Field Hockey, Handball, Judo, Modern Pentathlon, Rowing, Sailing, Shooting, Table Tennis, Tennis, Volleyball, Weight Lifting, and Wrestling
- 27,221 volunteers and 11,331 media/press credentials issued

The Korean War began with the invasion of South Korea by North Korean troops on June 25, 1950. A cease-fire agreement was put into effect in July 1951, and after two years of sporadic fighting, an armistice was signed on July 27, 1953. The armistice established a demilitarized zone, or DMZ, just 35 miles north of Seoul, the capital of South Korea. American forces continue to be stationed in South Korea to provide security against the North Koreans. The armistice between the two Koreas ended the war but not the hostilities, and peace talks between North and South Korea continue even today.

The people of South Korea are strongly anti-Communist and do not trust the North Koreans. The North Koreans have launched countless terrorist attacks against the South Koreans since the end of the war, which places the residents of Seoul on perpetual alert. Soldiers are everywhere in Seoul, and anti-tank walls line the highway from Seoul to the DMZ. With all the political turmoil in South Korea and the threat of terrorist activities from North Korea, it must have been a difficult decision for the IOC to award the 1988 Summer Olympiad to Seoul. The IOC did not want a repeat of the 1968 Mexico City Olympiad, when the government had to bring in troops to suppress dissident students who were opposed to the Olympics.

The South Koreans were looking forward to the Seoul Olympiad and did not want anything to detract from the games. To prevent the ugly politics of past Olympiads, the feuding political parties of South Korea agreed to a temporary truce.

Security Concerns and Olympic Politics

After 12 years of political exile, the Russians, Americans, and East Germans were once again going to compete in head-to-head Olympic competition. However, North Korean President Kim Il Sung continued to engage in saber rattling. North Korean agents blew up a South Korean jetliner in November 1987 to discourage other nations from attending the Seoul Olympiad. Sung announced that North Korea would boycott the games and

threatened to launch a campaign of terrorism to disrupt them. The 76-year-old Sung moved surface-to-air missiles to the DMZ, only 25 miles from the Olympic stadium. This did not sit well with the Russians or Chinese, who told their Communist comrades not to interfere in the games—or else! The South Koreans had 100,000 security forces at the games to guard against political demonstrations and terrorist attacks. It was feared that North Korea would employ the terrorist "Red Army" from Japan to ruin the games.

Japan and Korea have a history of confrontation over a thousand years old, so there were concerns about how Japanese Olympic fans would be treated in Korea. The focus of the tension between the Japanese and the Koreans was the judo competition. In this event, athletes from Korea and Japan competed in front of thousands of screaming Korean and Japanese fans. The possibility of fan violence between the Koreans and Japanese was a major concern, but it never materialized. In the end, the Japanese were humbled by the Russians, winning one gold medal; the Japanese had believed they would win four. The usually vocal Japanese judo fans were unusually quiet and speculated that their nation's athletes had been softened by affluence and no longer had the commitment necessary to win.

NBC Versus South Korea

The Seoul Olympics were, as Olympic Games go, peaceful. The only bomb threats were against National Broadcasting Corporation (NBC), which held the Olympic television rights. The South Koreans felt that NBC purposely set out to humiliate and embarrass South Korea in front of a world television audience of over a billion people. A brawl had broken out in the boxing arena that involved outraged South Koreans, who jumped into the boxing ring and attacked the referee because he declared that the South Korean boxer had lost the match. The defeated South Korean sulked and pouted in the corner of the ring for 67 minutes, refusing to move. NBC televised the replay of the brawl several times and periodically zoomed in on the brooding South Korean boxer who refused to leave the ring. "Saving face" is a cultural imperative in the Asian world, and the action of NBC thoroughly embarrassed the South Koreans. By Korean standards, the South Korean boxer was humiliated by NBC, as were the South Koreans who jumped into the ring and assaulted the referee. The situation became so inflamed that shop owners displayed signs that said they would not do business with NBC employees. The network sent a memo to all 1200 of its employees in Seoul stating that they should not display the NBC logo or other symbols linking them with NBC.

Banning Performance-Enhancing Drugs and Other Illicit Drugs at the Olympics

The IOC is adamant about eliminating drugs from the games. Prior to the 1988 Summer Games, IOC president Samaranch declared, "Doping equals death!"[166] Three million dollars were spent building and equipping the Doping Control Center in Seoul. A staff of 80 analyzed urine samples from the three medal winners in each of the 237 events on the Olympic program.[167] Drug testing was also administered to athletes on a random basis. Although the Canadians had a reputation for nailing drug users, it was Canadian Ben Johnson who was found "dirty" after his gold medal win in the 100-meters. Johnson's use of steroids was a national disgrace to Canada. The gold medal was awarded to Johnson's arch rival, Carl Lewis of the United States.

The Ultimate Incentive

The last vestige of amateurism all but vanished in Seoul when countries blatantly offered money to athletes who won Olympic medals. The Russians offered the equivalent of $20,200 to each athlete who won a gold medal. Poland offered $10,000 for a gold medal. Hungarian athletes were offered a pay scale ranging from $10,000 for a gold medal to a $4500 insurance policy for a sixth-place finish. East Germany's payout was $15,000 for a gold

medal. China would offer only $2700 for a gold medal, perhaps explaining to its athletes that it cost much less to live in China than East Germany.[168]

Notables

Athletes from the United States made a splash in the Olympics. The spectacular diving of Greg Louganis earned him four gold medals. Swimmer Janet Evans, a 17-year-old El Dorado High School student from Fullerton, California, won three individual gold medals: the 400-meter freestyle, the 500-meter freestyle, and the 400-meter individual medley. Matt Biondi, who had recently graduated from the University of California and specialized in the butterfly and freestyle, won seven medals—five gold, one silver, and one bronze—to pace the American men's "swimming machine." Not to be outdone, swimmer Kristin Otto of East Germany, who stood over 6 feet tall, won six gold medals for the always powerful East German women's team. Otto's performance broke the record for the most gold medals won by a woman in any sport at one Olympiad.

The United States men's volleyball team, led by Karch Kiraly and Steve Timmons, won another gold medal, defeating the Soviet Union 13–15, 15–10, 15–4, and 15–8. The U.S. women's volleyball team avoided last place by defeating South Korea. For the second time in Olympic history, the U.S. men's basketball team failed to win the gold medal, losing to the Soviet Union 82–76 in the semifinal game. While the Soviets played Yugoslavia for the gold, the United States played Australia for the bronze. The American team destroyed the Australian team 78–49.

The U.S. women's basketball team beat Yugoslavia 77–70 to win the gold medal. Kay Yow, the American coach, did a fabulous coaching job to neutralize the 6 foot 7 inch Razija Mujanovic, Yugoslavia's dominant player.

Florence Griffith Joyner of the United States won three gold medals and a silver in track and field. Her UCLA teammate and sister-in-law, Jackie Joyner-Kersee, won the heptathlon and the long-jump competition. The two athletes won or shared five-sixths of the gold medals won by the U.S. women in the track-and-field competition!

There were two new sports at the Seoul Olympiad. Table tennis, sometimes called "Ping-Pong," was introduced, and, after a 62-year hiatus, tennis was back on the Olympic program. After boycotting the 1984 Los Angeles Olympics, the Soviet Union and other Eastern European countries returned to the Olympics competition. Ten athletes failed drug tests.

The Seoul Olympics ended on Sunday, October 2. One hundred fifty-nine countries sent 8391 athletes to Seoul, and most returned home with fond memories and new friends. For the first time in Olympic history, the number of women athletes exceeded 2000 as 2194 participated in the games.[169] The political nature of the games was still in evidence, but less so than in previous games; this trend toward the depoliticization of the Olympics would continue. Amateurism was no longer an issue; it was now acceptable for Olympic athletes to earn huge sums of money from commercial endorsements or their government. With the diminishing role of politics, the amateurism issue all but dead, and the entry of professional athletes into the games, it appeared that some of the more controversial issues that had historically plagued the Olympics were either dead or close to dying. Unfortunately, this was not the case. Ergogenic aides, also known as performance-enhancing drugs, have been on the Olympic scene for a long time. Drug testing and the "Dream Team" were in the spotlight as the world turned its attention to Barcelona, Spain, for the Olympiad in 1992.

THE XVTH WINTER OLYMPICS: CALGARY, 1988

Economics

Calgary, Canada, home of the world-famous Calgary Stampede, was awarded the 1988 Winter Olympics in September 1981 at the XIth Olympic Congress in Baden-Baden, West Germany (Figure 16-1). Previously, Calgary had presented proposals to the IOC to host the 1964, 1968, and 1972 Winter Olympics but was unsuccessful. The cost of staging the Calgary Winter Olympics was staggering. The city of Calgary contributed $10 million to the Olympic effort, as did OCO '88, the committee organizing the Calgary Games. The federal government of Canada pledged $200 million to ensure the success of the Calgary Winter Olympics. The government allocated the money to the following projects:

1. Olympic Saddledome: $27.8 million. The Saddledome was the venue for figure skating and ice hockey.

Figure 16-1
Opening ceremonies, 1988 Winter Olympics, Calgary, Alberta.

2. Olympic Oval: $35 million. The Oval was the venue for speed skating.

3. Father David Bauer Olympic Arena: $2.2 million. The arena was the venue for figure skating, compulsory programs, and the demonstration sport of short-track speed skating.

4. Canada Olympic Park: $60 million. The park was the venue for ski jumping, Nordic combined jumping, bobsled, and luge. The demonstration sports of freestyle skiing and disabled Alpine skiing were also held at the park.

5. Olympic Endowment Fund: $30 million. This fund was to maintain and manage Canada Olympic Park and the Olympic Oval after the completion of the Winter Games.

6. Operational funding for the Calgary Olympic Organizing Committee: up to $45 million.[170]

In addition to the direct funding of $200 million, the Canadian government provided essential federal services such as the Royal Canadian Mounted Police (the legendary Mounties of Canada) for security.

Atmosphere

The hospitality extended to the Olympic athletes by Calgary's citizens was extraordinary. This city clearly had caught the "five-ring fever" that signified enthusiasm for and anticipation of Olympic competition. The Calgary Winter Olympics were broadcast to the world courtesy of the American Broadcasting Corporation (ABC), which paid the staggering amount of $309 million for the television rights. Just four years earlier, ABC had paid $91.5 million for television rights to broadcast the XIVth Winter Olympics. ABC mesmerized, and at times bored, Olympic fans with 94.5 hours of both comprehensive and mundane coverage of the Calgary Games. The American team did not perform well, and much of the coverage was considered desperation programming. At one point, programming executives went so far as to interview noted sex therapist Dr. Ruth relative to the merits of skiers having sex before competition.

Over 60,000 Olympic fans packed McMahon Stadium on the University of Calgary campus for the opening ceremonies. The Calgary Winter Games took 16 days to complete, the longest Winter Olympics yet.

Notables

Perhaps at no other time in the history of the Winter Olympics had countries entered Olympic athletes in "unnatural" events. This bizarre occurrence was in effect in the bobsled competition, when the traditional Olympic bobsledding countries of Switzerland, East Germany, Austria, and the United States had to share the track with teams from the Virgin Islands, Mexico, Jamaica (a real mecca for bobsledding enthusiasts), Portugal, Australia, and Taiwan. The Jamaicans were the talk of the games due to the team's ability to negotiate the course on the side of the sled, not upright on the runners, which is the preferred way.

The United States won six medals (two gold, one silver, and three bronze). Debi Thomas won the bronze medal in women's figure skating; Bonnie Blair won the gold medal in the women's 500-meter speed-skating competition and another bronze in the 1000-meters. Jill Watson and Peter

Oppergard won the bronze medal in the pairs figure skating, and Brian Boitano won the gold medal in men's figure skating, beating out Brian Orser of Canada. Eric Flaim won the silver medal in the men's 1500-meter speed-skating event. In

the unofficial medal count, the United States team placed ninth, as the Soviet Union with 29 medals (11 gold) and East Germany with 25 medals (nine gold) continued to dominate Winter Olympics competition.

SUMMARY

In 1968, for the first time since the end of World War II, Germany was represented by two separate teams. The East German team soon dominated the athletes from West Germany in both the Summer and Winter Olympics. The IOC and German Olympic officials realized the futility of forcing a "united German team" to compete in the Olympics. Not until 1992 in Barcelona would the Olympic community watch a unified German team compete under the same flag.

This situation was one of many political problems that confronted the IOC and the global community during the Cold War. During this era, the world would come close to war on several occasions. Olympic athletes from the United States and the Soviet Union became "soldiers of sport," political pawns who were expected to demonstrate the virtues of political ideology as well as athletic prowess. Nationalism was rampant and found a home in the Olympics. The initial vision that Baron de Coubertin had for the Olympics—a force for peace, international understanding, and friendship—morphed into a force for nationalism, a vehicle for the spreading of political ideology, and a forum for political propaganda.

There was anti-Olympic sentiment in the West, the East, and the Third World. Many said that the spirit of Olympism was dead. For a while, the Olympics, although not dead, seemed to be on "life support." As the Cold War grew "hot," it not only caused worry around the world but embroiled the Olympics as well. Judging was not always based on athletic performance; it could

be based on athletes' political ideology. Olympic judging was a disgrace at times.

The issue of racism was a factor in the Olympics and reflected the times. In the 1968 Mexico City Olympics, Tommie Smith and John Carlos from the United States used the victory platform to express their outrage at the racial situation in America. During the 1976 Montreal Olympiad, African nations boycotted the games because of racism—specifically, the policy of apartheid that was practiced in South Africa. There were other demonstrations of this nature that the IOC had to contend with as well.

The political turmoil and hostilities that to this day are manifest in the Middle East, especially between Israel and most of the Arab world, first surfaced in the 1948 London Olympiad. In 1972, the massacre of Israeli athletes by the Arab terrorist group Black September during the Munich Olympiad changed the face of the Olympics forever. Security of athletes, officials, and fans in future Olympics would be of paramount concern to the IOC and the host cities. The fear of terrorism in the Olympics would deter many athletes who were among the best in the world from trying out for a spot on their country's Olympic team.

The IOC, however, remained resolute. The Olympics survived the Cold War although there were many close calls. After the collapse of the Soviet Union and the fall of the Berlin Wall, the IOC and the Olympic games would enjoy renewed success under the leadership of President Juan Antonio Samaranch, albeit not without problems, scandals, and the ever-present threat of terrorism.

DISCUSSION QUESTIONS

1. Why does there seem to be more interest in the Summer Olympics than the Winter Olympics? Do the Summer Olympics attract more political controversy than the Winter Olympics?

2. What was the political nature of the Cold War Olympics? What political agendas and propaganda "victories" were advanced as a result of Olympic victories? How useful were the Olympic Games to

politicians? In general, how can we separate patriotism from nationalism in the Olympic Games?

3. How did politics and social issues manifest themselves during the 1968 Mexico City Olympiad? Should athletes be encouraged to make political statements during the Olympics?

4. Are Olympic athletes used as "political pawns" by politicians? If so, what examples can you draw on to support your position? In relation to the rest of the world, America's Olympic athletes are not supported with the resources that are available to athletes from other countries. Why does this situation exist?

5. What has sustained the Olympic spirit and the IOC through difficult times, such as Cold War politics, demonstrations, and boycotts?

6. In your opinion, what was the most despicable or repulsive political act or display during a particular Olympiad?

7. If you were the president of the IOC, how would you use the Olympics to further world peace and social justice issues, or would you choose not to do this?

8. Congratulations! You are the newly elected president of the IOC, having been elected in January 1968. What, if anything, would you have done to Tommie Smith and John Carlos? Considering the violent protests that took place in Mexico City before the Olympics began, would you have moved the games to another city, canceled the games, or continued as planned, holding the Olympics in Mexico City? Justify your position.

INTERNET RESOURCES

International Olympic Committee (IOC)
www.olympic.org
Includes links to and information about all aspects of the Olympic Games.

International Olympic Academy
www.ioa.org.gr
Is the home page of the International Olympic Academy.

United States Olympic Committee
www.usoc.org
Is the home page of the USOC; includes information on Olympic events and athletes.

International Center for Olympic Studies
www.uwo.ca/olympic/
Provides links for scholars interested in Olympic history and philosophy; also presents lectures and publishes the *International Journal of Olympic Studies—Olympika.*

Visit the *History and Philosophy of Sport and Physical Education* Online Learning Center (www.mhhe.com/mechikoff6e) for additional information and study tools.

SUGGESTED READING

David Clay Large. *Munich 1972.* Rowman & Littlefield, 2012. 372 pgs.

NOTES

1. Quoted in Bill Henry, *An Approved History of the Olympic Games* (Los Angeles: Southern California Committee for the Olympic Games, 1981), 195.

2. John Kieran and Arthur Daley, *The Story of the Olympic Games* (Philadelphia and New York: J. B. Lippincott, 1973), 184.

3. *London Times,* 1 July 1948, 4.

4. Ibid.

5. *London Times,* 24 July 1948, 5.

6. Kieran and Daley, *Story of the Olympic Games,* 188.

7. *The Olympic Movement* (Lausanne: International Olympic Committee, Chateau de Vidy, Switzerland, 1993), 62; Anita Defrantz, "The Olympic Games and Women," *Olympic Review* XXV (October–November 1995): 58.

8. *London Times,* 18 July 1948.

9. *London Times,* 27 July 1948.

10. Defrantz, "The Olympic Games and Women," 58.

11. Henry, *Approved History,* 202.

12. *The New York Times,* 1 July 1952, 2.

13. *The New York Times,* 2 July 1952, 3.

14. Henry, *Approved History,* 224; the Olympic bulletin at the end of the year 1949 as cited in Henry.

15. *The New York Times,* 11 July 1952, 3.

16. Kieran and Daley, *Story of the Olympic Games,* 226.

17. Ibid., 227.

18. Ibid.

19. *The New York Times,* 11 July 1952, 23; *The New York Times,* 13 July 1952, 2.

20. *The New York Times,* 18 July 1952, 1, 13.

21. *The New York Times,* 13 July 1952, 3.

22. *The New York Times,* 21 July 1952, 21.

23. Kieran and Daley, *Story of the Olympic Games,* 261.

24. Ibid., 265.

25. *The Olympic Movement,* 62; Defrantz, "Olympic Games and Women," 58.

26. Henry, *Approved History,* 226–27.

27. *The New York Times,* 1 November 1956, 1.

28. "Sport," *Newsweek,* 8 October 1956, 82.

29. "Periscope," *Newsweek,* 19 November 1956, 41–43.

30. Ibid., 43.

31. "Periscope," *Newsweek,* 2 July 1956, 33.

32. "Mau Mau Rebellion," *The New Republic,* 9 July 1956, 8.

33. *The New York Times,* 4 November 1956, 3.

34. Ibid.

35. *The New York Times,* 1 November 1956, 2.

36. "Sports," *Time,* 5 November 1956.

37. *The New York Times,* 6 November 1956, 42.

38. *The New York Times,* 7 November 1956, 43.

39. *The New York Times,* 10 November 1956, 22.

40. "They Won't Go Home Again," *Newsweek,* 17 December 1956, 96.

41. Henry, *Approved History,* 251.

42. *The Olympic Movement,* 74; Defrantz, "Olympic Games and Women," 58.

43. *The New York Times,* 10 August 1960, 40.

44. Curtis G. Pepper and Richard Schaap, "Men-Medals-Marxism, The 1960 Olympics," *Newsweek,* 29 August 1960, 77–81.

45. Ibid., 79.

46. Ibid., 80.

47. *The New York Times,* 17 August 1960, 28.

48. Kieran and Daley, *Story of the Olympic Games,* 348.

49. Ibid.

50. *The New York Times,* 31 August 1960, 21.

51. Ibid.

52. Ibid., 58, 62.

53. Henry, *Approved History,* 279.

54. David Wallechinsky, *The Complete Book of the Summer Olympics,* 2000 ed. (Woodstock, NY: Overlook Press, 2000), 287.

55. Henry, *Approved History,* 277.

56. *The New York Times,* 17 October 1964, 1.

57. Kieran and Daley, *Story of the Olympic Games,* 365.

58. Ibid., 366.

59. *The New York Times,* 9 October 1964, 24.

60. John C. Pooley and Arthur V. Webster, "Sport and Politics: Power Play," paper presented at Symposium on Sport, Man and Contemporary Society, Queens College of the City University of New York, March 10–11, 1974, 24.

61. Kieran and Daley, *Story of the Olympic Games,* 376.

62. Arthur Daley, "A Word to the Wise," *The New York Times,* 6 October 1964, 47.

63. Kieran and Daley, *Story of the Olympic Games,* 376.

64. Robert Trumbull, "Brundage Condemns Political Interference in Sports and Olympic Games," *The New York Times,* 8 October 1964, 56.

65. *The New York Times,* 28 September 1964, 24.

66. *The New York Times,* 2 October 1964, 48.

67. *The New York Times,* 12 October 1964, 40.

68. Kieran and Daley, *Story of the Olympic Games,* 377; *The New York Times,* 27 September 1964, 57.

69. *The New York Times,* 24 October 1964, 1.

70. Ibid., 58, 74.

71. Henry, *Approved History,* 300.

72. *The New York Times,* 1 June 1968, 22.

73. Avery Brundage, address to the International Olympic Committee, 67th Session, October 7, 1968, Mexico City.

74. *The New York Times,* 6 October 1968, 16.

75. *The New York Times,* 13 October 1968, 83.

76. Gerald C. Fraser, "Negroes Call Off Boycott, Reshape Olympic Protest," *The New York Times,* 1 September 1968, 1.

77. Ibid.

78. Ibid., 2.

79. *The New York Times,* 13 October 1968, 1.

80. Ibid., 2; Fraser, "Negroes Call Off Boycott," 1.

81. Fraser, "Negroes Call Off Boycott," 1.

82. *The New York Times,* 13 October 1968, 2.

83. "Black Complaint," *Time,* 25 October 1968, 62–63.

84. Ibid.

85. Ibid.

86. Kieran and Daley, *Story of the Olympic Games,* 419.

87. Ibid., 423.

88. *The Olympic Movement,* 74; Defrantz, "Olympic Games and Women," 58.

89. Henry, *Approved History,* 327.

90. *The New York Times,* 10 August 1972, 43.

91. *The New York Times,* 23 August 1972, 47.

92. Kieran and Daley, *Story of the Olympic Games,* 462.

93. *The New York Times,* 22 August 1972, 55.

94. *The New York Times,* 19 August 1972, 17.

95. Kieran and Daley, *Story of the Olympic Games,* 463.

96. "Terror at the Olympics," *Newsweek,* 18 September 1972, 24.

97. Ibid.

98. Ibid.

99. Ibid., 29.

100. Ibid.

101. Ibid., 33; *The New York Times,* 8 September 1972, 22.

102. *The New York Times,* 9 September 1972, 1; Henry, *Approved History,* 357.

103. *Olympic Movement,* 62; Defrantz, "Olympic Games and Women," 58.

104. Henry, *Approved History.*

105. *Olympic Movement,* 74; Defrantz, "Olympic Games and Women," 58.

106. *Long Beach Independent Press Telegram,* 8 July 1976, C1.

107. *Long Beach Independent Press Telegram,* 12 July 1976, C1.

108. *The New York Times,* 2 July 1976, A20.

109. Ibid.

110. *The New York Times,* 4 July 1976, 5, 1.

111. *Whittier News,* 12 July 1976, 1.

112. Pat Putnam, "It Was a Call to Colors," *Sports Illustrated,* 26 July 1976, 17.

113. Robert Trumbull, "Threat to Cancel Olympics Made over Taiwan Dispute," *The New York Times,* 10 July 1976, 17.

114. Robert Trumbull, "U.S., Canada: Diplomatic Rift," *The New York Times,* 16 July 1976, A17.

115. *Los Angeles Times,* 29 July 1976, III, 1.

116. Ibid.

117. Ibid.

118. *The New York Times,* 10 July 1976, 19.

119. Ibid.

120. Putnam, "Call to Colors," 16.

121. Ibid.

122. Ibid., 18.

123. *Long Beach Independent Press Telegram,* 12 July 1976, C1.

124. Ibid.

125. *Long Beach Independent Press Telegram,* 19 July 1976, C1.

126. *Whittier News,* 31 July 1976, 17.

127. *Los Angeles Times,* 1 August 1976, 1.

128. Ibid., 12.

129. *Long Beach Independent Press Telegram,* 3 August 1976, C1.

130. Ibid.

131. *Long Beach Independent Press Telegram,* 19 July 1976, C1.

132. Ibid.

133. Ibid.

134. Ibid.

135. Ibid., 62; Defrantz, "Olympic Games and Women," 58.

136. Henry, *Approved History,* 391.

137. Ibid., 74; Defrantz, "Olympic Games and Women," 58.

138. Henry, *Approved History,* 393.

139. Ibid., 392.

140. *U.S. News & World Report,* 14 January 1980, 22.

141. Laurel Brassy, "Boycott of the 1980 Olympic Games" (unpublished paper, San Diego State University, 1983), 3.

142. "Transcript of President's Speech," *The New York Times,* 4 January 1980; Henry, *Approved History,* 427.

143. Brassy, "Boycott," 5–6.

144. *Colorado Springs Gazette Telegraph,* 20 February 1980, 1.

145. Brassy, "Boycott," 7.

146. Ibid.

147. Ibid.

148. *Colorado Springs Gazette Telegraph,* 4 April 1980, 1.

149. Ibid.

150. Ibid.

151. Brassy, "Boycott," 8.

152. Ibid., 9.

153. Ibid.

154. Ibid., 9–10.

155. Ibid., 58, 62.

156. Ibid., 10–11.

157. Ibid., 12.

158. Henry, *Approved History,* 428.

159. Niccolò Machiavelli, *The Prince* and *The Discourses* (New York: Random House, 1950), 216.

160. Kenneth Reich, "An Outsider's View of the 1984 Olympic Games Preparations," in *Purposes, Principles, and Contradictions of the Olympic Movement: Proceedings of the United States Olympic Academy VI,* ed. Carolyn Vos Strache (Malibu, CA: Pepperdine University, 1982), 99.

161. Ibid.

162. Betty Spears and Richard Swanson, *History of Sport and Physical Education in the United States,* 3rd ed. (Dubuque, IA: Wm. C. Brown, 1988), 382.

163. *Olympic Movement,* 62; Defrantz, "Olympic Games and Women," 58.

164. Defrantz, "Olympic Games and Women," 58, 74.

165. Barry Hillenbrand, "Breaking into the Big Leagues," *Time,* 12 November 1988, 42.

166. William Oscar Johnson, "The Spirit Flames Anew," *Sports Illustrated,* 26 September 1988, 51.

167. Ibid.

168. Ibid., 52.

169. Ibid., 58, 62.

170. *Media Guide,* Calgary 1988 Olympic Winter Games, 26.

C H A P T E R 17

After the Cold War: 1992–2012

O B J E C T I V E S

Upon completing this chapter, you will be able to:

- Discuss the changes that were enacted by the IOC during the 1990s to enhance the Olympic movement and explain the IOC's decision to stage the Olympic Games every two years instead of every four years.
- Appreciate the atmosphere of the first post–Cold War Olympic Games held in Barcelona in 1992.
- Identify some of the new Olympic teams that competed in Barcelona as a result of the collapse of the Soviet Union.
- Recognize that, for the first time in decades, South Africa fielded an Olympic team because apartheid was no longer a social and political policy of the newly reformed nation.
- Understand that although the Barcelona Olympiad was the most peaceful Olympics in decades, there were still problems with performance-enhancing drugs.
- Explain the significance of the 1996 Atlanta Olympiad—the Centennial Olympiad.
- Understand the disappointment of Athens when the IOC awarded the Olympics to Atlanta and not Athens.
- Discuss the crass commercialism associated with the Atlanta Olympiad.
- Recognize the failure of the security measures taken to protect the fans and athletes in Atlanta against terrorist attacks.
- Recognize that the use of performance-enhancing drugs as well as recreational drug use among Olympic athletes was a major concern during the Atlanta Olympiad.
- Discuss the scandals associated with various cities' bids for the Summer and Winter Games.
- Explain why the IOC adopted a theme of environmental protection relative to the cities being considered to host the Olympic Games.
- Appreciate that during the 2000 Sydney Olympiad, North and South Korea entered the stadium during the opening ceremonies as Korea, a first for the two nations and a good omen for the Olympic movement.
- Discuss the protests in Sydney about the poor treatment of the Aboriginal population by the Australian government.
- Identify Cathy Freeman from Australia, an Aborigine, as the star of the Sydney Olympiad.

- Explain the rationale used by protesters at the Vancouver Winter Olympics to attack one of the biggest department stores in town.
- Understand that security was a critical concern and that there were terrorist threats.
- Understand that a major controversy occurred when NBC decided to provide tape-delayed coverage as opposed to live Olympic coverage to the United States during the 2000 games.
- Understand how the fast-food giant McDonald's capitalized on its association with the Olympic movement.
- Explain why the IOC is so reliant on television revenues to finance the Olympics.
- Identify the economic and social costs that host cities must incur to stage the Olympics, and explain why a number of individuals and organizations see no value in holding the Olympic Games.
- Understand that doping was once again a problem during the Sydney Olympiad.
- Discuss why some athletes hired lawyers when they were not selected to the American Olympic team.
- Appreciate the historical significance of holding the 2004 Olympiad in Athens.
- Understand how the international political arena affected the Athens Olympiad, especially in matters of security.
- Understand that doping was again a significant problem during the Athens Olympics and that the IOC and World Anti-Doping Agency (WADA) waged a war against the use of banned substances.
- Recognize that the economic costs Athens incurred to host the Olympics were enormous.
- Appreciate the Athens Olympiad as among the most spectacular in history.
- Understand the political climate during the 2006 Turin Winter Olympics. Was doping a serious problem?
- To what extent did issues of human rights and social justice surface during the Beijing Olympiad?
- To what extent did the Chinese invasion and occupation of Tibet manifest itself during the torch relay?
- Has the Cold War returned since Russia invaded Georgia?
- Identify the political acts that tooks place during Beijing Olympiad.

INTRODUCTION

The decade of the 1990s witnessed monumental events that had a significant impact on the world and the Olympics. The fall of the Berlin Wall that had been erected after World War II to separate East Germany from West Germany symbolically proclaimed that the Cold War was over. The Soviet Union soon collapsed and the Iron Curtain fell. The collapse of communism, the reunification of Germany, and autonomy for former Eastern Bloc countries were greeted with cheers in both the West and the East.

Although Olympic politics significantly declined as a result of the end of the Cold War, new problems arose that caused great concern within the Olympic community. The two most visible problems have been the use of drugs by Olympic athletes and the commercialization of the Olympic Games. Although drug use and the commercialization of the Olympics were alarming, the ensuing Olympic Games would enjoy an atmosphere that was essentially free from the kind of political bickering and boycotts that had been commonplace during the Cold War Olympics. Like a phoenix, the Olympic spirit emerged from the shadow of the Cold War stronger than ever. The Olympic flame once again became a symbol of peace and international goodwill, superpowers no longer looked at the Olympic flame as a "call to arms," and political disputes and boycotts no longer overshadowed the achievements of Olympic athletes, until 2008.

The IOC made the decision to stagger the Olympic Games on a two-year rotation instead of a four-year rotation. After the 1992 Barcelona Olympiad and 1992 Albertville Winter Olympics concluded, the Olympics would occur every two years. The 1994 Winter Olympics were held in Lillehammer, followed by the 1996 Atlanta Olympiad. It was a decision based partly on economics and partly on public interest. The interest level in the Olympic Games remains very high, and the IOC believes that the citizens of the world will support Olympics held on a two-year cycle. In addition, there is more of an economic benefit to the IOC and the Olympic movement when revenue is generated every two years as opposed to every four years.

THE XXVTH OLYMPIAD: BARCELONA, 1992

Barcelona had bid to host the Olympic Games in 1924 and 1936, which gave Baron de Coubertin the opportunity to visit Barcelona. In 1926, when he visited the Catalonian capital, he said, "Until I came to Barcelona, I thought I knew what a sporting city was."[1] The hometown of IOC president Juan Antonio Samaranch did indeed put on a spectacular Olympiad, perhaps the greatest Olympics ever. The financial outlay to ensure the success of the games was high—an estimated $7.5 billion to produce. The National Broadcasting Corporation (NBC) paid $350 million to secure broadcast rights to the games.[2] The Barcelona Olympiad featured the Commonwealth of Independent States, a team made up of athletes from the former Soviet Union, and a unified German team. The traditional and heated political rivalries between athletes from the West and the East were but a memory in Barcelona. There were 9356 athletes from

OLYMPIC SNAPSHOT

1992 Barcelona Olympiad:

Opening Day July 25; Closing Day August 9

- 169 countries sent teams
- 9356 athletes: 2704 women and 6652 men
- 25 sports, 257 events: Aquatics, Archery, Athletics, Badminton, Baseball, Basketball, Boxing, Canoe/Kayak, Cycling, Equestrian, Fencing, Soccer, Gymnastics, Field Hockey, Handball, Judo, Modern Pentathlon, Rowing, Sailing, Shooting, Table Tennis, Tennis, Volleyball, Weight Lifting, and Wrestling
- 1 demonstration sport: Basque Pelota
- 34,548 volunteers and 13,082 media/press credentials issued

169 nations participating in the Barcelona Olympiad, including 2704 women Olympians from 136 nations competing in 86 events.[3]

A Renewed Olympic Spirit

There were significant geopolitical changes throughout the world that showed up in the Barcelona Olympics. For the first time in decades, South Africa sent a team to the games. Namibia sent its first Olympic team, while the breakup of Yugoslavia resulted in three new Olympic teams: Croatia, Bosnia-Herzegovina, and Slovenia. With the collapse of the Soviet Union, the Baltic states were able to participate for the first time since World War II as separate countries. As a result, Estonia, Latvia, and Lithuania sent teams to Barcelona. The Barcelona Olympiad was indeed historic, and for all the right reasons!

The opening ceremonies, held in the Montjuic Stadium, were quite a sight for the 70,000 people in attendance. The Barcelona Olympiad did have a social theme, as it was declared "smoke free," a first in the history of the modern Olympics.

The Barcelona Games were the most peaceful in recent history, almost completely devoid of politics and volatile social issues. Five athletes did test positive for banned substances, but this was way down from the 17 who had tested positive in Los Angeles. There was some concern that Basques who want to separate from Spain would cause trouble, but this did not occur. The U.S. team won 108 medals in Barcelona, their greatest number in a nonboycotted Olympiad since the 1908 London Games. Athletes from the former Soviet Union, known as the Commonwealth of Independent States, once again collected the most medals. However, the athletic federation represented by the Commonwealth of Independent States was a one-time team, as it was dissolved after the Barcelona Olympiad.

The Barcelona sports program was the most extensive ever offered. There were 25 sports with 257 events. Baseball, badminton, and women's judo were officially included in the Olympic Games. The demonstration sports were rink hockey, Basque pelota (ball), and tae kwon do. However, these would be the last demonstration sports as the IOC made the decision in 1989 to no longer include demonstration sports during the Summer Games and Winter Olympics.

Notables

Much of the attention of the press and the public was on the basketball team from the United States. The issue of amateurism was a moot point, so the U.S. team was drawn primarily from the ranks of the National Basketball Association (NBA). The press was quick to note that the combined salary of the U.S. "Dream Team" was in the neighborhood of $100 million. With the likes of Magic Johnson, Michael Jordan, Charles Barkley, Larry Bird, and David Robinson, the U.S. team easily swept through the competition and won the gold medal, defeating Croatia in the championship game 117–85.

One of the more inspiring moments was in the women's 10,000-meter race. A South African athlete and an athlete from Ethiopia ran together for most of the race and then kept running together after they finished. This brought a wide smile to the face of IOC president Samaranch,

who personally selected "unity" as the theme for the Barcelona Olympiad. Vitali Chtcherbo from Minsk, representing the Commonwealth of Independent States, won six gold medals. Carl Lewis from the United States won his third consecutive gold medal in the long jump and won another gold medal in the 4 × 100 relay. The U.S. men's 4 × 400 relay team (Quincy Watts, Andrew Valmon, Steve Lewis, and Michael Johnson) won the gold medal and set a new world record of 2 minutes, 55.74 seconds, breaking the old record by 0.42 second. The U.S. men's 4 × 100 relay team (Mike Marsh, Leroy Burrell, Dennis Mitchell, and Carl Lewis) also won the gold medal in a world record time of 37.40. Gail Devers of the United States won the 100-meters. In tennis, the U.S. team of Gigi Fernandez and Mary Joe Fernandez won the gold medal in doubles play, while the men's basketball team from Lithuania upset the team from the Commonwealth of Independent States, 82–78, for third place and the bronze medal. The rivalry between South Korea and Japan went down to the wire in the men's marathon. Hwang Young-Cho of South Korea finished first with a time of 2 hours, 13 minutes, 23 seconds, edging Koichi Morishita of Japan by 22 seconds. In volleyball, the U.S. men's team won the bronze medal. In boxing, Cuba once again was the toast of the Olympics, winning seven gold medals. Oscar De La Hoya, a boxer from East Los Angeles, won the gold medal in the 132-pound division, defeating Marco Rudolph of Germany. De La Hoya had promised his dying mother that he would win the gold medal, and on the victory stand, he waved two flags, one from the United States and one from Mexico, in honor of his mother.

On August 9, 1992, the closing ceremonies took place in the magnificent Montjuic Stadium. The head of the Atlanta Committee for the Olympic Games (ACOG) that would play host to the world for the 1996 Olympiad was Billy Payne, who attended the Barcelona Olympics as an observer. Payne assured President Samaranch of the IOC that Atlanta was prepared to produce a splendid Olympiad.

THE XVIth WINTER OLYMPICS: ALBERTVILLE/SAVOIE, 1992

When the IOC awarded the Winter Olympics to Albertville/Savoie, it was a milestone of sorts because France is one of two countries that has had the opportunity to hold the Winter Olympics on three occasions: 1924 in Chamonix, 1968 in Grenoble, and 1992 in Albertville/Savoie. The other country that has been fortunate enough to have the Winter Olympics on its soil three times is the United States: 1932 in Lake Placid, 1960 in Squaw Valley, and Lake Placid again in 1980.

The organizing committee of the Albertville/ Savoie Winter Games was headed up by two people: Jean-Claude Killy, one of the most celebrated skiers in Olympic history, and his friend Michel Barnier. The XVIth Winter Olympics injected a positive social theme into the games; for the first time in Olympic history, the environment was an integral part of the Winter Games. Copresidents Killy and Barnier were given credit for bringing the theme of environmental responsibility to the Olympic movement. Environmental impact reports were ordered on each project to determine whether construction and renovation of facilities would harm the environment. The Albertville/ Savoie Organizing Committee recommended that all future cities applying to host the Olympic Games present to the IOC an environmental impact study to show the potential effects of their projects on the environment.[4]

Economics

The cost of security at the games was 64.4 million francs.[5] The broadcast rights for the Winter Olympics went for $292 million. The American media giant Columbia Broadcasting System (CBS) paid $243 million for broadcast rights, followed by the European Broadcast Union (EBU), which paid 27 million Swiss francs, and NHK of Japan, which paid $9 million.[6]

Atmosphere

The Alps provided a magnificent setting for the Winter Olympics and contributed to the festive mood among athletes and the thousands of spectators who flocked to see the athletes perform. It was not unusual to see people from Paris attending the games, having caught the high-speed bullet train that made the journey in about five hours. The trip from Lyon took about an hour, so many spectators were able to return home in the evening or stay in the hotels and guest houses in the Alps. The opening ceremonies were conducted on February 8 in Albertville; the closing ceremonies took place on February 23.

In the wake of the geopolitical changes that occurred in the late 1980s and early 1990s, a number of new National Olympic Committees (NOCs) had been formed and sent teams to the Winter Games. Germany sent one team composed of athletes from former East Germany (Deutsche Demokratische Republik—DDR) combined with their counterparts in West Germany (Federal Republic of Germany— FRG). The ex-Soviet athletes competed as the Unified Team, while Croatia, Slovenia, Estonia, Latvia, and Lithuania sent their own teams for the first time in decades.

The number of athletes who competed was 1801, including 488 women. These athletes represented 64 countries and in the end collected a total of 171 medals (57 gold, 58 silver, and 56 bronze).

OLYMPIC SNAPSHOT

1992 Albertville Winter Olympics:

Opening Day February 8; Closing Day February 23

- 64 countries sent teams
- 1801 athletes: 488 women and 1313 men
- 6 sports, 57 events: Biathlon, Bobsleigh, Ice Hockey, Luge, Skating, and Skiing
- 8647 volunteers and 5894 media/press credentials issued

The continent of Africa sent four teams, North and South America 14, Asia 9, Europe 35, and Oceania 2. The official program consisted of 6 sports and 57 events; the men had 32 events, the women had 23, and 2 were mixed.[7]

Notables

In the United States, the duel between America's two best figure skaters, Tonya Harding and Nancy Kerrigan, received a lot of attention, but not as much as they would receive two years later in Lillehammer. However, it was not Kerrigan or Harding who was "golden" in Albertville; that honor fell to 20-year-old Kristi Yamaguchi of Fremont, California. She won the gold medal in the women's figure skating, the first time an American had won the gold since Dorothy Hamill in 1976. Nancy Kerrigan won the bronze medal, while Tonya Harding finished in fourth place.

American football player Herschel Walker attempted to represent the United States as a member of the four-man bobsled team but was removed two days before the competition started. Alberto Tomba of Italy won the gold medal in the giant slalom and the silver medal in the slalom. Paul Wylie of the United States won the silver medal in men's figure skating, losing to Viktor Petrenko of the Unified Team. The U.S. hockey team lost to the Russian/Unified Team in the semifinals by a score of 5–2 and then lost 6–1 to Czechoslovakia, losing the bronze medal in the process. The team from Czechoslovakia may have had extra incentive because their NOC promised every athlete who won a medal a new car and some cash.[8] Kathi Turner of the United States won the gold medal in the 500-meter short-track speed-skating race, and teammate Bonnie Blair won gold medals in two events—the 500-meter and 1000-meter speed skating.

The Olympic movement had experienced enormous growth. The number of NOCs had grown as well, which, ironically, was causing the IOC serious problems. During the Winter Games, President Samaranch of the IOC stated his belief that modifications had to be made to the number of athletes competing in the Olympics, which might preclude the involvement of some countries in the games. Previously, the practice had been to allow all of the countries that belonged to the Olympic community the luxury of entering at least one athlete in each event, regardless of whether she or he was a world-class athlete. President Samaranch and the IOC were exploring the possibility of increasing the qualifying standards, saying, "That means some small countries will not be able to send athletes to the games. . . . We don't want a situation where an athlete finishes five laps behind the leaders. The Olympic Games are for the most important athletes."[9] This seemed to represent a significant departure from the philosophy espoused by Baron de Coubertin, who said that the object of the athlete was not necessarily to win, but to take part. However, the logistical reality of hosting upwards of 15,000 athletes during the 1996 Atlanta Olympiad served to alter the long-standing philosophy of Coubertin.

THE XVIITH WINTER OLYMPICS: LILLEHAMMER, 1994

The people of Norway and the 23,000 citizens of Lillehammer welcomed the world and 1737 athletes, including 522 women, from 67 countries to the 1994 Winter Games. There were 61 events: 34 for men, 25 for women, and 2 mixed. The opening ceremonies took place on February 12 and the closing ceremonies on February 27. The Lillehammer Organizing Committee, headed by Gerhard Heiberg, used the famous northern lights as the logo of the games. The Olympic mascots were two children, Kristin and Hakon. The Winter Games were another great success.[10]

Atmosphere

The Lillehammer Winter Olympics continued with the environmental theme established in Albertville/Savoie and became known as the "white-green" games. The Norwegians constructed venues that

OLYMPIC SNAPSHOT

1994 Lillehammer Winter Olympics:

Opening Day February 12; Closing Day February 27

- 67 countries sent teams
- 1737 athletes: 522 women and 1215 men
- 6 sports, 61 events: Biathlon, Bobsleigh, Ice Hockey, Luge, Skating, and Skiing
- 9054 volunteers and 6633 media/press credentials issued

blended in with the natural surroundings. The continent of Africa sent two teams, the Americas 11, Asia 9, Europe 41, and Oceania 4. Eight hundred fifteen medals were awarded.[11]

The facilities were first-rate and pleasing to the eye. Hamar Olympic Hall was designed to look like the upturned hull of a Viking ship. Gjovik Hall, one of the venues used to hold ice hockey competition, was built completely inside a mountain! It took nine months and the removal of 29,000 truckloads of rock to complete the hall. The weather was brisk, with an average temperature of 18 degrees. There was no lack of snow; in fact, the Lillehammer Organizing Committee had to remove over 7000 truckloads of snow because there was so much of the white stuff. The children of Lillehammer got a break from school as the authorities closed down the schools for the two weeks of the Winter Games so the region's 2000 school buses could be used as shuttle transportation.

Notables

About a month before the start of the Lillehammer Games, a despicable incident in the sport of figure skating occurred. Nancy Kerrigan was attacked by a thug allegedly hired by her rival, Tonya Harding, and her then-husband, in an effort to remove Kerrigan from the Olympic Team and ensure that

Harding would be on it. After the attack, Kerrigan was forced to withdraw from the U.S. Championships in Detroit due to injury. The U.S. Olympic Committee (USOC) removed Harding from any consideration relative to making the team, but Harding filed suit against the USOC and ended up in Lillehammer with Nancy Kerrigan. Kerrigan won the silver medal, but Harding was not able to win a medal, placing eighth. Kerrigan did not participate in the closing ceremonies; instead, she went to Disney World because she was under contract to the Walt Disney Company.

In the men's short-track 5000-meter relay, the U.S. team finished second to Italy, which set a new Olympic record. The U.S. bobsledding team had a difficult time in Lillehammer. The two-man sled was disqualified because of the sled's runners, while the four-man sled lost to the team from Jamaica and ended up in fifteenth place. At the time, the U.S. bobsled team had not won a medal in 38 years! In ice hockey, Sweden won the gold medal, defeating Canada 3–2, while the U.S. team placed eighth. In the men's downhill, American Tommy Moe won the gold medal and also captured the silver medal in the super G. In the women's downhill, Picabo Street won the silver medal. Perhaps the most sensational performance was turned in by Bonnie Blair, the speed skater from Wisconsin. She won gold medals in three events: the 500-meters, the 1000-meters, and the 1500-meters. Another speed skater from Wisconsin, Dan Jansen, won the gold medal in the men's 1000-meters, in a time of 1:12.43, setting a world record.

The U.S. team won 13 medals, while the Russians won 23. Baalentine Sich, head of the Russian sports delegation, was asked why the Russians always seem to do better than the Americans. He replied:

> Let's say you put an American and a Russian together. . . . The American is dressed very nicely, is well fed and has good equipment. The Russian is dressed poorly, is not fed and has no equipment [to speak of]. Now you put $1,000 at the end of 200 meters and you have them run for it. Who do you think will win?[12]

America's Olympic teams expend great effort to attract corporate sponsorships to help assemble and train the nation's Olympic athletes. Nevertheless, comparatively speaking, the United States does not do as well as other countries in the Winter or Summer Olympics. What do you think is missing from America's Olympic training program? Do you think Americans prefer to support their professional teams more than their Olympic team?

THE CENTENNIAL OLYMPIAD: ATLANTA, 1996

The XXVIth Olympiad, held in Atlanta, was a special occasion, marking the first 100 years of the modern Olympic Games. The two primary cities that were considered by the IOC to host this most important Olympiad were Atlanta and Athens. The Greeks made the forceful argument that Athens should be selected because Greece was the birthplace of the Olympic Games, and the first modern Olympiad was held in Athens in 1896. The symbolism and history of Athens in Olympic annals made the decision by the IOC very difficult. However, ultimately, Atlanta was selected. Athens later applied to the IOC to host the Olympic Games in 2004.

One of the most significant points that the Atlanta Committee for the Olympic Games (ACOG) made to the IOC in its bid was that the city of Atlanta was primarily populated by minorities; over 60 percent of the citizens of Atlanta were people of color. The IOC was impressed by the commitment and dedication of the ACOG and the fact that the host city was represented by people of all races and creeds. Atlanta was the ideal city to host the Olympic Games because the people of Atlanta embodied the spirit of achievement, harmony, and cooperation—the spirit of Olympism.

Although terrorist activity at the Olympics had significantly declined in recent years, it remained an issue of enormous concern. Over 30,000 security personnel were assigned to protect athletes and spectators. On July 17, a TWA jumbo jet carrying 229 people exploded over the waters

OLYMPIC SNAPSHOT

1996 Atlanta Olympiad:

Opening Day July 19; Closing Day August 4

- 197 countries sent teams
- 10,318 athletes: 3512 women and 6806 men
- 27 sports, 271 events: Aquatics, Archery, Athletics, Badminton, Baseball, Basketball, Boxing, Canoe/Kayak, Cycling, Equestrian, Fencing, Soccer, Women's Soccer, Gymnastics, Field Hockey, Handball, Judo, Modern Pentathlon, Mountain Biking, Rowing, Sailing, Shooting, Softball, Table Tennis, Tennis, Volleyball & Beach Volleyball, Weight Lifting, and Wrestling
- 47,466 volunteers and 15,108 media/press credentials issued

off Long Island, killing all aboard. Initially, it was speculated that the crash of TWA Flight 800 was due to a bomb. Security was immediately tightened in Atlanta because the opening ceremonies were scheduled to take place two days later; however, it would not be enough to prevent the explosion of a deadly pipe bomb during the games.

The Torch Relay

The Olympic torch relay started in Los Angeles at the Coliseum, the main venue of the 1932 and 1984 Olympic Games. The torch relay covered approximately 15,000 miles and visited 43 states. It was a huge success, drawing crowds and cheers in each city and town it passed through. The torch was the subject of media coverage, and almost every day, the nation's newspapers showed a map of where the torch was and where it was headed. The torch was carried by Americans from all walks of life, some running, some walking, and some in wheelchairs. It was a stirring sight and brought the Olympic spirit home for the many Americans who turned out to see the torch.

The Opening Ceremonies

The Atlanta Olympiad began on July 19 with a spectacular opening ceremony. 10,318 athletes from 197 countries took part in the opening ceremonies, held in the newly constructed Olympic Stadium. Muhammad Ali, who won the gold medal in boxing at the 1960 Rome Games as Cassius Clay, carried the Olympic flame up a flight of stairs and ignited the huge torch in Olympic Stadium. President Bill Clinton, on hand for the opening ceremonies, announced, "I declare open the Games of Atlanta celebrating the XXVIth Olympiad of the modern era."

Commercialization

NBC television broadcast the opening ceremonies live to the world, reaching an audience of about 3.5 billion viewers and providing more than 170 hours of Olympic coverage. Most of the broadcasts were live, but some events were shown on a delayed basis. The fees paid by television networks to the IOC for broadcast rights to the Olympics have increased dramatically over the years. NBC paid $456 million for the right to broadcast the 1996 games. In contrast, CBS paid $394,000 to the IOC to broadcast approximately 15 hours of the 1960 Rome Olympiad. To broadcast the Sydney Olympiad in 2000, NBC agreed to pay the IOC $715 million.

The commercialization of the Atlanta Olympiad was a topic of discussion not only in Atlanta but around the world. Especially noted were the seemingly endless commercials that NBC ran during the games. However, NBC is a corporate giant and, like other corporations, is in business to make a profit. As a result, NBC sold advertising time during the Olympics to recover the money paid to the IOC and to generate additional revenue.

There is an upside to having commercial television involved in broadcasting the Olympic Games. Although we must contend with what seem to be an overwhelming number of commercials, it costs us nothing to watch and enjoy the Olympic Games. When the IOC begins to sell broadcast rights to the

cable networks or to satellite TV, we will no longer be able to enjoy the Olympics for free.

The commercialization of the Atlanta Games went beyond television. If a business spent the money to become an official Olympic sponsor, its products were seen by a worldwide television audience. For example, during the opening ceremonies, General Motors products were featured in the form of 30 specially decked-out Chevrolet trucks used to deliver dancers and other entertainers to the field. In addition to the $40 million GM spent to become an official sponsor, it paid NBC over $50 million to advertise cars and trucks during televised events. Atlanta is the corporate home of soft drink giant Coca-Cola, which paid NBC over $60 million to advertise its products during the Olympics.

Centennial Olympic Park was a venue where the spectators could gather and "catch the Olympic spirit." It was also the location for many commercial interests to set up shop. The IOC and the USOC closely guarded the "turf" of the Olympics, making sure that there was no infringement on the Olympic name by organizations that did not pay sponsorship fees.

Many independent businesses as well as multinational corporations attempted to increase their product exposure and attendant profits by identifying with the Atlanta Olympiad in some way. Corporations that donated significant sums to the ACOG had their corporate logos and products prominently displayed in various venues. Many of the athletes who competed in the Olympics had sizable contracts with shoe and apparel companies. These athletes wore particular shoes and attire during competition so the brand name and logo were seen by millions of television viewers as well as those in attendance. Some of the more popular athletes had their own apparel companies and wore their products during Olympic competition, hoping that their fans would buy their product lines.

The commercialization of products like shoes and clothing did not stop with individual athletes. Many of the more recognizable footwear and clothing companies entered into contracts with various Olympic teams around the world. These teams were paid a sum of money to wear particular shoes and other clothing accessories. The commercial message was clear: "If you want to be the best, wear _____ shoes."

The Olympic Games are among the most expensive events to stage in the world. The cost of producing the Olympics continues to escalate, which eliminates many poor cities from hosting them (the Olympic Games are always awarded to a city, not a country). Host cities located in economically sound countries have turned to the private sector to help finance the Olympics. The private sector provides hundreds of millions of dollars to the host city in return for the commercial use of the games. Even though the media and the public may be opposed to the commercialization of the games, how many cities can afford to bid to host the Olympics if official sponsorships (generating millions of dollars) cannot be sold to commercial enterprises by the host city?

Drugs

Performance-enhancing drugs and, to an extent, recreational drugs are major problems in the Olympic Games. Anabolic steroids are used by many athletes and have been a source of frustration for IOC and USOC officials for many years. Athletes who believe in the benefits of performance-enhancing drugs become very skilled in avoiding detection.

The IOC publishes a list of banned substances, as does the USOC. However, the allure of the fame and possible financial rewards that accompany medals can be the reason why athletes have long used performance-enhancing drugs. For example, many Olympians are promised cash prizes and other incentives if they win an Olympic medal. In 1995, the French announced that any Olympian from France who won a gold medal would receive $68,952, tax free; a silver medal would be worth $33,124; and a bronze medal would fetch $21,632. During the 1996 Atlanta Olympiad, Somluck

Kamsing from Thailand won a gold medal in boxing—the first medal of any kind for Thailand. When he returned home, he was given a cash award of approximately $1.73 million, tax free! Windsurfer Lee Lai-shan from Hong Kong won a gold medal in Atlanta and returned home to claim cash and prizes worth approximately $405,600.[13] Certainly, these types of incentives tempt athletes to seek an "edge" that the competition doesn't have. Drugs are one way to gain an edge.

Drugs became an issue in Atlanta when swimmer Michelle Smith from Ireland came from relative obscurity and shocked the world by winning the gold medal in the 400-meter freestyle, the bronze in the 200-meter butterfly, the gold in the 200-meter individual medley, and another gold in the 400-meter individual medley. She was married to an athlete who had once admitted to using performance-enhancing drugs, which caused a great deal of suspicion among the swimmers, especially the Americans, who had not considered her a threat before the Olympics. Smith was "clean" and rightfully resented the accusations by the media that she may have used drugs to earn her Olympic medals.

To deter drug use among Olympic athletes, the IOC implemented a sophisticated drug detection system in Atlanta. The technology enabled the drug-testing professionals to detect drugs that had been taken into the body several months prior instead of just in the previous 30 days. Many athletes who used performance-enhancing drugs stopped taking them about 30 days prior to competition to "wash out" any sign of the drugs from their bodies. The new technology enabled the drug tests to "look back" 60 to 90 days using athletes' urine samples.

The drug-testing protocol in Atlanta was set up to take the top four finishers in each event plus others chosen at random. An escort took the athletes to the testing center, where they were required to provide a urine sample. If the test identified banned substances in an athlete's urine sample, he or she could appeal to the newly established Court of Arbitration for Sport (CAS). The CAS was set up to avoid the long and costly legal battles that had taken place previously when issues of drug use by athletes had arisen. Since there were 12 arbitrators on staff, it was hoped that all disputes regarding drug use could be resolved quickly.

The Closing Ceremonies

The closing ceremonies took place on August 4, after 16 days of competition that featured 271 events. Although many of the Olympic athletes had left Atlanta after their events were over, thousands stayed behind and gathered on the floor of the stadium on a hot August night. President Samaranch of the IOC called on the youths of the world to gather in Sydney, Australia, in four years to once again celebrate the Olympic Games. Samaranch heaped praise upon Billy Payne and the ACOG but stopped short of labeling the Atlanta Olympiad the "best ever." Perhaps he wanted the "best ever" Olympic Games label to remain identified with Barcelona, his hometown.

Notables

The Atlanta Olympiad was marred by a bomb attack that occurred on July 27 in Centennial Olympic Park. The bomb exploded at approximately 1:20 A.M. by a giant tower near a stage where thousands of tourists and spectators were enjoying a concert. Over 100 people were injured, and two people died. Security experts were called in to locate the individual or group responsible for the bombing, and the park was closed for a few days. However, the Olympic Games continued as scheduled. The people of Atlanta, the Olympic athletes, and the tens of thousands of Olympic spectators resolved not to be held hostage by the bombing and continued to uphold the Olympic spirit. Cooperation, which had been good prior to the bombing, was even better afterward because everybody was furious that such a tragic thing could happen. Although everyone grieved for the wounded and the dead, they went ahead and celebrated the Olympics. During the closing

ceremonies, Samaranch stated, "No act of terrorism has destroyed the Olympic movement and none ever will."[14]

In the race for Olympic medals, the United States, as expected, captured the most, 101 (44 gold, 32 silver, and 25 bronze). In second place was Germany, with 65 (20 gold, 18 silver, and 27 bronze). Although the mighty "Soviet sports machine" that won more Olympic medals during the Cold War than any other country was but a memory, the Russian Olympic team finished a strong third in the race for Olympic medals, with 61 (26 gold, 21 silver, and 14 bronze). Many experts believe it is simply a matter of time and money before the Russians once again compete head-to-head with the Americans for Olympic dominance.

There were two basketball "Dream Teams" in Atlanta: the NBA-led U.S. men's team and the U.S. women's team. The United States defeated Yugoslavia 95–69 for the gold medal in men's basketball with help from NBA stars David Robinson, Scottie Pippen, Karl Malone, and Shaquille O'Neal. The U.S. women, led by Dawn Staley, Lisa Leslie, and Sheryl Swoopes, demolished Brazil by a score of 111–87 to win the gold medal. The women's team had been assembled about a year before the Atlanta Olympics. Coached by Tara VanDerveer, the American women did not lose a single game during the year that they prepared for the Olympics, winning 60 straight. They then swept their Olympic competition.

The men's marathon was won by Josia Thugwane of South Africa, the first black South African to win a gold medal in the Olympic Games. Another black South African, Hezekiel Sepeng, won the silver medal in the men's 800-meters, another historic first in South African Olympic history. Remember that South Africa was banned by the IOC from participating in the Olympic Games in 1960 due to its policy of apartheid and was not allowed back in the games until 1992. Josia Thugwane dedicated his gold medal to Nelson Mandela, the first black president of South Africa.

In track and field, called "athletics" in Olympic circles, the United States was a dominant force. Michael Johnson of the United States wore gold shoes and won the gold medal in both the 200-meter and 400-meters, the first man to accomplish this amazing feat. Donovan Bailey of Canada won the men's 100-meter followed by Frank Fredericks of Namibia and Ato Boldoa of Trinidad.

In the 4 × 100 relay, the U.S. men finished second to Canada but did manage to win the gold medal in the 4 × 400 relay, beating Great Britain. The title of "world's best male athlete" was bestowed on American Dan O'Brien from Idaho, who won the decathlon. The amazing Carl Lewis of the United States, perhaps the best athlete ever to participate in track and field, won the long jump and added another gold medal to his collection. Lewis had won nine Olympic gold medals, and there was speculation he might run on the U.S. men's relay team in an effort to capture an unprecedented tenth, but he did not run.

The U.S. women's track-and-field team was sensational. Gail Devers won the 100-meter, while Gwen Torrence won the bronze medal in this event. In the 200-meter and 400-meter, Marie-José Perec from France was victorious, winning two gold medals. In the 800-meter and 1500-meter, Svetlana Masterkova from Russia was unbeatable, winning the gold medal in both. The American women won gold medals in the 4 × 100 relay and the 4 × 400 relay. Jackie Joyner-Kersee from the United States captured the bronze medal in the long jump. In the discus and shot put, the American women did not win any medals.

Volleyball is a popular American sport, both indoors and on the beach. In 1996, beach volleyball became an official Olympic sport. That same year, American Karch Kiraly was, without question, the greatest volleyball player in the world. He had played on the U.S. team that captured the gold medal in 1984 and had since turned his attention to the professional beach tour, where he remained a legend. Kiraly teamed up with Kent Steffes to play in the first Olympic two-man beach volleyball competition. The gold medal match pitted Kiraly and

Steffes against the team of Mike Dodd and Mike Whitmarsh. All four players were from California. Kiraly and Steffes prevailed over Dodd and Whitmarsh under a grueling sun and won the gold medal.

In women's beach volleyball, the American teams did not fare nearly as well. Jackie Silva and Sandra Pires from Brazil beat another team from Brazil to win the gold, while Natalie Cook and Kerri-Ann Pottharst from Australia captured the bronze medal.

Apart from the gold and silver medals won by the American men in beach volleyball, the nation's volleyball teams did not do nearly as well as expected. Both the men's and women's indoor volleyball teams were eliminated from medal competition. In men's volleyball, the Netherlands captured the gold medal, followed by Italy and Yugoslavia. Cuba won the gold medal in women's volleyball, followed by China and Italy.

In synchronized swimming, the battle was between the United States and Canada for the gold. The Canadians turned in what seemed to be a flawless performance, but the United States followed with an even better performance, edging out Canada for the gold medal.

In the men's swimming competition, the United States was expected to be strong, as were China and Russia. However, there were the usual surprises. Alexander Popov of Russia won both the 50-meter freestyle and 100-meter freestyle. Danyon Loader from New Zealand won gold medals in the 200-meter freestyle and 400-meter freestyle. Gary Hall of the United States won the silver in the 50-meter freestyle and the 100-meter freestyle, finishing second to Alexander Popov of Russia both times. Denis Pankratov of Russia won the gold medal in the 200-meter butterfly and 100 butterfly. American Tom Malchow won the silver medal in the 200-meter butterfly. The American men were victorious in the 400-meter medley relay, winning the gold medal ahead of Russia and Australia. They repeated as Olympic champions when they also won the 400-meter freestyle relay, beating Russia and Germany.

The American women did well in swimming. Perhaps the best story in women's swimming belonged to Michelle Smith of Ireland, who dispatched some of the best swimmers in the world in winning four Olympic medals—three gold and one bronze. Amy Van Dyken of the United States won gold medals in the 50-meter freestyle, 100-meter butterfly, 400-meter freestyle relay, and the 400-meter medley relay.

In baseball, Cuba was the toast of the Olympics, capturing the gold medal once again. Japan won the silver while the United States men's team had to settle for the bronze. In softball competition, the U.S. women dominated in winning the gold medal, followed by China and Australia.

In addition to beach volleyball, mountain biking was added to the Olympic program. The U.S. men's team did not earn a medal. The gold medal went to Bart Jan Brentjens of the Netherlands, the silver to Thomas Frishknecht of Switzerland, and the bronze to Miguel Martinez of France. North American women fared better than their male counterparts in this event. Although Paola Pezzo of Italy won the gold medal in mountain biking, the silver was won by Allison Sydor of Canada while American Susan DeMattei of Colorado won the bronze.

One of the more spectacular competitions in Atlanta was in women's gymnastics. The Russians and the Romanians had "owned" the gold medal in the team competition for as long as anybody could remember. In the final night of competition, it came down to the courage and dedication of American Kerri Strug, put into a "must do it" situation on the vault if the U.S. women were to capture the team championship. On her previous vault, she had suffered a severe sprain to her ankle and limped off the floor in pain. In the staging area, her coach, Bela Karolyi, kept saying, "You can do it—you can do it." And she did it! She sprinted to the vaulting horse, completed her routine, and "stuck" the landing, which she *had to do.* She could not waver, could not side-step. After the judges had indicated that her vault was good, she collapsed to the mat in pain and was helped off the floor by her teammates and medical personnel. She made a triumphant entry to the medal ceremony. With her ankle and shin wrapped, she was carried in by her coach

to the cheers of the thousands in attendance who witnessed her courage and determination. The U.S. women won the team championship and the gold medal, followed by Russia and Romania.

During the closing ceremonies, President Samaranch presented Muhammad Ali with a replacement gold medal because Ali had misplaced his 1960 gold medal won as a boxer in Rome. One of the most familiar faces in the world, Ali suffers from Parkinson's disease, which leaves him shaking and slow in speech. The ceremony was a touching and tasteful end to a grand Olympiad.

THE XVIIITH WINTER OLYMPICS: NAGANO, 1998

Seventy-two nations sent teams to Nagano, Japan, which hosted the Winter Olympics February 7–22. A worldwide audience of approximately 3 billion people followed the exploits of the athletes who competed in an extensive program that featured 8 sports and 68 events. There were 37 events for men, 29 for women, and 2 that featured men and women as a team. Of the 2176 athletes competing in Nagano, 727 were women. There were 1468 coaches and associated officials on hand to assist the athletes, and over 8000 media professionals reported their every move.

OLYMPIC SNAPSHOT

1998 Nagano Winter Olympics:

Opening Day February 7; Closing Day February 22

- 72 countries sent teams
- 2176 athletes: 787 women and 1389 men
- 8 sports, 68 events: Biathlon, Bobsleigh, Curling, Men's and Women's Ice Hockey, Luge, Skating, Skiing, and Snowboarding
- 32,000 volunteers and 8329 media/press credentials issued

Milestones

There were a number of "firsts" in Nagano. It was the first time that the nations of Azerbaijan, Kenya, Macedonia, Uruguay, and Venezuela sent teams to the Winter Olympics. Curling, women's ice hockey, and snowboarding were new sports. One hundred twenty-five professional athletes from the 26 teams in the National Hockey League (NHL) made their first appearance in the Winter Olympics, representing their home countries. Russia was represented by 22 NHL athletes, and defending Olympic champion Sweden had 18, while the teams from Canada and the United States consisted entirely of NHL players.

Goals and Outcomes

Nagano had three goals: (1) Promote the participation of children, (2) pay homage to nature, and (3) host a festival of peace and friendship. Some examples of how these three goals were implemented and their attendant outcomes warrant a brief discussion.

Goal 1

Each of the local schools was assigned a specific country and served as "host" to that country's athletes once they arrived in Nagano. The children made flags, studied the culture and customs of their assigned country, and cheered for the athletes of that country.

Goal 2

Protection of the environment was a critical concern. In this respect, the Nagano Organizing Committee performed admirably. The official uniforms of the host committee and staff were made from fully recyclable materials. Approximately 1000 tons of garbage from the games were recycled. Construction of the venues necessitated the removal of trees; however, "replacement trees" exceeded the number of trees cut down. For example, to build the new ski-jumping venue, 5500 trees were cut down, but in their place, 10,000 new trees were planted.

The city of Nagano sponsored a commemorative tree-planting program, and the citizens of Nagano responded by planting about 20,000 new trees to beautify the area.

The organizing committee paid close attention to the delicate balance between nature and the needs of the athletes and spectators. Topsoil was carefully preserved, and special precautions were taken to protect the green tree frog and the beautiful Gifu butterfly, which inhabit the area. Aesthetic concerns were not ignored, as all of the utility cables were carefully buried underground. The results were a beautiful location to welcome the world and the establishment of an environmental legacy that would benefit future generations.

Goal 3

For the most part, the atmosphere in Nagano was serene and peaceful, although there were legitimate security concerns. When a Japanese religious cult sprayed nerve gas in Nagano in 1994, IOC officials were justifiably worried that the 1998 Winter Olympics could be the target of a terrorist attack. This concern reflected the political reality of the times. Various political organizations and their factions could resort to extreme measures to call attention to their causes and send a message by engaging in acts of terrorism. Among the precautions taken to discourage would-be terrorists were the issuance of barcoded ID cards for staff and media, a fingerprint scanner at the accreditation center, and an eye scanner at the biathlon venue to control the rifles used in this event. The Nagano Organizing Committee used the services of over 3000 security personnel to ensure the safety of the athletes and spectators. In addition, cyberterrorists were a new problem that had to be addressed by security experts.

Notables

Drug testing was conducted on the athletes, and one snowboarder from Canada tested positive for marijuana. The athlete explained that several weeks before the start of the Winter Olympics, he had been at a ski resort in British Columbia and in the company of friends who were smoking marijuana. He did not use the drug, but the sophisticated drug-testing equipment detected the substance. This positive drug test on an athlete who allegedly did not use the drug but was in a room where cannabis was smoked opened a Pandora's box of legal and moral issues. The IOC Court of Arbitration of Sport (CAS) ruled that because marijuana was not on the list of banned performance-enhancing drugs, no rules had been broken. Many people had hoped that the IOC would send a message about drug use by severely punishing the Canadian athlete. This did not happen, and the IOC was once again subject to harsh criticism.

The U.S. men's hockey team was a favorite to win a medal. However, they were unceremoniously eliminated from competition, which led to some members of the team trashing a hotel room, once again reinforcing the image of the "ugly American." The Czech ice hockey team beat the Russians for the gold medal and returned home to Prague where they were greeted by over 100,000 jubilant fans. Women's ice hockey made its debut in Nagano, and the American women captured the inaugural gold medal by defeating the Canadian team. Germany won the medal count with 29, followed by Norway with 25, Russia with 18, Canada with 15, and the United States with 13. Out of the 72 nations that competed, 48 failed to win a medal.

The rich and powerful nations of the world, to no one's surprise, won more medals than countries at an economic disadvantage. If the IOC and the rest of the sporting world truly believe in fair play, it is essential that the poor nations of the Olympic family receive the necessary resources so they can compete—and not simply participate—in the Olympics. The IOC established the Olympic Solidarity program, which had a noble goal: to assist developing nations in their quest to field competitive teams for international competition. Judging from the medal count of the Nagano Winter Olympics, it fell far short of this goal.

The closing ceremonies were held on February 22, when the torch was passed to officials from Salt Lake City, where the next Winter Olympics were to take place.

SCANDALS AND ILL-GOTTEN GAINS

The 1990s were a painful decade for members of the IOC. In 1991, Toronto officials, unsuccessful in their bid to host the 1996 Olympics, claimed that 26 IOC members broke rules by bringing more than one guest when touring host cities and cashing in airline tickets. But this complaint paled in comparison to what was on the horizon. Scandalous behavior by some IOC members would cast a dark shadow over the entire Olympic movement. As it turned out, cities bidding for the Olympic Games had provided some IOC members with cash and gifts in exchange for their votes. These bribes made headlines and caused an uproar heard around the world. The IOC, federal governments, and the media launched inquiries. IOC vice president Dick Pound, a Canadian lawyer and former Olympic swimmer, was appointed as the IOC's chief investigator.

Records of the host cities were requested for review. The Nagano officials who hosted the 1998 Winter Olympic Games reported that they could not comply with the request because they had purposely burned the records. The Atlanta officials responsible for hosting the 1996 Summer Olympic Games were ordered to turn over their records for review as well. However, the biggest scandal would occur in Salt Lake City, Utah.

Salt Lake City had made previous bids to host the Winter Olympics, but to no avail. Undaunted, Salt Lake City decided to once again bid for the 2002 Winter Olympics. This time, their bid was successful, and there was jubilation in the streets of Salt Lake City.

The euphoria would be short-lived. In November 1998, a Salt Lake City television station obtained a leaked report that some IOC members had received cash and gifts worth more than $1 million from the Salt Lake City bid committee in exchange for their votes. For example, the IOC member from the Republic of Congo, Jean-Claude Ganga, was expelled from the IOC because he allegedly received more than $300,000 in cash and gifts. The Salt Lake City bid team also set up college scholarships for certain IOC members. Two weeks later, IOC member Marc Holder, a Swiss lawyer, said the scholarships were a bribe for votes. He was furious and went on to say that a certain part of the vote by IOC members had always been corrupt. Phil Coles, an IOC member from Australia, was accused of soliciting gifts from the committee. An avid skier, he took five trips to Salt Lake City—before voting. Coles also was accused of phoning Tom Welch, a former official of the Salt Lake City bid committee, in 1995 to arrange a ski holiday in Utah for his daughter and son-in-law—before voting. His former wife, Georgina, said that a businessperson closely connected with the unsuccessful bid by Athens to secure the 1996 Olympics provided Coles with jewelry worth about $10,000. At the time, the IOC allowed members to accept gifts worth $200 or less. IOC vice president Pound investigated the accusations against Coles. Pound did not find evidence to support the claims of Coles's ex-wife. Pound and the six-person committee that assisted him concluded that Coles had sullied the reputation of the IOC, but not enough to be expelled. Coles was severely reprimanded.

Investigators from the United States, which included the FBI, the USOC, and Congress, concluded that President Juan Antonio Samaranch expected IOC members to behave ethically and serve with honor. While the majority of IOC members did just that, some did not because the IOC did not exert firm control over its members. As a result of the scandals, the credibility of the IOC was called into question. Drastic reforms were called for as the media and the world waited for the IOC to "get its house in order."

They would not have to wait long. Four IOC members resigned and six others were expelled. Would it be enough to restore credibility?

Critics of the IOC demanded that Samaranch resign because the scandals had occurred under his watch. In March 1999, Samaranch asked the remaining IOC members to meet and decide his status in a vote. The vote was 86–2 in favor of Samaranch. He accepted responsibility for the problems and immediately called for reforms.

The IOC responded by instituting a program that identified 50 areas to be evaluated and reformed. Among these reforms was a rule that prohibits IOC members from visiting cities bidding for the Olympic Games. A committee established by the IOC would visit and evaluate candidate cities, and expensive and elaborate gifts would not be accepted. An IOC Ethics Committee was established to make certain the IOC remained above reproach.

Most people in the Olympic movement admired Samaranch as a skillful diplomat who rescued the Olympics from an abyss when he assumed the presidency in 1980. Critics remained disillusioned over his leadership, especially because of the scandals that permeated the 1990s. In 2001, Juan Antonio Samaranch retired as IOC president. He was replaced by Jacques Rogge, an orthopedic surgeon from Belgium.

The United States Department of Justice accused Salt Lake City bid leaders Tom Welch and Dave Johnson of providing cash and opulent gifts to IOC members in exchange for votes. The federal government's case against Welch and Johnson was dismissed by a Utah judge halfway through the trial. Mitt Romney took over the duties as chief organizer of the games and did a superb job. He later became governor of Massachusetts and campaigned for the presidency of the United States in 2008.

THE XXVIITH OLYMPIAD: SYDNEY, 2000

Although the IOC was implementing far-reaching reforms, the Salt Lake City scandal was still not resolved as the opening ceremonies of the Sydney Olympics took place on September 15. At one point, there was talk of a plea bargain arrangement that would have quickly resolved the criminal charges against the defendants. However, when a decision had to be made, the principal defendants in the case did not agree to the plea bargain. The IOC and the Salt Lake City Organizing Committee were hoping for a speedy resolution to the problem. As lawyers and other interested parties gazed into their crystal balls, it seemed likely that the actual trial of the accused individuals would be going on during the 2002 Winter Olympics in Salt Lake City. If this were to happen, it would cast yet another shadow on the Olympic movement. Needless to say, the IOC was banking that the Sydney Olympics would be an unqualified success that highlighted the positive aspects of Olympism.

In 1956, Melbourne had hosted the Olympics; as a city, it was the jewel of Australia. Sydney, on the other hand, was a city that had not matured in a cultural and aesthetic sense. In the latter 1960s, Sydney began its transformation from a second-class city and, over time, became the crown jewel of Australia. The harbor was developed, and beautiful parks and green belts were established. The world-renowned Sydney Opera House, built on the waterfront, anchors one of the most beautiful cities in the world. By the 1990s, Sydney had become the destination city for business and tourism and the choice of the IOC for the 2000 Olympics.

From the torch-lighting ceremony on, the Sydney Olympic Games were a spectacular success (Figure 17-1). Approximately 10,651 athletes who represented 199 countries participated in the games. The athletes were outnumbered by the media; approximately 16,000 members of the press and related concerns covered the Sydney Olympics.[15] The Olympic spirit soared when athletes from North Korea and South Korea entered the stadium as one team under the banner "KOREA." The opening ceremonies featured 12,600 performers who put on a spectacular show for the 11,600 athletes and officials who marched in the opening parade and the 110,000 who were lucky enough to get tickets to the festivities. When the Australian Olympic team marched into the stadium, they tossed stuffed kangaroos into the stands. The entire stadium began a celebration that did not end until the games drew to a close. Media experts predicted that close to 3.7 billion people around the world would watch the

OLYMPIC SNAPSHOT

2000 Sydney Olympiad:

Opening Day September 15; Closing Day October 1

- 199 countries sent teams—Note that four athletes from East Timor were classified by the IOC as Individual Olympic Athletes (IOA) and marched in the opening ceremonies while carrying the Olympic Flag.
- 10,651 athletes: 4069 women and 6582 men
- 29 sports, 300 events: Aquatics, Archery, Athletics, Badminton, Baseball, Basketball, Boxing, Canoe/Kayak, Cycling, Equestrian, Fencing, Soccer, Women's Soccer, Gymnastics, Field Hockey, Handball, Judo, Modern Pentathlon, Mountain Biking, Rowing, Sailing, Shooting, Softball, Table Tennis, Tae kwon do, Tennis, Triathlon, Volleyball & Beach Volleyball, Men's and Women's Weight Lifting, and Wrestling
- 46,967 volunteers and 16,033 media/press credentials issued

Olympic Games.[16] This would be an athletic festival that truly captivated the sporting world. During the closing ceremonies, which took place on October 1, IOC president Samaranch proclaimed that the Sydney Olympics were the best ever.

This is not to say that the Sydney Olympics were not without problems. There were some social protests, tasteless political remarks, nonlive television coverage in the United States, threats of violence, drug problems, and concern about a lethal arachnid known as the funnel web spider.

Social Protests

A sensitive issue in Australia historically has been the treatment of Australia's Aboriginal population. Most live in poverty and for the longest time were treated with disrespect and subject to insensitive social policies. In 1918, a form of social engineering was initiated that removed light-skinned

Figure 17-1

The Olympic flame. Thousands of spectators gathered in the ancient Olympic stadium to watch the torch-lighting ceremony and the first leg of the relay that carried the Olympic flame from ancient Olympia to Australia for the Sydney Olympic Games in 2000.

babies and youngsters from their parents. At that time, the Australian government believed it would be best if light-skinned Aboriginal children were removed from their homes and assimilated into the general population by way of foster homes or placement with white families instead of remaining in their homeland.

Many of these Aborigines never saw their families again and were called the "Lost Generation." The Aborigines have struggled to achieve equality and recognition within Australia for years. Some of the leaders of the Aborigines wanted to use the Sydney Olympics as a means to call attention to their situation through peaceful marches. One leader, Charles Perkins, even suggested that violent acts would take place. Perkins orchestrated "Freedom Rides" in the 1960s that brought to the attention of the public the harsh treatment of Aborigines and their miserable living conditions. He later was in charge of a federal agency responsible for overseeing Aboriginal affairs. Shortly before the opening ceremonies, he issued a warning to tourists planning on attending the Olympics: "If you want to see burning cars and burning buildings, then come over ... 'It's burn, baby, burn' from now on."[17]

This inflammatory prophecy did not come to pass. However, a peaceful protest was held in a park close to some of the venues that called attention to the situation of the Aboriginal population. On September 16, prior to the opening ceremonies, about 200 people marched from Victoria Park to the office of Prime Minister John Howard to focus attention on the Aborigines. The leaders of this march had anticipated a larger turnout. However, other Aboriginal leaders refused to join because they did not want to risk a confrontation with the authorities. Andrew Donnelley, one of the Aboriginal leaders, remarked that they did not participate in this protest because "we don't wish to disrupt the Games. . . . Our biggest goal is to gain recognition of Aboriginal sovereignty."[18]

It would be an Aborigine who captured everybody's heart in Sydney and the rest of the world. Cathy Freeman, an Aborigine and a sensational track-and-field athlete whose specialty was the 400-meters, was given the supreme honor of lighting the flame that symbolically opened the games of the XXVIIth Olympiad. The Lost Generation was a part of her history because members of her family had been taken by the government many years earlier. She was approached by some Aboriginal leaders about engaging in some form of protest, but she declined. Freeman won the gold medal in the 400-meter. Her smile and demeanor captivated the world, which quickly learned more about the Aborigines and their quest for a decent life. Australia, like most of the world's modern nations, still has much to do with regard to raising the standard of living and delivering health care to its indigenous population. For example, the mortality rate of Aboriginal children is three times higher than that of white children. Like many other Olympians over the years, Freeman promoted peace and raised issues that needed to be addressed. Some Olympians have engaged in socially and politically motivated demonstrations that, unfortunately, appear to have done more harm than good. However, the fact that these social protests take place in the Olympics demonstrates just how effective a forum the Olympics are. Because of Freeman's stature and accomplishments, an effort was launched to persuade her to run for the Australian parliament.

In another demonstration, about 30 people marched on September 15 to protest the corporate sponsorship of the Olympics and to express their displeasure over free trade. This demonstration was held in a suburb of Sydney.[19]

Terrorist Threats

The security forces at the Sydney Olympics received an average of 12 threats a day, ranging from bomb scares to extortion. Despite the threats, Sydney police did not locate one bomb during the games. However, a far more serious threat was uncovered in New Zealand.

Australian authorities announced in late August that a plot to blow up the country's only nuclear reactor had been uncovered. Police in New Zealand were working on a case in March and came across evidence that an organized crime ring with links to Afghanistan may have been planning to blow up the reactor during the Olympics. As a precaution, security was increased around the reactor, located in the Sydney suburb of Lucas Heights. The New Zealand police revealed that they had found street maps of Sydney that provided detailed entry and exit routes to and from the reactor, along with notes about the security setup at the reactor. Four men were arrested. There was speculation that those arrested were supporters of al Qaeda terrorist leader Osama bin Laden, who was reportedly hiding in Afghanistan.[20] In a less publicized incident, a van leased to the South Korean Olympic Committee was highjacked by two escaped convicts. The four people riding in the van were not harmed.

Politics

Although the North Korean and South Korean athletes marched as a unified group during the opening ceremonies, when it came to Olympic events, they competed as separate nations. However, the symbolic reunification of Olympic athletes from North and South Korea kept the hope alive that these two countries one day would unite, as had East and West Germany.

Tommy Lasorda, the 73-year-old coach of the U.S. baseball team, announced that he wanted his players to beat the mighty Cuban baseball team in honor of the many Cuban exiles living in south Florida. Although this kind of bravado is not in keeping with the spirit of the Olympics, the U.S. team did beat the Cuban team 4–0 to win the gold medal. This was an extraordinary achievement because since baseball became an official Olympic sport in 1992 in Barcelona, the Cubans had won the gold medal every time. In Sydney, it was expected that Cuba would once again bring home the gold, and no one except Lasorda believed that the Americans had a chance. As the manager of the Los Angeles Dodgers, he had won eight division championships and taken part in four World Series, winning twice. He also is in the baseball Hall of Fame. He has the ability to get 110 percent from his athletes. Lasorda was upset with Major League Baseball because it would not allow star players to represent the nation at the Olympics. Unlike basketball's "Dream Team," the U.S. baseball team was made up of minor league and college players.

So, how did the Cubans react back in Havana when it was announced that their beloved baseball team had lost to the Americans? In Havana's Central Park, baseball fans gathered daily to talk baseball. On September 28, the day after the loss, the Cuban fans "ripped apart their national team for allowing the Americans to topple them from their Olympic throne." Forty-year-old Lazaro Sanchez said, "They [Cubans] played like a high school team! Like kids just learning how to play baseball! They played badly in every way."[21]

Meanwhile, two Cuban athletes petitioned the IOC to compete under a flag other than Cuba's. Their request was denied.

The Tape-Delayed Olympics— Thank You, NBC!

Because of the time difference between Sydney and the United States, NBC and its cable outlets MSNBC and CNBC did not provide live coverage of the events. NBC covered the Sydney Olympics via "tape delay," which meant that on the West Coast, the event that was broadcast had taken place 18 hours earlier, and everyone already knew the outcome because the morning papers had already reported the results. Hours later, fans could turn on their televisions and watch Olympic events that had already been decided. Thanks to the Internet, people could log on to various websites and keep track of the events as they happened—live! Other countries did not have this situation and received their Olympic coverage live. Fans of the Olympics who lived in San Diego were able to tune in to some Mexican channels and see events live.

NBC believed that the number of Americans watching the tape-delayed Olympics would not drop off from previous Olympics that had been broadcast live. As a result, corporate sponsors paid enormous sums of money to NBC to advertise their products. To reassure sponsors that the money was well spent, NBC had guaranteed a specific audience rating (the number of viewers who would watch the tape-delayed coverage). If this number was not achieved, NBC agreed to run additional ads at no cost to the sponsors. The projected ratings did not materialize, and as a consequence, NBC was forced to air even more commercials. In any case, marketing the Olympics (the job of the IOC) and marketing products via the Olympics (the job of NBC) involved enormous economic assets and vast amounts of money.

Economics and Attendant Social Issues

Sydney is located in the most populous of Australia's six states—New South Wales. All of the venues were completed six months ahead of schedule, which was remarkable. This accomplishment was the result of the efforts of thousands of people working behind the scenes and one man in particular, Michael Knight, minister for the Olympics. He was granted sweeping powers that chief executives of past organizing committees could only have dreamed about. Minister Knight introduced legislation that imposed severe fines on people who parked their cars illegally ($6000 per day) or who used "ambush marketing"— unauthorized sponsorships using the Olympics as a means of commercial promotion. During the Atlanta Olympics, ambush marketing took the form of huge billboards erected close to venues that advertised unofficial products or the use of airplanes flying over venues to skywrite or tow banners touting everything from restaurants and clothing to beverages. In Sydney, ambush marketers faced fines as high as $150,000.

The Olympic Games are an expensive undertaking costing billions of dollars to produce. As an example, the venue used to hold the rowing, canoeing, and kayaking events in Sydney cost approximately $30 million![22] There is no doubt that wealthy cities like Sydney are in a better position to bid for the Olympics than municipalities located in the world's poor countries. Without vast sums of money, the Olympic Games as we have come to know them would likely disappear.

Money to stage the Olympics comes from several sources. In some countries, the national government provides significant funds to the host city. Since the 1984 Los Angeles Olympic Games returned a "surplus" or profit of over $250 million as a result of corporate sponsorships, the "LA model" has become the blueprint for each successive host city. Los Angeles sold exclusive advertising rights for millions of dollars to "official sponsors" who wanted to identify their products with the Olympic image. In 1984, for example, McDonald's paid the Los Angeles Organizing Committee millions of dollars so the swimming venue would be known as McDonald's Olympic Swim Stadium. The economic and public relations bonanza that McDonald's received as an Olympic sponsor in 1984 was so valuable that it decided to continue its relationship with the Olympic movement. The corporation extended its arrangement as an official sponsor of the Olympics by paying an estimated $50–60 million. What did McDonald's receive for this fee? It retained the coveted title of official sponsor of the 2002 Winter Olympics in Salt Lake City and the 2004 Olympics in Athens.[23] McDonald's apparently believed that it could turn the "golden arches" into Olympic gold in the form of profits and product exposure all over the world. According to Dean Barrett, vice president of global marketing for McDonald's, "This [Sydney Olympics] is a big opportunity for us. The Olympics are perceived as something that families look up to and kids look up to. It works very well for our customers."[24] How well did it work for McDonald's? In 2000, the fast-food giant served 43 million customers a day in 27,000 restaurants around the world. Barrett estimated that the month-long marketing effort during the Sydney Olympics would generate "billions of impressions" among customers. No wonder corporations pay millions of dollars to identify their products with the Olympics. However, as lucrative as corporate sponsorships are to the Olympics, it is the sale of television rights that fuels the Olympic movement.

The IOC makes most of its money by selling television rights to broadcast the Olympics. For example, NBC paid the IOC $705 million to broadcast the Sydney Olympics. NBC recovered this money and then some by selling advertising time. NBC charged an average of $615,000 for a 30-second advertising spot that ran during prime time. In comparison, during the Atlanta Olympics, NBC charged $420,000 per 30-second spot.[25] When all was said and done, NBC claimed that although it paid the IOC $705 million to broadcast the Sydney Olympics, it sold advertising time in excess of $900 million for a cool profit of $195 million!

Not surprisingly, executives at NBC have been very supportive of the Olympic movement. In 1995, NBC decided to negotiate with the IOC for exclusive rights to broadcast the Olympic Games for a long time to come. As a result, in 1995, NBC paid the IOC $2.3 billion for the broadcast rights to the 2004 Olympics in Athens, the 2006 Winter Olympics in Turin, Italy, and the 2008 Olympics in Beijing. Other nations also had to negotiate with the IOC to broadcast the Sydney Olympics back to their own countries. The amount of money paid to the IOC by NBC and other countries and television networks to broadcast the Sydney Olympics was a staggering $1.3 trillion.[26]

The popularity of the Olympics has become a double-edged sword. It is wonderful that the drama, excitement, and spirit of the Olympics have touched so many people over the past century. Billions of people follow the Olympics, and as each Olympiad draws to a close, the expectation for bigger and more lavish games only grows. This situation has resulted in the Olympics becoming gigantic. Each successive Olympics seems to include more sports, and the number of athletes and attendant "administrators" has increased dramatically. Thus, each city that bids for the Olympics must convince the IOC that it will produce the Olympic Games that will eclipse all previous ones. We can begin to understand the vast amounts of money required by noting a few details that must be addressed by a city bidding for the Olympics:

1. Prepare a bid for consideration, paying salary and expenses for the staff.
2. Prevail over other cities in the country that want to host the Olympics and are preparing bids. As an example, in the United States, at least eight cities established full-time bid committees to host the 2012 Summer Games. These bid committees then had to convince the USOC that their city should be the one selected and supported by the USOC to bid for the Olympics on behalf of the United States. The USOC charged each city $100,000 to review the bid.
3. Repair existing venues and build new venues so the bid city can show the IOC that its facilities are world-class.
4. Hold world championships in sports such as track and field, soccer, swimming, gymnastics, and archery to prove that the facilities and administration of these events are world-class.
5. Repair or build a civic infrastructure around the Olympic venues. Such things as transportation are vital. Is the existing airport a true international airport? Are the streets and surface transportation functioning properly? What new roads and transportation

networks (subways, freeways, streets, public buses) must be built to transport athletes and fans to the competition sites?

As noted previously, the economic costs associated with the Olympics are enormous. Sometimes, for cities in which streets are in disrepair, people are homeless, and the air and water in the vicinity of the city are polluted, many people seriously question the need to spend vast sums on an athletic festival. This happened in Sydney, but not to the same extent as in the past.

The cost to train and send a team to the Olympic Games runs into millions of dollars. The British Olympic Association relies on a steady stream of lottery money for this purpose in addition to enlisting the aid of sponsors and doing fundraising. The USOC relies on corporate sponsors to fund its wide range of programs and to send teams to international competitions in preparation for the Olympics. In 1996, the IOC paid countries $800 for each athlete sent to the Atlanta Olympic Games. The USOC received $523,200. In contrast, Peru, a relatively poor country, received $20,000 from the IOC because it could not afford to send many athletes to the Olympics. This situation is shameful.[27]

Third World nations, also known as developing countries, have a difficult time training their elite athletes. In 2000, the *Los Angeles Times* ran a story on Olympic athletes from poor countries. For example, in Peru, a wrestler came home from practice and joined his family for a dinner that consisted of bread and tea and perhaps some chicken left over from lunch. This Olympic hopeful did not have the advantage of a training table. In fact, sports administrators in Peru discovered that there were signs of malnutrition among the nation's best amateur athletes. The administrators began providing pasta to these athletes, who then sold the pasta to pay rent. Three-quarters of the countries that competed in Sydney struggled to provide basic equipment, coaching, and, at times, food, for their athletes.[28]

The IOC responded to this situation by establishing the Olympic Solidarity program. This program has administered grants to at least 154 developing countries in order to enhance their sports infrastructure, provide coaching clinics, send athletes to other countries to train, and help pay expenses so the Olympians from impoverished countries could participate in the Olympic Games. In 1999, Olympic Solidarity spent $28.4 million to promote sport and the Olympic movement in poor countries. This is a large amount of money; however, it represented a little over 3 percent of the Olympic revenue generated by the IOC in 1999, which was $901 million.[29]

The wrestler from Peru faced many hardships. Were things any better for women living in developing countries? No. Sirivanh Ketavong was a 29-year-old Laotian working as a secretary in the capital city of Vientiane. Laos is among the poorest countries in the world and is still feeling the aftermath of the Vietnam War. It was bombed heavily during the war, and the countryside is littered with thousands of tons of unexploded bombs. It is a difficult place to train, especially for a distance runner. And Sirivanh Ketavong was the best female distance runner in Laos. She earned $175 per month, an excellent salary compared to that of the average worker, who earned $20–30 per month. She competed in the 1996 Atlanta Olympics in the marathon. In preparation for the Sydney Olympics, she received less than $100 to take part in a half-marathon race in neighboring Cambodia. There was no money to send the best female distance runner in Laos to Europe to compete. She ran in the same shoes for nearly four years until an American aid worker in Laos purchased a new pair for her. The American also was able to provide her with a running magazine that had "training tips."[30]

It was not likely that she would receive lucrative commercial endorsements even though she was the best female distance runner in her country and a two-time Olympian. Laos is a Communist government, and Communist ideology is opposed to "commercial exploitation" of individuals. So Sirivanh Ketavong's only source of financial support was what her government was able to provide. Yet she trained and ran almost every day in a crumbling stadium, in a country littered with unexploded bombs. She, and thousands of other athletes who train in Third World countries, personify the Olympic spirit and bless the Olympic Games with their presence.

In contrast, most athletes from modern countries, with their state-of-the-art training centers and attendant economic support, do quite well at the Olympics. At the close of the 2000 Sydney Olympics, the media identified the top 10 countries that won the most gold, silver, and bronze medals. The Sydney top 10 were:

1. United States: 97
2. Russia: 88
3. People's Republic of China: 59
4. Australia: 58
5. Germany: 57
6. France: 38
7. Italy: 34
8. Cuba: 29
9. Great Britain: 28
10. South Korea: 28

Eight of the top 10 countries are considered to be modern. The People's Republic of China is rapidly transforming its economy and has joined the ranks of "modern nations." Cuba continues to struggle economically, as does Russia, a superpower prior to the collapse of the Soviet Union but still a modern nation. Laos did not win a single medal in Sydney. It takes money and technology to succeed at the Olympic Games.

Technology

Some followers of the Olympic movement referred to the Sydney Olympics as the Internet Olympics because anybody linked to the Net could follow the Olympics in real time. As interesting as the Internet was, it was the technological advances in sport that really captured the attention of the public.

Swimmers wore specially designed lightweight body suits designed to reduce drag and lower times. Some of the yacht races featured boats equipped with a device that allowed officials to accurately determine the position of a particular

boat to within 1-meter. Olympic fans who watched this event "live" could look at a nautical chart on the television (or on their computer screen) and see exactly where the boats were in relation to each other. Kayakers wore goggles equipped with sensors that displayed their vital signs. Rowers handled oars outfitted with sensors so their coaches would be able to determine how strong their strokes were and make appropriate adjustments. Marathoners had a tiny microchip implanted in their shoes that weighed about 5 grams, or 0.175 of an ounce. Antennas were placed on the course so that each marathoner could be tracked as to his or her position in the race. Olympians from France were provided with a message machine that appeared to be part robot and part vacuum cleaner. This machine was equipped with a motorized vacuum head that was applied to a spot on the athlete's body that was then massaged.[31]

Doping

There were six positive drug tests *during* the course of the Sydney Games. Considering that over 10,000 athletes competed, the problem of doping seemed to have been handled well by the IOC and the Sydney Organizing Committee. However, additional discoveries of doping were likely to be announced long after the end of the Olympics, because urine samples were taken from all Olympic medalists and stored for future analysis. Was anybody caught and stripped of their medal *after* the Sydney Olympics? Weeks after the closing ceremonies, Alexander Leipold of Germany, who initially was awarded the gold medal in freestyle wrestling, tested positive for the banned steroid nandrolone. He was stripped of his medal. Six weeks after the close of the Sydney Olympics, Anita Defrantz, vice president of the IOC, presided over a ceremony in New York and presented the gold medal to the new Olympic champion, Brandon Slay from the United States. She also awarded the silver medal to Moon Eui Jae of South Korea, while Adem Bereket of Turkey was presented with the bronze.

It may take several years after the Olympic Games for WADA (the World Anti-Doping Agency) and the IOC to rigorously test all Olympians. If it turns out that some of these athletes used banned substances, they will be stripped of their medals and punished. Olympians who believe that they have not been treated fairly can always appeal to the Court of Arbitration for Sport.

Notables

Several American athletes not selected for the Olympic team hired lawyers to argue their cases. Lisa Raymond, the top-ranked doubles player in the world, was not picked and filed for arbitration. The coach of the U.S. women's tennis team was none other than the legendary Billie Jean King. She used world rankings to select the singles players but not the doubles players. Instead of taking Raymond, King selected Serena Williams so she could play with her sister, Venus Williams, in doubles play. Raymond lost her appeal. In Greco-Roman wrestling, an arbitrator agreed to grant Matt Lindland a rematch against Keith Sieracki, the wrestler who had defeated him at the U.S. Olympic trials. In the rematch, Lindland defeated Sieracki, who in turn filed for arbitration to regain his spot on the Olympic team. Lindland's attorneys went to federal court in Chicago in an effort to block Sieracki's arbitration hearing. When the request was denied, Lindland's attorneys filed an appeal. Meanwhile, in the quadruple sculls, four women filed for arbitration and, they hoped, a spot on the Olympic team. They claimed they never had a fair chance to make the team because the coach, Igor Grinko, had promised other rowers earlier in the year that they (not the four who filed for arbitration) would make the team. The arbitrator ruled in favor of the four women.

We have already noted the accomplishments of Cathy Freeman, one of many highlights of the Sydney Olympics. A tragic story occurred when Glory Alozie from Nigeria arrived in Sydney with her fiancé. The couple was to be married after the Olympics. On the way to the store, her fiancé was struck and killed by a car. The determined Alozie, declining to drop out of the competition, instead repeated her performance in Atlanta by winning another silver medal in the 100-meter hurdles. She also ran the first leg of Nigeria's 4 × 100 relay team that won the bronze medal. When asked why she insisted on running, she replied, "To live up to the Olympic spirit."

Marie-José Perec, a sprinter from France, departed Sydney and returned to France before her event, the 400-meter sprint. It was reported that she did not want to compete against Freeman. The Australian press labeled Perec "Mademoiselle la Chicken." In Greco-Roman wrestling, Rulon Gardner from tiny Afton, Wyoming, beat the reigning world and Olympic champion, Alexander Karelin of Russia, who had not lost since 1987.

In swimming, the Americans and Australians ruled. Australian sensation Ian Thorpe was so good he became known as the "Thorpedo" because he sunk most of his competition. The pool at the Sydney Aquatic Center was so fast that five world records were set during the first night of the swimming finals. On September 16, the Thorpedo won two gold medals. Thirty-three-year-old Dara Tores from the United States became the oldest female swimmer to win a gold medal, while the U.S. men's 400-meter freestyle relay team lost the gold medal to the Australians. A few days later, on September 20, Olympic and world records tumbled as Inge de Bruijn from Holland won the 100-meter women's freestyle in 53.77 seconds. Misty Hyman, a 21-year-old student from Stanford University, won the 200-meter butterfly in 2 minutes, 5.88 seconds, a new Olympic record. Jenny Thompson of the United States won her seventh gold medal in swimming over a span of three Olympics: two in 1992 in Barcelona, three in Atlanta in 1996, and two in Sydney. All of her medals were in the relay events.

Gezahgne Abera of Ethiopia won the marathon in 2 hours, 10 minutes, 11 seconds. He dedicated his gold medal to himself, his remote village in the Southern Highlands, and Mamo Wolde, sitting in a jail cell in Ethiopia. Who was Mamo Wolde? He won the marathon in the 1968 Olympics in Mexico City and finished third in the 1972 Olympics in Munich. In the early 1990s, Wolde was jailed as a political prisoner by the Ethiopian authorities. In 1999, Wolde was charged with the shooting of a man that allegedly happened 21 years earlier. One Olympian sits in a jail cell while another one runs. Sadly, Wolde was not the only Olympian serving jail time. IOC president Samaranch lobbied the Indonesian government to secure the release of a jailed IOC member so he could attend the Sydney Olympics.[32]

There was a problem during the women's all-around gymnastics program. Prior to the women's all-around, the men had been using the same vaulting horse, and officials forgot to adjust the vaulting horse for the women. As a result, the greatest female gymnasts in the world appeared as if they had rarely practiced the vault because they made so many mistakes. The error was discovered and corrected. In water polo, two teams had dominated world competition since 1956. Once again, Hungary and Russia (formerly the Soviet Union) played for the gold. Hungary "edged" Russia 13–6 to win the gold medal. Athletes from the Netherlands did well. Inge de Bruijn won three gold medals in women's swimming, cyclist Leontien Zijlaard won three gold medals, and Pieter van den Hoogenband won four medals in men's swimming—two gold and two bronze. America's cycling sensation and former Tour de France champion Lance Armstrong raced but did not medal.

Marion Jones of the United States turned in a suspect performance in Sydney. She had predicted that by the end of the Olympics, five gold medals would be hanging from her neck. The track-and-field star did win five medals, three gold and two bronze. However, six years later in 2007, after repeatedly denying she had used performance-enhancing drugs, Jones admitted in court that she had done so. A few days later, the IOC took away her medals and removed her name from the Olympics; there is no mention of her any longer as an Olympic champion. In January 2008, Jones was sentenced to six months in prison. Her coach, Trevor Graham, was tried in a United States court on charges that he had provided illegal drugs to

athletes. His trial was scheduled to take place in 2008. Jones's former husband, C. J. Hunter, was also supposed to compete in the Sydney Olympics but tested positive for a banned substance.

As incredible as it may seem, Russian gymnast Alexei Nemov won six medals—two gold, one silver, and three bronze. Ian Thorpe, the Australian swimmer, won five medals—three gold and two silver.

The vaunted U.S. men's basketball team, typically referred to as the "Dream Team," came close to experiencing a nightmare when it played France for the gold medal. The Olympians from France gave the U.S. team all it could handle before losing 85–75. The American women had an easier time in beating host Australia 76–54 to win the gold medal in basketball. Meanwhile, the U.S. men won the 4×100 relay and then engaged in what the media believed was poor behavior. After the victory lap, several of the athletes wrapped themselves in the American flag and began an enthusiastic celebration. Some observers said that the celebration was no more than an "in your face" statement aimed at the teams that they beat—Brazil and Cuba. When the four U.S. victors climbed up to the victory stand to receive their gold medals, they flexed their muscles and posed like bodybuilders. It may not have been the dignified decorum that the IOC and the public were used to, but there is no doubt these athletes were elated at their victory. In the women's 4×100 relay, the team from the Bahamas won the gold, Jamaica the silver, and the United States the bronze.

The Sydney Olympics drew to a close on October 1, a rousing success. The IOC and the Olympic movement needed a "victory," and Sydney delivered in fine fashion.

THE XIXTH WINTER OLYMPICS: SALT LAKE CITY, 2002

The Political Atmosphere

When Sydney hosted the 2000 Summer Olympiad, the global political situation, especially in the Middle East, was tense and volatile. In the two years since the closing ceremonies in Sydney, political tensions and terrorist activities in the Middle East, Africa, Great Britain, Russia, and Chechnya had increased dramatically. Warfare had escalated in Africa, especially in Somalia. In the Sudan, thousands of refugees were dying each month in a civil war that was 15 years old. The Second Intifada (the First Intifada was from 1987 to 1993), a war against Israel launched by Palestinians and fueled by Islamic terrorists, was two years old and had claimed thousands of lives in Israel. The Palestinians, who harbored the terrorists/suicide bombers, had also suffered enormous loss of lives and property when Israel retaliated against them. There did not seem to be any end in sight, although the diplomatic community made many attempts to broker a peace treaty. In Great Britain, the Irish Republican Army and its supporters were still causing problems. The Russians, under the leadership of Vladimir Putin, were embroiled in a costly war in Chechnya against terrorists who would bring the war to Moscow, blowing up subways and spewing deadly poison gas in a central Moscow theater killing hundreds. Meanwhile, Americans breathed a sigh of relief. Apart from a failed attack on the World Trade Center in New York City in the early 1990s by Islamic terrorists and the bombing of the Murrah Federal Building in Oklahoma City by domestic terrorists, the nation seemed to have largely avoided the horrific attacks that were taking place in other parts of the world with increasing frequency. And then, on September 11, 2001, the unthinkable happened.

The 9/11 terrorist attacks on New York City and Washington cast a dark cloud over the United States. The nation was at war against the terrorist organization known as al Qaeda and its affiliates. Osama bin Laden was the "Most Wanted Man on Earth" in the eyes of President George W. Bush because it was bin Laden who financed al Qaeda and it was al Qaeda that trained and sent to the United States the terrorists who would highjack two American Airlines planes and two United Airlines planes. They crashed two of the fully loaded passenger planes into the Twin Towers of the World Trade Center in Manhattan, killing over 3000 civilians. The other plane crashed into

the Pentagon, killing everybody on board along with the Defense Department personnel who were working at the site of the impact. On the fourth plane, heroic passengers attacked the terrorists, and the plane crashed into an empty field, killing all aboard. The brave and resolute passengers fought to the death and saved countless more lives. It was speculated that the terrorists had planned to crash the plane into the White House. America, and the rest of the world, would never be the same.

The "War on Terror" began as President Bush enlisted the support of Great Britain, France, Germany, Russia, and other nations in a military campaign in Afghanistan against the Taliban, an extremist Islamic organization that gave aid and comfort to bin Laden and provided military training to al Qaeda. But France, Germany, Russia, and many others declined to provide military assistance and opposed the military action Bush demanded against Iraq and Saddam Hussein. Bush then formed a "Coalition of Nations" (Great Britain, Australia, Poland, Italy, Spain, and a number of smaller countries) and launched a war to rid Iraq of Hussein. Initially, the Bush administration claimed that Hussein was providing aid to bin Laden and al Qaeda. Then, the Bush administration and Great Britain suggested that Iraq had weapons of mass destruction and would use them against Israel and other nations that Hussein wanted to destroy. After the invasion of Iraq, it was determined that Iraq had

---

Olympic Snapshot

2002 Salt Lake City Winter Olympics:

Opening Day February 8; Closing Day February 24

- 77 countries sent teams
- 2399 athletes: 886 women and 1513 men
- 8 sports, 78 events: Biathlon, Bobsleigh, Curling, Men's and Women's Ice Hockey, Luge, Skating, Skiing, and Snowboarding
- 22,000 volunteers and 8730 media/press credentials issued

no weapons of mass destruction and that there was no link between Iraq and al Qaeda. To many Arabs, it appeared that the United States and Great Britain were waging another crusade against the Islamic world. This time, though, the supposed goal was not to wrest control of Jerusalem from the Muslims on behalf of Christendom, as with the original Crusades over a thousand years ago, but to dominate the Middle East and its vast oil reserves.

Security Concerns

The opening ceremonies for the Salt Lake City Winter Olympics were scheduled to take place the night of February 8, 2002. Only a few months had passed since the devastating attack of 9/11, and a frequently asked question was whether the games should be canceled due to security concerns. America was at war, and the possibility that the country would be attacked again was a legitimate concern. If terrorists sought to launch another attack on American soil, the Winter Olympics provided an ideal symbolic target. The IOC, USOC, and Salt Lake City Organizing Committee met and, with encouragement and support from the White House, decided that the Winter Games would take place as scheduled. For 17 days in February, the ravages of war and the cries of suffering would give way to the bright light of hope, joy, and goodwill as the Winter Olympics took center stage in the international arena. Tens of thousands would attend while billions more around the world watched the drama unfold.

To ensure that maximum security was in force, the federal government and the state of Utah provided manpower and resources that cost in excess of $1 billion. Barricades were erected to secure the safety of the citizens of Utah, fans, athletes, workers, and Olympic officials. The Little America Hotel in downtown Salt Lake City, home to the IOC, was heavily guarded, and the same security measures were taken at other sensitive venues. In addition, 14 nations brought their own security forces. What this meant, among other things, was that the lines were long at each venue because *everybody* was screened and checked. However,

the atmosphere was so electric and so exciting that very few people complained. Most of the time, the thousands of fans at each event expressed their thanks to the law enforcement and military professionals who patrolled the venues and surrounding areas.

The weather was made to order, the venues were all world-class, and the setting was spectacular. There were no terrorist threats or incidents. The thousands of volunteers were very helpful, and the competitions were thrilling. Overall, it was truly a magical 17 days for the fans and most of the athletes. However, there were glaring exceptions, especially when it came to a judging scandal in pairs ice skating, the use of performance-enhancing drugs by several athletes, and the "relativist" policies/laws of the IOC.

Drugs

In Salt Lake City, performance-enhancing drugs were once again a problem. The World Anti-Doping Agency (WADA), headed by IOC member Dick Pound, a lawyer from Canada, established a strong presence at the Winter Olympics. Olympic athletes can be drug tested "out-of-competition," which means medal winners can be tested several days after their medals have been awarded. In addition, "in-competition" testing is given to athletes, especially medal winners, immediately after their event is over. Even horses in the equestrian events are subjected to doping, so they are drug tested as well. In-competition testing also includes testing, usually in the form of a blood or urine sample, before the athletes compete. Most of the tests for doping, whether in-competition or out-of-competition, screen for a long list of banned substances, especially EPO (erythropoietin).

EPO is used to increase red blood cells far above normal levels in order to provide more oxygen to the muscles. It can be very difficult to detect. In addition, there are a number of EPO-like drugs that provide the cheating athlete with an unfair advantage. Sometimes WADA officials are able to detect these "designer" drugs, but other times, athletes who dope, aided by unethical scientists, are able to escape detection. However, three big-name athletes at the Winter Olympics were caught just a few hours before the closing ceremonies began. Johann Muehlegg, a cross-country skier who represented Spain, was caught using EPO. Interestingly, Muehlegg, originally from Germany, had competed for Germany in the Winter Olympics in Albertville/Savoie in 1992, in Lillehammer in 1994, and in Nagano in 1998. He never won a medal when he competed for Germany. He was lured to Spain where he was granted Spanish citizenship, even though he was not fluent in Spanish, and was immediately selected for the Spanish Winter Olympic team. During the Salt Lake City Games, Muehlegg finished first in the 10-kilometer freestyle, first in the 30-kilometer freestyle, and first in the 50-kilometer classic. Two Russian women, Larissa Lazutina and Olga Danilova, were caught using EPO as well. Between them, they had won a total of 14 medals over the course of their Olympic careers! Like Muehlegg, they were caught using a type of EPO, darbepoetin, that was supposed to be undetectable.

Philosophical Concerns and Legal Interpretations

Just when it appeared that justice would prevail, the three cheaters got the last laugh. Due to a loophole in the laws that the Olympic Games operate under, the three athletes actually were allowed to keep some of their medals. A legal technicality, drafted in language only a lawyer could love, allowed this to happen. The IOC and WADA had agreed, prior to the Winter Olympics, that if an athlete was caught cheating, all of the medals he or she might win *after* failing the drug tests would have to be returned. However, any medals that they "won" *before* the failed test was administered they would be allowed to keep.

Athletes who compete in grueling endurance events like the distance events in the biathlon and cross-country races are frequently checked for elevated levels of red blood cells, which supply oxygen to the muscles. These tests take place

before competition. If officials detect elevated or abnormally high levels of red blood cells, athletes are held out of competition because of concerns about their health. An elevated red blood cell count is not definitive proof that doping has taken place, but it does raise a big red flag that EPO may have been used. The test for EPO is very expensive, which is why it is not given after every event. All three athletes passed the mandatory basic drug test immediately after their events were over. However, an IOC doping scientist became skeptical because Muehlegg, who had already won two gold medals, had elevated levels of red blood cells, just a hair within acceptable limits.

On February 21, Muehlegg was escorted to an out-of-competition drug test that would, among other things, screen for EPO. Two days later, on February 23, Muehlegg won the grueling 50-kilometer classic cross-country race at Soldier Hollow. Later that night, the results of the EPO test were revealed. Muehlegg did indeed fail the test. However, since the test was given two days before the 50-kilometer event, the only gold medal he had to give up was for the latter race. Under IOC rules, he was able to keep the two gold medals he won before the drug test of February 21 because an athlete is penalized only in the events he or she competed in *after* the test. He won the gold medal in the 30-kilometer freestyle on February 9 and the gold medal in the 10-kilometer combined pursuit on February 14, almost a week *before* he would fail the drug test for EPO.

Lazutina and Danilova came under scrutiny when they, along with their teammates, arrived at Soldier Hollow on February 21 to compete in the 4 × 5-kilometer cross-country relay. Officials from WADA took blood samples from the two women and discovered that the levels of red blood cells in their bodies were far above acceptable limits. They were not allowed to compete, and when the more comprehensive test for EPO was administered, the two Russians were caught red-handed! The Russian women had dominated this event, winning the gold medal in the previous four Winter Games. There was not enough time to make substitutions for Lazutina and Danilova, so the Russian team was not able to compete. But once again, like Muehlegg, the two Russians were able to keep the medals they had won before they were tested for EPO. Danilova had won the silver medal in the 10-kilometer classic cross-country race on February 12 and the gold medal in the 5-kilometer combined pursuit on February 15. Lazutina had won the silver medal in the 15-kilometer freestyle race on February 9 and the silver medal in the 5-kilometer combined pursuit on February 15.

Ethical Decisions and the Decline of an Idea: Exercise in Critical Thinking

The use of performance-enhancing drugs has been a scourge on the Olympic Games for decades. Not so long ago, the IOC claimed that it was the only international sporting body capable of leading the war against doping in sport. However, given that the IOC permits athletes to keep medals even though they have been caught cheating, this claim is absurd. Philosophically, what message does the doping policy of the IOC, as revealed during the Salt Lake City Winter Games, send to the youths of the world? Seeing as how a number of lawyers are members of the IOC, perhaps some of them have redefined what it means to cheat and what penalties should be administered to those caught cheating. How would you respond to the following?

1. If an Olympic athlete is caught cheating and the evidence is conclusive, would you allow the athlete to keep any of her or his medals as the IOC did in Salt Lake City? Why or why not?

2. Has cheating become relative, and have situational ethics become the norm within the Olympics and American sport? Why or why not?

3. Are the ethical consequences of cheating in general, at least by IOC standards, minimal? Is it any different in U.S. society in general? Why or why not?

IOC members were caught accepting bribes and demanding goods and services from Salt Lake City officials in exchange for their vote to award the Winter Olympics to Salt Lake City. Some IOC officials were forced out, but others remain, to this day, as members of the IOC. They were reprimanded but kept their jobs. The responsibility of the IOC to serve as a role model to the youths of the world, to act as an institution with an impeccable reputation and capacity to render fair and just decisions, seems to have been shoveled into the dustbin of Olympic history.

Then again, perhaps the "new" culture of the IOC simply reflects postmodern thinking. How many politicians in our country accept money from supporters, and what do these supporters expect in return? Have American presidents, vice presidents, members of Congress, and other public servants been forced from office or jailed like their counterparts in the IOC? Perhaps it is not fair to expect the IOC to measure up to the ideals that traditionally we hold dear as a nation. But if not the IOC, then who?

Notables

The budget of the Salt Lake City Organizing Committee was in excess of $1 billion, with security costs picked up by the federal government and the state of Utah. Once again, NBC provided commercial television coverage, much of it live, especially in the Western Hemisphere—a vast improvement over the debacle in Sydney in 2000. NBC paid the IOC $555 million for the television rights to the Winter Olympics. The IOC has a sliding scale when it comes to the amount of money various nations pay to televise the games. Thus, for example, the Canadian Broadcasting Company paid $22 million while Korea paid $750,000. Corporate sponsors also paid millions of dollars to the Salt Lake City Organizing Committee in order to advertise their companies and products at the venues.

The sports program was the largest in Olympic history, featuring 78 events in 15 disciplines and eight sports. The 2002 Winter Olympics had ten more events, including additional women's events, than were featured at the 2000 games in Nagano. New or expanded events for 2002 included the skeleton for men and women, women's bobsled, the biathlon (added were men's 12.5-kilometer pursuit and women's 10-kilometer pursuit), cross-country skiing (added were men's and women's sprint, men's 15-kilometer classical, and women's 10-kilometer classical), Nordic combined (added individual event that included K120 jump and 7.5-kilometer cross-country race), short-track speed skating (added men's and women's 1500-meter race), curling (increased the number of men's and women's teams from eight to ten), ice hockey (increased the number of women's teams from six to eight), and snowboarding (changed men's and women's giant slalom to parallel giant slalom).

The opening ceremonies were held on the campus of the University of Utah, at Rice-Eccles Stadium. Over 50,000 fans celebrated a magnificent night capped off with the 1980 U.S. men's Olympic hockey team, led by Captain Mike Eruzione, lighting the Olympic flame. Recall that this team, made up of college players, defeated the mighty Soviet team and then went on to win the gold medal by defeating Finland. It was the astonishing and unexpected victory over the previously unbeaten Russians that caused ABC Sports anchor Al Michaels, who announced the game, to famously ask, "Do you believe in miracles?" The rest, as they say, is history.

The first gold medal was won by cross-country skier Stefania Belmondo from Italy, who won the 15-kilometer race. Derek Parra became the first Mexican-American to win a medal in the Winter Olympics, finishing second in the 5000-meter speed-skating event. On the fourth day of competition, a judging scandal in pairs figure skating surfaced. The French judge claimed she was bullied by another judge to award the gold medal to the Russian team of Elena Berezhnaya and Anton Sikharulidze over the Canadian team of Jamie Sale and David Pelletier, who were clearly the team the capacity crowd believed deserved to

win. Skating officials met several times after the judging scandal surfaced and, with the permission of the IOC, awarded the Canadians gold medals as well. They decided not to award a silver medal. The bronze medal was awarded to the Chinese team of Shen Xue and Zhao Hongbo.

Meanwhile, Russian ice hockey officials were furious at the fact that the referees for the ice hockey competition were from the National Hockey League (NHL). The Russian men's team complained bitterly that the NHL referees favored the American and Canadian teams. As it turned out, the Canadians did play the Americans for the gold medal. In one of the most exciting games since the 1980 "Miracle on Ice" game, the Canadians defeated the Americans 5–2 on the last night of competition. Canada had not won a gold medal in Olympic hockey in 50 years and understandably was elated. The Russians had to settle for the bronze medal, and their president, Vladimir Putin, was livid. Not to be outdone by their male counterparts, the Canadian women's ice hockey team defeated the American women to win the gold medal; the Swedish women's team won the bronze.

In alpine skiing, the Austrians, Germans, and French dominated. Bode Miller from the United States won the silver medal in the men's combined and another silver medal in the men's giant slalom. The American women's alpine team did not medal. In the popular bobsled competition, the American men won a silver in the four-man race, and the American women's team of Jill Bakken and Vonetta Flowers won the gold medal in the pairs event. Flowers was the first African-American woman to win a gold medal in the Winter Olympics. In figure skating, the Russian men's team captured the gold and silver medals while American Timothy Goebel won the bronze. Alexi Yagudin, who won the gold medal in men's figure skating, scored a record 6.0 from the judges in a magnificent display of athletic prowess and aesthetic brilliance. In women's figure skating, American teen sensation Sarah Hughes from Long Island won the gold medal. Her teammate Michelle Kwan took the bronze. American

Chris Klug, who had undergone a liver transplant, won the bronze medal in snowboarding. One of the more dramatic upsets occurred in the men's 1000-meter short-track speed-skating event. The favorite, Apolo Anton Ohno from the United States, stumbled and crashed as a result of a massive pileup on the track. Everybody fell except for an Australian skater who was far back in last place. He saw the pile of bodies ahead of him, easily skated around it, and won the gold medal! In the skeleton competition, the Americans did very well. Jim Shea, Jr., won the gold medal, and in the women's competition, Tristan Gale won the gold while her teammate Lea Ann Parsley won the silver.

In the final medal count, the unified German team led all nations with a total of 35 medals (12 gold). Close behind was the United States with 34 (10 gold), Norway with 24 (11 gold), and Canada with 17 (six gold). The Russians tied with Austria for fifth place in the medal standings with a total of 16 (six gold). The historic rivalry between the Americans and Russians burned bright during the Cold War. With the collapse of the Soviet Union, Russia's Olympic fortunes declined steeply save for a few great athletes. However, if history is any indication, it will not be long before the Russian Olympic team emerges out of the internal chaos that has crippled the nation and once again becomes an Olympic power, in both the Summer and Winter Games.

Next stop, Athens and the 2004 Summer Olympics.

THE XXVIIITH OLYMPIAD: ATHENS, 2004

The Political Atmosphere

In 2004, the geopolitical climate had not significantly changed from the time the Salt Lake City Winter Games were held in 2002. The United States was deeply involved in the War on Terror, both at home and abroad. On the domestic front, Congress passed and President George W. Bush signed into law the Patriot Act, which enabled

law enforcement agencies such as the FBI to utilize expanded means to thwart terrorist activities. People opposed to various aspects of the Patriot Act claimed that it could violate the civil rights of Americans. The Department of Homeland Security, headed by Tom Ridge, was a new cabinet-level office established by Bush to coordinate efforts to defend the United States against terrorist attacks. This department implemented a security stage alert system that when activated to "Orange" required passengers at the nation's airports and other transportation venues, such as cruise ship terminals, to undergo intensive searches prior to boarding. Cars were stopped before entering airports and thoroughly checked for weapons or explosives that could blow up terminals or planes. And people with Middle Eastern names or "Arabic" physical characteristics such as dress or appearance were almost always detained for questioning before being allowed on planes.

Islam, one of the world's four great religions, is based on the ideals of peace and devotion to God as outlined in the Koran, the holy book of Islam. Millions of devoted and peace-loving Muslims decried the brutal actions of the terrorists acting in the name of Islam. However, a large number of Muslims were persuaded to join terrorist or extremist organizations such as Hamas, the Taliban, and al Qaeda in a Holy War, or Jihad, against Israel, its allies, and Western culture. Islamic terrorists and their fellow extremists vowed to create hard-line Islamic fundamentalist nations, just as the Taliban had done in Afghanistan in the 1980s.

In 2004, the United States was still embroiled in Afghanistan and Iraq, and American casualties were mounting. By the time the Athens Olympics started, over a thousand American troops had died and thousands more had been seriously wounded. Islamic extremists also began to capture and execute workers who were hired from all parts of the world to repair and rebuild the infrastructure in Iraq. The brutal executions were then broadcast on websites run by the militants as the world watched in horror. The hoped-for "quick and decisive" victories in Afghanistan and Iraq were not going to happen. While a significant number of the citizens of Iraq and Afghanistan welcomed liberation from the Saddam Hussein and Taliban, respectively, many more hated the Americans and their allies and vowed to fight the Americans to the death.

It is not that far from Athens to Iraq; in fact, you can drive from Greece through Turkey and into Iraq, which shares a border with Turkey. The fear among Olympic officials was that the close proximity of Athens to Israel, the Palestinian Territory, and Iraq seemed to be an open invitation for a terrorist attack during the Olympics. Greece does not have a solid history of homeland security and has had major problems with domestic terrorists for years. One particular group known as "17 November" had murdered a number of diplomatic officials from Great Britain and the United States over the years. Not long before the opening ceremonies, Greek officials announced that they had caught the leader of 17 November, and Greece breathed a little easier. Nevertheless, the Greek border with Bulgaria and Turkey is, for the most part, rural

and isolated. In addition, the rugged coastline and many hundreds of islands concerned the experts planning and executing security measures for Athens. Sadly, on March 11, Islamic terrorists blew up and derailed a train in Madrid, Spain, killing 191 people. Spain had been a member of the coalition that was assisting the United States and Great Britain in Iraq.

In the Middle East, the Second Intifada was now four years old. Suicide bombers continued their attacks against Israel, blowing up buses, restaurants, and other targets. The Israelis responded by bombing suspected terrorist enclaves in Gaza and assassinating terrorists, especially members of Hamas. Yasser Arafat, leader of the Palestine Liberation Organization (PLO), was not able to secure peace. He had little, if any, influence on Hamas, the militant Palestinian organization that has waged war against Israel for years.

In Africa, the ongoing war in Somalia and the Sudan, especially in the Darfur region, was escalating. In March 2004, the World Health Organization estimated that 70,000 refugees had died in Darfur in the past year alone, mostly due to starvation and disease. Humanitarian groups from around the world, including the United Nations, attempted to send food and medical supplies to the Sudanese, but rival forces either blocked distribution, seized the supplies for their own people, or sold what little supplies actually got through to get more money to buy more guns.

In 2004 in the United States, the incumbent president, Republican George W. Bush, ran against Senator John Kerry, a Democrat from Massachusetts. Both President Bush and Senator Kerry made the War on Terror, especially American involvement in Iraq and Afghanistan, a primary issue in the campaign. The global political arena remained extremely tense. Americans were told that it was only a matter of time before al Qaeda or another terrorist group struck America again. Some American athletes from the National Basketball Association (NBA) refused to be considered for the U.S. Olympic basketball team because of the potential for terrorist attacks during the Olympics.

OLYMPIC SNAPSHOT

2004 Athens Olympiad:

Opening Day August 13; Closing Day August 29

- 201 countries sent teams
- 10,625 athletes: 4329 women and 6296 men
- 29 sports, 301 events: Aquatics, Archery, Athletics, Badminton, Baseball, Basketball, Boxing, Canoe/Kayak, Cycling, Equestrian, Fencing, Soccer, Women's Soccer, Gymnastics, Field Hockey, Handball, Judo, Modern Pentathlon, Mountain Biking, Rowing, Sailing, Shooting, Softball, Table Tennis, Tae kwon do, Tennis, Triathlon, Volleyball & Beach Volleyball, Men's and Women's Weight Lifting, and Men's & Women's Wrestling
- 45,000 volunteers and 21,500 media/press credentials issued

Everybody's crystal ball was cloudy when it came to forecasting the probability of a successful Athens Olympics. The big question was whether the Greeks could deliver and host a memorable Olympiad. There was a lot of speculation in the Western media that the Greeks would fail. Would they?

The Game Plan

Athens had bid for the 1996 Olympic Games that were awarded to Atlanta. To the Athenians, all that was needed, it had seemed, was for the city to present its bid to the IOC, and for sentimental and historical reasons, it would be a slam dunk vote: Athens in 1996. But it didn't happen as planned, and so the Athens bid committee drew up a new game plan to land the 2004 Olympic Games. This time they were successful. On September 5, 1997, in Lausanne, Switzerland, Athens was selected as the host city for the 2004 Olympics. Other cities in consideration were Buenos Aires, Cape Town, Rome, and Stockholm. Although there was opposition in Greece to hosting the Olympics, when the announcement was made that Athens had won the vote, the nation celebrated.

Ethical Dilemmas

Critics of the 2004 Athens Olympics argued that a host of social, humanitarian, and civic issues should be addressed before several billion dollars were allocated to an athletic festival that would last 17 days. For example, the nation's schools, state-run hospitals, and social-service agencies could have used this money to enhance the educational experience of students and care for more of the sick and elderly.

This was a serious issue that seemingly was ignored by the IOC, the Athens Organizing Committee, and the Greek government. It begs the question of whether the IOC has a moral obligation to consider the economic plight of the host city and the attendant costs that the host city and nation will incur as a result of hosting the Olympics. If you responded in the affirmative, you are not alone.

In the 1980s, the city of Denver was selected to host the Winter Olympics, but the citizens of Denver and Colorado voted not to host the games. Improving the schools, infrastructure, and fire and police services, and funding social programs were deemed more important than hosting the Winter Olympics. But Athens was not Denver.

In a previous chapter, we discussed the 1968 Mexico City Olympic Games. Mexico, to this day, is a very poor country. In 1968, thousands of students in Mexico City rioted in protest against government policies that allocated millions of dollars to stage the Olympic Games while all but ignoring the plight of the millions of poor Mexicans who were still living in huge slums and had little access to health care. The government called in the military, including snipers, who killed over 300 of the protesters and wounded many more. The games must go on, said the IOC and the Mexico City Organizing Committee. But at what cost? Again, Athens was not Mexico City.

Logistics and Security Concerns

The construction of 38 venues to accommodate 29 sports and their various events was subject to strikes, delays, and, in one case, a contractor declaring bankruptcy. This particular contractor had been hired to improve the roads and infrastructure for the marathon. Because he had not paid his workers for quite some time, they quit, and he went out of business. Another contractor was hired who managed to complete the project in the nick of time. In 2002, the leader of the Athens Organizing Committee, Gianna Angelopoulos, fired three senior members of her staff when an internal document calling attention to serious construction delays was made public. IOC president Jacques Rogge traveled to Athens to look into the matter; it would not be his last visit. Statements were made to the media by Rogge and other concerned individuals that Athens was making precious little progress and work needed to be accelerated.

Accommodations for the athletes were in the heavily guarded Olympic Village. The Olympic family, consisting of IOC members, members of National Olympic Committees (NOCs), and their respective employees, was housed in hotels in Athens and on cruise ships specifically brought in for the games. The Olympic family was able to use special traffic lanes in Athens marked for their personal use. Fans had to locate their own housing. One of the ambitious plans had been to build a high-speed bullet train from Corinth, where housing was available, to Athens, to significantly reduce traffic congestion, but it was not finished in time. The expanded highway from Athens to Corinth was completed, at least partially, about a week before the opening ceremonies. The author (Mechikoff), who was in Athens and Ancient Nemea for most of the summer of 2004, marveled at the ability of the Greeks to pull together at the last minute and complete massive projects.

However, not all of the plans and projects came to fruition. The World Wildlife Fund (WWF) delivered a scathing report about the lack of environmental precautions and the overall carelessness. The WWF labeled the 2004 Olympic Games the "Brown Olympics" because of missed opportunities to contribute to the greening of Athens. The environmental group complained that proper environmental impact reports were not filed and that the new venues significantly damaged the environment. Indeed, prior to the opening ceremonies, thousands of landscape plants and trees lined the roadways of Athens but never got watered, let alone planted, and simply died due to lack of care. It was indeed a missed opportunity, a waste of money, and, sadly, a waste of precious plants and trees.

Security was the main concern of Greece as well as the 201 Olympic teams that would travel to Athens to compete. The United States offered to assist in the security preparations, as did other nations. All told, approximately 45,000 security personnel were assigned to the Olympic Games. On July 21, 2004, *The New York Times* reported that American, British, and Israeli security officers would be allowed to carry guns during the Olympics. On July 23, less than a month before opening

ceremonies, the *Athens News,* an English-language newspaper published in Athens, reported that the Greek government insisted it would not allow foreign guards to carry weapons to protect athletes competing in the Olympics. However, among the security forces were 3500 "private contractors." George Voulgarakis, public order minister, told the *Athens News* that he had authorized private guards to carry guns in order to protect foreign dignitaries. He noted that this practice was in accord with established international protocols. What Greek security officials were concerned about, and rightly so, was the possibility of a shoot-out between foreign guards who didn't speak Greek and domestic security forces.

Colin Powell, Secretary of State in the Bush administration, had planned to attend the closing ceremonies. However, after police in Athens used tear gas and other means to disperse a crowd of several thousand who smashed windows and set fires to protest Powell's visit, he decided to remain in Washington, D.C. The protesters were attempting to march on the heavily fortified U.S. embassy in Athens. They shouted slogans, in Greek and English, condemning the invasion of Iraq by the United States and demanding the withdrawal of American troops from Iraq. This was the most violent protest during the Athens Olympiad. Security forces prevented the big crowd from doing considerable damage, and many arrests were made.

Greece spent over a billion euros ($1.25 billion) on security alone, four times the amount spent during the 2002 Sydney Olympics. The member countries from the North Atlantic Treaty Organization (NATO) provided air and sea patrols and marshaled military teams in neighboring nations that could provide immediate assistance with a single phone call. As it turned out, the complex and thorough security measures taken in Athens largely kept the peace. During the marathon, however, at mile 22, a defrocked and deranged priest from Ireland with a history of mental illness burst out of the crowd and attacked the lead runner, Valderlei de Lima from Brazil. Valderlei, visibly shaken, recovered and held off

Jon Brown of Great Britain to win the bronze medal. So much for crowd control.

Doping

Prior to the Olympics, American sprinter Torri Edwards was the reigning world champion in the 100-meters, and she finished second in that event in the Olympic trials. But in April, she tested positive for nikethamide, a stimulant. She blamed the positive result on a glucose supplement she had taken on the advice of her physician. She had not been feeling well, and the supplement was supposed to help. However, the supplement contained the banned drug. She fired her physician, but the damage had been done; she was given a two-year suspension. Her removal from the team opened the door for 37-year-old Gail Devers, who finished fourth at the trials, to take her place in the 100-meters.

After Greek track-and-field stars Kostas Kenteris and Katerina Thanou dropped out of competition as a result of a staged motorcycle accident that had no witnesses, Greeks began to cheer for Leonidas Sampanis, a weight lifter. He won the bronze medal but then was humiliated because of a failed drug test. He was not the only weight lifter to be expelled for drugs. Ferenc Gyurkovics from Hungary had to return his silver medal as well.

In rowing, the women's four from the Ukraine had to return their bronze medals because of doping. Other Eastern European athletes were caught doping as well. Robert Fazekas, the discus thrower from Hungary who won the gold medal, was ordered to return it after he failed a drug test. And shot-putter Irina Korzhanenko from Russia had to return her gold medal after failing a drug test.

Marion Jones, one of the fastest women in the world, was one American who was watched very closely because of her alleged association with a San Francisco–area lab known as the Bay Area Laboratory Co-Operative (BALCO). Government authorities, including the U.S. Anti-Doping Agency, believed that BALCO was providing supplements to athletes that contained banned pharmaceuticals. A serious investigation of BALCO was still going

on during the Athens Olympics, and Jones had been linked to BALCO. Although her former husband, C. J. Hunter, accused her of doping, she had always tested "clean." The USOC believed that Jones was playing by the rules (she wasn't), and she was selected to be a member of the U.S. Olympic team. She competed in the long jump and placed fifth. She also was on the 400-meter relay team but was disqualified after failing to pass the baton to teammate Lauryn Jones within the 20-meter exchange zone. As noted earlier; Jones would be convicted for doping in 2007—yet another embarrassment for the USOC.

Notables

A few days before the opening ceremonies, America's oldest Olympian, 102-year-old James Stillman Rockefeller, died. He had competed as a rower in the 1924 Paris Olympics. His teammate was fellow Yale University graduate Dr. Benjamin Spock, the world-renowned pediatrician who wrote a number of best-selling books on how to raise and nurture babies. Back then, the Yale rowers had been so dominating that the American Olympic Committee had simply sent the entire team to Paris where they beat the second-place Canadian team by 16 seconds!

By the time the Athens Olympiad was over, 10,625 athletes including 4329 women from 201 countries would compete for a medal. They were accompanied by over 5000 officials, and over 21,000 members of the media descended on Athens to cover the games. Several developments attracted special attention. One was the fact that the men's soccer team from Iraq qualified for the Olympics, the first Iraqi team to do so since 1988. Then, the day before the opening ceremonies, the underdog Iraqis defeated Portugal 4–2. They continued their winning streak for a while, eventually losing the bronze medal to Italy. The Iraqi Olympic team also featured a woman athlete, Alaa Jassim, the only woman on the team. She competed in the women's 100-meter race but did not medal. Still, it was a step forward for women's rights and women athletes in Iraq. Iraqis were proud of their soccer team's success. For a few weeks in August, there was soccer hysteria on the streets of Baghdad and in the villages of the war-ravaged country. The Olympics were a positive unifying force for a few wonderful weeks in Iraq.

The opening ceremonies were nothing less than spectacular, as was the setting for the games. The venues, clubs and restaurants, and magnificent archaeological sites dazzled fans and athletes, and the weather was perfect. One of the most memorable Olympiads of the modern era was in the making.

The host city was embarrassed when two of Greece's greatest Olympic track-and-field athletes—Kostas Kenteris, gold medal winner in the men's 200-meters, and Katerina Thanou, silver medal winner in the women's 100-meters—evaded a request by IOC officials for a drug test. IOC officials searched for them but could not find them anywhere. The two claimed they had been injured in a motorcycle accident that, after an intensive investigation, was determined to have been staged. They announced that they were too injured to compete further and dropped out of the competition. The Greeks suspected that the two athletes, who were expected to bring honor and glory to their country during the Olympics, were doping and used the alleged accident as an excuse to drop out of the competition and avoid drug testing. Both were eventually caught and convicted of doping.

In addition to Alaa Jassim from Iraq being the first woman Olympian to compete for that country, there were other "firsts" for women athletes from the Muslim world. All would compete in the 100-meter race, one of the premier events in women's track and field. Danah Al Nasrallah from Kuwait was the first woman Olympian to represent her country. Like Jassim, she competed in the 100-meters. Robina Muqimyar of Afghanistan also ran in the 100-meters, the first woman to compete from that country; her teammate, Friba Razayee, competed in judo. This would have been prohibited if the Taliban were still in power. Actually, the IOC banned Afghanistan from the Olympics in 1999 because of the Taliban's treatment of women, who essentially were forced to live as if they were

in the Dark Ages. Rakia Al Gassra from Bahrain, a devout Muslim, competed in the 100-meters wearing a headscarf, long-sleeved shirt, and long pants. None of the women from the Islamic world won an Olympic medal. However, as their country's first female Olympians, they were wonderful role models, and their pioneering efforts could pave the way for many other Muslim women athletes.

The American women's tennis team, which had dominated Olympic tennis since it returned as a medal sport during the Seoul Olympics in 1988, received bad news just hours before the team departed for Athens. Tennis great Serena Williams, sister of Venus Williams, a top-rate player herself, notified her coach and American Olympic officials that she had to pull out of the Athens Olympics because of an injured left knee. Venus Williams remained on the team and made the trip to Athens, but the American women did not medal. The men's team won one medal, a silver in singles play.

American swimming sensation Michael Phelps won a total of eight medals, including six gold, eclipsing the seven medals won by American swimmer Mark Spitz at the 1972 Munich Olympics. His chief rival, Ian Thorpe from Australia, won four medals including two gold. Natalie Coughlin of the United States led the women's swim team by winning five medals including two gold. Her rival Petria Thomas, from Australia, won four medals, three of them gold.

American gymnasts performed much better than they had in Sydney, winning nine medals. However, gymnast Paul Hamm from the United States was under constant criticism as a result of the gold medal he won because of a judging error. Yang Tae-young from South Korea was assigned a much lower difficulty level for a routine he performed in the all-around competition than he should have been. The South Koreans were outraged and appealed, but Hamm kept his medal. Later, in the horizontal bar competition, Hamm won a silver medal while Russian Alexei Nemov performed a near flawless routine but did not earn a medal. The crowd turned ugly, cheering for Nemov and booing Hamm. Once again, Hamm's medal was suspect. In October, six weeks after the closing ceremonies, the Court of Arbitration for Sport heard the case against Hamm filed by the South Korean Olympic team. The court ruled that Hamm could keep his gold medal.

In the men's 100-meter race, American sprinter Justin Gatlin won the gold medal, beating the fastest field in Olympic history. Maurice Green from the United States took the bronze. Deena Kastor from the United States won a bronze medal in the women's marathon while Meb Keflezighi from San Diego finished second in the men's marathon.

The women's soccer team from the United States, featuring the legendary Mia Hamm, won the gold medal with a dramatic overtime 2–1 victory over Brazil. The U.S. women's water polo team won the bronze with a 6–5 win over Australia; the men did not medal.

America was once again the softball power of the Olympic world. The mighty U.S. women won their third straight gold medal, outscoring their opponents 55–1! The Olympic baseball competition took place without the Americans, who failed to qualify. The U.S. women's basketball team won their third straight gold medal, beating Australia. The U.S. men's basketball team did not fare so well; the 2004 version of the Dream Team was more of a nightmare, stumbling to a bronze medal.

The U.S. men's volleyball team, an Olympic power in the 1980s, lost the bronze medal to long-time rival Russia, 3–0; Brazil beat Italy 3–1 to win the gold. In beach volleyball, the American women won two medals—Misty May and Kerri Walsh the gold, and Holly McPeak and Elaine Youngs the bronze.

In rowing, the United States won the gold medal in the men's eights while the American women won the silver in the eights. In women's gymnastics, Carly Patterson won the gold medal in the all-around competition. In the team gymnastics competition, both the American women and the American men won the silver. Finally, in the equestrian competition, the Americans faired well: The dressage team won the bronze, and in team jumping, the Americans won the silver.

According to the final tally, encompassing a total of 301 possible Olympic medals, the United States won more medals than any other country— a total of 103 (35 gold, 39 silver, and 29 bronze). Remember the Russians? They did not fare too well in the 2002 Winter Olympics, but they certainly made up for it in the 2004 Athens Olympiad, placing second in the medal count with a total of 92 (27 gold, 27 silver, and 38 bronze). China placed third with 63 medals (32 gold, 17 silver, and 14 bronze). The Greeks placed seventeenth with a total of 16 medals (6 gold, 6 silver, and 4 bronze).

On a warm August night, the 2004 Athens Olympics held closing ceremonies in the Olympic Stadium before approximately 70,000 fans. The Chinese Olympic delegation invited the world to Beijing where the 2008 Summer Olympics would be held. The Greeks had orchestrated one of the most memorable Olympics of the modern era. There were problems, to be sure, but overall, it was a smashing success!

The twenty-first century will provide many opportunities for the Olympic Movement. The IOC must make an objective assessment of its strengths and weaknesses. Among the most serious issues facing the IOC are the exorbitant costs that drown the host city in a sea of red ink. Athens, according to *The Economist* ("The World in 2005," p. 88) was saddled with mind-boggling cost overruns of $13 billion as a result of hosting the 2004 games.

At one point in time, cities bidding for the Olympics seemed resigned to the fact that they would have to incur significant debt in order to provide the type of atmosphere that the IOC demanded. The 1984 Los Angeles Olympic Games appeared to have changed this fate; it made money and hosted a spectacular Olympiad. However, this great accomplishment is in the past. Athens spent billions of dollars and will be repaying the debt for a long time to come. Beijing will spend more than Athens to host the 2008 Olympics. It is time for a change, a permanent change.

The birthplace of the Olympics is in Greece. Athens has the latest, most modern sports venues on earth. The Olympics should be permanently situated in Athens. The money that the IOC generates from "selling" the Olympic Games (television rights), combined with the dues (if this does not exist, start collecting) from the NOC's, international sports federations, and "related" organizations can be utilized to form a permanent endowment that will fund Athens as the eternal Home of the Summer Olympics. Existing venues and infrastructure can be maintained, regional and world championships can be situated in Athens that utilize the splendid facilities built for the 2004 games, and many jobs will be created to maintain the venues.

The IOC must face the fact that there are pressing social and humanitarian needs that nations, both rich and poor, must address before spending billions of dollars on an international athletic festival that lasts approximately three weeks. On the other hand, providing financial support to Athens for the purpose of keeping the Olympics in the Greek capital in perpetuity resolves this issue. The perpetual endowment and related income will assist Athens in retiring $13 billion of debt and establishing a sound financial base of which "surpluses," not debt, will be the order of the day.

Let history speak. Greece, the birthplace of the Olympics and Athens, birthplace of the Modern Olympic Games, is where the games belong. There will be no need for prospective cities bidding to host the games to engage in unsavory conduct or for less than honorable IOC members to sell their vote or allegiance to a particular city. Cities will prosper because they can spend precious monies improving their streets, educating their youth, providing food, medicine, and shelter for the less fortunate, and offering recreational and sports facilities for the populace.

THE XXTH WINTER OLYMPICS: TORINO, 2006

The Political Atmosphere

As the War on Terror entered its fourth year, America and Great Britain continued to lead the Coalition forces against Islamic terrorists and their supporters in Afghanistan and Iraq. As in wars of the past, this war escalated, this time into neighboring Pakistan.

Pakistan was governed by President Pervez Musharraf, a "friend" of the United States. He also was in charge of the Pakistani military and was often seen in public wearing his military uniform. Assassins had tried to kill him on six separate occasions. Terrorists belonging to al Qaeda were hiding in Pakistan's remote regions. Pakistani military forces would seek them out, but al Qaeda supporters would hide the terrorists and provide them with vital information on the whereabouts of the Pakistani military. Although the United States pressured Musharraf to increase the military presence in the remote tribal areas that harbored the terrorists, the outcome was always the same; some fighting, a few terrorists and Pakistanis dead but no significant victory. And all the while, more recruits were joining al Qaeda and receiving training in these lawless regions.

President Musharraf resisted pressure from the United States, who wanted to send its troops into Pakistan to do what it believed the Pakistanis couldn't or wouldn't do: destroy the leadership of al Qaeda, which was hiding in Pakistan. In January of 2006, American intelligence was certain that it had located al Qaeda's second in command, Aymam Al-Zawahiri, and fugitive Taliban leader Mullah Mohammed Omar.

Al-Zawahiri was born in Egypt and is a physician. He was jailed by Egyptian authorities for his efforts to overthrow the secular Egyptian government by violence. In response, Al-Zawahiri founded the Egyptian Islamic Jihad, which was dedicated to imposing radical Islamic rule in Muslim countries everywhere. In 1998 Al-Zawahiri was indicted in the United States for his alleged role in the August 7, 1998, bombings of American embassies in Dar es Salaam, Tanzania, and Kenya. Shortly after the bombings, Al-Zawahiri's Egyptian Islamic Jihad merged with al Qaeda, led by Osama bin Laden. The Federal Bureau of Investigation (FBI) offered a reward of $25 million for his capture or information leading to his conviction. Al-Zawahiri is clearly a wanted man.

Mullah Omar and bin Laden were resistance fighters against the Soviets when they invaded Afghanistan. They became close friends. The Taliban hid bin Laden and other al Qaeda leaders from the Coalition forces. Like Al-Zawahiri, Omar was a marked man.

Al-Zawahiri and Omar were supposed to be in a house located in the Bajur tribal area of Pakistan, long known as a safe haven for terrorists. The American military had no intention of asking Musharraf for permission to capture or kill these two terrorists. The Americans wanted Al-Zawahiri and Omar so much that every effort was made to capture or kill them; this effort would turn into a political crisis because the Americans did not notify their Pakistani counterparts that they were going to launch an attack inside Pakistan.

An unmarked Predator drone was launched and once inside Pakistan, searched and tracked what the Americans believed to be the two terrorists and their collaborators. Six missiles were fired at the house and surrounding area, killing at least 18 people. Pakistan was appalled by the American military strike, especially since most of the dead were women and children. To make matters worse, Al-Zawahiri and Omar were not among the dead. The Bajur region of Pakistan was already a radical Islamic stronghold. The attack only served to create more al Qaeda supporters and more hatred for America.

Close by, another radical Islamic nation was busy learning how to enrich uranium, allegedly to make nuclear bombs. Iran is led by President Mahmoud Ahmadinejad. He supports the terrorists in Iraq and Afghanistan. Western powers fear that the Iranians are "a loose cannon" and their possession of nuclear bombs and warheads could lead to yet another war in the Middle East. These fears may be well founded. Since Ahmadinejad came to power, he has called for the destruction of Israel and expressed doubts that the Holocaust happened. Iran is very worried that the United States and its allies might attack Iran, especially since Iran supplies terrorists with weapons, money, and supplies that kill Americans and Coalition forces in Afghanistan and Iraq. In addition, Israel is the only democracy in that part of the world and a close friend of the United States. In June 2005, Ahmadinejad opined that Israel should be wiped off the map.

The Cold War was over, but a new war—the War on Terror—would take its place. Instead of the Soviet Union and its Eastern European and Southeast Asian allies threatening the freedom and security of the West, radical Islamic countries and their supporters wage war against the West. Although the Cold War was brutal and costly, the War on Terror has spilled over to other countries. The entire world has taken notice that the risks have significantly increased and the war seems far from over.

In the United States, President Bush invoked emergency powers that authorized the Department of Justice and other law enforcement agencies to monitor phone calls and e-mails of Americans and foreigners living here and abroad who were suspected of involvement in terrorist activities. No warrant is necessary. President Bush defended this policy by saying it was needed to protect the nation from further terrorist attacks and for reasons of national security. At the other end of the issue was what many perceived to be the erosion

OLYMPIC SNAPSHOT

2006 Turin Winter Olympics:

Opening Day February 10; Closing Day February 26

- 80 countries sent teams
- 2508 athletes: 960 women and 1548 men
- 8 sports, 84 events: Biathlon, Bobsleigh, Curling, Men's and Women's Ice Hockey, Luge, Skating, Skiing, and Snowboarding
- 18,000 volunteers and 2688 media/press credentials issued

or outright attack on civil liberties; what evidence exists that only terrorists and their supporters are monitored/spied on by the government?

If you were president, would you enact the same domestic policy that permits the government to eavesdrop on phone and e-mail communications in the hope of preventing more attacks?

Notables

For the second time in Winter Olympics history, an Italian city was selected to host the games. Torino (*Turin* in English), is a large city of one million inhabitants nestled in the foothills of the Alps. The nearby ski resorts of Sestriere provided a magnificent setting for the alpine events. It was the largest and grandest Winter Olympics ever staged.

Once again, NBC broadcast 17 nights of tape-delayed coverage to American fans. Apparently the powers at NBC had not learned anything from the Sydney Olympiad. The television ratings of the Torino Winter Olympics were the worst in 38 years. Will NBC ever learn?

Germany took home the most gold medals, a total of 11. The United States was a close second and tied with Austria, each country winning nine gold medals. The Canadian team won seven gold medals while the Italian athletes won five.

What about the Russians? They were right behind the Americans and Austrians with seven gold medals. Estonia, a tiny but proud Baltic country that was under Soviet rule for many years before gaining its freedom, won three gold medals.

American skier Bode Miller was expected to medal in every race he competed in. The overrated Miller did not win one medal; he was disqualified and failed to finish some of his races and in others, he simply was not competitive. Snowboarding is a popular event, and no Olympian at Torino drew a bigger crowd than Shaun White, a 20-year-old from San Diego. Called the "Flying Tomato" because of his long red tresses, White became a crowd favorite with his engaging smile and outgoing personality. He won the gold medal in the half-pipe.

South Korea ruled short-track speed skating, winning ten of the possible 24 medals in this event. Sun-Yu Jin won three gold medals in women's speed skating while her male teammate, Hyun-soo Ahn, won three gold and one bronze. Canadian Cindy Klassen won five medals in the speed skating events: one gold, two silver, and two bronze.

In women's ice hockey, Canada won the gold medal, and in men's ice hockey, Sweden won the gold. A wonderful example of the spirit of the Olympics took place during the cross-country skiing competition. Sara Renner of Canada broke her pole. Close by, Norwegian cross-country coach Bjornar Hakensmoen saw what had happened and quickly came to her assistance. He handed Sara his pole, which was longer than her own pole but worked well enough to enable Renner and her Canadian team to win the silver medal. What must be known is that at the time Renner broke her pole, the Norwegian team was in a position to medal as long as Renner remained sidelined with a broken pole. When Coach Hakensmoen gave his pole to Renner so she could continue racing, it effectively ended the chance for the Norwegian team to medal. Hakensmoen's selfless act was the epitome of sportsmanship and a great example of what can happen in the Olympic Games. Would you have done the same thing?

The Austrian team was in the headlines because the police raided their headquarters. Italian authorities had reason to believe that Austrian coaches and athletes were involved in doping. Several athletes and a coach ran from the police and attempted to evade capture. The remaining athletes were tested for drugs and other banned substances and were declared eligible to compete.

Another notable story was the case of British Olympian Shelly Rudman. The 24-year-old competitor took up the skeleton after watching the 2002 Salt Lake Winter Olympics. She was a longshot to medal in the skeleton in Torino. She needed about $8,000 to buy a proper sled to compete with. In her hometown of Pewsey, the residents stepped up and raised the money. Rudman won the silver medal!

THE XXIX OLYMPIAD: BEIJING, 2008

Members of the IOC met on July 13, 2001, to select the host city for the 2008 Olympiad. Cities up for a vote were Istanbul, Osaka, Paris, Toronto, and Beijing. After two rounds of voting, Beijing was declared the winner. It would be the first Olympics held in the People's Republic of China and the second time the games were held in a Communist country, with Moscow having been the first in 1980.

The People's Republic of China (PRC) was established in 1949 after a fierce civil war that pitted the Communist guerillas led by Mao Tse-tung against the democratic forces of Nationalist China led by Chiang Kai-shek. The Communists emerged victorious, Chiang Kai-shek's remaining supporters fled to the island of Taiwan where they established the Republic of China (ROC). For the past six decades the Beijing government has continued to look upon Taiwan as part of the PRC, but the citizens of the ROC don't see it that way and tensions remain high to this day. At times, the real possibility of war between the two has set the world on edge, because the United States has vowed to defend the ROC.

Since Nationalist China cannot claim the name China, which belongs to the PRC, the ROC goes by Chinese Taipei when competing in the Olympics. Needless to say, there is a fierce rivalry between the two whenever their athletes are matched up in competition.

China is an economic powerhouse, one of the Asian Tigers. The opportunity to host the Olympics provided China with an unprecedented opportunity to showcase Beijing and the great economic progress it has made in the last 20 years. Although still ruled by the Communist Party, China has embraced economic reforms and monetary policies that would make Mao Tse-tung, Karl Marx, and Vladimir Lenin turn over in their respective mausoleums. There is a thriving stock market, and Chinese products have flooded Western countries. American companies are doing a brisk business in China, something that would have been unthinkable 20 years ago. Another noteworthy fact is that the Chinese government owns billions of dollars' worth of United States Treasury notes. There is frequent talk of what would happen to the American economy if China ever decided to "cash in" all or most of the notes they own. The Chinese exercise considerable leverage over the American economy. The economic climate in China has certainly changed for the better, but the same can't be said for their social policies.

Human Rights and Social Justice Concerns

The Chinese government still controls the media, and freedom of expression is very limited. Chinese authorities promised the IOC that unfettered media access would be available to the world press during the Olympics. Sadly, this promise was not kept. Public protests by Chinese citizens were also on the agenda of the IOC when it awarded Beijing the games. The Chinese government assured the IOC that designated places would be available for Chinese to demonstrate after the authorities approved the application that had to be filed by the would-be protesters. The IOC was buoyed by this decision, hoping it would be the catalyst for freedom of speech to take hold in China. Unfortunately, it became clear that the Chinese authorities had never intended to deliver on this promise.

The authorities may have feared another massive protest like the one in Tiananmen Square in 1989 where thousands of students and other civilians seeking democratic reforms gathered to air their grievances and make known their demands. The media was able to get this story out to the rest of the world, so for a while the Chinese military and police stayed in the shadows and let the protesters protest. But then on June 4, the brutal regime in Beijing ordered the military and police to crush the protesters, and the tanks and soldiers rolled into the huge square. By the time the bloodshed was over, upwards of 3000 civilian protesters were dead or injured. The democratic nations of the world were appalled and issued one condemnation after another directed at the Chinese government.

In 2008, Chinese authorities identified places in Beijing where those who wanted to protest or carry out peaceful demonstrations during the Olympics could assemble. Individuals or groups who wanted to protest were required to complete an application form that detailed the number of people involved and the nature of the demonstration. Although 77 applications were submitted by 149 people, not a single one was approved!

In the People's Republic of China, citizens can be detained indefinitely in prison, and there is no opportunity to appeal once a death sentence has been ordered by the courts. Execution is carried out immediately after the sentence, and it is not unusual for the vital organs to be stripped from the body and sold. To make matters more unsettling, the family of the deceased is usually charged for the bullet that is used to execute the criminal. Punishment is harsh and swift, and Chinese citizens are routinely spied on by the authorities. Human rights violations are a major concern of Western nations and also by groups who opposed Beijing as the host city of the 2008 Olympiad. To this day, many fans of the Olympic Games and the spirit of the Olympic ideal remain flummoxed by the IOC's decision to award Beijing the Olympic Games 12 years after the government of the People's Republic of China had ruthlessly crushed the dawn of democracy that was unfolding in Tiananmen Square in 1989. Tibet, a nation that China invaded in 1950 and still occupies, was another issue that would come to the fore during the run up to the Beijing Olympiad.

Politics and War

Prior to the opening ceremonies on August 8, there was plenty of tension and concern by the IOC and the Chinese authorities about "disruptions" to the games. The geopolitical situation in 2008 was as tense as it had been in 2004 prior to the Athens Olympiad—in fact, many parts of the world had actually become more dangerous than they had been in 2004.

OLYMPIC SNAPSHOT

2008 Beijing Olympiad:

Opening Day August 8; Closing Day August 24

- 204 countries sent teams—an Olympic record! 11,196 athletes: 4746 (42%) women and 6450 men.
- 35 sports—302 events: Aquatics, Archery, Athletics (Track and Field), Badminton, Baseball, Basketball, Boxing, Canoe/Kayak, Cycling, Equestrian, Fencing, Soccer, Gymnastics, Handball, Field Hockey, Judo, Modern Pentathlon, Rowing, Sailing, Shooting, Softball, Table Tennis, Tae kwon do, Tennis, Triathlon, Volleyball, Weight Lifting and Men's & Women's Wrestling.
- Baseball and Softball made their last Olympic appearance at the Beijing Olympiad. The IOC had voted earlier to eliminate these two sports from the Olympic Program after Beijing. Natalie du Toit of South Africa made Olympic history by becoming the first Paralympian to compete. An amputated leg did not stop her from finishing 16th in the Rough Water Swim, a new event on the program.
- By the close of the games on August 24, 132 new Olympic records were set and 43 world records had been broken. American swimmer Michael Phelps became the most decorated athlete in Olympic history by winning eight gold medals in Beijing. A record 87 countries won Olympic medals. Afghanistan, Mauritius, Tajikistan, and Togo won their first Olympic medals ever. The hometown Chinese athletes won 51 gold medals. The Americans were a distant second with 36 gold. Estimates are that upward of one million volunteers worked to make the Beijing Olympics the best ever. Four athletes were caught doping and 40 were caught before the games started.

The "War on Terror" that was largely confined to Iraq and Afghanistan continued unabated, with no end in sight. Thousands of innocent bystanders had died or been injured while they were shopping in a market, praying in a mosque, or sitting in their homes. Car bombs were a daily and deadly occurrence. The Taliban had become bolder in its attacks against the Coalition Forces that were led by the American military. Suicide bombers identified targets of opportunity in both countries as well as Pakistan where President Musharraf governed and supported the United States in the War on Terror. Having survived six assassination attempts, Musharraf resigned from the presidency during the Beijing Olympics. Most of Pakistan was elated when Musharraf announced his resignation. The majority of Pakistanis wanted to see the American military leave their country. A number of "mistakes" had been made by the military, leading to the destruction of homes and the deaths of civilians as American bombs went off target. Needless to say, Pakistan—a nuclear power—wanted the American military out of the country. With Musharraf gone, this was more likely to happen.

From 2003 to 2008 more than 3000 American military personnel had been killed and many more had been injured in the Middle East conflict. Other nations that had joined the Coalition also suffered heavy losses. The toll of civilian casualties, those people who are virtually "caught in the middle" between Coalition assaults and terrorist bombings, exceeded 100,000 killed or injured.

Al Qaeda and its allies were merciless in their quest for victory and imposition of Islamic rule in the Middle East and beyond. Would terrorists wreak havoc on the 2008 Beijing Olympics, as had occurred during the 1972 Munich Olympiad? This was a concern not only for the IOC and the Chinese authorities but also for the 204 countries who sent Olympic athletes to compete and for spectators around the world.

The Invasion of Tibet

The PRC has a history of harsh treatment of its citizens and those of nearby countries. The former Soviet Union and the PRC, although both Communist nations, did not get along and there were

a number of border disputes between the two. China also shares a border with India, and the two have had their share of disputes. Perhaps the most publicly recognizable transgression by the Chinese was the invasion of Tibet in 1950 by the People's Liberation Army. To this day, China occupies Tibet, which it claims is part of China. As you might imagine, the Tibetans don't see it this way and violent protests by the Tibetans over the years have left many dead and others injured. The Dalai Lama fled Tibet and has engendered support and goodwill around the world, all directed at the goal of a Free Tibet.

In March of 2008, hundreds of Tibetan monks and ordinary people attacked the Chinese police after the Chinese authorities demanded that the monks refute their spiritual leader, the Dalai Lama, and agree to participate in a Patriotic Education Program which had as its focal point the denouncement of the Dalai Lama once and for all. This demand did not sit well in a country where the Chinese had brutally subdued the population for more than half a century. There were several large anti-Chinese demonstrations throughout Tibet during March, and thanks to media outlets made available by the Internet and cell phones inside Tibet, the world watched as the Chinese once again cracked down on protests led by "political dissidents." The Chinese claimed that the Dalai Lama was behind the protests. Would the crisis in Tibet disrupt the Olympics? Unfortunately, it did.

Olympic Politics

The American press demanded that President Bush stay home and not attend the Beijing Olympiad in a symbolic protest of the Chinese repression in Tibet, but President Bush was in Beijing for the opening ceremonies. Several other world leaders said they would consider not attending the opening ceremonies as a form of protest against China's actions.

The Olympic Torch Relay is an event that most people look forward to seeing, especially if the torch passes through their city. Anti-China protesters and Free Tibet protesters showed up by the thousands throughout London and Paris and tried to disrupt the torch run. Security was high. In Paris, the torch runners were pelted with plastic bottles, rocks, and other objects. One protester attacked the runner with a fire extinguisher and tried to snuff out the flame. The protester was not able to snuff out the flame, but the French police did. They quickly recognized that the trouble was escalating so they wisely put the torch, sans flame, aboard the accompanying vehicle and cancelled the final leg of the torch relay.

San Francisco was the only scheduled stop for the torch in the United States. It is home to thousand of Chinese and because of this, was thought to be a relatively safe city in which to parade the torch. In retrospect, you have to wonder what the torch organizers were thinking when they made this decision. Arguably the most liberal city in America and minutes across the bay from Berkeley, the politics and attendant social justice views of this metropolitan area are decidedly liberal. As the torch entered the city, thousands of people who support democratic institutions and human rights in China showed up to protest along with groups who held up Tibetan flags and banners that proclaimed "Free Tibet." Others protested China's involvement in the Sudan where it supported a regime that had committed unspeakable atrocities including genocide. China also supported the brutal government in Myanmar that was created when a group of military staged a coup and like the Chinese, instituted a harsh and brutal crackdown against anybody or any group that was perceived as a threat to the new order.

San Francisco Mayor Gavin Newsom had closely watched how the authorities in London and Paris had planned for every possible problem. Several routes were identified and the flame made several sudden route alterations that left some of the fans and protesters disappointed. For example, the original route that the public expected was about six miles long. Less than 30 minutes before the torch relay began, the route was scaled down to about three miles due to security concerns. It must be said that although protesters and demonstrators

showed up in force, so did thousands of fans of the Olympic Games.

Zimbabwe is a nation in Africa that has been ruled by Robert Mugabe for decades. He and his cronies cling to power by eliminating any opposition that is a threat to his rule. In 2007, elections were held in Zimbabwe and this time the opposition won. However, Mugabe refused to step down and at first declared the election null and void. Protests and demonstrations soon become violent and Mugabe and his thugs crushed the supporters of the newly elected government. The global community was outraged, and this time their anger and disgust with Mugabe and his corrupt regime resulted in drastic actions. Observers were sent to Zimbabwe along with politicians to arrange a power-sharing agreement.

Mugabe decided that it would be in his and Zimbabwe's best interests to attend the Beijing Olympics. Zimbabwe's medal hopes rested in swimmer Kristy Coventry, who swims for Zimbabwe but lives in Austin, Texas, where she trains. In college, she competed for Auburn University and was a significant factor in Auburn winning several national championships. Mugabe was likely looking forward to watching Coventry swim and also gathering support for his failing regime since many of the world's leading politicians were attending the games. There was one insurmountable problem for Mugabe: the IOC notified him that he was not welcome in China. To add insult to injury, Beijing officials also told him that he was not welcome. Perhaps hard of hearing or confused, Mugabe traveled to Hong Kong and intended to continue traveling to Beijing. Chinese officials were waiting for him and immediately sent him back to Zimbabwe. Kristy Coventry did not disappoint. She won three silver medals and one gold medal in Beijing. For a country that had little to cheer about, her Olympic success put beaming smiles on the people of Zimbabwe.

As if the Iraqis hadn't suffered enough by enduring years of war and daily attacks by suicide bombers, two weeks before the opening ceremonies the IOC along with Beijing officials sent a letter notifying the Iraqi Olympic Committee in Baghdad that their Olympic Team was banned from competition. The problem had begun in June of 2008 when the Iraqi government decided it did not like the existing Olympic Committee and replaced the members with its own appointees. The IOC was outraged and told the government in Baghdad that they did not have the authority to do this. When all seemed lost, a few days before the opening ceremonies a deal was reached and Iraq was allowed to send their Olympic athletes to compete. These courageous athletes had trained for years, sometimes amid the din of gunfire and explosions, to compete in the Olympic Games.

Afghanistan had little to cheer about in the days preceding the Olympics. Soviets invaded the country in 1979 to support the communist government in power at that time. In 1989, the Soviets pulled out after suffering heavy losses, only to be immediately replaced by the Taliban who imposed harsh Islamic law and killed thousands who did not comply with their beliefs. In the wake of the September 11, 2001, attacks on the United States, Afghanistan was attacked by the United States and its Coalition partners in the War on Terror, meant in part to destroy the Taliban. This outcome had yet to happen, so when Rohullah Nikpai won the country's first Olympic medal in history, a bronze in the tae kwon do competition, the people cheered. For a few hours, Olympic success buoyed a nation that, like Iraq, had had little reason to cheer.

A student group based in New York traveled to Beijing to protest. As a result, eight students who were members of Students for a Free Tibet were detained by the authorities, sentenced to ten days in jail and then on the day of the closing ceremonies, were deported. In addition to the American students, protesters from England and Germany were rounded up and deported as well.

Two elderly Chinese women were cast in the media spotlight when it was learned that they were sentenced to a year of "reeducation" through labor after they made five visits to the local police station to inquire about the status of their protest application. The women were 77 and 79 years old

(Chicago Tribune and *San Diego Union Tribune,* August 24, 2008, p. F2).

The Cold War Returns

Just when it seemed the political situation could not get any worse, on August 8, the day of the opening ceremonies, Russia invaded Georgia, a country that had been part of the former Soviet Union and was governed by a lawyer, Mikheil Saakashvili, who had been educated in the United States. Georgia is pro-West, shares a border with Russia, and is closely aligned with the United States. On Thursday, August 7, just 24 hours before the opening ceremonies, Georgian military units launched an offensive against rebels in South Ossetia, which is part of Georgia. The rebels living in South Ossetia sought unification with North Ossetia, which is just across the border in Russia. So, with encouragement from Moscow, these rebels decided that it was a good time to break away from Georgia and be "annexed" into Russia. A few hours after the Georgian military rolled into South Ossetia to wrest control from the pro-Russian rebels, the Russian military, complete with tanks, ground troops, and air power, invaded Georgia during the Opening Ceremonies of the Olympics. So much for the Olympic Truce. The Russians crushed the Georgian military in a few days. The capital of South Ossetia, Tskhinvali, was destroyed and many civilians perished in the conflict.

To many observers, it seemed as if the Cold War had returned with a vengeance. The Russian bear has awakened from its long hibernation and appeared very hungry for territory and the raw materials it needed to once again become a feared Superpower. Relations between Washington and Moscow once again became tense even as former Russian President Vladimir Putin (prime minister at the time) and President Bush were attending the Olympic Games. Fortunately, the athletes from Russia and Georgia got along just fine during this crisis. The same can't be said for the politicians from Georgia and Russia.

Although the Russians gave assurances of withdrawing their military from Georgia, by the time the closing ceremonies took place on August 24 in Beijing, Russian forces were still occupying parts of Georgia. Poland, Ukraine, and other former Soviet Republics such as the Baltic nations of Latvia, Estonia, and Lithuania once again became fearful of Russian expansion and saber rattling. The day after Russia invaded Georgia, the Polish government eagerly signed a missile defense agreement with the United States that had been stalled for months. Part of this agreement permitted the United States to have a military presence in Poland.

The $41-Billion Olympics

The Chinese spared no expense to make the 2008 Olympics the most lavish in history. At least $41-Billion was spent to ensure that the venues and all services required to host the Olympics were first-class. The newly constructed venues were equipped with the latest technology. Architecturally the venues reflect the cultural heritage of China as well as the most modern and amazing facilities that have ever been built for athletic competition. The main stadium, known as the Bird's Nest because of its appearance, was magnificent, as was the swimming pool where American Michael Phelps won eight gold medals and became the most decorated Olympian in the history of the modern games. A record 11,196 athletes competed, and every moment was recorded and broadcast by the about 20,000 accredited media and press in attendance.

Several new sports were included: BMX bike competition, Men's and Women's Marathon Swimming, and the Women's 3000-meter steeplechase. Sadly, doping scandals did occur and athletes were stripped of their medals. In an athletic sense, the Beijing Olympics were the best ever, but from a philosophical/ethical perspective, Beijing was not the right choice—or was it?

Notables

With testing conducted by the most sophisticated pharmaceutical labs available, only four athletes were caught using drugs. However, there could be more "positive tests" long after the closing ceremony. Blood from every medal winner is kept for years, and many of the incredible performances that shattered Olympic records and world records could be revised when new ways to identify illegal drugs and other banned substances are discovered.

As noted earlier in this section, American swimming sensation Michael Phelps was the star of the Beijing Olympics. He won eight gold medals in Beijing. The previous best was by Mark Spitz, another American swimmer, who won seven at the 1972 Munich Olympiad. Another American swimmer, 41-year-old Dara Torres, also made history. Swimming in her fifth Olympic Games she won three silver medals in Beijing to tie her with American Jenny Thompson, each with 12 Olympic medals in swimming. Torres is also a mom and is the oldest Olympic swimmer in history to win medals.

Olympic history was made when Natalie du Toit from South Africa competed in the inaugural Rough Water Swim event. She has one leg. Before the Beijing Olympics she had competed successfully in the Paralympic Games as a swimmer. The Paralympic competitions feature athletes with physical disabilities and are held a few days after the closing ceremonies. Paralympic athletes, many who are in wheelchairs and missing an arm or leg, display incredible courage and emotion during competition. They use the same venues although their events are modified to accommodate their disability. Natalie du Toit finished sixteenth, beating a number of swimmers who were not disabled.

The Olympic athletes from Jamaica were unbeatable in the sprints. The fastest man in the world, Usain Bolt, was incredible! He won the 100-meter sprint in 9.69 seconds and set a new world record. Later, he ran the 200-meter sprint in 19.30 seconds and once again set a new world record. Not content with two gold medals and two world records, he ran on the Jamaican men's 4 × 100 relay which they won in 37.10, setting yet another new world record. The Jamaicans won a total of 11 Olympic medals, all in track and field. Veronica Campbell-Brown

Figure 17-2
The American men, led by Michael Phelps, dominated the swimming competition in Beijing. (L-R) Michael Phelps, Garrett Weber-Gale, Cullen Jones, and Jason Lezak hold up their gold medals after they won the 4 × 100 freestyle with a world record time of 3:08:24.

won, for the second time, the women's 200-meter sprint. She had first won the event in Athens during the 2004 Athens Olympiad. In short, the Jamaican athletes were phenomenal.

There were a number of athletes who, although not born in the country they competed for, were able to obtain citizenship and to compete as Olympic athletes. Case in point: the two female athletes who represented Georgia in beach volleyball were from Brazil. They couldn't speak Georgian, but it didn't matter. A female American basketball player from South Dakota played for the Russians. She had Russian citizenship as of 2007 but said she thought of herself as 100 percent American.

The American men's basketball team, nicknamed the "Redeem Team" for their quest to avenge their loss of the gold medal at the 2004 Athens Olympics, lived up to form and beat Spain 118 to 107 for the gold.

On a tragic note, the father-in-law of head coach Hugh McCutcheon of the United States men's indoor volleyball team was stabbed to death in Beijing. Todd Bachman and his wife Barbara were attacked by a knife-wielding assailant while touring the Drum Tower in Beijing. Todd died at the scene and Barbara was stabbed repeatedly. Their daughter, Elisabeth Bachman McCutcheon, who is the coach's wife and played volleyball in the 2004 Athens Olympics, was with them at the time. Fortunately she was not injured. The assailant leaped to his death after the attack. Coach McCutcheon left Beijing to help care for his mother-in-law who, after eight hours of surgery by a skilled Chinese physician, returned home to America to recover.

Coach McCutcheon later returned to Beijing where he coached the men to a thrilling victory over Brazil to win the gold medal. It was the same scenario that had taken place during the 1984 Los Angeles Olympics: an underdog American team facing perennial power Brazil for the gold. Nobody gave the Americans much of a chance. But in a stunning upset, the Americans coached by Doug Beal beat the mighty team from Brazil for the gold. The American women's volleyball team settled for a silver, losing the gold medal match to—who else?—Brazil!

Softball and baseball made their appearance for the last time in Beijing. The American women had pretty much owned the Olympic softball tournament. They had always won the gold and were expected to do so once again, especially this time—the last time. However, it was not to be. They settled for silver after losing to Japan 3–1. America's pastime, baseball, was also on the way out of the Olympic program. The Americans sat in the stands and watched South Korea beat Cuba 3–2 to win the gold. The United States had earlier defeated Japan 8–4 and captured the bronze medal.

The United States women's basketball team, led by Lisa Leslie, won another gold medal when the Americans routed the Australians 92–65. It was Leslie's fourth gold medal as an Olympic basketball player.

China, to nobody's surprise, won all six individual table tennis medals. There were two shocking moments. The first one was when Ara Abrahamian, a Greco-Roman wrestler from Sweden, removed his bronze medal at the medal ceremony and simply dropped it on the mat and walked away. He was protesting a decision by the referee that lowered his score. The IOC soon made a decision to strip him of the bronze medal and toss him out of the Olympic Village. The other shock was far more serious. The tae kwon do athlete from Cuba, Angel Valodia Matos, was disqualified in his match. He turned and seriously injured the referee who had disqualified him by kicking him in the head with his foot. The IOC banned him for life. Fortunately, the referee recovered.

Estonia's Gerd Kanter, who trained at the U.S. Olympic Training Center just south of San Diego, won the gold medal in the discus. The inaugural BMX competition was very popular. Maris Stromberg from Latvia won the gold medal and in the women's BMX, Anne-Caroline Chausson from France captured the gold. The Chinese women once again excelled in gymnastics. However, there were questions about the age of some of them.

Sixteen years is the minimum age to compete in Olympic gymnastics, but several of the Chinese athletes appeared to be much younger. An investigation was started, but no falsification was discovered.

NBC Coverage

Television coverage of the Beijing Olympics was better than it had been in Athens. Internet access enabled fans to see all of the events that were covered live. NBC did broadcast some of the events live, but many were delayed due to the time difference. Viewers during the first few days of the games saw lots of empty seats in lesser sport venues. Vacant seats are not good for the guardians of the Olympic flame, so thousands of eager Chinese were recruited to fill the empty seats. Beach volleyball must have been really important for NBC to promote. It would not be surprising to learn that NBC devoted more coverage to American beach volleyball players Misty May-Treanor and her partner Kerri Walsh playing in their bikinis than they did Michael Phelps. But then again, it's all about what will attract the most viewers, e.g., ratings. NBC had paid $894 million for exclusive broadcast rights. They more than recovered their investment from advertising revenues, and viewer ratings were the best in recent history.

Epilogue

The Beijing Olympics were, from an organizational and logistical standpoint, the best ever. Security was extraordinary. There were no terrorist attacks or major disruptions. The crowds were well behaved and the volunteers (some estimates put this figure at one million) were 100 percent invested in the success of the Olympics.

In the overall medal count, the United States garnered the most: 110 medals, 36 of which were gold. Close behind was China with 100 medals, including 51 gold! Russia was third with 72 medals, 23 of which were gold, and Great Britain finished a surprising fourth, winning 47 medals,

19 of them gold. Conventional thinking predicts China as the next sports superpower.

An American athlete who wins a gold medal is given $25,000 by the United States Olympic Committee. A silver medal is worth $15,000, and a bronze medal is worth $10,000. China pays much more. A gold medal is worth $150,000. The athlete from Afghanistan who won the bronze medal in tae kwon do, Rohullah Nikpai, received a new house, a new Toyota, and $20,000. (The *San Diego Union Tribune*, Monday, August 25, 2008, p. D6)

In 2012 London hosted the Olympic games for the third time. In 2014, Sochi, Russia will host the winter Olympics.

THE XXI WINTER OLYMPICS: VANCOUVER, 2010

The Political Atmosphere

Global politics and domestic issues in the year leading up to the Vancouver Winter Olympics (2009) were intense. The War on Terror intensified while in the United States history was made as American's elected Barack Obama, an African-American, as the nation's President. Obama's campaign featured social media and extensive

OLYMPIC SNAPSHOT

2010 Vancouver Winter Olympics:

Opening Day February 12; Closing Day February 28

- 82 countries sent teams
- 2566 athletes: 1044 women and 1522 men
- 7 sports - 86 events: Alpine Skiing, Biathlon, Bobsleigh, Cross Country Skiing, Curling, Figure Skating, Freestyle Skiing, Ice Hockey, Luge, Nordic
- Combined, Short Track Speed Skating, Skeleton, Ski Jumping, Snowboarding, and Speed Skating.
- 3 billion television viewers worldwide
- 18,500 volunteers, 9800 media credentials issued to 7000 broadcasters and 2800 written press.

Internet campaigns which appealed to young and old. The Obama & Biden ticket defeated Senator John McCain and Alaska Governor Sara Palin who ran for president and vice president respectively on the Republican ticket. President Obama became heir to the War on Terror and an economic crisis that rivaled the Great Depression.

President Obama appointed Hilary Rodham Clinton as Secretary of State. The wife of former President Bill Clinton, she waged a strong campaign to become the candidate the Democratic Party selected to run for President. The Democrats picked Barack Obama.

There were other historic political achievements on both the domestic front and in the international arena. Iceland elected Johanna Siguradardottir as their prime minister, the first time a woman has held this leadership position, while the Republican party elected Michael Steele, an African-American, as their Chairman. For the first time in 341 years, the United Kingdom appoints a woman, Carol Ann Duffy, as poet laureate.

North Korea convicts two American journalists for illegal entry and sentences them to 12 years in a labor prison camp. Former President Bill Clinton travels to North Korea and persuades the government to release Euna Lee and Laura Ling.

President Obama reduced the presence of the American military in Iraq; however, many of these same soldiers were sent to Afghanistan where the American military presence was increased. Suicide bombers and intense fighting were daily occurrences and resulted in horrific casualties and suffering.

The never-ending war between Israel and Palestinian terrorists led by Hamas continued unabated. In January Israeli troops crossed the border into Gaza, the stronghold of Hamas, and launched a "short war" against Hamas. Two weeks later, Israel announces a unilateral cease fire. Hamas will not stop fighting unless Israel leaves Gaza. A few days later, Israel and Hamas agree to a cease fire, for the time being.

In March, 12 assassins attacked the Sri Lanka national cricket team while the team was playing in Pakistan. The team was guarded by a police escort so everybody involved knew that there was a serious risk of attack by rebels. Six policemen were killed along with two people who happened to be in the wrong place at the wrong time.

Sudan, especially the Darfur area, was still embroiled in war. The International Criminal Court issues an arrest warrant for the President of Sudan, Omar Hassan Ahmad al Bashir charging him with crimes against humanity in the Darfur region where he ordered the massacre of anyone who opposed his rule.

Iranian President Mahmoud Ahmadinejad wins a second term amid widespread election fraud and vows to "wipe Israel off the map." He steps up Iran's nuclear research and development program which he insists is for peaceful purposes. Israel, the United States, and other nations don't believe him and impose more economic and political sanctions in the hope that Iran will stop its nuclear development.

As December 31, 2009, came to an end, much of the world waited in anticipation for the XXI Winter Olympic Games to begin. It would provide the international television audience with a brief respite from the endless wars and economic devastation that had defined 2009.

Notables

This was the third time that Canada was the home nation for the Olympic Games. The first time was in 1976 when Montreal was host city to the Summer Olympics. The second time was in [a year] when Calgary was host city for the Winter Olympics. Competition venues were located in the Vancouver metropolitan area and at the ski resort of Whistler Blackcomb.

The IOC awarded the 2010 Winter Olympics to Vancouver in 2003. Security was a priority and the legendary Royal Canadian Mounted Police took the lead to ensure the peace at a cost of one billion Canadian dollars, five times more than the original estimate.

In addition to the typical coins and stamps that serve as revenue generators and commemorative souvenirs, two video games were produced

and sold to eager fans who stood in long lines to buy them. Social media was a huge presence as athletes and fans posted their thoughts and action-packed video clips almost as fast as the television networks did.

Protests have become part of the Olympics and Vancouver was not spared. Before the opening ceremonies, Vancouver organized pre-Olympic festivals to generate excitement and enthusiasm. This plan was sabotaged in part by a week long counter Olympic demonstration called the Anti Olympic Convergence. On February 13, protesters smashed the windows of the Bay Department Store, which is the modem symbol of the Hudson Bay Company that explored and exploited North America several hundred years ago. In the Bay Department Store, protesters saw the colonial past of the Hudson Bay Company, which was a symbol of colonial oppression as well as a proud sponsor of the Vancouver Winter Olympics.

Low-income housing was promised but did not happen, which angered a lot of people and led to more protests. To complicate matters, protesters had reason to believe that forced human trafficking for purposes of prostitution would take place and so, they protested.

The budget for the Winter Olympics was in line with projections but still cost $1.84 billion dollars (US) This money was provided by the Canadian government and through marketing efforts. As Winter Olympics go, the Canadians were very frugal and careful. The final accounting made in December of 2010 showed that a surplus (profit) was not made and a deficit was not on the books. They broke even!

Before the competition began, Nodar Kumaritashvili who represented Georgia in the Luge was killed during a training run. Women ski jumpers had petitioned the IOC asking that women's ski jumping be added to the Olympic program. The IOC turned them down so they took their case to the Supreme Court of British Columbia who also denied their request. Undaunted, the women appealed to the Canadian Supreme Court who simply decided not to hear the appeal at all. Perhaps women's ski jumping

will be on the program during the next Winter Olympics in Sochi, Russia in 2014.

For the first time in Olympic history, ice hockey was played on a regulation National Hockey League (NHL) rink which is narrower. Teams from the rest of the world who play on international sized rinks complained that the Canadians and the Americans had an advantage. They were right but also knew way ahead of time that the competition would be on NHL rinks. It did not matter, the Canadian and the American teams ruled the ice from the first day and never complained when the Winter Olympics were held in Europe using international sized rinks.

Seven nations sent Olympic teams for the first time: the Cayman Islands, Colombia, Ghana, Montenegro, Pakistan, Peru, and Serbia marched in the opening ceremonies amid wild cheers and a somewhat confused audience. How much snow does the Cayman Islands get? To make it even more interesting, the South Pacific nation of Tonga (historically not much in the way of snowfall) sent a single athlete—a male who was attempting to qualify but crashed on the last day of qualifying and did not make the cut.

Canada won the most gold medals of any country, 14, and was the first host nation to do so since 1952 when Norway did it. The Canadians also eclipsed the former Soviet Union and Norway who had won 13 gold medals each. The United States won the most medals of any country, a total of 37, breaking the record of 36 held by Germany since 2002.

Arguably the premier event, the gold medal match in ice hockey, was standing room only as the Canadian men defeated their rivals, the American men 3–2. The two women's teams that absolutely dominate on the ice anywhere they play are, as you might expect, Canada and the United States. In a sold-out arena, the Canadian team beat the United States 2–0. The Canadians celebrated well into the night and the next morning. They won more gold medals than any other host nation in Olympic history although some would say they had the home field advantage.

THE XXX OLYMPIAD: LONDON, 2012 IN CHARGE: LORD SEBASTIAN COE

The Political Atmosphere

The war against terrorism continued unabated. The United States remained heavily involved in Iraq and Afghanistan although U.S. president Obama significantly reduced the U.S. presence in Iraq in 2012. It must be noted that U.S. military assets from Iraq were simply shifted to Afghanistan. Osama bin Laden was killed by a group of Navy SEALs who located his fortified home in Pakistan and arrived "locked and loaded" aboard two helicopters in the

OLYMPIC SNAPSHOT

2012 London Winter Olympics:

Opening Day July 27 2012; Closing Day August 12, 2012

- 10,500 athletes represented 204 countries: 4847 were women and 5653 were men
- 29 sports incorporated 39 different disciplines (e.g., Gymnastics is one sport that consists of several "events" formally called disciplines)
- 34 Olympic venues located around London were home to fans and athletes; nine venues were located in Olympic Park
- 21,000 media and press credentials were issued
- Worldwide television audience was in excess of 4 billion people, Internet viewers numbered in the hundreds of millions.
- 8.8 million tickets were available
- 2961 technical officials officiated
- 5770 team officials accompanied the 10,500 athletes
- 70,000 volunteers were selected from 240,000 applications
- 6000 paid staff members planned, implemented, and orchestrated the games that averaged 180,000 fans in attendance each day
- Approximately 45,000 meals served daily in the athlete's Olympic Village[33]

dead of night. One helicopter crashed but no one was hurt. The SEALs killed bin Laden and swiftly loaded his body aboard the remaining helicopter for burial at an undisclosed location at sea in a Muslim funeral. Americans celebrated this victory while many in the Muslim world became more hostile toward the United States than ever. Relations between Pakistan and the United States reached a new low because Pakistani intelligence claimed that they did not know where bin Laden was, even though many people in the village where bin Laden was hiding in Pakistan knew he was there.

The bloody civil war in Sudan claimed more lives. In 2011, the country split apart into two separate nations, the Republic of South Sudan broke away from Sudan. Sadly, peace is unknown in South Sudan as the new government based in Juba continues to fight paramilitary organizations determined to overthrow the new government.

In 2001 Guor Marial fled Sudan and ended up in the United States. He was issued a Green Card and eventually matriculated at Iowa State University where he became an All-American Cross Country Champion in 2009. In 2011, he entered his first marathon by registering for the Twin Cities Marathon. He finished in 2:14:32, fast enough to meet the Olympic qualifying time. That he had no country to compete for was the only problem. Although he had applied for U.S. citizenship as a naturalized citizen, his application was still not approved; he was not a U.S. citizen so he could not compete for the United States. South Sudan did not belong to the International Olympic Committee so they could not send a team. Sudan, the country that Mr. Marial fled from, was a member of the International Olympic Committee and offered him a spot on their Olympic Team. He declined.[34]

With the help of an attorney who Marial met during the Twin Cities Marathon, he was able to convince the IOC to let him compete as an independent athlete. Although many athletes in the past who fled the brutality of war and oppression in their homeland to seek a better life have petitioned the IOC to compete independently, the IOC has always refused, until now. The IOC also granted independent athlete status to three more athletes

in addition to Mr. Marial. So, how did Mr. Marial fair? He finished the marathon in 2:19:32, placing forty-seventh overall.[35]

The world economic situation continued to deteriorate. The European Union (EU) was in serious trouble as Greece was very close to declaring bankruptcy; Spain, Italy, and Ireland were waiting in the wings to possibly do the same. It appeared the EU was on the brink of breaking up with each EU nation abandoning the Euro and returning to their previous currencies. If this happened, the global economic system could unwind. Greece received billions of Euros from the EU to bailout the country in 2011 and 2012. The bailout came with a stiff price: reform Greece's financial system (many people and business concerns in Greece refused to pay or avoided paying taxes) and reduce or eliminate the many entitlements that Greeks had come to expect. It was not pretty. The EU insisted on harsh economic measures that would increase Greece's misery. The EU called it "tough love."

Riots broke out in Athens and other Greek cities, people and police were seriously injured, and deaths were not uncommon. The two most powerful EU countries, France and Germany, were lending the bulk of the money given to Greece came from France and Germany. Many citizens in France and Germany saw their tax money go to Greece instead of staying home. Bitterness and enmity toward the Greeks ensued and when the German chancellor paid a visit to Greece in October of 2012, thousands of Greeks demonstrated and waved Nazi flags as her motorcade made its way through Athens. Many economists and Olympic observers opined that the cost of Greece hosting the 2004 Olympic Games would return to haunt them a few years down the road. It had and the nation was economically in ruin.

Close by, Iran was working to produce an atomic bomb, while Israel was making preparations to make sure this would never happen, even if it meant attacking Iran. President Obama promised that the United States "will have Israel's back" in case the unthinkable should happen. Several weeks after the closing ceremonies ended the 2012 London Olympics, terrorists attacked the U.S. consulate in

Benghazi, Libya and murdered Chris Stevens, the U.S. ambassador to Libya and three other Americans who accompanied him. The Middle East remained the world's most dangerous place.

Presidential elections in France and the United States were on tap for 2012. In France, President Nikolas Sarkozy, a conservative married to supermodel Carla Brunei, lost the election to left-wing socialist (is there any other kind?) Francois Holland. In the United States, President Barack Obama was facing a serious threat from Republican challenger Mitt Romney, former governor of Massachusetts and savior of the 2002 Salt Lake City Winter Olympic Games. Romney is a multimillionaire, successful businessman, and devout Mormon.

The U.S. economy in 2012 was still digging out from the "Great Recession." Millions of people were out of work, business and factory operations were closing by the week, and the U.S. auto industry almost collapsed. Banks were also on the verge of collapse. Congress and the President agreed that the banks could not fail and loaned them billions of dollars to prop them up. In addition to loaning money to the banks, President Obama pumped billions of dollars into the economy by printing more money, which stimulated the economy for awhile. Like the banks, the auto industry was loaned billions of dollars, which saved Detroit for the time being. The housing collapse continued with home foreclosures increasing each week. Although interest rates were at an historic low, it was incredibly difficult to qualify for a home mortgage because lenders were reluctant to lend – even though they had money to lend.

After the fantastic closing ceremonies of the London Olympics on August 12, the U.S. economy started showing signs of life. President Obama claimed it was because his policies were beginning to work, while Republican challenger Romney said Obama's policies were failures. The 2012 U.S. presidential campaign was the most vicious, scurrilous, and negative in the history of the country. The accusations and finger pointing were not limited to the presidential debates or campaign ads; regional, state, and local political campaigns used the same vitriolic rhetoric that the presidential candidates did. It came as no surprise that poll after poll showed that the public's disgust with Congress was at an all-time high in 2012.

To make politics even more interesting, three leaders who intensely dislike the United States made the decision to endorse President Obama for a another term. Hugo Chavez, president of Venezuela, the ruling Castro family of Cuba, and President Vladimir Putin of Russia all endorsed President Obama for a second term.

Syria was still embroiled in a civil war. President Bashir Assad refused to step down after mass protests and riots by Syrians throughout the country. The protesters were inspired by the Arab Spring that toppled ruthless dictators in several Middle Eastern countries, notably Egypt (Mubarak) and Lybia (Quadaffi). Over 33,000 Syrians have died so far and cities have been destroyed; but there seems to be no end in sight.

In the world of sports, U.S. cyclist Lance Armstrong, winner of seven Tour de France championships, was stripped of his titles and banned for life by the Union Cyclists International (UCI), the governing body of cycling. Armstrong was accused of doping and the evidence, according to the UCI and the Unites States Anti-Doping Agency (USADA) was overwhelming. Sadly, Armstrong's fall from grace via doping was but a prologue to the doping violations that would surface during the 2012 London Olympic Games.

London Calling

The great and historical city of London previously hosted the Olympics at the request of the IOC in 1912 and again in 1948. On both occasions, London had not bid for these Olympiads, but a series of circumstances had unfolded that precluded the original cities from hosting the games. The IOC asking London to "step up" and save the Olympics. London, still digging out from the destruction of World War II and the Battle of Britain agreed to step up in 1948 as it had earlier agreed to step up in 1912 on the eve of World War I.

Bidding for the 2012 Olympic Games was a serious matter. London was the dark horse in the early selection of the five finalists: Paris, Madrid, Moscow, London, and New York. In the end, London won after four rounds of voting. Paris and London were neck and neck throughout the voting. On the fourth round, London secured enough votes to prevail and the celebration began. Parisians were devastated as the French had thought they had a lock on the 2012 Olympics.

There was an attempt by an IOC member to sell his vote to cities under consideration and a promise was made by this same IOC member to deliver additional votes for a price. Ivan Slavkov was the president of the Bulgarian Olympic Committee and in 2004 a British Broadcasting Corporation (BBC) investigation conducted a sting that exposed Slavkov's criminal intent. He engaged in discussions with three individuals who told Slavkov they represented East End business entrepreneurs, when in fact they were BBC investigative reporters.

Caught in the act on video tape, he was harshly reprimanded by the IOC and voted out. Several years earlier, when Cape Town, South Africa was bidding for the Olympics, Cape Town officials claimed that Slavkov approached them and offered to sell them his vote and promised several other votes could be bought as well. Cape Town officials were appalled and immediately reported their experience with Slavkov to the IOC who, after a thorough investigation, could not substantiate the claim by the South Africans and Slavkov was cleared of any wrongdoing.

Notables

The opening ceremonies were spectacular! Very different from the sensational opening ceremonies that Beijing orchestrated in 2008, London focused on all things British including James Bond, Queen Elizabeth II, Harry Potter, and of course, London itself! The closing ceremonies were no less spectacular and featured the Spice Girls reunion as well as famous British musicians, including former Beatle Paul McCartney. The Rolling Stones declined the invitation to appear.[36]

Coming into the London Olympics, the media discounted the ability of U.S. swimming sensation Michael Phelps to repeat the amazing performance that he displayed in Beijing four years earlier. They said he didn't train hard enough and missed workouts. His teammate, Ryan Lochte, was the early media darling and everyone expected him to defeat Phelps every time they went head-to-head in the pool for swimming supremacy; everyone, that is, but Michael Phelps!

The first head-to-head meeting matched Lochte and Phelps in the 400-meter individual medley. Lochte beat Phelps for the gold medal while Phelps finished in fourth place, the first time Phelps did not win an Olympic medal since the Sydney Olympics in 2000. The media and swimming fans everywhere said Phelps was "history" and anointed Lochte as swimming's newest "King of the Pool"; everyone, that is, but Michael Phelps! As it turned out, Lochte was "one and done." He had his brief moment in the media spotlight and then it was all Phelps from then on. Four gold and two silver medals later, Michael Phelps became the most decorated Olympian of all time. His 22 Olympic medals, 18 of them gold, was an amazing achievement. Prior to Phelps's arrival on the Olympic scene, the record for most Olympic medals was held by former Soviet gymnast Larisa Latynina, who won a total of 18. Latynina's record lasted for 48 years. How long Phelps's record will last is anybody's guess.[37]

An epic and inspiring historical first unfolded in London as Oscar Pistorius of South Africa became the first double amputee to compete in the Olympic Games. Known as "The Blade Runner" because of the two carbon fiber "legs" he wears, Oscar advanced to the semifinals of the 400-meter sprint where he finished last with a time of 46.54. Detractors claimed his carbon fiber legs gave him an advantage as he could "spring" where others had to affect the typical "step."

Pistorius is a legend in the Paralympics where he has won several gold medals as a sprinter. After the London Olympic Games finished, Oscar competed in the 2012 London Summer Paralympics and won two gold medals (400-meter sprint and

4×100 relay) and one silver medal (200-meter sprint). It gets better. During the Olympics, Pistorius also found time to date a supermodel!

In basketball, the Americans continued their Olympic domination. LeBron James led the way in a hard fought 107–100 victory over Spain for the gold medal while Candace Parker scored 21 points as the women defeated France 86–50. Then there was the unusual story of Becky Harmon.

Harmon played basketball at Colorado State University and for eight seasons in the Women's National Basketball Association (WNBA) during which time she was selected to the All-WNBA First Team in 2008 and 2009. Her lifelong dream was to play in the Olympics and she came close to making the cut for the U.S. team in 2008. When she didn't make the cut, she executed Plan B and contacted a Russian professional team from Moscow and was given a contract to play for CSKA Moscow. With this contract came an understanding that if she applied for Russian citizenship and became a naturalized Russian citizen she could possibly make the Russian Olympic team. Harmon became a Russian citizen and became a star on the Russian Olympic team. She led the Russian women to a bronze medal win over China in Beijing, and in London she helped the Russians reach the bronze medal round where they lost to Australia 73–84.

Beach volleyball is a very popular sport worldwide and was especially popular during the Olympics. In London, tickets for women's beach volleyball were in great demand. It was an all-American final where the reigning world and Olympic championship team of Misty May Treanor and Kerri Walsh Jennings defeated the team of Jen Kessy and April Ross for their third Olympic gold medal.

In other volleyball action, the U.S. men failed to advance to the medal round while the women's team had to settle for the silver medal after a tough loss to Brazil. In men's beach volleyball, the team of Julius Brink and Jonas Reckermann from Germany won the gold medal by defeating the Brazilian team. Where did the U.S. beach volleyball team finish? They made it all the way to the quarter finals where they blew a lead and lost to Latvia, a tiny but proud

Baltic nation where they are probably still celebrating as you read this.

Gabby Douglas, 4' 11" tall, was the talk of the gymnastics world. The 16-year-old high school student from the United States won the gold medal in the women's allaround competition propelling the U.S. women to win the team gold medal and a third-place finish behind second place China and first place Russia.

In a great win for Mexico, their men's soccer team defeated Latin American rival Brazil 2–1 to win the gold medal. This victory may well be the greatest achievement in the history of Mexican sports. In women's soccer, the U.S. women defeated Japan 2–1 for the gold medal while Canada defeated France 1–0 for the bronze medal. In earlier action, the U.S. and Canadian teams went head to head in the women's semifinal. In a game for the ages, the U.S. team beat the Canadians 4–3.

The team of Venus and Serena Williams continued their domination of tennis doubles with a resounding 6–4 gold medal win over the team from the Czech Republic, while London's own Andy Murray defeated top-ranked Roger Fededer 6–2, 6–1, and 6–4 for the gold.

Iceland, an island nation in the North Atlantic that speaks Danish and fluent English is obsessed with the sport of handball. Their national team is revered. With short summers and harsh winters, indoor sports are the norm. No wonder handball and other racket sports flourish in Iceland where winter cross-country skiing is a national pastime. During the 2008 Beijing Olympiad, Iceland reached the finals of the handball competition where it lost to France and "settled" for the silver medal. This achievement made Iceland the smallest country to ever to medal in an Olympic team sport![38] History did not repeat itself in 2012. Iceland's handball team failed to reach the medal round and returned empty-handed.

Badminton is among the last sports one would identify with Olympic scandals and disqualified athletes, but it happened, much to the dismay of the IOC and badminton fans the world over. On August 1, eight teams were kicked out of the

Olympics for demonstrating a lack of effort and shaming the sport. As it turned out, one team from China, two teams from South Korea, and one team from Indonesia hatched a strategy to play so badly and purposely loose in order to receive a better seed during the rest of the qualifying rounds. These teams played so badly that fans began booing and screaming for them to seriously compete. The teams ignored the thousands in attendance and continued to make a mockery of the competition. The team from China were the reigning Olympic and World champions. The embarrassed officials called an end to the charade and after a formal inquiry, threw them out![39]

Doping, always a serious cheating problem during elite athletic competition, reared its ugly head in London. Shot putter Nadezhda Ostapchuk from Belarus was stripped of her gold medal when she tested positive for steroids. U.S. and British Olympic athletes claimed that doping was a serious problem in London. They said that a number of athletes who were competing in London were at some point in their career banned from competition because of doping. These former drug cheats "served their time" and immediately became eligible to compete internationally and in the Olympics. A number of these formerly disgraced athletes won gold medals in London.[40] China has produced incredible athletes as of late. Their success in the Olympic Games has been met with suspicion that doping plays a large part in their recent dominance. Ye Shiwen swims the 400 individual medley (400 IM) for China. In London, her time in the freestyle leg of the women's 400 IM was faster than Ryan Lochte's, who won the gold medal in the men's 400 IM.

By any measure, the London Olympic Games was a spectacular success. In 2016, Rio de Janeiro will host the Summer Olympics. In 2014, the Winter Olympics will be hosted by the Russian city of Sochi.

SUMMARY

The Olympic Games tend to reflect the day-to-day activities of large cities that can be found anywhere in the world. The games, like big cities, are good, bad, glorious, uplifting, hypocritical, inspirational, and memorable. The Olympic flag waving in the breeze is an inspiring sight. The five interlocking rings are symbolic of the world's only true international athletic festival. No matter where you travel in this world, the mere mention of the Olympic Games remains one of the few things that generates positive excitement and animated discussions focused on the performances of the best athletes in the world. The Olympics represent a belief system that emphasizes the high ideals of achievement, understanding, and goodwill. However, the recent deplorable behavior of some IOC members has damaged the credibility of the IOC.

The Olympic ideal has survived world wars, terrorist attacks, boycotts, and meddling by politicians. During the Cold War era, the Olympic Games often deteriorated into competition between nations for the purpose of enhancing national prestige and promoting political ideologies. International relations, social policy, and economic considerations represent elements of political power that sometimes determined who could compete in the games; power politics, in the form of the boycotts of the XXIst, XXIInd, and XXIIIrd Olympiads, served to dim, but did not extinguish, the Olympic flame.

It has been demonstrated that bickering between nations does not confine itself to the political or diplomatic arenas. From time to time, the Olympic Games have become a preferred platform for political confrontations. Olympic athletes have been pawns of their governments and targets of terrorists. Security precautions costing billions of dollars are now needed to deter political terrorists from attacking the Olympics. At various times, Olympic athletes who have trained for years have been relegated to the role of soldiers of sport. From 1936 to 1988, it was sometimes difficult to separate the political arena from the Olympic arena. Nationalism has always been a part of the Olympics.

Following the collapse of communism in Eastern Europe, the propaganda war between the United States and the former Soviet Union ended. One of the chief beneficiaries of the end of the Cold War has been the Olympic movement. The Olympic Games have entered a period of prosperity and incredible growth, and today, the Olympic flame burns brighter than ever. The Olympic Games have always endeavored to bring people together from different parts of the world to foster international understanding and to enhance the prospects for peace. Perhaps this millennium will usher in a new era in which athletes and the Olympics will truly make a difference in promoting goodwill and international understanding.

The use of drugs by Olympic athletes has replaced politics as the scourge of the games. Blood doping by distance runners and steroid use among weight-lifters and track-and-field athletes have been a plague on the Olympics. The use of ergogenic aids and their detection will no doubt be a recurring story in future Olympics. Still, the use of illicit drugs by unscrupulous athletes is a measure of the importance of an Olympic victory and what athletes will do to achieve it. The ancient Greeks

had to deal with cheating in the Olympic Games, and the IOC has inherited this problem. Niccolò Machiavelli, who wrote the classic book *The Prince,* asserted that "The end justifies the means." Drugs have become the means that some athletes resort to in order to achieve their end—an Olympic medal. These athletes are not worthy to be honored as Olympians.

It has been said that "nothing is forever." If the Olympics once again fall prey to power politics, the Olympic flame may be extinguished once and for all. The IOC has been effective in breathing new life into the Olympics despite the social and political agendas that have tainted the games. We can only hope that the IOC will continue to do what many detractors have termed "mission impossible": Keep the Olympic flame burning bright for a long time to come.

DISCUSSION QUESTIONS

1. How have social issues affected the Olympic Games?

2. To what extent did the issue of apartheid and the political act of terrorism have an impact on the 1972 Munich Olympiad? Did the IOC have a moral obligation to make sure the Olympics continued after the massacre of the Israeli athletes? If so, why? Do you believe the IOC should have canceled the games after the massacre? Why or why not?

3. Considering the exorbitant costs associated with holding the Olympic Games, what benefits are derived by the host city and country?

4. What could be done to remove politics from the Olympics? Do you believe that the end of the Cold War and the breakup of the Soviet Union will result in all future Olympiads becoming more peaceful and friendly?

5. What changes would you suggest that the IOC make to ensure that future Olympiads promote

international understanding and goodwill? Should the Olympic Games be permanently located in one place? Where and why? Will American athletes ever again dominate the Olympic Games as they did prior to 1960? With the global changes underway, who will be the dominant Olympic power of this century?

6. To what extent do you believe that commercialization of the Olympics has a negative impact?

7. To what extent, if any, will the War on Terror affect the Olympics?

8. If you were a member of the IOC when the vote was taken to select the city to host the 2008 Olympic Games, would you have voted for Beijing? Give reasons to justify your decision.

9. Can nationalism be separated from patriotism or are they the same thing?

INTERNET RESOURCES

International Olympic Committee (IOC)
www.olympic.org
Includes links and information about all aspects of the Olympic Games.

International Olympic Academy
www.ioa.org.gr
Is the home page of the International Olympic Academy.

United States Olympic Committee
www.usoc.org
Is the home page of the U.S. Olympic Committee; includes information on Olympic events and athletes.

Olympic Studies Center
http://olympicstudies.uab.es/eng/yellow/dir/om.html
Provides historical and philosophical information about the modern Olympic Games.

Pierre de Coubertin Committee
www.decoubertin.org
Is the home page of the de Coubertin Committee.

International Center for Olympic Studies
www.uwo.ca/olympic/
Provides links for scholars interested in Olympic history and philosophy; also presents lectures and publishes the *International Journal of Olympic Studies—Olympika.*

Visit the *History and Philosophy of Sport and Physical Education* Online Learning Center (www.mhhe.com/mechikoff6e) for additional information and study tools.

SUGGESTIONS FOR FURTHER READING

The author recommends that students interested in the Olympic movement read the critically acclaimed book by John A. Lucas, *Future of the Olympic Games.*

Albanidis, E., R. K. Barney, and N. Choutas. "An Olympian Sanctuary: The Quest to Permanently Host the Olympic Games in Greece." *Journal of Olympic History,* Vol. 14, No. 2, July 2007, pp. 28–39.

Camper, R. *Encyclopedia of the Olympic Games.* New York: McGraw-Hill, 1972.

Durance, J. *Highlights of the Olympics.* New York: Hastiness House, 1965.

Gray, W., and R. Knight Barony. "Devotion to Whom? German-American Loyalty on the Issue of Participation in the 1936 Olympic Games." *Journal of Sport History* 17, no. 2 (Summer 1990): 214–31.

Killanin, Lord, and J. Rod, eds. *The Olympic Games 1980.* New York: Macmillan, 1979.

Kretchmar, R. S. "Ethics and Sport: An Overview." *Journal of the Philosophy of Sport* X (1983): 21–32.

Leiper, J. M. "The International Olympic Committee: The Pursuit of Olympicism 1894–1970." Doctoral dissertation, University of Alberta, 1976.

Lucas, J. A. *Future of the Olympic Games.* Champaign, IL: Human Kinetics, 1992.

Real, M. R. *Super Media: A Cultural Studies Approach.* Newbury Park, CA: Sage, 1989.

NOTES

1. John Huxley, "Barcelona a Searing, Surprising Success," *Los Angeles Times,* 10 August 1992, 2w.

2. Ibid.

3. *The Olympic Movement* (Lausanne: International Olympic Committee, Chateao de Vidy, Switzerland, 1993), 62; Anita Defrantz, "The Olympic Games and Women," *Olympic Review* XXV (October–November 1995): 58.

4. Official Report of the XVI Olympic Winter Games of Albertville and Savoie—Comite d'Organization des XVI Jeux Olympiques d'Hiver d'Albertville et de la Savoie, 73200 Albertville, France, 1992, 124.

5. Ibid., 235.

6. Fact Sheet #B-1 from Olympic Museum, Lausanne, Switzerland, 30 June 1995, 3.

7. Ibid., 2.

8. *San Diego-Union Tribune,* 23 February 1992, H13.

9. *Los Angeles Times,* 8 February 1992, C9.

10. Fact Sheet #B-3 from Olympic Museum, Lausanne, Switzerland, 30 June 1995, 2.

11. Ibid., 2.

12. *San Diego Union-Tribune,* 28 February 1994, D13.

13. *San Diego Union-Tribune,* 13 August 1996, C2.

14. *Jackson Hole Daily Guide,* 5 August 1996, 21.

15. *USA Today,* 12 April 2000, C3.

16. *San Diego Union Tribune,* 16 September 2000, E6.

17. *USA Today,* 12 April 2000, C3.

18. *San Diego Union Tribune,* 16 September 2000, C4.

19. Ibid.

20. *San Diego Union Tribune,* 27 August 2000, A21.

21. *San Diego Union Tribune,* 28 September 2000, C1, C2.

22. *USA Today,* 12 April 2000, C3.

23. *USA Today,* 8 August 2000, B8.

24. Ibid.

25. *Los Angeles Times,* 13 August 2000, A1; *International Herald Tribune,* 15 September 2000, "Sydney 2000 An Olympic Special," 1.

26. *Los Angeles Times,* 13 August 2000, A1.

27. *Los Angeles Times,* 16 July 2000, A24.

28. Ibid., 1.

29. Ibid., 1, A24, A25.

30. Ibid., A24.

31. *International Herald Tribune,* 15 September 2000, II.

32. *San Diego Union Tribune,* 2 October 2000, C3; *International Herald Tribune,* 15 September 2000, 22.

33. International Olympic Committee website: http://www.olympic.org?london-2012-summer-olympics FACTS

34. "Unflagged and Unflagging. Guor Marials Marathon." *Time,* 13 August 2012, 20.

35. Ibid., 21.

36. 2012 Summer Olympics closing ceremony. (October 18, 2012). In *Wikipedia, The Free Encyclopedia.* Retrieved October 24, 2012, from http://en.wikipedia.org/w/index.php?title=2012_Summer_Olympics_closing_ceremony&oldid=518597219

37. *Time,* p. 9.

38. Ibid., 18.

39. http://articles.latimes.com/2012/aug/01/sports/la-sp-on-badminton-scandal-20120801

40. http://www.dailymail.co.uk/sport/olympics/article-2190409/London-2012-Olympics-Drug-cheats-prospering–Dick-Pound.html

CREDITS

Section-Opening Pages

Left and center: Anthony Saint James/Getty Images
Right: Lawrence M. Sawyer/Getty Images

Chapter-Opening Pages

PhotoLink/Getty Images

Chapter 2

p. 27: Dennis Sherman, *Western Civilization: Sources, Images, and Interpretations,* vol. 1, to 1700 (5th ed.) (Boston: McGraw-Hill, 2000).
p. 32: British Museum
p. 40: Photo by Linda Ginsburg
p. 41: Royalty-Free/Corbis

Chapter 3

p. 46: Dennis Sherman, *Western Civilization: Sources, Images, and Interpretations,* vol. 1, to 1700 (5th ed.) (Boston: McGraw-Hill, 2000).
p. 49: Robert C. Lamin, Neal M. Cross, and Rudy H. Turk, *The Search for Personal Freedom,* vol. 1 (Dubuque, IA: Wm. C. Brown, 1984).
p. 53: From E. W. Gerber, *Innovators and Institutions in Physical Education* (Philadelphia: Lea & Febiger, 1971).
p. 56, top: Courtesy Mary Pavlich Roby, University of Arizona
p. 56, bottom: Courtesy of University of Iowa Photographic Service
p. 62: From Repository at Knossos, Crete
p. 71, top, middle left, bottom left: From the Museum at Ancient Nemea, Greece

Chapter 4

p. 79: Source: Dennis Sherman, *Western Civilization: Sources, Images, and Interpretations,* vol. 1, to 1700 (5th ed.) (Boston: McGraw-Hill, 2000).
p. 95: From the Archeological Museum of Barcelona

Chapter 5

p. 121: The British Library

Chapter 6

p. 134: From E. W. Gerber, *Innovators and Institutions in Physical Education* (Philadelphia: Lea & Febiger, 1971).
p. 139: Source: Emma Lee/Life File/Getty Images

Chapter 8

p. 182: From E. W. Gerber, *Innovators and Institutions in Physical Education* (Philadelphia: Lea & Febiger, 1971).
p. 183, p. 188: From Charles Beek, *A Treatise on Gymnastiks.* Taken from the German of F. L. Jahn (Northampton, MA.: Simeon Butler, 1828).
p. 189: From E. W. Gerber, *Innovators and Institutions in Physical Education* (Philadelphia: Lea & Febiger, 1971).

Chapter 9

p. 203, top: Courtesy of the Library of Congress.
p. 203, bottom: From Betty Spears and Richard A. Swanson, *History of Sport and Physical Education in the United States,* 3rd ed. (Dubuque, IA: Wm. C. Brown, 1988).
p. 204, top left: Courtesy of Department of Library Services, American Museum of Natural History.
p. 204, bottom: From an engraving after a drawing by George Catlin, *North American Indian Portfolio.* London, 1814.

Chapter 10

p. 219: Courtesy Enoch Pratt Free Library, Baltimore, Maryland.
p. 220, top left: 1834 painting by Edward Troy, from New York Historical Society.
p. 221: From Frank Leslie's *Illustrated Newspaper,* June 28, 1856.
p. 225: Courtesy Spalding Archives, Chicopee, Massachusetts.

Chapter 11

p. 239: From E. W. Gerber, *Innovators and Institutions in Physical Education* (Philadelphia: Lea & Febiger, 1971).

p. 245: Courtesy of Mount Holyoke College Library/Archives
p. 250, p. 253: From E. W. Gerber, *Innovators and Institutions in Physical Education* (Philadelphia: Lea & Febiger, 1971).

Chapter 14

p. 291, all: Courtesy of the University of Michigan.
p. 292, top and bottom: Photo courtesy of Cumberland County Historical Society, Carlisle, PA.
p. 295: Photo by Culver Pictures, Inc. Courtesy of Cumberland County Historical Society, Carlisle, PA.
p. 297: From Betty Spears and Richard A. Swanson, *History of Sport and Physical Education in the United States,* 3rd ed. (Dubuque, IA: Wm. C. Brown, 1988).
p. 298: Smith College Archives, Smith College. Photo by Katherine E. McClellan.
p. 301, All: Courtesy of American Alliance for Health, Physical Education, Recreation, and Dance
p. 302: From Betty Spears and Richard A. Swanson, *History of Sport and Physical Education in the United States,* 3rd ed. (Dubuque, IA: Wm. C. Brown, 1988).

Chapter 15

p. 314: From E. W. Gerber, *Innovators and Institutions in Physical Education* (Philadelphia: Lea & Febiger, 1971).
p. 324: Photo by Culver Pictures, Inc. Courtesy of Cumberland County Historical Society, Carlisle, PA.
p. 325: Courtesy of University of Michigan

Chapter 16

p. 394: Photo by F. Scott Grant. Courtesy of Athlete Information Bureau and Canadian Olympic Association

Chapter 17

p. 418: Photo by Ruth Beck-PerrenoudCredits
p. 447: © Getty Images/Mike Hewitt

INDEX

C